MASTERWORKS
OF
CHILDREN'S
LITERATURE

MASTERWORKS

OF

CHILDREN'S

LITERATURE

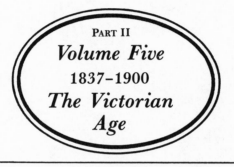

PART II
Volume Five
1837–1900
The Victorian Age

EDITED BY **Robert Lee Wolff**

GENERAL EDITOR: *Jonathan Cott*

THE STONEHILL PUBLISHING COMPANY
IN ASSOCIATION WITH
CHELSEA HOUSE PUBLISHERS
NEW YORK

GENERAL EDITOR: Jonathan Cott
ADVISORY EDITOR: Robert G. Miner, Jr.
VOLUME EDITOR: Robert Lee Wolff
PROJECT DIRECTOR: Esther Mitgang
DESIGNER: Paul Bacon
EDITORIAL STAFF: Joy Johannessen, Philip Minges III, Claire Bottler
PRODUCTION: Coco Dupuy, Heather White, Sandra Su, Susan Lusk,
   Christopher Newton, Carol McDougall

First Printing
Printed and Bound in the United States of America
ISBN: 0-87754-380-1
LC: 79-89986

Chelsea House Publishers
   Harold Steinberg, Chairman and Publisher
   Andrew E. Norman, President
   Susan Lusk, Vice President
A Division of Chelsea House Educational Communications, Inc.
133 Christopher Street, New York, NY 10014

Contents

4

Eric;
or
Little by Little

A Tale of Roslyn School

By FREDERIC W. FARRAR

ERIC

OR

LITTLE BY LITTLE

A TALE OF ROSLYN SCHOOL

BY

FREDERIC W. FARRAR

ILLUSTRATED BY

GORDON BROWNE

LONDON ADAM & CHARLES BLACK

mdcccxcviii

I N ITS OWN DAY, *Eric; or, Little by Little* was a schoolboy story even more popular than *Tom Brown's School Days* (reprinted in Volume 5, Part I); it went through thirty-six editions. Nowadays it is remembered as mawkishly pious and is seldom read. It is often noted that by 1899 the schoolboys in Kipling's *Stalky & Co.* were poking fun at *Eric*; but it comes as a surprise to find that thirty years earlier, in 1869, Charlotte M. Yonge, herself so deeply religious, called the boisterous and somewhat rowdy *Tom Brown* so good as to be "unapproachable," but condemned *Eric* outright. She hoped no mother or boy would ever read it: all it could do was make them "unhappy or suspicious" and convince them that "the sure reward of virtue is a fatal accident." Knowing how popular it was, she also warned girls against it: "It enters upon schoolboy trials" that they had no business to hear about. Yonge had doctrinal as well as moral reasons for her derogatory opinions.

Eric appeared in 1858, just a year after *Tom Brown*. The two celebrated stories have always invited comparison and contrast. *Eric*'s author, Frederic William Farrar (1831–1903), attended the Evangelical King William's College on the Isle of Man. He immortalized this institution in his schoolboy story as "Roslyn School," just as Thomas Hughes immortalized his alma mater, Rugby, in *Tom Brown's School Days*. Like Hughes, but a few years later, Farrar fell under the influence of the "Broad Church" leader Frederick Denison Maurice; but unlike Hughes, he went on to make a career as parson and schoolmaster, becoming headmaster of Marlborough, a large public school, and eventually dean of Canterbury. *Eric* appeared while he was a master at Harrow. Farrar wrote many articles on theology and education, as well as a popular *Life of Christ* (1874). Although identified with F. D. Maurice and Charles Kingsley in the Broad Church movement, which was based on a belief in the infinite love of God for all created beings, Farrar remained strongly Evangelical in outlook. He was formed by King's College, London, and Trinity College, Cambridge; he strongly approved of John Wesley. The Oxford Tractarians, like the Tractarian Charlotte M. Yonge, would have disapproved of his views, while Miss Newmarsh, the Duff's Evangelical governess in *The Fairy Bower* (also reprinted in Volume 5, Part I), would have largely applauded them.

Evangelicals tended to distrust fiction on principle, believing it permissible only when it taught a religious lesson: an Evangelical author felt obliged to intervene anxiously to point the moral to the reader, and to reassure him that he was dealing with fact and not with imagined events. And, in introducing so many children's deaths, for example, Farrar *was* dealing with facts; Victorian children *did* often die, leaving their families emotionally devastated, and the moralizing over their deathbeds *was* in fact a staple of ordinary life, not mere fictional imagining. The very greatest Victorian writers (Dickens himself, for example, with Little Nell and Paul Dombey, to name only the most obvious) slew their child characters in hecatombs. Somehow it gratified grieving parents to weep again when reading of an experience like their own; surely it edified, and probably terrified, surviving children. Such scenes were almost obligatory in Victorian fiction: even Tom Brown almost loses young Arthur, and has a saccharine reunion with him after his recovery. And, in portraying emotional relationships between boys at school, and between men and boys, Farrar, as he said, was also dealing in facts. He often receives the blame for the morbidity of an entire age because *Eric* is so exaggerated an example of the genre. True: Farrar overdid it, as Charlotte Yonge rightly pointed out when she wrote that in *Eric* good behavior is always rewarded by a fatal accident.

Rugby's "small friend" system, with all its evils, is mirrored in Roslyn School's "taking-up" practice. Bullying and cheating and drinking pervade both schools. There is nothing in *Tom Brown*, however, to correspond with the appalling series of beatings that fill the pages of Eric, sometimes delivered by the noblest and most high-minded of schoolmasters, and often described in such loving detail that the reader suspects Farrar of a strong sadistic streak. Nor was this uncommon among Victorian schoolmasters, those godlike figures who sometimes combined the most savage corporal punishment with floods of tears and later kisses of forgiveness. What twentieth-century readers regard as super-heated demonstrations of mutual affection between males, and the free use of the term "love" for male friendships, were common features of the brutal atmosphere of the Victorian boys' school, perhaps making it more tolerable. Often we are assured that the homosexual relations we suspect in such episodes did not in fact occur.

Careful readers of both books will note that Rugby Chapel and the sermons of the headmaster, Dr. Rowlands, play an important part in *Tom Brown;* while in *Eric*, despite its religiosity, school religious services are never once described: the Evangelical emphasis is on private prayer. "Little by little" Eric falls from virtue; though it must be noted that he does not commit the worst sin of all—lying—and a boy who does lie receives an overpoweringly brutal thrashing from a master. Yet Eric is doomed; he cannot redeem himself even if he tries; he must leave school for a crime of which he is innocent because his past record is so murky that he cannot clear himself of the charges.

Aboard the ship on which he is then shanghaied, he suffers the ghastliest beating of all; it nearly kills him. Only then can he be redeemed. Eric experiences, in the very last pages of the novel, a "conversion," that great religious experience without which, the Evangelicals believed, salvation was impossible. Each of his previous punishments has been too slight to turn his steps back into the paths of righteousness. It is only when he has been beaten to a pulp that in the

> valley of the shadow of death, a Voice had come to him—a still small voice—at whose holy and healing utterance Eric had bowed his head, and had listened to the messages of God, and learned His will; and now, in humble resignation, in touching penitence, with solemn self-devotion, he had cast himself at the feet of Jesus, and prayed to be helped, and guided, and forgiven. . . . Yes, for Jesus' sake he was washed, he was cleansed, he was sanctified, he was justified; he would fear no evil, for God was with him. . . .

Eric; or, Little by Little, then, is not just a religious novel for boys, but a very special kind of religious novel, illustrating the harsh and relentless side of the Evangelical spirit: the recalcitrant and erring human being must be bent and bent again; and if he will not relent in his wickedness, he must be broken. He must be broken to be converted and converted to avoid damnation.

Yet, when one sets aside the Evangelical fervor and the preaching that almost from the first made *Eric* seem stiff and even laughable to the admirers of *Tom Brown*, one realizes that Farrar, in the ideals he held up for Eric—attention to learning, industriousness, enjoyment of the out-of-doors and exercise, moral purity, and earnest piety—had in his emphasis come far closer to the ideals cherished and promulgated by Dr. Arnold, headmaster of Rugby, than had Arnold's loyal admirer, Thomas Hughes. *Eric*, as Hugh Kingsmill once wittily remarked, "is the kind of book Dr. Arnold might have written had he taken to drink" and become intoxicated with romanticism. This final paradox alone justifies a new reprinting of these two remarkable Victorian books for boys.

The text of Eric; or, Little by Little, *with illustrations by Gordon Browne, is reprinted from an English edition (London: Adam and Charles Black, 1898).*

'Tis one thing to be tempted, Escalus,
Another thing to fall.
Measure for Measure, Act ii, Scene I

TO
THE RIGHT REVEREND
G. E. L. COTTON, D.D.
LORD BISHOP OF CALCUTTA
THIS STORY OF SCHOOL LIFE
IS
AFFECTIONATELY DEDICATED
IN
GRATEFUL MEMORY OF THE PAST

PREFACE
TO TWENTY FOURTH EDITION

THE STORY OF 'ERIC' was written with but one single object—the vivid inculcation of inward purity and moral purpose, by the history of a boy who, in spite of the inherent nobleness of his disposition, falls into all folly and wickedness, until he has learnt to seek help from above. I am deeply thankful to know—from testimony public and private, anonymous and acknowledged—that this object has, by God's blessing, been fulfilled.

The fact that new editions are still called for thirty-one years after its publication, shows, I trust, that the story has been found to be of real use. I have not thought it right to alter in any way the style or structure of the narrative, but I have so far revised it as to remove a few of the minor blemishes. I trust that the book may continue to live so long—and so long only—as it may prove to be a source of moral benefit to those who read it.

APRIL 21, 1889

Part I

CHAPTER THE FIRST

CHILDHOOD

Ah dear delights, that o'er my soul
On memory's wing like shadows fly!
Ah flowers that Joy from Eden stole,
While Innocence stood laughing by.
COLERIDGE

'HURRAH! HURRAH! HURRAH!' cried a young boy, as he capered vigorously about, and clapped his hands. 'Father and mother will be home in a week now, and then we shall stay here a little time, and *then*, and *then*, I shall go to school.'

The last words were enunciated with immense importance, as he stopped his impromptu dance before the chair where his sober cousin Fanny was patiently working at her crochet; but she did not look so much affected by the announcement as the boy seemed to demand, so he again exclaimed, 'And then, Miss Fanny, I shall go to school.'

'Well, Eric,' said Fanny, raising her matter-of-fact quiet face from her endless work, 'I doubt, dear, whether you will talk of it with quite as much joy a year hence.'

'Oh ay, Fanny, that's just like you to say so; you're always talking and prophesying; but never mind, I'm going to school, so, hurrah! hurrah! hurrah!' and he again began his capering,—jumping over the chairs, trying to vault the tables, singing and dancing with an exuberance of delight, till, catching a sudden sight of his little spaniel Flo, he sprang through the open window into the garden, and disappeared behind the trees of the shrubbery; but Fanny still heard his clear, ringing, silvery laughter, as he continued his games in the summer air.

She looked up from her work after he had gone, and sighed. In spite of the sunshine and balm of the bright weather, a sense of heaviness and foreboding oppressed her. Everything looked smiling and beautiful, and there was an almost irresistible contagion in the mirth of her young cousin, but still she could not help feeling sad. It was not merely that she would have to part with Eric, 'but that bright boy,' thought Fanny, 'what will become of him? I have heard strange things of schools; oh, if he should be spoilt and ruined, what misery it would be. Those baby lips, that pure young heart, a year may work sad change in their words and thoughts!' She sighed again, and her eyes glistened as she raised them upwards, and breathed a silent prayer.

She loved the boy dearly, and had taught him from his earliest years. In most things she found him an apt pupil. Truthful, ingenuous, quick, he would acquire almost without effort any subject that interested him, and a word was often enough to bring the impetuous blood to his cheeks, in a flush of pride or indignation. He required the gentlest teaching, and had received it, while his mind seemed cast in such a mould of stainless honour, that he avoided most of the weaknesses to which children are prone. But he was far from blameless. He was proud to a fault; he well knew that few of his fellows had gifts like his, either of mind or person, and his fair face often showed a clear impression of his own superiority. His passion, too, was imperious, and though it always met with prompt correction, his cousin had latterly found it difficult to subdue. She felt, in a word, that he was outgrowing her rule. Beyond a certain age no boy of spirit can be safely guided by a woman's hand alone.

Eric Williams was now twelve years old. His father was a civilian in India, and was returning on furlough to England, after a long absence. Eric had been born in India, but had been sent to England by his parents at an early age, in charge of a lady friend of his mother. The parting, which had been agony to his father and mother, he was too young to feel; indeed the moment itself passed by without his being conscious of it. They took him on board the ship, and, after a time, gave him a hammer and some nails to play with. These had always been to him a supreme delight, and while he hammered away, Mr. and Mrs. Williams, denying themselves, for the child's sake, even one more tearful embrace, went ashore in the boat and left him. It was not till the ship sailed that he was told he would not see them again for a long, long time. Poor child, his tears and cries were piteous when he first understood it; but the sorrows of four years old are very transient, and before a week was over, little Eric felt almost reconciled to his position, and had become the universal pet and plaything of every one on board, from Captain Broadland down to the cabin-boy, with whom he very soon struck up an acquaintance. Yet twice a day at least his mirth would be checked as he lisped his little prayer, kneeling at Mrs. Munro's knee, and asked God 'to bless his dear, dear father and mother, and make him a good boy.'

When Eric arrived in England, he was entrusted to the care of a widowed aunt, whose daughter, Fanny, had the main charge of his early teaching. At first, the wayward little Indian seemed likely to form no accession to the quiet household, but he soon became its brightest ornament and pride. Everything was in his favour at the pleasant home of Mrs. Trevor. He was treated with motherly kindness and tenderness, yet firmly checked when he went wrong. From the first he had a well-spring of strength against temptation, in the long letters which every mail brought from his parents; and all his childish affections were entwined round the fancied image of a brother born since he had left India. In his bedroom there hung a cherub's head, drawn in pencil by his mother, and this winged child was inextricably identified in his imagination with his 'little brother Vernon.' He loved it dearly, and whenever he went astray, nothing weighed on his mind so strongly as the thought, that if he were naughty he would teach little Vernon to be naughty too when he came home.

And Nature also—wisest, gentlest, holiest of teachers—was with him in his childhood. Fairholm Cottage, where his aunt lived, was situated in the beautiful Vale of Ayrton, and a clear stream ran through the valley at the bottom of Mrs. Trevor's orchard. Eric loved this stream, and was always happy as he roamed by its side, or over the low green hills and scattered dingles which lent unusual loveliness to every winding of its waters. He was allowed to go about a good deal by himself, and it did him good. He grew up fearless and self-dependent, and never felt the want of amusement. The garden and orchard supplied him a theatre for endless games and romps, sometimes with no other companion than his cousin and his dog, and sometimes with the few children of his own age whom he knew in the hamlet. Very soon he forgot all about India; it only hung like a distant golden haze on the horizon of his memory. When asked if he remembered it, he would say thoughtfully, that in dreams and at some other times, he saw a little boy, with long curly hair, running about in a flower-garden, near a great river, in a place where the air was very bright. But whether the little boy was himself or his brother Vernon, whom he had never seen, he couldn't quite tell.

But, above all, it was happy for Eric that his training was religious and enlightened. With Mrs. Trevor and her daughter, religion was not a system but a habit—not a theory but a continued act of life. All was simple, sweet, and unaffected, about their charity and their devotions. They loved God, and they did all the good they could to those around them. The floating gossip and ill-nature of the little village never affected them; it melted away insensibly in the presence of their cultivated minds; so that friendship with them was a bond of union among all, and from the vicar to the dairyman every one loved and respected them, asked their counsel, and sought their sympathy.

They called themselves by no sectarian name, nor could they have told to what 'party' they belonged. They troubled themselves with no theories of education, but mingled gentle nurture with 'wholesome neglect.' There was nothing exotic or constrained in the growth of Eric's character. He was not one of the angelically good children at all, and knew none of the phrases of which infant prodigies are supposed to be so fond. But to be truthful, to be honest, to be kind, to be brave, these lessons had been taught him, and he never *quite* forgot them; nor amid the sorrows of after life did he ever quite lose the

sense—learnt at dear quiet Fairholm—of a present loving God, of a tender and long-suffering Father.

As yet he could be hardly said to know what school was. He had been sent indeed to Mr. Lawley's grammar school for the last half-year, and had learned a few declensions in his Latin grammar. But as Mr. Lawley allowed his upper class to hear the little boys their lessons, Eric had managed to get on pretty much as he liked. Only *once* in the entire half-year had he said a lesson to the dreadful master himself, and of course it was a ruinous failure, involving some tremendous pulls of Eric's hair, and making him tremble like a leaf. Several things combined to make Mr. Lawley terrific to his imagination. Ever since he was quite little, he remembered hearing the howls which proceeded from the 'Latin school' as he passed by, whilst some luckless youngster was getting caned; and the reverend pedagogue was notoriously passionate. Then, again, he spoke so indistinctly with his deep gruff voice, that Eric never could and never did understand a word he said, and this kept him in a perpetual terror. Once Mr. Lawley had told him to go out, and see what time it was by the church clock. Only hearing that he was to do something, too frightened to ask what it was, and feeling sure that even if he did, he should not make out what the master meant, Eric ran out, went straight to Mr. Lawley's house, and, after having managed by strenuous jumps to touch the knocker, informed the servant 'that Mr. Lawley wanted his man.'

'What man?' said the maid-servant, 'the young man? or the butler? or is it the clerk?'

Here was a puzzler! all Eric knew was, that he was in the habit of sending sometimes for one or other of these functionaries; but he was in for it, so with a faltering voice he said 'the young man' at hazard, and went back to the Latin school.

'Why have you been so long?' roared Mr. Lawley, as he timidly entered. Fear entirely prevented Eric from hearing the exact question, so he answered at random, 'He's coming, sir.' The master seeing by his scared look that something was wrong, waited to see what would turn up.

Soon after in walked 'the young man,' and coming to the astonished Mr. Lawley, bowed, scraped, and said, 'Master Williams said you sent for me, sir.'

'A mistake,' growled the schoolmaster, turning on Eric a look which nearly petrified him; he quite expected a book at his head, or at best a great whack of the cane; but Mr. Lawley had naturally a kind heart, soured as it was, and pitying perhaps the child's white face, he contented himself with the effects of his look.

The simple truth was, that poor Mr. Lawley was a little wrong in the head. A scholar and a gentleman, early misfortunes and an imprudent marriage had driven him to the mastership of the little country grammar school; and here the perpetual annoyance caused to his refined mind by the coarseness of clumsy or spiteful boys, had gradually unhinged his intellect. Often did he tell the boys 'that it was an easier life by far to break stones by the roadside than to teach them'; and at last his eccentricities became too obvious to be any longer overlooked.

The denouement of his history was a tragic one, and had come a few days before the time when our narrative opens. It was a common practice among the Latin-school boys, as I suppose among all boys, to amuse themselves by putting a heavy book on the top of a door left partially ajar, and to cry out, 'Crown him!' as the first luckless youngster who happened to come in received the book thundering on his head. One day, just as the trap had been adroitly laid, Mr. Lawley walked in unexpectedly. The moment he entered the schoolroom, down came an Ainsworth's Dictionary on the top of his hat, and the boy, concealed behind the door, unconscious of who the victim was, enunciated with mock gravity, 'Crown him! three cheers!'

It took Mr. Lawley a second to raise from his eyebrows the battered hat, and recover from his confusion; the next instant he was springing after the boy who had caused the mishap, and who, knowing the effects of the master's fury, fled with precipitation. In one minute the offender was caught, and Mr. Lawley's heavy hand fell recklessly on his ears and back, until he screamed with terror. At last, by a tremendous writhe, wrenching himself free, he darted towards the door, and Mr. Lawley, too much tired to pursue, snatched his large gold watch out of his fob, and hurled it at the boy's retreating figure. The watch flew through the air;—crash! it had missed its aim, and, striking the wall above the lintel, fell smashed into a thousand shivers.

The sound, the violence of the action, the sight of the broken watch, which was the gift of a cherished friend, instantly awoke the master to his senses. The whole school had seen it; they sate there pale and breathless with excitement and awe. The poor man could bear it no longer. He flung himself into his chair, hid his face with his hands, and burst into hysterical tears. It was the outbreak of feelings long pent up. In that instant all his life passed before him—its hopes, its failures, its miseries, its madness. 'Yes!' he thought, 'I am mad.'

Raising his head, he cried wildly, 'Boys, go, I am mad!' and sank again into his former position, rocking himself to and fro. One by one the boys stole out, and he was left alone. The end is soon told. Forced to leave Ayrton, he had no means of earning his daily bread; and the weight of this new anxiety hastening the crisis, the handsome proud scholar became an inmate of the Brerely Lunatic Asylum. A few years afterwards, Eric heard that he was dead. Poor broken human heart! may he rest in peace.

Such was Eric's first school and schoolmaster. But although he learnt little there, and gained no experience of the character of others or of his own, yet there was one point about Ayrton Latin School which he never regretted. It was the mixture there of all classes. On those benches gentlemen's sons sat side by side with plebeians, and no harm, but only good, seemed to come from the intercourse. The neighbouring gentry, most of whom had begun their education there, were drawn into closer and kindlier union with their neighbours and dependants, from the fact of having been their associates in the days of their boyhood. Many a time afterwards, when Eric, as he passed down the streets, interchanged friendly greetings with some young glazier or tradesman whom he remembered at school, he felt glad that thus early he had learnt practically to despise the accidental and nominal differences which separate man from man.

CHAPTER THE SECOND

A NEW HOME

Life hath its May, and all is joyous then;
The woods are vocal, and the flowers breathe odour,
The very breeze hath mirth in't.
OLD PLAY

At LAST THE LONGED-FOR yet dreaded day approached, and a letter informed the Trevors that Mr. and Mrs. Williams would arrive at Southampton on 5th July, and would probably reach Ayrton the evening after. They particularly requested that no one should come to meet them on their landing. 'We shall reach Southampton,' wrote Mrs. Williams, 'tired, pale, and travel-stained, and had much rather see you first at Fairholm, where we shall be spared the painful constraint of a meeting in public. So please expect our arrival at about seven in the evening.'

Poor Eric! although he had been longing for the time ever since the news came, yet now he was too agitated for enjoyment. Exertion and expectation made him restless, and he could settle down to nothing all day, every hour of which hung most heavily on his hands.

At last the afternoon wore away, and a soft summer evening filled the sky with its gorgeous calm. Far off they caught the sound of wheels; a carriage dashed up to the door, and the next moment Eric sprang into his mother's arms.

'O mother! mother!'

'My own darling, darling boy!'

And as the pale sweet face of the mother met the bright and rosy child-face, each of them was wet with a rush of unbidden tears. In another moment Eric had been folded to his father's heart, and locked in the arms of his little brother Vernon. Who shall describe the emotions of those few moments? they did not seem like earthly moments; they seemed to belong not to time, but to eternity.

The first evening of such a scene is too excited to be happy. The little party at Fairholm retired early, and Eric was soon fast asleep with his arm round his new-found brother's neck.

Quiet steps entered the chamber, and noiselessly the father and mother sat down by the bedside of their children. Earth could have shown no scene more perfect in its beauty than that which met their eyes. The pure moonlight flooded the little room, and showed distinctly the forms and countenances of the sleepers, whose soft regular breathing was the only sound that broke the stillness of the July night. The small shining flower-like faces, with their fair hair—the trustful loving arms folded round each brother's neck—the closed lids and parted lips—made an exquisite picture, and one never to be forgotten. Side by side, without a word, the parents knelt down, and with eyes wet with tears of joyfulness, poured out their hearts in passionate prayer for their young and beloved boys.

Very happily the next month glided away; a new life seemed opened to Eric in the world of rich affections which had unfolded itself before him. His parents—above all, his mother—were everything that he had longed for; and Vernon more than fulfilled to his loving heart the ideal of his childish fancy. He was never tired of playing with and patronising his little brother, and their rambles by stream and hill made those days appear the happiest he had ever spent. Every evening (for having lived all his life at home, he had not yet laid aside the habits of early childhood) he said his prayers by his mother's knee; and at the end of one long summer's day, when prayers were finished, and full of life and happiness he lay down to sleep, 'Oh, mother,' he said, 'I am so happy—I like to say my prayers when you are here.'

'Yes, my boy, and God loves to hear them.'

'Aren't there some who never say prayers, mother?'

'Very many, love, I fear.'

'How unhappy they must be! *I* shall *always* love to say my prayers.'

'Ah, Eric, God grant that you may.'

And the fond mother hoped he always would. But these words often came back to Eric's mind in later and less happy days—days when that gentle hand could no longer rest lovingly on his head—when those mild blue eyes were dim with tears, and the poor boy, changed in heart and life, often flung himself down with an unreproaching conscience to prayerless sleep.

It had been settled that in another week Eric was to go to school in the Isle of Roslyn. Mr. Williams had hired a small house in the town of Ellan, and intended to stay there for his year of furlough, at the end of which period Vernon was to be left at Fairholm, and Eric in the house of the headmaster of the school. Eric enjoyed the prospect of all things, and he hardly fancied that Paradise itself could be happier than a life at the seaside with his father and mother and Vernon, combined with the commencement of schoolboy dignity. When the time for the voyage came, his first glimpse of the sea, and the sensation of sailing over it with only a few planks between him and the deep waters, struck him silent with admiring wonder. It was a cloudless day; the line of blue sky melted into the line of blue wave, and the air was filled with sunlight. At evening they landed, and the coach took them to Ellan. On the way Eric saw for the first time the strength of the hills, so that when they reached the town and took possession of their cottage, he was dumb with the inrush of new and marvellous impressions.

Next morning he was awake early, and jumping out of bed, so as not to disturb the sleeping Vernon, he drew up the window-blind, and gently opened the window. A very beautiful scene burst on him, one destined to be long mingled with all his most vivid reminiscences. It had been too dark on their arrival the evening before to get any definite impression of their residence, so that this first glimpse of it filled him with delighted surprise. Not twenty yards below the garden, in front of the house, lay Ellan Bay, at that moment rippling with golden laughter in the fresh breeze of sunrise. On either side of the bay was a bold headland, the one stretching out in a series of broken crags, the other terminating in a huge mass of rock, called from its shape The Stack. To the right lay the town, with its gray old castle, and the mountain stream running through it into the sea; to the left, high above the beach, rose the crumbling fragment of a picturesque fort, behind which towered the lofty buildings of Roslyn School. Eric learnt the whole landscape by heart, and thought himself a most happy boy to come to such a place. He fancied that he should never be tired of looking at the sea, and could not take his eyes off the great buoy that rolled about in the centre of the bay, and flashed in the sunlight at every move. He turned round full of hope and spirits, and, after watching for a few moments the beautiful face of his sleeping brother, awoke him with boisterous mirth.

'Now, Verny,' he cried, as the little boy sprang eagerly out of bed, 'don't look till I tell you;' and putting his hands over Vernon's eyes, he led him to the window. Then he threw up the sash, and embodied all his sensations in the one word—

'There!'

To which apostrophe Vernon, after a long gaze, could make no other answer than, 'Oh, Eric! oh, I say!'

That day Eric was to have his first interview with Dr. Rowlands. The school had already re-opened, and one of the boys passed by the window while they were breakfasting. He looked very happy and engaging, and was humming a tune as he strolled along. Eric started up and gazed after him with the most intense curiosity. At that moment the

unconscious schoolboy was to him the most interesting person in the whole world, and he couldn't realise the fact that, before the day was over, he would be a Roslyn boy himself. He very much wondered what sort of a fellow the boy was, and whether he should ever recognise him again, and make his acquaintance. Yes, Eric, the thread of that boy's destiny is twined for many a day with yours; his name is Montagu, as you will know very soon.

At nine o'clock Mr. Williams started towards the school with his son. The walk led them by the seaside, over the sands, and past the ruin, at the foot of which the waves broke at high tide. At any other time Eric would have been overflowing with life and wonder at the murmur of the ripples, the sight of the ships in the bay or on the horizon, and the numberless little shells, with their bright colours and sculptured shapes, which lay about the beach. But now his mind was too full of a single anxiety; and when, after crossing a green playground, they stood by the headmaster's door, his heart fluttered, and it required all his energy to keep down the nervous trembling which shook him.

Mr. Williams gave his card, and they were shown into Dr. Rowlands's study. He was a kind-looking gentlemanly man, and when he turned to address Eric, after a few minutes' conversation with his father, the boy felt instantly reassured by the pleasant sincerity and frank courtesy of his manner. A short examination showed that Eric's attainments were very slight as yet, and he was to be put in the lowest form of all, under the superintendence of the Rev. Henry Gordon. Dr. Rowlands wrote a short note in pencil, and giving it to Eric, directed the servant to show him to Mr. Gordon's schoolroom.

The bell had just done ringing when they had started for the school, so that Eric knew that all the boys would be by this time assembled at their work, and that he should have to go alone into the middle of them. As he walked after the servant through the long corridors and up the broad stairs, he longed to make friends with him, so as, if possible, to feel less lonely. But he had only time to get out, 'I say, what sort of a fellow is Mr. Gordon?'

'Terrible strict, sir, I hear," said the man, touching his cap with a comic expression, which didn't at all tend to enliven the future pupil. 'That's the door,' he continued, 'and you'll have to give him the Doctor's note;' and, pointing to a door at the end of the passage, he walked off.

Eric stopped irresolutely. The man had disappeared, and he was by himself in the great silent building. Afraid of the sound of his own footsteps, he ran along the passage, and knocked timidly. He heard a low, a very low murmur in the room, but there was no answer. He knocked again a little louder; still no notice: then, overdoing it in his fright, he gave a very loud tap indeed.

'Come in!' said a voice, which to the new boy sounded awful; but he opened the door, and entered. As he came in every head was quickly raised, he heard a whisper of 'New fellow,' and the crimson flooded his face, as he felt himself the cynosure of some forty intensely-inquisitive pairs of eyes.

He found himself in a high airy room, with three large windows opening towards the sea. At one end was the master's throne, and facing it, all down the room, were desks and benches, along which the boys were sitting at work. Every one knows how very confusing it is to enter a strange room full of strange people, and especially when you enter it from a darker passage. Eric felt dazzled, and not seeing the regular route to the master's desk, went towards it between two of the benches. As these were at no great distance from each other, he stumbled against several legs on his way, and felt pretty sure that they were put out on purpose to trip him, especially by one boy, who pretended to be much hurt, drew up his leg, and began rubbing it, ejaculating *sotto voce,* 'Awkward little fool.'

In this very clumsy way he had at last reached the desk, and presented his missive. The master's eye was on him, but all Eric had time to observe was, that he looked rather stern, and had in his hand a book which he seemed to be studying with the deepest interest. He glanced first at the note, and then looked full at the boy, as though determined to read his whole character by a single perusal of his face.

'Williams, I suppose?'

'Yes, sir,' said Eric, very low, still painfully conscious that all the boys were looking at him, as well as the master.

'Very well, Williams, you are placed in the lowest form—the fourth. I hope you will work well. At present they are learning their Cæsar. Go and sit next to that boy,' pointing towards the lower end of the room; 'he will show you the lesson, and let you look over his book. Barker, let Williams look over you!'

Eric went and sat down at the end of a bench by the boy indicated. He was a rough-looking fellow with a shock head of black hair, and a very dogged look. Eric secretly thought that he wasn't a very nice-looking specimen of Roslyn School. However, he sate by him, and glanced at the Cæsar which the boy shoved about a quarter of an inch in his direction. But Barker didn't seem inclined to make any futher advances, and presently Eric asked in a whisper—

'What's the lesson?'

The boy glanced at him, but took no further notice.

Eric repeated, 'I say, what's the lesson?'

Instead of answering, Barker stared at him, and grunted—

'What's your name?'

'Eric—I mean Williams.'

'Then why don't you say what you mean?'

Eric moved his foot impatiently at this ungracious reception; but as he seemed to have no redress, he pulled the Cæsar nearer towards him.

'Drop that; 'tisn't yours.'

Mr. Gordon heard a whisper, and glanced that way. 'Silence!' he said, and Barker pretended to be deep in his work, while Eric, resigning himself to his fate, looked about him.

He had plenty to occupy his attention in the faces round him. He furtively examined Mr. Gordon, as he bent over his high desk, writing, but couldn't make out the physiognomy. There had been something reserved and imperious in the master's manner, yet he thought he should not dislike him on the whole. With the countenances of his future schoolfellows he was not altogether pleased, but there were one or two which thoroughly attracted him. One boy, whose side face was turned towards him as he sat on the bench in front, took his fancy particularly, so, tired of doing nothing, he plucked up courage, and leaning forward, whispered, 'Do lend me your Cæsar for a few minutes.' The boy at once handed it to him with a pleasant smile, and as the lesson was marked, Eric had time to hurry over a few sentences, when Mr. Gordon's sonorous voice exclaimed—

'Fourth form, come up!'

Some twenty of the boys went up, and stood in a large semicircle round the desk. Eric of course was placed last, and the lesson commenced.

'Russell, begin,' said the master; and immediately the boy who had handed Eric his Cæsar began reading a few sentences, and construed them very creditably, only losing a place or two. He had a frank open face, bright intelligent fearless eyes, and a very taking voice and manner. Eric listened admiringly, and felt sure he should like him.

Barker was put on next. He bungled through the Latin in a grating, irresolute sort of way, with several false quantities, for each of which the next boy took him up. Then he began to construe;—a frightful confusion of nominatives without verbs, accusatives translated as ablatives, and adverbs turned into prepositions, ensued, and after a hopeless flounder, during which Mr. Gordon left him entirely to himself, Barker came to a full stop; his catastrophe was so ludicrous, that Eric could not help joining in the general titter. Barker scowled.

'As usual, Barker,' said the master, with a curl of the lip. 'Hold out your hand!'

Barker did so, looking sullen defiance, and the cane immediately descended on his open palm. Six similar cuts followed, during which the form looked on, not without terror; and Barker, squeezing his hands tight together, went back to his seat.

'Williams, translate the piece in which Barker has just failed!'

Eric did as he was bid, and got through it pretty well. He had now quite recovered his ordinary bearing, and spoke out clearly and without nervousness. He afterwards won several places by answering questions, and at the end of the lesson was marked about half-way up the form. The boys' numbers were then taken down in the weekly register, and they went back to their seats.

On his desk Eric found a torn bit of paper, on which was clumsily scrawled, 'I'll teach you to grin when I'm turned, you young brute.'

The paper seemed to fascinate his eyes. He stared at it fixedly, and augured ominously of Barker's intentions, since that worthy obviously alluded to his having smiled in form, and chose to interpret it as an intentional provocation. He felt that he was in for it, and that Barker meant to pick a quarrel with him. This puzzled and annoyed him, and he felt very sad to have found an enemy already.

While he was looking at the paper the great school-clock struck twelve; and the captain of the form getting up, threw open the folding doors of the schoolroom.

'You may go,' said Mr. Gordon; and leaving his seat, disappeared by a door at the farther end of the room.

Instantly there was a rush for caps, and the boys poured out in a confused and noisy stream, while at the same moment the other schoolrooms disgorged their inmates. Eric naturally went out among the last; but just as he was going to take his cap, Barker seized it, and flung it with a whoop to the end of the passage, where it was trampled on by a number of the boys as they ran out.

Eric, gulping down his fury with a great effort, turned to his opponent, and said coolly, 'Is that what you always do to new fellows?'

'Yes, you bumptious young owl, it is, and that too;' and a tolerably smart slap on the face followed—leaving a red mark on a cheek already aflame with anger and indignation,— 'should you like a little more?'

He was hurt and offended, but was too proud to cry. 'What's that for?' he said, with flashing eyes.

'For your conceit in laughing at me when I was caned.'

Eric stamped. 'I did nothing of the kind, and you know it as well as I do.'

'What? I'm a liar, am I? Oh, we shall take this kind of thing out of you, you young cub; take that!' and a heavier blow followed.

'You brutal cowardly bully,' shouted Eric; and in another moment he would have sprung upon him. It was lucky for him that he did not, for Barker was three years older than he, and very powerful. Such an attack would have been most unfortunate for him in every way. But at this instant some boys hearing the quarrel ran up, and Russell among them.

'Hallo, Barker,' said one; 'what's up?'

'Why, I'm teaching this new fry to be less bumptious, that's all.'

'Shame!' said Russell, as he saw the mark on Eric's cheek; 'what a fellow you are, Barker. Why couldn't you let him alone for the first day at any rate?'

'What's that to you? I'll kick you too if you say much.'

'Cavé! cavé!' whispered half a dozen voices, and instantly the knot of boys dispersed in every direction, as Mr. Gordon was seen approaching. He had caught a glimpse of the scene without understanding it, and seeing the new boy's red and angry face, he only said, as he passed by, 'What, Williams! fighting already? Take care.'

This was the cruellest cut of all. 'So,' thought Eric, 'a nice beginning! it seems both boys and masters are against me;' and very disconsolately he walked to pick up his cap.

The boys were all dispersed on the playground at different games, and as he went home he was stopped perpetually, and had to answer the usual questions, 'What's your name? Are you a boarder or a day scholar? What form are you in?' Eric expected all this, and it therefore did not annoy him. Under any other circumstances, he would have answered cheerfully and frankly enough; but now he felt miserable at his morning's rencontre, and his answers were short and sheepish, his only desire being to get away as soon as possible. It was an additional vexation to feel sure that his manner did not make a favourable impression.

Before he had got out of the playground, Russell ran up to him. 'I'm afraid you won't like this, or think much of us, Williams,' he said. 'But never mind. It'll only last a day or two, and the fellows are not so bad as they seem; except that Barker. I'm sorry you've come across him, but it can't be helped.'

It was the first kind word he had had since the morning, and after his troubles kindness melted him. He felt half inclined to cry, and for a few moments could say nothing in reply to Russell's soothing words. But the boy's friendliness went far to comfort him, and at last, shaking hands with him, he said—

'Do let me speak to you sometimes, while I am a new boy, Russell.'

'Oh yes,' said Russell, laughing, 'as much as ever you like. And as Barker hates me pretty much as he seems inclined to hate you, we are in the same box. Good-bye.'

So Eric left the field, and wandered home, like Calchas in the Iliad, 'sorrowful by the side of the sounding sea.' Already the purple mantle had fallen from his ideal of schoolboy life. He got home later than they expected, and found his parents waiting for him. It was rather disappointing to them to see his face so melancholy, when they expected him to be full of animation and pleasure. Mrs. Williams drew her own conclusions from the red mark on his cheek, as well as the traces of tears welling to his eyes; but, like a wise mother, she asked nothing, and left the boy to tell his own story,—which in time he did, omitting all the painful part, speaking enthusiastically of Russell, and only admitting that he had been a little teased.

CHAPTER THE THIRD

BULLYING

Give to the morn of life its natural blessedness.
WORDSWORTH

W HY IS IT THAT new boys are almost invariably ill-treated? I have often fancied that there must be in boyhood a pseudo-instinctive cruelty, a sort of 'wild trick of the ancestral savage,' which no amount of civilisation can entirely repress. Certain it is, that to most boys the first term is a trying ordeal. They are being tested and weighed. Their place in the general estimation is not yet fixed, and the slightest circumstances are seized upon to settle the category under which the boy is to be classed. A few apparently trivial accidents of his first few weeks at school often decide his position in the general regard for the remainder of his boyhood. And yet these are *not* accidents; they are the slight indications which give an unerring proof of the general tendencies of his character and training. Hence much of the apparent cruelty with which new boys are treated is not exactly intentional. At first, of course, as they can have no friends worth speaking of, there are always plenty of coarse and brutal minds that take a pleasure in their torment, particularly if they at once recognise any innate superiority to themselves. Of this class was Barker. He hated Eric at first sight, simply because his feeble mind could only realise one idea about him, and that was the new boy's striking contrast with his own imperfections. Hence he left no means untried to vent on Eric his low and mean jealousy. He showed undisguised pleasure when he fell in form, and signs of disgust when he rose; he fomented every little source of disapproval or quarrelling which happened to arise against him; he never looked at him without a frown or a sneer; he waited for him to kick and annoy him as he came out of, or went in to, the schoolroom. In fact, he did his very best to make the boy's life miserable, and the occupation of hating him seemed in some measure to fill up the vacuity of an ill-conditioned and degraded mind.

Hatred is a most mysterious and painful phenomenon to the unhappy person who is the object of it, and more especially if he have incurred it by no one assignable reason. Why it happens that no heart can be so generous, no life so self-denying, no intentions so honourable and pure, as to shield a man from the enmity of his fellows, must remain a dark question for ever. But certain it is, that to bear the undeserved malignity of the evil-minded, to hear unmoved the sneers of the proud and the calumnies of the base, is one of the hardest lessons in life. And to Eric this opposition was peculiarly painful; he was utterly unprepared for it. In his bright joyous life at Fairholm, in the little he saw of the boys at the Latin school, he had met with nothing but kindness and caresses, and the generous nobleness of his character had seemed to claim them as a natural element. 'And now, why,' he asked impatiently, 'should this bulldog sort of fellow have set his whole aim to annoy, vex, and hurt me?' Incapable himself of so mean a spirit of jealousy at superior excellence, he could not make it out; but such was the fact, and the very mysteriousness of it made it more intolerable to bear.

But it must be admitted that he made matters worse by his own bursts of passion. His was not the temper to turn the other cheek; but, brave and spirited as he was, he felt how utterly hopeless would be any attempt on his part to repel force by force. He would have tried some conciliation, but it was really impossible with such a boy as his enemy. Barker never gave him even so much as an indifferent look, much less a civil word. Eric loathed him, and the only good and happy part of the matter to his own mind was, that conscientiously his only desire was to get rid of him, and be left alone, while he never cherished a particle of revenge.

While every day Eric was getting on better in form, and winning himself a very good position with the other boys, who liked his frankness, his mirth, his spirit, and cleverness, he felt this feud with Barker like a dark background to all his enjoyment. He even had to manœuvre daily how to escape him, and violent scenes were of constant occurrence between them. Eric could not, and would not, brook his bullying with silence. His resentment was loud and stinging, and, Ishamaelite as Barker was, even *his* phlegmatic temperament took fire when Eric shouted his fierce and uncompromising retorts in the hearing of the others.

Meanwhile Eric was on the best of terms with the rest of the form, and such of the other boys as he knew, although, at first, his position as a home-boarder prevented his knowing many. Besides Russell, there were three whom he liked best, and respected most—Duncan, Montagu, and Owen. They were very different boys, but all of them had qualities which well deserved his esteem. Duncan was the most boyish of boys, intensely full of fun, good nature, and vigour; with fair abilities, he never got on well, because he could not be still for two minutes; and even if, in some fit of sudden ambition, he got up high in the form, he was sure to be put to the bottom again before the day was over, for trifling or talking. But out of school he was the soul of every game; whatever *he* took up was sure to be done pleasantly, and no party of amusement was ever planned without endeavouring to secure him as one of the number.

Montagu's chief merit was, that he was such a thorough little gentleman; 'such a jolly little fellow,' every one said of him. Without being clever or athletic, he managed to do very fairly both at work and at the games, and while he was too exclusive to make many *intimate* friends, everybody liked walking about or talking with him. Even Barker, blackguard as he was, seemed to be a little uneasy when confronted with Montagu's naturally noble and chivalrous bearing. In nearly all respects his influence was thoroughly good, and few boys were more generally popular.

Owen, again, was a very different boy. His merit was a ceaseless diligence, in which it was doubtful whether ambition or conscientiousness had the greatest share. Reserved and thoughtful, unfitted for or indifferent to most games, he was anything but a favourite with the rest, and Eric rather respected than liked him. When he first came he had been one of the most natural butts for Barker's craving ill-nature, and for a time he had been tremendously bullied. But gradually his mental superiority asserted itself. He took everything without tears and without passion, and this diminished the pleasure of annoying him. One day when Barker had given him an unprovoked kick, he quietly said—

'Barker, next time you do that I'll tell Mr. Gordon.'

'Sneak! do it if you dare.' And he kicked him again; but the moment after he was sorry for it, for there was a dark look in Owen's eyes, as he turned instantly into the door of the master's room, and laid a formal complaint against Barker for bullying.

Mr. Gordon didn't like 'telling,' and he said so to Owen, without reserve. An ordinary boy would have broken into a flood of explanations and palliations, but Owen simply bowed, and said nothing. 'He stood there for justice,' and he had counted the cost. Strong-minded and clear-headed, he calculated correctly that the momentary dislike of his schoolfellows, with whom he well knew that he never could be popular, would be less unbearable than Barker's villainous insults. The consequence was, that Mr. Gordon caned Barker soundly, although, with some injustice, he made no attempt to conceal that he did it unwillingly.

Of course the fellows were very indignant with Owen for sneaking, as they called it, and for a week or two he had the keen mortification of seeing 'Owen is a sneak' written up all about the walls. But he was too proud or too cold to make any defence till called upon, and bore it in silence. Barker threatened eternal vengeance, and the very day after had seized Owen with the avowed intention of 'half murdering him.' But before he could once strike him, Owen said in the most chill tone, 'Barker, if you touch me, I shall go straight to Dr. Rowlands.' The bully well knew that Owen never broke his word, but he could not govern his rage, and first giving Owen a violent shake, he proceeded to thrash him without limit or remorse.

Pale but unmoved, Owen got away, and walked straight to Dr. Rowlands's door. The thing was unheard of, and the boys were amazed at his temerity, for the Doctor was to all their imaginations a regular *Deus ex machinâ*. That afternoon, again, Barker was publicly caned, with the threat that the next offence would be followed by instant and public expulsion. This punishment he particularly dreaded, because he was intended for the army, and he well knew that it might ruin his prospects. The consequence was, that Owen never suffered from him again, although he daily received a shower of oaths and curses, which he passed over with silent contempt.

Now, I do not recommend any boy to imitate Owen in this matter. It is a far better and braver thing to bear bullying with such a mixture of spirit and good humour, as in time to disarm it. But Owen was a peculiar boy, and remember he had *no* redress. He bore for a time, until he felt that he *must* have the justice and defence, without which it would have been impossible for him to continue at Roslyn School.

But why, you ask, didn't he tell the monitors? Unfortunately at Roslyn the monitorial system was not established. Although it was a school of 250 boys, the sixth form, with all their privileges, had no prerogative of authority. They hadn't the least right to interfere, because no such power had been delegated to them, and therefore they felt themselves merely on a par with the rest, except for such eminence as their intellectual superiority gave them. The consequence was, that any interference from them would have been of a simply individual nature, and was exerted very rarely. It would have done Owen no more good to tell a sixth-form boy than to tell any other boy; and as he was not a favourite, he was not likely to find any champion to fight his battles or maintain his just rights.

All this happened before Eric's time, and he heard it from his best friend Russell. His heart clave to that boy. They became friends at once by a kind of electric sympathy; the first glance of each at the other's face prepared the friendship, and every day of acquaintance more firmly cemented it. Eric could not have had a better friend; not so clever as himself, not so diligent as Owen, not so athletic as Duncan, or so fascinating as Montagu, Russell combined the best qualities of them all. And, above all, he acted invariably from the highest principle; he presented that noblest of all noble spectacles—one so rare that many think it impossible—the spectacle of an honourable, pure-hearted, happy boy, who, as his early years speed by, is ever growing in wisdom and stature, and favour with God and man.

'Did that brute Barker ever bully you as he bullies me?' said Eric one day, as he walked on the seashore with his friend.

'Yes,' said Russell; 'I slept in his dormitory when I first came, and he has often made me so wretched that I have flung myself on my knees at night in pretence of prayer, but really to get a little quiet time to cry like a child.'

'And when was it he left off at last?'

'Why, you know, Upton in the fifth is my cousin, and very fond of me; he heard of it, though I didn't say anything about it, and told Barker that if ever he caught him at it, he would thrash him within an inch of his life; and that frightened him for one thing. Besides, Duncan, Montagu, and other friends of mine, began to cut him in consequence, so he thought it best to leave off.'

'How is it, Russell, that fellows stand by and let him do it?'

'You see, Williams,' said Russell, 'Barker is an enormously strong fellow, and that makes the younger chaps, whom he fags, look up to him as a great hero. And there isn't one in our part of the school who can thrash him. Besides, people never do interfere, you know—at least not often. I remember once seeing a street-row in London, at which twenty people stood by, and let a drunken beast of a husband strike his wife without ever stirring to defend her.'

'Well,' sighed Eric, 'I hope my day of deliverance will come soon, for I can't stand it much longer, and "tell" I won't, whatever Owen may do.'

Eric's deliverance came very soon. It was afternoon; the boys were playing at different games in the green playground, and he was waiting for his turn at rounders. At this moment Barker lounged up, and calmly snatching off Eric's cap, shied it over Dr. Rowlands's garden-wall. 'There, go and fetch that.'

'You blackguard,' said Eric, standing irresolutely for a few minutes; and then with tears in his eyes began to climb the wall. It was not very high, but boys were peremptorily forbidden to get over it under any circumstances, and Eric broke the rule not without trepidation. However, he dropped down on one of Mrs. Rowlands's flower-beds, got his cap in a hurry, and clambered back undiscovered.

He thought this would have satisfied his tormentor for one day; but Barker was in a mischievous mood, so he again came up to Eric, and calling out, 'Who'll have a game at football?' again snatched the cap, and gave it a kick; Eric tried to recover it, but every time he came up Barker gave it a fresh kick, and finally kicked it into a puddle.

Eric stood still, trembling with rage, while his eyes lightened scorn and indignation. 'You hulking, stupid, cowardly bully'—here Barker seized him, and every word brought a tremendous blow on the head; but blind with passion Eric went on—'you despicable bully, I won't touch that cap again; you shall pick it up yourself. Duncan, Russell, here! do help me against this intolerable brute.'

Several boys ran up, but they were all weaker than Barker, who besides was now in a towering fury, and kicked Eric unmercifully.

'Leave him alone,' shouted Duncan, seizing Barker's arm; 'what a confounded bully you are—always plaguing some one.'

'I shall do as I like; mind your own business,' growled Barker, roughly shaking himself free from Duncan's hand.

'Barker, I'll never speak to you again from this day,' said Montagu, turning on his heel, with a look of withering contempt.

'What do I care? puppy, you want taking down too,' was the reply, and some more kicks at Eric followed.

'Barker, I won't stand this any longer,' said Russell, 'so look out;' and grasping Barker by the collar, he dealt him a swinging blow on the face.

The bully stood in amazement, and dropped Eric, who fell on the turf nearly fainting, and bleeding at the nose. But now Russell's turn came, and in a moment Barker, who was twice his weight, had tripped him up,—when he found himself collared in an iron grasp.

There had been an unobserved spectator of the whole scene, in the person of Mr. Williams himself, and it was his strong hand that now gripped Barker's shoulder. He was greatly respected by the boys, who all knew his tall handsome figure by sight, and he frequently stood a quiet and pleased observer of their games. The boys in the playground came crowding round, and Barker in vain struggled to escape. Mr. Williams held him firmly, and said in a calm voice, 'I have just seen you treat one of your schoolfellows with the grossest violence. It makes me blush for you, Roslyn boys,' he continued, turning to the group that surrounded him, 'that you can even for a moment stand by unmoved, and see such things done. You know that you despise any one who tells a master, yet you allow this bullying to go on, and that, too, without any provocation. Now, mark; it makes no difference that the boy who has been hurt is my own son; I would have punished this scoundrel whoever it had been, and I shall punish him now.' With these words, he lifted the riding-whip which he happened to be carrying, and gave Barker by far the severest castigation he had ever undergone; the boys declared that Dr.

Rowlands's 'swishings' were nothing to it. Mr. Williams saw that the offender was a tough subject, and determined that he should not soon forget the punishment he then received. He had never heard from Eric how this boy had been treating him, but he had heard it from Russell, and now he had seen one of the worst specimens of it with his own eyes. He therefore belaboured him till his sullen obstinacy gave way to a roar for mercy, and promises never so to offend again.

At this crisis he flung the boy from him with a 'phew' of disgust, and said, 'I give nothing for your word; but if ever you do bully in this way again, and I see or hear of it, your present punishment shall be a trifle to what I shall then administer. At present, thank me for not informing your master.' So saying, he made Barker pick up the cap, and, turning away, walked home with Eric leaning on his arm.

Barker, too, carried himself off with the best grace he could; but it certainly didn't mend matters when he heard numbers of fellows, even little boys, say openly, 'I'm so glad; serves you right.'

From that day Eric was never troubled with personal violence from Barker or any other boy. But rancour smouldered deep in the mind of the baffled tyrant, and, as we shall see hereafter, there are subtler means of making an enemy wretched than striking or kicking him.

CHAPTER THE FOURTH

CRIBBING

Et nos ergo manum ferulæ subduximus.
JUV. i, 15

I<small>T MUST NOT</small> be thought that Eric's year as a home-boarder was made up of dark experiences. Roslyn had a very bright as well as a dark side, and Eric enjoyed it 'to the finger-tips.' School life, like all other life, is an April day of shower and sunshine. Its joys may be more childish, its sorrows more trifling, than those of after years;—but they are more keenly felt.

And yet, although we know it to be a mere delusion, we all idealise and idolise our childhood. The memory of it makes pleasant purple in the distance, and as we look back on the sunlight of its blue far-off hills, we forget how steep we sometimes found them.

Upon Barker's discomfiture, which took place some three weeks after his arrival, Eric liked the school more and more, and got liked by it more and more. This might have been easily foreseen, for he was the type of a thoroughly boyish nature in its more genial and honourable characteristics, and his round of acquaintances daily increased. Among others, a few of the sixth, who were also day-scholars, began to notice and walk home with him. He looked on them as great heroes, and their condescension much increased his dignity both in his own estimation and that of his equals.

Now, too, he began to ask some of his most intimate acquaintances to spend an evening with him sometimes at home. This was a pleasure much coveted, for no boy ever saw Mrs. Williams without loving her, and they felt themselves humanised by the friendly interest of a lady who reminded every boy of his own mother. Vernon, too, now a lively and active child of nine, was a great pet among them, so that every one liked Eric who 'knew him at home.' A boy generally shows his best side at home; the softening shadows of a mother's tender influence play over him, and tone down the roughnesses of boyish character. Duncan, Montagu, and Owen were special favourites in the home circle, and Mrs. Williams felt truly glad that her son had singled out friends who seemed, on the whole, so desirable. But Montagu and Russell were the most frequent visitors, and the latter became almost like one of the family; he won so much on all their hearts that Mrs. Williams was not surprised when Eric confided to her one day that he loved Russell almost as well as he loved Vernon.

As Christmas approached, the boys began to take a lively interest in the half-year's prizes, and Eric was particularly eager about them. He had improved wonderfully, and as both his father and mother prevented him from being idle, even had he been so inclined, he had soon shown that he was one of the best in the form. Two prizes were given half-yearly to each remove; one for 'marks,' indicating the boy who had generally been highest throughout the half-year, and the other for the best proofs of proficiency in a special examination. It was commonly thought in the form that Owen would get the first of these prizes, and Eric the other; and towards the approach of the examination, he threw his whole energy into the desire to win. The desire was not selfish. Some ambition was of course natural; but he longed for the prize chiefly for the delight which he knew his success would cause at Fairholm, and still more to his own family.

During the last week an untoward circumstance happened, which, while it increased his popularity, diminished a good deal (as he thought) his chance of success. The fourth form were learning a Homer lesson, and Barker, totally unable to do it by his own resources, was trying to borrow a crib. Eric, much to their mutual disgust, still sat next to him in school, and would have helped him if he had chosen to ask; but he never did choose, nor did Eric care to volunteer. The consequence was, that unless he could borrow a crib, he was invariably turned, and he was now particularly anxious to get one, because the time was nearly up.

There was a certain idle, good-natured boy, named Llewellyn, who had 'cribs' to every book they did, and who, with a pernicious *bonhommie*, lent them promiscuously to the rest, all of whom were only too glad to avail themselves of the help, except the few at the top of the form, who found it a slovenly way of learning the lesson, which was sure to get them into worse difficulties than an honest attempt to master the meaning for themselves. Llewellyn sat at the farther end of the form in front, so Barker scribbled in the fly-leaf of his book, 'Please send us your Homer crib,' and got the book passed on to Llewellyn, who immediately shoved his crib in Barker's direction. The only danger of the transaction being noticed was when the book was being handed from one bench to another, and as Eric unluckily had an end seat, he had got into trouble more than once.

On this occasion, just as Graham, the last boy on the form in front, handed Eric the crib, Mr. Gordon happened to look up, and Eric, very naturally anxious to screen another from trouble, popped the book under his own Homer.

'Williams, what are you doing?'

'Nothing, sir,' said Eric, looking up innocently.

'Bring me that book under your Homer.'

Eric blushed, hesitated—but at last, amid a dead silence, took up the book. Mr. Gordon looked at it for a minute, let it fall on the ground, and then, with an unnecessary affectation of disgust, took it up with the tongs, and dropped it into the grate. There was a titter round the room.

'Silence!' thundered the master; 'this is no matter for laughing. So, sir, *this* is the way you get up to the top of the form?'

'I wasn't using it, sir,' said Eric.

'Not using it! Why, I saw you put it, open, under your Homer.'

'It isn't mine, sir.'

'Then whose is it?' Mr. Gordon, motioning to Eric to pick up the book, looked at the fly-leaf, but of course no name was there; in those days it was dangerous to write one's name in a translation.

Eric was silent.

'Under the circumstances, Williams, I must punish you,' said Mr. Gordon. 'Of course I am *bound* to believe you, but the circumstances are very suspicious. You had no business with such a book at all. Hold out your hand.'

As yet Eric had never been caned. It would have been easy for him in this case to clear himself without mentioning names, but (very rightly) he thought it unmanly to clamour about being punished, and he felt nettled at Mr. Gordon's merely official belief of his word. He knew that he had his faults, but certainly want of honour was not among

them. Indeed, there were only three boys out of the twenty in the form who did not resort to modes of unfairness far worse than the use of cribs, and those three were— Russell, Owen, and himself; even Duncan, even Montagu, inured to it by custom, were not ashamed to read their lesson off a concealed book, or copy a date from a furtive piece of paper. They would have been ashamed of it before they came to Roslyn School, but the commonness of the habit had now made them blind or indifferent to its meanness. It was peculiarly bad in the fourth form, because the master treated them with implicit confidence, and being scrupulously honourable himself, was unsuspicious of others. He was therefore extremely indignant at this apparent discovery of an attempt to overreach him in a boy so promising and so much of a favourite as Eric Williams.

'Hold out your hand,' he repeated.

Eric did so, and the cane tingled sharply across his palm. He could bear the pain well enough, but he was keenly alive to the disgrace; he, a boy at the head of his form, to be caned in this way by a man who didn't understand him, and unjustly too! He mustered up an indifferent air, closed his lips tight, and determined to give no further signs. The defiance of his look made Mr. Gordon angry, and he inflicted in succession five hard cuts on either hand, each one of which was more excruciating than the last.

'Now, go to your seat.'

Eric did go to his seat, with all his bad passions roused, and he walked in a jaunty and defiant kind of way, that made the master really grieve at the disgrace into which he had fallen. But he instantly became a hero with the form, who unanimously called him a great brick for not telling, and admired him immensely for bearing up without crying under so severe a punishment. The punishment *was* most severe, and for some weeks after there were dark weals visible across Eric's palm, which rendered the use of his hands painful.

'Poor Williams,' said Duncan, as they went out of school, 'how very plucky of you not to cry.'

'Vengeance deep brooding o'er the *cane*,
Had locked the source of softer woe:
And burning pride and high disdain
Forbade the gentler tear to flow,'

said Eric, with a smile.

But he only bore up till he got home, and there, while he was telling his father the occurrence, he burst into a storm of passionate tears, mingled with the fiercest invectives against Mr. Gordon for his injustice.

'Never mind, Eric,' said his father; 'only take care that you never get a punishment *justly*, and I shall always be as proud of you as I am now. And don't cherish this resentment, my boy; it will only do you harm. Try to forgive and forget.'

'But, father, Mr. Gordon is so hasty. I have indeed been rather a favourite of his, yet now he shows that he has no confidence in me. It is a great shame that he shouldn't believe my word. I don't mind the pain; but I shan't like him any more, and I'm sure now I shan't get the examination prize.'

'You don't mean, Eric, that he will be influenced by partiality in the matter?'

'No, father, not exactly; at least I dare say he won't *intend* to be. But it is unlucky to be on bad terms with a master, and I know I shan't work so well.'

On the whole the boy was right in thinking this incident a misfortune. Although he had nothing particular for which to blame himself, yet the affair had increased his pride, while it lowered his self-respect; and he had an indistinct consciousness that the popularity in his form would do him as much harm as the change of feeling in his master. He grew careless and dispirited, nor was it till in the very heat of the final competition that he felt his energies fully revived.

Half the form were as eager about the examination as the other half were indifferent; but none were more eager than Eric. He was much hindered by Barker's unceasing attempt to copy his papers surreptitiously; and very much disgusted at the shameless way in which many of the boys 'cribbed' from books, and from each other, or used torn leaves concealed in their sleeves, or dates written on their wristbands and on their nails. He saw how easily much of this might have been prevented; but Mr. Gordon was fresh at his work, and had not yet learned the practical lesson (which cost him many a qualm of sorrow and disgust), that to trust young boys to any great extent is really to increase their temptations. He *did* learn the lesson afterwards, and then almost entirely suppressed the practice, partly by increased vigilance, and partly by forbidding *any* book to be brought into the room during the time of examination. But meanwhile much evil had been done by the habitual abuse of his former confidence.

I shall not linger over the examination. At its close, the day before the breaking up, the list was posted on the door of the great schoolroom, and most boys made an impetuous rush to see the result. But Eric was too nervous to be present at the hour when this was usually done, and he had asked Russell to bring him the news.

He was walking up and down the garden, counting the number of steps he took, counting the number of shrubs along each path, and devising every sort of means to beguile the time, when he heard hasty steps, and Russell burst in at the back gate, breathless with haste and bright with excitement.

'Hurrah! old fellow!' he cried, seizing both Eric's hands; 'I never felt so good in my life;' and he shook his friend's arms up and down, laughing joyously.

'Well! tell me,' said Eric.

'First, $\left\{ \begin{array}{l} \text{Owen} \\ \text{Williams} \end{array} \right\}$ Æquales,' said he; 'you've got head remove, you see, in spite of your forebodings, as I always said you would; and I congratulate you with all my heart.'

'No?' said Eric, 'have I really?—you're not joking? Oh! hurrah!—I must rush in and tell them;' and he bounded off.

In a second he was back at Russell's side. 'What a selfish animal I am! Where are you placed, Russell?'

'Oh! magnificent; I'm third—far higher than I expected.'

'I'm so glad,' said Eric. 'Come in with me and tell them. I'm head remove, mother,' he shouted, springing into the parlour where his father and mother sat.

In the lively joy that this announcement excited, Russell stood by for the moment unheeded; and when Eric took him by the hand to tell them that he was third, he hung his head, and a tear was in his eye.

'Poor boy! I'm afraid you're disappointed,' said Mrs. Williams kindly, drawing him to her side.

'Oh, no, no! it's not *that*,' said Russell hastily, as he lifted his swimming eyes to her face.

'What's the matter, Russell?' asked Eric, surprised.

'Oh, nothing; don't ask me; I'm only foolish to-day;' and with a burst of sorrow he bent down, and hid his face. Mrs. Williams guessed the source of his anguish, and soothed him tenderly; nor was she surprised when, as soon as his sobs would let him speak, he kissed her hand, and whispered in a low tone, 'It is but a year since I became an orphan.'

'Dearest child,' she said, 'I know how to sympathise with you. But I am sure, my boy, that you have learnt to feel Who is the Father of the fatherless.'

Russell's eye brightened, but his only answer was a look of intelligence and gratitude, as he hastily dried his tears.

Gradually he grew calmer. They made him stay to dinner and spend the rest of the day there, and by the evening he had recovered all his usual sprightliness. Towards sunset he and Eric went for a stroll down the bay, and talked over the term and the examination.

They sat down on a green bank just beyond the beach, and watched the tide come in, while the sea-distance was crimson with the glory of evening. The beauty and the murmur filled them with a quiet happiness, not untinged with the melancholy thought of parting the next day.

At last Eric broke the silence. 'Russell, let me always call you Edwin, and call me Eric.'

'Very gladly, Eric. Your coming here has made me so happy.' And the two boys squeezed each other's hands, and looked into each other's faces, and silently promised that they would be loving friends for ever.

CHAPTER THE FIFTH

THE SECOND TERM

Take us the foxes, the little foxes that spoil our vines; for our vines have tender grapes.
Cant. ii. 15

THE SECOND TERM at school is generally the great test of the strength of a boy's principles and resolutions. During the first term the novelty, the loneliness, the dread of unknown punishments, the respect for authorities, the desire to measure himself with his companions—all tend to keep him right and diligent. But many of these incentives are removed after the first brush of novelty, and many a lad who has given good promise at first, turns out, after a short probation, idle or vicious, or indifferent.

But there was little comparative danger for Eric, so long as he continued to be a home-boarder, which was for another half-year. On the contrary, he was anxious to support in his new remove the prestige of having been head-boy; and as he still continued under Mr. Gordon, he really wished to turn over a new leaf in his conduct towards him, and recover, if possible, his lost esteem.

His popularity was a fatal snare. He enjoyed and was very proud of it, and was half inclined to be angry with Russell for not fully sharing his feelings; but Russell had a far larger experience of school life than his new friend, and dreaded with all his heart lest 'he should follow a multitude to do evil.'

The 'cribbing,' which had astonished and pained Eric at first, was more flagrant than even in the Upper Fourth, and assumed a chronic form. In all the repetition lessons one of the boys used to write out in a large hand the passage to be learnt by heart, and dexterously pin it to the front of Mr. Gordon's desk. There any boy who chose could read it off with little danger of detection, and, as before, the only boys who refused to avail themselves of this trickery were Eric, Russell, and Owen.

Eric did *not* yield to it; never once did he suffer his eyes to glance at the paper when his turn to repeat came round. But although this was the case, he never spoke against the practice to the other boys, even when he lost places by it. Nay more, he would laugh when any one told him how he had escaped 'skewing' (*i.e.* being turned) by reading it off; and he even went so far as to allow them to suppose that he wouldn't himself object to take advantage of the master's unsuspicious confidence.

'I say, Williams,' said Duncan, one morning as they strolled into the school-yard, 'do you know your Rep.?'

'No,' said Eric, 'not very well; I haven't given more than ten minutes to it.'

'Oh, well, never mind it now; come and have a game at racquets. Russell and Montagu have taken the court.'

'But I shall skew.'

'Oh no, you needn't, you know. I'll take care to pin it upon the desk near you.'

'Well, I don't much care. At any rate I'll chance it.' And off the boys ran to the racquet-court, Eric intending to occupy the last quarter of an hour before school-time in learning his lesson. Russell and he stood the other two, and they were very well matched. They had finished two splendid games, and each side had been victorious in turn, when Duncan, in the highest spirits, shouted, 'Now, Russell, for the conqueror.'

'Get some one else in my place,' said Russell; 'I don't know my Rep., and must cut and learn it.'

'Oh, bother the Rep.,' said Montagu, 'somebody's sure to write it out in school, and old Gordon'll never see.'

'You forget, Montagu, I don't deign to crib. It isn't fair.'

'Oh ay, I forgot. Well, after all, you're quite right; I only wish I was as good.'

'What a capital fellow he is,' continued Montagu, leaning on his racquet and looking after him, as Russell left the court. 'But I say, Williams, you're not going too, are you?'

'I think I must, I don't know half my lesson.'

'Oh no! don't go; there's Llewellyn; he'll take Russell's place, and we *must* have the conquering game.'

Again Eric yielded; and when the clock struck, he ran into school, hot, vexed with himself, and certain to break down, just as Russell strolled in, whispering, 'I've had lots of time to get up the Horace, and know it pat.'

Still he clung to the little thistledown of hope that he should have plenty of time to cram it before the form were called up. But another temptation waited him. No sooner was he seated than Graham whispered, 'Williams, it's your turn to write out the Horace; I did last time, you know.'

Poor Eric! He was reaping the fruits of his desire to keep up popularity, which had prevented him from expressing a manly disapproval of the general cheating. Everybody seemed to assume now that *he* at any rate didn't think much of it, and he had never claimed his real right up to that time of asserting his innocence. But this was a step farther than he had ever gone before. He drew back—

'My *turn*, what do you mean?'

'Why, you know as well as I do that we all write it out by turns.'

'Do you mean to say Owen or Russell ever wrote it out?'

'Of course not; you wouldn't expect the saints to be guilty of such a thing, would you?'

'I'd rather not, Graham,' he said, getting very red.

'Well, that *is* cowardly,' answered Graham angrily; 'then I suppose I must do it myself.'

'Here, I'll do it,' said Eric suddenly; 'shy us the paper.'

His conscience smote him bitterly. In his silly dread of giving offence, he was doing what he heartily despised, and he felt most uncomfortable.

'There,' he said, pushing the paper from him in a pet; 'I've written it, and I'll have nothing more to do with it.'

Just as he finished, they were called up, and Barker, taking the paper, succeeded in pinning it as usual on the front of the desk. Eric had never seen it done so carelessly and clumsily before, and firmly believed, what was indeed a fact, that Barker had done it badly on purpose, in the hope that it might be discovered, and so Eric be got once more into a scrape. He was in an agony of apprehension, and when put on, was totally unable to say a word of his Rep. But far as he had yielded, he would not cheat like the rest; in this respect, at any rate, he would not give up his claim to chivalrous and stainless honour; he kept his eyes resolutely turned away from the guilty paper, and even refused to repeat the words which were prompted in his ear by the boys on each side. Mr. Gordon, after waiting a moment, said—

'Why, sir, you know nothing about it; you can't have looked at it. Go to the bottom, and write it out five times.'

'*Write it out*,' thought Eric; 'this is retribution, I suppose;' and, covered with shame and vexation, he took his place below the malicious Barker at the bottom of the form.

It happened that during the lesson the fire began to smoke, and Mr. Gordon told Owen to open the window for a moment. No sooner was this done than the mischievous whiff of sea-air which entered the room began to trifle and coquet with the pendulous half-sheet pinned in front of the desk, causing thereby an unwonted little pattering crepitation. In alarm, Duncan thoughtlessly pulled out the pin, and immediately the paper floated gracefully over Russell's head, as he sat at the top of the form, and, after one or two gyrations, fluttered down in the centre of the room.

'Bring me that piece of paper,' said Mr. Gordon, full of vague suspicion.

Several boys moved uneasily, and Eric looked nervously round.

'Did you hear? fetch me that half-sheet of paper.'

A boy picked it up, and handed it to him. Mr. Gordon held it for a full minute in his hands without a word, while vexation, deep disgust, and rising anger, struggled in his countenance. At last, he suddenly turned full on Eric, whose writing he recognised, and broke out—

'So, sir! a second time caught in gross deceit. I should not have thought it possible. Your face and manners belie you. You have lost my confidence for ever. I *despise* you.'

'Indeed, sir,' said the penitent Eric, 'I never meant——'

'Silence—you are detected, as cheats always will be. I shall report you to Dr. Rowlands.'

The next boy was put on, and broke down. The same with the next, and the next, and the next; Montagu, Graham, Llewellyn, Duncan, Barker, all hopeless failures; only two boys had said it right—Russell and Owen.

Mr. Gordon's face grew blacker and blacker. The deep undisguised pain which the discovery caused him was swallowed up in unbounded indignation. 'Deceitful, dishonourable boys,' he exclaimed, 'henceforth my treatment of you shall be very different. The whole form, except Russell and Owen, shall have an extra lesson every half-holiday; not one of the rest of you will I trust again. I took you for gentlemen. I was mistaken. Go.' And so saying, he motioned them to their seats with imperious disdain.

They went, looking sheepish and ashamed. Eric, deeply vexed, kept twisting and untwisting a bit of paper, without raising his eyes, and even Barker thoroughly repented his short-sighted treachery; the rest were silent and miserable.

At twelve o'clock two boys lingered in the room to speak to Mr. Gordon; they were Eric Williams and Edwin Russell, but they were full of very different feelings.

Eric stepped to the desk first. Mr. Gordon looked up.

'You! Williams, I wonder that you have the audacity to speak to me. Go—I have nothing to say to you.'

'But, sir, I want to tell you that——'

'Your guilt is only too clear, Williams. You will hear more of this. Go, I tell you.'

Eric's passion overcame him; he stamped furiously on the ground, and burst out, 'I *will* speak, sir; you have been unjust to me for a long time, but I will *not* be——'

Mr. Gordon's cane fell sharply across the boy's back; he stopped, glared for a moment, and then saying, 'Very well, sir! I shall tell Dr. Rowlands that you strike before you hear me,' he angrily left the room, and slammed the door violently behind him.

Before Mr. Gordon had time to recover from his astonishment, Russell stood by him.

'Well, my boy,' said the master, softening in a moment, and laying his hand gently on Russell's head, 'what have you to say? You cannot tell how I rejoice, amid the vexation and disgust that this has caused me, to find that *you* at least are honourable. But I *knew*, Edwin, that I could trust you.'

'Oh, sir, I come to speak for Eric—for Williams.' Mr. Gordon's brow darkened again and the storm gathered, as he interrupted vehemently, 'Not a word, Russell; not a word. This is the *second* time that he has wilfully deceived me; and this time he has involved others too in his base deceit.'

'Indeed, sir, you wrong him. I can't think how he came to write the paper, but I *know* that he did not and would not use it. Didn't you see yourself, sir, how he turned his head quite another way when he broke down?'

'It is very kind of you, Edwin, to defend him,' said Mr. Gordon coldly, 'but at present, at any rate, I must not hear you. Leave me; I feel deeply vexed, and must have time to think over this disgraceful affair.'

Russell went away disconsolate, and met his friend striding up and down the passage, waiting for Dr. Rowlands to come out of the library.

'Oh, Eric,' he said, 'how came you to write that paper?'

'Why, Russell, I did feel very much ashamed, and I would have explained it, and said so; but that Gordon spites me so. It is such a shame; I don't feel now as if I cared one bit.'

'I am sorry you don't get on with him; but remember you have given him in this case good cause to suspect. You never crib, Eric, I know, so I can't help being sorry that you wrote the paper.'

'But then Graham asked me to do it, and called me cowardly because I refused at first.'

'Ah, Eric,' said Russell, 'they will ask you to do worse things if you yield so easily. I wouldn't say anything to Dr. Rowlands about it, if I were you.'

Eric took the advice, and, full of mortification, went home. He gave his father a true and manly account of the whole occurrence, and that afternoon Mr. Williams wrote a note of apology and explanation to Mr. Gordon. Next time the form went up, Mr. Gordon said, in his most freezing tone, 'Williams, at present I shall take no further notice of your offence beyond including you in the extra lesson every half-holiday.'

From that day forward Eric felt that he was marked and suspected, and the feeling worked on him with the worst effects. He grew more careless in work, and more trifling and indifferent in manner. Several boys now got above him in form whom he had easily surpassed before, and his energies were for a time entirely directed to keeping that supremacy in the games which he had won by his activity and strength.

It was a Sunday afternoon, toward the end of the summer term, and the boys were sauntering about in the green playground, or lying on the banks reading and chatting. Eric was with a little knot of his chief friends, enjoying the sea-breeze as they sat on the grass. At last the bell of the school chapel began to ring, and they went in to the afternoon service. Eric usually sat with Duncan and Llewellyn, immediately behind the benches allotted to chance visitors. The bench in front of them happened on this afternoon to be occupied by some rather odd people, viz. an old man with long white hair, and two ladies remarkably stout, who were dressed with much juvenility, although past middle age. Their appearance immediately attracted notice, and no sooner had they taken their seats than Duncan and Llewellyn began to titter. The ladies' bonnets, which were of white, trimmed with long green leaves and flowers, just peered over the top of the boys' pew, and excited much amusement; particularly when Duncan, in his irresistible sense of the ludicrous, began to adorn them with little bits of paper. But Eric had not yet learnt to disregard the solemnity of the place, and the sacred act in which they were engaged. He tried to look away and attend to the service, and for a time he partially succeeded, although, seated as he was between the two triflers, who were

perpetually telegraphing to each other their jokes, he found it a difficult task, and secretly he began to be much tickled.

At last the sermon commenced, and Llewellyn, who had imprisoned a grasshopper in a paper cage, suddenly let it hop out. The first hop took it to the top of the pew; the second perched it on the shoulder of the stoutest lady. Duncan and Llewellyn tittered louder, and even Eric could not resist a smile. But when the lady, feeling some irritation on her shoulder, raised her hand, and the grasshopper took a frightened leap into the centre of the green foliage which enwreathed her bonnet, none of the three could stand it, and they burst into fits of laughter, which they tried in vain to conceal by bending down their heads and cramming their fists into their mouths. Eric, having once given way, enjoyed the joke uncontrollably, and the lady made matters worse by her uneasy attempts to dislodge the unknown intruder, and discover the cause of the tittering, which she could not help hearing. At last all three began to laugh so violently that several heads were turned in their direction, and Dr. Rowlands's stern eye caught sight of their levity. He stopped short in his sermon, and for one instant transfixed them with his indignant glance. Quiet was instantly restored, and alarm reduced them to the most perfect order, although the grasshopper still sat imperturbable among the artificial flowers. Meanwhile the stout lady had discovered that for some unknown reason she had been causing considerable amusement, and attributing it to intentional ridicule, looked around, justly hurt. Eric, with real shame, observed the pained uneasiness of her manner, and bitterly repented his share in the transaction.

Next morning Dr. Rowlands, in full academicals, sailed into the fourth-form room. His entrance was the signal for every boy to rise, and after a word or two to Mr. Gordon, he motioned them to be seated. Eric's heart sank within him.

'Williams, Duncan, and Llewellyn, stand out!' said the Doctor. The boys, with downcast eyes and burning cheeks, stood before him.

'I was sorry to notice,' said he, 'your shameful conduct in chapel yesterday afternoon. As far as I could observe, you were making yourselves merry in that sacred place with the personal defects of others. The lessons you receive here must be futile indeed if they do not teach you the duty of reverence to God, and courtesy to man. It gives me special pain, Williams, to have observed that you, too, a boy high in your remove, were guilty of

this most culpable levity. You will all come to me at twelve o'clock in the library.'

At twelve o'clock they each received a flogging. The pain inflicted was not great, and Duncan and Llewellyn, who had got into similar trouble before, cared very little for it, and went out laughing to tell the number of swishes they had received to a little crowd of boys who were lingering outside the library door. But not so Eric. It was his *first* flogging, and he felt it deeply. To his proud spirit the disgrace was intolerable. At that moment he hated Dr. Rowlands, he hated Mr. Gordon, he hated his school-fellows, he hated everybody. He had been flogged; the thought haunted him; he, Eric Williams, had been forced to receive this most degrading corporal punishment. He pushed fiercely through the knot of boys, and strode as quickly as he could along the playground, angry and impenitent.

At the gate Russell met him. Eric felt the meeting inopportune; he was ashamed to meet his friend, ashamed to speak to him, envious of him, and jealous of his better reputation. He wanted to pass him by without notice, but Russell would not suffer this. He came up to him and took his arm affectionately. The slightest allusion to his late disgrace would have made Eric flame out into a passion; but Russell was too kind to allude to it then. He talked as if nothing had happened, and tried to turn his friend's thoughts to more pleasant subjects. Eric appreciated his kindness, but he was still sullen and fretful, and it was not until they parted that his better feelings won the day. But when Russell said to him, 'Good-bye, Eric, and don't be down in the mouth,' it was too much for him, and seizing Edwin's hand, he wrung it hard, and exclaimed impetuously—

'How I wish I was like you, Edwin! If all my friends were like you, I should never get into these rows.'

'Nay, Eric,' said Russell, 'it's I who ought to envy you; you are no end cleverer and stronger, and you can't think how glad I am that we are friends.'

They parted by Mr. Williams's door, and Russell walked home sad and thoughtful; but Eric, barely answering his brother's greeting, rushed up to his room, and, flinging himself on his bed, brooded alone over the remembrance of his disgrace. Still nursing a fierce resentment, he felt something hard at his heart, and, as he prayed neither for help nor forgiveness, it was pride and rebellion, not penitence, that made him miserable.

CHAPTER THE SIXTH

HOME AFFECTIONS

Keep the spell of home affection
Still alive in every heart;
May its power, with mild direction,
Draw our love from self apart,
Till thy children
Feel that thou their Father art.
SCHOOL HYMN

'I HAVE CAUGHT such a lot of pretty sea-anemones, Eric,' said little Vernon Williams, as his brother strolled in after morning school; 'I wish you would come and look at them.'

'Oh, I can't come now, Verny; I am going out to play cricket with some fellows directly.'

'But it won't take you a minute; do come.'

'What a little bore you are. Where are the things?'

'Oh, never mind, Eric, if you don't want to look at them,' said Vernon, hurt at his brother's rough manner.

'First, you ask me to look, and then say "never mind," ' said Eric impatiently; 'here, show me them.'

The little boy brought a large saucer, round which the crimson sea-flowers were waving their long tentacula in the salt water.

'Oh ay; very pretty indeed. But I must be off to cricket.'

Vernon looked up at his brother sadly.

'You aren't so kind to me, Eric, as you used to be.'

'What nonsense! and all because I don't admire those nasty red-jelly things, which one may see on the shore by thousands any day. What a little goose you are, Vernon.'

Vernon made no reply, but was putting away his sea-anemones with a sigh, when in came Russell to fetch Eric to the cricket.

'Well, Verny,' he said, 'have you been getting those pretty sea-anemones? come here and show me them. Ah, I declare you've got one of those famous white plumosa fellows among them. What a lucky little chap you are!'

Vernon was delighted.

'Mind you take care of them,' said Russell. 'Where did you find them?'

'I have been down the shore getting them.'

'And have you had a pleasant morning?'

'Yes, Russell, thank you. Only it is rather dull being always by myself, and Eric never comes with me now.'

'Hang Eric,' said Russell playfully. 'Never mind, Verny; you and I will cut him, and go by ourselves.'

Eric had stood by during the conversation, and the contrast of Russell's unselfish kindness with his own harsh want of sympathy struck him. He threw his arms round his brother's neck, and said, 'We will both go with you, Verny, next half-holiday.'

'Oh, thank you, Eric,' said his brother; and the two schoolboys ran out. But when the next half-holiday came, warm and bright, with the promise of a good match that afternoon, Eric repented his promise, and left Russell to amuse his little brother, while he went off, as usual, to the playground.

There was one silent witness of scenes like these, who laid them up deeply in her heart. Mrs. Williams was not unobservant of the gradual but steady falling off in Eric's character, and the first thing she noticed was the blunting of his home affections. When they first came to Roslyn, the boy used constantly to join his father and mother in their walks; but now he went seldom or never; and even if he did go, he seemed ashamed, while with them, to meet any of his schoolfellows. The spirit of false independence was awake and growing in her darling son. The bright afternoons they had spent together on the sunny shore, or seeking for sea-flowers among the lonely rocks of the neighbouring headlands—the walks at evening and sunset among the hills, and the sweet counsel they had together, when the boy's character opened like a bud in the light and warmth of his mother's love—the long twilights when he would sit on a stool with his young head resting on her knees, and her loving hand in his fair hair—all these things were becoming to Mrs. Williams memories, and nothing more.

It was the trial of her life, and very sad to bear; the more so because they were soon to be parted—certainly for years, perhaps for ever. The time was drawing nearer and nearer; it was now June, and Mr. Williams's term of furlough ended in two months. The holidays at Roslyn were the months of July and August, and towards their close Mr. and Mrs. Williams intended to leave Vernon at Fairholm, and start for India—sending back Eric by himself as a boarder in Dr. Rowlands's house.

After morning school, on fine days, the boys used to run straight down to the shore and bathe. A bright and joyous scene it was. They stripped off their clothes on the shingle that adjoined the beach, and then, running along the sands, would swim out far into the bay till their heads looked like small dots glancing in the sunshine. This year Eric had learned to swim, and he enjoyed the bathing more than any other pleasure.

One day after they had dressed, Russell and he began to amuse themselves on the sea-shore. The little translucent pools left on the sands by the ebbing tide always swarm with life, and the two boys found great fun in hunting audacious little crabs, or catching the shrimps that shuffled about in the shallow water. At last Eric picked up a piece of wood which he found lying on the beach, and said, 'What do you say to coming crab-fishing, Edwin? this bit of stick will do capitally to thrust between the rocks in the holes where they lie?'

Russell agreed, and they started to the rocks of the Ness to seek a likely place for their purpose. The Ness was a mile off, but in the excitement of their pleasure they were oblivious of time.

The Williamses, for the boys' convenience, usually dined at one, but on this day they waited half an hour for Eric. Since, however, he didn't appear, they dined without him, supposing that he was accidentally detained, and expecting him to come in every minute. But two o'clock came, and no Eric; half-past two, and no Eric; three, but still no Eric. Mrs. Williams became seriously alarmed, and even her husband grew uneasy.

Vernon was watching for his brother at the window, and seeing Duncan pass by, ran down to ask him, 'If he knew where Eric was?'

'No,' said Duncan; 'last time I saw him was on the shore. We bathed together, and I remember his clothes were lying by mine when I dressed. But I haven't seen him since. If you like, we'll go and look for him. I daresay he's on the beach somewhere.'

But they found no traces of him there; and when they returned with this intelligence, his mother got so agitated that it required all her husband's firm gentleness to support her sinking spirits. There was enough to cause anxiety, for Vernon repeatedly ran out to ask the boys who were passing if they had seen his brother, and the answer always was, that they had left him bathing in the sea.

Meanwhile our young friends, having caught several crabs, suddenly noticed by the sun that it was getting late.

'Good gracious, Edwin,' said Eric, pulling out his watch, 'it's half-past three; what have we been thinking of? How frightened they'll be at home;' and running back as fast as they could, they reached the house at five o'clock, and rushed into the room.

'Eric, Eric,' said Mrs. Williams faintly, 'where have you been? has anything happened to you, my child?'

'No, mother, nothing. I've only been crab-fishing with Russell, and we forgot the time.'

'Thoughtless boy,' said his father; 'your mother has been in an agony about you.'

Eric saw her pale face and tearful eyes, and flung himself in her arms, and mother and son wept in a long embrace. 'Only two months,' whispered Mrs. Williams, 'and we shall leave you, dear boy, perhaps for ever. Oh do not forget your love for us in the midst of new companions.'

The end of the term arrived; this time Eric came out eighth only instead of first, and therefore, on the prize-day, was obliged to sit among the crowd of undistinguished boys. He saw that his parents were disappointed, and his own ambition was grievously mortified. But he had full confidence in his own powers, and made the strongest resolutions to work hard the next half-year, when he had got out of 'that Gordon's' clutches.

The Williamses spent the holidays at Fairholm, and now, indeed, in the prospect of losing them, Eric's feelings to his parents came out in all their strength. Most happily the days glided by, and the father and mother used them wisely. All their gentle influence, all their deep affection, were employed in leaving on the boy's heart lasting impressions of godliness and truth. He learnt to feel that their love would encircle him for ever with its heavenly tenderness, and their pure prayers rise for him night and day to the throne of God.

The day of parting came, and most bitter and heartrending it was. In the wildness of their passionate sorrow, Eric and Vernon seemed to hear the sound of everlasting farewells. It is God's mercy that ordains how seldom young hearts have to endure such misery.

At length it was over. The last sound of wheels had died away; and during those hours the hearts of parents and children felt the bitterness of death. Mrs. Trevor and Fanny, themselves filled with grief, still used all their unselfish endeavours to comfort their dear boys. Vernon, weary of crying, soon sank to sleep; but not so Eric. He sat on a low stool, his face buried in his hands, breaking the stillness every now and then with his convulsive sobs.

'Oh, Aunty,' he cried, 'do you think I shall ever see them again? I have been so selfish, and so little grateful for all their love. Oh, I wish I had thought at Roslyn how soon I was to lose them.'

'Yes, dearest,' said Mrs. Trevor, 'I have no doubt we shall all meet again soon. Your father is only going for five years, you know, and that will not seem very long. And then they will be writing continually to us, and we to them. Think, Eric, how gladdened their hearts will be to hear that you and Vernon are good boys, and getting on well.'

'Oh, I *will* be a better boy, I *will* indeed,' said Eric; 'I mean to do great things, and they shall have nothing but good reports of me.'

'God helping you, dear,' said his aunt, pushing back his hair from his forehead, and kissing it softly; 'without His help, Eric, we are all weak indeed.'

She sighed. But how far deeper her sigh would have been had she known the future. Merciful is the darkness that shrouds it from human eyes!

CHAPTER THE SEVENTH

ERIC A BOARDER

We were, fair queen,
Two lads that thought there was no more behind,
But such a day to-morrow as to-day,
And to be boy eternal.
Winter's Tale, i. 2

T HE HOLIDAYS were over. Vernon was to have a tutor at Fairholm, and Eric was to return alone, and be received into Dr. Rowlands's house.

As he went on board the steam-packet, he saw numbers of the well-known faces on deck, and merry voices greeted him.

'Hullo, Williams! here you are at last,' said Duncan, seizing his hand. 'How have you enjoyed the holidays? It's so jolly to see you again.'

'So you're coming as a boarder,' said Montagu, 'and to our noble house, too. Mind you stick up for it, old fellow. Come along, and let's watch whether the boats are bringing any more fellows; we shall be starting in a few minutes.'

'Ha! there's Russell,' said Eric, springing to the gangway, and warmly shaking his friend's hand as he came on board.

'Have your father and mother gone, Eric?' said Russell, after a few minutes' talk.

'Yes,' said Eric, turning away his head, and hastily brushing his eyes. 'They are on their way back to India.'

'I'm so sorry,' said Russell; 'I don't think any one has ever been so kind to me as they were.'

'And they loved you, Edwin, dearly, and told me almost the last thing that they hoped we should always be friends. Stop! they gave me something for you.' Eric opened his carpet-bag, and took out a little box carefully wrapped up, which he gave to Russell. It contained a pretty silver watch, and inside the case was engraved—'Edwin Russell, from the mother of his friend Eric.'

The boy's eyes glistened with joyful surprise. 'How good they are,' he said; 'I shall write and thank Mrs. Williams directly we get to Roslyn.'

They had a fine bright voyage, and arrived that night. Eric, as a new-comer, was ushered at once into Dr. Rowlands's drawing-room, where the headmaster was sitting with his wife and children. His greeting was dignified, but not unkindly; and, on saying 'good-night,' he gave Eric a few plain words of affectionate advice.

At that moment Eric hardly cared for advice. He was full of life and spirits, brave, bright, impetuous, tingling with hope, in the very flush of boyhood. He bounded down the stairs, and in another minute entered the large room where all Dr. Rowlands's boarders assembled, and where most of them lived, except the few privileged sixth form, and other boys who had 'studies.' A cheer greeted his entrance into the room. By this time most of the Rowlandites knew him, and were proud to have him among their number. They knew that he was clever enough to get them credit in the school, and, what was better still, that he would be a capital accession of strength to the cricket and football. Except Barker, there was not one who had not a personal liking for him, and on this occasion even Barker was gracious.

The room in which Eric found himself was large and high. At one end was a huge fireplace, and there was generally a throng of boys round the great iron fender, where, in cold weather, a little boy could seldom find room. The large windows opened on the green playground; and iron bars prevented any exit through them. This large room, called 'the boarders' room,' was the joint habitation of Eric and some thirty other boys; and at one side ran a range of shelves and drawers, where they kept their books and private property. There the younger Rowlandites breakfasted, dined, had tea, and, for the most part, lived. Here, too, they had to get through all such work as was not performed under direct supervision. How many and what varied scenes had not that room beheld! had those dumb walls any feeling, what worlds of life and experience they would have acquired! If against each boy's name, as it was rudely cut on the oak panels, could have been also cut the fate that had befallen him, the good that he had there learnt, the evil that he there had suffered—what *noble* histories would the records unfold of honour and success, of baffled temptations and hard-won triumphs; what *awful* histories of hopes blighted and habits learned, of wasted talents and ruined lives!

The routine of school life was on this wise:—At half-past seven the boys came down to prayers, which were immediately followed by breakfast. At nine they went into school, where they continued, with little interruption, till twelve. At one they dined, and, except on half-holidays, went into school again from two till five. The lock-up bell rang at dusk; at six o'clock they had tea—which was a repetition of breakfast, with leave to add to it whatever else they liked—and immediately after sat down to 'preparation,' which lasted from seven till nine. During this time one of the masters was always in the room, who allowed them to read amusing books or employ themselves in any other quiet way they liked, as soon as ever they had learnt their lessons for the following day. At nine Dr. Rowlands came in and read prayers, after which the boys were dismissed to bed.

The arrangement of the dormitories was peculiar. They were a suite of rooms, exactly the same size, each opening into the other; six on each side of a lavatory, which occupied the space between them, so that, when all the doors were open, you could see from one end of the whole range to the other. The only advantage of this arrangement was, that one master walking up and down could keep all the boys in order while they were getting into bed. About a quarter of an hour was allowed for this process, and then the master went along the rooms putting out the lights. A few of the 'study-boys' were allowed to sit up till half-past ten, and their bedrooms were elsewhere. The consequence was, that in these dormitories the boys felt perfectly secure from any interruption. There were only two ways by which a master could get at them—one up the great staircase, and through the lavatory; the other by a door at the extreme end of the range, which led into Dr. Rowlands's house, but was generally kept locked.

In each dormitory slept four or five boys, distributed by their order in the school list, so that, in all the dormitories, there were nearly sixty; and of these a goodly number were, on Eric's arrival, collected in the boarders' room, the rest being in their studies, or in the class-rooms, which some were allowed to use in order to prevent too great a crowd in the room below.

At nine o'clock the prayer-bell rang. This was the signal for all the boarders to take their seats for prayers, each with an open Bible before him; and when the school servants had also come in, Dr. Rowlands read a chapter, and offered up an extempore prayer. While reading, he generally interspersed a few pointed remarks or graphic explanations, and Eric learnt much in this simple way. The prayer, though short, was always well suited to the occasion, and calculated to carry with it the attention of the worshippers.

Prayers over, the boys noisily dispersed to their bedrooms, and Eric found himself placed in a room immediately to the right of the lavatory, occupied by Duncan, Graham, Llewellyn, and two other boys named Ball and Attlay, all in the same form with himself. They were all tired with their voyage and the excitement of coming back to school, so that they did not talk much that night, and before long Eric was fast asleep, dreaming, dreaming, dreaming that he should have a very happy life at Roslyn School, and seeing himself win no end of distinctions, and make no end of new friends.

CHAPTER THE EIGHTH

'TAKING UP'

We are not worst at once; the course of evil
Beings so slowly, and from such slight source,
An infant's hand might stop the breach with clay;
But let the stream grow wider, and Philosophy—
Ay, and Religion too—may strive in vain
To stem the headlong current!
ANON.

W ITH INTENSE DELIGHT Eric heard it announced next morning, when the new school list was read, that he had got his remove into the 'Shell,' as the form was called which intervened between the fourth and the fifth. Russell, Owen, and Montagu also got their removes with him, but his other friends were left for the present in the form below.

Mr. Rose, his new master, was in every respect a great contrast with Mr. Gordon. He was not so brilliant in his acquiremenets, nor so vigorous in his teaching, and therefore clever boys did not catch fire from him so much as from the fourth-form master. But he was a far truer and deeper Christian; and, with no less scrupulous a sense of honour and detestation of every form of moral obliquity, he never yielded to those storms of passionate indignation which Mr. Gordon found it impossible to control. Disappointed in early life, subjected to the deepest and most painful trials, Mr. Rose's fine character had come out like gold from the flame. He now lived in and for the boys alone, and his whole life was one long self-devotion to their service and interests. The boys felt this, and even the worst of them, in their worst moments, loved and honoured Mr. Rose. But

he was not seeking for gratitude, which he neither expected nor required; he asked no affection in return for his self-denials; he worked with a pure spirit of human and self-sacrificing love, happy beyond all payment if ever he were instrumental in saving one of his charge from evil, or turning one wanderer from the error of his ways.

He was an unmarried man, and therefore took no boarders himself, but lived in the school buildings, and had the care of the boys in Dr. Rowlands's house.

Such was the master under whom Eric was now placed, and the boy was sadly afraid that an evil report would have reached his ears, and given him already an unfavourable impression. But he was soon happily undeceived. Mr. Rose at once addressed him with much kindness, and he felt that, however bad he had been before, he would now have an opportunity to turn over a new leaf, and begin again a career of hope. He worked admirably at first, and even beat, for the first week or two, his old competitors, Owen and Russell.

From the beginning, Mr. Rose took a deep interest in him. Few could look at the boy's bright blue eyes and noble face without doing so, and the more when they knew that his father and mother were thousands of miles away, leaving him alone in the midst of so many dangers. Often the master asked him, and Russell and Owen and Montagu, to supper with him in the library, which gave them the privilege of sitting up later than usual, and enjoying a more quiet and pleasant evening than was possible in the noisy rooms. Boys and master were soon quite at home with each other, and in this way Mr. Rose had an opportunity of instilling many a useful warning without the formality of regular discipline or stereotyped instruction.

Eric found the life of the 'boarders' room' far rougher than he had expected. Work was out of the question there, except during the hours of preparation, and the long dark winter evenings were often dull enough. Sometimes, indeed, they would all join in some regular indoor boys' game like 'baste the bear,' or 'high-cockolorum'; or they would have amusing 'ghost hunts,' as they called them, after some dressed-up boy among the dark corridors and staircases. This was good fun, but at other times they got tired of games, and could not get them up, and then numbers of boys felt the idle time hang heavy on their hands. When this was the case, some of the worst sort, as might have been expected, would fill up their leisure with bullying or mischief.

For some time they had a form of diversion which disgusted and annoyed Eric exceedingly. On each of the long iron-bound deal tables were placed two or three tallow candles in tin candlesticks, and this was the only light the boys had. Of course these candles often wanted snuffing, and as snuffers were sure to be thrown about and broken as soon as they were brought into the room, the only resource was to snuff them with the fingers, at which all the boys became great adepts from necessity. One evening Barker, having snuffed the candle, suddenly and slyly put the smouldering wick unnoticed on the head of a little quiet inoffensive fellow named Wright, who happened to be sitting next to him. It went on smouldering for some time without Wright's perceiving it, and at last Barker, highly delighted, exclaimed—

'I see a chimney,' and laughed.

Four or five boys looked up, and very soon every one in the room had noticed the trick except little Wright himself, who unconsciously toiled on at the letter he was sending home.

Eric did not like this, but not wishing to come across Barker again, said nothing, and affected not to have observed. But Russell said quietly, 'There's something on your head, Wright,' and the little boy, putting up his hand, hastily brushed off the horrid wick.

'What a shame,' he said, as it fell on his letter, and made a smudge.

'Who told you to interfere?' said Barker, turning fiercely to Russell. Russell, as usual, took not the slightest notice of him, and Barker, after a little more bluster, repeated the trick on another boy. This time Russell thought that every one might be on the lookout for himself, and so went on with his work. But when Barker again chanted maliciously—

'I see a chimney!' every boy who happened to be reading or writing, uneasily felt to discover whether this time he were himself the victim or no; and so things continued for half an hour.

Ridiculous and disgusting as this folly was, it became, when constantly repeated, very annoying. A boy could not sit down to any quiet work without constant danger of having some one creep up behind him and put the offensive fragment of smoking snuff on his head; and neither Barker nor any of his little gang of imitators seemed disposed to give up their low mischief.

One night, when the usual exclamation was made, Eric felt sure, from seeing several boys looking at him, that this time some one had been treating him in the same way. He indignantly shook his head, and sure enough the bit of wick dropped off. Eric was furious, and, springing up, he shouted—

'By Jove! I *won't* stand this any longer.'

'You'll have to sit it, then,' said Barker.

'Oh, it was you who did it, was it? Then take that!' and seizing one of the tin candlesticks, Eric hurled it at Barker's head. Barker dodged, but the edge of it cut open his eyebrow as it whizzed by, and the blood flowed fast.

'I'll kill you for that,' said Barker, leaping at Eric, and seizing him by the hair.

'You'll get killed yourself then, you brute,' said Upton, Russell's cousin, a fifth-form boy, who had just come into the room—and he boxed Barker's ears as a premonitory admonition. 'But I say, young un,' continued he to Eric, 'this kind of thing won't do, you know. You'll get into rows if you shy candlesticks at fellows' heads at that rate.'

'He has been making the room intolerable for the last month by his filthy tricks,' said Eric hotly; 'some one must stop him, and I will somehow, if no one else does.'

'It wasn't I who put the thing on your head, you passionate young fool,' growled Barker.

'Who was it, then? how was I to know? You began it.'

'You shut up, Barker,' said Upton; 'I've heard of your ways before, and when I catch you at your tricks, I'll teach you a lesson. Come up to my study, Williams, if you like.'

Upton was a fine sturdy fellow of eighteen, immensely popular in the school for his prowess and good looks. He hated bullying, and often interfered to protect little boys, who accordingly idolised him, and did anything he told them very willingly. He meant to do no harm, but he did great harm. He was full of misdirected impulses, and had a great notion of being manly, which he thought consisted in a fearless disregard of all school rules, and the performance of the wildest tricks. For this reason he was never very intimate with his cousin Russell, whom he liked very much, but who was too scrupulous and independent to please him. Eric, on the other hand, was just the boy to take his fancy, and to admire him in return; his life, strength, and pluck made him a ready pupil in all schemes of mischief, and Upton, who had often noticed him, would have been the first to shudder had he known how far his example went to undermine all Eric's lingering good resolutions, and injure permanently the boy of whom he was so fond.

From this time Eric was much in Upton's study, and constantly by his side in the playground. In spite of their disparity in age and position in the school, they became sworn friends, though their friendship was broken every now and then by little quarrels, which united them all the more closely after they had not spoken to each other perhaps for a week.

'Your cousin Upton has "taken up" Williams,' said Montagu to Russell one afternoon, as he saw the two strolling together on the beach, with Eric's arm in Upton's.

'Yes, I am sorry for it.'

'So am I. We shan't see so much of him now.'

'Oh, that's not my only reason,' answered Russell, who had a rare habit of always going straight to the point.

'You mean you don't like the "taking up" system.'

'No, Montagu; I used once to have fine theories about it. I used to fancy that a big fellow would do no end of good to one lower in the school, and that the two would stand to each other in the relation of knight to squire. You know what the young knights were taught, Monty—to keep their bodies under, and bring them into subjection; to love God, and speak the truth always. That sounds very grand and noble to me. But when a big fellow takes up a little one *you* know pretty well that *those* are not the kind of lessons he teaches.'

'No, Russell; you're quite right. It's bad for a fellow in every way. First of all, it keeps him in an unnatural sort of dependence; then ten to one it makes him conceited, and prevents his character from really coming out well. And besides, the young chap generally gets paid out in kicks and abuse from the jealousy and contempt of the rest; and if his protector happens to leave, or anything of that kind, woe betide him!'

'No fear for Eric in that line, though,' said Russell; 'he can hold his own pretty well against any one. And after all, he is a most jolly fellow. I don't think even Upton would spoil him; it's chiefly the soft self-indulgent fellows, who are all straw and no iron, who get spoilt by being "taken up." '

Russell was partly right. Eric learned a great deal of harm from Upton, and the misapplied hero-worship led to bad results. But he was too manly a little fellow, and had too much self-respect, to sink into the dependent condition which usually grows on the foolish little boys who have the misfortune to be 'taken up.'

Nor did he in the least drop his old friends, except Owen. A coolness grew up between the latter and Eric, not unmingled with a little mutual contempt. Eric sneered at Owen as a fellow who did nothing but grind all day long, and had no geniality in him; while Owen pitied the love of popularity which so often led Eric into delinquencies, which he himself despised. Owen had, indeed, but few friends in the school; the only boy who knew him well enough to respect and like him thoroughly was Russell, who found in him the only one who took the same high ground with himself. But Russell loved the good in every one, and was loved by all in return, and Eric he loved most of all, while he often mourned over his increasing failures.

One day as the two were walking together in the green playground, Mr. Gordon passed by; and as the boys touched their caps, he nodded and smiled pleasantly at Russell, but hardly noticed, and did not return Eric's salute. He had begun to dislike the latter more and more, and had given him up altogether as one of the reprobates. Barker, who happened to pass at the same moment, received from him the same cold glance that Eric had done.

'What a surly devil that is,' said Eric, when he had passed; 'did you see how he purposely cut me?'

'A surly . . . ? Oh, Eric, that's the first time I ever heard you swear.'

Eric blushed. He hadn't meant the word to slip out in Russell's hearing, though similar and worse expressions were common enough in his talk with other boys. But he didn't like to be reproved, even by Russell, and in the ready spirit of self-defence, he answered—

'Pooh, Edwin, you don't call that swearing, do you? You're so strict, so religious, you know. I love you for it, but then, there are none like you. Nobody thinks anything of swearing here,—even of *real* swearing, you know.'

Russell was silent.

'Besides, what can be the harm of it? it means nothing. I was thinking the other night, and I made out that you and Owen are the only two fellows here who don't swear.'

Russell still said nothing.

'And, after all, I didn't swear; I only called that fellow a surly devil.'

'Oh, hush! Eric, hush!' said Russell sadly. 'You wouldn't have said so half a year ago.'

Eric knew what he meant. The image of his father and mother rose before him, as they sate far away in their lonely Indian home, thinking of him, praying for him, centring all their hopes in him. In him!—and he knew how many things he was daily doing and saying, which would cut them to the heart. He knew that all his moral consciousness was fast vanishing, and leaving him a bad and reckless boy.

In a moment all this passed through his mind. He remembered how shocked he had been at swearing at first; and even when it became too familiar to shock him, how he determined never to fall into the habit himself. Then he remembered how gradually it had become quite a graceful sound in his ears—a sound of entire freedom and independence of moral restraint; an open casting off, as it were, of all authority, so that he had begun to admire it, particularly in Duncan, and, above all, in his new hero, Upton; and he recollected how, at last, an oath had one day slipped out suddenly in his own words, and how strange it sounded to him, and how Upton smiled to hear it, though his own conscience had reproached him bitterly; but now that he had done it once, it became less dreadful, and grew common enough, till even conscience hardly reminded him that he was doing wrong.

He thought of all this, and hung his head. Pride struggled with him for a moment, but at length he answered, 'Oh, Edwin, you're quite right, and I'm all in the wrong as usual. But I shall never be like you,' he added in a low sad tone.

'Dear Eric, don't think that I'm always sermonising. But I hope that I know the difference between what's right and what's wrong, and do let me say that you will be so much happier, if you try not to yield to all the bad things round us. Remember, I know more of school than you.'

The two boys strolled on silently. That night Eric knelt at his bedside, and prayed as he had not done for many a long day.

And here let those scoff who deny 'the sinfulness of little sins'; but I remember the words of one who wrote, that

> The most childish thing which man can do,
> Is yet a sin which Jesus never did
> When Jesus was a child,—and yet a sin
> For which in lowly pain he came to die;
> That for the *bravest* sin that e'er was praised
> The King Eternal wore the crown of thorns.

CHAPTER THE NINTH

'DEAD FLIES,' OR 'YE SHALL BE AS GODS'

In the twilight, in the evening, in the black and dark night.
Prov. vii. 9

ATT ROSLYN, even in summer, the hour for going to bed was half-past nine. It was hardly likely that so many boys, overflowing with turbulent life, should lie down quietly, and get to sleep. They never dreamt of doing so. Very soon after the masters were gone, the sconces were often relighted, sometimes in separate dormitories, sometimes in all of them, and the boys amused themselves by reading novels or making a row. They would play various games about the bedrooms, vaulting or jumping over the beds, running races in sheets, getting through the windows upon the roofs, to frighten the study-boys with sham ghosts, or playing the thousand other pranks which suggested themselves to the fertile imagination of fifteen. But the favourite amusement was a bolstering match. One room would challenge another, and stripping the covers off their bolsters, would meet in mortal fray. A bolster well wielded, especially when dexterously applied to the legs, is a very efficient instrument to bring a boy to the ground; but it doesn't hurt very much, even when the blows fall on the head. Hence these matches were excellent trials of strength and temper, and were generally accompanied with shouts of laughter, never ending until one side was driven back to its own room. Many a long and tough struggle had Eric enjoyed, and his prowess was now so universally acknowledged, that his dormitory, No. 7, was a match for any other, and far stronger in this warfare than most of the rest. At bolstering, Duncan was a perfect champion; his strength and activity were marvellous, and his mirth uproarious. Eric and Graham backed him up brilliantly; while Llewellyn and Attlay, with sturdy vigour, supported the skirmishers. Ball, the sixth boy in No. 7, was the only *fainéant* among them, though he did occasionally help to keep off the smaller fry.

Happy would it have been for all of them if Ball had never been placed in No. 7; happier still if he had never come to Roslyn School. Backward in work, overflowing with vanity at his supposed good looks, of mean disposition and feeble intellect, he was the very worst specimen of a boy that Eric had ever seen. Not even Barker so deeply excited Eric's repulsion and contempt. And yet, since the affair of Upton, Barker and Eric were declared enemies, and, much to the satisfaction of the latter, never spoke to each other; but with Ball—much as he inwardly loathed him—he was professedly and apparently on good terms. His silly love of universal popularity made him accept and tolerate the society even of this worthless boy.

Any two boys talking to each other about Ball would probably profess to like him 'well enough,' but if they were honest, they would generally end by allowing their contempt.

'We've got a nice set in No. 7, haven't we?' said Duncan to Eric one day.

'Capital. Old Llewellyn's a stunner, and I like Attlay and Graham.'

'Don't you like Ball, then?'

'Oh yes; pretty well.'

'BALL'.

The two boys looked each other in the face, and then, like the confidential augurs, burst out laughing.

'You know you detest him,' said Duncan.

'No, I don't. He never did me any harm that I know of.'

'Hm!—well, *I* detest him.'

'Well!' answered Eric, 'on coming to think of it, so do I. And yet he's popular enough in the school. I wonder how that is.'

'He's not *really* popular. I've often noticed that fellows pretty generally despise him, yet somehow don't like to say so.'

'Why do you dislike him, Duncan?'

'I don't know. Why do you?'

'I don't know either.'

Neither Eric nor Duncan meant this answer to be false, and yet if they had taken the trouble to consider, they would have found out in their secret souls the reasons of their dislike.

Ball had been to school before, and of this school he often bragged as the acme of desirability and wickedness. He was always telling boys what they did at 'his old school,' and he quite inflamed the minds of such as fell under his influence by marvellous tales of the wild and wilful things which he and his former schoolfellows had done. Many and many a scheme of sin and mischief at Roslyn was suggested, planned, and carried out, on the model of Ball's reminiscences of his previous life.

He had tasted more largely of the tree of the knowledge of evil than any other boy, and, strange to say, this was the secret why the general odium was never expressed. He claimed his guilty experience so often as a ground of superiority, that at last the claim was silently allowed. He spoke from the platform of more advanced iniquity, and the others listened first curiously, and then eagerly to his words.

'Ye shall be as gods, knowing good and evil.' Such was the temptation which assailed the other boys in dormitory No. 7; and Eric among the number. Ball was the tempter. Secretly, gradually, he dropped into their too willing ears the poison of his immorality.

In brief, this boy was cursed with a degraded and corrupting mind.

I hurry over a part of my subject inconceivably painful; I hurry over it, but if I am to perform my self-imposed duty of giving a true picture of what school life *sometimes* is, I must not pass it by altogether.

The first time that Eric heard indecent words in dormitory No. 7, he was shocked beyond bound or measure. Dark though it was, he felt himself blushing scarlet to the roots of his hair, and then growing pale again, while a hot dew was left upon his, forehead. Ball was the speaker; but this time there was a silence, and the subject instantly dropped. The others felt that a 'new boy' was in the room; they did not know how he would take it; they were unconsciously abashed.

Besides, though they had themselves joined in such conversation before, they did not love it, and, on the contrary, felt ashamed of yielding to it.

Now, Eric, now or never! Life and death, ruin and salvation, corruption and purity, are perhaps in the balance together, and the scale of your destiny may hang on a single word of yours. Speak out, boy! Tell these fellows that unseemly words wound your conscience; tell them that they are ruinous, sinful, damnable; speak out and save yourself and the rest. Virtue is strong and beautiful, Eric, and vice is downcast in her awful presence. Lose your purity of heart, Eric, and you have lost a jewel which the whole world, if it were 'one entire and perfect chrysolite,' cannot replace.

Good spirits guard that young boy, and give him grace in this his hour of trial! Open his eyes that he may see the fiery horses and the fiery chariots of the angels who would defend him, and the dark array of spiritual foes who throng around his bed. Point a pitying finger to the yawning abyss of shame, ruin, and despair that even now perhaps is being cleft under his feet. Show him the garlands of the present and the past, withering at the touch of the Erinnys in the future. In pity, in pity, show him the canker which he is introducing into the sap of the tree of life, which shall cause its root to be hereafter as bitterness, and its blossom to go up as dust.

But the sense of sin was on Eric's mind. How *could* he speak? was not his own language sometimes profane? How—how could he profess to reprove another boy on the ground of morality, when he himself said and did things less dangerous perhaps, but equally forbidden?

For half an hour, in an agony of struggle with himself, Eric lay silent. Since Ball's last words nobody had spoken. They were going to sleep. It was too late to speak now, Eric thought. The moment passed by for ever; Eric had listened without objection to foul words, and the irreparable harm was done.

How easy it would have been to speak! With the temptation, God had provided also a way to escape. Next time it came, it was far harder to resist, and it soon became, to men, impossible.

Ah, Eric, Eric! how little we know the moments which decide the destinies of life. We live on as usual. The day is a common day, the hour a common hour. We never thought twice about the change of intention which by one of the accidents—(accidents!)—of life determined for good or for evil, for happiness or misery, the colour of our remaining years. The stroke of the pen was done in a moment which led unconsciously to our ruin; the word was uttered quite heedlessly on which turned for ever the decision of our weal or woe.

Eric lay silent. The darkness was not broken by the flashing of an angel's wing, the stillness was not syllabled by the sound of an angel's voice; but to his dying day Eric never forgot the moments which passed, until, weary and self-reproachful, he fell asleep.

Next morning he awoke, restless and feverish. He at once remembered what had passed. Ball's words haunted him; he could not forget them; they burnt within him like the flame of a moral fever. He was moody and petulant, and for a time could hardly conceal his aversion. Ah, Eric! moodiness and petulance cannot save you, but prayerfulness would; one word, Eric, at the throne of grace—one prayer before you go down among the boys, that God in His mercy would wash away, in the blood of His dear Son, your crimson stains, and keep your conscience and memory clean.

The boy knelt down for a few minutes, and repeated to himself a few formal words. Had he stayed longer on his knees, he might have given way to a burst of penitence and supplication—but he heard Ball's footstep, and getting up he ran downstairs to breakfast; so Eric did not pray.

Conversations did not generally drop so suddenly in dormitory No. 7. On the contrary, they generally flashed along in the liveliest way, till some one said 'good-night'; and then the boys turned off to sleep. Eric knew this, and instantly conjectured that it was only a sort of respect for him, and ignorance of the manner in which he would consider it, that prevented Duncan and the rest from taking any further notice of Ball's remark. It was therefore no good disburdening his mind to any of them; but he determined to speak about the matter to Russell in their next walk.

They usually walked together on Sunday. Dr. Rowlands had discontinued the odious and ridiculous custom of the younger boys taking their exercise under a master's inspection. Boys are not generally fond of constitutionals, so that on the half-holidays they almost entirely confined their open-air exercise to the regular games, and many of them hardly left the playground boundaries once a week. But on Sundays they often went walks, each with his favourite friend or companion. When Eric first came as a boarder, he invariably went with Russell on Sunday, and many a pleasant stroll they had taken together, sometimes accompanied by Duncan, Montagu, or Owen. The latter, however, had dropped even this intercourse with Eric, who for the last few weeks had more often gone with his new friend Upton.

'Come a walk, boy,' said Upton, as they left the dining-room.

'Oh, excuse me to-day, Upton,' said Eric, 'I'm going with your cousin.'

'Oh, very well,' said Upton, in high dudgeon; and hoping to make Eric jealous, he went a walk with Graham, whom he had 'taken up' before he knew Williams.

Russell was rather surprised when Eric came to him and said, 'Come a stroll to Fort Island, Edwin—will you?'

'Oh yes,' said Russell cheerfully; 'why, we haven't seen each other for some time lately! I was beginning to fancy that you meant to drop me, Eric.'

He spoke with a smile and in a rallying tone, but Eric hung his head; for the charge was true. Proud of his popularity among all the school, and especially at his friendship with so leading a fellow as Upton, Eric had *not* seen much of his friend since their last conversation about swearing. Indeed, conscious of failure, he felt sometimes uneasy in Russell's company.

He faltered, and answered humbly, 'I hope you will never drop *me*, Edwin, whatever happens to me. But I particularly want to speak to you to-day.'

In an instant Russell had twined his arm in Eric's as they turned towards Fort Island;

and Eric, with an effort, was just going to begin when they heard Montagu's voice calling after them—

'I say, you fellows, where are you off to? may I come with you?'

'Oh yes, Monty, do,' said Russell; 'it will be quite like old times; now that my cousin Horace has got hold of Eric, we have to sing "When shall we three meet again?" '

Russell only spoke in fun; but, unintentionally, his words jarred in Eric's heart. He was silent and answered in monosyllables, so the walk was provokingly dull. At last they reached Fort Island, and sate down by the ruined chapel looking on the sea.

'Why, what's the row with you, old boy?' said Montagu, playfully shaking Eric by the shoulder; 'you're as silent as Zimmerman on Solitude, and as doleful as Harvey on the Tombs. I expect you've been going through a select course of Blair's Grave, Young's Night Thoughts, and Drelincourt on Death.'

To his surprise Eric's head was still bent, and, at last, he heard a deep suppressed sigh.

'My dear fellow, what is the matter with you?' said Russell, affectionately taking his hand; 'surely you're not offended at my nonsense?'

Eric had not liked to speak while Montagu was by, but now he gulped down his rising emotion, and briefly told them of Ball's vile words the night before. They listened in silence.

'I knew it must come, Eric,' said Russell at last, 'and I am so sorry you didn't speak at the time.'

'Do the fellows ever talk in that way in either of your dormitories?' asked Eric.

'No,' said Russell.

'Very little,' said Montagu.

A pause followed, during which all three plucked the grass and looked away.

'Let me tell you,' said Russell solemnly; 'my father (he is dead now, you know, Eric), when I was sent to school, warned me of this kind of thing. I had been brought up in utter ignorance of such coarse knowledge as is forced upon one here, and with my reminiscences of home, I could not bear even that much of it which it was impossible to avoid. But the very first time such talk was begun in my dormitory, I spoke out. What I said I don't know, but I felt as if I was trampling on a slimy poisonous adder, and, at any rate, I showed such pain and distress that the fellows dropped it at the time. Since then I have absolutely refused to stay in the room if ever such talk is begun. So it never is now, and I do think the fellows are very glad of it themselves.'

'Well,' said Montagu, 'I don't profess to look on it from the religious ground, you know, but I thought it blackguardly, and in bad taste, and said so. The fellow who began it threatened to kick me for a conceited little fool, but he didn't; and they hardly ever venture on that line now.'

'It is more than blackguardly, it is deadly,' answered Russell; 'my father said it was the most fatal curse which could ever become rife in a public school.'

'Why do masters never give us any help or advice on these matters?' asked Eric thoughtfully.

'In sermons they do. Don't you remember Rowlands's sermon not two weeks ago on Kibroth-Hattaavah? But I for one think them quite right not to speak to us privately on such subjects, unless we invite confidence. Besides, they cannot know that any boys talk in this way. After all, it is only a very few of the worst who ever do.'

They got up and walked home, but from day to day Eric put off performing the duty which Russell had advised, viz.—a private request to Ball to abstain from his offensive communications, and an endeavour to enlist Duncan into his wishes.

One evening they were telling each other stories in No. 7. Ball's turn came, and in his story the vile element again appeared. For a while Eric said nothing, but as the strain grew worse, he made a faint remonstrance.

'Shut up there, Williams,' said Attlay, 'and don't spoil the story.'

'Very well. It's your own fault, and I shall shut my ears.'

He did for a time, but a general laugh awoke him. He pretended to be asleep, but he listened. Iniquity of this kind was utterly new to him; his curiosity was awakened; he no longer feigned indifference, and the poison of evil communication flowed deep into his veins.

Oh, young boys, if your eyes ever read these pages, pause and beware. The knowledge of evil is ruin, and the continuance in it is moral death. That little matter—that beginning of evil—it will be like the snowflake detached by the breath of air from the mountaintop, which, as it rushes down, gains size and strength and impetus, till it has swollen to the mighty and irresistible avalanche that overwhelms garden and field and village in a chaos of undistinguishable death.

Kibroth-Hattaavah! Many and many a young Englishman has perished there! Many and many a happy English boy, the jewel of his mother's heart—brave and beautiful and strong—lies buried there. Very pale their shadows rise before us—the shadows of our young brothers who have sinned and suffered. From the sea and the sod, from foreign graves and English churchyards, they start up and throng around us in the paleness of their fall. May every schoolboy who reads this page be warned by the waving of their wasted hands, from that burning marle of passion where they found nothing but shame and ruin, polluted affections, and an early grave.

CHAPTER THE TENTH

DORMITORY LIFE

Ἀσπασίη τρίλλιστος ἐπήλυθε νύξ ἐρεβένη.
HOMER

FOR A FEW DAYS AFTER the Sunday walk narrated in the last chapter, Upton and Eric cut each other dead. Upton was angry at Eric's declining the honour of his company, and Eric was piqued at Upton's unreasonableness. In the 'taking up' system, such quarrels were of frequent occurrence, and as the existence of a misunderstanding was generally indicated in this very public way, the variations of good-will between such friends generally excited no little notice and amusement among the other boys. But both Upton and Eric were too sensible to carry their differences so far as others similarly circumstanced;

each thoroughly enjoyed the other's company, and they generally seized an early opportunity for effecting a reconciliation, which united them more firmly than ever.

As soon as Eric had got over his little pique, he made the first advances by writing a note to Upton, which he slipped under his study door, and which ran as follows:—

'DEAR HORACE—Don't let us quarrel about nothing. Silly fellow, why should you be angry with me because for once I wanted to go a walk with Russell, who, by the bye, is twice as good a fellow as you? I shall expect you to make it up directly after prayers.—Yours, if you are not silly, E.W.'

The consequence was, that as they came out from prayers Upton seized Eric's hand, and slapped him on the back, after which they had a good laugh over their own foolish fracas, and ran upstairs, chattering merrily.

'There's to be an awful lark in the dormitories to-night,' said Eric; 'the Doctor's gone to a dinner-party, and we're going to have no end of fun.'

'Are you? Well, if it gets amusing, come to my study and tell me, and I'll come and look on.'

'Very well; depend upon it I'll come.' And they parted at the foot of the study stairs.

It was Mr. Rose's night of duty. He walked slowly up and down the range of dormitories until every boy seemed ready to get into bed, and then he put out all the candles. So long as he was present the boys observed the utmost quiet and decorum. All continued quite orderly until he had passed away through the lavatory, and one of the boys, following him as a scout, had seen the last glimmer of his candle disappear round the corner at the foot of the great staircase, and heard the library door close behind him.

After that, particularly as Dr. Rowlands was absent, the boys knew that they were safe from disturbance, and the occupants of No. 7 were the first to stir.

'Now for some fun,' said Duncan, starting up, and by way of initiative, pitching his pillow at Eric's head.

'I'll pay you out for that when I'm ready,' said Eric, laughing; 'but give us a match first.'

Duncan produced some vestas, and no sooner had they lighted their candle, than several of the dormitory doors began to be thrown open, and one after another all requested a light, which Duncan and Eric conveyed to them in a sort of emulous torch-race, so that at length all the twelve dormitories had their sconces lit, and the boys began all sorts of amusement, some in their night-shirts, and others with their trousers slipped on. Leap-frog was the prevalent game for a time, but at last Graham suggested theatricals, and they were agreed on.

'But we're making a regular knock-me-down shindy,' said Llewellyn; 'somebody must keep cavé.'

'Oh, old Rose is safe enough at his Hebrew in the library; no fear of disturbing him if we were dancing hippopotami,' answered Graham.

But it was generally considered safe to put some one at the top of the stairs, in case of an unexpected diversion in that direction, and little Wright consented to go first. He had only to leave the lavatory door open, and stand at the top of the staircase, and he then commanded for a great distance the only avenue in which danger was expected. If any master's candle appeared in the hall, the boys had full three minutes' warning, and

a single loudly-whispered 'cavé' would cause some one in each dormitory instantly to
'douse the glim,' and shut the door; so that by the time of the adversary's arrival they
would all be (of course) fast asleep in bed, some of them snoring in an alarming
manner. Whatever noise the master might have heard, it would be impossible to fix it on
any of the sleepers.

So at the top of the stairs stood little Wright, shoeless, and shivering in his nightgown, but keenly entering into the fun, and not unconscious of the dignity of his
position. Meanwhile the rest were getting up a scenic representation of Bombastes
Furioso, arranging a stage, piling a lot of beds together for a theatre, and dressing up
the actors in the most fantastic apparel.

The impromptu Bombastes excited universal applause, and just at the end Wright ran
in through the lavatory.

'I say,' said the little fellow, 'it's jolly cold standing at the top of the stairs. Won't some
one relieve guard?'

'Oh, I will,' answered Eric good-naturedly; 'it's a shame that one fellow should have all
the bother and none of the fun;' and he ran to take Wright's post.

After watching a minute or two, he felt sure that there was no danger, and therefore
ran up to Upton's study for a change.

'Well, what's up?' said the study-boy approvingly, as he glanced at Eric's laughing
eyes.

'Oh, we've been having leap-frog, and then Bombastes Furioso. But I'm keeping
"cavé" now; only it's so cold that I thought I'd run up to your study.'

'Little traitor; we'll shoot you for a deserting sentinel.'

'Oh no!' said Eric, 'it's all serene; Rowley's out, and dear old Rose'd never dream of
supposing us elsewhere than in the arms of Morpheus. Besides, the fellows are making
less row now.'

'Well, look here! let's go and look on, and I'll tell you a dodge; put one of the tin
washing-basins against the iron door of the lavatory, and then if any one comes he'll
make clang enough to wake the dead; and while he's amusing himself with this, there'll
be lots of time to "extinguish the superfluous abundance of the nocturnal illuminators."
Eh?'

'Capital!' said Eric; 'come along.'

They went down and arranged the signal very artistically, leaving the iron door ajar a
little, and then neatly poising the large tin basin on its edge, so as to lean against it.
Having extremely enjoyed this part of the proceedings, they went to look at the
theatricals again, the boys being highly delighted at Upton's appearance among them.

They at once made Eric take a part in some very distant reminiscences of Macbeth,
and corked his cheeks with whiskers and mustachios to make him resemble Banquo, his
costume being completed by a girdle round his night-shirt, consisting of a very fine
crimson silk handkerchief, richly broidered with gold, which had been brought to him
from India, and which at first, in the innocence of his heart, he used to wear on
Sundays, until it acquired the soubriquet of 'the Dragon.' Duncan made a superb
Macbeth.

They were doing the dagger-scene, which was put on the stage in a most novel
manner. A sheet had been pinned from the top of the room, on one side of which stood

a boy with a broken dinner-knife, the handle end of which he was pushing through a hole in the middle of the sheet at the shadow of Duncan on the other side.

Duncan himself, in an attitude of intensely-affected melodrama, was spouting—

> 'Is this a dagger which I see before me?
> The handle towards me now? come, let me clutch thee:'

And he snatched convulsively at the handle of the protruded knife; but as soon as he nearly touched it, this end was immediately withdrawn and the blade end substituted, which made the comic Macbeth instantly draw back again, and recommence his apostrophe. This scene had tickled the audience immensely, and Duncan, amid shouts of laughter, was just drawing the somewhat unwarrantable conclusion that it was

> 'A dagger of the mind, a false creation,'

when a sudden grating, followed by a reverberated clang, produced a dead silence.

'Cavé,' shouted Eric, and took a flying leap into his bed. Instantly there was a bolt in different directions; the sheet was torn down, the candles dashed out, the beds shoved aside, and the dormitories at once plunged in profound silence, only broken by the heavy breathing of sleepers, when in strode—not Mr. Rose or any of the under-masters—but—Dr. Rowlands himself!

He stood for a moment to survey the scene. All the dormitory doors were wide open; the sheet which had formed the stage curtain lay torn on the floor of No.7; the beds in all the adjoining rooms were in the strangest positions; and half-extinguished wicks still smouldered in several of the sconces. Every boy was in bed, but the extraordinary way in which the bed-clothes were huddled about told an unmistakable tale.

He glanced quickly round, but the moment he had passed into No. 8 he heard a run, and, turning, just caught sight of Upton's figure vanishing into the darkness of the lavatory, towards the study stairs.

He said not a word, but stalked hastily through all the dormitories, again stopping at No. 7 on his return. He heard nothing but the deep snores of Duncan, and instantly fixed on him as a chief culprit.

'Duncan!'

No reply; but calm stertorous music from Duncan's bed.

'Duncan!' he said, still louder and more sternly; 'you sleep soundly, sir, too soundly; get up directly,' and he laid his hand on the the boy's arm.

'Get away, you old donkey,' said Duncan sleepily, ' 'taint time to get up yet. First bell hasn't rung.'

'Come, sir, this shamming will only increase your punishment;' but the imperturbable Duncan stretched himself lazily, gave a great yawn, and then awoke with such an admirably-feigned start at seeing Dr. Rowlands, that Eric, who had been peeping at the scene from over his bed-clothes, burst into an irresistible explosion of laughter.

Dr. Rowlands swung round on his heel—'What! Williams! get out of bed, sir, this instant.'

Eric, forgetful of his disguise, sheepishly obeyed, but when he stood on the floor, he looked so odd in his crimson girdle and corked cheeks, with Dr. Rowlands surveying him in intense astonishment, that the scene became overpoweringly ludicrous to Duncan,

who now in his turn was convulsed with a storm of laughter, faintly echoed in stifled titterings from other beds.

'*Very* good,' said Dr. Rowlands, now thoroughly angry; 'you will hear of this to-morrow;' and he walked away with a heavy step, stopping at the lavatory door to restore the tin basin to its proper place, and then mounting to the studies.

Standing in the passage into which the studies opened, he knocked at one of the doors, and told a boy to summon all their occupants at once to the library.

Meanwhile the dormitory boys were aghast, and as soon as they heard the Doctor's retreating footsteps, began flocking in the dark to No. 7, not daring to relight their candles.

'Good gracious!' said Attlay, 'only to think of Rowley appearing! How could he have twigged?'

'He must have seen our lights in the window as he came home,' said Eric.

'I say, what a row that tin-basin dodge of yours made! What a rage the Doctor will be in to-morrow!'

'Won't you just catch it!' said Barker to Duncan, but intending the remark for Eric.

'Just like your mean chaff,' retorted Duncan. 'But I say, Williams,' he continued, laughing, 'you *did* look so funny in the whiskers.'

At this juncture they heard all the study-boys running downstairs to the library, and, lost in conjecture, retired to their different rooms.

'What do you think he'll do to us?' asked Eric.

'I don't know,' said Duncan uneasily; 'flog us for one thing, that's certain. I'm so sorry about that basin, Eric; but it's no good fretting. We've had our cake, and now we must pay for it, that's all.'

Eric's cogitations began to be unpleasant, when the door opened, and somebody stole noiselessly in.

'Who's there?'

'Upton. I've come to have a chat. The Doctor's like a turkey-cock at the sight of a red handkerchief. Never saw him in such a rage.'

'Why, what's he been saying?' asked Eric, as Upton came and took a seat on his bed.

'Oh! he's been rowing us like six o'clock,' said Upton, 'about "moral responsibility," "abetting the follies of children," "forgetting our position in the school," and I don't know what all; and he ended by asking who'd been in the dormitories. Of course, I confessed the soft impeachment, whereon he snorted, "Ha! I suspected so. Very well, sir, you don't know how to use a study; you shall be deprived of it till the end of term." '

'Did he really, Horace?' said Eric. 'And it's all my doing that you've got into the scrape. Do forgive me.'

'Bosh! My dear fellow,' said Upton, 'it's twice as much my fault as yours; and, after all, it was only a bit of fun. It's rather a bore losing the study, certainly; but never mind, we shall see all the more of each other. Good-night; I must be off.'

Next morning, prayers were no sooner over than Dr. Rowlands said to the boys, 'Stop! I have a word to say to you.'

'I find that there was the utmost disorder in the dormitories yesterday evening. All the candles were relighted at forbidden hours, and the noise made was so great that it was heard through the whole building. I am grieved that I cannot leave you, even for a few hours, without your taking such advantage of my absence; and that the upper boys, so far from using their influence to prevent these infractions of discipline, seem inclined rather to join in them themselves. On this occasion I have punished Upton, by depriving him of a privilege which he has abused; and as I myself detected Duncan and Williams, they will be flogged in the library at twelve. But I now come to the worst part of the proceeding. Somebody had been reckless enough to try and prevent surprise by the dangerous expedient of putting a tin basin against the iron door. The consequence was, that I was severely hurt, and *might* have been seriously injured in entering the lavatory. I must know the name of the delinquent.'

Upton and Eric immediately stood up. Dr. Rowlands looked surprised, and there was an expression of grieved interest in Mr. Rose's face.

'Very well,' said the Doctor, 'I shall speak to you both privately.'

Twelve o'clock came, and Duncan and Eric received a severe caning. Corporal punishment, however necessary and desirable for some dispositions, always produced on Eric the worst effects. He burned not with remorse or regret, but with shame and violent indignation, and listened, with an affectation of stubborn indifference, to Dr. Rowlands's warnings. When the flogging was over, he almost rushed out of the room, to choke in solitude his sense of humiliation, nor would he suffer any one for an instant to allude to his disgrace. Dr. Rowlands had hinted that Upton was doing him no good; but he passionately resented the suggestion, and determined, with obstinate perversity, to cling more than ever to the boy whom he had helped to involve in the same trouble with himself.

Any attempt on the part of masters to interfere in the friendships of boys is usually unsuccessful. The boy who has been warned against his new acquaintance not seldom repeats to him the fact that Mr. So-and-so doesn't like seeing them together, and after that they fancy themselves bound in honour to show that they are not afraid of continuing their acquaintance. It was not strange, therefore, that Eric and Upton were thrown more than ever into each other's society, and consequently that Eric, while he improved daily in strength, activity, and prowess, neglected more and more his school duties and honourable ambitions.

Mr. Rose sadly remarked the failure of promise in his character and abilities, and did all that could be done, by gentle firmness and unwavering kindness, to recall his pupil to a sense of duty. One night he sent for him to supper, and invited no one else. During the evening he drew out Eric's exercise, and compared it with those of Russell and Owen, who were now getting easily ahead of him in marks. Eric's was careless, hurried, and untidy; the other two were neat, spirited, and painstaking, and had, therefore, been marked much higher. They displayed all the difference between conscientious and perfunctory work.

'Your exercises *used* to be far better—even incomparably better,' said Mr. Rose; 'what is the cause of this falling off?'

Eric was silent.

Mr. Rose laid his hand gently on his head. 'I fear, my boy, you have not been improving lately. You have got into many scrapes, and are letting boys beat you in form who are far your inferiors in ability. That is a very bad *sign*, Eric; in itself it is a discouraging fact, but I fear it indicates worse evils. You are wasting the golden hours, my boy, that can never return. I only hope and trust that no other change for the worse is taking place in your character.'

And so he talked on till the boy's sorrow was undisguised. 'Come,' he said gently, 'let us kneel down together before we part.'

Boy and master knelt down humbly side by side, and from a full heart, the young man poured out his fervent petitions for the boy beside him. Eric's soul seemed to catch a glow from his words, and he loved him as a brother. He rose from his knees full of the strongest resolutions, and earnestly promised amendment for the future.

But poor Eric did not yet know his own infirmity. For a time, indeed, there was a marked improvement; but daily life flowed on with its usual allurements, and when the hours of temptation came, his good intentions melted away like the morning dew, so that, in a few more weeks, the prayer, and the vows that followed it, had been obliterated from his memory without leaving any traces in his life.

CHAPTER THE ELEVENTH

ERIC IN COVENTRY

And either greet him not,
Or else disdainfully, which shall shake him more
Than if not looked on.
Troilus and Cressida, iii. 3

UPTON, EXPATRIATED FROM his study, was allowed to use one of the smaller class-rooms which were occupied during play-hours by those boys who were too high in the school for 'the boarders' room,' and who were waiting to succeed to the studies as they fell vacant. There were three or four others with him in this class-room, and although it was less pleasant than his old quarters, it was yet far more comfortable than the Pandemonium of the Shell and fourth-form boys.

As a general rule, no boys were allowed to sit in any of the class-rooms except their legitimate occupants. The rule, however, was very generally overlooked, and hence, Eric, always glad of an opportunity to escape from the company of Barker and his associates, became a constant frequenter of his friend's new abode. Here they used to make themselves very comfortable. Joining the rest, they would drink coffee or chocolate, and amuse themselves over the fire with *Punch,* or some warlike novel in a green or yellow cover. One of them very often read aloud to the rest; and Eric, being both a good reader and a merry intelligent listener, soon became quite a favourite among the other boys.

Mr. Rose had often seen him sitting there, and left him unmolested; but if ever Mr. Gordon happened to come in and notice him, he invariably turned him out, and after the first offence or two, had several times set him an imposition. This treatment gave fresh intensity to his now deeply-seated disgust at his late master, and his expressions of indignation at 'Gordon's spite' were loud and frequent.

One day Mr. Gordon had accidentally come in, and found no one there but Upton and Eric; they were standing very harmlessly by the window, with Upton's arm resting kindly on Eric's shoulder, as they watched with admiration the network of rippled sunbeams that flashed over the sea. Upton had just been telling Eric the splendid phrase ἀνήριθμον γέλασμα πόνου which he had stumbled upon in an Æschylus lesson that morning, and they were trying which would hit on the best rendering of it. Eric stuck up for the literal sublimity of 'the innumerable laughter of the sea,' while Upton was trying to win him over to 'the many-twinkling smile of ocean.' They were enjoying the discussion, and each stoutly maintaining his own rendering, when Mr. Gordon entered.

On this occasion he was particularly angry: he had an especial dislike of seeing the two boys together, because he fancied that the younger had grown more than usually conceited and neglectful since he had been under the fifth-form patronage; and he saw in Eric's presence there a new case of wilful disobedience.

'Williams, here *again!*' he exclaimed sharply; 'why, sir, you seem to suppose that you may defy rules with impunity! How often have I told you that no one is allowed to sit here, except the regular occupants?'

His voice startled the two boys from their pleasant discussion.

'No other master takes any notice of it, sir,' said Upton.

'I have nothing to do with other masters. Williams, you will bring me the fourth Georgic, written out by Saturday morning, for your repeated disobedience. Upton, I have a great mind to punish you also, for tempting him to come here.'

This was a mistake on Mr. Gordon's part, of which Upton took immediate advantage.

'I have no power to prevent it, sir, if he wishes it. Besides,' he continued with annoying blandness of tone, 'it would be inhospitable; and I am too glad of his company.'

Eric smiled; and Mr. Gordon frowned. 'Williams, leave the room instantly.'

The boy obeyed slowly and doggedly. 'Mr. Rose never interferes with me, when he sees me here,' he said as he retreated.

'Then I shall request Mr. Rose to do so in future; your conceit and impertinence are getting intolerable.'

Eric only answered with a fiery glance; for of all charges the one which a boy resents most is an accusation of conceit. The next minute Upton joined him on the stairs, and Mr. Gordon heard them laughing a little ostentatiously, as they ran out into the playground together. He went away full of strong contempt, and from that moment began to look on the friends as two of the worst boys in the school.

This incident had happened on Thursday, which was a half-holiday, and instead of being able to join in any of the games, Eric had to spend that weary afternoon in writing away at the fourth Georgic; Upton staying in a part of the time to help him a little, by dictating the lines to him—an occupation not unfrequently interrupted by storms of furious denunciation against Mr. Gordon's injustice and tyranny; Eric vowing, with the usual vagueness of schoolboy intention, 'that he would pay him out somehow yet.'

The imposition was not finished that evening, and it again consumed some of the next day's leisure, part of it being written between schools in the forbidden class-room. Still it was not quite finished on Friday afternoon at six, when school ended, and Eric stayed a few minutes behind the rest to scribble off the last ten lines; which done, he banged down the lid of the desk, not locking it, and ran out.

The next morning an incident happened which involved considerable consequences to some of the actors in my story.

Mr. Rose and several other masters had not a schoolroom to themselves, like Mr. Gordon, but heard their forms in the great hall. At one end of this hall was a board used for the various school notices, to which there were always affixed two or three pieces of paper containing announcements about examinations and other matters of general interest.

On Saturday morning (when Eric was to give up his Georgic), the boys, as they dropped into the hall for morning school, observed a new notice on the board, and thronging round to see what it was, read these words, written on a half-sheet of paper attached by wafers to the board—

'GORDON IS A SURLY DEVIL.'

As may be supposed, so completely novel an announcement took them all very much by surprise, and they wondered who had been so audacious as to play this trick. But their wonder was cut short by the entrance of the masters, and they all took their seats, without any one tearing down the dangerous paper.

After a few minutes the eye of the second master, Mr. Ready, fell on the paper, and, going up, he read it, stood for a moment transfixed with astonishment, and then called Mr. Rose.

Pointing to the inscription he said, 'I think we had better leave that there, Rose, exactly as it is, till Dr. Rowlands has seen it. Would you mind asking him to step in here?'

Just at this juncture Eric came in, having been delayed by Mr. Gordon, while he rigidly inspected the imposition. As he took his seat, Montagu, who was next him, whispered—

'I say, have you seen the notice-board?'

'No. Why?'

'Why, some fellow has been writing up an opinion of Gordon not very favourable.'

'And serve him right, too, brute!' said Eric, smarting with the memory of his imposition.

'Well, there'll be no end of a row; you'll see.'

During this conversation, Dr. Rowlands came in with Mr. Rose. He read the paper, frowned, pondered a moment, and then said to Mr. Rose—'Would you kindly summon the lower school into the hall? As it would be painful to Mr. Gordon to be present, you had better explain to him how matters stand.'

'Hulloa! here's a rumpus!' whispered Montagu; 'he never has the lower school down for nothing.'

A noise was heard on the stairs, and in flocked the lower school. When they had ranged themselves on the vacant forms, there was a dead silence and hush of expectation.

'I have summoned you all together,' said the Doctor, 'on a most serious occasion. This morning, on coming into the schoolroom, the masters found that the notice-board had been abused for the purpose of writing up an insult to one of our number, which is at once coarse and wicked. As only a few of you have seen it, it becomes my deeply painful duty to inform you of its purport; the words are these—"Gordon is a surly devil." ' A *very* slight titter followed this statement, which was instantly succeeded by a sort of thrilling excitement; but Eric, when he heard the words, started perceptibly, and coloured as he caught Montagu's eye fixed on him.

Dr. Rowlands continued—'I suppose this dastardly impertinence has been perpetrated by some boy out of a spirit of revenge. I am perfectly amazed at the audacity and meanness of the attempt, and it may be very difficult to discover the author of it. But, depend upon it, discover him *we will*, at whatever cost. Whoever the offender may be, and he must be listening to me at this moment, let him be assured that he shall *not* be unpunished. His guilty secret shall be torn from him. His punishment can only be mitigated by his instantly yielding himself up.'

No one stirred, but during the latter part of this address Eric was so uneasy, and his cheek burned with such hot crimson, that several eyes were upon him, and the suspicions of more than one boy were awakened.

'Very well,' said the headmaster, 'the guilty boy is not inclined to confess. Mark then; if his name has not been given up to me by to-day week, every indulgence to the school will be forfeited, the next whole holiday stopped, and the coming cricket-match prohibited.'

'The handwriting may be some clue,' suggested Mr. Ready. 'Would you have any objection to my examining the note-books of the Shell?'

'None at all. The Shell boys are to show their books to Mr. Ready immediately.'

The head-boy of the Shell collected the books, and took them to the desk; the three masters glanced casually at about a dozen, and suddenly stopped at one. Eric's heart beat loud, as he saw Mr. Rose point towards him.

'We have discovered a handwriting which remarkably resembles that on the board. I give the offender one more chance of substituting confession for detection.'

No one stirred; but Montagu felt that his friend was trembling violently.

'Eric Williams, stand out in the room!'

Blushing scarlet, and deeply agitated, the boy obeyed.

'The writing on the notice is exactly like yours. Do you know anything of this shameful proceeding?'

'Nothing, sir,' he murmured in a low tone.

'Nothing whatever?'

'Nothing whatever, sir.'

Dr. Rowlands's look searched him through and through, and seemed to burn into his heart. He did not meet it, but hung his head. The Doctor felt certain from his manner that he was guilty. He chained him to the spot with his glance for a minute or two, and then said slowly, and with a deep sigh—

'Very well; I *hope* you have spoken the truth, but whether you have or no, we shall soon discover. The school, and especially the upper boys, will remember what I have said. I shall now tear down the insulting notice, and put it into your hands, Avonley, as head of the school, that you may make further inquiries.' He left the room, and the boys resumed their usual avocation till twelve o'clock. But poor Eric could hardly get through his ordinary pursuits; he felt sick and giddy, until everybody noticed his strange embarrassed manner and random answers.

No sooner had twelve o'clock struck than the whole school broke up into knots of buzzing and eager talkers.

'I wonder who did it,' said a dozen voices at once.

'The writing was undoubtedly Williams's,' suggested some.

'And did you notice how red and pale he got when the Doctor spoke to him, and how he hung his head?'

'Yes; and one knows how he hates Gordon.'

'Ay; by the bye, Gordon set him a Georgic only on Thursday, and he has been swearing at him ever since.'

'I noticed that he stayed in after all the rest last night,' said Barker pointedly.

'Did he? By Jove, that looks bad.'

'Has any one charged him with it?' asked Duncan.

'Yes,' answered one of the group; 'but he's as proud about it as Lucifer, and is furious if you mention it to him. He says we ought to know him better than to think him capable of such a thing.'

'And quite right, too,' said Duncan. 'If he did it, he's done something totally unlike what one would have believed possible of him.'

The various items of evidence were put together, and certainly they seemed to prove a strong case against Eric. In addition to the probabilities already mentioned, it was found that the ink used was of a violet colour, and a peculiar kind, which Eric was known to patronise; and not only so, but the wafers with which the paper had been attached to the board were yellow, and exactly of the same size with some which Eric was said to possess. How the latter facts had been discovered, nobody exactly knew, but they began to be very generally whispered throughout the school.

In short, the almost universal conviction among the boys proclaimed that he was guilty, and many urged him to confess it at once, and save the school from the threatened punishment. But he listened to such suggestions with the most passionate indignation.

'What!' he said angrily, 'tell a wilful lie to blacken my own innocent character? Never!'

The consequence was, they all begun to shun him. Eric was put into Coventry. Very few boys in the school still clung to him, and maintained his innocence in spite of appearances, but they were the boys whom he had most loved and valued, and they were most vigorous in his defence. They were Russell, Montagu, Duncan, Owen, and little Wright.

On the evening of the Saturday, Upton had sought out Eric, and said, in a very serious tone, 'This is a bad business, Williams. I cannot forget how you have been abusing Gordon lately, and though I won't believe you guilty, yet you ought to explain.'

'What? even *you*, then, suspect me?' said Eric, bursting into proud and angry tears. 'Very well. I shan't condescend to *deny* it. I won't speak to you again till you have repented of mistrusting me;' and he resolutely rejected all further overtures on Upton's part.

He was alone in his misery. Some one, he perceived, had plotted to destroy his character, and he saw too clearly how many causes of suspicion told against him. But it was very bitter to think that the whole school could so readily suppose that he would do a thing which from his soul he abhorred. 'No,' he thought; 'bad I may be, but I *could* not have done such a base and cowardly trick.'

Never in his life had he been so wretched. He wandered alone to the rocks, and watched the waves dashing against them with the rising tide. The tumult of the weather seemed to relieve and console the tumult of his heart. He drank in strength and defiance from the roar of the waters, and climbed to their very edge along the rocks, where every fresh rush of the waves enveloped him in white swirls of cold salt spray. The look of the green, rough, hungry sea harmonised with his feelings, and he sat down and stared into it, to find relief from the torment of his thoughts.

At last, with a deep sigh, he turned away to go back and meet the crowd of suspicious and unkindly companions, and brood alone over his sorrow in the midst of them. He had not gone many steps when he caught sight of Russell in the distance. His first impulse was to run away and escape; but Russell determined to stop him, and when he came up, said, 'Dear Eric, I have sought you out on purpose to tell you that *I* don't suspect you, and have never done so for a moment. I know you too well, my boy, and be sure that *I* will always stick to you, even if the whole school cut you.'

'Oh, Edwin, I am *so* wretched. I needn't tell you that I am quite innocent of this. What have I done to be so suspected? Why, even your cousin Upton won't believe me.'

'But he does, Eric,' said Russell; 'he told me so just now, and several others said the same thing.'

A transient gleam passed over Eric's face.

'Oh, I do so long for home again,' he said. 'I hate this place. Except you, I have no friend.'

'Don't say so, Eric. This cloud will soon blow over. Depend upon it, as the Doctor said, we shall discover the offender yet, and the fellows will soon make you reparation for their false suspicions. And you *have* one friend, Eric,' he continued, pointing reverently upwards.

Eric was overcome; he sat down on the grass, while intense pride and the consciousness of innocence struggled with the burning sense of painful injustice. Russell sat silent and pitying beside him, till at last Eric, with sudden energy, sprang to his feet, and said, 'Now, Edwin! I've been conquering my cowardice, thanks to you, so come along home. After all, the fellows are in the wrong, not I;' and so saying he took Russell's arm, and walked across the playground with almost a haughty look.

When they got home, Eric found three notes in his drawer. One was from Mr. Gordon, and ran thus:—

'I have little doubt, Williams, that you have done this act. Believe me, I feel no anger, only pity for you. Come to me and confess, and I promise, by every means in my power, to befriend and save you.'

This note he read, and then, stamping on the floor, tore it up furiously into twenty pieces, which he scattered about the room.

Another was from Mr. Rose:—

'DEAR ERIC—I *cannot, will* not, believe you guilty, although appearances look very black. You have many faults, but I feel sure that I cannot be mistaken in supposing you too noble-minded for a revenge so petty and so mean. Come to me, my boy, if I can help you in any way. I *trust you*, Eric, and will use every endeavour to right you in the general estimation. You are innocent; pray to God for help under this cruel trial, and be sure that your character will yet be cleared.—Affectionately yours,

'WALTER ROSE.

'*P.S.*—I can easily understand that just now you will like quiet; come and sit with me in the library as much as you like.'

He read this note two or three times with grateful emotion, and at that moment would have died for Mr. Rose. The third note was from Owen, as follows:—

'DEAR WILLIAMS—We have been cool to each other lately; naturally, perhaps. But yet I think that it will be some consolation to you to be told, even by a rival, that I, for one, feel certain of your innocence,—and, moreover, think that I can *prove* it, as I will tell you in time. If you want company, I shall be delighted to have a walk.—Yours truly,

'D. OWEN.'

This note, too, brought much comfort to the poor boy's lonely and passionate heart. He put it into his pocket, and determined at once to accept Mr. Rose's kind offer of allowing him to sit for the present in the library.

There were several boys in the room while he was reading his notes, but none of them spoke to him, and he was too proud to notice them, or interrupt the constrained silence. As he went out he met Duncan and Montagu, who at once addressed him in the hearing of the rest.

'Ha! Williams,' said Duncan, 'we have been looking everywhere for you, old fellow. Cheer up, you shall be cleared yet. I for one, and Monty for another, will maintain your innocence before the whole school.'

Montagu *said* nothing, but Eric understood full well the trustful kindness of his pressure of the hand. His heart was too full to speak, and he went on towards the library.

'I wonder at your speaking to that fellow,' said Ball, as the two new-comers joined the group at the fireplace.

'You will be yourself ashamed of having ever suspected him before long,' said Montagu warmly; 'ay, the whole lot of you; and you are very unkind to condemn him before you are certain.'

'I wish you joy of your *friend*, Duncan,' sneered Barker.

'Friend?' said Duncan, firing up; 'yes! he is my friend, and I'm not ashamed of him. It would be well for the school if *all* the fellows were as honourable as Williams.'

Barker took the hint, and although he was too brazen to blush, thought it better to say no more.

CHAPTER THE TWELFTH

THE TRIAL

A plot, a plot, a plot, to ruin all.
TENNYSON, *The Princess*

O N THE MONDAY EVENING the head-boy reported to Dr. Rowlands that the perpetrator of the offence had not been discovered, but that one boy was very generally suspected, and on grounds that seemed plausible. 'I admit,' he added, 'that from the little I know of him, he seems to me a very unlikely sort of boy to do it.'

'I think,' suggested the Doctor, 'that the best way would be for you to have a regular trial on the subject and hear the evidence. Do you think that you can be trusted to carry on the investigation publicly, with good order and fairness?'

'I think so, sir,' said Avonley.

'Very well. Put up a notice, asking all the school to meet by themselves in the boarders' room to-morrow afternoon at three, and see what you can do among you.'

Avonley did as the Doctor suggested. At first, when the boys assembled, they seemed inclined to treat the matter as a joke, and were rather disorderly; but Avonley briefly begged them, if they determined to have a trial, to see that it was conducted sensibly; and by general consent he was himself voted into the desk as president. He then got up and said—

'There must be no sham or nonsense about this affair. Let all the boys take their seats quietly down the room.'

They did so, and Avonley asked, 'Is Williams here?'

Looking round, they discovered he was not. Russell instantly went to the library to fetch him, and told him what was going on. He took Eric's arm kindly as they entered, to show the whole school that he was not ashamed of him, and Eric deeply felt the delicacy of his goodwill.

'Are you willing to be tried, Williams,' asked Avonley, 'on the charge of having written the insulting paper about Mr. Gordon? Of course we know very little how these kind of things ought to be conducted, but we will see that everything done is open and above ground, and try to manage it properly.'

'There is nothing I should like better,' said Eric.

He had quite recovered his firm manly bearing. A quiet conversation with his dearly loved friend and master had reassured him in the confidence of innocence, and though the colour on his cheeks had through excitement sunk into two bright red spots, he looked wonderfully noble and winning as he stood before the boys in the centre of the room, modest, and yet with the proud consciousness of innocence in his bearing. His appearance caused a little reaction in his favour, and a murmur of applause followed his answer.

'Good,' said Avonley; 'who will prosecute on the part of the school?'

There was a pause. Nobody seemed to covet the office.

'Very well; if no one is willing to prosecute, the charge drops.'

'I will do it,' said Gibson, a Rowlandite, one of the study-boys at the top of the fifth form. He was a clever fellow, and Eric liked the little he had seen of him.

'Have you any objection, Williams, to the jury being composed of the sixth form? or are there any names among them which you wish to challenge?'

'No,' said Eric, glancing round indifferently.

'Well, now, who will defend the accused?'

Another pause, and Upton got up.

'No,' said Eric at once. 'You were inclined to distrust me, Upton, and I will only be defended by somebody who never doubted my innocence.'

Another pause followed, and then, blushing crimson, Russell got up. 'I am only a Shell boy,' he said; 'but if Eric doesn't mind trusting his cause to me, I will defend him since no other fifth-form fellow stirs.'

'Thank you, Russell, I *wanted* you to offer; I could wish no better defender.'

'Will Owen, Duncan, and Montagu help me, if they can?' asked Russell.

'Very willingly,' they all said, and went to take their seats by him. They conversed eagerly for a few minutes, seeming to make more than one discovery during their discussion, and then declared themselves ready.

'All I have got to do,' said Gibson rising, 'is to bring before the school the grounds for suspecting Williams, and all the evidence which makes it probable that he is the offender. Now, first of all, the thing must have been done between Friday evening and Saturday morning; and since the schoolroom door is generally locked soon after school, it was probably done in the short interval between six and a quarter-past. I shall now examine some witnesses.'

The first boy called upon was Pietrie, who deposed that on Friday evening, when he left the room, having been detained a few minutes, the only boy remaining in it was Williams.

Carter, the school servant, was then sent for, and deposed that he had met Master Williams hastily running out of the room, when he went at a quarter-past six to lock the door.

Examined by Gibson.—'Was any boy in the room when you did lock the door?'

'No one.'

'Did you meet any one else in the passage?'

'No.'

Cross-examined by Russell.—'Do boys ever get into the room after the door is locked?'

'Yes.'

'By what means?'

'Through the side windows.'

'That will do.'

Russell here whispered something to Duncan, who at once left the room, and on returning, after a few minutes' absence, gave Russell a nod so full of significance that, like Lord Burleigh's shake of the head, it seemed to speak whole volumes at once.

Barker was next brought forward, and questioned by Gibson.

'Do you know that Williams is in the habit of using a particular kind of ink?'

'Yes; it is of a violet colour, and has a peculiar smell.'

'Could you recognise anything written with it?'

'Yes.'

Gibson here handed to Barker the paper which had caused so much trouble.

'Is that the kind of ink?'

'Yes.'

'Do you know the handwriting on that paper?'

'Yes; it is Williams's hand.'

'How can you tell?'

'He makes his r's in a curious way.'

'Turn the paper over. Have you ever seen wafers of that kind before?'

'Yes; Williams has a box of them in his desk.'

'Has any other boy, that you are aware of, wafers like them?'

'No.'

Cross-examined by Duncan.—'*How* do you know that Williams has wafers like those?'

'I have seen him use them.'

'For what purpose?'

'To fasten letters.'

'I can't help remarking that you seem very well acquainted with what he does. Several of those who know him best, and have seen him oftenest, never heard of these wafers. May I ask,' he said, 'if any one else in the school will witness to having seen Williams use these wafers?'

No one spoke, and Barker, whose malice seemed to have been changed into uneasiness, sat down.

Upton was the next witness. Gibson began—

'You have seen a good deal of Williams?'

'Yes,' said Upton, smiling.

'Have you ever heard him express any opinions of Mr. Gordon?'

'Often.'

'Of what kind?'

'Dislike and contempt,' said Upton, amidst general laughter.

'Have you ever heard him say anything which implied a desire to injure him?'

'The other day Mr. Gordon gave him a Georgic as an imposition, and I heard Williams say that he would like to pay him out.'

This last fact was new to the school, and excited a great sensation.

'When did he say this?'

'On Friday afternoon.'

Upton had given his evidence with great reluctance, although, being simply desirous that the truth should come out, he concealed nothing that he knew. He brightened up a little when Russell rose to cross-examine him.

'Have you ever known Williams do any mean act?'

'Never.'

'Do you consider him a boy *likely* to have been guilty on this occasion?'

'Distinctly the reverse. I am convinced of his innocence.'

The answer was given with vehement emphasis, and Eric felt greatly relieved by it.

One or two other boys were then called on as witnesses to the great agitation which Eric had shown during the investigation in the schoolroom, and then Gibson, who was a sensible self-contained fellow, said, 'I have now done my part. I have shown that the accused had a grudge against Mr. Gordon at the time the thing was done, and had threatened to be revenged on him; that he was the last boy in the room during the time when the offence must have been committed; that the handwriting is known to be like his, and that the ink and wafers employed were such as he, and he only, was known to possess. In addition to all this, his behaviour, when the matter was first publicly noticed, was exactly such as coincides with the supposition of his guilt. I think you will all agree in considering these grounds of suspicion very strong; and leaving them to carry their full weight with you, I close the case for the prosecution.'

The school listened to Gibson's quiet unmoved formality with a kind of grim and gloomy satisfaction, and when he had concluded, there were probably few but Eric's own immediate friends who were not fully convinced of his guilt, however sorry they might be to admit so unfavourable an opinion of a companion whom they all admired.

After a minute or two Russell rose for the defence, and asked, 'Has Williams any objection to his desk being brought, and any of its contents put in as evidence?'

'Not the least; there is the key, and you will find it in my place in school.'

The desk was brought, but it was found to be already unlocked, and Russell looked at some of the note-paper which it contained. He then rose—nervously at first, and with a deep blush lighting up his face, but soon showing a warmth and sarcasm, which few expected from his gentle nature. 'In spite of the evidence adduced,' he began, 'I think I can show that Williams is not guilty. It is quite true that he dislikes Mr. Gordon, and would not object to any open way of showing it; it is quite true that he used the expressions attributed to him, and that the ink and wafers are such as may be found in his desk, and that the handwriting is not unlike his. But is it probable that a boy intending to post up an insult such as this, would do so in a manner and at a time so likely to involve him in immediate detection and certain punishment? At any rate, he would surely disguise his usual handwriting. Now, I ask any one to look at this paper, and tell me whether it is not clear, on the contrary, that these letters were traced slowly and with care, as would be the case with an elaborate attempt to imitate?' Russell here handed the paper to the jury, who again narrowly examined it.

'Now, the evidence of Pietrie and Carter is of no use, because Carter himself admitted that boys often enter the room by the window—a fact to which we shall have to allude again.

'We admit the evidence about the ink and wafers. But it is rather strange that Barker should know about the wafers, since neither I, nor any other friend of Williams, often as we have sat by him when writing letters, have ever observed that he possessed any like them."

Several boys began to look at Barker, who was sitting very ill at ease on the corner of a form, in vain trying to appear unconcerned.

'There is another fact which no one yet knows, but which I must mention. It will explain Eric's—I mean Williams's—agitation when Dr. Rowlands read out the words on that paper; and, confident of his innocence, I am indifferent to its appearing to tell against him. I myself once heard Eric—I beg pardon, I mean Williams' (he said, correcting himself with a smile)—'use the very words written on that paper, and not only heard them, but expostulated with him strongly for the use of them. I need hardly say how very unlikely it is that, remembering this, he should thus publicly draw my suspicions on him, if he meant to insult Mr. Gordon undiscovered. But, besides myself there was another boy who accidentally overheard that expression. That boy was Barker.

'I have to bring forward a new piece of evidence, which at least ought to go for something. Looking at this half-sheet of note-paper, I see that the printer's name on the stamp in the corner is "Graves, York." Now, I have just found that there is no paper at all like this in Williams's desk; all the note-paper it contains is marked "Blakes, Ayrton."'

'I might bring many witnesses to prove how very unlike Williams's general character a trick of this kind would be. But I am not going to do this. We think we know the real offender. We have had one trial, and now demand another. It is our painful duty (but depend upon it we shall not shirk it,' he added with unusual passion) 'to prove Williams's innocence by proving another's guilt. That other is a known enemy of mine, and of Montagu's, and of Owen's. We therefore leave the charge of stating the case against him to Duncan, with whom he has never quarrelled.'

Russell sat down amid general applause; he had performed his task with a wonderful modesty and self-possession, which filled every one with admiration, and Eric warmly pressed his hand.

The interest of the school was intensely excited, and Duncan, after a minute's pause, starting up, said—

'Williams has allowed his desk to be brought in and examined. Will Barker do the same?'

The real culprit now saw at once that his plot to ruin Eric was recoiling on himself. He got up, swore and blustered at Russell, Duncan, and Montagu, and at first flatly refused to allow his desk to be brought. He was, however, forced to yield, and when opened, it was immediately seen that the note-paper it contained was identical with that on which the words had been written. At this he affected to be perfectly unconcerned, and merely protested against what he called the meanness of trying to fix the charge on him.

'And what have you been doing the whole of the last day or two,' asked Gibson quietly, 'but endeavouring to fix the charge on another?'

'We have stronger evidence against you,' said Duncan, confronting him with an undaunted look, before which his insolence quailed. 'Russell, will you call Graham?'

Graham was called, and put on his honour.

'You were in the sick-room on Friday evening?'

'Yes.'

'Did you see any one get in to the schoolroom through the side window?'

'That's a leading question,' interrupted Barker.

'Stuff!' said Graham contemptuously, not vouchsafing further reply to the objection. 'I'll just tell you all I know. I was sitting doing nothing in the sick-room, when I suddenly saw Barker clamber into the schoolroom by the window, which he left open. I was looking on simply from curiosity, and saw him search Williams's desk, from which he took out something, I could not make out what. He then went to his own desk, and wrote for about ten minutes, after which I observed him go up and stand by the notice-board. When he had done this, he got out by the window again, and ran off.'

'Didn't this strike you as extraordinary?'

'No; I thought nothing more about it till some one told me in the sick-room about this row. I then mentioned privately what I had seen, and it wasn't till I saw Duncan, half an hour ago, that I thought it worth while to make it generally known.'

Duncan turned an inquiring eye to Barker (who sat black and silent), and then pulled out some bits of torn paper from his pocket, put them together, and called Owen to

stand up. Showing him the fragments of paper, he asked, 'Have you ever seen these before?'

'Yes. On Saturday, when the boys left the schoolroom, I stayed behind to think a little over what had occurred, feeling convinced that Williams was *not* guilty, spite of appearances. I was standing by the empty fireplace, when these bits of paper caught my eye. I picked them up, and, after a great deal of trouble, fitted them together. They are covered apparently with failures in an attempt at forgery, viz. first, "Gordon is a sur——" and then a stop as though the writer were dissatisfied, and several of the words written over again for practice, and then a number of r's made in the way that Williams makes them.'

'There you may stop,' said Barker, stamping fiercely; 'I did it all.'

A perfect yell of scorn and execration followed this announcement.

'What! *you* did it, and caused all this trouble, you ineffable blackguard!' shouted Upton, grasping him with one hand, while he struck him with the other.

'Stop!' said Avonley; 'just see that he doesn't escape, while we decide on his punishment.'

It was very soon decided by the sixth form that he should run the gauntlet of the school. The boys instantly took out their handkerchiefs, and knotted them tight. They then made a double line down each side of the corridor, and turned Barker loose. He stood stock-still at one end while the fellows nearest him thrashed him unmercifully with the heavy knots. At last the pain was getting severe, and he moved on, finally beginning to run. Five times he was forced up and down the line, and five times did every boy in the line give him a blow, which, if it did not hurt much, at least spoke of no slight anger and contempt. He was dogged and unmoved to the last, and then Avonley hauled him into the presence of Dr. Rowlands. He was put in a secure room by himself, and the next morning was first flogged and then publicly expelled. Thenceforth, he disappears from the history of Roslyn School.

I need hardly say that neither Eric nor his friends took any part in this retributive act; indeed they tried (though in vain) to prevent it. They sat together in the boarders' room till it was over, engaged in exciting discussion of the recent events. Most warmly did Eric thank them for their trustfulness. 'Thank you,' he said, 'with all my heart, for proving my innocence; but thank you, even more a great deal, for first believing it.'

Upton was the first to join them, and since he had but wavered for a moment, he was soon warmly reconciled with Eric. They had hardly shaken hands when the rest came flocking in. 'We have all been unjust,' said Avonley; 'let's make up for it as well as we can. Three cheers for Eric Williams!'

They gave not three, but a dozen, till they were tired; and meanwhile every one was pressing round him, telling him how sorry they were for the false suspicion, and doing all they could to show their regret for his recent troubles. His genial, boyish heart readily forgave them, and his eyes shone with joy. The delicious sensation of returning esteem made him almost think it worth while to have undergone his trial.

Most happily did he spend the remainder of that afternoon, and it was no small relief to all the Rowlandites in the evening to find themselves finally rid of Barker, whose fate no one pitied, and whose name no one mentioned without disgust. He had done more than any other boy to introduce meanness, quarrelling, and vice, and the very atmosphere of the rooms seemed healthier in his absence. One boy only forgave him, one boy only prayed for him, one boy only endeavoured to see him for one last kind word. That boy was Edwin Russell.

After prayers, Mr. Gordon, who had been at Dr. Rowlands's to dinner, apologised to Eric amply and frankly for his note, and did and said all that could be done by an honourable man to repair the injury of an unjust doubt. Eric felt his generous humility, and from thenceforth, though they were never friends, he and Mr. Gordon ceased to be enemies.

That night Mr. Rose crowned his happiness by asking him and his defenders to supper in the library. A most bright and joyous evening they passed, for they were in the highest spirits; and when the master bade them 'good-night,' he kindly detained Eric, and said to him, 'Keep an innocent heart, my boy, and you need never fear trouble. Only think if you had been guilty, and were now in Barker's place!'

'Oh, I *couldn't* be guilty, sir,' said Eric, gaily.

'Not of such a fault, perhaps. But,' he added solemnly, 'there are many kinds of temptation, Eric; many kinds. And they are easy to fall into. You will find it no light battle to resist them.'

'Believe me, sir, I will try,' he answered with humility.

'Jehovah-Nissi!' said Mr. Rose. 'Let the Lord be your banner, Eric, and you will win the victory. God bless you.'

And as the boy's graceful figure disappeared through the door, Mr. Rose drew his arm-chair to the fire, and sat and meditated long. He was imagining for Eric a sunny future—a future of splendid usefulness, of reciprocated affection, of brilliant fame.

CHAPTER THE THIRTEENTH

THE ADVENTURE AT THE STACK

> Ten cables from where green meadows
> And quiet homes could be seen,
> No greater space
> From peril to peace;—
> But the savage sea between!
> EDWIN ARNOLD

THE EASTER HOLIDAYS at Roslyn lasted about ten days, and as most of the boys came from a distance, they usually spent them at school. Many of the ordinary rules were suspended during this time, and the boys were supplied every day with pocket money; consequently the Easter holidays passed very pleasantly, and there was plenty of fun.

It was the great time for excursions all over the island, and the boys would often be out the whole day long among the hills, or about the coast. Eric enjoyed the time particularly, and was in great request among all the boys. He was now more gay and popular than ever, and felt as if nothing were wanting to his happiness. But this brilliant prosperity was not good for him, and he felt continually that he cared far less for the reproaches of conscience than he had done in the hours of his trial; sought far less for help from God than he had done when he was lonely and neglected.

He always knew that his great safeguard was the affection of Russell. For Edwin's sake, and for shame at the thought of Edwin's disapproval, he abstained from many things into which he would otherwise have insensibly glided in conformation to the general looseness of the school morality. But Russell's influence worked on him powerfully, and tended to counteract a multitude of temptations.

Among other undesirable lessons Upton had taught Eric to smoke; and he was now one of those who often spent a part of their holidays in lurking about with pipes in their mouths at places where they were unlikely to be disturbed, instead of joining in some hearty and healthy game. When he began to 'learn' smoking, he found it anything but pleasant; but a little practice had made him an adept, and he found a certain amount of enjoyable excitement in finding out cosy places by the river, where he and Upton might go and lounge for an hour to enjoy the forbidden luxury.

In reality, he, like most boys, at first disliked the habit; but it seemed a fine thing to do, and to some, at any rate, it was a refuge from vacuity. Besides, they had a confused notion that there was something 'manly' in it, and it derived an additional zest from the stringency of the rules adopted to put it down. So a number of the boys smoked, and some few of them to such excess as seriously to injure their health, and form a habit which they could never afterwards abandon.

One morning of the Easter holidays, Eric, Montagu, and Russell started for an excursion down the coast to Rilby Head. As they passed through Ellan, Eric was deputed to go and buy Easter eggs and other provisions, as they did not mean to be back for dinner. In about ten minutes he caught up the other two, just as they were getting out of the town.

'What an age you've been buying a few Easter eggs,' said Russell, laughing; 'have you been waiting till the hens laid?'

'No; they're not the *only* things I've got.'

'Well, but you might have got all the grub at the same shop.'

'Ay; but I've procured a more refined article. Guess what it is.'

The two boys didn't guess, and Eric said, to enlighten them, 'Will you have a whiff, Monty?'

'A whiff! Oh! I see you've been wasting your tin on cigars—*alias,* rolled cabbage-leaves. O fumose puer!'

'Well, will you have one?'

'If you like,' said Montagu, wavering; 'but I don't much care to smoke.'

'Well, *I* shall, at any rate,' said Eric, keeping off the wind with his cap, as he lighted a cigar, and began to puff.

They strolled on in silence; the smoking didn't promote conversation, and Russell thought that he had never seen his friend look so ridiculous, and entirely unlike himself, as he did while strutting along with the weed in his mouth. The fact was, Eric didn't guess how much he was hurting Edwin's feelings, and he was smoking more to 'make things look like the holidays,' by a little bravado, than anything else. But suddenly he caught the expression of Russell's face, and instantly said—

'Oh, I forgot, Edwin; I know you don't like smoking;' and he instantly flung the cigar over the hedge, being really rather glad to get rid of it. With the cigar, he seemed to have flung away the affected manner he displayed just before, and the spirits of all three rose at once.

'It isn't that I don't *like* smoking only, Eric, but I think it wrong—for *us* I mean.'

'Oh, my dear fellow! surely there can't be any harm in it. Why, everybody smokes.'

'It may be all very well for men, although I'm not so sure of that. But, at any rate, it does nothing but harm to growing boys. You know yourself what harm it does in every way.'

'Oh, it's a mere school rule against it. How can it be wrong? Why, I even know clergymen who smoke.'

Montagu laughed. 'Well, clergymen ain't immaculate,' said he; 'but I have seldom met a man yet who didn't tell you that he was *sorry* he'd acquired the habit.'

'I'm sure you won't thank that rascally cousin of mine for having taught you,' said Russell; 'but seriously, isn't it a very moping way of spending the afternoon, to go and lie down behind some haystack, or in some frowsy tumble-down barn, as you smokers do, instead of playing racquets or football?'

'Oh, it's pleasant enough sometimes,' said Eric, speaking rather against his own convictions.

'As for me, I've pretty nearly left it off,' said Montagu, 'and I think Rose convinced me that it was a mistake. Not that he knows that I ever did smoke. I should be precious sorry if he did, for I know how he despises it in boys. Were you in school the other day when he caught Pietrie and Booking?'

'No.'

'Well, when Booking went up to have his exercise corrected, Rose smelt that he had been smoking, and charged him with it. Booking stoutly denied it, but after he had told the most robust lies, Rose made him empty his pockets, and there, sure enough, were a pipe and a cigar-case half full! You *should* have heard how Rose thundered and lightened at him for his lying, and then sent him to the Doctor. I never saw him so terrific before.'

'You don't mean to say you were convinced it was wrong because Booking was caught, and told lies—do you? *Non sequitur.*'

'Stop—not so fast. Very soon after Rose twigged Pietrie, who at once confessed, and was caned. I happened to be in the library when Rose sent for him, and Pietrie said mildly that "he didn't see the harm of it." Rose smiled in his kind way, and said, "Don't see the *harm* of it! Do you see any good in it?"

' "No, sir."

' "Well, isn't it forbidden?"

' "Yes, sir."

' "And doesn't it waste your money?"

' "Yes, sir."

' "And tempt you to break rules, and tell lies to screen yourself?"

' "Yes, sir," said Pietrie, looking unusually crestfallen.

' "And don't your parents disapprove it? And doesn't it throw you among some of the worst boys, and get you into great troubles? Silly fellow," he said, pulling Pietrie's ear (as he sometimes does, you know), "don't talk nonsense; and remember next time you're caught, I shall have you punished." So off went Pietrie, ἀχρεῖον ἰδών, as our friend Homer says. And your humble servant was convinced.'

'Well, well!' said Eric, laughing, 'I suppose you're right. At any rate, I give in. Two to one ain't fair:—πρὸς δύο οὐδ' ὁ Ἡρακλῆς, since you're in a quoting humour.'

Talking in this way they got to Rilby Head, where they found plenty to amuse them. It was a splendid headland, rising bluff four hundred feet out of the sea, and presenting magnificent reaches of rock scenery on all sides. The boys lay on the turf at the summit, and flung innocuous stones at the sea-gulls as they sailed far below them over the water and every now and then pounced at some stray fish that came to the surface; or they watched the stately barques as they sailed by on the horizon, wondering at their cargo and destination; or chaffed the fisherman, whose boats heaved on the waves at the foot of the promontory. When they were rested, they visited a copper-mine by the side of the Head, and filled their pockets with bits of bright quartz or red shining spar, which they found in plenty among the rocks.

In the afternoon they strolled towards home, determining to stop a little at the Stack on their way. The Stack formed one of the extremities of Ellan Bay, and was a huge mass of isolated schist, accessible at low water, but entirely surrounded at high tide. It was a very favourite resort of Eric's, as the coast all about it was bold and romantic; and he often went there with Russell on a Sunday evening to watch the long line of golden radiance slanting to them over the water from the setting sun—a sight which they agreed to consider one of the most peaceful and mysteriously beautiful in nature.

They reached the Stack, and began to climb to its summit. The sun was just preparing to set, and the west was gorgeous with red and gold.

'We shan't see the line on the waters this evening,' said Eric; 'there's too much of a breeze. But look, what a glorious sunset!'

'It is indeed,' said Russell; 'it reminds me of what Rose said the other day; we were standing on the top of Brada, leaning against a heap of stones to keep off the north-easter, and Rose suddenly exclaimed, "Look, Edwin, how that crimson sunset burns itself away like a thought of death, judgment, and eternity, all in one!" I wonder what he meant?'

'It'll be stormy to-morrow,' said Montagu; 'but come along, let's get to the top; the wind's rising, and the waves will be rather grand.'

'Ay, we'll sit and watch them; and let's finish our grub; I've got several eggs left, and I want to get them out of my pocket.'

They devoured the eggs, and then stood enjoying the sight of the waves, which sometimes climbed up the rock almost to their feet, and then fell back, hissing and discomfited. Suddenly they remembered that it was getting late, and that they ought to get home for tea at seven.

'Hallo!' said Russell, looking at his watch, 'it's half-past six. We must cut back as hard as we can. By the bye, I hope the tide hasn't been coming in all this time.'

'My goodness!' said Montagu, with a violent start, 'I'm afraid it has, though! What asses we have been, with our waves and sunsets. Let's set off as hard as we can pelt.'

Immediately they scrambled, by the aid of hands and knees, down the Stack, and made their way for the belt of rock which joined it to the mainland; but to their horror, they at once saw that the tide had come in, and that a narrow gulf of sea already divided them from the shore.

'There's only one way for it,' said Eric; 'if we're plucky, we can jump that; but we mustn't wait till it gets worse. A good jump will take us *nearly* to the other side—far enough, at any rate, to let us flounder across somehow.'

As fast as they could they hurried along down to the place where the momentarily increasing zone of water seemed as yet to be narrowest; and where the rocks on the other side were lower than those on which they stood. Their situation was by no means pleasant. The wind had been rising more and more, and the waves dashed into this little channel with such violence, that to swim it would have been a most hazardous experiment, particularly as they could not dive in from the ledge on which they stood, from their ignorance of the depth of water.

Eric's courage supported the other two. 'There's no good *thinking* about it,' said he, 'jump we *must*; the sooner the better. We can but be a little hurt at the worst. Here, I'll set the example.'

He drew back a step or two, and sprang out with all his force. He was a practised and agile jumper, and, to their great relief, he alighted near the water's edge, on the other side, where, after slipping once or twice on the wet and seaweed-covered rocks, he effected a safe landing, with no worse harm than a wetting up to the knees.

'Now then, you two,' he shouted, 'no time to lose.'

'Will you jump first, Monty?' said Russell; 'both of you are better jumpers than I, and to tell the truth, I'm rather afraid.'

'Then I won't leave you,' said Montagu; 'we'll both stay here.'

'And perhaps be drowned or starved for our pains. No, Monty, *you* can clear it, I've no doubt.'

'Couldn't we try to swim it together, Edwin?'

'Madness! look there.' And as he spoke, a huge furious wave swept down the entire length of the gulf by which he stood, roaring and surging along till the whole water seethed, and tearing the seaweeds from their roots in the rock.

'Now's your time,' shouted Eric again. 'What *are* you waiting for? For God's sake, jump before another wave comes.'

'Monty, you *must* jump now,' said Russell, 'if only to help me when I try.'

Montagu went back as far as he could, which was only a few steps, and leapt wildly forward. He lighted into deep water, nearly up to his neck, and at first tried in vain to secure a footing on the sharp slippery schist; but, after a complete ducking, he stumbled forwards vigorously, and in half a minute, Eric leaning out as far as he could, caught his hand, and just pulled him to the other side in time to escape another rush of tumultuous and angry foam.

'Now, Edwin,' they both shouted, 'it'll be too late in another minute. Jump for your life.'

Russell stood on the rock pale and irresolute. Once or twice he prepared to spring, and stopped from fear at the critical instant. In truth, the leap was now most formidable;

to clear it was hopeless; and the fury of the rock-tormented waves rendered the prospect of a swim on the other side terrible to contemplate. Once in the grasp of one of those billows, even a strong man must have been carried out of the narrow channel, and hurled against the towering sweep of rocks which lay beyond it.

'O Edwin, Edwin—dear Edwin—*do* jump!' cried Eric with passionate excitement. 'We will rush in for you.'

Russell now seemed to have determined on running the risk; he stepped back, ran to the edge, missed his footing, and with a sharp cry of pain, fell heavily forward into the water. For an instant Eric and Montagu stood breathless,—but the next instant, they saw Russell's head emerge, and then another wave foaming madly by, made them run backwards for their lives, and hid him from their view. When it had passed, they saw him clinging with both hands, in the desperate instinct of self-preservation, to a projecting bit of rock, by the aid of which he gradually dragged himself out of the water, and grasping at crevices or bits of seaweed, slowly and painfully reached the ledge on which they had stood before they took the leap. He presented a pitiable spectacle; his face, pale as death, was dabbled with blood; his head drooped on his breast; his clothes were torn, and streamed with the salt water; his cap was gone, and the wet hair, which he seemed too exhausted to push aside, hung in heavy masses over his forehead and eyes. He was evidently dizzy, and in pain; and they noticed that he only seemed to use one foot.

While he was regaining the ledge, neither of the boys spoke, lest their voices should startle him, and make him fall; but now they both cried out, 'Are you hurt, Edwin?'

He did not answer, but supported his pale face on one hand, while he put the other to his head, from which the blood was flowing fast.

'O Edwin, for the love of God, try once more!' said Montagu; 'you will die if you spend the night on that rock.'

They could not catch the reply, and called again. The wind and waves were both rising fast, and it was only by listening intently, that they caught the faint words, 'I can't, my leg is hurt.' Besides, they both saw that a jump was no longer possible; the channel was more than double the width which it had been when Eric leaped, and from the rapid ascent of the rocks on both sides, it was now far out of depth.

'O God, what can we do?' said Montagu, bursting into tears. 'We can never save him, and all but the very top of the Stack is covered at high tide.'

Eric had not lost his presence of mind, 'Cheer up, Edwin,' he shouted, 'I *will* get back to you somehow. If I fail, crawl up to the top again.'

Again the wind carried away the reply, and Russell had sunk back on the rock.

'Monty,' said Eric, 'just watch for a minute or two. When I have got across, run to Ellan as hard as you can tear, and tell them that we are cut off by the tide on the Stack. They'll bring round the lifeboat. It's our only chance.'

'What are you going to do?' asked Montagu, terrified. 'Why, Eric, it's death to attempt swimming that. Good heavens!' And he drew Eric back hastily, as another vast swell of water came rolling along, shaking its white curled mane, like a sea-monster bent on destruction.

'Monty, it's no use,' said Eric, hastily tearing off his jacket and waistcoat; 'I'm not going to let Russell die on that ledge of rock. I shall try to reach him, whatever happens to me. Here; I want to keep these things dry. Be on the look-out; if I get across, fling them over to me if you can, and then do as I told you.'

He turned round; the wave had just spent its fury, and knowing that his only chance was to swim over before another came, he plunged in, and struck out like a man. He was a strong and expert swimmer, and as yet the channel was not more than a dozen yards across. He dashed over with the speed and strength of despair, and had just time to clutch the rocks on the other side before the next mighty swirl of the tide swept up in its white and tormented course. In another minute he was on the ledge by Russell's side.

He lifted him tenderly, and called to Montagu for the dry clothes. Montagu tied them skillfully with his neck-handkerchief round a fragment of rock, adding his own wet jacket to the bundle, and then flung it over. Eric wrapped up his friend in the clothes, and once more shouted to Montagu to go on his errand. For a short time the boy lingered, reluctant to leave them. Then he started off at a run. Looking back after a few minutes, he caught, through the gathering dusk, his last glimpse of the friends in their perilous situation. Eric was seated supporting Russell across his knees. When he saw Montagu turn, he waved his cap over his head as a signal of encouragement, and then began to carry Edwin higher up the rock for safety. It soon grew too dark to distinguish them, and Montagu at full speed flew to Ellan, which was a mile off. When he got to the harbour he told some sailors of the danger in which his friends were, and then ran on to the school. It was now eight o'clock, and quite dark. Tea was over, and lock-up time long past, when he stood wet through, excited, breathless, and without cap or jacket, at Dr. Rowlands's door.

'Good gracious! Master Montagu,' said the servant; 'what's the matter; have you been robbed?'

He pushed the girl aside, and ran straight to Dr. Rowlands's study. 'Oh, sir!' he exclaimed, bursting in, 'Eric and Russell are on the Stack, cut off by the tide.'

Dr. Rowlands started up hastily. 'What! on this stormy night? Have you raised the alarm?'

'I told the lifeboat people, sir, and then ran on.'

'I will set off myself at once,' said the Doctor, seizing his hat. 'But, my poor boy, how pale and ill you look, and you are wet through too. You had better change your clothes at once, or go to bed.'

'Oh no, sir,' said Montagu pleadingly; 'do take me with you.'

'Very well; but you must change first, or you may suffer in consequence. Make all haste, and directly you are dressed, a cup of tea shall be ready for you down here, and we will start.'

Montagu was off in an instant, and only stopped on his way to tell Duncan and the others of the danger which threatened their companions. The absence of the three boys from tea and lock-up had already excited general surmise, and Montagu's appearance, jacketless and wet, at the door of the boarders' room, at once attracted a group round him. He rapidly told them how things stood, and, hastening off, left them nearly as much agitated as himself. In a very short time he presented himself again before Dr. Rowlands, and when he had with difficulty swallowed the cup of tea, they sallied out.

It was pitch dark, and only one or two stars were seen at intervals struggling through the ragged masses of cloud. The wind howled in fitful gusts, and as their road led by the seaside, Montagu shuddered to hear how rough and turbulent the sea was, even on the sands. He stumbled once or twice, and then the Doctor kindly drew his trembling arm through his own, and made him describe the whole occurrence; while the servant went on in front with the lantern. When Montagu told how Eric had braved the danger of reaching his friend at the risk of his life, Dr. Rowlands's admiration was unbounded. 'Fine lad!' he exclaimed, with enthusiasm; 'I shall find it hard to believe any evil of him after this.'

They reached Ellan, and went to the boathouse.

'Have you put out the lifeboat?' said Dr. Rowlands anxiously.

'Ill luck, sir,' said one of the sailors, touching his cap; 'the lifeboat went to a wreck at Port Vash two days ago, and she hasn't been brought round again yet.'

'Indeed! but I do trust you have sent out another boat to try and save those poor boys.'

'We've been trying, sir, and a boat has just managed to start; but in a sea like that it's very dangerous, and it's so dark and gusty that I doubt it's no use, so I expect they'll put back.'

The Doctor sighed deeply. 'Don't alarm any other people,' he said; 'it will merely raise a crowd to no purpose. Here, George,' he continued to the servant, 'give me the lantern; I will go with this boy to the Stack; you follow us with ropes, and order a carriage from the King's Head. Take care to bring anything with you that seems likely to be useful.'

Montagu and Dr. Rowlands again started, and with difficulty made their way through the storm to the shore opposite the Stack. Here they raised the lantern and shouted; but the wind was now screaming with such violence that they were not sure that they heard any answering shout. Their eyes, accustomed to the darkness, could just make out the huge black outline of the Stack rising from the yeast of boiling waves, and enveloped every moment in blinding sheets of spray. On the top of it Montagu half thought that he saw something, but he was not sure.

'Thank God, there is yet hope,' said the Doctor, with difficulty making his young companion catch his words amid the uproar of the elements; 'if they can but keep warm in their wet clothes, we may perhaps rescue them before morning.'

Again he shouted to cheer them with his strong voice, and Montagu joined his clear ringing tones to the shout. This time they fancied that in one of the pauses of the wind they heard a faint cheer returned. Never was sound more welcome, and as they paced up and down they shouted at intervals, and held up the lantern, to show the boys that friends and help were near.

Eric heard them. When Montagu left, he had carried Russell to the highest point of the rock, and there, with gentle hands and soothing words, made him as comfortable as he could. He wrapped him in every piece of dry clothing he could find, and supported his head, heedless of the blood which covered him. Very faintly Russell thanked him, and pressed his hand; but he moaned with pain continually, and at last fainted away.

Meanwhile the wind rose higher, and the tide gained on the rocks, and the sacred darkness came down. At first Eric could think of nothing but storm and sea. Cold, and cruel, and remorseless, the sea beat up, drenching them to the skin continually with its clammy spray; and the storm shrieked round them pitilessly, and flung about the wet hair on Eric's bare head, and forced him to plant himself firmly, lest the rage of the gusts should hurl them from their narrow resting-place. The darkness made everything more fearful, for his eyes could distinguish nothing but the gulfs of black water glistening here and there with hissing foam, and he shuddered as his ears caught the unearthly noises that came to him in the mingled scream of weltering tempest and plangent wave. It was fearful to be isolated on the black rent rock, and see the waves gaining on them, higher, higher, higher, every moment; and he was in ceaseless terror lest they should be swept away by the violence of the breakers. 'At least,' thought he, as he looked down and saw that the ledge on which they had been standing had long been covered with deep and agitated waves—'at least I have tried to save Edwin's life.' And he bravely made up his mind to keep up heart and hope, and to weather the comfortless night as best he could.

And then his thoughts turned to Russell, who was still unconscious; and stooping down he folded his arms around the boy's breast. He felt *then* how deeply he loved him, how much he owed him; and no mother could have nursed a child more tenderly than he did his fainting friend. Russell's head rested on his breast, and the soft hair, tangled with welling blood, stained his clothes. Eric feared that he would die, his fainting-fit continued so long, and from the helpless way in which one of his legs trailed on the ground, he felt sure that he had received some dangerous hurt.

At last Russell stirred and groaned. 'Where am I?' he said, and half opened his eyes; he started up frightened, and fell back heavily. He saw only the darkness; felt only the fierce wind and salt mist; heard only the relentless fury of the blast. Memory had no time to wake, and he screamed and fainted once more.

Poor Eric knew not what to do but to shelter him to the best of his power; and when he showed any signs of consciousness again, he bent over him, and said, 'Don't you remember, Edwin? We're quite safe. I'm with you, and Monty's gone for help.'

'Oh! I daren't jump,' sobbed Russell; 'O mother, I shall be drowned. Save me! save me! I'm so glad they're safe, mother; but my leg hurts so.' And he moaned again. He was delirious.

'How cold it is, and wet too! where's Eric? are we bathing? run along, we shall be late. But stop, you're smoking. Dear Eric, don't smoke. Poor fellow, I'm afraid he's getting spoilt, and learning bad ways. Oh save him.' And as he wandered on, he repeated a prayer for Eric, which evidently had been often on his lips.

Eric was touched to the heart's core, and in one rapid lightning-like glance, his memory revealed to him the faultful past, in all its sorrowfulness. And *he* too prayed wildly for help both for soul and body. Alone on the crag, with the sea tumbling and plashing round them, growing and gaining so much on their place of refuge, that his terror began to summon up the image of certain death; alone, wet, hungry, and exhausted, with the wounded and delirious boy, whose life depended on his courage, he prayed as he had never prayed before, and seemed to grow calmer by his prayer, and to feel God nearer him than ever he had done in the green cricket-field, or the safe dormitories of Roslyn School.

A shout startled him. Lights on the water heaved up and down, now disappearing, and now lifted high, and at intervals there came the sound of voices and the plash of irregular oars. Thank God! help was near; they were coming in a boat to save them.

But the lights grew more distant; he saw them disappearing towards the harbour. Yes; it was of no use; no boat could live in the surf at the foot of the Stack cliffs, and the sailors had given it up in despair. His heart sank again, all the more for its glimpse of hope, and his strength began to give way. Russell's delirium continued, and he grew too frightened even to pray.

A light from the land. The sound of shouts—yes, he could be sure of it; it was Dr. Rowlands's voice and Montagu's. He got convinced of this, and summoned all his strength to shout in return. The light kept moving up and down on the shore, not a hundred yards off. His fear vanished; they were no longer alone. The first moment that the tide suffered any one to reach them they would be rescued. His mind grew calm again, and he determined to hold up for Russell's sake until help should come; and every now and then, to make it feel less lonely, he answered the shouts which came from the friendly voices in the fitful pauses of the storm.

But Dr. Rowlands and Montagu paced up and down, and the master soothed the boy's fears, and talked to him so kindly, so gently, that Montagu began to wonder if this really could be the awful headmaster, whose warm strong hand he was grasping, and who was comforting him as a father might. What a depth of genuine human kindness that stern exterior concealed! And every now and then, when the storm blew loudest, the Doctor would stand still for a moment, and offer up a short intense prayer or ejaculation, that help and safety might come to his beloved charge in their exposure and peril.

Six or seven hours passed away; at last the wind began to sink, and the sea to be less violent. The tide was on the turn. The carriage drove up with more men and lights, and the thoughtful servant brought with him the school surgeon, Dr. Underhay. Long and anxiously did they watch the ebbing tide, and when it had gone out sufficiently to allow of two stout planks being fastened securely to the rocks and laid across the channel, an active sailor ventured over with a light, and in a few moments stood by Eric's side. Eric saw him coming, but was too weak and numb to move; and when the sailor lifted up the unconscious Russell from his knees, Eric was too much exhausted even to speak. The man returned for him, and lifting him on his back, crossed the plank once more in safety. Then he carried Russell first and Eric afterwards to the carriage, where Dr. Underhay had taken care to have everything likely to revive and sustain them. They were driven rapidly to the school, and the Doctor raised to God tearful eyes of gratitude as the boys were taken to the rooms prepared for them. Mrs. Rowlands was anxiously awaiting their arrival, and the noise of wheels was the signal for twenty heads to be put through the dormitory windows, with many an anxious inquiry, 'Are they safe?'

'Yes, thank God!' called Dr. Rowlands; 'so now, boys, shut the windows, and get to sleep.'

Russell was carefully undressed, and put to bed in the Doctor's own house, and the wound in his head was dressed. Eric and Montagu had beds provided them in another room by themselves, away from the dormitories; the room was bright and cheerful with a blazing fire, and looked like home; and when the two boys had drunk some warm wine, and cried for weariness and joy, they sank to sleep after their dangers and fatigues, and slept the deep, calm, dreamless sleep of tired children.

So ended the perilous adventure of that eventful night of the Easter holidays.

CHAPTER THE FOURTEENTH

THE SILVER CORD BROKEN

Calm on the bosom of thy God,
Fair spirit rest thee now!
E'en while with us thy footsteps trod,
His seal was on thy brow.
MRS. HEMANS

THEY DID NOT AWAKE till noon. Montagu opened his eyes, and at first could not collect his thoughts, as he saw the carpeted little room, the bright fire, and the housekeeper seated in her arm-chair before it. But turning his head he caught a glimpse of Eric, who was still asleep, and he then remembered all. He sprang out of bed, refreshed and perfectly well, and the sound of his voice woke Eric; but Eric was still languid and weak, and did not get up that day, nor was he able to go to work again for some days; but he was young and strong, and his vigorous constitution soon threw off the effects of this fast and exposure.

Their first inquiry was for Edwin. The nurse shook her head sadly. 'He is very dangerously ill.'

'Is he?' said they both anxiously. And then they preserved a deep silence; and when Montagu, who immediately began to dress, knelt down to say his prayers, Eric, though unable to get up, knelt also over his pillow, and the two felt that their young earnest prayers were mingling for the one who seemed to have been taken while they were left.

The reports grew darker and darker about Edwin. At first it was thought that the blow on his head was dangerous, and that the exposure to wet, cold, fear, and hunger had permanently weakened his constitution; and when his youth seemed to be triumphing over these dangers, another became more threatening. His leg never mended; he had both sprained the knee badly, and given the tibia an awkward twist, so that the least motion was agony to him.

In his fever he was constantly delirious. No one was allowed to see him, though many of the boys tried to do so, and many were the earnest inquiries for him day by day. It then became more fully apparent than ever, that, although Edwin was among them without being *of* them, no boy in the school was more deeply honoured and fondly loved than he. Even the elastic spirits of boyhood could not quite throw off the shadow of gloom which his illness cast over the school.

Very tenderly they nursed him. All that human kindness could do was done for him by the stranger hands. And yet not all; poor Edwin had no father, no mother, hardly any relatives. His only aunt, Mrs. Upton, would have come to nurse him, but she was an invalid, and he was often left alone in his delirium and agony.

Alone, yet not alone. There was One with him—always in his thoughts, always leading, guiding, blessing him unseen—not deserting the hurt lamb of His flock; one who was once a boy Himself, and who, when He was a boy, did His Father's business, and was subject unto His parents in the obscure home of the despised village. Alone! nay, to them whose eyes were opened, the room of sickness and pain was thronged and beautiful with angelic presences.

Often did Eric, and Upton, and Montagu talk of their loved friend. Eric's life seemed absorbed in the thought of him, and in passionate, unspeakable longings for his recovery. Now he valued more than ever the happy hours which he had spent with him; their games, and communings, and walks, and Russell's gentle influence, and brave kindly rebukes. Yet he must not even see him, must not smooth his pillow, must not whisper one word of soothing to him in his anguish; he could only pray for him, and that he did with a depth of hope.

At last Upton, in virtue of his relationship, was allowed to visit him. His delirium had become more unfrequent, but he could not yet even recognise his cousin, and the visits to the sick-room were so sad and useless, that Upton forbore. 'And yet you should hear him talk in his delirium,' he said to Eric; 'not one evil word, or bad thought, or wicked thing, ever escapes him. I'm afraid, Eric, it would hardly be so with you or me.'

'No,' said Eric, in a low and humble tone; and guilty conscience brought the deep colour, wave after wave of crimson, into his cheeks.

'And he talks with such affection of you, Eric. He speaks sometimes of all of us very gently; but you seem to be always in his thoughts, and every now and then he prays for you quite unconsciously.'

Eric turned his head to brush away a tear. 'When do you think I shall be allowed to see him?'

'Not just yet, I fear.'

After a week or two of most anxious suspense, Russell's mind ceased to wander, but the state of his sprain gave more cause for alarm. Fresh advice was called in, and it was decided that the leg must be amputated.

When Eric was told this, he burst into passionate complaints. 'Only think, Monty, isn't it hard, isn't it cruel? When we see our brave, bright Edwin again he will be a cripple.' Eric hardly understood that he was railing at the providence of a merciful God.

The day for the operation came. When it was over, poor Russell seemed to amend, and the removal of the perpetual pain gave him relief. They were all deeply moved at his touching resignation; no murmur, no cry escaped him; no words but the sweetest thanks for every little office of kindness done to him. A few days after, he asked Dr. Underhay 'if he might see Eric?'

'Yes, my boy,' said the Doctor kindly, 'he, and one or two others of your particular friends may see you if you like, provided you don't excite yourself too much. I trust that you will get better now.'

So Eric and Montagu were told by Dr. Rowlands that at six they might go and see their friend. 'Be sure,' he added, 'that you don't startle or excite him.'

They promised, and after school on that beautiful evening of early summer they went to the sick-room door. Stopping, they held their breath, and knocked very gently. Yes! it was the well-known voice which gave the answer, but it was faint and low. Full of awe, they softly opened the door, which admitted them into the presence of the dear companion whom they had not seen for so long. Since then it seemed as though gulfs far deeper than the sea had been flowing between him and them.

Full of awe, and hand in hand, they entered the room on tiptoe—the darkened room where Russell was. What a hush and oppression there seemed to them at first in the dim, silent chamber; what an awfulness in all the appliances which showed how long and deeply their schoolfellow had suffered. But all this vanished directly they caught sight of his face. There he lay, so calm, and weak, and still, with his bright, earnest eyes turned towards them as though to see whether any of their affection for him had ceased or been forgotten!

In an instant they were kneeling in silence by the bed with bowed foreheads; and the sick boy tenderly put his hands on their heads, and pushed his thin white fingers through their hair, and looked at them tearfully without a word, till they hid their faces with their hands, and broke into deep suppressed sobs of compassion.

'Oh, hush, hush!' he said, as he felt their tears dropping on his hands; 'dear Eric, dear Monty, why should you cry so for me? I am very happy.'

But they caught the outline of his form as he lay on the bed, and had now for the first time realised that he was a cripple for life; and as the throng of memories came on them—memories of his skill and fame at cricket, and racquets, and football—of their sunny bathes together in sea and river, and all their happy holiday wanderings—they could not restrain their emotion, and wept uncontrollably. Neither of them could speak a word, or break the holy silence; and as he patted their heads and cheeks, his own tears flowed fast in sympathy and self-pity. But he felt the comforting affection which they could not utter; he felt it in his loneliness, and it did him good.

The nurse broke in upon the scene, which she feared would agitate Edwin too much; and with red eyes and heavy hearts the boys left, only whispering, 'We will come again to-morrow, Edwin!'

They came the next day and many days, and got to talk quite cheerfully with him, and read to him. They loved this occupation more than any game, and devoted themselves to it. The sorrow of the sick-room more than repaid them for the glad life without, when they heard Russell's simple and heartfelt thanks. 'Ah! how good of you, dear fellows,' he would say, 'to give up the merry playground for a wretched cripple;' and he would smile cheerfully to show that his trial had not made him weary of life. Indeed, he often told them that he believed they felt for him more than he did himself.

One day Eric brought him a little bunch of primroses and violets. He seemed much better, and Eric's spirits were high with the thoughts and hopes of the coming holidays. 'There, Edwin,' he said, as the boy gratefully and eagerly took the flowers, 'don't they make you glad? They are one of our *three* signs, you know, of the approaching holidays. One sign was the first sight of the summer steamer going across the bay; another was May eve, when these island-fellows light big gorse fires all over the mountains, and throw yellow marsh-lilies at their doors to keep off the fairies. Do you remember, Eddy, gathering some last May eve, and sitting out in the playground till sunset, watching the fires begin to twinkle on Cronck-Irey and Barrule for miles away? What a jolly talk we had that evening about the holidays; but my father and mother were here then, you know, and we were all going to Fairholm. But the third sign—the first primrose and violet—was always the happiest, as well as quite the earliest. You can't think how I *grabbed* at the first primrose this year; I found it by a cave on the Ness. And though these are rather the last than the first, yet I knew you'd like them, Eddy, so I hunted for them everywhere. And how much better you're looking too; such shining eyes, and yes! I positively declare, quite a ruddy cheek like your old one. You'll soon be out among us again, that's clear——'

He stopped abruptly: he had been rattling on just in the merry way that Russell now most loved to hear, but, as he was talking, he caught the touch of sadness on Russell's face, and saw his long, abstracted, eager look at the flowers.

'Dear fellow, you're not worse, are you?' he said quickly. 'What a fool I am to chatter so; it makes you ill.'

'No, no, Eric, talk on; you can't think how I love to hear you. Oh, how very beautiful these primroses are! Thank you for bringing them.' And he again fixed on them the eager dreamy look which had startled Eric—as though he were learning their colour and shape by heart.

'I wish I hadn't brought them though,' said Eric; 'they are filling your mind with regrets. But, Eddy, you'll be well by the holidays—a month hence, you know—or else I shouldn't have talked so gladly about them.'

'No, Eric,' said Russell sadly, 'these dear flowers are the last spring blossoms that I shall see—*here* at least. Yes, I will keep them, for your sake, Eric, till I die.'

'Oh, don't talk so,' said Eric, shocked and flustered; 'why, everybody knows and says that you're getting better.'

Russell smiled and shook his head. 'No, Eric, I shall die. There stop, dear fellow, don't cry,' said he, raising his hands quietly to Eric's face; 'isn't it better for me so? I own it seemed sad at first to leave this bright world and the sea—yes, even that cruel sea,' he continued, smiling; 'and to leave Roslyn, and Upton, and Monty, and, above all, to leave *you*, Eric, whom I love best in all the world. Yes, remember, I've no home, Eric, and no prospects. There was nothing to be sorry for in this, so long as God gave me health and strength; but health went for ever into those waves at the Stack, where you saved my life, dear gallant Eric; and what could I do now? It doesn't look so happy to *halt* through life. O Eric, Eric, I am young, but I am dying—dying. Eric,' he said solemnly, 'my brother— let me call you brother—I have no near relations, you know, to fill up the love in my yearning heart, but I *do* love *you*. I wish you were my brother,' he said, as Eric took his hand between both his own. 'There, that comforts me; I feel as if I *were* a child again, and had a brother; and I *shall* be a child again soon, Eric, in the courts of a Father's house.'

Eric could not speak. These words startled him; he never dreamt *recently* of Russell's death, but had begun to reckon on his recovery, and now life seemed darker to him than ever.

But Russell was pressing the flowers to his lips. 'The grass withereth,' he murmured, 'the flower fadeth, and the glory of his beauty perisheth; but—*but* the word of the Lord endureth for ever.' And here he too burst into natural tears, and Eric pressed his hand, with more than a brother's fondness, to his heart.

'O Eddy, Eddy, my heart is full,' he said, 'too full to speak to you. Let me read to you;' and with his arm round Russell's neck, he sat down beside his pillow, and read to him about the 'pure river of water of life, clear as crystal, proceeding out of the throne of God and of the Lamb.' At first sobs choked his voice, but it gathered firmness as he went on.

'In the midst of the street of it, and on either side of the river, was there the tree of life, which bare twelve manner of fruits, and yielded her fruit every month; and the leaves of the tree were for the healing of the nations.

'And there shall be no more curse'—and here the reader's musical voice rose into deeper and steadier sweetness—'but the throne of God and of the Lamb shall be in it;

and his servants shall serve him; and they shall see his face; and his name shall be in their foreheads.'

'And they shall see his face,' murmured Russell, *'and they shall see his face.'* Eric paused and looked at him; a sort of rapture seemed to be lighted in his eyes, as though they saw heavenly things, and his countenance was like an angel's to look upon. Eric closed the book reverently, and gazed.

'And now pray for me, Eric, will you?' Eric knelt down, but no prayer would come; his breast swelled, and his heart beat fast, but emotion prevented him from uttering a word. But Russell laid his hand on his head and prayed.

'O gracious Lord God, look down, merciful Father, on us, two erring, weak, sinful boys; look down and bless us, Lord, for the love Thou bearest unto Thy children. One Thou art taking; Lord, take me to the green pastures of Thy home, where no curse is; and one remains—O Lord! bless him with the dew of Thy blessing; lead and guide him, and keep him for ever in Thy fear and love, that he may continue Thine for ever, and hereafter we may meet together among the redeemed, in the immortal glory of the resurrection. Hear us, O Father, for Thy dear Son's sake. Amen! Amen!'

The childlike, holy, reverent voice ceased, and Eric rose. One long brotherly kiss he printed on Russell's forehead, and, full of sorrowful forebodings, bade him good-night.

He asked Dr. Underhay whether his fears were correct. 'Yes,' he said, 'he may die at any time; he *must* die soon. It is even best that he should; besides the loss of a limb, that blow on the head would certainly affect the brain and the intellect if he lived.'

Eric shuddered—a long cold shudder.

The holidays drew on; for Russell's sake, and at his earnest wish, Eric had worked harder than he ever did before. All his brilliant abilities, all his boyish ambition, were called into exercise; and to the delight of every one, he gained ground rapidly, and seemed likely once more to dispute the palm with Owen. No one rejoiced more in this than Mr. Rose, and he often gladdened Russell's heart by telling him about it; for every day he paid a long visit to the sick boy's room, which refreshed and comforted them both.

In other respects too, Eric seemed to be turning over a new leaf. He and Upton, by common consent, had laid aside smoking, and every bad habit or disobedient custom which would have grieved the dying boy whom they both loved so well. And although Eric's popularity, after the romantic Stack adventure, and his chivalrous daring, was at its very zenith,—although he had received a medal and flattering letter from the Humane Society, who had been informed of the transaction by Dr. Rowlands,—although his success, both physical and intellectual, was higher than ever,—yet the dread of the great loss he was doomed to suffer, and the friendship which was to be snapped, overpowered every other feeling, and his heart was ennobled and purified by contact with his suffering friend.

It was a June evening, and he and Russell were alone; he had drawn up the blind, and through the open window the summer breeze, pure from the sea and fragrant from the garden, was blowing refreshfully into the sick boy's room. Russell was very, very happy. No doubt, no fear assailed him; all was peace and trustfulness. Long and earnestly that evening did he talk to Eric, and implore him to shun evil ways, striving to lead him gently to that love of God which was his only support and refuge now. Tearfully and humbly Eric listened, and every now and then the sufferer stopped to pray aloud.

'Good-night, Eric,' he said, 'I am tired, *so* tired. I hope we shall meet again; I shall give you my desk and all my books, Eric, except a few for Horace, Owen, Duncan, and Monty. And my watch, that dear watch your mother, *my* mother, gave me, I shall leave to Rose as a remembrance of us both. Good-night, dear old boy.'

A little before ten that night Eric was again summoned with Upton and Montagu to Russell's bedside. He was sinking fast; and as he had but a short time to live, he expressed a desire to see them, though he could see no others.

They came, and were amazed to see how bright, how beautiful, the dying boy looked. They received his last farewells—he would die that night. Sweetly he blessed them, and made them promise to avoid all evil, and read the Bible, and pray to God. But he had only strength to speak at intervals. Mr. Rose, too, was there; it seemed as though he held the boy by the hand, as fearlessly now, yea, joyously, he entered the waters of the dark river.

'Oh, I should *so* like to stay with you, Monty, Horace, dear, dear Eric, but God calls me. I am going—a long way—to my father and mother—and to the light. I shall not be a cripple there—nor be in pain.' His words grew slow and difficult. 'God bless you, dear fellows; God bless you, dear Eric; I am going—to God.'

He sighed very gently; there was a slight sound in his throat, and he was dead. The gentle, holy, pure spirit of Edwin Russell had passed into the presence of its Saviour and its God. O happy and blameless boy, no fairer soul has ever stood in the light of the rainbow-circled throne.

A terrible scene of boyish anguish followed, as they bent over the lifeless brow. But quietly, calmly, Mr. Rose checked them, and they knelt down with streaming eyes while he prayed.

They rose a little calmer, and as they turned back again and again to take one last fond look at the pale yet placid face, Mr. Rose said in a solemn tone—

> 'For ever with the Lord,
>   Amen! so let it be!
> Life from the dead is in that word,
>   And Immortality.'

CHAPTER THE FIFTEENTH

HOME AGAIN

> O far beyond the waters
>   The fickle feet may roam,
> But they find no light so pure and bright
>   As the one fair star of home:
> The star of tender hearts, lady,
>   That glows in an English home.

THAT NIGHT, when Eric returned to his dormitory, full of grief, and weighed down with the sense of desolation and mystery, the other boys were silent from sympathy in his sorrow. Duncan and Llewellyn both knew and loved Russell themselves, and they were awestruck to hear of his death; they asked some of the particulars, but Eric was not calm enough to tell them that evening. The one sense of infinite loss agitated him, and he indulged his paroxysms of emotion unrestrained, yet silently. Reader, if ever the life has been cut short which you most dearly loved, if ever you have been made to feel absolutely lonely in the world, then, and then only, will you appreciate the depth of his affliction.

But, like all affliction, it purified and sanctified. To Eric, as he rested his aching head on a pillow wet with tears, and vainly sought for the sleep whose blessing he had never learned to prize before, how odious seemed all the vice which he had seen and partaken in since he became an inmate of that little room. How his soul revolted with infinite disgust from the language which he had heard, and the open glorying in sin of which he had so often been a witness. The stain and the shame of sin fell heavier than ever on his heart; it rode on his breast like a nightmare; it haunted his fancy with visions of guilty memory, and shapes of horrible regret. The ghosts of buried misdoings, which he had thought long lost in the mists of recollection, started up menacingly from their forgotten graves, and made him shrink with a sense of their awful reality. Behind him, like a wilderness, lay years which the locust had eaten; the entrusted hours which had passed away, and been reckoned to him as they passed.

And the thought of Russell mingled with all—Russell, as he fondly imaged him now, glorified with the glory of heaven, crowned, and in white robes, and with a palm in his hand. Yes, he had walked and talked with one of the Holy Ones. Had Edwin's death quenched his human affections, and altered his human heart? If not, might not he be there even now, leaning over his friend with the beauty of his invisible presence? The thought startled him, and seemed to give an awful lustre to the moonbeam which fell into the room. No! he could not endure such a presence now, with his weak conscience and corrupted heart; and Eric hid his head under the clothes, and shut his eyes.

Once more the pang of separation entered like iron into his soul. Should he ever meet Russell again? What if *he* had died instead of Edwin, where would he have been? 'Oh no! no!' he murmured aloud, as the terrible thought came over him of his own utter unfitness for death, and the possibility that he might never never again hear the beloved accents, or gaze on the cherished countenance of his school friend.

In this tumult of accusing thoughts he fell asleep; but that night the dew of blessing did not fall for him on the fields of sleep. He was frightened by unbidden dreams, in all of which his conscience obtruded on him his sinfulness, and his affection called up the haunting lineaments of the dear dead face. He was wandering down a path, at the end of which Russell stood with beckoning hand inviting him earnestly to join him there; he saw his bright ingenuous smile, and heard, as of old, his joyous words, and he hastened to meet him; when suddenly the boy-figure disappeared, and in its place he saw the stern brow, and gleaming garments, and drawn flaming sword of the Avenger. And then he was in a great wood alone, and wandering, when the well-known voice called his name, and entreated him to turn from that evil place; and he longed to turn,—but, whenever he tried, ghostly hands seemed to wave him back again, and irresistible cords to drag him into the dark forest, amid the sound of mocking laughs. Then he was sinking, sinking, sinking into a gulf, deep and darker even than the inner darkness of a sin-desolated heart; sinking, helplessly, hopelessly, everlastingly; while far away, like a star, stood the loved figure in light infinitely above him, and with pleading hands implored his deliverance, but could not prevail; and Eric was still sinking, sinking infinitely, when the agony awoke him with a violent start and stifled scream.

He could sleep no longer. Whenever he closed his eyes he saw the pale, dead, holy features of Edwin, and at last he fancied that he was praying beside his corpse, praying to be more like *him,* who lay there so white and calm; sorrowing beside it, sorrowing that he had so often rejected his kind warnings, and pained his affectionate heart. So Eric began again to make good resolutions about all his future life. Ah! how often he had done so before, and how often they had failed. He had not yet learned the lessons which David learned by sad experience: 'Then I said, it is mine own infirmity, *but I will remember the years of the right hand of the Most High.*'

That too, was an eventful night for Montagu. He had grown of late far more thoughtful than before; under Edwin's influence he had been laying aside, one by one, the careless sins of school life, and his tone was nobler and manlier than it had ever been. Montagu had never known or heard much about godliness; his father, a gentleman, a scholar, and a man of the world, had trained him in the principles of refinement and good taste, and given him a high standard of conventional honour; but he passed through life lightly, and had taught his son to do the same. Possessed of an ample fortune, which Montagu was to inherit, he troubled himself with none of the deep mysteries of life, and

> Pampered the coward heart
> With feelings all too delicate for use;
> Nursing in some delicious solitude
> His dainty loves and slothful sympathies.

But Montagu in Edwin's sickroom and by his death-bed; in the terrible storm at the Stack, and by contact with Dr. Rowlands's earnestness, and Mr. Rose's deep, unaffected, sorrow-mingled piety; by witnessing Eric's failures and recoveries; and by beginning to take in his course the same heartfelt interest which Edwin taught him—Montagu, in consequence of these things, had begun to see another side of life, which awoke all his dormant affections and profoundest reasonings. It seemed as though, for the first time, he began to catch some of

> The still sad music of humanity,

and to listen with deep eagerness to the strain. Hitherto, to be well dressed, handsome, agreeable, rich, and popular, had been to him a realised ideal of life; but now he awoke to higher and worthier aims; and once, when Russell, whose intelligent interest in his work exceeded that of any other boy, had pointed out to him that solemn question—

> Οἴει σὺ τοὺς θανόντας ὦ Νικήρατε
> Τρυφῆς ἁπάσης μεταλαβόντας ἐν βίῳ
> Πεφευγέναι τὸ θεῖον;

he had entered into its meaning with wonderful vividness. So that, without losing any of that winning gracefulness of address which made him so great a favourite with the school, it became evident to all that he combined with it a touching earnestness. Sometimes when he read the Bible to Edwin he began to wonder at his past ignorance and selfishness, and humbly hope for better things. All that night of death he had truer comfort than Eric—for he cast his cares on God; more calm than Eric—for he fixed his hopes on the Son of God; greater strength granted him than Eric—because he had learned not to rely upon his own; less fear and torment than Eric—because he laid the burden of his sins before the cross, and, as a child, believed in their forgiveness for His sake who died thereon.

The holidays were approaching. Eric, to escape as much as possible from his sorrow, plunged into the excitement of working for the examination, and rapidly made up for lost ground. He now spent most of his time with the best of his friends, particularly Montagu, Owen, and Upton; for Upton, like himself, had been much sobered by sorrow at their loss. This time he came out *second* in his form, and gained more than one prize. This was his first glimpse of real delight since Russell's death; and when the prize-day came, and he stood with his companions in the flower-decorated room, and went up amid universal applause to take his prize-books, and receive a few words of compliment from the governor who took the chair, he felt almost happy, and keenly entered into the pleasure which his success caused, as well as into the honours won by his friends. One outward sign only remained of his late bereavement—his mourning dress. All the prize-boys wore rosebuds or lilies of the valley in their button-holes on the occasion, but on this day Eric would not wear them. Little Wright, who was a great friend of theirs, had brought some as a present both to Eric and Montagu, as they stood together on the prize-day morning; they took them with thanks, and, as their eyes met, they understood each other's thought.

'No,' said Eric to Wright, 'we won't wear these to-day, although we have both got prizes. Come along; I know what we will do with them.'

They all three walked together to the little green quiet churchyard, where, by his own request, Edwin had been buried. Many a silent visit had the friends paid to that grave, on which the turf was now green again and the daisies had begun to blossom. A stone had recently been placed to mark the spot, and they read—

SACRED TO THE MEMORY

OF

EDWIN RUSSELL,

AN ORPHAN BOY

WHO DIED AT ROSLYN SCHOOL, MAY 1847,

AGED FIFTEEN YEARS.

Is it well with the child? It is well.
I KINGS iv, 26.

The three boys stood by the grave in silence and sorrow for a time.

'He would have been the gladdest at our success, Monty,' said Eric; 'let us leave the signs of it upon his grave.'

And, with reverent hand, scattering over that small mound the choice rosebuds and fragrant lilies with their green leaves, they turned away without another word.

The next morning the great piles of corded boxes which crowded the passage were put on the coach, and the boys, gladly leaving the deserted building, drove in every sort of vehicle to the steamer. What joyous, triumphant mornings those were! How the heart exulted and bounded with the sense of life and pleasure, and how universal was the gladness and good-humour of every one. Never were voyages so merry as those of the steamer that day, and even the 'good-byes' that had to be said at Southpool were lightly borne. From thence the boys quickly scattered to the different railways, and the numbers of those who were travelling together got thinner and thinner as the distance increased. Wright and one or two others went nearly all the way with Eric, and when he got down at the little roadside station, from whence started the branch rail to Ayrton, he

bade them a merry and affectionate farewell. The branch train soon started, and in another hour he would be at Fairholm.

It was not till then that his home feelings woke in all their intensity. He had not been there for a year. At Roslyn the summer holidays were nine weeks, and the holidays at Christmas and Easter were short, so that it had not been worth while to travel so far as Fairholm, and Eric had spent his Christmas with friends in another part of the island. But now he was once more to see dear Fairholm, and his aunt, his cousin Fanny, and above all his little brother. His heart was beating fast with joy, and his eyes sparkling with pleasure and excitement. As he thrust his head out of the window, each well-remembered landmark gave him the delicious sensation of meeting again an old friend. 'Ah! there's the white bridge, and there's the canal, and the stile; and *there* runs the river, and there's Velvet Lawn. Hurrah! here we are.' And springing out of the train before it had well stopped, he had shaken hands heartily with the old coachman, who was expecting him, and jumped up into the carriage in a moment.

Through the lanes he knew so well, by whose hedgerows he had so often plucked sorrel and wild roses; past the old church with its sleeping churchyard; through the quiet village, where every ten yards he met old acquaintances who looked pleased to see him, and whom he greeted with glad smiles and nods of recognition; past the Latin school, from which came murmurs and voices as of yore (what a man he felt himself now by comparison!)—by the old Roman camp, where he had imagined such heroic things when he was a little child; through all the scenes so rich with the memories and associations of his happy childhood, they flew along; and now they had entered the avenue, and Eric was painfully on the look-out.

Yes! there they were all three—Mrs. Trevor, and Fanny, and Vernon, on the mound at the end of the avenue; and the younger ones ran to meet him. It was a joyous meeting; he gave Fanny a hearty kiss, and put his arm round Vernon's neck, and then held him in front to have a look at him.

'How tall you've grown, Verny, and how well you look,' he said, gazing proudly at him; and indeed the boy was a brother to be justly proud of. And Vernon quite returned the admiration as he saw the healthy glow of Eric's features, and what a tall strong boy he had grown to be.

And so they quickly joined Mrs. Trevor, who embraced her nephew with a mother's love; and, amid all that nameless questioning of delightful trifles, that 'blossoming vein' of household talk, which gives such an incommunicable charm to the revisiting of home, they all three turned into the house, where Eric, hungry with his travels, enjoyed at leisure the 'jolly spread' prepared for him, luxurious beyond anything he had seen for his last year at school. When he and Vernon went up to their room at night—the same little room in which they slept on the night when they first had met—they marked their heights on the door again, which showed Eric that in the last year he had grown two inches, a fact which he pointed out to Vernon with no little exultation. And then they went to bed, and to a sleep over which brooded the indefinite sensation of a great unknown joy;—that rare heavenly sleep which only comes once or twice or thrice in life, on occasions such as this.

He was up early next morning, and, opening his window, leaned out with his hands among the green vine-leaves which encircled it. The garden looked beautiful as ever, and he promised himself an early enjoyment of those currants which hung in ruby clusters over the walls. Everything was bathed in the dewy balm of summer morning, and he felt very happy as, with his little spaniel frisking around him, he visited the great Newfoundland in his kennel, and his old pet the pony in the stable. He had barely finished his rounds when breakfast was ready, and he once more met the home circle from which he had been separated for a year. And yet over all his happiness hung a sense of change and half melancholy; they were not changed, but *he* was changed. Mrs. Trevor, and Fanny, and Vernon were the same as ever, but over *him* had come an alteration of feeling and circumstance; an unknown or half-known *something* which cast a shadow between them and him, and sometimes made him half shrink and start as he met their loving looks. Can no schoolboy, who reads his history, understand and explain the feeling which I mean?

By that mail he wrote to his father and mother an account of Russell's death, and he felt that they would guess why the letter was so blurred. 'But,' he wrote, 'I have some friends still; especially Mr. Rose among the masters, and Monty and Upton among the boys. Monty you know; he is more like Edwin than any other boy, and I like him very much. You didn't know Upton, but I am a great deal with him, though he is much older than I am. He is a fine handsome fellow, and one of the most popular in the school. I hope you will know him some day.'

The very next morning Eric received a letter which he at once recognised to be in Upton's handwriting. He eagerly tore off the envelope, and read—

   'MY DEAREST ERIC—I have got bad news to tell you, at least I feel it to be bad news for me, and I flatter myself that you will feel it to be bad news for you. In short, I am going to leave Roslyn, and probably we shall never meet there again. The reason is, I have had a cadetship given me, and I am to sail for India in September. I have already written to the school to tell them to pack up and send me all my books and clothes.

   'I feel leaving very much; it has made me quite miserable. I wanted to stay at school another year at least; and I will honestly tell you, Eric, one reason; I'm very much afraid that I've done you, and Graham, and other fellows no good; and I wanted, if I possibly could, to undo the harm I had done. Poor Edwin's death opened my eyes to a good many things, and now I'd give all I have never to have taught or encouraged you in wrong things. Unluckily it's too late;—only, I hope that you already see, as I do, that the things I mean lead to evil far greater than we ever used to dream of.

'Good-bye now, old fellow! Do write to me soon, and forgive me, and believe me ever—Your most affectionate,

HORACE UPTON.

'*P.S.*—Is that jolly little Vernon going back to school with you this time? I remember seeing him running about the shore with my poor cousin when you were a home boarder, and thinking what a nice little chap he looked. I hope you'll look after him as a brother should, and keep him out of mischief.'

Eric folded the letter sadly, and put it into his pocket; he didn't often show them his school letters, because, like this one, they often contained allusions to things which he did not like his aunt to know. The thought of Upton's leaving made him quite unhappy, and he wrote him a long letter that post, indignantly denying the supposition that his friendship had ever done him anything but good.

The postscript about Vernon suggested a thought that had been often in his mind. He could not but shudder in himself, when he thought of that bright little brother of his being initiated in the mysteries of evil which he himself had learnt, and sinking like himself into slow degeneracy of heart and life. It often puzzled and perplexed him, and at last he determined to open his heart, partially at least, in a letter to Mr. Rose. The master fully understood his doubts, and wrote him the following reply:—

'MY DEAR ERIC—I have just received your letter about your brother Vernon, and I think that it does you honour. I will briefly give you my own opinion.

'You mean, no doubt, that from your own experience, you fear that Vernon will hear at school many things which will shock his modesty, and much language which is evil and blasphemous; you fear that he will meet with many bad examples, and learn to look on God and godliness in a way far different from that to which he has been accustomed at home. You fear, in short, that he must pass through the same painful temptations to which you have yourself been subjected; to which, perhaps, you have even succumbed.

'Well, Eric, this is all true. Yet, knowing this, I say, by all means let Vernon come to Roslyn. The innocence of mere ignorance is a poor thing; it *cannot*, under any circumstances, be permanent, nor is it at all valuable as a foundation of character. The true preparation for life, the true basis of a manly character, is not to have been ignorant of evil, but to have known it and avoided it; not to have been sheltered from temptation, but to have passed through it and overcome it by God's help. Many have drawn exaggerated pictures of the lowness of public school morality; the best answer is to point to the good and splendid men that have been trained in public schools, and who lose no opportunity of recurring to them with affection. It is quite possible to be *in* the little world of school-life, and yet not *of* it. The ruin of human souls can never be achieved by enemies from without unless they be aided by traitors from within. Remember our lost friend; the peculiar lustre of his piety was caused by the circumstances under which he was placed. He often told me before his last hour, that he rejoiced to have been at Roslyn; that he had experienced there much real happiness, and derived in every way lasting good.

'I hope you have been enjoying your holidays, and that you will come back with the "spell of home affection" alive in your heart. I shall rejoice to make Vernon's acquaintance, and will do for him all I can. Bring him with you to me in the library as soon as you arrive.—Ever, dear Eric,

'Affectionately yours,

'WALTER ROSE.'

END OF PART I

Part II

Sed revocare gradum . . . !
VIRGIL

CHAPTER THE FIRST

ABDIEL

Φθείρουσιν ἤθη χρησθ' ὁμιλίαι κακα!
MENANDER

A YEAR HAD PASSED since the events narrated in the last chapter, and had brought with it many changes.

To Eric the changes were not for good.

The memories of Russell were getting dim; the resolutions made during his friend's illness had vanished; the bad habits laid aside after his death had been resumed. All this took place very gradually; there were many inward struggles, much occasional remorse, but the struggles by degrees grew weaker, and remorse lost its sting, and Eric Williams soon learned again to follow the multitude to do evil.

He was now sixteen years old, and high in the fifth form, and, besides this, he was captain of the school eleven. In work he had fallen off, and no one now expected the fulfilment of that promise of genius which he had given them when he first came. But in all school sports he had improved, and was the acknowledged leader and champion in matters requiring boldness and courage. His popularity made him giddy; favour of man led to forgetfulness of God; and even a glance at his countenance showed a self-sufficiency and arrogance which ill became the refinement of his features, and ill replaced the ingenuous modesty of former days.

And Vernon Williams was no longer a new boy. The worst had happened to him, which Eric in his better moments could have feared. He had fallen into thoroughly bad hands, and Eric, who should have been his natural guardian and guide, began to treat him with indifference, and scarcely ever had any affectionate intercourse with him. It is by no means unfrequent that brothers at school see but little of each other, and follow their several pursuits, and choose their various companions, with small regard to the relationship between them.

Yet Eric could not overlook or be blind to the fact, that Vernon's chief friend or leader was the most undesirable whom he could have chosen. It was a new boy named Brigson. This boy had been expelled from one of the most ill-managed schools in Ireland, although, of course, the fact had been treacherously concealed from the authorities at Roslyn; and now he was let loose, without warning or caution, among the Roslyn boys. Better for them if their gates had been open to the pestilence! the pestilence could but have killed the body, but this boy—this fore-front fighter in the devil's battle—did much to ruin many an immortal soul. He systematically, from the very first, called evil good, and good evil, put bitter for sweet, and sweet for bitter. He openly threw aside the admission of any one moral obligation. Never did some of the Roslyn boys, to their dying day, forget the deep, intolerable, unfathomable flood of moral turpitude and iniquity which he bore with him; a flood, which seemed so irresistible, that the influence of such boys as Montagu and Owen to stay its onrush seemed as futile as the weight of a feather to bar the fury of a mountain stream. Eric might have done much, Duncan might have done much, to aid the better cause had they tried; but they resisted at first but faintly, and then not at all, until they too were swept away in the broadening tide of degeneracy and sin.

Big, burly, and strong, though much younger than he looked (if he stated his age correctly, which I doubt), Brigson, being low in the school, naturally became the bully and the leader of all the lower forms—the bully if they opposed him, the leader if they accepted his guidance. A little army of small boys attended him, and were ever ready for the schemes of mischief to which he deliberately trained them, until they grew almost as turbulent, as disobedient, and as wicked as himself. He taught both by precept and example, that towards masters neither honour was to be recognised, nor respect to be considered due. To cheat them, to lie to them, to annoy them in every possible way—to misrepresent their motives, mimic their defects, and calumniate their actions—was the conduct which he inaugurated towards them; and for the time that he continued at Roslyn the whole lower school was a Pandemonium of evil passions and despicable habits.

Every one of the little boys became more or less amenable to his influence, and among them Vernon Williams. Had Eric done his duty, this would never have been; but he was half ashamed to be often with his brother, and disliked to find him so often creeping to his side. He flattered himself that in this feeling he was only anxious that Vernon should grow spirited and independent; but, had he examined himself, he would have found selfishness at the bottom of it. Once or twice his manner showed harshness to Vernon, and his younger brother both observed and resented it. Montagu and others noticed him for Eric's sake; but, being in the same form with Brigson, Vernon was thrown much

with him, and feeling, as he did, deserted and lonely, he was easily caught by the ascendency of his physical strength and reckless daring. Before three months were over, he became, to Eric's intolerable disgust, a ringleader in the band of troublesome scapegraces, whose increasing numbers were the despair of all who had the interest of the school at heart.

Unfortunately, Owen was now head of the school, and from his constitutional want of geniality, he was so little of a boy that he had no sympathy with the others, and little authority over them. He simply kept aloof, holding his own way, and retiring into his own tastes and pursuits, and the society of one or two congenial spirits in the school, so as in no way to come in contact with the spreading corruption.

Montagu, now Owen's chief friend, was also in the sixth, and fearlessly expressed at once his contempt for Brigson, and his dread of the evil he was effecting. Had the monitorial system existed, that contagion could have been effectually checked; but, as it was, brute force had unlimited authority. Ill indeed are those informed who raise a cry, and join in the ignorant abuse of that noble safeguard of English schools. Any who have had personal and intimate experience of how schools work *with* it and *without* it, know what a Palladium it is of happiness and morality; how it prevents bullying, upholds manliness, is the bulwark of discipline, and makes boys more earnest and thoughtful, often at the most critical periods of their lives, by enlisting all their sympathies and interests on the side of the honourable and the just.

Brigson knew at a glance whom he had most to fear; Ball, Attlay, Llewellyn, Graham, all tolerated or even approved of him. Owen did not come in his way, so he left him unmolested. To Eric and Duncan he was scrupulously civil, and by flattery and deference managed to keep apparently on excellent terms with them. Eric pretended to be

ignorant of the harm he was bringing about, and in answer to the indignant and measureless invectives of Montagu and others, professed to see in Brigson a very good fellow.

Brigson hated Montagu, because he read on his features the unvarying glance of undisguised contempt. He dared not come across him openly since Montagu was so high in the school; and besides, though much the bigger of the two, Brigson was decidedly afraid of him. But he chose sly methods of perpetual annoyance. He nick-named him 'Rosebud,' he talked *at* him whenever he had an opportunity; he poisoned the minds of the gang of youngsters against him; he spread malicious reports about him; he diminished his popularity, and embittered his feelings, by every secret and underhand means which lay in his power.

One method of torment was most successful. As a study-boy, Montagu did not come to bed till an hour later than the lower part of the school, and Brigson taught some of the little fellows to play all kinds of tricks to his bed and room, so that when he came down, it was with the certainty of finding everything in confusion. Sometimes his bed would be turned right on end, and he would have to put it to the ground and remake it before he could lie down. Sometimes all the furniture in the room would be thrown about in different corners, with no trace of the offender. Sometimes he would find all sorts of things put inside the bed itself. The intolerable part of the vexation was, to be certain that this was done at Brigson's instigation, or by his own hand, without having the means of convicting or preventing him. Poor Monty grew very sad at heart, and this perpetual dastardly annoyance weighed the more heavily on his spirits, from its being of a kind which peculiarly grated on his refined taste, and his natural sense of what was gentlemanly and fair.

One night, coming down, as usual, in melancholy dread, he saw a light under the door of his room. It struck him that he was earlier than usual, and he walked up quickly and noiselessly. There they were at it! The instant he entered, there was a rush through the opposite door, and he felt convinced that one of the retreating figures was Brigson's. In a second he had sprung across the room, so as to prevent the rest from running, and with heaving breast and flashing eyes, glared at the intruders as they stood there, sheepish and afraid.

'What!' he said angrily, 'so *you* are the fellows who have had the cowardice to annoy me thus, night after night, for weeks; you miserable, degraded young animals!' and he looked at the four or five who had not made their escape. 'What! and *you* among them,' he said with a start, as he caught the eye of Vernon Williams. 'Oh, this is too bad.' His tone showed the deepest sorrow and vexation, and for a moment he said no more. Instantly Vernon was by him.

'*Do* forgive me, *do* forgive me, Montagu,' he said; 'I really didn't know it teased you so much.'

But Montagu shook him off, and at once recovered himself. 'Wretched boys! let me see what you have been doing to-night. Oh, as usual,' he said, glancing at the complete disorder which they had been effecting. 'Ha! but what is this? So Brigson has introduced another vile secret among you. Well, he shall rue it!' and he pointed to some small, almost invisible flakes of a whitish substance, scattered here and there over his pillow. It was a kind of powder which, if once it touched the skin, caused the most violent and painful irritation.

'By heavens, this is *too* bad!' he exclaimed, stamping his foot with anger. 'What have I ever done to you young blackguards, that you should treat me thus? Have I ever been a bully? Have I ever harmed one of you? And *you*, too, Vernon Williams!'

The little boy trembled and looked ashamed under his glance of sorrow and scorn.

'Well, I *know* who has put you up to this; but you shall not escape so. I shall thrash you every one.'

Very quietly he suited the action to the word, sparing none. They took it patiently enough, conscious of richly deserving it; and when it was over, Vernon said, 'Forgive me, Montagu. I am very sorry, and will never do so again.' Montagu, without deigning a reply, motioned them to go, and then sat down, full of grief, on his bed. But the outrage was not over for that night, and no sooner had he put out the light than he became painfully aware that several boys were stealing into the room, and the next moment he felt a bolster fall on his head. He was out of bed in an instant, and with a few fierce and indignant blows, had scattered the crowd of his cowardly assailants, and driven them away. A number of fellows had set on him in the dark—on *him* of all others. Oh, what a change must have happened in the school that this should be possible! He felt that the contagion of Brigson's baseness had spread far indeed.

He fought like a lion, and several of the conspirators had reason to repent their miscalculation in assaulting so spirited an antagonist. But this did not content him; his blood was up, and he determined to attack the evil at its source. He strode through his discomfited enemies straight into Brigson's room, struck a match, and said, 'Brigson, get out of bed this instant.'

'Hullo!' grunted Brigson, pretending to be only just awake.

'None of that, you blackguard! Will you take a thrashing?'

'No!' roared Brigson, 'I should think not.'

'Well, then, take *that!*' he shouted, striking him in the face.

The fight that followed was very short. In a single round Montagu had utterly thrashed, and stricken to the earth, and forced to beg for mercy, his cumbrous and brutal opponent. He seemed to tower above him with a magnificent superiority, and there was a self-controlled passion about him which gave tremendous energy to every blow. Brigson was utterly dashed, confounded, and cowed, and took without a word the parting kick of contempt which Montagu bestowed on him.

'There,' he said to the fellows, who had thronged in from all the dormitories at the first hint of a fight, 'I, a sixth-form fellow, have condescended to thrash that base coward there, whom all you miserable lower boys have been making an idol and hero of, and from whom you have been so readily learning every sort of blackguardly and debasing trick. But let me tell you and your hero, that if any of you dare to annoy or lift a finger at me again, you shall do it at your peril. I despise you all; there is hardly one gentlemanly or honourable fellow left among you since that fellow Brigson has come here; yes, I despise you, and you know that you deserve it.' And every one of them *did* shrink before his just and fiery rebuke.

The scene was not over when the door suddenly opened, and Mr. Rose appeared. He stood amazed to see Montagu there in his night-shirt, the boys all round, and Brigson standing over a basin, washing his nose, which was bleeding profusely.

Montagu instantly stepped up to him. 'You can trust me, sir; may I ask you kindly to say nothing of this? I have been thrashing some one that deserved it, and teaching these fellows a lesson.'

Mr. Rose saw and allowed for his excited manner. 'I can trust you,' he said, 'Montagu, and shall take no further notice of this irregularity. And now get instantly to your beds.'

But Montagu, slipping on his clothes, went straight up to the studies, and called the upper boys together. He briefly told them what had occurred, and they rejoiced greatly, binding themselves for the future to check, if they could, by all fair means, Brigson's pernicious influence and abominable example.

But it was too late now; the mischief was done.

'O Eric,' said Montagu, 'why did you not make a stand against all this before? Your own brother was one of them.'

'Little wretch. I'll kick him well for it,' said Eric.

'No, no!' said Montagu, 'that'll do no good. Try rather to look after him a little more.'

'I hope *you* will forgive him, and try and rescue him.'

'I will do what I can,' said Montagu coldly.

Eric sighed, and they parted.

Montagu had hoped that after this, Eric would at least break off all open connection with Brigson; and, indeed, Eric had meant to do so. But that personage kept carefully out of his way until the first burst of indignation against him had subsided, and after a time began to address Eric as if nothing had happened. Meanwhile he had completely regained his ascendency over the lower part of the school, which was not difficult, because they were wincing under Montagu's contempt, and mingled no little dislike with it; a dislike which all are too apt to feel towards those whose very presence and moral superiority are a tacit rebuke of their own failings. But while Montagu was hated, Eric was at the zenith of popular favour, a favour which Brigson ostentatiously encouraged. He was openly flattered and caressed, and if ever he got a large score at cricket, it was chalked triumphantly over the walls. All this he was weak enough to enjoy immensely, and it was one of the reasons why he did not wish to risk his popularity by breaking with Brigson. So, after a little constraint and coldness, he began to stand in much the same relation to him as before.

The best disposed of the upper boys disliked all this very much, and the sixth and fifth forms began to be split up into two main parties—the one headed by Eric, and, to a much less degree, by Duncan, who devoted themselves to the games and diversions of the school, and troubled themselves comparatively little about anything else; the other headed by Montagu, who took the lead in intellectual pursuits, and endeavoured, by every means in their power, to counteract the pernicious effects of the spreading immorality.

And so at Roslyn, owing mainly to the wickedness of one depraved boy, and the weak fear of man which actuated others, all was disunion, misery, and deterioration. The community which had once been peaceful, happy, and united, was filled with violent jealousy and heartburnings; every boy's hand seemed to be against his neighbour; lying, bad language, dishonesty, grew fearfully rife, and the few who, like Owen and Montagu, remained uncontaminated by the general mischief, walked alone and despondent amid their uncongenial and degraded schoolfellows.

CHAPTER THE SECOND

WILDNEY

That punishment's the best to bear
That follows soonest on the sin,
And guilt's a game where losers fare
Better than those who seem to win.
COV. PATMORE

At the beginning of this quarter, Eric and Duncan had succeeded to one of the studies, and Owen shared with Montagu the one which adjoined it.

Latterly the small boys, in the universal spirit of disobedience, had frequented the studies a good deal, but it was generally understood that no study-boy might ask any one to be a regular visitor to his room without the leave of its other occupant.

So one evening Duncan said to Eric, 'Do you know little Wildney?'

'You mean that jolly fearless-looking little fellow, with the great black eyes, who came at the beginning of the quarter? No, I don't know him.'

'Well he's a very nice little fellow; a regular devil.'

'Humph!' said Eric, laughing, 'I shall bring out a new Duncan-dictionary, in which κερκοκερώνυχος = very nice little fellow.'

'Pooh!' said Duncan; 'you know well enough what I mean; I mean he's not one of your white-faced, lily-hearted new boys, but has lots of fun in him.'

'Well, what of him?'

'Have you any objection to my asking him to sit in the study when he likes?'

'Not the least in the world.'

'Very well, I'll go and fetch him now. But wouldn't you like to ask your brother Vernon to come in too, whenever he's inclined?'

'No,' said Eric, 'I don't care. He does come every now and then.'

Duncan went to fetch Wildney, and while he was gone, Eric was thinking *why* he didn't give Vernon the free run of his study. He would not admit to himself the true reason, which was, that he had too much ground to fear that his example would do his brother no good.

Eric soon learned to like Wildney, who was a very bright, engaging, spirited boy, with a dash of pleasant impudence about him which took Eric's fancy. He had been one of the most mischievous of the lower fellows, but, although clever, did little or nothing in school, and was in the worst repute with the masters. Until he was 'taken up' by Eric, he had been a regular little hero among his compeers, because he was game for any kind of mischief, and, in the new tone of popular morality, his fearless disregard of rules made him the object of general admiration. From this time, however, he was much in the studies, and unhappily carried with him to those upper regions the temptation to worse and more injurious follies than had yet penetrated there.

It was an ill day for General Wildney when he sent his idolised little son to Roslyn; it was an ill day for Eric when Duncan first asked the child to frequent their study.

It was past nine at night, and the lower school had gone to bed, but there was Wildney quietly sitting by the study fire, while Duncan was doing some Arnold's verses for him to be shown up next day.

'Bother these verses,' said Duncan, 'I shall have a whiff. Do you mind, Eric?'

'No; not at all.'

'Give me a weed too,' said Wildney.

'What! young un—you don't mean to say you smoke?' asked Eric, in surprise.

'Don't I, though? Let me show you. Why, a whole lot of us went and smoked two or three pipes by Riverbend only yesterday.'

'Phew!' said Eric; 'then I suppose I must smoke too to keep you in countenance;' and he took a cigar. It was the first time he had touched one since the day at the Stack. The remembrance made him gloomy and silent. 'Tempora mutantur,' thought he, 'nos et mutamur in illis.'

'Why, how glum you are,' said Wildney, patting him on the head.

'Oh no!' said Eric, shaking off unpleasant memories. 'Look,' he continued, pointing out of the window to change the subject, 'what a glorious night it is! Nothing but stars, stars, stars.'

'Yes,' said Duncan, yawning, 'this smoking makes one very thirsty. I wish I'd some beer.'

'Well, why shouldn't we get some?' said Wildney; 'it would be very jolly.'

'Get some! What! at this time of night?'

'Yes; I'll go now, if you like, to Ellan, and be back before ten.'

'Nonsense,' said Eric; 'it ain't worth while.'

'I believe you think I'm afraid,' said Wildney, laughing, and looking at Eric with his dark eyes; 'and what's more, I believe *you're* afraid.'

'Little whippersnapper!' said Eric, colouring, 'as if I was afraid to do anything *you* dare do. I'll go with you at once, if you like.'

'What are you thinking of?' asked Duncan; 'I don't care twopence about the beer, and I hope you won't go.'

'But I will, though,' said Eric, a little nettled that Wildney, of all people, should think him wanting in pluck.

'But how will you get out?'

'Oh, *I'll* show you a dodge there,' said Wildney. 'Come along. Have you a dark lantern?'

'No, but I'll get Llewellyn's.'

'Come along, then.'

So the little boy of twelve took the initiative, and, carrying the dark lantern, initiated the two study-boys of sixteen into a secret which had long been known to the lower part of the school.

'Ibant obscuri dubiâ sub luce.' He led them quietly down stairs, stole with them noiselessly past the library door, and took them to a window in the passage, where a pane was broken.

'Could you get through that?' he whispered to Eric, 'if we broke away the rest of the glass?'

'I don't know. But then, there's the bar outside.'

'Oh, I'll manage that. But will you go and peep through the key-hole of the library, and see who's there, Duncan?'

'No,' said Duncan bluntly, 'no key-holes for me.'

'Hush! Then *I* will,' and he glided away, while Eric, as quietly as he could, broke away the glass until it was all removed.

'There's only old Stupid,' whispered he, irreverently designating an under-master named Harley, 'and he's asleep before the fire. Now, then, just lift me up, Eric, will you?'

Eric lifted him, and he removed the nails which fastened the end of the bar. They looked secure enough, and were nails an inch long driven into the mortar; but they had been successfully loosened, and only wanted a little pull to bring them out. In one minute Wildney had unfastened and pushed down one end of the bar. He then got through the broken pane and dropped down outside. Eric followed with some little difficulty, for the aperture would only just admit his passage; and Duncan, going back to the study, anxiously awaited their return.

It was a bright moonlight night, and the autumn air was pleasant and cool. But Eric's

first thought, as he dropped on to the ground, was one of shame that he should suffer his new friend, a mere child, so easily to tempt him into disobedience and sin. He had hardly thought till then of what their errand was to be, but now he couldn't help so strongly disapproving of it, that he was half inclined to turn back. He did not, however, dare to suggest this, lest Wildney should charge him with cowardice, and betray it to the rest. Besides, the adventure had its own excitement, the stars looked splendid, and the stolen waters were sweet.

'I hope we shan't be seen crossing the playground,' said Wildney. 'My eye, shouldn't we catch it!'

He was obviously beginning to be afraid; so Eric assumed an air of nonchalance, and played the part of protector.

'Here, take my arm,' he said; and as Wildney grasped it tight, instead of feeling angry and ashamed at having been misled by one so much his junior, Eric felt strongly drawn towards him by community of danger and interest. Reaching Ellan, it suddenly struck him that he did not know where they were going to buy the beer. He asked Wildney.

'Oh, I see you're not half up to snuff,' said Wildney, whose courage had risen; 'I'll show you.'

He led to a little low public-house, whence tipsy songs were booming, and tapped at a side door three times. As they looked in they saw some sailors boozing in a dirty taproom, and enveloped in tobacco smoke.

The side door was opened, and a cunning wicked-looking man held up a light to see who they were.

'Hallo, Billy,' said Wildney confidentially, 'all serene; give us two bottles of beer—on tick, you know.'

'Yessir—d'reckly,' said the man, with a hateful twinkle of the eyes. 'So you're out for a spree,' he continued, winking in a knowing way. 'Won't you walk into the back parlour while I get them?' And he showed them into a dingy horrid room behind the house, stale with smoke, and begrimed with dust.

Eric was silent and disgusted, but Wildney seemed quite at home. The man soon returned with the beer. 'Wouldn't you like a glass of summat now, young gen'leman?' he asked in an insinuating way.

'No, Billy! don't jabber—we must be off. Here, open the door.'

'Stop, I'll pay,' said Eric. 'What's the damage?'

'Three shilling, sir,' said the man. 'Glad to see a new customer, sir.' He pocketed the money and showed them out, standing to look after them with a malicious leer as they disappeared, and jerking his left thumb over his shoulder.

'Faugh!' said Eric, taking a long breath as they got out again into the moonlight, 'what a poisonous place! Good gracious, Charlie, who introduced you there?'

'Oh, I don't think much of going *there*,' said Wildney carelessly, 'we go every week almost.'

'We! who?'

'Oh, Brigson and a lot of us. We have a club there which we call "the Anti-muffs," and that's our smoking-room.'

'And is that horrid beast the landlord?'

'Yes; he was an old school-servant, and there's no harm in him that I know of.'

But Eric only 'phewed' again two or three times, and thought of Montagu.

Suddenly Wildney clutched him by the arm, and pulled him into the deep shadow of a porch, whispering in a low tone, 'Look!'

Under a lamp-post directly opposite them, stood Mr. Rose. He had heard voices and footsteps a moment before, and, puzzled at their sudden cessation in the noiseless street, he was looking round.

'We must run for it,' whispered Wildney hastily, as Mr. Rose approached the porch; and the two boys took to their heels, and scampered away as hard as they could, Eric helping on Wildney by taking his hand, and neither of them looking behind. They heard Mr. Rose following them at first, but soon distanced him, and reached a place where two roads met, either of which would lead to the school.

'We won't go by the road; I know a short cut by the fields. What fun!' said Wildney, laughing.

'What an audacious little monkey you are; you know all sorts of dodges,' said Eric.

They had no time to talk, but with a speed winged by fear got to the school, sprang on the buttress beneath the window, effected their entrance, and vanished after replacing the bar—Eric to his study, and Wildney to his dormitory.

'Here's a go!' said the latter, as they ran up stairs; 'I've smashed one of the beer bottles in getting through the window, and my trousers are deluged with the stuff.'

They had hardly separated when Mr. Rose's step was heard on the stairs. He was just returning from a dinner-party, when the sight of two boys and the sound of their voices startled him in the street, and their sudden disappearance made him sure that they were Roslyn boys, particularly when they began to run. He strongly suspected that he recognised Wildney as one of them, and therefore made straight for his dormitory, which he entered, just as that worthy had thrust the beer-stained trousers under his bed.

Mr. Rose walked up quietly to his bedside, and observed that he was not asleep, and that he still had half his clothes on. He was going away when he saw a little bit of the trousers protruding under the mattress, and giving a pull, out they came wringing wet with the streams of beer. He could not tell at first what this imported, but a fragment of the bottle fell out of the pocket with a crash on the floor, and he then discovered. Taking no notice of Wildney's pretended sleep, he said quietly, 'Come to me before breakfast to-morrow, Wildney,' and went down stairs.

Eric came in soon after, and found the little fellow vainly attempting to appear indifferent as he related to his admiring auditors the night's adventure; being evidently rather proud of the 'Eric and I,' which he introduced every now and then into his story.

'Has he twigged you?'

'Yes.'

'And me?'

'I don't know; we shall see to-morrow.'

'I hope not,' said Eric; 'I'm sorry for you, Charlie.'

'Can't be cured, must be endured,' said Wildney.

'Well, good-night! and don't lose heart.'

Eric went back to Duncan in the study, and they finished the other bottle of beer between them, though without much enjoyment, because they were full of surmises as to the extent of the discovery, and the nature of the punishment.

Eric went in to tell Montagu of their escapade.

He listened very coldly, and said, 'Well, Eric, it would serve you right to be caught. What business have you to be going out at night at the invitation of contemptible small fry, like this little Wildney?'

'I beg you won't speak of any friend of mine in those terms,' said Eric, drawing up haughtily.

'I hope you don't call a bad little boy like Wildney, who'd be no credit to any one, *your* friend, Eric?'

'Yes, I do though. He's one of the pluckiest, finest, most promising fellows in the lower school.'

'How I begin to hate that word plucky,' said Montagu; 'it's made the excuse here for everything that's wrong, base, and unmanly. It seems to me it's infinitely more "plucky" just now to do your duty and not be ashamed of it.'

'You've certainly required *that* kind of pluck to bear you up lately, Monty,' said Owen, looking up from his books.

'Pluck!' said Montagu scornfully; 'you seem to me to think it consists in lowering yourself down to the level of that odious Brigson, and joining hand and glove with the dregs of the school.'

'Dregs of the school! Upon my word, you're cool, to speak of any of my associates in that way,' said Eric, now thoroughly angry.

'Associates!' retorted Montagu hotly; 'pretty associates! How do you expect anything good to go on, when fellows high in the school like you have such dealings with the refined honourable Brigson, and the exemplary intellectual Wildney?'

'You're a couple of confounded muffs!' shouted Eric, banging the door and flinging into his own study again without further reply.

'Haven't you been a little hard on him, considering the row he's in?' asked Owen.

Montagu's head was resting on his hand as he bent over the table. 'Perhaps I have, indeed. But who could help it, Owen, in the present state of things? Yes, you're right,' he said, after a pause; '*this* wasn't the time to speak. I'll go and talk to him again. But how utterly changed he is!'

He found Eric on the stairs going down to bed with an affectation of noise and gaiety. He ran after him, and said—

'Forgive me my passion and sarcasm, Williams. You know I am apt to express myself strongly.' He could not trust himself to say more, but held out his hand.

Eric got red, and hesitated for a moment.

'Come, Eric, it isn't *wholly* my fault, is it, that we are not so warm to each other as we were when——'

'O Monty, Monty!' said Eric, softened by the allusion; and he warmly grasped his friend's proffered hand.

'O Eric!'

The two shook hands in silence, and as they left each other they felt that while things continued thus their friendship could not last. It was a sad thought for both.

Next morning Wildney received a severe flogging, but gained great reputation by not betraying his companion, and refusing to drop the least hint as to their means of getting out, or their purpose in visiting Ellan. So the secret of the bar remained undiscovered, and when any boy wanted to get out at night—(unhappily the trick now became common enough)—he had only to break a pane of glass in that particular window, which, as it was in the passage, often remained unmended and undiscovered for weeks.

After the flogging, Mr. Rose said shortly to Eric, 'I want to speak to you.'

The boy's heart misgave him as they entered the familiar library.

'I think I suspect who was Wildney's companion.'

Eric was silent.

'I have no proof, and shall not therefore act on vague suspicion; but the boy whom I *do* suspect is one whose course lately has given me the deepest pain; one who has violated all the early promise he gave; one who seems to be going farther and farther astray, and sacrificing all moral principle to the ghost of a fleeting and most despicable popularity—to the approval of those whom he cannot himself approve.'

Eric still silent.

'Whatever you do *yourself*, Williams'—(it was the first time for two years that Mr. Rose had called him 'Williams,' and he winced a little)—'whatever you do *yourself*, Williams, rests with *you*; but remember it is a ten-thousandfold heavier and more accursed crime to set stumbling-blocks in the way of others, and abuse your influence to cause any of Christ's little ones to perish.'

'I wasn't the tempter, however,' thought Eric, still silent;—it was the silence of pride and unwilling conviction.

'Well, you seem hardened, and give no sign. Believe me, Williams, I grieve for you, and that bitterly. My interest in you is no less warm, though my affection for you cannot be the same. You may go.'

'Another friend alienated, and oh, how true a one! He has not asked me to see him once this term,' thought Eric sadly; but a shout of pleasure greeted him directly he joined the football in the playground, and half consoled, he hoped Mr. Rose had heard it, and understood that it was meant for the boy whom he had just been rebuking. 'Well, after all,' he thought, 'I have *some* friends still.'

Yes, friends, such as they were! Except Duncan, hardly one boy whom he really respected ever walked with him now. Even little Wright, one of the very few lower boys who had risen superior to Brigson's temptations, seemed to keep clear of him as much as he could: and in absolute vacuity, he was obliged to associate with fellows like Attlay, and Graham, and Llewellyn, and Ball.

Even with Ball! All Eric's repugnance for this boy seemed to have evaporated; they were often together, and, to all appearance, were sworn friends. Eric did not shrink now from such conversation as was pursued unchecked in his presence by nearly every one; nay, worse, it had lost its horror, and he was neither afraid nor ashamed to join in it himself. This plague-spot had fretted more deeply than any other into the heart of the school morality, and the least boys seemed the greatest proficients in unbaring, without a blush, its hideous ugliness.

CHAPTER THE THIRD

'THE JOLLY HERRING'

Velut unda supervenit undam.
HORACE

'THE ANTI-MUFFS REQUEST the honour of Eric Williams's company to a spread they are going to have to-morrow evening at half-past four, in their smoking-room.'

A note to this effect was put into Eric's hands with much *empressement* by Wildney after prayers. He read it when he got into his study, and hardly knew whether to be pleased or disgusted at it.

He tossed it to Duncan, and said, 'What shall I do?'

Duncan turned up his nose, and chucked the note into the fire.

'I'd give them that answer, and no other.'

'Why?'

'Because, Eric,' said Duncan, with more seriousness than was usual with him, 'I can't help thinking things have gone too far lately.'

'How do you mean?'

'Well, I'm no saint myself, Heaven knows; but I do think that the fellows are worse now than I have ever known them—far worse. Your friend Brigson reigns supreme out of the studies; he has laid down a law that *no work* is to be done down stairs ever under any pretence, and it's only by getting into one of the studies that good little chaps like Wright can get on at all. Even in the classrooms there's so much row and confusion that the mere thought of work is ridiculous.'

'Well, there's no great harm in a little noise, if that's all.'

'But it isn't all. The talk of nearly the whole school is getting most blackguardly; shamelessly so. Only yesterday Wildney was chatting with Vernon up here (you were out, or Vernon would not have been here) while I was reading; they didn't seem to mind me, and I'm sure you'd have been vexed to the heart if you'd heard how they talked to each other. At last I couldn't stand it any longer, and bouncing up, I boxed both their ears smartly, and kicked them down stairs.'

As Eric said nothing, Duncan continued, 'And I wish it ended in talk, but——'

'But I believe you're turning Owenite. Why, bless me, we're only schoolboys; it'll be lots of time to turn saint some other day.'

Eric was talking at random, and in the spirit of opposition. 'You don't want to make the whole school such a muffish set as the Rosebuds, do you?'

There was something of assumed bravado in Eric's whole manner which jarred on Duncan exceedingly. 'Do as you like,' he said curtly, and went into another study.

Immediately after came a rap at the door, and in walked Wildney, as he often did after the rest were gone to bed, merely slipping his trousers over his night-shirt, and running up to the studies.

'Well, you'll come to the Anti-muffs, won't you?' he said.

'To that pestilential place again?—not I.'

Wildney looked offended. 'Not after we've all asked you? The fellows won't half like your refusing.'

He had touched Eric's weak point.

'Do come,' he said, looking up in Eric's face.

'Confound it all,' answered Eric, hastily. 'Yes, I've no friends, I'll come, Charlie. Anything to please you, boy.'

'That's a brick. Then I shall cut down and tell the fellows. They'll be no end glad. No friends! what bosh! why, all the school like you.' And he scampered off, leaving Eric ill at ease.

Duncan didn't re-enter the study that evening.

The next day, about half-past four, Eric found himself on the way to Ellan. As he was starting, Ball caught him up and said—

'Are you going to the Anti-muffs?'

'Yes; why? are you going too?'

'Yes; do you mind our going together?'

'Not at all.'

In fact, Eric was very glad of some one—no matter who—to keep him in countenance, for he felt considerably more than half ashamed of himself.

They went to 'The Jolly Herring,' as the pot-house was called, and passed through the dingy beery taproom into the back parlour, to which Eric had already been introduced by Wildney. About a dozen boys were assembled, and there was a great clapping as the two new-comers entered. A long table was laid down the room, which was regularly spread for dinner.

'Now then, Billy; make haste with the goose,' called Brigson. 'I vote, boys, that Eric Williams takes the chair.'

'Hear! hear!' said half a dozen; and Eric, rather against his will, found himself ensconced at the end of the table, with Brigson and Ball on either hand. The villainous low-foreheaded man, whom they called Billy, soon brought in a tough goose at one end of the table, and some fowls at the other; and they fell to, doing ample justice to the δαὶς ἐΐση, while Billy waited on them. There was immense uproar during the dinner, every one eating as fast, and talking as loud, as he could.

The birds soon vanished, and were succeeded by long roly-poly puddings, which the boys called Goliahs; and they, too, rapidly disappeared. Meanwhile beer was circling only too plentifully.

'Now for the dessert, Billy,' called several voices; and that worthy proceeded to put on the table some figs, cakes, oranges, and four black bottles of wine. There was a general grab for these dainties, and one boy shouted, 'I say, I've had no wine.'

'Well, it's all gone. We must get some brandy—it's cheaper,' said Brigson; and accordingly some brandy was brought in, which the boys diluted with hot water, and soon despatched.

'Here! before you're all done swilling,' said Brigson, 'I've got a health: "Confound muffs and masters, and success to the antis." '

'And their chairman,' suggested Wildney.

'And their chairman, the best fellow in the school,' added Brigson.

The health was drunk with due clamour, and Eric (ridiculous and meaningless as he thought the toast) got up to thank them.

'I'm not going to spout,' he said; 'but boys must be boys, and there's no harm in a bit of fun. I for one have enjoyed it, and am much obliged to you for asking me; and now I call for a song.'

'Wildney! Wildney's song,' called several.

Wildney had a good voice, and struck up without the least bashfulness—

> 'Come, landlord, fill the flowing bowl
>   Until it does run over!
> Come, landlord, fill, etc.

'Now,' he said, 'join in the chorus!' The boys, all more or less excited, joined in heartily and uproariously—

'For to-night we'll merry merry be!
For to-night we'll merry merry be!
For to-night we'll merry merry be!
To-morrow we'll be sober!'

While Wildney sang, Eric had time to think. As he glanced round the room at the flushed faces of the boys, some of whom he could not recognise in the dusky atmosphere, a qualm of disgust and shame passed over him. Several of them were smoking, and, with Ball and Brigson heading the line on each side of the table, he could not help observing what a bad set they looked. The remembrance of Russell came back to him. Oh, if Edwin could have known that he was in such company at such a place! And by the door stood Billy, watching them all like an evil spirit, with a leer of saturnine malice on his evil face.

But the bright little Wildney, unconscious of Eric's bitter thoughts, sang on with overflowing mirth. As Eric looked at him, shining out like a sunbeam among the rest, he felt something like blood-guiltiness on his soul, when he felt that he was sanctioning the young boy's presence in that degraded assemblage.

Wildney meanwhile was just beginning the next verse, when he was interrupted by a general cry of 'Cavé, cavé.' In an instant the room was in confusion; some one dashed the candles upon the floor, the table was overturned with a mighty crash, and plates, glasses, and bottles rushed on to the ground in shivers. Nearly every one bolted for the door, which led through the passage into the street; and in their headlong flight and selfishness, they stumbled over each other, and prevented all egress, several being knocked down and bruised in the crush. Others made for the taproom; but, as they opened the door leading into it, there stood Mr. Ready and Mr. Gordon! and as it was impossible to pass without being seen, they made no further attempt at escape. All this was the work of a minute. Entering the back parlour, the two masters quickly took down the names of full half the boys who, in the suddenness of the surprise, had been unable to make their exit.

And Eric?

The instant that the candles were knocked over, he felt Wildney seize his hand, and whisper, 'This way; all serene;' following, he groped his way in the dark to the end of the room, where Wildney, shoving aside a green baize curtain, noiselessly opened a door, which at once led them into a little garden. There they both crouched down under a lilac tree beside the house, and listened intently.

There was no need for this precaution; their door remained unsuspected, and in five minutes the coast was clear. Creeping into the house again, they whistled, and Billy coming in, told them that the masters had gone, and all was safe.

'Glad ye're not twigged, gen'lemen,' he said; 'but there'll be a pretty sight of damage for all this glass and plates.'

'Shut up with your glass and plates,' said Wildney. 'Here, Eric, we must cut for it again.'

It was the dusk of a winter evening when they got out from the close room into the open air, and they had to consider which way they would choose to avoid discovery. They happened to choose the wrong, but escaped by dint of hard running, and Wildney's old short cut. As they ran they passed several boys (who, having been caught, were walking home leisurely), and managed to get back undiscovered, when they both answered their names quite innocently at the roll-call, immediately after lock-up.

'What lucky dogs you are to get off,' said many boys to them.

'Yes; it's precious lucky for me,' said Wildney. 'If I'd been caught at this kind of thing a second time, I should have got something worse than a swishing.'

'Well it's all through you I escaped,' said Eric, 'you knowing little scamp.'

'I'm glad of it, Eric,' said Wildney, in his fascinating way, 'since it was all through me you went. It's rather too hazardous though; we must manage better another time.'

During tea-time Eric was silent, as he felt pretty sure that none of the sixth form or other study-boys would particularly sympathise with his late associates. Since the previous evening he had been cool with Duncan, and the rest had long rather despised him as a boy who'd do anything to be popular; so he sat there silent, looking as disdainful as he could, and not touching the tea, for which he felt disinclined after the recent potations. But the contemptuous exterior hid a self-reproving heart, and he felt how far more worthy Owen and Montagu were than he. How gladly would he have changed places with them; how much he would have given to recover some of their forfeited esteem.

The master on duty was Mr. Rose, and after tea he left the room for a few minutes while the tables were cleared for 'preparation,' and the boys were getting out their books and exercises. All the study and classroom boys were expected to go away during this interval; but Eric, not noticing Mr. Rose's entrance, sat gossiping with Wildney about the dinner and its possible consequences to the school.

He was sitting on the desk carelessly, with one leg over the other, and bending down towards Wildney. He had just told him that he looked like a regular little sunbeam in the smoking-room of 'The Jolly Herring,' and Wildney was pretending to be immensely offended by the simile.

'Hush! no more talking,' said Mr. Rose, who did everything very gently and quietly. Eric heard him, but he was inclined to linger, and had always received such mild treatment from Mr. Rose, that he didn't think he would take much notice of the delay. For the moment he did not, so Wildney began to chatter again.

'All study-boys to leave the room,' said Mr. Rose.

Eric just glanced round and moved slightly; he might have gone away, but that he caught a satirical look in Wildney's eye, and besides wanted to show off a little indifference to his old master, with whom he had had no intercourse since their last-mentioned conversation.

'Williams, go away instantly; what do you mean by staying after I have dismissed you?' said Mr. Rose sternly.

Every one knew what a favourite Eric had once been, so this speech created a slight titter. The boy heard it just as he was going out of the room, and it annoyed him, and called to arms all his proud and dogged obstinacy. Pretending to have forgotten something, he walked conceitedly back to Wildney, and whispered to him, 'I shan't go if he chooses to speak like that.'

A red flush passed over Mr. Rose's cheek; he took two strides to Eric, and laid the cane sharply once across his back.

Eric was not quite himself, or he would not have acted as he had done. His potations, though not deep, had, with the exciting events of the evening, made his head giddy, and the stroke of the cane, which he had not felt now for two years, roused him to madness. He bounded up, sprang towards Mr. Rose, and almost before he knew what he was about, had wrenched the cane out of his hands, twisted it violently in the middle until it broke, and flung one of the pieces furiously into the fire.

For one instant, boy and master—Eric Williams and Mr. Rose—stood facing each other amid breathless silence, the boy panting and passionate, with his brain swimming, and his heart on fire; the master pale, grieved, amazed beyond measure, but perfectly self-collected.

'After that exhibition,' said Mr. Rose, with cold and quiet dignity, 'you had better leave the room.'

'Yes, I had,' answered Eric bitterly; 'there's your cane.' And, flinging the other fragment at Mr. Rose's head, he strode blindly out of the room, sweeping books from the table, and overturning several boys in his way. He then banged the door with all his force, and rushed up into his study.

Duncan was there, and remarking his wild look and demeanour, asked, after a moment's awkward silence, 'Is anything the matter, Williams?'

'Williams!' echoed Eric with a scornful laugh; 'yes, that's always the way with a fellow when he's in trouble. I always know what's coming when you begin to leave off calling me by my Christian name.'

'Very well, then,' said Duncan good-humouredly, 'what's the matter, Eric?'

'Matter?' answered Eric, pacing up and down the little room with an angry to-and-fro like a caged wild beast, and kicking everything which came in his way; 'matter? hang you all, you are all turning against me, because you are a set of muffs, and——'

'Take care!' said Duncan; but suddenly he caught Eric's look, and stopped.

'——And I've been breaking Rose's cane over his head, because he had the impudence to touch me with it, and——'

'Eric, you're not yourself to-night,' said Duncan, interrupting, but speaking in the kindest tone; and taking Eric's hand, he looked him steadily in the face.

Their eyes met; the boy's false self once more slipped off. By a strong effort he repressed the rising passion which the fumes of drink had caused, and flinging himself on his chair, refused to speak again, or even to go down stairs when the prayer-bell rang.

Seeing that in his present mood there was nothing to be done with him, Duncan, instead of returning to the study, went after prayers into Montagu's, and talked with him over the recent events, of which the boys' minds were all full.

But Eric sat lonely, sulky, and miserable, in his study, doing nothing, and when Montagu came in to visit him, felt inclined to resent his presence.

'So!' he said, looking up at the ceiling, 'another saint come to cast a stone at me! Well! I suppose I must be resigned,' he continued, dropping his cheek on his hand again; 'only don't let the sermon be long.'

But Montagu took no notice of his sardonic harshness, and seated himself by his side, though Eric pettishly pushed him away.

'Come, Eric,' said Montagu, taking the hand which was repelling him; 'I won't be repulsed in this way. Look at me. What? won't you even look? O Eric, one wouldn't have fancied this in past days, when we were so much together with one who is dead. It's a long long time since we've even alluded to him, but *I* shall never forget those happy days.'

Eric heaved a deep sigh.

'I'm not come to reproach you. You don't give me a friend's right to reprove. But still, Eric, for your own sake, dear fellow, I can't help being sorry for all this. I did hope you'd have broken with Brigson after the thrashing I gave him for the foul way in which he treated me. I don't think you *can* know the mischief he is doing.'

The large tears began to soften the fire of Eric's eye. 'Ah!' he said, 'it's all of no use; you're all giving me the cold shoulder, and I'm going to the bad, that's the long and short of it.'

'O Eric! for your own sake, for your parents' sake, for the school's sake, for all your real friends' sake, don't talk in that bitter, hopeless way. You are too fine a fellow to be made the tool or the patron of the boys who lead, while they seem to follow you. I *do* hope you'll join us even yet in resisting them.'

Eric had laid his head on the table, which shook with his emotion. 'I can't talk, Monty,' he said, in an altered tone; 'but leave me now; and if you like, we will have a walk to-morrow.'

'Most willingly, Eric.' And, again warmly pressing his hand, Montagu returned to his own study.

Soon after, there came a timid knock at Eric's door. He expected Wildney as usual; a little before, he had been looking out for him, and hoping he would come, but he didn't want to see him now, so he answered rather peevishly, 'Come in; but I don't want to be bothered to-night.'

Not Wildney, but Vernon appeared at the door. 'May I come in? not if it bothers you, Eric,' he said gently.

'Oh, Verny, I didn't know it was you; I thought it would be Wildney. You *never* come now.'

The little boy came in, and his pleading look seemed to say, 'Whose fault is that?'

'Come here, Verny;' and Eric drew him towards him, and put him on his knee, while the tears trembled large and luminous in the child's eyes.

It was the first time for many a long day that the brothers had been alone together, the first time for many a long day that any acts of kindness had passed between them. Both seemed to remember this, and, at the same time, to remember home, and their absent parents, and their mother's prayers, and all the quiet half-forgotten vista of innocent pleasures, and sacred relationships, and holy affections. And why did they see each other so little at school? Their consciences told them both that either wished to conceal from the other his wickedness and forgetfulness of God.

They wept together; and once more, as they had not done since they were children, each brother put his arm round the other's neck. And remorseful Eric could not help being amazed, how, in his cruel, heartless selfishness, he had let that fair child go so far far astray; left him as a prey to such boys as were his companions in the lower school.

'Eric, did you know I was caught to-night at the dinner?'

'You!' said Eric, with a start and a deep blush. 'Good heavens! I didn't notice you, and should not have dreamt of coming, if I'd known you were there. Oh, Vernon, forgive me for setting you such a bad example.'

'Yes, I was there, and I was caught.'

'Poor boy! but never mind; there are such a lot that you can't get much done to you.'

'It isn't *that* I care for; I've been flogged before, you know. But—may I say something?'

'Yes, Vernon, anything you like.'

'Well, then,—oh, Eric! I'm *so so* sorry that you did that to Mr. Rose to-night. All the fellows are praising you up, of course; but I could have cried to see it, and I did. I wouldn't have minded if it had been anybody but Rose.'

'But why?'

'Because, Eric, he's been so good, so kind to both of us. You've often told me about him, you know, at Fairholm, and he's done such lots of kind things to me. And only to-night, when he heard I was caught, he sent for me to the library, and spoke so firmly, yet so gently, about the wickedness of going to such low places, and about so young a boy as I am learning to drink, and the ruin of it——and—and——' His voice was choked by sobs for a time,—'and then he knelt down and prayed for me, so as I have never heard any one pray but mother; and do you know, Eric, it was strange, but I thought, I *did* hear our mother's voice praying for me too, while he prayed, and——' He tried in vain to go on; but Eric's conscience continued for him; 'and just as he had ceased doing this for one brother, the other brother, for whom he has often done the same, treated him with coarseness, violence, and insolence.'

'Oh, I am utterly wretched, Verny. I hate myself. And to think that while I'm like this they are yet loving and praising me at home. And, O Verny, I was so sorry to hear from Duncan how you were talking the other day.'

Vernon hid his face on Eric's shoulder; and as his brother stooped over him and folded him to his heart, they cried in silence, for there seemed no more to say, until, wearied with sorrow, the younger fell asleep; and then Eric carried him tenderly down stairs, and laid him, still half sleeping, upon his bed.

He laid him down, and looked at him as he slumbered. The other boys had not been disturbed by their noiseless entrance, and he sat down on his brother's bed to think, shading off the light of the candle with his hand. It was rarely now that Eric's thoughts were so rich with the memories of childhood, and sombre with the consciousness of sin, as they were that night, while he gazed on his brother Vernon's face. He did not know what made him look so long and earnestly; an indistinct sorrow, an unconjectured foreboding, passed over his mind, like the shadow of a summer cloud. Vernon was now slumbering deeply; his soft bright hair fell over his forehead, and his head nestled in the pillow; but there was an expression of uneasiness on his sleeping features, and the long eyelashes were still wet with tears.

'Poor child,' thought Eric; 'dear little Vernon: and he is to be flogged, perhaps birched, to-morrow.'

He went off sadly to bed, and hardly once remembered that *he* too would come in for very severe and certain punishment the next day.

CHAPTER THE FOURTH

MR. ROSE AND BRIGSON

Raro antecedentem scelestum
Deseruit pede Pœna claudo.
HORACE

AFTER PRAYERS the next morning Dr. Rowlands spoke to his boarders on the previous day's discovery, and in a few forcible vivid words, set before them the enormity of the offence. He ended by announcing that the boys who were caught would be birched, —'except the elder ones, who will bring me one hundred lines every hour of the half-holidays till further notice. There are some,' he said, 'I am well aware, who, though present yesterday, were not detected. I am sorry for it for *their* sakes; they will be more likely to sin again. In cases like this, punishment is a blessing, and impunity a burden.' On leaving the room he bade Eric follow him into his study. Eric obeyed, and stood before the head-master with downcast eyes.

'Williams,' he said, 'I have had a great regard for you, and felt a deep interest in you from the day I first saw you, and knew your excellent parents. At one time I had conceived great hopes of your future course, and your abilities seemed likely to blossom into excellent fruit. But you fell off greatly, and grew idle and careless. At last an event happened, in which for a time you acted worthily of yourself, and which seemed to arouse you from your negligence and indifference. All my hopes in you revived; but as I continued to watch your course (more closely perhaps than you supposed), I observed with pain that those hopes must be again disappointed. It needs but a glance at your countenance to be sure that you are not so upright or right-minded a boy as you were two years ago. I can judge only from your outward course; but I deeply fear, Williams—I deeply fear, that in *other* respects also you are going the down-hill road. And what am I to think now, when, on the *same* morning, you and your little brother *both* come before me for such serious and heavy faults? I cannot free you from blame even for *his* misdoings, for you are his natural guardian here; I am only glad that you were not involved with him in that charge.'

'Let *me* bear the punishment, sir, instead of him,' said Eric, by a sudden impulse; 'for I misled him, and was there myself.'

Dr. Rowlands paced the room in deep sorrow. 'You, Williams! on the verge of the sixth form. Alas! I fear, from this, that the state of things among you is even worse than I had supposed.'

Eric again hung his head.

'No; you have confessed the sin voluntarily, and therefore at present I shall not notice it; only, let me entreat you to beware. But I must turn to the other matter. What excuse have you for your intolerable conduct to Mr. Rose, who, as I know, has shown you from the first the most unusual and disinterested kindness?'

'I cannot defend myself, sir. I was excited, and could not control my passion.'

'Then you must sit down here, and write an apology, which I shall make you read aloud before the whole school at twelve to-day.'

Eric, with trembling hand, wrote his apology, and Dr. Rowlands glanced at it. 'That will do,' he said; 'I am glad you take a right view of the matter. Come to me again at twelve.'

At twelve all the school were assembled, and Eric, pale and miserable, followed the Doctor into the great schoolroom. The masters stood at one end of the room, and among them Mr. Rose, who, however, appeared an indifferent and uninterested spectator of the transaction. Every glance was fixed on Eric, and every one pitied him.

'We are assembled,' said Dr. Rowlands, 'for an act of justice. One of your number has insulted a master publicly, and is ashamed of his conduct, and has himself written the apology which he will read. I had intended to add a still severer punishment, but Mr. Rose has earnestly begged me not to do so, and I have succumbed to his wishes. Williams, read your apology.'

There was a dead hush, and Eric tried once or twice in vain to utter a word. At last, by a spasmodic effort, he regained his voice, and read, but in so low and nervous a tone, that not even those nearest him heard what he was saying.

Dr. Rowlands took the paper from him. 'Owing,' he said, 'to a very natural and pardonable emotion, the apology has been read in such a way that you could not have understood it. I will therefore read it myself. It is to this effect—

' "I, Eric Williams, beg humbly and sincerely to apologise for my passionate and ungrateful insult to Mr. Rose."

'You will understand that he was left quite free to choose his own expressions; and as he has acknowledged his shame and compunction for the act, I trust that none of you will be tempted to elevate him into a hero, for a folly which he himself so much regrets. This affair—as I should wish all bad deeds to be after they have once been punished—will now be forgiven, and I hope forgotten.'

They left the room and dispersed, and Eric fancied that all shunned and looked coldly on his degradation. But not so: Montagu came, and taking his arm in the old friendly way, went a walk with him. It was a constrained and silent walk, and they were both glad when it was over, although Montagu did all he could to show that he loved Eric no less than before. Still it was weeks since they had been much together, and they had far fewer things in common now than they used to have before. Eric's sprightliness, once the delight of all his friends, was now rarely exhibited, except in the company of Wildney and Graham.

'I'm so wretched, Monty,' said Eric at last; 'do you think Rose despises me?'

'I am *sure* of the contrary. Won't you go to him, Eric, and say all you feel?'

'Heigh ho! I shall never get right again. Oh, to recover the last two years!'

'You can redeem them, Eric, by a wiser present. Let the same words comfort you that have often brought hope to me—"I will restore the years which the locust hath eaten." '

They reached the school-door, and Eric went straight to the library. Mr. Rose was there alone. He received him kindly, as usual, and Eric went up to the fireplace where he was standing. They had often stood by that library fire on far different terms.

'Forgive me, sir,' was all Eric could say, as the tears rushed to his eyes.

'Freely, my boy,' said Mr. Rose sadly. 'I wish you could feel how fully I forgive you; but,' he added, laying his hand for the last time on Eric's head, 'you have far more, Eric, to forgive yourself. I will not talk to you, Eric; it would be little good, I fear; but you little know how much I pity and tremble for you.'

While these scenes were being enacted with Eric, a large group was collected round the fireplace in the boarders' room, and many tongues were loudly discussing the recent events.

Alas for gratitude! There was not a boy in that group to whom Mr. Rose had not done many an act of kindness; and to most of them far more than they ever knew. Many a weary hour had he toiled for them in private, when his weak frame was harassed by suffering; many a sleepless night had he wrestled for them in prayer, when, for their sakes, his own many troubles were laid aside. Work on, Walter Rose, and He who seeth in secret will reward you openly! but expect no gratitude from those for whose salvation you, like the great tender-hearted apostle, would almost be ready to wish yourself accursed.

Nearly every one in that noisy group was abusing Mr. Rose. It had long been Brigson's cue to do so; he derided him on every opportunity, and delighted to represent him as hypocritical and insincere. Even his weak health was the subject of Brigson's coarse ridicule, and the bad boy paid in deep hatred the natural tribute which vice must ever accord to excellence.

'You see how he turns on his pets if they offend him,' said Brigson; 'why, even that old beast Gordon isn't as bad.'

'Yes; while poor Eric was reading, Rose reminded me of Milton's serpent,' observed Ball sententiously—

> 'Hope elevates, and joy
> Brightens his crest.'

'He-e-ar! he-e-ar!' said Pietrie; '*vide* the last fifth form Rep.'

'I expect Eric won't see everything so much *couleur de rose* now, as the French frog hath it,' remarked Graham.

'Turn him out for his bad pun,' said Wildney.

'That means you're jealous of it, old fellow,' answered Graham.

'I can't say either you or he *rose* in my estimation in consequence,' said Wildney, chuckling, as he dodged away to escape Graham's pursuit.

'It was too bad to stand by and triumph, certainly,' observed Llewellyn.

'I say, you fellows,' remonstrated the sober little Wright, who, with Vernon, was sitting reading a book at one of the desks, 'all that isn't fair. I'm sure you all saw how really sorry Rose looked about it; and he said, you know, that it was merely for the sake of school discipline that he put the matter in Rowlands's hands.'

'Discipline be hanged,' shouted Brigson; 'we'll have our revenge on him yet, discipline or no.'

'I hope you won't though,' said Vernon; 'I know Eric will be sorry if you do.'

'The more muff he. We shall do as we like.'

'Well, I shall tell him; and I'm sure he'll ask you not. You know how often he tries to stick up for Rose.'

'If you say a word more,' said Brigson, unaccustomed to being opposed among his knot of courtiers, 'I'll kick you out of the room; you and that wretched little fool there with you.'

'You may do as you like,' answered Wright quietly; 'but you won't go on like this long, I can tell you.'

Brigson tried to seize him, but failing, contented himself with flinging a big coal at him as he ran out of the room, which narrowly missed his head.

'I have it!' said Brigson; 'that little donkey's given me an idea. We'll *crust* Rose to-night.'

'To crust,' gentle reader, means to pelt an obnoxious person with crusts.

'Capital!' said some of the worst boys present; 'we will.'

'Well, who'll take part?'

No one offered. 'What! are we all turning sneaks and cowards? Here, Wildney, won't you? you were abusing Rose just now.'

'Yes, I will,' said Wildney, but with no great alacrity. 'You'll not have done till you've got us all expelled, I believe.'

'Fiddlestick-end! and what if we are? besides, he can't expel half the school.'

First two or three more offered, and then a whole lot, gaining courage by numbers. So the plot was regularly laid. Pietrie and Graham were to put out the lights at each end of one table immediately after tea, and Wildney and Booking at the other, when the study fellows had gone out. There would then be only Mr. Rose's candle burning, and the two middle candles, which in so large a room would just give enough light for their purpose. Then all the conspirators were to throng around the door, and from it aim their crusts at Mr. Rose's head. Not nearly so many would have volunteered to join, but that they fancied Mr. Rose was too gentle to take up the matter with vigour, and they were encouraged in their project by his quiet leniency towards Eric the night before. It was agreed that no study-boy should be told of the intention, lest any of them should interfere.

The hearts of many beat fast at tea that night as they observed that numbers of boys, instead of eating all their bread, were cutting off the crusts, and breaking them into good-sized bits.

Tea finished, Mr. Rose said grace, and then sat down quietly reading in his desk. The signal agreed on was the (accidental) dropping of a plate by Brigson. The study-boys left the room.

Crash!—down fell a plate on the floor, breaking to pieces in the fall.

Instantly the four candles went out, and there was a hurried movement towards the door, and a murmur of voices.

'Now then,' said Brigson, in a loud whisper; 'what a wretched set you are! Here goes!'

The master, surprised at the sudden gloom and confusion, had just looked up, unable to conjecture what was the matter. Brigson's crust caught him a sharp rap on the forehead as he moved.

In an instant he started up, and ten or twelve more crusts flew by or hit him on the head as he strode out of the desk towards the door. Directly he stirred, there was a rush of boys into the passage, and if he had once lost his judgment or temper, worse harm might have followed. But he did not. Going to the door, he said, 'Preparation will be in five minutes; every boy not then in his place will be punished.'

During that five minutes the servants had cleared away the tea, full of wonder; but Mr. Rose paced up and down the room, taking no notice of any one. Immediately after, all the boys were in their places, with their books open before them, and in the thrilling silence you might have heard a pin drop. Every one felt that Mr. Rose was master of the occasion, and awaited his next step in terrified suspense.

They all perceived how thoroughly they had mistaken their subject. The ringleaders would have given all they had to be well out of the scrape. Mr. Rose ruled by kindness, but he never suffered his will to be disputed for an instant. He governed with such consummate tact, that they hardly felt it to be government at all, and hence arose their stupid miscalculation. But he felt that the time was now come to assert his paramount authority, and determined to do so at once and for ever.

'Some of you have mistaken me,' he said, in a voice so strong and stern that it almost startled them. 'The silly display of passion in one boy yesterday has led you to presume that you may trifle with me. You are wrong. For Williams's sake, as a boy who has, or at least once *had*, something noble in him, I left that matter in the Doctor's hands. I shall *not* do so to-night. Which of you put out the candles?'

Dead silence. A pause.

'Which of you had the audacity to throw pieces of bread at me?'

Still silence.

'I warn you that I *will* know, and it will be far worse for all the guilty if I do not know at once.' There was unmistakable decision in the tone.

'Very well. I know many boys who were *not* guilty, because I saw them in parts of the room where to throw was impossible. I shall now *ask* all the rest, one by one, if they took any part in this. And beware of telling me a lie.'

There was an uneasy sensation in the room, and several boys began to whisper aloud, 'Brigson! Brigson!' The whisper grew louder, and Mr. Rose heard it. He turned on Brigson indignantly, and said—

'They call your name; stand out!'

The awkward, big, ungainly boy, with his repulsive countenance, shambled out of his place into the middle of the room. Mr. Rose swept him with one flashing glance. '*That* is the boy,' thought he to himself, 'who has been like an ulcer to this school. These boys shall have a good look at their hero.' It was but recently that Mr. Rose knew all the harm which Brigson had been doing, though he had discovered, almost from the first, what *sort* of character he had.

So Brigson stood out in the room, and as they looked at him, many a boy cursed him in their hearts. And it was *that* fellow, that stupid, clumsy, base compound of meanness and malice, that had ruled like a king among them. Faugh!

'They call your name! Do you know anything of this?'

'No!' said Brigson: 'I'll swear I'd nothing to do with it.'

'Oh-h-h-h!'—the long, intense, deep-drawn expression of disgust and contempt ran round the room.

'You have told me a lie!' said Mr. Rose slowly, and with strong contempt. 'No words can express my loathing for your false and dishonourable conduct. Nor shall your lie save you, as you shall find immediately. Still you shall escape if you can or dare to deny it again. I repeat my question—Were you engaged in this?'

He fixed his full, piercing eye on the culprit, whom it seemed to scorch and wither. Brigson winced back, and said nothing. 'As I thought,' said Mr. Rose.

'Not one boy only, but many were engaged. I shall call you up one by one to answer me. Wildney, come here.'

The boy walked in front of the desk.

'Were you one of those who threw?'

Wildney, full as he was of dangerous and deadly faults, was no coward, and not a liar. He knew, or at least feared, that this new scrape might be fatal to him, but raising his dark and glistening eyes to Mr. Rose, he said penitently—

'I didn't throw, sir, but I *did* put out one of the candles that it might be done.'

The contrast with Brigson was very great; the dark cloud hung a little less darkly on Mr. Rose's forehead, and there was a very faint murmur of applause.

'Good! stand back. Pietrie, come up.'

Pietrie, too, confessed, and indeed all the rest of the plotters except Booking. Mr. Rose's lip curled with scorn as he heard the exclamation which his denial caused; but he suffered him to sit down.

When Wright's turn came to be asked, Mr. Rose said—'No! I shall not even ask you, Wright. I know well that your character is too good to be involved in such an attempt.'

The boy bowed humbly, and sat down. Among the last questioned was Vernon Williams, and Mr. Rose seemed anxious for his answer.

'No,' he said at once,—and seemed to wish to add something.

'Go on,' said Mr. Rose encouragingly.

'Oh, sir! I only wanted to say that I hope you won't think Eric knew of this. He would have hated it, sir, more even than I do.'

'Good,' said Mr. Rose; 'I am sure of it. And now,' turning to the offenders, 'I shall teach you never to dare again to be guilty of such presumption and wickedness as to-night. I shall punish you according to my notion of your degrees of guilt. Brigson, bring me a cane from that desk.'

He brought it.

'Hold out your hand.'

The cane fell, and instantly split up from top to bottom. Mr. Rose looked at it, for it was new that morning.

'Ha! I see; more mischief; there is a hair in it.'

The boys were too much frightened to smile at the complete success of the trick.

'Who did this? I must be told at once.'

'*I* did, sir,' said Wildney, stepping forward.

'Ha! very well,' said Mr. Rose, while, in spite of his anger, a smile hovered at the corner of his lips. 'Go and borrow me a cane from Mr. Harley.'

While he went there was unbroken silence.

'Now, sir,' said he to Brigson, 'I shall flog you.'

Corporal punishment was avoided with the bigger boys, and Brigson had never undergone it before. At the first stroke he writhed and yelled; at the second he retreated, twisting like a serpent, and blubbering like a baby; at the third he flung himself on his knees, and as the strokes fell fast, clasped Mr. Rose's arm, and implored and besought for mercy.

'*Miserable* coward,' said Mr. Rose, throwing into the word such ringing scorn that no one who heard it ever forgot it. He indignantly shook the boy off, and caned him till he rolled on the floor, losing every particle of self-control, and calling out, 'The devil—the devil—the devil!' ('invoking his patron saint,' as Wildney maliciously observed).

'There! cease to blaspheme, and get up,' said the master, blowing out a cloud of fiery indignation. 'There, sir. Retribution comes at last, leaden-footed but iron-handed. A long catalogue of sins is visited on you to-day, and not only on your shrinking body, but on your conscience too, if you have one left. Let those red marks be token that your reign is ended. Liar and tempter, you have led boys into the sins which you then meanly deny! And now, you boys, *there* in that coward, who cannot even endure his richly-

merited punishment, see the boy whom you have suffered to be your *leader* for well-nigh six months!'

'Now, sir'—again he turned upon Brigson—'that flogging shall be repeated with interest on your next offence. At present you will take each boy on your back while I cane him. It is fit that they should see where *you* lead them to.'

Trembling violently, and cowed beyond description, he did as he was bid. No other boy cried, or even winced; a few sharp cuts was all which Mr. Rose gave them, and even they grew fewer each time, for he was tired, and displeased to be an executioner.

'And now,' he said, 'since that disgusting but necessary scene is over, *never* let me have to repeat it again.' But his authority was established like a rock from that night forward. No one ever ventured to dispute it again, or forgot that evening. Mr. Rose's noble moral influence gained tenfold strength from the respect and wholesome fear that he then inspired.

But, as he said, Brigson's reign was over. Looks of the most unmitigated disgust and contempt were darted at him, as he sat alone and shunned at the end of the table; and the boys seemed now to loathe and nauseate the golden calf they had been worshipping. He had not done blubbering even yet, when the prayer-bell rang. No sooner had Mr. Rose left the room than Wildney, his dark eyes sparkling with rage, leaped on the table, and shouted—

'Three groans, hoots, and hisses for a liar and a coward,' a sign of execration which he was the first to lead off, and which the boys echoed like a storm.

Astonished at the tumult, Mr. Rose reappeared at the door. 'Oh, we're not hissing you, sir,' said Wildney excitedly; 'we're all hissing at lying and cowardice.'

Mr. Rose thought the revulsion of feeling might do good, and he was striding out again without a word when—

'Three times three for Mr. Rose,' sang out Wildney.

Never did a more hearty or spontaneous cheer burst from the lips and lungs of fifty boys than that. The news had spread like wildfire to the studies, and the other boys came flocking in during the uproar, to join in it heartily. Cheer after cheer rang out like a sound of silver clarions from the clear boy-voices; and in the midst of the excited throng stood Eric and Montagu, side by side, hurrahing more lustily than all the rest.

But Mr. Rose, in the library, was on his knees, with moving lips and lifted hands. He coveted the popular applause as little as he had dreaded the popular opposition; and the evening's painful experiences had taught him anew the bitter lesson to expect no gratitude, and hope for no reward, but simply, and contentedly, and unmurmuringly, to work on in God's vineyard so long as life and health should last.

Brigson's brazen forehead bore him through the disgrace which would have crushed another. But still he felt that his position at Roslyn could never be what it had been before, and he therefore determined to leave at once. By grossly calumniating the school, he got his father to remove him, and announced, to every one's great delight, that he was going in a fortnight. On his last day, by way of bravado, he smashed and damaged as much of the school property as he could, a proceeding which failed to gain him any admiration, and merely put his father to ruinous expense.

The day after his exposure Eric had cut him dead, without the least pretense of concealment; an example pretty generally followed throughout the school.

In the evening Brigson went up to Eric and hissed in his ear, 'You cut me, curse you; but, *never fear, I'll be revenged on you yet.*'

'Do your worst,' answered Eric contemptuously; 'and never speak to me again.'

CHAPTER THE FIFTH

RIPPLES

Our echoes roll from soul to soul,
And live for ever and for ever.
TENNYSON

Owen and Montagu were walking by Silverburn, and talking over the affairs of the school. During their walk they saw Wright and Vernon Williams in front of them.

'I am so glad to see those two together,' said Montagu; 'I really think Wright is one of the best little fellows in the school, and he'll be the saving of Vernon. He's already persuaded him to leave off smoking and other bad things, and has got him to work a little harder, and turn over a new leaf altogether.'

'Yes,' answered Owen; 'I've seen a marvellous improvement in little Williams lately. I think that Duncan gave him a rough lesson the other night which did him good, and dear old Rose too has been leading him by the hand; but the best thing is that, through Wright, he sees less of Eric's *friend*, that young scapegrace Wildney.'

'Yes; that little wretch has a good deal to answer for. What a pity that Eric spoils him so, or rather suffers himself to be spoilt by him. I'm glad Vernon's escaped his influence now; he's too fine a nature to be made as bad as the general run of them. What a brilliant little fellow he is; just like his brother.'

'Just like what his brother *was*,' said Owen; 'his face, like his mind, has suffered lately.'

'Too true,' answered Montagu, with a sigh; 'and yet, cool as we now are in our outward intercourse, he little knows how I love him, and yearn for the Eric I once knew—Eric the fair-haired, as Russell and I used sometimes to call him in fun. Would to God poor Russell had lived, and then I believe that he wouldn't have gone so far wrong.'

'Well, I think there's another chance for him now that—that—what name is bad enough for that Brigson?—is gone.'

'I hope so. But'—he added after a pause—'his works do follow him. Look there!' He took a large stone and threw it into the Silverburn stream; there was a great splash, and the ever-widening circles of blue ripple broke the surface of the water, dying away one by one in the sedges on the bank. 'There,' he said, 'see how long those ripples last, and how numerous they are.'

Owen understood him. 'Poor Eric! What a gleam of new hope there was in him after Russell's death!'

'Yes, for a time,' said Montagu; 'heigh ho! I fear we shall never be warm friends again. We can't be while he goes on as he is doing. And yet I love him.'

A sudden turn of the stream brought them to the place called Riverbend.

'If you want a practical comment on what we've been talking about, you'll see it there,' said Montagu.

He pointed to a party of boys, four or five, all lying on a pleasant grass bank, smoking pipes. Prominent among them was Eric, stretched at ease, and looking up at the clouds, towards which curled the puffed fumes of his meerschaum—a gift of Wildney's. That worthy was beside him similarly employed.

The two sixth form boys hoped to pass by unobserved, as they did not wish for a rencontre with our hero under such circumstances. But they saw Wildney pointing to them, and, from the fits of laughter which followed his remarks, they had little doubt that they were the subject of the young gentleman's wit. This is never a pleasant sensation; but they observed that Eric made a point of not looking their way, and went on in silence.

'How very sad!' said Montagu.

'How very contemptible!' said Owen. 'Harfagher among his subjects!'

'Did you observe what they were doing?'

'Smoking?'

'Worse than that a good deal. They were doing something which, if Eric doesn't take care, will one day be his ruin.'

'What?'

'I saw them drinking. I have little doubt it was brandy.'

'Good heavens!'

'It is getting a common practice with some fellows. One of the ripples, you see, of Brigson's influence.'

Before they got home they caught up Wright and Vernon, and walked in together.

'We've been talking,' said Wright, 'about a bad matter. Vernon here says that there's no good working for a prize in his form, because the cribbing's so atrocious. Indeed, it's very nearly as bad in my form. It always is under Gordon; he *can't* understand fellows doing dishonourable things.'

'It's a great bore in the weekly examinations,' said Vernon; 'every now and then Gordon will even leave the room for a few minutes, and then out come dozens of books.'

'Well, Wright,' said Montagu, 'if that happens again next examination, I'd speak out about it.'

'How?'

'Why, I'd get every fellow who disapproves of it to give me his name, and get up and read the list, and say that you at least have pledged yourselves not to do it.'

'Humph! I don't know how that would answer. They'd half kill me for one thing.'

'Never mind; do your duty. I wish I'd such an opportunity, if only to show how sorry I am for my own past unfairness.'

And so talking, the four went in, and the two elder went to their study.

It was too true that drinking had become a common vice at Roslyn School. Accordingly, when Eric came in with Wildney about half an hour after, Owen and Montagu heard them talk about ordering some brandy, and then arrange to have a 'jollification,' as they called it, that evening.

They got the brandy through 'Billy.' One of Brigson's most cursed legacies to the school was the introduction of this man to a nefarious intercourse with the boys. His character was so well known that it had long been forbidden, under the strictest penalty, for any boy ever to speak to him; yet, strange to say, they seemed to take a pleasure in doing so, and just now particularly, it was thought a fine thing, a sign of 'pluck' and 'anti-muffishness,' to be on familiar and intimate terms with that degraded and villainous scoundrel.

Duncan had made friends again with Eric; but he did not join him in his escapades

and excesses, and sat much in other studies. He had not been altogether a good boy, but yet there was a sort of rough honesty and good sense in him which preserved him from the worst and most dangerous failings, and his character had been gradually improving as he mounted higher in the school. He was getting steadier, more diligent, more thoughtful, more manly; he was passing through that change so frequent in boys as they grow older, to which Eric was so sad an exception. Accordingly Duncan, though sincerely fond of Eric, had latterly disapproved vehemently of his proceedings, and had therefore taken to snubbing his old friend Wildney, in whose favour Eric seemed to have an infatuation, and who was the means of involving him in every kind of impropriety and mischief. So that night Duncan, hearing of what was intended, sat in the next study, and Eric, with Ball, Wildney, Graham, and Pietrie, had the room to themselves. Several of them were lower boys still, but they came up to the studies after bed-time, according to Wildney's almost nightly custom.

A little pebble struck the study window.

'Hurrah!' said Wildney, clapping his hands, 'here's the grub.'

They opened the window and looked out. Billy was there, and they let down to him a long piece of cord, to which he attached a basket, and, after bidding them 'Good-night, and a merry drink,' retired. No sooner had they shut the window, then he grimaced as usual towards them, and shook his fist in a sort of demoniacal exultation, muttering, 'Oh, I'll have you all under my thumb yet, you fine young fools!'

Meanwhile the unconscious boys had opened the basket, and spread its contents on the table. They were bread, butter, a large dish of sausages, a tart, beer, and, alas! a bottle of brandy.

They soon got very noisy, and at last uproarious. The snatches of songs, peals of laughter, and rattle of plates at last grew so loud that the other study-boys were afraid lest one of the masters should come up and catch the revellers. All of them heard every word that was spoken by Eric and his party; as the walls between the rooms were very thin; and very objectionable much of the conversation was.

'This *won't* do,' said Duncan emphatically, after a louder burst of merriment than usual; 'those fellows are getting drunk; I can tell it to a certainty from the confused and random way in which some of them are talking.'

'We'd better go in and speak to them,' said Montagu; 'at any rate, they've no right to disturb us all night. Will you come?'

'I'll join you,' said Owen; 'though I'm afraid my presence won't do you much good.'

The three boys went to the door of Eric's study and their knock could not at first be heard for the noise. When they went in they found a scene of reckless disorder; books were scattered about, plates and glasses lay broken on the floor, beer was spilt on all sides, and there was an intolerable smell of brandy.

'If you fellows don't take care,' said Duncan sharply, 'Rose or somebody'll be coming up and catching you. It's ten now.'

'What's that to you?' answered Graham, with an insolent look.

'It's something to me that you nice young men have been making such a row that none of the rest of us can hear our own voices, and that between you you've made this study in such a mess that I can't endure it.'

'Pooh!' said Pietrie; 'we're all getting such saints, that one can't have the least bit of spree nowadays.'

'Spree!' burst in Montagu indignantly; 'fine spree to make sots of yourselves with spirits; fine spree to——'

'Amen!' said Wildney, who was perched on the back of a chair; and he turned up his eyes and clasped his hands with a mock-heroic air.

'There, Williams,' continued Montagu, pointing to the mischievous-looking little boy; 'see that spectacle, and be ashamed of yourself, if you can. That's what you lead boys to! Are you anxious to become the teacher of drunkenness?'

In truth, there was good ground for his sorrowful apostrophe, for the scene was very painful to a high-minded witness.

They hardly understood the look on Eric's countenance; he had been taking far more than was good for him; his eyes sparkled fiercely, and though as yet he said nothing, he seemed to be resenting the intrusion in furious silence.

'How much longer is this interesting lecture to last?' asked Ball, with his usual insufferable tone; 'for I want to finish my brandy.'

Montagu rather looked as if he intended to give the speaker a box on the ear; but he was just deciding that he wasn't worth the trouble, when Wildney, who had been grimacing all the time, burst into a fit of satirical laughter.

'Here, Wildney,' said Graham; 'just hand me *The Whole Duty of Man,* or something of that sort, from the shelf, will you? That's a brick.'

'Certainly. Let's see; Watts's Hymns;—*I* bag those for myself,' said Wildney; 'they'll just suit—

'How doth the little——'

'Let's turn out these impudent lower-school fellows,' said Montagu, speaking to

Duncan. 'Here! you go first,' he said, seizing Wildney by the arm, and giving him a swing, which, as he was by no means steady on his legs, brought him sprawling to the ground, and sent Watts's Hymns flying open-leaved under the table.

'By Jove, I won't stand this any longer,' shouted Eric, springing up ferociously. 'What on earth do you mean by daring to come in like this? Do you hear?'

Montagu took no sort of notice of his threatening gesture, for he was looking to see if Wildney was hurt, and finding he was not, proceeded to drag him out, struggling and kicking frantically.

'Drop me, you fellow, drop me, I say. I won't go for you,' cried Wildney, clinging tight to a chair. 'Eric, why do you let him bully me?'

'You let him go this minute,' repeated Eric hoarsely.

'I shall do no such thing. You don't know what you're about.'

'Don't I? Well then, take *that,* to show whether I do or no!' And suddenly leaning forward, he struck Montagu a violent back-handed blow on the mouth.

Everybody saw it, everybody heard it; and it instantly astounded them into silence. That Montagu should have been so struck in public, and that by Eric—by a boy who had been his schoolfellow for three years now, and whose whole life seemed bound to him by so many associations; it was strange and sad indeed.

Montagu sprang straight upright; for an instant he took one stride towards his striker with lifted hand and lightening eyes, while the blood started to his lips in consequence of the blow. But he stopped suddenly, and his hand fell to his side; by a strong effort of self-control he contrived to master himself, and sitting down quite quietly on a chair, he put his white handkerchief to his wounded mouth, and took it away stained with blood.

No one spoke; and rising with quiet dignity, he went back into his study without a word.

'Very well,' said Duncan; 'you may all do as you like; only I heartily hope now you will be caught. Come, Owen.'

'O Williams,' said Owen, 'you are changed indeed, to treat your best friend so.'

But Eric was excited with drink, and the slave of every evil passion at that moment. 'Serve him right,' he said; 'what business has he to interfere with what I choose to do?'

There was no more noise that night. Wildney and the rest slunk off ashamed and frightened, and Eric, leaving his candle flaring on the table, went down to his bedroom, where he was very sick. He had neither strength nor spirit to undress, and flung himself into bed just as he was. When they heard that he was gone, Owen and Duncan (for Montagu was silent and melancholy) went into his study, put out the candle, and only just cleared away, to the best of their power, the traces of the carouse, when Dr. Rowlands came up stairs on his usual nightly rounds. They had been lighting brown paper to take away the fumes of the brandy, and the Doctor asked them casually the cause of the smell of burning. Neither of them answered, and seeing Owen there, in whom he placed implicit trust, the Doctor thought no more about it.

Eric awoke with a bad headache, and a sense of shame and sickness. When he got up he felt most wretched; and while washing he thought to himself, 'Ah! that I could thus wash away the memory of last night!' Of course, after what had occurred, Eric and Montagu were no longer on speaking terms, and miserable as poor Eric felt when he saw how his blow had bruised and disfigured his friend's face, he made no advances. He longed, indeed, from his inmost heart, to be reconciled to him; but feeling that he had done grievous wrong, he dreaded a repulse, and his pride would not suffer him to run the risk. So he pretended to feel no regret, and supported by his late boon companions, represented the matter as occurring in the defence of Wildney, whom Montagu was bullying.

Montagu, too, was very miserable; but he felt that, although ready to forgive Eric, he could not, in common self-respect, take the first step to a reconciliation; indeed, he rightly thought that it was not for Eric's good that he should do so.

'You and Williams appear never to speak to each other now,' said Mr. Rose. 'I am sorry for it, Monty; I think you are the only boy who has any influence over him.'

'I fear you are mistaken, sir, in that. Little Wildney has much more.'

'Wildney?' asked Mr. Rose, in sorrowful surprise. 'Wildney more influence than *you?*'

'Yes, sir.'

'Ah, that our poor Edwin had lived!'

So, with a sigh, Walter Rose and Harry Montagu buried their friendship for Eric until happier days.

CHAPTER THE SIXTH

ERIC AND MONTAGU

And constancy lives in realms above;
    And life is thorny; and youth is vain;
And to be wroth with one we love
    Doth work like madness in the brain. . . .
Each spoke words of high disdain,
    And insult to his heart's best brother.
                        COLERIDGE, *Christabel*

WRIGHT HAD NOT forgotten Montagu's advice, and had endeavoured to get the names of boys who weren't afraid to scout publicly the disgrace of cheating in form. But he could only get one name promised him—the name of Vernon Williams; and feeling how little could be gained by using it, he determined to spare Vernon the trial, and speak, if he spoke at all, on his own responsibility.

As usual, the cribbing at the next weekly examination was well-nigh universal, and when Mr. Gordon went out to fetch something he had forgotten, merely saying, 'I trust to your honour not to abuse my absence,' books and papers were immediately pulled out with the coolest and most unblushing indifference.

This was the time for Wright to deliver his conscience; he had counted the cost, and, rightly or wrongly, considering it to be his duty, he had decided that speak he would. He well knew that his interference would be attributed to jealousy, meanness, sneaking, and every kind of wrong motive, since he was himself one of the greatest sufferers from the prevalent dishonesty; but still he had come to the conclusion that he *ought* not to draw back, and therefore he bravely determined that he would make his protest, whatever happened.

So, very nervously, he rose and said, 'I want to tell you all that I think this cheating very wrong and blackguardly. I don't mind losing by it myself; but if Vernon Williams loses the prize in the lower fourth, and any one gets it by copying, I've made up my mind to tell Gordon.'

His voice trembled a little at first, but he spoke fast, and acquired firmness as he went on. Absolute astonishment and curiosity had held the boys silent with amazement, but by the end of this sentence they had recovered themselves, and a perfect burst of derision and indignation followed.

'Let's see if *that*'ll cut short his oration,' said Wildney, throwing a book at his head, which was instantly followed by others from all quarters.

'My word! we've had nothing but lectures lately,' said Booking. 'Horrid little Owenite saint.'

'Saint!—sneak, you mean. I'll teach him,' growled Pietrie, and jumping up, he belaboured Wright's head with the Latin Grammar out of which he had just been cribbing.

The whole room was in confusion and hubbub, during which Wright sat stock-still, quietly enduring without bowing to the storm.

Only one boy sympathised with him, but he did so deeply—poor little penitent Vernon. He felt his position hard because Wright had alluded so prominently to him, and he knew how much he must be misconstrued; but he had his brother's spirit, and would not shrink. Amid the tumult he got up in his seat, and they heard his pleasant childish voice saying boldly, 'I hope Wright won't tell; but he's the best fellow in the room, and cribbing *is* a shame, as he says.'

What notice would have been taken of this speech is doubtful, for at the critical moment Mr. Gordon reappeared, and the whispered cavé caused instantaneous quiet.

Poor Wright awaited with some dread the end of school; and many an angry kick and blow he got, though he disarmed malice by the spirit and heroism with which he endured them. The news of his impudence spread like wildfire, and not five boys in the school approved of what he had done, while most of them were furious at his ill-judged threat of informing Mr. Gordon. There was a general agreement to thrash him after roll-call that afternoon.

Eric had lately taken a violent dislike to Wright, though he had been fond of him in better days. He used to denounce him as a disagreeable and pragmatical little muff, and was as loud as any of them in condemning his announced determination to 'sneak.' Had he known that Wright had acted under Montagu's well-meant, though rather mistaken advice, he might have abstained from having anything more to do with the matter, but now he promised to kick Wright himself after the four o'clock bell.

Four o'clock came; the names were called; the master left the room. Wright, who perfectly knew what was threatened, stood there pale but fearless. His indifferent look was an additional annoyance to Eric, who walked up to him carelessly, and boxing his ears, though without hurting him, said contemptuously, 'Conceited little sneak.'

Montagu had been told of the intended kicking, and had determined even single-handed to prevent it. He did *not*, however, expect that Eric would have taken part in it, and was therefore unprepared. The colour rushed into his cheeks; he went up, took Wright quietly by the hand, and said with firm determination, 'No one in the school shall touch Wright again.'

'What? no one! just hark to that,' said Graham; 'I suppose he thinks himself cock of the school.'

Eric quite misunderstood Montagu's proceeding; he took it for a public challenge. All the Rowlandites were round, and to yield would have looked like cowardice. Above all, his evil genius Wildney was by, and said, 'How very nice! I say, Eric, you and I will have to get *The Whole Duty of Man* again.'

A threatening circle had formed round Montagu, but his closed lips and flushing brow and dilated nostrils betrayed a spirit which made them waver, and his noble face glowed with a yet nobler expression in the consciousness of an honourable cause, as he quietly repeated, 'No one shall touch you, Wright.'

'They *will*, though,' said Eric instantly; '*I* will, for one, and I should like to see you prevent me.' And so saying he gave Wright another slight blow.

Montagu dropped Wright's hand, and said slowly, 'Eric Williams, I have taken one unexpected blow from you without a word, and bear the marks of it yet. It is time to show that it was *not* through cowardice that I did not return it. Will you fight?'

The answer was not prompt by any means, though every one in the school knew that Eric was not afraid. So sure was he of this, that, for the sake of 'auld lang syne,' he would probably have declined to fight with Montagu had it been left to his own impulses.

'I have been in the wrong, Montagu, more than once,' he answered falteringly, 'and we have been friends——'

But it was the object of many of the worst boys that the two should fight—not only that they might see the fun, but that Montagu's authority, which stood in their way, might be flung aside. So Booking whispered in an audible voice—

'Faith! he's showing the white feather.'

'You're a liar!' flung in Eric; and turning to Montagu, he said, 'There! I'll fight you this moment.'

Instantly they had stripped off their coats and prepared for action. A ring of excited boys crowded round them. Fellows of sixteen, like Montagu and Eric, rarely fight, because their battles have usually been decided in their earlier schooldays; and it was also but seldom that two boys so strong, active, and prominent (above all, so high in the school) took this method of settling their differences.

The fight began, and at first the popular favour was entirely on the side of Eric, while Montagu found few or none to back him. But he fought with a fire and courage which soon won applause; and as Eric, on the other hand, was random and spiritless, the cry was soon pretty fairly divided between them.

After a sharp round they paused for breath, and Owen, who had been a silent and disgusted spectator of such a combat between boys of such high standing, said with much feeling—

'This is not a very creditable affair, Montagu.'

'It is necessary,' was Montagu's laconic reply.

Among other boys who had left the room before the fracas had taken place was Vernon Williams, who shrank away to avoid the pain of seeing his new friend Wright bullied and tormented. But curiosity soon took him back, and he came in just as the second round began. At first he only saw a crowd of boys in the middle of the room, but jumping on a desk he had a full view of what was going on.

There was a tremendous hubbub of voices, and Eric, now thoroughly roused by the remarks he overheard, and especially by Wildney's whisper that 'he was letting himself be licked,' was exerting himself with more vigour and effect. It was anything but a pleasant sight; the faces of the combatants were streaked with blood and sweat, and as the miserable gang of lower-school boys backed them on with eager shouts of —'Now Eric, now Eric,' 'Now Montagu, go it sixth form,' etc., both of them fought under a sense of deep disgrace, increased by the recollections which they shared in common.

All this Vernon marked in a moment, and, filled with pain and vexation, he said in a voice which, though low, could be heard amid all the uproar, 'O Eric, Eric, fighting with Montagu!' There was reproach and sorrow in the tone, which touched more than one boy there, for Vernon, spite of the recent change in him, could not but continue a popular favourite.

'Shut up there, you little donkey,' shouted one or two, looking back at him for a moment.

But Eric heard the words, and knew that it was his brother's voice. The thought rushed on him how degraded his whole position was, and how different it might have been. He felt that he was utterly in the wrong, and Montagu altogether in the right; and from that moment his blows once more grew feeble and ill-directed. When they again stopped to take rest, the general shout for Montagu showed that he was considered to have the best of it.

'I'm getting so tired of this,' muttered Eric, during the pause.

'Why, you're fighting like a regular muff,' said Graham; 'you'll have to acknowledge yourself thrashed in a minute.'

'That I'll *never* do,' he said, once more firing up.

Just as the third round began, Duncan came striding in, for Owen, who had left the room, told him what was going on. He had always been a leading fellow, and quite recently his influence had several times been exerted in the right direction, and he was very much looked up to by all the boys alike, good or bad. He determined, for the credit of the sixth, that the fight should not go on, and bursting into the ring, with his strong shoulders he hurled on each side the boys who stood in his way, and struck down the lifted arms of the fighters.

'You *shan't* fight,' he said doggedly, thrusting himself between them; 'so there's an end of it. If you do, you'll both have to fight me first.'

'Shame!' said several of the boys, and the cry was caught up by Ball and others.

'Shame, is it?' said Duncan, and his lip curled with scorn. 'There's only one way to argue with you fellows. Ball, if you or any other boy repeat that word, I'll thrash him. Here, Monty, come away from this disgraceful scene.'

'I'm sick enough of it,' said Montagu, 'and am ready to stop if Williams is,—provided no one touches Wright.'

'I'm sick of it too,' said Eric sullenly.

'Then you two shall shake hands,' said Duncan.

For one instant—an instant which he regretted till the end of his life—Montagu drew himself up and hesitated. He had been deeply wronged, deeply provoked, and no one could blame him for the momentary feeling; but Eric had observed the gesture, and his passionate pride took the alarm. 'It's come to this then,' he thought; 'Montagu doesn't think me good enough to be shaken hands with.'

'Pish!' he said aloud, in a tone of sarcasm; 'it may be an awful honour to shake hands with such an immaculate person as Montagu, but I'm not proud on the subject;' and he turned away.

Montagu's hesitation was but momentary, and without a particle of anger or indignation he sorrowfully held out his hand. It was too late; that moment had done the mischief, and it was now Eric's turn coldly to withdraw.

'You don't think me worthy of your friendship, and what's the good of grasping hands if we don't do it with cordial hearts?'

Montagu's lip trembled, but he said nothing, and quietly putting on his coat, motioned back the throng of boys with a sweep of his arm, and left the room with Duncan.

'Come along, Wright,' he said.

'Nay, leave him,' said Eric, with a touch of remorse. 'Much as you think me beneath you, I have honour enough to see that no one hurts him.'

The group of boys gradually dispersed, but one or two remained with Eric, although he was excessively wearied by their observations.

'You didn't fight half like yourself,' said Wildney.

'Can't you tell why? I had the wrong side to fight for.' And getting up abruptly, he left the room, to be alone in his study, and bathe his swollen and aching face.

In a few minutes Vernon joined him, and at the mere sight of him Eric turned away in shame. That evening with Vernon in the study, after the dinner at 'The Jolly Herring,' had revived all his really warm affection for his little brother; and as he could no longer conceal the line he took in the school, they had been often together since then; and Eric's moral obliquity was not so great as to prevent him from feeling deep joy at the change for the better in Vernon's character.

'Verny, Verny,' he said, as the boy came up and affectionately took his hand, 'it was you that lost me that fight.'

'Oh, but Eric, you were fighting with Montagu. Don't you remember the days, Eric,' he continued, 'when we were home boarders, and how kind Monty used to be to me even then, and how mother liked him, and thought him quite your truest friend, except poor Russell?'

'I do indeed. I didn't think then that it would come to this.'

'I've always been *so* sorry,' said Vernon, 'that I joined the fellows in playing him tricks. I can't think how I came to do it, except that I've done such lots of bad things here. But he's forgiven and forgotten that long ago, and is very kind to me now.'

It was true; but Eric didn't know that half the kindness which Montagu showed to his brother was shown solely for *his* sake.

'Do you know, I've thought of a plan for making you two friends again? I've written to Aunt Trevor to ask him to Fairholm with us next holidays.'

'Oh, have you? Good Verny! Yes; *there* we might be friends. Perhaps there,' he added, half to himself, 'I might be more like what I was in better days.'

'But it's a long time to look forward to. Easter hasn't come yet,' said Vernon.

So the two young boys proposed; but God had disposed it otherwise.

CHAPTER THE SEVENTH

THE PIGEONS

Et motæ ad Lunam trepidabis arundinis umbram.
JUV x. 21

'How awfully dull it is, Charlie,' said Eric, a few weeks before Easter, as he sat with Wildney in his study one holiday afternoon.

'Yes; too late for football, too early for cricket.' And Wildney stretched himself and yawned.

'I suppose this is what they call ennui,' said Eric again, after a pause. 'What's to be done, Sunbeam?'

'You *shan't* call me that, Eric the fair-haired; you *shan't* call me that, so there's an end of it,' said Wildney, hitting him on the arm.

'Hush, Charlie, don't call *me* that either; it is a name that—never mind; only don't— that's a good fellow.'

'By the bye, Eric, I've just remembered to-morrow's my birthday, and I've got a parcel coming this afternoon full of grub from home. Let's go and see if it's come.'

'Capital! We will.'

So Eric and Wildney started off to the coach-office, where they found the hamper, and ordered it to be brought at once to the school, and carried up to Eric's study.

On opening it they found it rich in dainties, among which were a pair of fowls and a large plum-cake.

'Hurrah!' said Wildney; 'you were talking of nothing to do; I vote we have a carouse to-morrow.'

'Very well; only let's have it *before* prayers, because we so nearly got caught last time.'

'Ay, and let it be in one of the classrooms, Eric; not up here, lest we have another incursion of the "Rosebuds." I shall have to cut preparation, but that don't matter. It's Harley's night, and old Stupid will never twig.'

'Well, whom shall we ask?' said Eric.

'Old Llewellyn for one,' said Wildney. 'We haven't seen him for an age, and he's getting too lazy even for a bit of fun.'

'Good; and Graham?' suggested Eric. He and Wildney regarded their possessions so much as common property, that he hadn't the least delicacy in mentioning the boys whom he wanted to invite.

'Yes; Graham's a jolly bird; and Ball?'

'I've no objection; and Pietrie?'

'Well; and your brother Vernon?'

'No!' said Eric emphatically. 'At any rate I won't lead *him* into mischief any more.'

'Attlay, then; and what do you say to Booking?'

'No, again,' said Eric; 'he's a blackguard.'

'I wonder you haven't mentioned Duncan,' said Wildney.

'Duncan! why, my good fellow, you might as well ask Owen, or even old Rose at once. Bless you, Charlie, he's a great deal too correct to come now.'

'Well; we've got six already, that's quite enough.'

'Yes; but two fowls isn't enough for six hungry boys.'

'No, it isn't,' said Wildney. He thought a little, and then, clapping his hands, danced about, and said, 'Are you game for a *regular* lark, Eric?'

'Yes; anything to make it less dull. I declare I've very nearly been taking to work again to fill up the time.'

Eric often talked now of work in this slighting way, partly as an excuse for the low places in form to which he was gradually sinking. Everybody knew that had he properly exerted his abilities he was capable of beating almost any boy; so, to quiet his conscience, he professed to ridicule diligence as an unboyish piece of muffishness, and was never slow to sneer at the 'grinders,' as he contemptuously called all those who laid themselves out to win school distinctions.

'Ha, ha!' said Wildney, 'that's rather good! No, Eric, it's too late for you to turn "grinder" now. I might as well think of doing it myself, and I've never been higher than five from lag in my form yet.'

'Haven't you? But what's the regular lark you hinted at?'

'First of all, I hope you won't think the *lark* less larky because it's connected with *pigeons*,' said Wildney.

'Ridiculous little Sphinx! What do you mean?'

'Why, we'll go and seize the Gordonites' *pigeons*, and make another dish of them.'

'Seize the Gordonites' pigeons! Why, when do you mean?'

'To-night.'

Eric gave a long whistle. 'But wouldn't it be st—st——?'

'Stealing?' said Wildney, with a loud laugh. 'Pooh! "*convey* the wise it call." '

But Eric still looked serious. 'Why, my dear old boy,' continued Wildney, 'the Gordonites'll be the first to laugh at the trick when we tell them of it next morning, as of course we will do. There, now, don't look grumpy. I shall cut away and arrange it with Graham, and tell you the whole dodge ready prepared to-night at bed-time.'

After lights were put out, Wildney came up to the study according to promise, and threw out hints about the proposed plan. He didn't tell it plainly, because Duncan was there, but Duncan caught quite enough to guess that some night excursion was intended, and said, when Wildney had gone—

'Take my advice, and have nothing to do with this, Eric.'

Eric had grown very touchy lately about advice, particularly from any fellow of his own standing; and after the checks he had recently received, a coolness had sprung up between him and nearly all the study-boys, which made him more than ever inclined to assert his independence, and defy and thwart them in every way.

'Keep your advice to yourself, Duncan, till it's asked for,' he answered roughly. 'You've done nothing but *advise* lately, and I'm rather sick of it.'

'Comme vous voulez,' replied Duncan, with a shrug. 'Gang your own gait; I'll have nothing more to do with trying to stop you since you *will* ruin yourself.'

Nothing more was said in the study that evening, and when Eric went down he didn't even bid Duncan good-night.

'Charlie,' he said, as he stole on tiptoe into Wildney's dormitory.

'Hush!' whispered Wildney, 'the other fellows are asleep. Come and sit by my bedside, and I'll tell you what we are going to do.'

Eric went and sat by him, and he sat up in his bed. 'First of all, *you're* to keep awake till twelve to-night,' he whispered; 'old Rowley'll have gone round by that time, and it'll be all safe. Then come and awake me again, and I'll watch till one, Pietrie till two, and Graham till three. Then Graham'll awake us all, and we'll dress.'

'Very well. But how will you get the key of the lavatory?'

'Oh, I'll manage that,' said Wildney, chuckling. 'But come again and awake me at twelve, will you?'

Eric went to his room and lay down, but he didn't take off his clothes, for fear he should go to sleep. Dr. Rowlands came round as usual at eleven, and then Eric closed his eyes for a few minutes, till the headmaster had disappeared. After that he lay awake thinking for an hour, but his thoughts weren't very pleasant.

At twelve he went and awoke Wildney.

'I don't feel very sleepy. Shall I sit with you for your hour, Charlie?'

'Oh, do! I should like it of all things. But douse the glim there; we shan't want it, and it might give the alarm.'

'All right.'

So Eric went and sat by his dangerous little friend, and they talked in low voices until they heard the great school clock strike one. They then woke Pietrie, and Eric went off to bed again.

At three Graham awoke him, and dressing hastily, he joined the others in the lavatory.

'Now I'm going to get the key,' said Wildney, 'and mean to feel very poorly for the purpose.'

Laughing quietly, he went up to the door of Mr. Harley's bedroom, which opened out of the lavatory, and knocked.

No answer.

He knocked a little louder.

Still no answer.

Louder still.

'Bother the fellow,' said Wildney; 'he sleeps like a grampus. Won't one of you try to wake him?'

'No,' said Graham; ' 'tain't dignified.'

'Well, I must try again.' But it seemed no use knocking, and Wildney at last, in a fit of impatience, thumped a regular tattoo on the bedroom door.

'Who's there?' said the startled voice of Mr. Harley.

'Only me, sir!' answered Wildney, in a mild and innocent way.

'What do you want?'

'Please, sir, I want the key of the lavatory. I want to see the doctor. I'm indisposed,' said Wildney again, in a tone of such disciplined suavity, that the others shook with laughing.

Mr. Harley opened the door about an inch, and peered out suspiciously.

'Oh, well, you must go and awake Mr. Rose. I don't happen to have the key to-night.' And so saying, he shut the door.

'Phew! Here's a go!' said Wildney, recovering immediately. 'It'll never do to awake old Rose. He'd smell a rat in no time.'

'I have it,' said Pietrie. 'I've got an old nail, with which I believe I can open the lock quite simply. Let's try.'

'Quietly and quick, then,' said Eric.

In ten minutes he had silently shot back the lock with the old nail, and the boys were on the landing. They carried their shoes in their hands, ran noiselessly down stairs, and went to the same window at which Eric and Wildney had got out before. Wildney had taken care beforehand to break the pane and move away the glass, so they had only to loosen the bar and slip through one by one.

It was cold and very dark, and as on the March morning they stood out in the playground, all four would rather have been safely and harmlessly in bed. But the novelty and the excitement of the enterprise bore them up, and they started off quickly for the house at which Mr. Gordon and his pupils lived, which was about half a mile from the school. They went arm in arm to assure each other a little, for at first in their fright they were inclined to take every post and tree for a man in ambush, and to hear a recalling voice in every sound of cold wind and murmuring wave.

Not far from Mr. Gordon's was a carpenter's shop, and outside of this there was generally a ladder standing. They had arranged to carry this ladder with them (as it was only a short one), climb the low garden wall with it, and then place it against the house, immediately under the dovecot which hung by the first-story windows. Wildney, as the lightest of the four, was to take the birds, while the others held the ladder.

Slanting it so that it should be as far from the side of the window as possible, Wildney ascended and thrust both hands into the cot. He succeeded in seizing a pigeon with each hand, but in doing so threw the other birds into a state of such alarm that they fluttered about in the wildest manner, and the moment his hands were withdrawn, flew out with a great flapping of hurried wings.

The noise they made alarmed the plunderer, and he hurried down the ladder as fast as he could. He handed the pigeons to the others, who instantly wrung their necks.

'I'm nearly sure I heard somebody stir,' said Wildney; 'we haven't been half quiet enough. Here! let's crouch down in this corner.'

All four shrank up as close to the wall as they could, and held their breath. Some one was certainly stirring, and at last they heard the window open.

A head was thrust out, and Mr. Gordon's voice asked sternly—'Who's there?'

He seemed at once to have caught sight of the ladder, and made an endeavour to reach it; but though he stretched out his arm at full length he could not manage to do so.

'We must cut for it,' said Eric; 'it's quite too dark for him to see who we are, or even to notice that we are boys.'

They moved the ladder to the wall, and sprang over, one after the other, as fast as they could. Eric was last, and just as he got on the top of the wall he heard the back door open, and some one run out into the yard.

'Run for your lives,' said Eric hurriedly; 'it's Gordon, and he's raising the alarm.'

They heard footsteps following them, and an occasional shout of 'Thieves! thieves!'

'We must separate and run different ways, or we've no chance of escape. We'd better turn towards the town to put them off the right scent,' said Eric again.

'Don't leave me,' pleaded Wildney; 'you know I can't run very fast.'

'No, Charlie, I won't;' and grasping his hand, Eric hurried him over the stile and through the fields as fast as he could, while Pietrie and Graham took the opposite direction.

Some one (they did not know who it was, but suspected it to be Mr. Gordon's servant-man) was running after them, and they could distinctly hear his footsteps, which seemed to be half a field distant. He carried a light and they heard him panting. They were themselves tired, and in the utmost trepidation; the usually courageous Wildney was trembling all over, and his fear communicated itself to Eric. Horrible visions of a trial for burglary, imprisonment in the castle jail, and perhaps transportation, presented themselves to their excited imaginations, as the sound of the footsteps came nearer and nearer.

'I can't run any farther, Eric,' said Wildney. 'What shall we do? don't leave me, for Heaven's sake.'

'Not I, Charlie. We must hide the minute we get t'other side of this hedge.'

They scrambled over the gate, and plunged into the thickest part of a plantation close by, lying down on the ground behind some bushes, and keeping as still as they possibly could, taking care to cover over their white collars.

The pursuer reached the gate, and no longer hearing footsteps in front of him, he paused. He went a little distance up the hedge on both sides, and held up his light, but did not detect the cowering boys, and at last giving up the search in despair, went slowly home. They heard him plodding back over the field, and it was not until the sound of his footsteps had died away, that Eric cautiously broke cover, and looked over the hedge. He saw the man's light gradually getting more distant, and said, 'All right now, Charlie. We must make the best of our way home.'

'Are you sure he's gone?' said Wildney, who had not yet recovered from his fright.

'Quite; come along. I only hope Pietrie and Graham ain't caught.'

They got back about half-past four, and climbed in unheard and undetected through the window pane. They then stole upstairs with beating hearts, and sate in Eric's room to wait for the other two. To their great relief they heard them enter the lavatory about ten minutes after.

'Were you twigged?' asked Wildney eagerly.

'No,' said Graham; 'precious near it though. Old Gordon and some men were after us, but at last we doubled rather neatly, and escaped them. It's all serene, and we shan't be caught. But it's a precious long time before I run such a risk again for a brace of rubbishing pigeons.'

'Well, we'd best to bed now,' said Eric; 'and to my thinking, we should be wise to keep a quiet tongue in our heads about this affair.'

'Yes, we had better tell *no one*.' They agreed, and went off to bed again. So, next morning, they all four got up quite as if nothing had happened, and made no allusion to the preceding night, although they could not help chuckling inwardly a little when the Gordonites came to morning school, brimful of a story about their house having been attacked in the night by thieves, who after bagging some pigeons, had been chevied by Gordon and the servants. Wildney professed immense interest in the incident, and asked many questions, which showed that there was not a shadow of suspicion in any one's mind as to the real culprits.

Carter, the school servant, didn't seem to have noticed that the lavatory door was unlocked, and Mr. Harley never alluded again to his disturbance in the night. So the theft of the pigeons remained undiscovered, and remains so till this day. If any old Roslyn boy reads this veracious history, he will doubtless be astounded to hear that the burglars on that memorable night were Eric, Pietrie, Graham, and Wildney.

CHAPTER THE EIGHTH

SOWING THE WIND

Præpediuntur
Crura vacillanti, tardescit lingua, madet mens,
Nant oculi.
LUCR. iii. 417

NEXT EVENING when preparation began, Pietrie and Graham got everything ready for the carouse in their classroom. Wildney, relying on the chance of names not being called over (which was only done in case any one's absence was observed), had absented himself altogether from the boarders' room, and helped busily to spread the table for the banquet. The cook had roasted for them the fowls and pigeons, and Billy had brought an ample supply of beer and some brandy for the occasion. A little before eight o'clock everything was ready, and Eric, Attlay, and Llewellyn were summoned to join the rest.

The fowls, pigeons, and beer had soon vanished, and the boys were in the highest spirits. Eric's reckless gaiety was kindled by Wildney's frolicsome vivacity and Graham's sparkling wit; they were all six in a roar of perpetual laughter at some fresh sally of fun elicited by the more phlegmatic natures of Attlay or Llewellyn, and the dainties of Wildney's parcel were accompanied by draughts of brandy and water, which were sometimes exchanged for potations of the raw liquor. It was not the first time, be it remembered, that the members of that young party had been present at similar scenes, and even the scoundrel Billy was astonished, and occasionally alarmed, at the quantities of spirits and other inebriating drinks that of late had found their way to the studies. The disgraceful and deadly habit of tippling had already told physically on both Eric and Wildney. The former felt painfully that he was losing his clear-headedness, and that his intellectual tastes were getting not only blunted but destroyed; and while he perceived in himself the terrible effects of his sinful indulgence, he saw them still more indisputably in the gradual coarseness which seemed to be spreading, like a gray lichen, over the countenance, the mind, and the manners of his younger companion. Sometimes the vision of a Nemesis breaking in fire out of his darkened future, terrified his guilty conscience in the watches of the night; and the conviction of some fearful Erinnys, some discovery dawning out of the night of his undetected sins, made his heart beat fast with agony and fear. But he fancied it too late to repent. He strangled the half-formed resolutions as they rose, and trusted to the time when, by leaving school, he should escape, as he idly supposed, the temptations to which he had yielded. Meanwhile, the friends who would have rescued him had been alienated by his follies, and the principles which might have preserved him had been eradicated by his guilt. He had long flung away the shield of prayer and the helmet of holiness, and the sword of the Spirit, which is the word of God; and now, unarmed and helpless, Eric stood alone, a mark for the fiery arrows of his enemies, while, through the weakened inlet of every corrupted sense, temptation rushed in upon him perpetually and unawares.

As the classroom they had selected was in a remote part of the building, there was little immediate chance of detection. So the laughter of the party grew louder and sillier; the talk more foolish and random; the merriment more noisy and meaningless. But still most of them mingled some sense of caution with their enjoyment, and warned Eric and Wildney more than once that they must look out, and not take too much that night for fear of being caught. But it was Wildney's birthday, and Eric's boyish mirth, suppressed by his recent troubles, was blazing out unrestrained. In the riot of their feasting the caution had been utterly neglected, and the two boys were far from being sober when the sound of the prayer-bell ringing through the great hall startled them into momentary consciousness.

'Good heavens!' shouted Graham, springing up; 'there's the prayer-bell; I'd no notion it was so late. Here, let's shove these brandy bottles and things into the cupboards and drawers, and then we must run down.'

There was no time to lose. The least muddled of the party had cleared the room in a moment, and then addressed themselves to the more difficult task of trying to quiet Eric and Wildney, and conduct them steadily into the prayer-room.

Wildney's seat was near the door, so there was little difficulty in getting him to his place comparatively unobserved. Llewellyn took him by the arm, and after a little stumbling helped him safely to his seat, where he assumed a look of preternatural gravity. But Eric sat near the head of the first table, not far from Dr. Rowlands's desk, and none of the others had to go to that part of the room. Graham grasped his arm tight, led him carefully down stairs, and, as they were reaching the door, said to him, in a most earnest and imploring tone—

'Do try and walk sensibly to your place, Eric, or we shall all be caught.'

It was rather late when they got down. Everybody was quietly seated, and most of the Bibles were already open, although the Doctor had not yet come in. Consequently, the room was still, and the entrance of Graham and Eric after the rest attracted general notice. Eric had just sense enough to try and assume his ordinary manner; but he was too giddy with the fumes of drink to walk straight or act naturally.

Vernon was sitting next to Wright, and stared at his brother with great eyes and open lips. He was not the only observer.

'Wright,' whispered he in a timid voice; 'just see how Eric walks. What can be the matter with him? Good gracious, he must be ill!' he said, starting up, as Eric suddenly made a great stagger to one side, and nearly fell in the attempt to recover himself.

Wright pulled the little boy down with a firm hand.

'Hush!' he whispered; 'take no notice; he's been drinking, Verny, and I fear he'll be caught.'

Vernon instantly sat down, and turned deadly pale. He thought, and he had hoped, that since the day at 'The Jolly Herring' his brother had abandoned all such practices, for Eric had been most careful to conceal from him the worst of his failings. And now he trembled violently with fear for his discovery, and horror at his disgraceful condition.

The sound of Eric's unsteady footsteps had made Mr. Rose quickly raise his head; but at the same moment Duncan hastily made room for the boy on the seat beside him, and held out his hand to assist him. It was not Eric's proper place; but Mr. Rose, after one long glance of astonishment, looked down at his book again, and said nothing.

It made other hearts besides Vernon's ache to see the unhappy boy roll to his place in that helpless way.

Dr. Rowlands came in and prayers commenced.

When they were finished, the names were called, and Eric, instead of quietly answering his 'adsum,' as he should have done, stood up, with a foolish look, and said, 'Yes, sir.' The head-master looked at him for a minute; the boy's glassy eyes and jocosely stupid appearance told an unmistakable tale; but Dr. Rowlands only remarked, 'Williams, you don't look well. You had better go at once to bed.'

It was hopeless for Eric to attempt getting along without help so Duncan at once got up, took him by the arm, and with much difficulty (for Eric staggered at every step) conducted him to his bedroom, where he left him without a word.

Wildney's condition was also too evident; and Mr. Rose, while walking up and down the dormitories, had no doubt left on his mind that both Eric and Wildney had been drinking. But he made no remarks to them, and merely went to the Doctor, to talk over the steps which were to be taken.

'I shall summon the school,' said Dr. Rowlands, 'on Monday, and by that time we will decide on the punishment. Expulsion, I fear, is the only course open to us.'

'Is not that a *very* severe line to take?'

'Perhaps; but the offence is of the worst character. I must consider the matter.'

'Poor Williams!' sighed Mr. Rose, as he left the room.

The whole of the miserable Sunday that followed was spent by Eric and his companions in vain inquiries and futile restlessness. It seemed clear that two of them at least were detected, and they were inexpressibly wretched with anxiety and suspense. Wildney, who had to stay in bed, was even more depressed; his head ached violently, and he was alone with his own terrified thoughts. He longed for the morrow, that at least he might have the poor consolation of knowing his fate. No one came near him all day. Eric wished to do so, but as he could not have visited the room without express leave, the rest dissuaded him from asking, lest he should excite further suspicion. His apparent neglect made poor Wildney even more unhappy, for Wildney loved Eric as much as it was possible for his volatile mind to love any one; and it seemed hard to be deserted in the moment of disgrace and sorrow by so close a friend.

At school the next morning the various masters read out to their forms a notice from Dr. Rowlands, that the whole school were to meet at ten in the great schoolroom. The object of the summons was pretty clearly understood; and few boys had any doubt that it had reference to the drinking on Saturday night. Still nothing had been *said* on the subject as yet; and every guilty heart among those 250 boys beat fast lest *his* sin too should have been discovered, and he should be called out for some public and heavy punishment.

The hour arrived. The boys, thronging into the great schoolroom, took their places according to their respective forms. The masters in their caps and gowns were all seated on a small semicircular bench at the upper end of the room, and in the centre of them, before a small table, sate Dr. Rowlands.

The sound of whispering voices sank to a dead and painful hush. The blood was tingling consciously in many cheeks, and not even a breath could be heard in the deep expectation of that anxious and solemn moment.

Dr. Rowlands spread before him the list of the school, and said, 'I shall first read out the names of the boys in the first-fifth and upper-fourth forms.'

This was done to ascertain formally whether the boys were present on whose account the meeting was convened; and it at once told Eric and Wildney that *they* were the boys to be punished, and that the others had escaped.

The names were called over, and an attentive observer might have told, from the sound of the boys' voices as they answered, which of them were afflicted with a troubled conscience.

Another slight pause and breathless hush.

'Eric Williams and Charles Wildney, stand forward.'

The boys obeyed. From his place in the fifth, where he was sitting with his head propped on his hand, Eric rose and advanced; and Wildney, from the other end of the room, where the younger boys sat, getting up, came and stood by his side.

Both of them fixed their eyes on the ground, whence they never once raised them; and in the deadly pallor of their haggard faces you could scarcely have recognised the joyous high-spirited friends, whose laugh and shout had often rung so merrily through the playground, and woke the echoes of the rocks along the shore. Every eye was on them, and they were conscious of it, though they could not see it—painfully conscious of it, so that they wished the very ground to yawn beneath their feet for the moment and swallow up their shame. Companionship in disgrace increased the suffering; had either of them been alone, he would have been less acutely sensible to the trying nature of his position; but that they, so different in their ages and position in the school, should thus have their friendship and the results of it blazoned, or rather branded, before their friends and enemies, added keenly to the misery they felt. So with eyes bent on the floor, Eric and Charlie awaited their sentence.

'Williams and Wildney,' said Dr. Rowlands in a solemn voice, of which every articulation thrilled to the heart of every hearer, 'you have been detected in a sin most disgraceful and most dangerous. On Saturday night you were both drinking, and you were guilty of such gross excess, that you were neither of you in a fit state to appear among your companions—least of all to appear among them at the hour of prayer. I shall not waste many words on an occasion like this; only I trust that those of your school-fellows who saw you staggering and rolling into the room on Saturday evening in a manner so unspeakably shameful and degrading, will learn from that melancholy sight the lesson which the Spartans taught their children by exhibiting a drunkard before them—the lesson of the brutalising and fearful character of this most ruinous vice. Eric Williams and Charles Wildney, your punishment will be public expulsion, for which you will prepare this very evening. I am unwilling that for a single day, either of you—especially the elder of you—should linger, so as possibly to contaminate others with the danger of so pernicious an example.'

Such a sentence was wholly unexpected; it took boys and masters equally by surprise. The announcement of it caused an uneasy sensation, which was evident to all present, though no one spoke a word; but Dr. Rowlands took no notice of it, and only said to the culprits—

'You may return to your seats.'

The two boys found their way back instinctively, they hardly knew how. They seemed confounded and thunderstruck by their sentence, and the painful accessories of its publicity. Eric leaned over the desk with his head resting on a book, too stunned even to think; and Wildney looked straight before him, with his eyes fixed in a stupid and unobservant stare.

Form by form the school dispersed, and the moment he was liberated Eric sprang away from the boys, who would have spoken to him, and rushed wildly to his study, where he locked the door. In a moment, however, he re-opened it, for he heard Wildney's step, and, after admitting him, locked it once more.

Without a word Wildney, who looked very pale, flung his arms round Eric's neck, and, unable to bear up any longer, burst into a flood of tears. Both of them felt relief in giving the reins to their sorrow, and silently satiating the anguish of their hearts.

'Oh, my father! my father!' sobbed Wildney at length, 'what will he say? He will disown me, I know; he is so stern always with me when he thinks I bring disgrace on him.'

Eric thought of Fairholm, and of his own far-distant parents, and of the pang which *his* disgrace would cause their loving hearts; but he could say nothing, and only stroked Wildney's dark hair again and again with a soothing hand.

They sat there long, hardly knowing how the time passed; Eric could not help thinking how very very different their relative positions might have been; how, while he might have been aiding and ennobling the young boy beside him, he had alternately led and followed him into wickedness and disgrace. His heart was full of misery and bitterness, and he felt almost indifferent to all the future, and weary of his life.

A loud knocking at the door disturbed them. It was Carter, the school servant.

'You must pack up to go this evening, young gentlemen.'

'Oh no! no! no!' exclaimed Wildney; 'I *cannot* be sent away like this. It would break my father's heart. Eric, *do* come and entreat Dr. Rowlands to forgive us only this once.'

'Yes,' said Eric, starting up with sudden energy; 'he *shall* forgive us—*you* at any rate. I will not leave him till he does. Cheer up, Charlie, cheer up, and come along.'

Filled with an irresistible impulse, he pushed Carter aside, and sprang down stairs three steps at a time, with Wildney following him. They went straight for the Doctor's study, and without waiting for the answer to their knock at the door, Eric walked up to Dr. Rowlands, who sate thinking in his arm-chair by the fire, and burst out passionately, 'Oh, sir, forgive us, forgive us this once.'

The Doctor was completely taken by surprise, so sudden was the intrusion, and so intense was the boy's manner. He remained silent a moment from astonishment, and then said with asperity—

'Your offence is one of the most dangerous possible. There could be no more perilous example for the school, than the one you have been setting, Williams. Leave the room,' he added with an authoritative gesture; 'my mind is made up.'

But Eric was too excited to be overawed by the master's manner; an imperious passion blinded him to all ordinary considerations, and, heedless of the command, he broke out again—

'Oh, sir, try me but once, *only* try me. I promise you most faithfully that I will never again commit the sin. Oh, sir, do, do trust me, and I will be responsible for Wildney too.'

Dr. Rowlands, seeing that in Eric's present mood he must and would be heard, unless he were ejected by actual force, began to pace silently up and down the room in perplexed and anxious thought; at last he stopped and turned over the pages of a thick school register, and found Eric's name.

'It is not your first offence, Williams, even of this very kind. That most seriously aggravates your fault.'

'Oh, sir! give us one more chance to mend. Oh, I feel that I *could* do such great things, if you will but be merciful, and give me time to change. Oh, I entreat you, sir, to forgive us only this once, and I will never ask again. Let us bear *any* other punishment but this. Oh, sir,' he said, approaching the Doctor in an imploring attitude, 'spare us this one time for the sake of our friends.'

The head-master made no reply for a time, but again paced the room in silence. He was touched, and seemed hardly able to restrain his emotion.

'It was my deliberate conclusion to expel you, Williams. I must not weakly yield to entreaty. You must go.'

Eric wrung his hands in agony. 'Oh, sir, then if you must do so, expel me only, and not Charlie. *I* can bear it, but do not let me ruin him also. Oh, I implore you, sir, for the love of God, do, do forgive him! It is I who have misled him;' and he flung himself on his knees, and lifted his hands entreatingly towards the Doctor.

Dr. Rowlands looked at him—at his blue eyes drowned with tears, his agitated gesture, his pale, expressive face, full of passionate supplication. He looked at Wildney too, who stood trembling with a look of painful and miserable suspense, and occasionally added his wild word of entreaty, or uttered sobs more powerful still, that seemed to come from the depth of his heart. He was shaken in his resolve, wavered for a moment, and then once more looked at the register.

'Yes,' he said, after a long pause, 'here is an entry which shall save you this time. I find written here against your name, "April 3. Risked his life in the endeavour to save Edwin Russell at the Stack." That one good and noble deed shall be the proof that you are capable of better things. It may be weak perhaps—I know that it will be called weak— and I do not feel certain that I am doing right; but if I err it shall be on the side of mercy. I shall change expulsion into some other punishment. You may go.'

Wildney's face lighted up as suddenly and joyously as when a ray of sunlight gleams for an instant out of a dark cloud.

'Oh, thank you, thank you, sir,' he exclaimed, drying his eyes, and pouring into the words a world of expression, which it was no light pleasure to have heard. But Eric spoke less impulsively, and while the two boys were stammering out their deep gratitude, a timid hand knocked at the door, and Vernon entered.

'I have come, sir, to speak for poor Eric,' he said in a voice low and trembling with emotion, as, with downcast eyes, he modestly approached towards Dr. Rowlands, not even observing the presence of the others in the complete absorption of his feelings. He stood in a sorrowful attitude, not venturing to look up, and his hand played nervously with the ribbon of his straw hat.

'I have just forgiven him, my little boy,' said the Doctor kindly, patting his stooping head; 'there he is, and he has been speaking for himself.'

'O Eric, I am so, so glad, I don't know what to say for joy. O Eric, thank God that you are not to be expelled;' and Vernon went to his brother and embraced him with the deepest affection.

Dr. Rowlands watched the scene with moist eyes. He was generally a man of prompt decision, and he well knew that he would incur by this act the charge of vacillation. It was a noble self-denial in him to be willing to do so, but it would have required an iron heart to resist such earnest supplications, and he was more than repaid when he saw how much anguish he had removed by yielding to their entreaties.

Once more humbly expressing their gratitude, the boys retired.

They did not know that other influences had been also exerted in their favour, which, although ineffectual at the time, had tended to alter the Doctor's intention. Immediately after school Mr. Rose had been strongly endeavouring to change the Doctor's mind, and had dwelt forcibly on all the good points in Eric's character, and the promise of his earlier career. And Montagu had gone with Owen and Duncan to beg that the expulsion might be commuted into some other punishment. They had failed to convince him; but perhaps, had they not thus exerted themselves, Dr. Rowlands might have been unshaken, though he could not be unmoved, by Vernon's gentle intercession and Eric's passionate prayers.

Wildney, full of joy, and excited by the sudden revulsion of feeling, only shook Eric's hands with all his might, and then darted out into the playground to announce the happy news. The boys all flocked round him, and received the intelligence with unmitigated pleasure. Among them all there was not one who did not rejoice that Eric and Wildney were yet to continue of their number.

But the two brothers returned to the study, and there, sorrowful in his penitence, with his heart still aching with remorse, Eric sat down on a chair facing the window, and drew Vernon to his side. The sun was setting behind the purple hills, flooding the green fields and silver sea with the crimson of his parting rays. The air was full of peace and coolness, and the merry sounds of the cricket-field blended joyously with the whisper of the evening breeze. Eric was fond of beauty in every shape, and his father had early taught him a keen appreciation of the glories of nature. He had often gazed before on that splendid scene, as he was now gazing on it thoughtfully with his brother by his side. He looked long and wistfully at the gorgeous pageantry of quiet clouds, and passed his arm more fondly round Vernon's shoulder.

'What are you thinking of, Eric? Why, I declare you are crying still,' said Vernon playfully, as he wiped away a tear which had overflowed on his brother's cheek; 'aren't you glad that the Doctor has forgiven you?'

'Gladder, far gladder than I can say, Verny. O Verny, Verny, I hope your school-life may be happier than mine has been. I would give up all I have, Verny, to have kept free from the sins I have learnt. God grant that I may yet have time and space to do better.'

'Let us pray together, Eric,' whispered his brother reverently, and they knelt down and prayed; they prayed for their distant parents and friends; they prayed for their schoolfellows and for each other, and for Wildney, and they thanked God for all His goodness to them; and then Eric poured out his heart in a fervent prayer that a holier and happier future might atone for his desecrated past, and that his sins might be forgiven for his Saviour's sake.

The brothers rose from their knees calmer and more light-hearted in the beauty of holiness, and gave each other a solemn affectionate kiss, before they went down again to the playground. But they avoided the rest of the boys, and took a stroll together along the sands, talking quietly and happily, and hoping bright hopes for future days.

CHAPTER THE NINTH

WHOM THE GODS LOVE DIE YOUNG

Oh is it weed, or fish, or floating hair?
A tress of maiden's hair,
Of drownèd maiden's hair,
Above the nets at sea!
KINGSLEY

ERIC AND WILDNEY were flogged and confined to gates for a time instead of being expelled, and they both bore the punishment in a manly and penitent way, and set themselves with all their might to repair the injury which their characters had received. Eric especially seemed to be devoting himself with every energy to regain, if possible, his long-lost position, and by the altered complexion of his remaining school-life, to atone in some poor measure for its earlier sins. And he carried Wildney with him, influencing others also of his late companions in a greater or less degree. It was not Eric's nature to do things by halves, and it became obvious to all that his exertions to resist and abandon his old temptations were strenuous and unwavering. He could no longer hope for the school distinctions, which would have once lain so easily within his reach, for the ground lost during weeks of idleness cannot be recovered by a wish; but he succeeded sufficiently, by dint of desperately hard work, to acquit himself with considerable credit, and in the Easter examination came out high enough in the upper fifth to secure his remove into the sixth form after the holidays.

He felt far happier in the endeavour to do his duty, than he had ever done during the last years of recklessness and neglect, and the change for the better in his character tended to restore unanimity and goodwill to the school. Eric no longer headed the party which made a point of ridiculing and preventing industry; and sharing as he did the sympathy of nearly all the boys, he was able quietly and unobtrusively to calm down the jealousies and allay the heartburnings which had for so long a time brought discord and disunion into the school society. Cheerfulness and unanimity began to prevail once more at Roslyn, and Eric had the intense happiness of seeing how much good lay still within his power.

So the Easter holidays commenced with promise, and the few first days glided away in innocent enjoyments. Eric was now reconciled again to Owen and Duncan, and, therefore, had a wider choice of companions more truly congenial to his higher nature than the narrow circle of his late associates.

'What do you say to a boat excursion to-morrow?' asked Duncan, as they chatted together one evening.

'I won't go without leave,' said Eric; 'I should only get caught, and get into another mess. Besides, I feel myself pledged now to strict obedience.'

'Ay, you're quite right. We'll get leave easily enough though, provided we agree to take Jim the boatman with us; so I vote we make up a party.'

'By the bye, I forgot; I'm engaged to Wildney to-morrow.'

'Never mind. Bring him with you, and Graham too, if you like.'

'Most gladly,' said Eric, really pleased; for he saw by this that Duncan observed the improvement in his old friends, and was falling in with the endeavour to make all the boys really cordial to each other, and destroy all traces of the late factions.

'Do you mind my bringing Montagu?'

'Not at all. Why should I?' answered Eric, with a slight blush. Montagu and he had never been formally reconciled, nor had they, as yet, spoken to each other. Indeed, Duncan had purposely planned the excursion to give them an opportunity of becoming friends once more, by being thrown together. He knew well that they both earnestly wished it, although, with the natural shyness of boys, they hardly knew how to set about effecting it. Montagu hung back lest he should seem to be patronising a fallen enemy, and Eric lest he should have sinned too deeply to be forgiven.

The next morning dawned gloriously, and it was agreed that they should meet at Starhaven, the point where they were to get the boat, at ten o'clock. As they had supposed, Dr. Rowlands gave a ready consent to the row, on condition of their being accompanied by the experienced sailor whom the boys called Jim. The precaution was by no means unnecessary, for the various currents which ran round the island were violent at certain stages of the tide, and extremely dangerous for any who were not aware of their general course.

Feeling that the day would pass off very unpleasantly if any feeling of restraint remained between him and Montagu, Eric, by a strong effort, determined to 'make up with him' before starting, and went into his study for that purpose after breakfast. Directly he came in, Montagu jumped up and welcomed him cordially, and when without any allusion to the past, the two shook hands with all warmth, and looked the old proud look into each other's faces, they felt once more that their former affection was unimpaired, and that in heart they were real and loving friends. Most keenly did they both enjoy the renewed intercourse, and they found endless subjects to talk about on their way to Starhaven, where the others were already assembled when they came.

With Jim's assistance they shoved a boat into the water, and sprang into it in the highest spirits. Just as they were pushing off they saw Wright and Vernon running down to the shore towards them, and they waited to see what they wanted.

'Couldn't you take us with you?' asked Vernon, breathless with his run.

'I'm afraid not, Verny,' said Montagu; 'the boat won't hold more than six, will it, Jim?'

'No, sir, not safely.'

'Never mind, you shall have my place, Verny,' said Eric, as he saw his brother's disappointed look.

'Then Wright shall take mine,' said Wildney.

'Oh dear, no,' said Wright, 'we wouldn't turn you out for the world. Vernon and I will take an immense walk down the coast instead, and will meet you here as we come back.'

'Well, good-bye, then; off we go;' and with light hearts the boaters and the pedestrians parted.

Eric, Graham, Duncan, and Montagu took the first turn at the oars, while Wildney steered. Graham's 'crabs,' and Wildney's rather crooked steering, gave plenty of opportunity for chaff, and they were full of fun, as the oar-blades splashed and sparkled in the waves. Then they made Jim sing them some of his old sailor-songs as they rowed, and joined vigorously in the choruses. They had arranged to make straight for St. Catharine's Head, and land somewhere near it to choose a place for their picnic. It took them nearly two hours to get there, as they rowed leisurely, and enjoyed the luxury of the vernal air. It was one of the sunniest days of early spring; the air was pure and delicious, and the calm sea-breeze, just strong enough to make the sea flame and glister in the warm sunlight, was exhilarating as new wine. Underneath them the water was transparent as crystal, and far below they could see the green and purple seaweeds rising like a many-coloured wood, through which occasionally they saw a fish, startled by their oars, dart like an arrow. The sky overhead was a cloudless blue, and as they kept not far from shore, the clearly cut outline of the coast, with its rocks and hills standing out in the vivid atmosphere, made a glowing picture, to which the golden green of the spring herbage, bathed in its morning sunlight, lent the magic of enchantment. Who could have been otherwise than happy in such a scene and at such a time? but these were boys with the long bright holiday before them, and happiness is almost too quiet a word to express the bounding exultation of heart, the royal and tingling sense of vigorous life, which made them shout and sing, as their boat rustled through the ripples, from a mere instinct of inexpressible enjoyment.

They had each contributed some luxury to the picnic, and it made a very tempting display as they spread it out under a sunny pebbled cave, by St. Catharine's Head; although, instead of anything more objectionable, they had thought it best to content themselves with ginger beer and lemonade. When they had done eating, they amused themselves on the shore; and had magnificent games among the rocks, and in every fantastic nook of the romantic promontory. And then Eric suggested a bathe to wind up with, as it was the first day when it had been quite warm enough to make bathing pleasant.

'But we've got no towels.'

'Oh! chance the towels. We can run about till we're dry.' So they bathed, and then getting in the boat to row back again, they all agreed that it was the very jolliest day they'd ever had at Roslyn, and voted to renew the experiment before the holidays were over, and take Wright and Vernon with them in a larger boat.

It was afternoon—an afternoon still warm and beautiful—when they began to row home; so they took it quietly, and kept near the land for variety's sake, laughing, joking, and talking as merrily as ever.

'I declare I think this is the prettiest, or anyhow the grandest bit of the whole coast,' said Eric, as they neared a glen through whose narrow gorge a green and garrulous little river gambolled down with noisy turbulence into the sea. He might well admire that glen; its steep and rugged sides were veiled with lichens, moss, and wild-flowers, and the sea-birds found safe refuge in its lonely windings, which were coloured with topaz and emerald by the pencillings of nature and the rich stains of time.

'Yes,' answered Montagu, 'I always stick up for Avon Glen as the finest scene we've got about here. But, I say, who's that gesticulating on the rock there to the right of it? I verily believe it's Wright, apostrophising the ocean for Vernon's benefit. I only see one of them though.'

'I bet you he's spouting

'Roll on, thou deep and dark blue ocean, roll!
Ten thousand fleets, etc.,'

said Graham, laughing.

'What do you say to putting in to shore there?' said Duncan. 'It's only two miles to Starhaven, and I daresay we could make shift to take them in for that distance. If Jim says anything we'll chuck him overboard.'

They rowed towards Avon Glen, and to their surprise Wright, who stood there alone (for with a pocket telescope they clearly made out that it *was* Wright), still continued to wave his arms and beckon them in a manner which they at first thought ridiculous, but which soon made them feel rather uneasy.

Jim took an oar, and they soon got within two hundred yards of the beach. Wright had ceased to make signals, but appeared to be shouting to them, and pointing towards one corner of the glen; but though they caught the sound of his voice, they could not hear what he said.

'I wonder why Vernon isn't with him,' said Eric anxiously; 'I hope—why, what *are* you looking at, Charlie?'

'What's that in the water there?' said Wildney, pointing in the direction to which Wright was also looking.

Montagu snatched the telescope out of his hand and looked. 'Good God!' he exclaimed, turning pale; 'what can be the matter?'

'Oh, *do* let me look,' said Eric.

'No! stop, stop, Eric; you'd better not, I think; pray don't, it may be all a mistake. You'd better not—but it looked—nay, you really *mustn't*, Eric,' he said, and, as if accidentally, he let the telescope fall into the water, and they saw it sink down among the seaweeds at the bottom.

Eric looked at him reproachfully. 'What's the fun of that, Monty? you let it drop on purpose.'

'Oh, never mind; I'll get Wildney another. I really daren't let you look, for fear you should *fancy* the same as I did, for it must be fancy. Oh, *don't* let us put in there—at least not all of us.'

What *was* that thing in the water?—

When Wright and Vernon left the others, they walked along the coast, following the direction of the boat, and agreed to amuse themselves in collecting eggs. They were very successful, and, to their great delight, managed to secure some rather rare specimens. When they had tired themselves with this pursuit, they lay on the summit of one of the cliffs which formed the sides of Avon Glen, and Wright, who was very fond of poetry, read Vernon a canto of *Marmion* with great enthusiasm.

So they wiled away the morning, and when the canto was over, Vernon took a great stone and rolled it for amusement over the cliff's edge. It thundered over the side, bounding down till it reached the strand, and a large black cormorant, startled by the reverberating echoes, rose up suddenly, and flapped its way with protruded neck to a rock on the farther side of the little bay.

'I bet you that animal's got a nest somewhere near here,' said Vernon eagerly. 'Come, let's have a look for it; a cormorant's egg would be a jolly addition to our collection.'

They got up, and looking down the face of the cliff, saw, some eight feet below them, a projection half hidden by the branch of a tree on which the scattered pieces of stick clearly showed the existence of a rude nest. They could not, however, see whether it contained eggs or no.

'I must bag that nest; it's pretty sure to have eggs in it,' said Vernon, 'and I can get at it easy enough.'

He immediately began to descend towards the place where the nest was built, but he found it harder than he expected.

'Hallo,' he said, 'this is a failure. I must climb up again to reconnoitre if there isn't a better dodge for getting at it.'

He reached the top, and, looking down, saw a plan of reaching the ledge which promised more hope of success.

'You'd better give it up, Verny,' said Wright. 'I'm sure it's harder than we fancied. *I* couldn't manage it, I know.'

'Oh, no, Wright, never say die. Look; if I get down more toward the right the way's plain enough, and I shall have reached the nest in no time.'

Again he descended in a different direction, but again he failed. The nest could only be seen from the top, and he lost the proper route.

'You must keep more to the right.'

'I know,' answered Vernon; 'but, bother take it, I can't manage it, now I'm so far down. I must climb up *again*.'

'*Do* give it up, Verny, there's a good fellow. You *can't* reach it, and really it's dangerous.'

'Oh no, not a bit of it. My head's very steady and I feel as cool as possible. We mustn't give up; I've only to get at the tree, and then I shall be able to reach the nest from it quite easily.'

'Well, do take care, that's a dear fellow.'

'Never fear,' said Vernon, who was already commencing his third attempt.

This time he got to the tree, and placed his foot on a part of the root, while with his hands he clung on to a clump of heather.

'Hurrah!' he cried, 'it's got two eggs in it, Wright;' and he stretched downwards to take them. Just as he was doing so, he heard the root on which his foot rested give a great crack, and with a violent start he made a spring for one of the lower branches. The motion caused his whole weight to rest for an instant on his arms;——unable to sustain the wrench, the heather gave way, and with a wild shriek he fell headlong down the surface of the cliff.

With a wild shriek!——but silence followed it.

'Vernon! Vernon!' shouted the terrified Wright, creeping close up to the edge of the precipice. 'O Vernon! for Heaven's sake, speak.'

There was no answer, and leaning over, Wright saw the young boy outstretched on the stones three hundred feet below. For some minutes he was horror-struck beyond expression, and made wild attempts to descend the cliff and reach him. But he soon gave up the attempt in despair. There was a tradition in the school that the feat had once been accomplished by an adventurous and active boy, but Wright at any rate found it hopeless for himself. The only other way to reach the glen was by a circuitous route which led to the entrance of the narrow gorge, along the sides of which it was possible to make way with difficulty down the bank of the river to the place where it met the sea. But this would have taken him an hour and a half, and was far from easy when the river was swollen with high tide. There was no house within moderate distance at which assistance could be procured, and Wright, in a tumult of conflicting emotions, deter-

mined to wait where he was, on the chance of seeing the boat as it returned from St. Catharine's Head. It was already three o'clock, and he knew that the boys could not now be longer than an hour at most; so with eager eyes he sat watching the headland, round which he knew they would first come in sight. He watched with wild eager eyes, absorbed in the one longing desire to catch sight of them; but the leaden-footed moments crawled on like hours, and he could not help shivering with agony and fear. At last he caught a glimpse of them, and springing up, began to shout at the top of his voice, and wave his handkerchief and his arms in the hope of attracting their attention. Little thought those blithe, merry-hearted boys, in the midst of the happy laughter which they sent ringing over the waters, little they thought how terrible a tragedy awaited them.

At last Wright saw that they had perceived him, and were putting inland, and now, in his fright, he hardly knew what to do; but feeling sure that they could not fail to see Vernon, he ran off as fast as he could to Starhaven, where he rapidly told the people at a farmhouse what had happened, and asked them to get a cart ready to convey the wounded boy to Roslyn School.

Meanwhile the tide rolled in calmly and quietly in the rosy evening, radiant with the diamond and gold of reflected sunlight and transparent wave. Gradually, gently it crept up to the place where Vernon lay; and the little ripples fell over him wonderingly, with the low murmur of their musical laughter, and blurred and dimmed the vivid splashes and crimson streaks upon the white stone on which his head had fallen, and washed away some of the purple bells and green sprigs of heather round which his fingers were closed in the grasp of death, and played softly with his fair hair as it rose, and fell, and floated on their undulations like a leaf of golden-coloured weed, until they themselves

were faintly discoloured by his blood. And then, tired with their new plaything, they passed on, until the swelling of the water was just strong enough to move rudely the boy's light weight, and in a few moments more would have tossed it up and down with every careless wave among the boulders of the glen. And then it was that Montagu's horror-stricken gaze had identified the object at which they had been gazing. In strange foreboding silence they urged on the boat, while Eric at the prow seemed wild with the one intense impulse to verify his horrible suspicion. The suspicion grew and grew:—it *was* a boy lying in the water;—it was Vernon;—he was motionless;—he must have fallen there from the cliff.

Eric could endure the suspense no longer. The instant that the boat grated on the shingle, he sprang into the water, and rushed to the spot where his brother's body lay. With a burst of passionate affection, he flung himself on his knees beside it, and took the cold hand in his own—the little rigid hand in which the green blades of grass, and fern, and heath, so tightly clutched, were unconscious of the tale they told.

'O Verny, Verny, darling Verny, speak to me!' he cried in anguish, as he tenderly lifted up the body, and marked how little blood had flowed. But the child's head fell back heavily, and his arms hung motionlessly beside him, and with a shriek, Eric suddenly caught the look of dead fixity in his blue open eyes.

The others had come up. 'O God, save my brother, save him, save him from death,' cried Eric; 'I cannot live without him. O God! O God! Look! look!' he continued, 'he has fallen from the cliff with his head on this cursed stone,' pointing to the block of quartz, still red with blood-stained hair; 'but we must get a doctor. He is not dead! no, no, he *cannot* be dead. Take him quickly, and let us row home. O God! why did I ever leave him?'

The boys drew round in a frightened circle, and lifted Vernon's corpse into the boat; and then, while Eric still supported the body, and moaned, and called to him in anguish, and chafed his cold pale brow and white hands, and kept saying that he had fainted and was not dead, the others rowed home with all speed, while a feeling of terrified anxiety lay like frost upon their hearts.

They reached Starhaven, and lifted the lifeless boy into the cart, and heard from Wright how the accident had taken place. Few boys were about the playground, so they got unnoticed to Roslyn, and Dr. Underhay, who had been summoned, was instantly in attendance. He looked at Vernon for a moment, and then shook his head in a way that could not be mistaken.

Eric saw it, and flung himself with uncontrollable agony on his brother's corpse. 'O Vernon, Vernon, my own darling brother! O God, then he is dead!' And, unable to endure the blow, he fainted away.

I cannot dwell on the miserable days that followed when the very sun in heaven seemed dark to poor Eric's wounded and crushed spirit. He hardly knew how they went by. And when they buried Vernon in the little green churchyard by Russell's side, and the patter of the earth upon the coffin—that most terrible of all sounds—struck his ear, the iron entered into his soul, and he had but one wish as he turned away from the open grave, and that was, soon to lie beside his beloved little brother, and to be at rest.

CHAPTER THE TENTH

THE LAST TEMPTATION

Ἡ δ' ''Ατη σθεναρή τε καὶ ἀρτιπος · οὕνεκα πασας
Πολλὸν ὑπεκπροθέει, φθανέει δέ τε πᾶσαν ἐπ' αἶαν
Βλάπτουσ' ἀνθρώπους.

HOM. *Il.* ix. 505

TIME, THE GREAT GOOD ANGEL, Time, the merciful healer, assuaged the violence of Eric's grief, which seemed likely to settle down into a sober sadness. At first his letters to his parents and to Fairholm were almost unintelligible in their fierce abandonment of sorrow; but they grew calmer in time,—and while none of his schoolfellows ever ventured in his presence to allude to Vernon, because of the emotion which the slightest mention of him excited, yet he rarely wrote any letters to his relations in which he did not refer to his brother's death, in language which grew at length both manly and resigned.

A month after, in the summer term, he was sitting alone in his study in the afternoon (for he could not summon up spirit enough to play regularly at cricket), writing a long letter to his aunt. He spoke freely and unreservedly of his past errors,—more freely than he had ever done before,—and expressed not only deep penitence, but even strong hatred of his previous unworthy courses. 'I can hardly even yet realise,' he added, 'that I am alone here, and that I am writing to my aunt Trevor about the death of my little brother, my noble, only brother, Vernon. Oh, how my whole soul yearns towards him. I *must* be a better boy, I *will* be better than I have been, in the hopes of meeting him again. Indeed, indeed, dear aunt, though I have been so guilty, I am laying aside, with all my might, idleness and all bad habits, and doing my very best to redeem the lost years. I do hope that the rest of my time at Roslyn will be more worthily spent than any of it has been as yet.'

He finished the sentence, and laid his pen down to think, gazing quietly on the blue hills and sunlit sea. A feeling of hope and repose stole over him;—when suddenly he saw at the door, which was ajar, the leering eyes and villainously cunning countenance of Billy.

'What do you want?' he said angrily, casting at the intruder a look of intense disgust.

'Beg pardon, sir,' said the man, pulling his hair. 'Anything in my line, sir, to-day?'

'No!' answered Eric, rising up in a gust of indignation. 'What business have you here? Get away instantly.'

'Not had much custom from you lately, sir,' said the man.

'What do you mean by having the insolence to begin talking to me? If you don't make yourself scarce at once, I'll——'

'Oh, well,' said the man; 'if it comes to that, I've business enough. Perhaps you'll just pay me this debt,' he continued, changing his fawning manner into a bullying swagger. 'I've waited long enough.'

Eric, greatly discomfited, took the dirty bit of paper. It purported to be a bill for various items of drink, all of which Eric *knew* to have been paid for, and among other things, a charge of £6 for the dinner at 'The Jolly Herring.'

'Why, you scoundrel, these have all been paid. What! six pounds for the dinner! Why, Brigson collected the subscriptions to pay for it before it took place.'

'That's now't to me, sir. He never paid me; and as you was the young gen'leman in the cheer, I comes to you.'

Now Eric knew for the first time what Brigson had meant by his threatened revenge. He saw at once that the man had been put up to act in this way by some one, and had little doubt that Brigson was the instigator. Perhaps it might be even true, as the man said, that he had never received the money. Brigson was quite wicked enough to have embezzled it for his own purposes.

'Go,' he said to the man; 'you shall have the money in a week.'

'And mind it bean't more nor a week. I don't chuse to wait for my money no more,' said Billy impudently, as he retired with an undisguised chuckle, which very nearly made Eric kick him down stairs. With a heartrending sigh Eric folded and directed his letter to Mrs. Trevor, and then ran out into the fresh air to relieve the qualm of sickness which had come over him.

What was to be done? To mention the subject to Owen or Montagu, who were best capable of advising him, would have been to renew the memory of unpleasant incidents, which he was most anxious to obliterate from the memory of all. He had not the moral courage to face the natural consequences of his past misconduct, and was now ashamed to speak of what he had not then been ashamed to do. He told Graham and Wildney, who were the best of his old associates, and they at once agreed that they ought to be responsible for at least a share of the debt. Still, between them they could only muster three pounds out of the six which were required, and the week had half elapsed before there seemed any prospect of extrication from the difficulty; so Eric daily grew more miserable and dejected.

A happy thought struck him. He would go and explain the source of his trouble to Mr. Rose, his oldest, his kindest, his wisest friend. To him he could speak without scruple and without reserve, and from him he knew that he would receive nothing but the noblest advice and the warmest sympathy.

He went to him after prayers that night, and told his story.

'Ah, Eric, Eric!' said Mr. Rose; 'you see, my boy, that sin and punishment are twins.'

'Oh but, sir, I was just striving so hard to amend, and it seems cruel that I should be checked at once.'

'Let it teach you a life-long lesson, dear Eric;—the lesson that when a sin is committed *we* may have done with *it*, but *it* has by no means done with *us*. It is always so, Eric; when we drink the wine it is red and sparkling, but we come afterwards to the ragged and bitter dregs.'

'But what shall I do, sir?' said Eric sadly.

'There is only one way that I see, Eric. You must write home for the money, and confess the truth to them honestly, as you have to me.'

It was a hard course for Eric's proud and loving heart to write and tell his aunt the full extent of his guilt. But he did it faithfully, extenuating nothing, and entreating her, as she loved him, to send the money by return of post.

It came, and with it a letter full of deep and gentle affection. Mrs. Trevor knew her nephew's character, and did not add by reproaches to the bitterness which she perceived he had endured; she simply sent him the money, and told him, that in spite of his many failures, 'she still had perfect confidence in the true heart of her dear boy.'

Touched by the affection which all seemed to be showing him, it became more and more the passionate craving of Eric's soul to be worthy of that love. But it is far far harder to recover a lost path than to keep in the right one all along; and by one more terrible fall the poor errring boy was to be taught for the last time the fearful strength of temptation, and the only source in earth and heaven from which deliverance can come. Theoretically he knew it, but as yet not practically. Great as his trials had been, and deeply as he had suffered, it was God's will that he should pass through a yet fiercer flame ere he could be purified from pride and passion and self-confidence, and led to the cross of a suffering Saviour, there to fling himself down in heartrending humility, and cast his great load of cares and sins upon Him who cared for him through all his wanderings, and was leading him back through thorny places to the green pastures and still waters, where at last he might have rest.

The money came, and walking off straight to 'The Jolly Herring,' he dashed it down on the table before Billy, and imperiously bade him write a receipt.

The man did so, but with so unmistakable an air of cunning and triumph that Eric was both astonished and dismayed. Could the miscreant have any further plot against him? At first he fancied that Billy might attempt to extort money by a threat of telling

Dr. Rowlands; but this supposition he banished as unlikely, since it might expose Billy himself to very unpleasant consequences.

Eric snatched the receipt, and said contemptuously, 'Never come near me again; next time you come up to the studies I'll tell Carter to turn you out.'

'Ho, ho, ho!' sneered Billy. 'How mighty we young gents are all of a sudden. Unless you buy of me sometimes, you shall hear of me again; never fear, young gen'leman.' He shouted out the latter words, for Eric had turned scornfully on his heel, and was already in the street.

Obviously more danger was to be apprehended from this quarter. At first the thought of it was disquieting, but three weeks glided away, and Eric, now absorbed heart and soul in school work, began to remember it as a mere vague and idle threat.

But one afternoon, to his horror, he again heard Billy's step on the stairs, and again saw the hateful iniquitous face at the door.

'Not much custom from you lately, sir,' said Billy mockingly. 'Anything in my line to-day?'

'Didn't I tell you never to come near me again, you foul villain?' cried Eric, springing up in a flame of wrath. 'Go this instant, or I'll call Carter;' and opening the window, he prepared to put his threat into execution.

'Ho, ho, ho! Better look at summat I've got first.' It was a printed notice to the following effect:—

'FIVE POUNDS REWARD

'WHEREAS some evil-disposed persons stole some pigeons on the evening of April 6th from the Rev. H. Gordon's premises; the above reward will be given for any such information as may lead to the apprehension of the offenders.'

Soon after the seizure of the pigeons there had been a rumour that Gordon had offered a reward of this kind, but the matter had been forgotten, and the boys had long fancied their secret secure, though at first they had been terribly alarmed.

'What do you show me that for?' he asked, reddening and then growing pale again.

Billy's only answer was to pass his finger slowly along the words, 'Five pounds reward!'

'Well?'

'I thinks I knows who took they pigeons.'

'What's that to me?'

'Ho, ho, ho! that's a good un,' was Billy's reply; and he continued to cackle as though enjoying a great joke.

'Unless you gives me five pound, anyhow, I knows where to get 'em. I know who them evil-disposed persons be! So I'll give ye another week to decide.'

Billy shambled off in high spirits; but Eric sank back into his chair. Five pounds! The idea haunted him. How could he ever get them? To write home again was out of the question. The Trevors, though liberal, were not rich, and after just sending him so large a sum, it was impossible, he thought, that they should send him five pounds more at his mere request. Besides, how could he be sure that Billy would not play upon his fears to extort further sums? And to explain the matter to them fully was more than he could endure. He remembered now how easily his want of caution might have put Billy in possession of the secret, and he knew enough of the fellow's character to feel quite sure of the use he would be inclined to make of it. Oh, how he cursed that hour of folly!

Five pounds! He began to think of what money he could procure. He thought again and again, but it was no use; only one thing was clear—he *had* not the money and could not get it. Miserable boy! It was too late then? for him repentance was to be made impossible; every time he attempted it he was to be thwarted by some fresh discovery. And, leaning his head on his open palms, poor Eric sobbed like a child.

Five pounds! And all this misery was to come upon him for the want of five pounds! Expulsion was *certain*, was *inevitable* now, and perhaps for Wildney too as well as for himself. After all his fine promises in his letters home,—yes, that reminded him of Vernon. The grave had not closed for a month over one brother, and the other would be *expelled*. Oh, misery, misery! He was sure it would break his mother's heart. Oh, how cruel everything was to him!

Five pounds! He wondered whether Montagu would lend it him, or any other boy? But then it was late in the quarter, and all the boys would have spent the money they brought with them from home. There was no chance of any one having five pounds, and to a master he *dare* not apply, not even to Mr. Rose. The offence was too serious to be overlooked, and if noticed at all, he fancied that, after his other delinquencies, it *must*, as a matter of notoriety, be visited with expulsion. He could not face that bitter thought; he could not thus bring open disgrace upon his father's and his brother's name; this was the fear which kept recurring to him with dreadful iteration.

Suddenly he remembered that if he had continued captain of the school eleven, he would have had easy command of the money, by being treasurer of the cricket subscriptions. But at Vernon's death he lost all interest in cricket for a time, and had thrown up his office, to which Montagu had been elected by the general suffrage.

He wondered whether there was as much as five pounds of the cricketing money left! He knew that the box which contained it was in Montagu's study, and he also knew where the key was kept. It was merely a feeling of curiosity—he would go and look.

All this passed through Eric's mind as he sat in his study after Billy had gone. It was a sultry summer day; all the study doors were open, and all their occupants were absent in the cricket-field, or bathing. He stole into Montagu's study, hastily got the key, and took down the box.

'Oh, put it down, put it down, Eric,' said Conscience; 'what business have you with it?'

'Pooh! it is merely curiosity; as if I couldn't trust myself!'

'Put it down,' repeated Conscience authoritatively, deigning no longer to argue or entreat.

Eric hesitated, and did put down the box; but he did not instantly leave the room. He began to look at Montagu's books and then out of the window. The gravel playground was deserted, he noticed, for the cricket-field. Nobody was near therefore. Well, what of that? he was doing no harm.

'Nonsense! I *will* just look and see if there's five pounds in the cricket-box.' Slowly at first he put out his hand, and then, hastily turning the key, opened the box. It contained three pounds in gold, and a quantity of silver. He began to count the silver, putting it on the table, and found that it made up three pounds ten more. 'So that, altogether, there's six pounds ten; that's thirty shillings more than——and it won't be wanted till next summer term, because all the bats and balls are bought now. I dare say

Montagu won't even open the box again. I know he keeps it stowed away in a corner, and hardly ever looks at it, and I can put back the five pounds the very first day of next term, and it will save me from expulsion.'

Very slowly Eric took the three sovereigns and put them in his pocket, and then he took up one of the heaps of shillings and sixpences which he had counted, and dropped them also into his trousers; they fell into the pocket with a great jingle. . . .

'Eric, you are a thief!' He thought he heard his brother Vernon's voice utter the words thrillingly distinct, but it was conscience who had borrowed the voice, and, sick with horror, he began to shake the money out of his pockets again into the box. He was only just in time; he had barely locked the box, and put it in its place, when he heard the sound of voices and footsteps on the stairs. He had no time to take out the key and put it back where he found it, and hardly time to slip into his own study again, when the boys had reached the landing.

They were Duncan and Montagu, and as they passed the door, Eric pretended to be plunged in books.

'Hallo, Eric! grinding as usual,' said Duncan good-humouredly; but he only got a sickly smile in reply.

'What! are you the only fellow in the studies?' asked Montagu. 'I was nearly sure I heard some one moving about as we came upstairs.'

'I don't think there's any one here but me,' said Eric, 'and I'm going a walk now.'

He closed his books with a bang, flew down stairs, and away through the playground towards the shore, vaulting with one hand the playground gate. But he could not so escape his thoughts. 'Eric, you are thief! Eric, you are a thief!' rang in his ear. 'Yes,' he thought; 'I am even a thief. Oh, good God, yes, *even a thief,* for I *had* actually stolen the money, until I changed my mind. What if they should have heard the jingle of money, or should discover the key in the box, knowing that I was the only fellow up stairs? Oh, mercy, mercy, mercy!'

It was a lonely place, and he flung himself down and hid his face in the coarse grass, trying to cool the wild burning of his brow. And as he lay he thrust his hand into the guilty pocket! Good heavens there was something still there. He pulled it out; it was a sovereign. Then he was a thief, even actually. Oh, everything was against him; and starting to his feet, he flung the accursed gold over the rocks far into the sea.

When he got home, he felt so inconceivably wretched, that, unable to work, he begged leave to go to bed at once. It was long before he fell asleep; but when he did, the sleep was more terrible than the haunted wakefulness. For he had no rest from tormenting and horrid dreams. Brigson and Billy, their bodies grown to gigantic proportions, and their faces fierce with demoniacal wickedness, seemed to be standing over him, and demanding five pounds on pain of death. Flights of pigeons, darkening the air, settled on him, and flapped about him. He fled from them madly through the dark midnight, but many steps pursued him. He saw Mr. Rose, and running up, seized him by the hand, and implored protection. But in his dream Mr. Rose turned from him with a cold look of sorrowful reproach. And then he saw Wildney, and cried out to him, 'O Charlie, do speak to me!' but Charlie ran away, saying, "*You*, Eric! what? *you* a thief!' and then a chorus of voices took up that awful cry—voices of expostulation, voices of contempt, voices of indignation, voices of menace; they took up the cry, and repeated and re-echoed it; but most unendurable of all, there were voices of wailing and voices of gentleness among them, and his soul died within him as he caught, amid the confusion of condemning sounds, the voices of Russell and Vernon, and they, too, were saying to him, in tender pity and agonised astonishment, 'Eric, Eric, you are a thief!'

CHAPTER THE ELEVENTH

REAPING THE WHIRLWIND

For alas! alas! with me
The light of life is o'er;
No more—no more—no more!
(Such language holds the solemn sea
To the sands upon the shore)
Shall bloom the thunder-blasted tree,
Or the stricken eagle soar!
EDGAR POE

THE LANDLORD OF 'THE JOLLY HERRING' had observed, during his visits to Eric, that at mid-day the studies were usually deserted, and the doors for the most part left unlocked. He very soon determined to make use of this knowledge for his own purposes, and, as he was well acquainted with the building (in which for a short time he had been a servant), he laid his plans without the least dread of discovery.

There was a back entrance into Roslyn School behind the chapel, and it could be reached by a path through the fields without any chance of being seen, if a person set warily to work and watched his opportunity. By this path Billy came, two days after his last visit, and walked straight up the great staircase, armed with the excuse of business with Eric in case any one met or questioned him. But no one was about, since between twelve and one the boys were pretty sure to be amusing themselves out of doors; and after glancing into each of the studies, Billy finally settled on searching Montagu's (which was the neatest and most tastefully furnished), to see what he could get.

The very first thing which caught his experienced eye was the cricket-fund box, with the key temptingly in the lock, just where Eric had left it when the sounds of some one coming had startled him. In a moment Billy had made a descent on the promising looking booty, and opening his treasure, saw, with lively feelings of gratification, the unexpected store of silver and gold. This he instantly transferred to his own pocket, and then replacing the box where he had found it, decamped with the spoil unseen, leaving the study in all other respects exactly as he had found it.

Meanwhile the unhappy Eric was tossed and agitated with apprehension and suspense. Unable to endure his misery in loneliness, he had made several boys to a greater or less degree participators in the knowledge of his difficult position; and in the sympathy which his danger excited, the general nature of his dilemma with Billy (though not its special circumstances) was soon known through the school.

At the very time when the money was being stolen, Eric was sitting with Wildney and Graham under the ruin by the shore, and the sorrow which lay at his heart was sadly visible in the anxious expression of his face, and the deep dejection of his attitude and manner.

The other two were trying to console him. They suggested every possible topic of hope; but it was too plain that there was nothing to be said, and that Eric had real cause to fear the worst. Yet though their arguments were futile, he keenly felt the genuineness of their affection, and it brought a little alleviation to his heavy mood.

'Well, well; at least *do* hope the best, Eric,' said Graham.

'Yes!' urged Wildney; 'only think, dear old fellow, what lots of worse scrapes we've been in before, and how we've always managed to get out of them somehow.'

'No, my boy; not worse scrapes,' answered Eric. 'Depend upon it this is the last for me; I shall not have the chance of getting into another at *Roslyn,* anyhow.'

'Poor Eric! what shall I do if you leave?' said Wildney, laying his arm on Eric's shoulder. 'Besides it's all my fault, hang it, that you got into this cursed row.'

> 'The curse is come upon me, cried
> The Lady of Shalott,

'those words keep ringing in my ears,' murmured Eric.

'Well, Eric, if *you* are sent away, I know I shall get my father to take me too, and then we'll join each other somewhere. Come, cheer up, old boy—being sent isn't such a very frightful thing after all.'

'No,' said Graham; 'and besides the bagging of the pigeons was only a lark, when one comes to think of it. It wasn't like stealing, you know; *that*'d be quite a different thing.'

Eric winced visibly at this remark, but his companions did not notice it. 'Ah,' thought he, 'there's *one* passage of my life which I never shall be able to reveal to any human soul.'

'Come now, Eric,' said Wildney, 'I've got something to propose. You shall play cricket to-day; you haven't played for an age, and it's high time you should. If you don't, you'll go mooning about the shore all day, and that'll never do, for you'll come back glummer than ever.'

'No!' said Eric, with a heavy sigh, as the image of Vernon instantly passed through his mind; 'no more cricket for me.'

'Nay, but you *must* play to-day. Come, you shan't say no. You won't say no to me, will you, dear old fellow?' And Wildney looked up to him with that pleasant smile, and the merry light in his dark eyes, which had always been so charming to Eric's fancy.

'There's no refusing you,' said Eric, with the ghost of a laugh, as he boxed Wildney's ears. 'Oh, you dear little rogue, Charlie, I wish I were you.'

'Pooh! pooh! now you shan't get sentimental again. As if you weren't fifty times better than me every way. I'm sure I don't know how I shall ever thank you enough, Eric,' he added more seriously, 'for all your kindness to me.'

'I'm so glad you're going to play, though,' said Graham; 'and so will everybody be, and I'm certain it'll be good for you. The game will divert your thoughts.'

So that afternoon Eric, for the first time since Verny's death, played with the first eleven, of which he had been captain. The school cheered him vigorously as he appeared again on the field, and the sound lighted up his countenance with some gleam of its old joyousness. When one looked at him that day with his straw hat on and its neat light blue ribbon, and the cricket dress (a pink jersey, and leather belt, with a silver clasp in front), showing off his well-built and graceful figure, one little thought what an agony was gnawing like a serpent at his heart. But that day, poor boy, in the excitement of the game he half forgot it himself, and more and more as the game went on.

The other side, headed by Montagu, went in first, and Eric caught out two and bowled several. Montagu was the only one who stayed in long, and when at last Eric sent his middle wicket flying with a magnificent ball, the shouts of 'Well bowled! well bowled *indeed!*' were universal.

'Just listen to that, Eric,' said Montagu; 'why, you're outdoing everybody to-day, yourself included, and taking us by storm.'

'Wait till you see me come out for a duck,' said Eric, laughing.

'Not you. You're too much in luck to come out with a duck,' answered Montagu. 'You see I've already become the poet of your triumphs, and prophesy in rhyme.'

And now it was Eric's turn to go in. It was long since he had stood before the wicket, but now he was there, looking like a beautiful picture as the sunlight streamed over him, and made his fair hair shine like gold. In the triumph of success his sorrows were flung to the winds, and his blue eyes sparkled with interest and joy.

He contented himself with blocking Duncan's balls until his eye was in; but then, acquiring confidence, he sent them flying right and left. His score rapidly mounted, and there seemed no chance of getting him out, so that there was every probability of his carrying out his bat.

'Oh, *well* hit! *well* hit! A three'r for Eric,' cried Wildney to the scorer; and he began to clap his hands and dance about with excitement at his friend's success.

'Oh, well hit! well hit in—deed!' shouted all the lookers on, as Eric caught the next ball half-volley, and sent it whizzing over the hedge, getting a sixer by the hit.

At the next ball they heard a great crack, and he got no run, for the handle of his bat broke right off.

'How unlucky!' he said, flinging down the handle with vexation. 'I believe this was our best bat.'

'Oh, never mind,' said Montagu; 'we can soon get another; we've got lots of money in the box.'

What had come over Eric? if there had been a sudden breath of poison in the atmosphere he could hardly have been more affected than he was by Montagu's simple remark. Montagu could not help noticing it, but at the time merely attributed it to some unknown gust of feeling, and made no comment. But Eric, hastily borrowing another bat, took his place again quite tamely; he was trembling, and at the very next ball, he spooned a miserable catch into Graham's hand, and the shout of triumph from the other side proclaimed that his innings was over.

He walked dejectedly to the pavilion for his coat, and the boys, who were seated in crowds about it, received him, of course, after his brilliant score, with loud and continued plaudits. But the light had died away from his face and figure, and he never raised his eyes from the ground.

'Modest Eric!' said Wildney chaffingly, 'you don't acknowledge your honours.'

Eric dropped his bat in the corner, put his coat across his arm, and walked away. As he passed Wildney, he stooped down and whispered again in a low voice—

> 'The curse has come upon me, cried
> The Lady of Shalott.'

'Hush, Eric, nonsense,' whispered Wildney; 'you're not going away,' he continued aloud, as Eric turned towards the school. 'Why, there are only two more to go in!'

'Yes, thank you, I must go.'

'Oh, then, I'll come too.'

Wildney at once joined his friend. 'There's nothing more the matter, is there?' he asked anxiously, when they were out of hearing of the rest.

'God only knows.'

'Well, let's change the subject. You've been playing brilliantly, old fellow.'

'Have I?'

'I should just think so, only you got out in rather a stupid way.'

'Ah well! it matters very little.'

Just at this moment one of the servants handed Eric a kind note from Mrs. Rowlands, with whom he was a very great favourite, asking him to tea that night. He was not much surprised, for he had been asked several times lately, and the sweet womanly kindness which she always showed him caused him the greatest pleasure. Besides, she had known his mother.

'Upon my word, honours *are* being showered on you!' said Wildney. 'First to get *the* score of the season at cricket, and bowl out about half the other side, and then go to tea with the head-master. Upon my word! Why, any of us poor wretches would give our two ears for such distinctions. Talk of curse indeed! Fiddlestick-end!'

But Eric's sorrow lay too deep for chaff, and only answering with a sigh he went to dress for tea.

Just before tea-time Duncan and Montagu strolled in together. 'How splendidly Eric played,' said Duncan.

'Yes, indeed. I'm so glad. By the bye, I must see about getting a new bat. I don't know exactly how much money we've got, but I know there's plenty. Let's come and see.'

They entered his study, and he looked about everywhere for the key. 'Hallo,' he said, 'I'm nearly sure I left it in the corner of this drawer, under some other things; but it isn't there now. What can have become of it?'

'Where's the box?' said Duncan; 'let's see if any of my keys will fit it. Hallo! why *you're* a nice treasurer, Monty! here's the key in the box!'

'No, is it though?' asked Montagu, looking serious. 'Here, give it me; I hope nobody's been meddling with it.'

He opened it quickly, and stood in dumb and blank amazement to see it empty.

'Phew-w-w-w!' Montagu gave a long whistle.

'By Jove!' was Duncan's only comment.

The boys looked at each other, but neither dared to express what was in his thoughts.

'A bad, bad business! what's to be done, Monty?'

'I'll rush straight down to tea, and ask the fellows about it. Would you mind requesting Rose not to come in for five minutes? Tell him there's a row.'

He ran down stairs hastily and entered the tea-room, where the boys were talking in high spirits about the match, and liberally praising Eric's play.

'I've got something unpleasant to say,' he announced, raising his voice.

'Hush! hush! hush! what's the row?' asked half a dozen at once.

'The whole of the cricket money, some six pounds at least, has vanished from the box in my study!'

For an instant the whole room was silent; Wildney and Graham interchanged anxious glances.

'Does any fellow know anything about this?'

All, or most, had a vague suspicion, but no one spoke.

'Where is Williams?' asked one of the sixth form casually.

'He's taking tea with the Doctor,' said Wildney.

Mr. Rose came in, and there was no opportunity for more to be said, except in confidential whispers.

Duncan went up with Owen and Montagu to their study. 'What's to be done?' was the general question.

'I think we've all had a lesson once before not to suspect too hastily. Still, in a matter like this,' said Montagu, 'one *must* take notice of apparent cues.'

'I know what you're thinking of, Monty,' said Duncan.

'Well, then, did you hear anything when you and I surprised Eric suddenly two days ago?'

'I heard some one moving about in your study, as I thought.'

'I heard more, though at the time it didn't strike me particularly. I distinctly heard the jingle of money.'

'Well, it's no good counting up suspicious circumstances; we must *ask* him about it and act accordingly.'

'Will he come up to the studies again to-night?'

'I think not,' said Owen; 'I notice he generally goes straight to bed after he has been out to tea; that's to say, directly after prayers.'

The three sat there till prayer-time, taciturn and thoughtful. Their books were open, but they did little work, and it was evident that Montagu was filled with the most touching grief. During the evening he drew out a little likeness which Eric had given him, and looked at it long and earnestly. 'Is it possible?' he thought. 'O Eric, Eric! can that face be the face of a thief?'

The prayer-bell dispelled his reverie. Eric entered with the Rowlandses, and sat in his accustomed place. He had spent a pleasant, quiet evening, and, little knowing what had happened, felt far more cheerful and hopeful than he had done before, although he was still ignorant how to escape the difficulty which threatened him.

He couldn't help observing that as he entered he was the object of general attention; but he attributed it either to his playing that day, or to the circumstances in which he was placed by Billy's treachery, of which he knew that many boys were now aware. But when prayers were over, and he saw that every one shunned him, or looked and spoke in the coldest manner, his most terrible fears revived.

He went off to his dormitory, and began to undress. As he sat half abstracted on his bed doing nothing, Montagu and Duncan entered, and he started to see them, for they were evidently the bearers of some serious intelligence.

'Eric,' said Duncan, 'do you know that some one has stolen all the cricket money?'

'Stolen—what—*all?*' he cried, leaping up as if he had been shot. 'Oh, what new retribution is this?' and he hid his face, which had turned ashy pale, in his hands.

'To cut matters short, Eric, do you know anything about it?'

'If it is all gone, it is not I who stole it,' he said, not lifting his head.

'Do you know anything about it?'

'No!' he sobbed convulsively. 'No, no, no! Yet stop; don't let me add a lie—— Let me think. No, Duncan!' he said, looking up, 'I do *not* know who stole it.'

They stood silent, and the tears were stealing down Montagu's averted face.

'O Duncan, Monty, be merciful, be merciful,' said Eric. 'Don't *yet* condemn me. I am guilty, not of *this*, but of something as bad. I admit I was tempted; but if the money really is all gone, it is *not* I who am the thief.'

'You must know, Eric, that the suspicion against you is very strong, and rests on some definite facts.'

'Yes, I know it must. Yet, oh, do be merciful, and don't yet condemn me. I have denied it. Whatever else I am, am I a liar, Monty? O Monty, Monty, believe me in this!'

But the boys still stood silent.

'Well then,' he said, 'I will tell you all. But I can only tell it to you, Monty. Duncan, indeed, you mustn't be angry; you are my friend, but not so much as Monty. I can tell him, and him only.'

Duncan left the room, and Montagu sat down beside Eric on the bed, and put his arm round him to support him, for he shook violently. There, with deep and wild emotion, and many interruptions of passionate silence, Eric told to Montagu his miserable tale. 'I am the most wretched fellow living,' he said; 'there must be some fiend that hates me, and drives me to ruin. But let it all come: I care nothing, nothing, what happens to me now. Only, dear, dear Monty, forgive me, and love me still.'

'O Eric, it is not for one like me to talk of forgiveness; you were sorely tempted. Yet God will forgive you if you ask Him. Won't you pray to Him to-night? I love you, Eric, still, with all my heart, and do you think God can be less kind than man? And *I*, too, will pray for you, Eric. Good-night, and God bless you.' He gently disengaged himself—for Eric clung to him, and seemed unwilling to lose sight of him—and a moment after he was gone.

Eric felt terribly alone. He knelt down and tried to pray, but somehow it didn't seem as if the prayer came from his heart, and his thoughts began instantly to wander far away. Still he knelt—knelt even until his candle had gone out, and he had nearly fallen asleep, thought-wearied, on his knees. And then he got into bed still dressed. He had been making up his mind that he could bear it no longer, and would run away to sea that night.

He waited till eleven, when Dr. Rowlands took his rounds. The Doctor had been told all the circumstances of suspicion, and they amounted in his mind to certainty. It made him very sad, and he stopped to look at the boy from whom he had parted on such friendly terms so short a time before. Eric did not pretend to be asleep, but opened his eyes, and looked at the head-master. Very sorrowfully Dr. Rowlands shook his head, and went away. Eric never saw him again.

The moment he was gone Eric got up. He meant to go to his study, collect the few presents, which were his dearest mementos of Russell, Wildney, and his other friends—above all, Vernon's likeness—and then make his escape from the building, using for the last time the broken pane and loosened bar in the corridor, with which past temptations had made him so familiar.

He turned the handle of the door and pushed, but it did not yield. Half contemplating the possibility of such an intention on Eric's part, Dr. Rowlands had locked it behind him when he went out.

'Ha!' thought the boy, 'then he too knows and suspects. Never mind. I must give up my treasures—yes, even poor Verny's picture; perhaps it is best I should, for I'm only disgracing his dear memory. But they shan't prevent me from running away.'

Once more he deliberated. Yes, there could be no doubt about the decision. He *could* not endure another public expulsion, or even another birching; he *could* not endure the cold faces of even his best friends. No, no! he *could* not face the horrible phantom of

detection, and exposure, and shame. But worse than all this, he could not endure *himself;* he must fly away from the sense that *he,* Eric Williams, the brother of Vernon, the friend of Edwin Russell, was sunk in all degradation. Could it really, really be, that *he,* once the soul of chivalrous honour, who once would have felt a stain like a wound,—was it possible that he should have been a thief? It was too dreadful a thought. Escape he must.

After using all his strength in long-continued efforts, he succeeded in loosening the bar of his bedroom window. He then took his two sheets, tied them together in a firm knot, wound one end tightly round the remaining bar, and let the other fall down the side of the building. He took one more glance round his little room, and then let himself down by the sheet, hand under hand, until he could drop to the ground. Once safe, he ran towards Starhaven as fast as he could, and felt as if he were flying for his life. But when he got to the end of the playground he could not help stopping to take one more longing, lingering look at the scenes he was leaving for ever. It was a chilly and overclouded night, and by the gleams of struggling moonlight, he saw the whole buildings standing out black in the night air. The past lay behind him like a painting. Many and many unhappy or guilty hours had he spent in that home, and yet those last four years had not gone by without their own wealth of life and joy. He remembered how he had first walked across that playground, hand in hand with his father, a little boy of twelve. He remembered his first troubles with Barker, and how his father had at last delivered him from the annoyances of his old enemy. He remembered how often he and Russell had sat there, looking at the sea, in pleasant talk, especially the evening when he had got his first prize and head-remove in the lower-fourth; and how, on the night of Russell's death, he had gazed over that playground from the sick-room window. He

remembered how often he had got cheered there for his feats at cricket and football, and how often he and Upton, in old days, and he and Wildney afterwards, had walked there on Sundays, arm in arm. Then the stroll to Fort Island, and Barker's plot against him, and the evening at the Stack, passed through his mind; and the dinner at 'The Jolly Herring,' and, above all, Vernon's death. Oh! how awful it seemed to him now, as he looked through the darkness at the very road along which they had brought Verny's dead body. Then his thoughts turned to the theft of the pigeons, his own drunkenness, and then his last cruel, cruel experiences, and this dreadful end of the day which, for an hour or two, had seemed so bright on that very spot where he stood. Could it be that this (oh, how little he had ever dreamed of it)—that this was to be the conclusion of his schooldays?

Yes, in those rooms, of which the windows fronted him, there they lay, all his schoolfellows—Montagu, and Wildney, and Duncan, and all whom he cared for best. And there was Mr. Rose's light still burning in the library window; and he was leaving the school and those who had been with him there so long, in the dark night, by stealth, penniless, and broken-hearted, with the shameful character of a thief.

Suddenly Mr. Rose's light moved, and fearing discovery or interception, he roused himself from the bitter reverie and fled to Starhaven through the darkness. There was still a light in the little sailors' tavern, and entering, he asked the woman who kept it, 'if she knew of any ship which was going to sail next morning?'

'Why, your'n is, bean't it, Maister Davey?' she asked, turning to a rough-looking sailor who sat smoking in the bar.

'Ees,' grunted the man.

'Will you take me on board?' said Eric.

'You be a runaway, I'm thinking?'

'Never mind. I'll come as cabin-boy—anything.'

The sailor glanced at his striking appearance and neat dress. 'Hardly in the cabun-buoy line, I should say.'

'Will you take me?' said Eric. 'You'll find me strong and willing enough.'

'Well—if the skipper don't say no. Come along.'

They went down to a boat, and 'Maister Davey' rowed to a schooner in the harbour, and took Eric on board.

'There,' he said, 'you may sleep there for tonight,' and he pointed to a great heap of sailcloth beside the mast.

Weary to death, Eric flung himself down, and slept deep and sound till the morning, on board the *Stormy Petrel.*

CHAPTER THE TWELFTH

THE 'STORMY PETREL'

They hadna sailed a league, a league,
  A league but barely three,
When the lift grew dark, and the wind grew high,
And gurly grew the sea.
  SIR PATRICK SPENS

'HILLOA!' exclaimed the skipper with a sudden start, next morning, as he saw Eric's recumbent figure on the ratlin stuff, 'who be this young varmint?'

'Oh, I brought him aboord last night,' said Davey; 'he wanted to be cabun-boy.'

'Precious like un *he* looks. Never mind, we've got him and we'll use him.'

The vessel was under way when Eric woke and collected his scattered thoughts to a remembrance of his new position. At first, as the *Stormy Petrel* dashed its way gallantly through the blue sea, he felt one absorbing sense of joy to have escaped from Roslyn. But before he had been three hours on board, his eyes were opened to the trying nature of his circumstances, which were, indeed, *so* trying that *anything* in the world seemed preferable to enduring them. He had escaped from Roslyn, but, alas! he had not escaped from himself. He had hardly been three hours on board when he would have given everything in his power to be back again; but such regrets were useless, for the vessel was now fairly on her way for Corunna, where she was to take in a cargo of cattle.

There were eight men belonging to the crew; and as the ship was only a little trading schooner, these were sailors of the lowest and coarsest grade. They all seemed to take their cue from the captain, who was a drunken, blaspheming, and cruel vagabond.

This man from the first took a savage hatred to Eric, partly because he was annoyed with Davey for bringing him on board. The first words he addressed to him were—

'I say, you young lubber, you must pay your footing.'

'I've got nothing to pay with. I brought no money with me.'

'Well, then, you shall give us your gran' clothes. Them things isn't fit for a cabin-boy.'

Eric saw no remedy, and making a virtue of necessity, exchanged his good cloth suit for a rough sailor's shirt and trousers, not over clean, which the captain gave him. His own clothes were at once appropriated by that functionary, who carried them into his cabin. But it was lucky for Eric that, seeing how matters were likely to go, he had succeeded in secreting his watch.

The day grew misty and comfortless, and towards evening the wind rose to a storm. Eric soon began to feel very sick, and, to make his case worse, could not endure either the taste, smell, or sight of such coarse food as was contemptuously flung to him.

'Where am I to sleep?' he asked, 'I feel very sick.'

'Babby,' said one of the sailors, 'what's your name?'

'Williams.'

'Well, Bill, you'll have to get over yer sickness pretty soon, *I* can tell ye. Here,' he added, relenting a little, 'Davey's slung ye a hammock in the forecastle.'

He showed the way, but poor Eric in the dark, and amid the lurches of the vessel, could hardly steady himself down the companion-ladder, much less get into his hammock. The man saw his condition, and, sulkily enough, hove him into his place.

And there, in that swinging bed, where sleep seemed impossible, and in which he was unpleasantly shaken about, when the ship rolled and pitched through the dark, heaving, discoloured waves, and with dirty men sleeping round him at night, until the atmosphere of the forecastle became like poison, hopelessly and helplessly sick, and half-starved, the boy lay for two days. The crew neglected him shamefully. It was nobody's business to wait on him, and he could procure neither sufficient food nor any water; they only brought him some grog to drink, which in his weakness and sickness was nauseous to him as medicine.

'I say, you young cub down there,' shouted the skipper to him from the hatchway, 'come up and swab this deck.'

He got up, and after bruising himself severely, as he stumbled about to find the ladder, made an effort to obey the command. But he staggered from feebleness when he reached the deck, and had to grasp for some fresh support at every step.

'None of that 'ere slobbering and shamming, Bill. Why, d—— you, what d'ye think you're here for, eh? You swab this deck, and in five minutes, or I'll teach you, and be d——d.'

Sick as death, Eric slowly obeyed, but did not get through his task without many blows and curses. He felt very ill—he had no means of washing or cleaning himself; no brush, or comb or soap, or clean linen; and even his sleep seemed unrefreshful when the waking brought no change in his condition. And then the whole life of the ship was odious to him. His sense of refinement was exquisitely keen, and now to be called Bill, and kicked and cuffed about by these gross-minded men, and to hear their rough, coarse, drunken talk, and sometimes endure their still more intolerable patronage, filled him with deeply-seated loathing. His whole soul rebelled and revolted from them all, and, seeing his fastidious pride, not one of them showed him the least glimpse of open kindness, though he observed that one of them did seem to pity him in heart.

Things grew worse and worse. The perils which he had to endure at first, when ordered about the rigging, were what affected him least; he longed for death, and often contemplated flinging himself into those cold deep waves which he gazed on daily over the vessel's side. Hope was the only thing which supported him. He had heard from one of the crew that the vessel would be back in not more than six weeks, and he made a deeply-seated resolve to escape the very first day that they again anchored in an English harbour.

The homeward voyage was even more intolerable, for the cattle on board greatly increased the amount of necessary menial and disgusting work which fell to his share, as well as made the atmosphere of the close little schooner twice as poisonous as before. And to add to his miseries, his relations with the crew got more and more unfavourable, and began to reach their climax.

One night the sailor who occupied the hammock next to his heard him winding up his watch. This he always did in the dark, as secretly and silently as he could, and never looked at it, except when no one could observe him; while, during the day, he kept both watch and chain concealed in his trousers.

Next morning the man made proposals to him to sell the watch, and tried by every species of threat and promise to extort it from him. But the watch had been his mother's gift, and he was resolute never to part with it into such hands.

'Very well, you young shaver, I shall tell the skipper, and he'll soon get it out of you as your footing, depend on it.'

The fellow was as good as his word, and the skipper demanded the watch as pay for Eric's feed, for he maintained that he'd done no work, and was perfectly useless. Eric, grown desperate, still refused, and the man struck him brutally on the face, and at the same time aimed a kick at him, which he vainly tried to avoid. It caught him on the knee-cap, and put it out, causing him the most excruciating agony.

He now could do no work whatever, not even swab the deck. It was only with difficulty that he could limp along, and every move caused him violent pain. He grew listless and dejected, and sat all day on the vessel's side, eagerly straining his eyes to catch any sight of land, or gazing vacantly into the weary sameness of sea and sky.

Once, when it was rather gusty weather, all hands were wanted, and the skipper ordered him to furl a sail.

'I can't,' said Eric, in an accent of despair, barely stirring, and not lifting his eyes to the man's unfeeling face.

'Can't, d—— you! Can't! We'll soon see whether you can or no! You do it, or *I* shall have to mend your leg for you;' and he showered down a storm of oaths.

Eric rose, and resolutely tried to mount the rigging, determined at least to give no ground he could help to their wilful cruelty. But the effort was vain, and with a sharp cry of suffering he dropped once more on deck.

'Cursed young brat! I suppose you think we're going to bother ourselves with you, and yer impudence, and get victuals for nothing. It's all sham. Here, Jim, tie him up.'

A stout sailor seized the unresisting boy, tied his hands together, and then drew them up above his head, and strung them to the rigging.

'Why didn't ye strip him first, d—— you?' roared the skipper.

'He's only got that blue shirt on, and that's soon mended,' said the man, taking hold of the collar of the shirt on both sides, and tearing it open with a great rip.

Eric's white back was bare, his hands tied up, his head hanging, and his injured leg slightly lifted from the ground. 'And now for some rope-pie for the stubborn young lubber,' said the skipper, lifting a bit of rope as he spoke.

Eric, with a shudder, heard it whistle through the air, and the next instant it had descended on his back with a dull thump, rasping away a red line of flesh. Now Eric knew for the first time the awful reality of intense pain; he had determined to utter no sound, to give no sign; but when the horrible rope fell on him, griding across his back, and making his body literally creak under the blow, he quivered like an aspen-leaf in every limb, and could not suppress the harrowing murmur, 'O God, help me, help me.'

Again the rope whistled in the air, again it grided across the boy's naked back, and once more the crimson furrow bore witness to the violent laceration. A sharp shriek of inexpressible agony rang from his lips, so shrill, so heartrending, that it sounded long in the memory of all who heard it. But the brute who administered the torture was untouched. Once more, and again, the rope rose and fell, and under its marks the blood first dribbled, and then streamed from the white and tender skin.

But Eric felt no more; that scream had been the last effort of nature; his head had dropped on his bosom, and though his limbs still seemed to creep at the unnatural infliction, he had fainted away.

'Stop, master, stop, if you don't want to kill the boy outright,' said Roberts, one of the crew, stepping forward, while the hot flush of indignation burned through his tanned and weather-beaten cheek. The sailors called him 'Softy Bob,' from that half-gentleness of disposition which had made him, alone of all the men, speak one kind or consoling word for the proud and lonely cabin-boy.

'Undo him then, and be ——,' growled the skipper, and rolled off to drink himself drunk.

'I doubt he's wellnigh done for him already,' said Roberts, quickly untying Eric's hands, round which the cords had been pulled so tight as to leave two blue rings round his wrists. 'Poor fellow, poor fellow! it's all over now,' he murmured soothingly, as the boy's body fell motionless into his arms, which he hastily stretched to prevent him from tumbling on the deck.

But Eric heard not; and the man, touched with the deepest pity, carried him down tenderly into his hammock, and wrapped him up in a clean blanket, and sat by him till the swoon should be over.

It lasted very long, and the sailor began to fear that his words had been prophetic.

'How is the young varmint?' shouted the skipper, looking into the forecastle.

'You've killed him, I think.'

The only answer was a volley of oaths; but the fellow was sufficiently frightened to order Roberts to do all he could for his patient.

At last Eric woke with a moan. To think was too painful, but the raw state of his back, ulcerated with the cruelty he had undergone, reminded him too bitterly of his situation. Roberts did for him all that could be done, but for a week Eric lay in that dark and fœtid place, in the languishing of absolute despair. Often and often the unbidden tears flowed from very weakness from his eyes, and in the sickness of his heart, and the torment of his wounded body, he thought that he should die.

But youth is very strong, and it wrestled with despair, and agony, and death, and after a time, Eric could rise from his comfortless hammock. The news that land was in sight first roused him, and with the help of Roberts, he was carried on deck, thankful, with childlike gratitude, that God suffered him to breathe once more the pure air of heaven, and sit under the canopy of its gold-pervaded blue. The breeze and the sunlight refreshed him, as they might a broken flower; and, with eyes upraised, he poured from his heart a prayer of deep unspeakable thankfulness to a Father in heaven.

Yes! at last he had remembered his Father's home. There, in the dark berth, where every move caused irritation, and the unclean atmosphere brooded over his senses like lead, when his forehead burned, and his heart melted within him, and he had felt almost inclined to curse his life, or even to end it by crawling up and committing himself to the deep cold water which he heard rippling on the vessel's side; then, even then, in that valley of the shadow of death, a Voice had come to him—a still small voice—at whose holy and healing utterance Eric had bowed his head, and had listened to the messages of God, and learned His will; and now, in humble resignation, in touching penitence, with solemn self-devotion, he had cast himself at the feet of Jesus, and prayed to be helped, and guided, and forgiven. One little star of hope rose in the darkness of his solitude, and its rays grew brighter and brighter, till they were glorious now. Yes, for Jesus' sake he was washed, he was cleansed, he was sanctified, he was justified; he would fear no evil, for God was with him, and underneath were the everlasting arms.

And while he sat there, undisturbed at last, and unmolested by harsh word or savage blow, recovering health with every breath of the sea wind, the skipper came up to him, and muttered something half like an apology.

The sight of him, and the sound of his voice, made Eric shudder again, but he listened meekly, and, with no flash of scorn or horror, put out his hand to the man to shake. There was something touching and noble in the gesture, and thoroughly ashamed of himself for once, the fellow shook the proffered hand, and slunk away.

They entered the broad river at Southpool.

'I must leave the ship when we get to port, Roberts,' said Eric.

'I doubt whether yon'll let you,' answered Roberts, jerking his finger towards the skipper's cabin.

'Why?'

'He'll be afeared you might take the law on him.'

'He needn't fear.'

Roberts only shook his head.

'Then I must run away somehow. Will you help me?'

'Yes, that I will.'

That very evening Eric escaped from the *Stormy Petrel,* unknown to all but Roberts. They were in the dock, and he dropped into the water in the evening, and swam to the

pier, which was only a yard or two distant; but the effort almost exhausted his strength, for his knee was still painful, and he was very weak.

Wet and penniless, he knew not where to go, but spent the sleepless night under an arch. Early the next morning he went to a pawnbroker's, and raised £2:10s. on his watch, with which money he walked straight to the railway station.

It was July, and the Roslyn summer holidays had commenced. As Eric dragged his slow way to the station, he suddenly saw Wildney on the other side of the street. His first impulse was to spring to meet him, as he would have done in old times. His whole heart yearned towards him. It was six weeks now since Eric had seen one loving face, and during all that time he had hardly heard one kindly word. And now he saw before him the boy with whom he had spent so many happy hours of schoolboy friendship, with whom he had gone through so many schoolboy adventures, and who, he believed, was still his friend.

Forgetful for the moment of his condition, Eric moved across the street. Wildney was walking with his cousin, a beautiful girl, some four years older than himself, whom he was evidently patronising immensely. They were talking very merrily, and Eric over-heard the word Roslyn. Like a lightning-flash the memory of the theft, the memory of his ruin, came upon him; he looked down at his dress—it was a coarse blue shirt, which Roberts had given him in place of his old one, and the back of it was stained and saturated with blood from his unhealed wounds; his trousers were dirty, tarred, and ragged, and his shoes, full of holes, barely covered his feet. He remembered too that for weeks he had not been able to wash, and that very morning, as he saw himself in a looking-glass at a shop window, he had been deeply shocked at his own appearance. His face was white as a sheet, the fair hair matted and tangled, the eyes sunken and surrounded with a dark colour, and dead and lustreless. No! he could not meet Wildney as a sick and ragged sailor boy; perhaps even he might not be recognised if he did. He drew back, and hid himself till the merry-hearted pair had passed, and it was almost with a pang of jealousy that he saw how happy Wildney could be while *he* was thus; but he cast aside the unworthy thought at once. 'After all, how is poor Charlie to know what has happened to me?'

CHAPTER THE THIRTEENTH

HOME AT LAST

I will arise and go to my Father.

Ach! ein Schicksal droht,
Und es droht nicht lange!
Auf der holden Wange
Brennt ein böses Roth!

TIEDGE

ERIC WILLIAMS pursued his disconsolate way to the station, and found that his money only just sufficed to get him something to eat during the day, and carry him third class by the parliamentary train to Charlesbury, the little station where he had to take the branch line to Ayrton.

He got into the carriage, and sat in the far corner, hiding himself from notice as well as he could. The weary train—(it carried poor people for the most part, so, of course, it could matter but little how tedious or slow it was!)—the weary train, stopping at every station, and often waiting on the rail until it had been passed by trains that started four or five hours after it,—dragged its slow course through the fair counties of England. Many people got in and out of the carriage, which was generally full, and some of them tried occasionally to enter into conversation with him. But poor Eric was too sick and tired, and his heart was too full to talk much, and he contented himself with civil answers to the questions put to him, dropping the conversation as soon as he could.

At six in the evening the train stopped at Charlesbury, and he got down.

'Ticket,' said the station-man.

Eric gave it, turning his head away, for the man knew him well from having often seen him there. It was of no use; the man looked hard at him, and then, opening his eyes wide, exclaimed—

'Well, I never! what, Master Williams of Fairholm, can that be you?'

'Hush, John, hush! yes, I am Eric Williams. But don't say a word, that's a good fellow; I'm going on to Ayrton this evening.'

'Well, sir, I *am* hurt like to see you looking so ragged and poorly. Let me give you a bed to-night, and send you on by first train to-morrow.'

'Oh no, thank you, John, I've got no money, and——'

'Tut, tut, sir; I thought you'd know me better nor that. Proud I'd be any day to do anything for Mrs. Trevor's nephew, let alone a young gentleman like you. Well, then, let me drive you, sir, in my little cart this evening.'

'No, thank you, John, never mind; you are very, very good, but,' he said, and the tears were in his eyes, 'I want to walk in alone to-night.'

'Well, God keep and bless you, sir,' said the man, 'for you look to need it;' and touching his cap he watched the boy's painful walk across some fields to the main road.

'Who'd ha' thought it, Jenny!' he said to his wife. 'There's that young Master Williams, whom we've always thought so noble like, just been here as ragged as ragged, and with a face the colour o' my white signal flag.'

'Lawks!' said the woman; 'well, well! poor young gentleman, I'm afeard he's been doing something bad.'

Balmily and beautiful the evening fell, as Eric, not without toil, made his way along the road towards Ayrton, which was ten miles off. The road wound through the valley, across the low hills that encircled it, sometimes spanning or running parallel to the bright stream that had been the delight of Eric's innocent childhood. There was something enjoyable at first to the poor boy's eyes, so long accustomed to the barren sea, in resting once more on the soft undulating green of the summer fields, which were intertissued with white and yellow flowers, like a broidery of pearls and gold. The whole scene was bathed in the exquisite light, and rich with the delicate perfumes of a glorious evening, which filled the sky over his head with every perfect gradation of rose and amber and amethyst, and breathed over the quiet landscape a sensation of unbroken peace. But peace did not remain long in Eric's heart; each well-remembered landmark filled his soul with recollections of the days when he had returned from school, oh! how differently; and of the last time when he had come home with Vernon by his side. 'O Verny, Verny, dear little Verny, would to God that I were with you now! But you are resting, Verny, in the green grave by Russell's side, and I—O God, be merciful to me now!'

It was evening, and the stars came out and shone by hundreds, and Eric walked on by the moonlight. But the exertion had brought on the pain in his knee, and he had to sit down a long time by the roadside to rest. He reached Ayrton at ten o'clock, but even then he could not summon up courage to pass through the town where he was so well known, lest any straggler should recognise him,—and he took a detour in order to get to Fairholm. He did not arrive there till eleven o'clock; and then he could not venture into the grounds, for he saw through the trees of the shrubbery that there was no light in any of the windows, and it was clear that they were all gone to bed.

What was he to do? He durst not disturb them so late at night. He remembered that they would not have heard a syllable of or from him since he had run away from Roslyn, and he feared the effect of so sudden an emotion as his appearance at that hour might excite.

So, under the starlight he lay down to sleep on a cold bank beside the gate, determining to enter early in the morning. It was long before he slept, but at last weary nature demanded her privilege with importunity, and gentle sleep floated over him like a dark dewy cloud, and the sun was high in heaven before he woke.

It was about half-past nine in the morning, and Mrs. Trevor, with Fanny, was starting to visit some of her poor neighbours, an occupation full of holy pleasure to her kind heart, and in which she had found more than usual consolation during the heavy trials which she had recently suffered; for she had loved Eric and Vernon as a mother does her own children, and now Vernon, the little cherished jewel of her heart, was dead— Vernon was dead, and Eric, she feared not dead but worse than dead, guilty, stained, dishonoured. Often had she thought to herself, in deep anguish of heart, 'Our darling little Vernon dead—and Eric fallen and ruined!'

'Look at that poor fellow asleep on the grass,' said Fanny, pointing to a sailor boy, who lay coiled up on the bank beside the gate. 'He has had a rough bed, mother, if he has spent the night there, as I fear.'

Mrs. Trevor had grasped her arm. 'What is Flo doing?' she said, stopping, as the pretty little spaniel trotted up to the boy's reclining figure, and began snuffing about it, and then broke into a quick short bark of pleasure, and fawned and frisked about him, and leapt upon him, joyously wagging his tail.

The boy rose with the dew wet from the flowers upon his hair;—he saw the dog, and at once began playfully to fondle it, and hold its little silken head between his hands; but as yet he had not caught sight of the Trevors.

'It is—O good heavens! it is Eric,' cried Mrs. Trevor, as she flew towards him. Another moment and he was in her arms, silent, speechless, with long arrears of pent-up emotion.

'Oh, my Eric, our poor, lost, wandering Eric—come home; you are forgiven, more than forgiven, my own darling boy. Yes, I knew that my prayers would be answered; this is as though we received you from the dead.' And the noble lady wept upon his neck, and Eric, his heart shaken with accumulated feelings, clung to her and wept.

Deeply did that loving household rejoice to receive back their lost child. At once they procured him a proper dress and a warm bath, and tended him with every gentle office of female ministering hands. And in the evening, when he told them his story in a broken voice of penitence and remorse, their love came to him like a sweet balsam, and he rested by them, 'seated, and clothed, and in his right mind.'

The pretty little room, fragrant with sweet flowers from the greenhouse, was decorated with all the refinement of womanly taste, and its glass doors opened on the pleasant garden. It was long, long since Eric had seen anything like it, and he had never hoped to see it again. 'Oh, dearest aunty,' he murmured, as he rested his weary head upon her lap, while he sat on a low stool at her feet, 'O aunty, you will never know how different this is from the foul horrible hold of the *Stormy Petrel,* and its detestable inmates.'

When Eric was dressed once more as a gentleman, and once more fed on nourishing and wholesome food, and was able to move once more about the garden by Fanny's side, he began to recover his old appearance, and the soft bloom came back to his cheek again, and the light to his blue eye. But still his health gave most serious cause for apprehension; weeks of semi-starvation, bad air, sickness, and neglect, followed by two nights of exposure and wet, had at last undermined the remarkable strength of his constitution, and the Trevors soon became aware of the painful fact that he was sinking to the grave, and had come home only to die.

Above all, there seemed to be some great load at his heart which he could not remove; a sense of shame, the memory of his disgrace at Roslyn, and of the dark suspicion that rested on his name. He avoided the subject, and they were too kind to force it on him, especially as he had taken away the bitterest part of their trial in remembering it, by explaining to them that he was far from being so wicked in the matter of the theft as they had at first been (how slowly and reluctantly!) almost forced to believe.

'Have you ever heard—oh, how shall I put it?—have you ever heard, aunty, how things went on at Roslyn after I ran away?' he asked one evening, with evident effort.

'No, love, I have not. After they had sent home your things, I heard no more; only two most kind and excellent letters—one from Dr. Rowlands, and one from your friend Mr. Rose—informed me of what had happened about you.'

'Oh, have they sent home my things?' he asked eagerly. 'There are very few among them that I care about; but there is just one——'

'I guessed it, my Eric, and, but that I feared to agitate you, should have given it you before;' and she drew out of a drawer the little likeness of Vernon's sweet childish face.

Eric gazed at it till the sobs shook him, and tears blinded his eyes.

'Do not weep, my boy,' said Mrs. Trevor, kissing his forehead. 'Dear little Verny, remember, is in a land where God Himself wipes away all tears from all eyes.'

'Is there anything else you would like?' asked Fanny, to divert his painful thoughts. 'I will get you anything in a moment.'

'Yes, Fanny dear, there is the medal I got for saving Russell's life, and one or two things which he gave me;—ah, poor Edwin, you never knew him!'

He told her what to fetch, and when she brought them it seemed to give him great pleasure to recall his friends to mind by name, and speak of them—especially of Montagu and Wildney.

'I have a plan to please you, Eric,' said Mrs. Trevor. 'Shall I ask Montagu and Wildney here? we have plenty of room for them.'

'Oh, thank you,' he said, with the utmost eagerness. 'Thank you, dearest aunt.' Then suddenly his countenance fell. 'Stop—shall we?—yes, yes, I am going to die soon, I know; let me see them before I die.'

The Trevors did not know that he was aware of the precarious tenure of his life, but they listened to him in silence, and did not contradict him; and Mrs. Trevor wrote to both the boys (whose directions Eric knew), telling them what had happened, and begging them, simply for his sake, to come and stay with her for a time. She hinted clearly that it might be the last opportunity they would ever have of seeing him.

Wildney and Montagu accepted the invitation; and they arrived together at Fairholm on one of the early autumn evenings. They both greeted Eric with the utmost affection; and he seemed never tired of pressing their hands, and looking at them again. Yet every now and then a memory of sadness would pass over his face, like a dark ripple on the clear surface of a lake.

'Tell me, Monty,' he said one evening, 'all about what happened after I left Roslyn.'

'Gladly, Eric; now that your name is cleared, there is——'

'My name cleared!' said Eric, leaning forward eagerly. 'Did you say that?'

'Yes, Eric. Didn't you know, then, that the thief had been discovered?'

'No,' he murmured faintly, leaning back again; 'oh, thank God, thank God! Do tell me all about it, Monty.'

'Well, Eric, I will tell you all from the beginning. You may guess how utterly astonished we were in the morning, when we heard that you had run away. Wildney here was the first to discover it, for he went early to your bedroom——'

'Dear little Sunbeam,' interrupted Eric, resting his hand against Wildney's cheek; but Wildney shook his fist at him when he heard the forbidden name.

'He found the door locked,' continued Montagu, 'and called to you, but there came no answer; this made us suspect the truth, and we were certain of it when some one caught sight of the sheet hanging from your window. The masters soon heard the report, and sent Carter to make inquiries, but they did not succeed in discovering anything definite about you. Then, of course, everybody assumed as a certainty that you were guilty, and I fear that my bare assertion on the other side had little weight.'

Eric's eyes glistened as he drank in his friend's story.

'But, about a fortnight after, *more* money and several other articles disappeared from the studies, and all suspicion as to the perpetrator was baffled; only now the boys began to admit that, after all, they had been premature in condemning you. It was a miserable time; for every one was full of distrust, and the more nervous boys were always afraid

lest any one should on some slight grounds suspect *them*. *Still* things kept disappearing.

'We found out at length that the time when the robberies were effected must be between twelve and one, and it was secretly agreed that some one should be concealed in the studies for a day or two during those hours. Carter undertook the office, and was ensconced in one of the big cupboards in a study which had not yet been touched. On the third day he heard some one stealthily mount the stairs. The fellows were more careful now, and used to keep their doors shut, but the person was provided with keys, and opened the study in which Carter was. He moved about for a little time—Carter watching him through the key-hole, and prepared to spring on him before he could make his escape. Not getting much, the man at last opened the cupboard door, where Carter had just time to conceal himself behind a greatcoat. The greatcoat took the plunderer's fancy; he took it down off the peg, and—there stood Carter before him! Billy—for it was he—stood absolutely confounded, as though a ghost had suddenly appeared; and Carter, after enjoying his unconcealed terror, collared him, and hauled him off to the police station. He was tried soon after, and finally confessed that it was he who had taken the cricket-money too; for which offences he was sentenced to transportation. So, Eric, dear Eric, at last your name was cleared.'

'As I always knew it would be, dear old boy,' said Wildney.

Montagu and Wildney found plenty to make them happy at Fairholm, and were never tired of Eric's society, and of his stories about all that befell him on board the *Stormy Petrel*. They perceived a marvellous change in him. Every trace of recklessness and arrogance had passed away; every stain of passion had been removed; every particle of hardness had been calcined in the flame of trial. All was gentleness, love, and dependence, in the once bright, impetuous, self-willed boy; it seemed as though the lightning of God's anger had shattered and swept away all that was evil in his heart and life, and left all his true excellence, all the royal prerogatives of his character, pure and unscathed. Eric, even in his worst days, was, as I well remember, a lovable and noble boy; but at this period there must have been something about him for which to thank God, something unspeakably winning and irresistibly attractive. During the day, as Eric was too weak to walk with them, Montagu and Wildney used to take boating and fishing excursions by themselves, but in the evening the whole party would sit out reading and talking in the garden till twilight fell. The two visitors began to hope that Mrs. Trevor had been mistaken, and that Eric's health would still recover; but Mrs. Trevor would not deceive herself with a vain hope, and the boy himself shook his head when they called him convalescent.

Their hopes were never higher than one evening about a week after their arrival, when they were all seated, as usual, in the open air, under a lime-tree on the lawn. The sun was beginning to set, and the rain of golden sunlight fell over them through the green ambrosial foliage of the tree, whose pale blossoms were still murmurous with bees. Eric was leaning back in an easy chair, with Wildney sitting on the grass beside his feet, while Montagu, resting on one of the mossy roots, read to them the *Midsummer Night's Dream,* and the ladies were busy with their work.

'There—stop now,' said Eric, 'and let's sit out and talk until we see some of "the fiery a'es and o'es of light" which he talks of.'

'I'd no idea Shakespeare was such immensely jolly reading,' remarked Wildney naïvely. 'I shall take to reading him through when I get home.'

'Do you remember, Eric,' said Montagu, 'how Rose used to chaff us in old days for our ignorance of literature, and how indignant we used to be when he asked if we'd ever heard of an obscure person called William Shakespeare?'

'Yes, very well,' answered Eric, laughing heartily. And in this strain they continued to chat merrily, while the ladies enjoyed listening to their schoolboy mirth.

'What a perfectly delicious evening. It's almost enough to make me wish to live,' said Eric.

He did not often speak thus; and it made them sad. But Eric half sang, half murmured to himself, a hymn with which his mother's sweet voice had made him familiar in their cottage-home at Ellan—

> 'There is a calm for those who weep,
>   A rest for weary pilgrims found;
> They softly lie, and sweetly sleep,
>   Low in the ground.

> 'The storm that wrecks the winter sky,
>   No more disturbs their deep repose,
> Than summer evening's latest sigh
>   That shuts the rose.'

The last two lines lingered pleasantly in his fancy, and he murmured to himself again in low tones—

> 'Than summer evening's latest sigh
>   That shuts the rose.'

'Oh, hush, hush, Eric!' said Wildney, laying his hand upon his friend's lips; 'don't let's spoil to-night by forebodings.'

It seemed, indeed, a shame to do so, for it was almost an awful thing to be breathing the splendour of the transparent air, as the sun broadened and fell, and a faint violet glow floated over soft meadow and silver stream. One might have fancied that the last rays of sunshine loved to linger over Eric's face, now flushed with a hectic tinge of pleasure, and to light up sudden glories in his bright hair, which the wind just fanned off his forehead as he leaned back and inhaled the luxury of evening perfume, which the flowers of the garden poured on the gentle breeze. Ah, how sad that such scenes should be so rare and so short-lived!

'Hark—tirra-la-lirra-lirra!' said Wildney, 'there goes the postman's horn! Shall I run and get the letter-bag as he passes the gate?'

'Yes, do,' they all cried; and the boy bounded off full of fun, greeting the postman with such a burst of merry apostrophe, that the man shook with laughing at him.

'Here it is at last,' said Wildney. 'Now, then, for the key. Here's a letter for me, hurrah!—two for you, Miss Trevor—*what* people you young ladies are for writing to each other! None for you, Monty—oh yes! I'm wrong, here's one; but none for Eric.'

'I expected none,' said Eric, sighing; but his eye was fixed earnestly on one of Mrs. Trevor's letters. He saw that it was from India, and directed in his father's hand.

Mrs. Trevor caught his look. 'Shall I read it aloud to you, dear? Do you think you can stand it? Remember it will be in answer to ours, telling them of——'

'Oh yes, yes,' he said eagerly, 'do let me hear it.'

With instinctive delicacy Montagu and Wildney rose, but Eric pressed them to stay. 'It will help me to bear what mother says, if I see you by me,' he pleaded.

God forbid that I should transcribe that letter. It was written from the depths of such sorrow as He only can fully sympathise with, who for thirty years pitched his tent in the valley of human misery. By the former mail Mrs. Williams had heard of Verny's melancholy death; by the next she had been told that her only other child, Eric, was not dead indeed, but a wandering outcast, marked with the brand of terrible suspicion. Let her agony be sacred; it was God who sent it, and He only enabled her to endure it. With bent head, and streaming eyes, and a breast that heaved involuntarily with fitful sobs, Eric listened as though to his mother's voice, and only now and then he murmured low to himself, 'O mother, mother, mother—but I am forgiven now. O mother, God and man have forgiven me, and we shall be at peace again once more.'

Mrs. Trevor's eyes grew too dim with weeping to read it all, and Fanny finished it. 'Here is a little note from your father, Eric, which dropped out when we opened dear aunt's letter. Shall I read it too?'

'Perhaps not now, love,' said Mrs. Trevor. 'Poor Eric is too tired and excited already.'

'Well, then, let me glance at it myself, aunty,' he said. He opened it, read a line or two, and then, with a scream, fell back swooning, while it dropped out of his hands.

Terrified, they picked up the fallen paper; it told briefly, in a few heartrending words, that, after writing the letter, Mrs. Williams had been taken ill; that her life was absolutely despaired of, and that before the letter reached England, she would, in all human probability, be dead. It conveyed the impression of a soul resigned indeed, and humble, but crushed down to the very earth with the load of mysterious bereavement and irretrievable sorrow.

'Oh, I have killed her, I have killed my mother!' said Eric, in a hollow voice, when he came to himself. 'O God, forgive me, forgive me!'

They gathered round him; they soothed, and comforted, and prayed for him; but his soul refused comfort, and all his strength appeared to have been broken down at once like a feeble reed. At last a momentary energy returned; his eyes were lifted to the gloaming heaven where a few stars had already begun to shine, and a bright look illuminated his countenance. They listened deeply—'Yes, mother,' he murmured, in broken tones, 'forgiven now, for Christ's dear sake. Oh, Thou merciful God! Yes, there they are, and we shall meet again. Verny—oh, happy, happy at last—too happy!'

The sounds died away, and his head fell back; for a transient moment more the smile and the brightness played over his fair features like a lambent flame. It passed away, and Eric was with those he dearliest loved, in the land where there is no more curse.

'Yes, dearest Eric, forgiven and happy now,' sobbed Mrs. Trevor; and her tears fell fast upon the dead boy's face, as she pressed upon it a long, last kiss.

But Montagu, as he consoled the poignancy of Wildney's grief, was reminded by Mrs. Trevor's words of that sweet German verse—

Doch sonst an keinem Orte
Wohnt die ersehnte Ruh',
Nur durch die dunkle Pforte
Geht man der Heimat zu.

CHAPTER THE FOURTEENTH

CONCLUSION

And hath that early hope been blessed with truth?
Hath he fulfilled the promise of his youth?
And borne unscathed through danger's stormy field
Honour's white wreath and virtue's stainless shield?
HARROW, A Prize Poem

THE OTHER DAY I was staying with Montagu. He has succeeded to his father's estate, and is the best loved landlord for miles around. He intends to stand for the county at the next general election, and I haven't the shadow of a doubt that he will succeed. If he does, Parliament will have gained a worthy addition. Montagu has the very soul of honour, and he can set off the conclusions of his vigorous judgment, and the treasures of his cultivated taste, with an eloquence that rises to extraordinary grandeur when he is fulminating his scorn at any species of tyranny or meanness.

It was very pleasant to talk with him about our old schooldays in his charming home. We sate by the open window (which looks over his grounds, and then across one of the richest plains in England) one long summer evening, recalling all the vanished scenes and figures of the past, until we almost felt ourselves boys again.

'I have just been staying at Trinity,' said I, 'and Owen, as I suppose you know, is doing brilliantly. He has taken a high first class, and they have already elected him fellow and assistant tutor.'

'Is he liked?'

'Yes, very much. He always used to strike me at school as one of those fellows who are much more likely to be happy and successful as men than they had ever any chance of being as boys. I hope the *greatest* things of him; but have you heard anything of Duncan lately?'

'Yes, he's just been gazetted as lieutenant. I had a letter from him the other day. He's met two old Roslyn fellows, Wildney and Upton, the latter of whom is now Captain Upton; he says that there are not two finer or manlier officers in the whole service, and Wildney, as you may easily guess, is the favourite of the mess-room. You know, I suppose, that Graham is making a great start at the bar.'

'Is he? I'm delighted to hear it.'

'Yes. He had a "mauvais sujet" to defend the other day, in the person of our old enemy Brigson, who having been at last disowned by his relations, is at present a policeman in London.'

'On the principle, I suppose, of "Set a thief to catch a thief," ' said Montagu, with a smile.

'Yes; but he exemplifies the truth, "chassez le naturel, il revient au galop;" for he was charged with abetting a street fight between two boys, which very nearly ended fatally. However, he was penitent, and Graham got him off with wonderful cleverness.'

'Ah!' said Montagu, sighing, 'there was *one* who would have been the pride of Roslyn had he lived. Poor, poor Eric!'

We talked long of our loved friend; his bright face, his winning words, his merry smile, came back to us with the memory of his melancholy fate, and a deep sadness fell over us.

'Poor boy, he is at peace now,' said Montagu; and he told me once more the sorrowful particulars of his death. 'Shall I read you some verses,' he asked, 'which he must have composed, poor fellow, on board the *Stormy Petrel,* though he probably wrote them at Fairholm afterwards?'

'Yes, do.'

And Montagu, in his pleasant musical voice, read me, with much feeling, these lines, written in Eric's boyish hand, and signed with his name—

ALONE, YET NOT ALONE

Alone, alone! ah, weary soul,
　In all the world alone I stand,
With none to wed their hearts to mine,
　Or link in mine a loving hand.

Ah! tell me not that I have those
　Who own the ties of blood and name;
Or pitying friends who love me well,
　And dear returns of friendship claim.

I have, I have! but none can heal,
　And none shall see my inward woe,
And the deep thoughts within me veiled
　No other heart but mine shall know.

And yet amid my sins and shames
　The shield of God is o'er me thrown;

> And 'neath its awful shade I feel
>   Alone,—yet, ah, not all alone!
>
> Not all alone! and though my life
>   Be dragged along the stained earth,
> O God! I feel thee near me still,
>   And thank thee for my birth!
>
> E.W.

Montagu gave me the paper, and I cherish it as my dearest memorial of my erring but noble schoolboy friend.

Knowing how strong an interest Mr. Rose always took in Eric, I gave him a copy of these verses when last I visited him at his pleasant vicarage of Seaford, to which he was presented a year or two ago by Dr. Rowlands, now Bishop of Roslyn, who has also appointed him examining chaplain. I sat and watched Mr. Rose while he read them. A mournful interest was depicted on his face, his hand trembled a little, and I fancied that he bent his gray hair over the paper to hide a tear. We always knew at school that Eric was one of his greatest favourites, as indeed he and Vernon were with all of us; and when the unhappy boy had run away without even having the opportunity for bidding any one farewell, Mr. Rose displayed such real grief, that for weeks he was like a man who went mourning for a son. After those summer holidays, when we returned to school, Montagu and Wildney brought back with them the intelligence of Eric's return to Fairholm, and of his death. The news plunged many of us in sorrow, and when, on the first Sunday in chapel, Mr. Rose alluded to this sad tale, there were few dry eyes among those who listened to him. I shall never forget that Sunday afternoon. A deep hush brooded over us, and before the sermon was over, many a face was hidden to conceal the emotion which could not be suppressed.

'I speak,' said Mr. Rose, 'to a congregation of mourners, for one who but a few weeks back was sitting among you as one of yourselves. But, for myself, I do *not* mourn over his death. Many a time have I mourned for him in past days, when I marked how widely he went astray—but I do not mourn now, for after his fiery trials he died penitent and happy, and at last his sorrows are over for ever, and the dreams of ambition have vanished, and the fires of passion have been quenched, and for all eternity the young soul is in the presence of its God. Let none of you think that his life has been wasted. Possibly, had it pleased Heaven to spare him, he might have found great works to do among his fellow-men, and he would have done them as few else could. But do not let us fancy that our work must cease of necessity with our lives. Not so; far rather must we believe that it will continue for ever, seeing that we are all partakers of God's unspeakable blessing, the common mystery of immortality. Perhaps it may be the glorious destiny of very many here to recognize that truth more fully when we meet and converse with our dear departed brother in a holier and happier world.'

I have preserved some faint echo of the words he used, but I can give no conception of the dignity and earnestness of his manner, or the intense pathos of his tones.

The scene passed before me again as I looked at him, while he lingered over Eric's verses, and seemed lost in a reverie of thought.

At last he looked up and sighed. 'Poor Eric!— But no, I will not call him poor! after

all, he is happier now than we. You loved him well,' he continued; 'why do you not try and preserve some records of his life?'

The suggestion took me by surprise, but I thought over it, and at once began to accomplish it. My own reminiscences of Eric were numerous and vivid, and several of my schoolfellows and friends gladly supplied me with other particulars, especially the Bishop of Roslyn, Mr. Rose, Montagu, and Wildney. So the story of Eric's ruin has been told, and told, as he would have wished it done, with simple truth. Poor Eric! I do not fear that I have wronged your memory, and you I know would rejoice to think how sorrowful hours have lost something of their sorrow, as I wrote the scenes in so many of which we were engaged together in our schoolboy days.

I visited Roslyn a short time ago, and walked for hours along the sands, picturing in my memory the pleasant faces, and recalling the joyous tones of the many whom I had known and loved. Other boys were playing by the sea-side, who were strangers to me and I to them; and as I marked how wave after wave rolled up the shore, with its murmur and its foam, each sweeping farther than the other, each effacing the traces of the last, I saw an emblem of the passing generations, and was content to find that my place knew me no more.

> Ah me! the golden time!—
>   But its hours have passed away,
> With the pure and bracing clime,
>   And the bright and merry day.
> And the sea still laughs to the rosy shells ashore,
>   And the shore still shines in the lustre of the wave;
> But the joyaunce and the beauty of the boyish days is o'er
>   And many of the beautiful lie quiet in the grave;
>   And he who comes again
>   Wears a brow of toil and pain,
> And wanders sad and silent by the melancholy main.

ΤΩ ΘΕΩ ΔΟΞΑ

5

The Rival Kings; or, Overbearing

By ANNIE KEARY

Although ANNIE KEARY'S *Rival Kings* is the least familiar of all the children's books chosen for this collection, it is surely one of the most distinguished as a work of art and of psychology. Annie Keary (1825–1879) led a life of self-sacrifice and suffering of a kind not uncommon among Victorian women, yet unusually full of pathos. Sixth child in a large family born to a Low Church minister of Irish origins, she was brought up chiefly in the Yorkshire industrial seaport of Hull. Uneventful, confined, and governed by rigid Evangelical principles, her childhood was peopled by the imaginary beings about whom she told stories in the nursery, and by the personages of *Pilgrim's Progress* and of Mrs. Sherwood's stories. The Keary children's greatest entertainment was the annual meeting of the Church Missionary Society, and next best was the weekly Bible discussion meeting on Fridays. Annie was slightly deaf, and—though she was a handsome girl—her parents told her she was ugly, in order to discourage pride. So she suffered from wholly unwarranted feelings of inadequacy.

Her one serious love affair was interrupted when she had to go to live with an elder brother whose wife had died, leaving him with three young boys. Annie's lover either died or the engagement was broken: the memoir of Annie written by her sister Eliza is ambiguous. Other family deaths saddened her deeply, but she remained cheerful. And her three young nephews adored her. Long afterwards, one of them remembered how, with Aunt Annie, the drawing-room sofa became a sledge on which they were drawn at a gallop across the snow; how with her they looked at illustrated editions of Shakespeare and Dickens, and had the stories told to them even before they could read; how she sympathized with them, "penetrating behind the barriers" that children erect between themselves and adults, encouraging their natural "faculties of thought and fancy." He pronounced Annie Keary's training "better and more precious than a thousand well-ordered kindergartens." It was for these children that she began to write: *Sidney Grey* (1857) dealt with their Staffordshire region and its brick kilns.

Interrupted by the need to take care of her invalid mother, and again by a summons to look after four little girl-cousins whose parents were going to India, Annie Keary's career as a writer never brought her the kind of appreciation for which she longed. Like so many of her generation, brought up on the harsh Evangelical teachings of eternal hellfire for the unregenerate, she was tortured by religious malaise. For a time she found comfort in the Broad Church teachings of Maurice and Kingsley, which offered hope of salvation to all mankind; but this too eventually left her dissatisfied, and she tried Spiritualism, Swedenborgianism, and—after a brief flirtation with Rome itself—High Church Anglicanism. Then she began to feel that in confession she was abdicating her right as an individual Christian to address God directly, and in her last years she returned to something very like the Evangelical belief in the necessity of a personal conversion: she was joyous in the conviction that she had had a revelation of Christ's personal friendship for herself. Her life was anguished in its emotional and spiritual stress, and full of harsh external experience, and yet she gave comfort to many by her friendship and her eagerness to help in times of trouble, and to many more, children and adults, by her fiction.

With her sister Eliza, Annie Keary in 1857 produced the first children's version of Norse mythology, quarrying from the most scholarly available compendia for adults. Published as *Heroes of Asgard and the Giants of Jotunheim; or, The Week and Its Story*, the first edition presents these grim tales in the setting of a Victorian family Christmas

201

party, with the uncle each day telling a new story to eager children. As the Norse gods went down into the twilight of *Götterdämmerung* at the end, the Kearys gave their young readers a prophetic vision of the dawn of Christianity. In the same year Annie Keary alone published *The Rival Kings*. Like her other forgotten books for adults and for children, it richly deserves rediscovery.

Perhaps the effort to adapt for children the semi-savage Norse myths, full of violence, direct action, and unrestrained passions, suggested to Annie Keary that intense hatred and the catastrophes to which it leads were not the sole property of heroic past ages, but could be seen every day around the domestic hearth. Perhaps in observing her own small nephews she became aware that, even in the best brought-up youngsters with the best religious training, savagery lay not far beneath the surface. She may well have felt that a warning against hatred might be made more palatable if presented in the form of an exciting and credible story. Whatever its inspiration, *The Rival Kings* stands out from the great mass of contemporary fiction for the young, and even from Annie Keary's own other stories, because its children move so unmistakably in their own emotional world, virtually beyond the reach even of the most sympathetic adults.

Next door to the comfortable rectory where the Lloyd family lives with their five children in a remote Welsh seaside village, moves an English farmer's family, the Fletchers, with their three children. At first disposed to be friendly, the young Lloyds find the young Fletchers uncongenial and given to making anti-Welsh remarks. Before long, Maurice Lloyd, the eldest son, perhaps about twelve, grows almost obsessed with his dislike for young Roger Fletcher. Into the Lloyd household, and into the midst of this childhood feud, come three more children, the Maynes, recently orphaned. Despite their best intentions, the Lloyds, especially Maurice, find it impossible to be hospitable, friendly, and sympathetic to the newcomers. And the Maynes—stunned by grief, strangers in a household that cannot seem like home to them despite the efforts of the senior Lloyds and the initial endeavors of the Lloyd children—cling only to one another, and grow increasingly wretched. Each attempt at reconciliation only heightens the new feud between Maurice Lloyd and Walter Mayne, and each new failure of understanding widens the breach. The hated Roger Fletcher makes an ally of the much younger Mayne children. Unrestrained self-will and passionate hatred—"overbearing" behavior, Maurice's besetting sin—bring on a series of dramatic episodes whose climax leads the children to the very edge of disaster.

None of this is at all incredible. All of it takes place in an exotic and delightful setting, in which an isolated rocky island plays a major part, as so often in the best children's stories. The loving and attentive and devout Lloyd parents—whose kindness has prompted them to take in the Maynes after consulting their own children and obtaining an enthusiastic consent, who teach their own children in person, and who are fully aware of the mounting tensions—are helpless before the tide of childhood passions. Even a cautionary tale that Mrs. Lloyd writes for the express purpose of warning Maurice remains ineffectual. *The Rival Kings*, then, whose title itself comes out of a violent heroic age, is a most unusual children's story. Among its morals it teaches that deception—concealment of the truth from one's parents—is a fault likely to be visited with retribution: but the "overbearing" Maurice goes his own way, precipitates a nearly fatal catastrophe, and, having excluded his parents from his confidence, leaves them powerless to turn the tide. Not for more than twenty years, when Flora Shaw in 1878 published *Castle Blair*, was such an autonomous group of fictional children allowed to make their own mistakes, and to suffer the consequences.

The text of The Rival Kings; or, Overbearing *is reprinted from the first edition (London: W. Kent and Co., 1857).*

"He that is slow to anger is better than the mighty;
and he that ruleth his spirit than he that taketh a city."

CHAPTER I

GARDEN HOMES

I DO NOT THINK there ever was a pleasanter place for children to play in than the garden at the back of Gorphwysfa House, where Mr. and Mrs. Lloyd lived. There was another garden in front, carefully kept and laid out in ornamental beds and flower baskets; but the children did not care much for going there, where they were obliged to be careful not to tread on the borders or wear away the grass. The back garden sloped down the little hill on which the house was built, and, as it was not much seen from any of the windows, it was not at all carefully kept, and the children were allowed to follow their own devices in it. The borders on the three sides they called their own, to be cultivated diligently when their zeal for gardening happened to be strong, and to become overgrown with weeds when some other amusement was in favour. The great grass plot in the middle was only mown twice or thrice in the summer. It looked generally like a meadow very full of daisies, and the children changed their name for it every week. Sometimes it was a savannah, and the children were Indians and hunted buffaloes over it; sometimes it was the Sahara, or Great Desert, and they played at the story of the Eagle and the Lion, which their mamma had read out loud to them one winter's evening; sometimes it was the Mediterranean Sea, and they had invented an ingenious way of rowing themselves up and down it in boats made of garden chairs, with old matting for sails.

These, however, at the time we are now speaking of, were rather old-fashioned plays, which had been in greater favour last summer. The three elder children, Maurice, Emma, and Owen, were beginning to look down upon them, and to care for the grass plot only because it was a safe place where little Gwen and the baby could be left while they carried out other schemes. The garden was large enough for plenty of these—it was so full of winding walks, and bushy hiding places, and gnarled old trees. All the children, including Gwen, had favourite places in the garden, which they called their homes. Gwen's home was a corner between two arbutus trees and the wall. It was small and dark, and no one knew why she had chosen it; but there was room in it for her, and for her family of dolls, and, with a good deal of squeezing, for Maurice when he was kind enough to come and play with her, or for the baby when he would not stay on the grass plot alone, and had to be propped up against the wall in Gwen's corner with a footstool and two rag dolls. Emma's home was a seat under a weeping willow. She kept her workbox there and one or two of her books, and she did not much like the boys even to look in. Owen's home varied between the dry ditch at the bottom of the garden and a dark, deserted tool-shed near the house; but Maurice was always quite constant to his—the one broad, even place at the top of the garden wall, where he could walk up and down without any fear of falling, or sit at his ease with his carpenter's tools about him, working at his boats, or at the set of tea-things he was making for Gwen.

All the children thought Maurice's home the best; but as he was the eldest he had, of course, a right to choose. There was certainly a great deal to be seen from his seat; it overlooked the steep road leading down to the sea, and the shore itself, with its one landing place of yellow sand, and its endless piles of gleaming white stones, against which the waves broke in foam, and which in some places jutted far into the sea. No fishing boat could put out on a still evening but Maurice could see the whole process, from the time when the fisherman waded into the water to push the boat from the sand till it had dropped down so far that the white sail looked no bigger than a sea-gull's wing; and, if he were only up early enough in the morning to see the boats return, he might almost have counted the fish as the men threw them out of the boats to the women, who had driven their donkeys down to have their panniers filled on the shore.

These sights had been what Maurice had cared most to see last summer; but lately he had found it more interesting to turn his back on the sea, and give his chief attention to watching the doings of his new neighbours the Fletchers, who had lately come to live at a large farm-house, which was only separated by a paddock and a narrow road from the Gorphwysfa garden. Of course the children had known long ago that they could see from the wall everything that went on in the farm-yard, and even any visitors that came up to the front door; but when old farmer Williams had lived opposite they had seldom troubled themselves to look, except when they knew that something unusual was going to happen, that a hive of bees was expected to swarm, or that a kite was hovering over a brood of young chickens. But now, through one cause or another, the farm-house and its new inhabitants had come to fill a large place in their thoughts, and to excite a great deal of curiosity; and Emma and Owen were rather sorry to be obliged to be satisfied with only having Maurice's account of the peculiar things that Tom, Roger, and Nancy Fletcher were constantly discovered to be doing.

When Mr. Fletcher had first taken the farm six months ago, Mr. and Mrs. Lloyd, finding that he was a superior man to the surrounding Welsh farmers, hoped that there might be a pleasant acquaintance between the children of the two families; but a few interviews showed them that the young Fletchers were by no means the kind of friends they should choose for their children, and, though Mr. Fletcher himself proved a friendly neighbour, there was, for several reasons, little intercourse maintained between the two houses. The children met often on the shore, and by the little stream where both parties went to sail their boats. The little Lloyds had been advised by their parents to speak civilly and pleasantly on these occasions, and to lose no opportunity of doing a kind action; but Maurice found that it was very difficult to go on asking civil questions when he was almost sure of having nothing for an answer but a titter or a rude stare. Besides, the Fletchers did not only titter and stare, they could talk sometimes, and when they did it was to make sneering remarks about Wales and Welsh people, as compared with English, such as Maurice found it very difficult to seem not to hear.

He wished his father had not been so particular in his injunctions to him to avoid all quarrelling, and he thought it really a grievance that these people should have come all the way from England to plant themselves in the only respectable house in Gorphwysfa village, and come always in his way.

Considering his growing dislike to the Fletchers, it was strange that he would spend so much of his time in looking at them; but Maurice had not yet learnt the wisdom of putting away irritating thoughts. He encouraged himself and his brother and sisters in listening to all the stories which the village people told about Mr. Fletcher's odd English ways, and Mrs. Fletcher's temper, and their children's overbearing manners, till at last nothing wrong could happen in the village without the little Lloyds feeling sure that the Fletchers had somehow or other something to do with it.

At first Mr. Lloyd used sometimes to laugh at these histories, and sometimes to take the trouble to contradict them. Before long, however, a very sad story reached his ears of Roger Fletcher's misconduct towards an old woman who lived on a lonely part of Gorphwysfa Hill, whose garden he robbed of the early strawberries she had intended to sell at the next market; and he felt so angry about it, and joined so heartily in his children's expressions of indignation, that it was difficult for him afterwards to take the Fletcher side in the conversations that were apt to begin at teatime and last through the greater part of the evening.

The children heard and talked a great deal more about Roger Fletcher's bad behaviour to widow Hughes than Mrs. Lloyd thought at all necessary. It was natural that they should be especially interested in her behalf, for widow Hughes had a grandson who was a great ally of Maurice's, and who just then, for want of better employment, was engaged to work in the Rectory garden. A certain amount of talk with Griffith Hughes about his grandmother's disappointment was to be expected; but after they had done all they could to make up for it by taking her the ripe strawberries from their own gardens, Mrs. Lloyd thought they might as well have dropped the subject. She began to look grave when either widow Hughes' or Roger Fletcher's name reached her ears; and it would have been better if Maurice, who was generally so observant of the changes in his mother's face, had taken the trouble to inquire into the cause of that.

There was another thing, too, which he might have remarked if he had been so inclined. Since the Fletcher feud had been gaining ground in the family it was remarkable how much there had been said about forgiving offences and judging kindly of others in the Sunday sermons. Maurice listened, and wrote very good abstracts of them in his sermon-book; but it never occurred to him that such grave words as those about "forgiving men their trespasses," and "judging not, that ye be not judged," could apply to such trifles as his own habit of catching up idle stories about the Fletchers, or to the harsh constructions he put on the doings he spied from the garden wall. On the contrary, he availed himself of the liberty brought by the lengthening summer days to be more vigilant than ever. The home on the garden wall changed its name, and became a Welsh watchtower, from which Maurice, as Prince Llewellyn, overlooked the country ravaged by an invading English army. Griffith Hughes learned a great deal of early Welsh history from Maurice's present conversation, and nourished his hatred of English farmers and new agricultural methods on descriptions of King David's death and scraps of Grey's Bard. He was quite as apt a pupil as Maurice could have wished for, and he by no means kept his convictions to himself.

Mr. Fletcher complained to Mr. Lloyd of the unreasonable prejudice against his family and his plans, which prevented him from being of any use to his poor neighbours or the labourers on his own farm; and Mr. Lloyd, while sympathising with him and doing all he could to bring about a better state of feeling, would have been much grieved and surprised to learn that a part at least of the ill-will might have been traced to his own household. Dislike resembles a serpent's egg: it looks very harmless at first, and people keep it warm in their hearts without knowing how by and by the serpent within will break forth and sting them.

CHAPTER II

THE MOTE AND THE BEAM

ONE SATURDAY, towards the end of May, Emma discovered that she had a little cold and headache, and, as none of the children liked to be kept in on Sunday, mamma prescribed a day's quiet and nursing. It was considered rather a privilege to be ill at Gorphwysfa, and, as no one had claimed it for a long time, Emma was quite ready to enjoy the freedom from lessons, mamma's pleasant nursing, the dignity of sitting alone with papa in the study while he wrote his sermons, and the privilege of choosing a story-book from the invalid's bookshelf, of which mamma kept the key.

It was, however, rather a drawback to her enjoyment that the headache occurred on a Saturday, for that was always the stillest day of the week inside the house, and the most bustling without. In the house every one moved about his work methodically under Mrs. Lloyd's eye, who had the interest of the Sunday sermons too much at heart to allow any disturbing noises; but in the garden and yard Maurice and Griffith Hughes had it pretty much their own way. From twelve till two Maurice, with Owen under him, worked hard to assist Griffith in what he called his finishing-up work. After dinner Mrs. Lloyd walked round the premises, and, if she found everything in Sunday trim, Griffith had leave to spend the afternoon in helping Maurice and Owen in any of their hut-building, or fishing, or kite-flying schemes, in which his strong hands were wanted. Whatever they were doing, and wherever they went, the girls must of course accompany them. Emma's neat hands were often as useful as Griffith's strong ones, and Maurice used to say that Gwen's clever little head was worth more than either. He never cared much, indeed, to do anything unless Gwen was there to see and to tell her odd thoughts about all that occurred, and it never seemed to tire him to carry her two miles home on his shoulder after ever such a hard afternoon's work.

Pleasant as these Saturday expeditions were, the children were generally punctual to the same hour in coming home, for Maurice was always anxious to be at a particular turn in the road by six o'clock, that he might meet the market-cart from Carregllwyd, and persuade William Williams to let him drive it up to the Rectory gate. Every one in the house, from Mr. Lloyd to Gwen, always expected something interesting to come by the cart, and Maurice liked to be the person to bring the good things, and to have every one running out to meet him. He sometimes allowed Gwen to sit on the driving-board by his side, but he took care never to see the wistful look with which Owen saw him

jump into the cart. He said to himself that it was quite foolish in Owen even to think of taking his place, as he was so much the elder, and that, two years ago, even he had never been trusted to drive a cart.

On the Saturday when Emma had been advised to remain quietly at home she saw the rest of the party set out on their walk without much regret; for she was very happily employed in making some ends of silk and beads, which her mamma had given her, into a pincushion; but she felt a little mortified some hours afterwards when she heard the cart drive up to the gate, and when she knew that every one in the house had run out into the yard to see it unpacked. Her headache would have allowed her to join them, but she did not like to resign the dignity of invalid so suddenly. She resolutely kept her feet on the sofa, and only listened. Soon she heard her papa's step in the hall, and Gwen's pattering feet running after him. She knew he was carrying the book box into the study, and that Gwen was following him to see if she could find some of the little red or yellow-covered books among the larger volumes, which she loved next best to her dolls.

By and by a servant came into the drawing-room with an armful of parcels, and Emma felt proud of her resolution when she kept her place, and did not jump up to look at them. There was one large brown paper parcel which puzzled Emma very much. She hoped she should not have to wait long to know what was in it, and before her patience failed her papa and mamma entered the room together.

Emma expected some praise for having kept quiet during the bustle; but Mr. and Mrs. Lloyd were talking so busily that they did not see her as she sat on the high sofa; and Emma, though she would not knowingly have listened to anything she was not intended to hear, remained out of sight, because she was mortified at not being remembered, and it did not occur to her at once that her papa and mamma were talking as they would not have done if they had known that she was in the room.

The first part of the conversation was nothing particular; it appeared to be about the large brown parcel, and Emma discovered that it contained chintz; then there was something said about expense, and Emma found out that they were settling how to furnish two upper rooms in the house which had always been lumber-rooms in the children's recollection; then came a sentence which made Emma listen eagerly. Mrs. Lloyd was speaking.

"It will be a great change for the children," she said; "they are all very happy together now, and I do not know when there has been anything like a quarrel. I hope they will get on as well under the new circumstances—that the change will be for good."

"I think it will be for good," Mr. Lloyd said; "you know how often we have regretted the want of companions of their own age, and lately I have considered it a serious evil. Since the Fletchers came there has certainly been a change in Maurice and Emma. I see now more clearly than I did the tendency to overbearing in Maurice's character which you noticed long ago; and though Emma is an obedient, sensible——"

"Papa, I am here," said Emma, looking over the back of the sofa.

"An obedient, sensible, honest little girl," papa went on, coming to the sofa and kissing her; "and I will keep what I have to say about her faults till some day when she has not a headache."

Emma returned her papa's kiss gratefully, and thought that, as the headache had lost her so many pleasant things, it might as well spare her the talk about faults, which, to confess the truth, Emma always found it a difficult task to bear well.

Nothing more was said. Emma was allowed the great privilege of making tea as a compensation of her solitary afternoon, and every one had a great deal to say to her; but, though the evening passed pleasantly, she could not forget the knowledge she had gained that her papa and mamma were not quite satisfied with her, and that there was a grave conversation in store. It made her feel so sober, that for some time she had no thoughts to spare for the wonderful news about the lumber-rooms, or for the change that might or might not be good for the children. She even refrained from mentioning what she had overheard to Maurice all through the Sunday morning and afternoon, though they were often alone together; and when it came out at last she really thought that she only told it because she was quite obliged.

In the evening she and Maurice walked home from service together so slowly, that the rest of the party had entered the house while they were still sauntering in the lane. Maurice was repeating to her the poem he had learned during the week to say to his papa on Sunday evening. It was Heber's Palestine, and, as Maurice liked it very much, he was saying it slowly and rather loud. Emma wished him to stop repeating when he entered the Fletchers' lane; but Maurice never liked to be interrupted in anything that interested him. He went on louder and louder, and was just spouting his favourite passage with great emphasis when a shower of small stones came clattering down upon the top of his Sunday cap, and, looking up, he saw Roger Fletcher's red face, with a broad grin on it, peeping over the garden wall. It disappeared as soon as Maurice looked up, but Nancy Fletcher's most provoking giggle was distinctly heard below. Maurice was half way up the garden wall, with some intention of throwing himself over, before Emma could make him hear.

"Oh, Maurice!" she called out, "what are you thinking of on a Sunday evening, and when you are just out of church?"

The reflection cooled Maurice a little; he dropped down from the wall again, settled his cap on his head, and let Emma lead him safely out of hearing through the little door into the back garden. Then he began, "Just like the Fletchers! I declare there is no place anywhere now where one can speak above a whisper without their overhearing one."

Emma was accustomed to Maurice's style of speaking of the Fletchers; but to-day she thought it sounded rather exaggerated.

"I don't know about that, Maurice," she said: "you know you were speaking very loud close under their garden wall."

"What has that to do with it? Why, Emma, surely *you* are not going to take the Fletchers' part?"

"Oh, indeed, no! But now, Maurice, I want to tell you something very particular;" and, with this opening, Emma thought herself called upon to repeat yesterday evening's conversation, with a few additional reflections of her own on the Fletcher question which had occurred during the day. Her communication had rather a different effect from what she anticipated. Maurice's face grew hotter and hotter as she went on, and he had to fan himself with his cap.

"Just like the Fletchers!" he said at last. "They are not content with spoiling our walks and our play and everything; they must get us into disgrace with papa and mamma."

"Oh, Maurice!" said Emma, "I don't think that's quite the way to put it."

But, though Emma saw the unfortunate turn Maurice's thoughts were taking, she was too much afraid of bringing on herself another accusation of taking the Fletchers' part to be very earnest in putting it in any truer light. She tried, instead, to turn the conversation to more agreeable subjects, and hoped that Maurice would forget his anger in curiosity about the lumber-rooms. But no, the mischief had been done; Maurice was thoroughly angry, and everything that Emma said only made him worse. He was not at all curious about the lumber-rooms, he said; it would be horrid to have them furnished, for they were the only places now where it was possible to play without hearing or seeing the Fletchers, and, if any change were coming, Maurice was certain that it would be something disagreeable, and that it would turn out that the Fletchers were at the bottom of it.

Emma ventured to remark that coming into supper with a cross face on Sunday evening was not the way to make papa and mamma alter their opinion about his faults of temper. Maurice answered that, if people *were* to think badly of him *because of the Fletchers,* he could not help it; and Emma found that there was nothing to be done but watch him as he walked up and down the garden, switching the heads off his own flowers, and wish that she had chosen a better time for telling him what she had overheard, or, perhaps, as she had heard what she was not intended to know, refrained from repeating it altogether. At last the supper-bell rang, and Maurice and Emma went into the drawing-room, feeling not at all as if it were Sunday evening.

Owen and Gwen were seated at the table when they came in, mamma was dividing the strawberries and pouring out the milk, and papa talking to her with his very brightest Sunday evening's looks. Everything was bright, as it always was on a summer Sunday evening; but Maurice felt as if he were under a cloud. He did not choose to talk all supper time, or to smile at any of Gwen's or papa's sayings, although they were discussing one of Gwen's dear little red books, and a great many pleasant things were said. He was thinking about that giggle of Nancy Fletcher's, and feeling as if he never could repeat the poem he had learned without hearing it again. All the pleasure of saying it would be quite lost now, he considered; and when Gwen, having finished her strawberries, bustled down from her high chair to fetch her hymn book, Maurice got up too, with an idea of escaping the repetition altogether. Mr. Lloyd, who had been looking at him, called him back.

"Don't run away yet, Maurice," he said; "and Gwen, never mind the hymns for to-night. Mamma and I have something very particular to talk to you about."

Emma's face fell; Maurice's could not lengthen further; but a glance at mamma's smiling face, and a recollection how unlike papa it would be to choose Sunday evening for fault-finding, reassured them both.

"I must have Maurice to sit by me," said mamma, holding out her kind hand, with a look that no ill humour could withstand, "for he is the eldest, and we want to consult you all."

To consult! Emma looked important at the word, and Maurice's discontent was blown away like a cloud before a strong west wind.

"Yes, to consult," Mr. Lloyd went on when Maurice was seated. "We are thinking of making a change in our household, which will affect you children more than any one else, and so it is only fair that you should give your opinion about it. Now listen, all of you, and let me finish my story before you decide. You have often heard me speak of my old school friend, Walter Mayne?"

"The boy who was so kind to you when you first went to school, and helped you out of so many scrapes?" said Maurice.

"But he is dead," said Gwen, looking at the black bows on her lilac frock.

"Yes," said Mr. Lloyd; "I daresay you remember my going to London in the winter to see him when he was ill, and what I told you, when I came home, about the three children whom his death had made orphans. Directly after their father's funeral they were taken to the house of a distant relation, an old lady in rather poor circumstances, who promised to be kind to them and do what she could for them. She appears to have found the change a greater burden than she expected, for some days ago I had a letter from her, in which she says that she feels it impossible to keep the children in her own house any longer. She says that they are delicate in health and very difficult to manage, and that she has not strength to teach them or look after them. She wants me to help her to send them to some cheap school, where they can stay all the year round, and not give her any further trouble."

"And never come home for the holidays?" said Maurice.

"They have no home," said Mrs. Lloyd.

"Oh, mamma!" said Gwen, "why don't they come home to us?"

"That is just the question, Gwen; and I told you not to decide till you had heard all I have got to say. You have often heard me tell you about my early days, and describe to you what I felt when I was a friendless orphan, sent to school to be out of the way. I found kind friends who helped me in my loneliness. Walter Mayne was one of them; and as, since then, God has made my life prosperous and happy, I always feel that I have a debt to pay to all unfortunate people. It seems as if I were especially called upon to remember it now; but, as I shall not be the person who will have to give up the most comfort or convenience if we decide on bringing these children to share our home, I should like to hear what you all think about it, and how far you are willing to bear a part of the self-denial we must all exercise."

"Self-denial! Why, it would be the best fun in the world to have them to live with us," said Maurice; "they shall learn lessons with us and share all that we have."

"Ah! now I understand about the lumber-rooms and the pretty pink chintz," said Emma.

"It will be delightful," cried Gwen, clapping her hands. "It is like the story of the orphans in my red book. You know, papa, the children I have been telling you about had their cousins from India to live with them, and they were perfectly happy."

"In the red book I daresay, Gwen; but I cannot promise you that if the Maynes come to live here you will find everything perfectly charming and happy. You must consider it well; there will be many things to be given up. It will cost me more to feed and clothe eight children than five, and I am not rich. We must make up the difference by doing without many luxuries that we have now. There will be fewer new frocks, Emma; fewer toys and presents at Christmas and on birthdays, Owen; no more expeditions to Carregllwyd, Maurice; very few story books, Gwen. Griffith Hughes cannot be allowed to spend half his time in waiting on you; and in lessons and in plays, when there are more to share them, there must be more giving up, more exercise of self-denial, or all will not go on well. I should like you to consider it seriously, for almost the worst thing you could do would be to let me bring these children here, and fail to make them feel that they are really at home."

"Papa," said Maurice, his face suddenly flushing up, "why do you look at me? I hope you don't mean that I am the least likely to give up things?"

"O no, indeed!" said Gwen; "papa could not mean that, for there is nothing Maurice would not give away."

"That I believe," said Mr. Lloyd; "but, Maurice, when I looked at you I was not talking of *things*. I quite believe that you would cheerfully give up luxuries and pleasures; but that is not all; there is something else that I am afraid you don't at all like giving up—your own way. You have always been first hitherto, and ruled all the others. Now, the eldest of these children is only a few months younger than you, and, if I judge rightly by the little I saw of him, much cleverer than you are, and more forward in learning. Can you, do you think, yield the first place to him when he ought to have it, and be just and generous to him as a brother should?"

Maurice pondered. "He is not at all like Roger Fletcher I suppose?"

"No; but he is just as little like you."

"Very well, papa," said Maurice, lifting up his head and speaking decidedly, "you shall see; let the children come here, and you shall see."

Mrs. Lloyd was rather disappointed in the tone of voice. She could have wished that there had been less self-confidence in it, but she did not think it wise to say anything just then, and Mr. Lloyd turned to Emma and Owen.

"What do you say to the thought of sharing everything with a new sister, Emma?"

"She will have *some* things of her own, I suppose," said Emma; "and I do not think I shall mind doing without many new frocks, because I shall take great care of all my old ones."

"I choose what Maurice chooses, of course," said Owen.

"And how will Gwen do without story books?" asked Mrs. Lloyd.

"Why, it will *be* a story, you know, mamma," cried Gwen; "and I have always been wanting something of that kind to happen."

"You are all agreed then?" asked Mr. Lloyd.

"Yes, of course," said Maurice decidedly; "and now, papa, when will they come?"

"I have business that must take me to London to-morrow," his father answered. "When I am there I shall call on this lady, and if I can settle the business as I wish I shall probably bring the children home with me on Saturday night. You and mamma will have a busy week preparing the house for them while I am away."

"How very nice!" said Gwen. "Tell us their names, papa, and all about them."

"The all I know is not much, Gwen; I only saw the poor children during the one week I stayed in London before their father died. Mr. Mayne lived abroad from the time he married till within a few years of his death, so that I had seen nothing of him for many years. I noticed how attentive his children were to him, and how still and quiet their life in his sick room had made them. The eldest boy appeared very clever and well taught, and I could see that he did not look upon books and lessons in quite the same light that a friend of mine called Maurice does. The rest you will have to learn for yourself, except the names, which I think I can tell you. The eldest boy is called Walter, and is a few months younger than Maurice; then there is a girl, Constance—she will come between Emma and Owen; the youngest is a little boy called Clive, who will be just the sort of playfellow to suit Gwen. Now go to bed and dream about them; for, if I am really to start for London to-morrow, mamma and I have a great deal to talk about."

It had been a very short Sunday evening conversation, but the children for once were not unwilling to say "good night," for they were eager to talk over the wonderful news with each other. Instead of going to bed they stood for a long time in the school-room window conjecturing and making plans. Maurice, who generally took the lead in all their talks, was this night the most silent of the party. He did not look vexed or out of humour, but he appeared to be pondering something in his mind. When his mamma peeped into his room, three hours after, at her own going to bed, she was surprised to find him still wide awake. She had her Bible in her hand, and she came in and sat down by his bedside, and read a few verses to him, as she had often done before when she thought him restless or unhappy. Maurice heard, but without attending very carefully.

"It is of no use, mamma," he said, when she had done; "though you have read, there is something I must say before I can go to sleep."

"You had better say it at once then, my dear, but it must not be long."

"Papa thinks me overbearing," said Maurice, tossing himself over in the bed. "Why did not you tell me so before? and why *does* he think so? O dear!"

"We have told you often when we have seen you do overbearing things, or heard you speak in an overbearing way; and if we did not say more it is because we don't think it helps people to talk to them about their dispositions. You have heard it now; and, Oh! Maurice, how is it that all your care seems to be about our thinking you overbearing?"

"Mamma," said Maurice, interrupting her, "I'll tell you what I mean to do. When these children come I'll show you and papa what a mistake you have made about my disposition. You will find that I am not the least bit overbearing, and that you never would have thought so if it had not been for the Fletchers. I am glad the eldest boy is nearly my own age and so clever."

"So am I; but, Maurice, don't make it your chief object to justify yourself with us; it makes me uneasy to see you so determined to shut your eyes to your own faults. If you will not believe us when we warn you of them I am afraid you will have to learn the truth about yourself in some more painful way—that it will be you, not us, who will have to learn lessons about your character from these children's coming."

Mrs. Lloyd's voice was almost sad as she spoke, and Maurice fancied there were tears in her eyes. He felt very uncomfortable, for he did not know exactly what to say. He was not inclined to admit that he was over-confident, and he felt that it would not do just then to begin the long explanatory conversation about the Fletchers, which he felt convinced was all that was wanted to reinstate him in his papa's good opinion.

His mamma did not wait long for an answer. When she found that he was not inclined to say more she bade him good night cheerfully, and hoped that he would follow his papa's advice, and dream pleasant dreams about his new companions.

It was, however, still a long time before Maurice could get to sleep; and then, though he did dream, all the events of the evening were mixed up in disagreeable confusion in his fancies. He was climbing up walls all night to speak to Walter Mayne, who sat at the top, and who, as soon as he reached him, invariably turned into Roger Fletcher, and knocked him down with his own poetry book.

CHAPTER III

WAYS OF GIVING

M R. LLOYD set off for London the next morning, and two days after a letter came to say that the Maynes might be expected on Saturday evening. Mrs. Lloyd was extremely busy in consequence, and had very little time to attend to lessons, which, indeed, were apt to fall to the ground when papa was away. Owen, Emma, and Gwen found plenty of employment in watching and assisting in the different arrangements that had to be made; but whether it was owing to the confusion of his dreams, or to the disagreeable Fletcher associations of the Sunday evening, Maurice certainly did not show his usual anxiety to make himself useful on this occasion. He left Owen and Griffith Hughes to look after the carpenter and paper-hanger who came to work in the unfurnished rooms, and devoted himself to an energetic digging of the strip of garden that lay under his own wall. By Thursday evening, however, he appeared to have dug his disturbing thoughts well down into the soil; for he got up the next morning in one of his most energetic humours, and threw himself into the work with a zeal that cast every one else into the shade. He found that nothing had been done exactly as it would have been if he had been there to help, and he discovered so many oversights in the arrangements that Owen and Griffith began to think it might be necessary that all the work should be done over again. As this could not be permitted, however, and as Mrs. Lloyd declared that she must now have the rooms entirely to herself, Maurice called a parliament of his subjects, including Griffith Hughes, to meet in the back garden, and take into consideration the most important part of the preparations, which, of course, had not occurred to any one but him.

"It is all very well," he said, "for you to stand watching the carpenters and people, and call *that* helping. The rooms must be made ready somehow, and I don't see any particular good in our doing it; but there is one thing that no one can do but ourselves. You know I told papa that we would share all our things with the Maynes. I meant, of course, our toys and books, and our gardens. Now, I think that we had better begin at once, and collect all we have, and make a fair division. I will be judge."

The idea of a general turn out of treasures was quite to Gwen's taste, and she clapped her hands, but Emma ventured on a faint opposition.

"I thought you meant all the toys and books we shall have given us for the future," she said.

"What! and keep all we have now for ourselves? How dreadfully shabby!" cried Maurice, hotly.

"Oh, Maurice! of course I did not mean to be shabby," said Emma, alarmed; "only do you think that mamma will like us to give our things away without leave?"

"I'll run and ask leave," said Gwen, twisting herself down from the high stool where Maurice had perched her.

"That's just Gwen," said Maurice, looking at Emma; "she never lets a plan be stopped by little stupid difficulties."

"But, Maurice," said Owen, who had wanted all this time to take in the full force of Maurice's proposition, "I don't see how an exact division of all our toys *will* be fair, for you have nothing to divide; you always say you don't care for toys or presents, and you almost always lose or give away everything that is given to you."

"So he do," said Griffith, feeling that it was time for him to put in a word; "Master Maurice he's like that great capting that he tell us about last Saturday, who give everything away to his soldiers, and leave nothing for himself."

"Alexander the Great. Yes, that's quite true, Griffith," said Maurice; "but he was a king, not a captain; and I wish you would learn not to make mistakes in your verbs, and put g's at the end of your words in that way, when I tell you about it so often. As for the toys, Owen, of course I mean to give something as well as any one else. I mean to give up the whole of my garden to Walter Mayne, and you know I do care about that. I have been digging it and putting it into thorough order, and I shall expect him to keep it so; for I see the Fletchers are working very hard in their back garden, and I should not like ours to look less tidy than theirs."

"I suppose, then, Maurice," said Emma, "that you will think I ought to share my workbox and my little chest of drawers with Constance; but I do hope she will keep them as tidy as I have always done, for I shall not like at all to see them spoiled."

"I only hope Master Mayne like work," said Griffith, who was notorious for not liking it himself; "for there'll be enough to do if Master Maurice has set it in his mind to have the garden put up in Mr. Fletcher's new English way."

There was something in this speech that grated very much on Maurice's ear; he was glad to cut it short by running forward to meet Gwen, and swinging her up on the high seat again, that she might proclaim the answer she had brought.

"Mamma says," said Gwen, "that we may do as we like with our own toys, but she thinks we had better wait till the Maynes come, and we have found out what they really care for; and we are to remember, she says, that giving is giving."

"Of course," said Maurice; "but it would spoil all to wait till they come: there would be no surprise, and the presents must be all properly arranged."

"Yes," said Emma, "and then we can show them how to take proper care of them."

"I think we had better divide the toys ourselves," said Owen, "because, if we wait for them to choose, they might wish for the very things that it would be most inconvenient to let them have."

"But one would not like to give what one did not care for," said Gwen.

"I care for all my toys," said Owen, rather dolefully.

"And you and Emma have such a hoard of rubbish," said Maurice, "that we may as well begin at once to look it over. Bring everything out of the nursery toy-cupboard and show it to me."

Owen and Emma obeyed with a tolerably good grace, for, when Maurice considered a plan as settled, there could be no good in talking any more about it; but the division was a much more serious thing to them than Maurice could at all understand. His patience was soon exhausted by the time they spent in discussing the merits of each separate toy, and before long, to their great relief, he left them to their own devices; and having made short work of his own affairs by throwing everything that was called his into the common fund, he gave all the rest of his attention to Gwen, who was by far the happiest and most important of the party. The collection she produced, from various odd corners, of dolls, wooden dogs, lambs, cats, and parrots, all more or less the worse for wear, was a sight to be seen; and, as each separate animal had a history of its own, and relationships and attachments of the most complicated kind, it required Maurice's and Gwen's united ingenuity to devise such a scheme of division as should give them the least pain and satisfy their little mistress of their future welfare.

Late in the evening, when everything was settled, Maurice brought his mamma to look at their arrangements.

Such thoughtful preparation for strangers was certainly pleasant to see. Mrs. Lloyd's smile showed that she thought so, and all the children felt satisfied with their own doings.

Gwen's bright face was brightest when she pointed out to her mamma Maurice's newly-dug garden and the bright green watering-pot, like Roger Fletcher's—his last purchase—on which he had with some trouble altered the letters M. L. to W. M.

"You know, mamma, Maurice has really cared for his garden lately," said Gwen, "and for having it better kept than the Fletchers have theirs, so it is very generous in him to give it away."

"Yes," said mamma; "I know that Maurice would never give anything away that he did not value; but to secure its being a true gift there is one other thing that I hope he means to let go with it."

"Do tell me what it is, mamma," said Maurice; "you know I like giving."

"If only rivalship with the Fletchers could be thrown in among all these garden tools," said Mrs. Lloyd, smiling.

"Only it would be a pity for Walter Mayne to pick it up," said Gwen.

Maurice felt quite obliged to her for answering instead of him; he did not at all know what to say, and he walked away, thinking it a great pity that his mamma never would understand about the Fletchers.

CHAPTER IV

FIRST IMPRESSIONS

THE NEXT DAY was Saturday. It was a very hot day, and Maurice, who was always very lazy when he was not very industrious, decided that there was nothing to be done but wait. He lounged about the garden all the morning, and as soon as dinner was over he stretched himself at full length on the nursery floor, with his head propped against one rocker of the rocking-horse, while Gwen sat upon the other, ready to fetch him anything he might want, or, when there was nothing else to do, act the Lady Sheherazade, and tell stories to the Sultan Haroun el Reschid. If Maurice had not wanted her Gwen would have preferred following her mamma about the house, as Emma and Owen were doing; for she was restless from what she called the Carregllwyd feeling—a touch of the same excitement that always preceded the half-yearly visits to Carregllwyd, and which Gwen described as having the carriage and horses in her head.

Maurice said he only hoped she had the Maynes in her head, for then nothing could be easier than for her to take them out one by one and show them to him—it would be better than a story.

Gwen made many attempts to satisfy him, but though her descriptions grew more minute every time, she never succeeded in saying exactly what Maurice expected. Her ideas about Constance and Clive were all very well, but she was always turned back when she came to Walter. She felt rather puzzled herself to know what to say about him. A boy, to be worth anything in Gwen's eyes, must be like Maurice; and yet it sounded rather flat to be able to say nothing but that he would be nearly as tall, and nearly as strong, and nearly as clever as Maurice himself.

"Why not cleverer, and taller, and stronger, Gwen?" said Maurice.

"But that would not do at all, Maurice," said Gwen, shaking her head; "I assure you it would not do at all."

Maurice felt somehow or other as if he, too, thought it would not do. The idea even was not particularly pleasant, though he had started it himself. He found that on a hot afternoon it made him rather cross to think so much about one thing; he would forget the Maynes, and talk about something else.

"You are not so clever as usual in describing, Gwen," he said. "Let us pass on to the story."

Patient Queen Sheherazade was used to such sudden changes, and could accommodate herself to all the Sultan's moods. She covered her eyes with her hands for a few minutes, and then, with a preparatory "once upon a time," plunged into Maurice's favourite tale of the "Palace that stood upon Golden Pillars," and managed to spin out all the details of the talking cat's conversation with its mistress; and the giant who saw the loaf sticking in the keyhole, and cried, "Unlock, unlock!" and the loaf that would tell its story—"First they kneaded me as if they would knead me to death; then they floured me as if they would flour me to death"—to such good purpose that Maurice was surprised when he found that the hot part of the afternoon was over, and that nurse had come in to dress Emma and Gwen for tea.

"Well, Master Maurice," she said, "you *are* a kind brother to have kept Miss Gwen quiet and cool the whole afternoon, instead of letting her tire herself to death. She *ought* to be obliged to you."

Gwen ran after Maurice, who was leaving the room, to give him a kiss, and say that she believed she should have had a headache if it had not been for him, and Maurice received her thanks very graciously; for, as every one took his kindness for granted, it never occurred to him to consider whether he had been quiet for Gwen's sake or for his own.

The travellers were expected at seven o'clock, and Mrs. Lloyd allowed the children to wait tea for them. They had a good hour and a half of watching, but it was a very merry time. Maurice had recovered his energy, and raced Gwen in and out of the house and round and round the garden, saying they were trying to find the place from which they could see furthest down the road.

Emma said she knew there could not be any better place than the front gate, and she proved herself right, for she saw something that Maurice did not see.

"What do you think?" she said, when at last Maurice stood still at the front gate. "The three Fletchers have gone down to the turnstile, and are standing on it, looking down the road, that they may be the first to see into the carriage. I can see the red ribbon of Nancy Fletcher's best bonnet from where I stand."

"As if it were anything to them," said Maurice, aghast at the intelligence. "How very interfering! I wonder *we* did not think of going to the turnstile."

"The Maynes will take them for us," said Emma. "Only think how provoking."

"It is the same with everything," said Maurice, feeling suddenly as if all the pleasure of receiving visitors was destroyed, since the Fletchers would see them first.

"There's Roger Fletcher waving his cap," cried Owen; "the carriage must be in sight."

"What can it matter to him?" said Maurice. "Well, I shall not stay at the gate just for the Fletchers to stare at me; I shall go home;" and Maurice turned into the house, leaving it to Griffith Hughes to open the gate and be the first to greet the travellers.

A sudden fit of shyness had, perhaps, something to do with this retreat; the other children shared it, and, instead of running down the steps to meet their father, they all huddled together behind the door, and stayed there till his cheerful voice in the hall calling them obliged them to come out. Mrs. Lloyd was stooping down to kiss a little pale girl much smaller than Emma; and Mr. Lloyd was putting down a curly-haired boy whom he had carried from the carriage.

"There!" he said, looking at his own children, "come and shake hands, all of you; you are brothers and sisters. Clive, here is another big brother for you."

Maurice held out his hand, but the little fellow shrank back. "Walter is my brother," he said, retreating towards an older-looking boy who was standing behind Mr. Lloyd, and clinging to him nervously with both hands.

"Oh, Walter! you must not put yourself out of sight," said Mr. Lloyd, briskly; "here's Maurice."

Walter was stooping down to whisper to his brother: when he had done he looked up, got very red in the face, and held out his hand shyly. Maurice took it without a word, and the two groups of children stood stock still staring at each other in silence.

"Come, come," said Mr. Lloyd; "let us go into the drawing-room and have tea; that will set us all to rights. We are very tired."

Mr. Lloyd led the way, and the children followed, but as soon as they reached the drawing-room they separated again. The little Maynes crowded together into the window-seat like frightened sheep, and none of the other children could think of anything to do but look at them.

At last, on a hint from Mrs. Lloyd, Emma and Maurice offered to help the younger boy and girl to take off their walking things, and then they found their voices for the first time; but Constance only said that she would rather undress herself, and pulled her bonnet-strings into such a hard knot that Mrs. Lloyd had to come and undo it; and Clive squeezed himself still closer against the wall, and stammered out something which Maurice understood to mean that no one could do anything for him but Walter.

"Leave them alone just now," whispered Mrs. Lloyd, who saw the blank look on Maurice's face, "and go and help Jane to take the luggage upstairs. You must expect them to be shy at first; it will be better to-morrow."

Maurice found it quite a relief to escape out of the room, and to talk as loudly as he liked on the stairs, and feel at his ease again. He spun out the business of taking up the luggage as long as he could, and when he came back into the drawing-room tea was made, and the children seated round the table. There was plenty of time to have a good look at the new comers during tea, but no opportunity of knowing more of them than could be learned by looking, for they seldom spoke above a whisper, or raised their eyes from their cups and plates. Once, however, there was a little gleam of something like sociability, but it passed away too soon for Maurice to hope much from it. When tea was half over, Gwen, who had been for some time staring very earnestly, ventured on a direct remark.

"What large eyes you all have," she said; and Clive looked up, and smiled, and whispered something to his brother.

"What does he say?" asked Gwen, eagerly.

"He said, 'The better to see with, my dear,'" answered Walter, smiling too—and he looked very pleasant when he smiled—"'like Red Ridinghood's grandmother.'"

"Oh! I know all about that," cried Gwen; "I am so glad you do." But Clive turned his large eyes full of tears on his brother, as if to reproach him for repeating his words, and Walter's face grew graver than ever again—graver and sadder, Maurice thought, than any other young face he had ever seen.

Very soon after tea Mrs. Lloyd advised that the young travellers should go to bed. She herself went up with them to their new rooms, and told Maurice he might follow to see if he could be of any use to Walter or Clive. Emma, Owen, and Gwen assembled in the school-room to watch for Maurice's coming down, and hear his opinion of the Maynes before they ventured to form their own.

He was not absent long. In about five minutes they heard him come running downstairs, and Gwen knew by his step that he was feeling impatient.

"Well," he said, shutting the door with his foot, "there was nothing for *me* to do; they did not seem to care about my help; they would not let me do anything for them."

"What do you think of them, Maurice?" said Emma.

Maurice pushed his hair back from his forehead and fanned himself.

"They are not the least bit in the world like the Fletchers, at all events," he said.

"They are a great deal shorter than any of the Fletchers," said Owen.

"No chance of Walter ever being taller or stronger than you, Maurice," cried Gwen.

"The Fletchers will think him very short," said Emma. "Roger will call him Miss Nancy, I have no doubt, the first time he sees him with us—he is so very pale."

"Roger Fletcher had better not," said Maurice, rubbing his hands, and feeling more complacently towards Walter than he had yet done, now that the idea of defending him against the Fletchers had presented itself to his mind.

"After all," said Owen, "people may be disagreeable without being like the Fletchers. Did you see how nearly Clive cried at tea, and what a grimace Constance made when she tasted the bread and milk?"

"Yes," said Emma; "and mamma took it away directly and gave her tea. I was very much surprised. Fancy any of us having tea given us for pulling faces at the milk!"

"I was still more surprised by something that happened upstairs," said Maurice. "Mamma offered to help Clive to undress, and he began to whine in a very disagreeable way; and Walter said, rather rudely, I thought, 'Let him alone, please; he never lets any one but me do anything for him.' I expected mamma to say she could not allow such fancies; but, instead of that, she only wished them good night, and said they should make themselves comfortable in their own way."

"And she has sent for a night-light for Constance's room because she is afraid of the dark," added Emma.

"We should be called silly if we were afraid. It is certainly odd," observed Owen.

"But it is mamma," said Gwen.

"And, of course, she has a good reason for all she does: where's the use in talking?" added Maurice.

"You have not said yet whether you like or dislike them, Maurice," asked Emma.

"Let's hear what Gwen thinks," said Maurice. "There, stand on this chair and speak out. You look as grave as an owl, Mrs. Wisehead."

"I was thinking of what mamma said to the Maynes when they came in about Gorphwysfa meaning 'the house of peace,'" said Gwen.

"As if that were an answer," exclaimed Owen.

"Yes, it's one of Gwen's answers," said Maurice; "and she is quite right. She means that there is no use in our talking about whether we like them or not, for we have chosen to have them here at home with us, and we must like them."

"If only Clive would not whine," said Owen.

"And Walter look so very grave," added Emma. "He looks more like old Dr. Scot at Carregllwyd than any one else."

"Only he is a great deal prettier," cried Gwen.

"Prettier! Don't let the Fletchers hear you say that for all the world," cried Maurice; "it is dreadfully soft for a boy to be pretty."

"At all events you are not," said Gwen, triumphantly. "Till I saw Walter Mayne I did not quite understand what a tall, strong, plain boy you are, my dear Maurice."

CHAPTER V

THE HOUSE, NOT HOME

THE LITTLE MAYNES were a shade less grave and shy when they came down to breakfast the next morning, and before the day was over just so much improvement had been made that Clive would consent to walk in the garden or stand in the nursery without having hold of his brother's hand, and Constance could answer a question of Mr. Lloyd's without crying.

Maurice said it was all nonsense any one pretending to be frightened or shy at Gorphwysfa—he would soon teach the Maynes to know better; and for two days he gave up all his time to very energetic efforts to promote their amusement, and to persuade them to be interested in Gorphwysfa doings. He could not always make out whether he was succeeding or not, and he felt worried and cross when his mamma every now and then called him aside, and begged him to be less vehement, warning him that his new friends would never feel at home while he allowed them no choice of their own employments, and insisted on their taking an active part in games they did not understand.

Maurice complained to himself that he was hardly used. His mamma had found fault with him for being overbearing, and now, when he was doing all he could to prove that she was mistaken, and to give the first place to Walter Mayne in all his own games, she appeared as far as ever from being convinced of his amiability. What more, Maurice asked himself, could any one do? The more he dwelt on this thought the less success he had in any of his plans for making the Maynes feel at home with him. Even the division of toys, which he had suggested and entered into so heartily, was not as well received as he had expected. There was no surprise or gratitude on the part of the Maynes at all: it was quite a failure.

Emma and Owen introduced their guests to the toy-cupboard with much ceremony the evening of the first day after their arrival; and, as it had really cost them some effort to part with their treasures, they could not help being disappointed at the indifferent way in which they were received. Walter scarcely looked into the cupboard, and, before they had an opportunity of explaining that any part of its contents were meant for him, he remarked that he had left off playing with toys for a long time, and could not understand what pleasure any one had in them. Constance and Clive brightened at the first sight of the pretty things, but they looked grave and frightened again as soon as ever Emma began to explain that it was nurse's rule that every one should put by all the toys they took out in their exact places, and that for her part she certainly should be sorry to see anything that had been hers broken or spoiled.

Constance put down a pretty moss hermitage that she had been examining when Emma began to speak, and said, in a helpless way, that she thought it would be very difficult to put everything by exactly in the right place, and that, if Emma pleased, she would never take down any of her things from the shelf, and then they could not be broken.

The days passed on, and there was still the same languid, indifferent spirit displayed about everything that the little Lloyds thought rational, and every now and then an eagerness about what they called trifles that made it the more provoking.

Walter, when he declared himself too tired to work in the garden, would spend hours in searching through the rubbish shelf in the nursery bookcase for some missing leaves of the old "Philip Quarle" which Maurice had tossed away as a baby book a year before; and Conny and Clive seemed to prefer sauntering up and down the gravel walks looking for coloured stones to the most amusing games that Maurice could suggest.

How were they ever to get on with playfellows who showed such unaccountable tastes? Maurice asked. Mrs. Lloyd, when appealed to, could only advise patience, and assure her children that they would gain nothing by forcing more active pleasures on their companions when they were not in a mood to enjoy them. They would grow into a better understanding of each other soon, she said, and like each other all the better for having become acquainted by degrees.

Unluckily, Maurice could not understand doing anything by degrees; it must be all or nothing. At the end of a week he declared that he was tired out. He began to think of taking to his own pursuits again, and leaving the Maynes to take their chance, when he made a discovery that wounded his self-importance more than anything else had done. He observed that the Maynes, in spite of their shyness and indifference to his plans of amusement, could laugh, and talk, and look quite at home in Gwen's corner. Perhaps it was the darkness that set them at their ease; perhaps it was because no one ever thought of minding what he said or did to Gwen; but certainly Gwen's gifts and Gwen's attentions received greater favour than any others had done. She had taken a favourable opportunity of making Clive acquainted with the histories and relationships of all the wooden animals that she had made over to his care, and she easily persuaded him that it was necessary to have a meeting between all the old friends in the corner every day. Clive could not go without Walter, and Constance must not be left behind, so some branches of the arbutus trees had to be broken away to make more room; and Maurice, Emma, and Owen, while engaged in other parts of the garden, heard more whispering and laughing come from behind the trees than they were regaled with during all the rest of the day. Gwen told Maurice in confidence that Walter Mayne was the most wonderful person for stories that ever lived, and Maurice thought it so very absurd that anything really interesting should go on without him, that he could not help poking his head into the corner every now and then to ask what they were all talking about. Gwen did her very best to make him welcome, but the result of Maurice's coming usually was, that the play or story, whatever it might be, had to be begun over again—he was so sure to see some better way of carrying it on than any one else had thought of. Clive and Constance were sometimes rather loud in expressions of disappointment at his appearance, and, to prevent a quarrel, Gwen was at last obliged to bring Clive to agree that the corner was not large enough for big boys, and that he could stay in it for a part of the playhours without Walter.

Clive and Conny being now out of the way, Walter showed less objection to joining in Maurice's pursuits than he had done before; and Maurice's spirits revived at the prospect of having some one cleverer than Owen and more active than Griffith Hughes to help him in his schemes, and work vigorously at the grand object of eclipsing the Fletchers in the cultivation of the back garden. Walter was willing enough to work, and did not seem to mind much doing as Maurice bid him; but his acquiescence was something very different from the admiring obedience of Owen and Griffith Hughes, and Maurice soon began to feel dissatisfied with it. It really seemed as if Walter only followed his lead because he did not think it worth his while to suggest anything himself. Most unsatisfactory of all was the way in which he talked about the garden. Maurice saw plainly that his generosity about that was as much thrown away as Emma's about the toys. Walter could not or would not understand that it belonged to him; and Maurice thought he saw a provoking sort of smile on his face one day, when he, after giving some very particular directions about it to Griffith, found fault with him for forgetting to call the garden Master Mayne's.

Before long another source of dissatisfaction arose. One day, when Maurice was trying to interest Walter in something that was going on in the Fletchers' garden, Walter asked, with a very long yawn, if they always talked as much about the Fletchers at Gorphwysfa as they had done since he came. Maurice denied indignantly that they talked more about the Fletchers than about any one else, and he was excessively provoked when Walter proved past contradiction that the obnoxious name had been on his own lips ten times in the course of the morning. Walter cut the dispute short before it had gone very far, but the subject seemed to have an unfortunate knack of recurring again and again, and it soon became a sore point which never came up without calling forth angry feelings. It was always coming up, too, and Maurice found the inconvenience of having given such a warlike character to all his games. He could no longer enjoy his watch-tower on the wall in comfort, or instruct Griffith in Welsh history in comfort, for Walter seemed to think himself called on to point out any little inaccuracies that occurred in Maurice's statements, and to insist on a fair hearing for the English side. He was quite as quick, too, in detecting exaggerations about the Fletchers as he was in finding out mis-statements about Edward I., and he had a provoking way of laughing quietly at things Maurice said, which was harder to bear than any contradiction—very hard indeed to Maurice, who had never been laughed at in his life before. Disputes between the two elder boys were very apt to spread into family quarrels, in which every one was drawn to take a share, Conny and Clive being always as sure that Walter was right as Owen, Emma, and Gwen were ready to prove that Maurice could not possibly be mistaken. It was astonishing how many hours passed in this unsatisfactory kind of talk, and how little enjoyment or profit the children now got out of the long bright June days and the pleasant old garden.

Still, if Maurice had been asked, he would not have willingly confessed that the change had not been for good. He liked very much to hear visitors say how thankful the little orphans must be to have come among such kind people, and he would have felt very much aggrieved if his papa or mamma had questioned him as to how far he was keeping his promise, and making the homeless children feel really at home. The idea that the Maynes were not happy at Gorphwysfa, and that he might possibly have something to do with it, only came once to disturb his self-complacency. It was brought about by a little conversation between the Maynes and Gwen which he overheard accidentally one Sunday evening when they had been more than a month at the Rectory.

Rather more disputing than usual had gone on during the day, and Maurice had been provoked by Walter's defence of Nancy Fletcher's behaviour at church, which he condemned, into saying some very angry things about "disagreeable English people, who came to Wales, where no one wanted them." He forgot his words as soon as they were said, and came to supper in as happy a temper as usual. The Maynes were late in coming in, as they often were on Sunday evening. Gwen was sent to call them in from the garden, and Maurice took it into his head to follow her. They were found standing all together, looking out at the back garden door with wistful faces turned away from the house, as if the road that led out into the world were more attractive than anything else.

"Why don't you come home?" cried Gwen, running up to them.

Walter turned round at the sound of her voice with a sigh, and shut the door.

"It is not *home*," he said, half to himself, "only *the house*."

Gwen checked her running pace, and walked down the gravelled path with him gravely, and Maurice followed behind.

"I know why you said that," Maurice heard Gwen say as they came near the open study window. "Home is where one's father and mother are, and, as your father and mother are *there*, I don't wonder at your not liking to call any other place *home*."

Gwen looked up as she spoke, and all the children's eyes followed hers towards the soft clear evening sky, where the stars were just beginning to shine.

"I did not mean what you mean," said Walter, quickly; "but I wish I had, for it is very nice."

"It is true, you know," said Gwen.

Conny turned around suddenly and kissed Gwen, and then they all went in through the window together, while Maurice stayed for a minute behind in the garden, for he felt sure that none of the children would have said what they did if they had known that he was near enough to hear them. He thought a good deal about this when he got to bed, and wondered how it was that all his presents and his patronage failed to make the Maynes at home with him. He had a painful feeling, quite at the bottom of his mind, that the reason lay in himself, and that he could find it out if he looked deep enough; but Maurice had been busied for a long time in looking at other people's faults, and therefore it was not likely that his eyes should be in a good condition for discovering his own.

His thoughts soon wandered off into the usual train, and, though he felt partly willing to allow that things were not going on quite as they ought to do, he found plenty of outward circumstances on which to lay the blame. He settled it to his own satisfaction that the Maynes were dull and out of spirits because nothing really amusing had happened at Gorphwysfa since they came. They had all been working too hard at lessons, and perhaps talking too much about the Fletchers. The best thing he could do would be to remedy this, and procure some pleasure for the whole party, which would prevent them from dwelling on old grievances, and turn their thoughts into a more agreeable channel.

Maurice was famous for thinking of pleasant holiday schemes, and before he went to sleep he made quite a new plan for putting every one in a good humour.

CHAPTER VI

EXCUSES FOR A HOLIDAY

THE NEXT MORNING when Maurice awoke, it was bright and fine. He got up in high spirits, and was heard, under the nursery window, calling to Gwen to come out into the garden long before any one else had thought of getting up. Gwen came out as soon as she was dressed, and Maurice jumped her down the three tall steps that led into the back garden, and wheeled her over the grass plot in the wheelbarrow in his most good-humoured way. When he had pushed Gwen and the wheelbarrow under the arbutus trees and seated himself in front he began to unfold his project.

"Gwen, I am certain that this is somebody's birthday," he said.

"O dear, no," said Gwen; "I am afraid not. Emma's birthday is in April, and mine is not till October, and yours—"

"Oh! of course I know about our birthdays; but I have made up my mind that this must be some one's, and you must find out. The Maynes—"

"My dear Maurice," said Gwen, looking solemn, "we are never to mention their birthdays."

"Never to mention their birthdays!" cried Maurice.

"No. Yesterday was Walter's birthday. Clive told me for a great secret, and said it would vex him dreadfully to have it talked about."

"Well, I never heard anything so foolish," said Maurice; "such a mystery about nothing. And for you to be told a thing and not me!"

"That part of it is very bad," said Gwen; "but I am not sure that I should like to talk about my birthday if so many sad things had happened to me since last year—"

"It is all very well to be sorry for people," said Maurice; "but all this sort of melancholy has been going on too long. I am sure it is a bad thing, and I want to make the Maynes more sociable. My dear Gwen, we must find out that it is some one's birthday."

"I should not wonder if it were the queen's," said Gwen, brightening suddenly.

"Gwen, you really are the cleverest girl," said Maurice. "Here's my pocket-book: let us look in the almanack."

Gwen's little finger travelled slowly down the pages.

"Adam Smith born. Who was he?"

"Oh! he invented something—he would do," said Maurice.

"Virgil born. There now," said Gwen, "you often talk about him."

"Horrible fellow!" cried Maurice, "we won't keep his birthday; besides, my dear Gwen, you are looking at April. Give the book to me. July 21st, *Spanish Armada defeated.* What a very extraordinary thing! I said there would be something about to-day. Now, am I not always right?"

"Will it do?" asked Gwen.

"Of course it ought to be kept," said Maurice. "Only think, the Spanish Armada! Why, we should all have been slaves at this very moment in the West Indies if it had not been defeated, and all this time we have never been taking any notice of the day. I think it's quite wrong. Come with me to papa, and you shall hear what I will say about it."

"But what do you want to do—Carregllwyd?" whispered Gwen, anxiously.

"No, no, no," said Maurice, with an admonitory shake of the head; "you know we gave up Carregllwyd for the Maynes (not that they seem to know or care anything about it), and we must not tease papa by asking to go where we know he cannot afford to take us. My plan will not cost anything. Do you remember one day in May that the Fletchers had a pic-nic to Şt. David's Island? We saw them set off, a large party, in their boat."

"And you said what a foolish, stupid scheme it was, I remember," said Gwen.

"For the Fletchers, yes; for what do they know about Welsh islands? and what is St. David's Cave to them? But it would be a capital way for us to keep 'the defeat of the Spanish Armada'—going on the sea, you know—so appropriate. Old Rollo will take us to the island in his boat if I ask him; and only think what a treat it will be for the Maynes. It will put them in good spirits, and make them forget all the queer fancies they seem to have."

"Do you think they will like it?" said Gwen. "Clive is afraid of the sea, and Walter never likes anything that vexes Clive."

"Clive must learn not to be such a coward, then," said Maurice. "It is quite absurd the way in which Walter seems to think everything ought to give way to his whims. I declare it's spoiling him; mamma says so, and we ought not to allow it."

"Only will it be a treat?" said Gwen, doubtfully.

"It will do him all the good in the world," said Maurice. "When he has once been in a boat he will like it, and then there will be no more crying on bathing days. Just run back to the house, Gwen, and see if papa is in the study, and tell me how he looks."

Gwen soon brought back a good report. Papa was in the study and did not look busy, and Maurice made haste to seize the favourable moment, for the voices of the other children were heard on the stairs, and he wanted to have all the honour and glory of arranging the plan before any one else heard of it.

Mr. Lloyd was so ready with his promise of a holiday, that Maurice had no occasion to make any allusion to the Spanish Armada; but when he heard further particulars of the scheme he looked a little grave.

"Could not you think of any other equally pleasant excursion?" he said.

"Oh, papa, why?" cried Maurice, in a very disturbed tone of voice.

"I do not much like taking frightened children in a sailing-boat on the sea."

"*Frightened children!*"

"Softly, Maurice; I was not thinking of you, but of Clive and Conny Mayne, who have not lived all their lives by the sea."

"Indeed, papa," said Maurice, eagerly, "it was chiefly for their pleasure that I thought of the plan."

"Did you consult them about it?"

"Why no; of course I never consult *them*," cried Maurice.

"Suppose you do so, then, for once; talk it all over together, and when you have thought of a way of spending the day that will be equally pleasant to all come and tell me, and I will do what I can to help you. I shall have no objection to go to the island if the Maynes really like it; but I thought I heard something about Clive's crying when he was desired to bathe."

"It is often very difficult to say why he cries," said Maurice, contemptuously.

"Possibly," said Mr. Lloyd; "but let us have no danger of any one crying if we are to have a treat. Clive deserves a holiday more than any of you; he gets on very fast with his lessons. Look how correctly all these sums are worked."

Maurice just glanced at the slate his papa held, and looked away rather gravely. He had reasons for thinking that Walter helped Clive with his lessons a great deal more than was at all right, and he felt provoked at hearing what seemed to him very unjust praises.

"Why, Maurice, you surely are not jealous?" cried Mr. Lloyd, sharply.

Maurice answered with an indignant "Of course not, papa," and turned and left the room in a very discontented state of mind.

Emma and Owen were waiting for him in the hall; but Gwen, after explaining Maurice's plan to the other two, had run upstairs to help Conny, who was generally late.

"Well, well, well," they cried.

"We are to have a holiday," Maurice began; "but we are to consult the Maynes. We are not to go to the island unless they choose."

"Then we certainly shall not go," cried Owen; "we may make up our minds to stay at home at once. Conny will say she has a headache—she always has a headache if one asks her to go beyond the garden—and Clive will be frightened about the boat. I almost wonder you ever thought of our going, Maurice; we shall never go anywhere if it is to depend on the Maynes."

"How very provoking!" said Maurice, walking up and down, and becoming more angry as he walked and talked. "Yes, it is very provoking—it's a shame. There, we gave up Carregllwyd and everything for them, and now all our plans are to depend upon the whims of that little whining Clive, who is made to seem so much cleverer than he is. It is dreadful. What deceitful ways they have! And for papa to call me jealous! I declare I shall get to hate Walter if—"

Maurice stopped short here, startled at the ugly sound of the word his passion was bringing to light; and then he saw that Emma was making a sign to him, and that Clive was standing on the last step of the stairs, with the large eyes Gwen wondered at fixed gravely on him.

"You should not come here listening," said Maurice, stammering, and feeling ashamed of himself under the child's gaze.

Clive slipped down the last step of the stairs, and came closer up to Maurice than he had ever yet deigned to do.

"I am not a coward!" he said resolutely, drawing up his small figure, and opening his brown eyes widely. "Tell me what you want to do. There is nothing I would not rather do than make any one hate Walter."

"You—you should not come listening," said Maurice, not knowing anything else to say.

"But you *are* a coward," said Owen, who could not understand the change in Maurice's face; "and Maurice is angry with you because you are afraid of the sea, and that prevents papa letting us go to the island."

"Hold your tongue, Owen," said Maurice, gruffly; "you never understand anything;" and he turned away as he spoke, and went out of the garden door.

"There now," said Owen; "Maurice is angry, and there will be no more pleasure all the rest of the day for any one: we might just as well not have a holiday."

"It is all your fault, Clive," said Emma; "you are a very strange, fretful-tempered child. Nurse says so, and if you give way to these tempers, and Walter goes on encouraging you in them, as nurse says he does, you will be unhappy all your lives, both of you, and no one will ever love you. I don't now, I assure you; and I shall go away, and not talk to you any more."

After delivering this speech Emma turned her back on Clive, and walked away with a dignified air, such as she had seen her cousin's governess assume when she had been giving a lecture. Owen followed, and little Clive stood alone in the middle of the hall. The ever-ready tears were filling his eyes and rolling over his cheeks; but he brushed them quickly away with his hands, and walked up to the study door with a resolute step.

"He has gone to complain of us to papa," said Owen, looking back.

"What has he to complain of?" said Emma, rather anxiously; and she stopped in the doorway, casting nervous glances at the study door, where her father was now standing talking to Clive.

In a minute the talk ended, and Mr. Lloyd, holding Clive's hand, came towards them. Emma thought he looked grave, and the speech she had just thought so appropriate did not please her quite so well when she imagined having to repeat it to him.

"Did Maurice or any of you send Clive to ask for leave to go to the island?" Mr. Lloyd asked anxiously.

"No, indeed," cried Emma, much relieved; "we none of us knew what he was going to say to you."

"He came *quite* of his own accord, then?"

"Yes, certainly, quite," said Emma and Owen together, both too eager to have done with the subject to weigh the exact truth of their answers.

"I am very glad to hear it," said Mr. Lloyd. "I should be extremely displeased if I thought he had been persuaded or teased into wishing to go. As he asked of his own accord it is all right. He knows best what he and his sister will like I suppose, and since you are all agreed I see no objection to Maurice's plan. Get me my hat, Owen; I will run down to Rollo's and see what can be done. Maurice shall have the pleasure of telling mamma and making all the arrangements with her; I know that is what he likes. Run and tell him the good news, Clive, and that it was your vote that settled it."

Mr. Lloyd walked briskly down the hall and out at the front door; but Clive stood stock still, with his hands behind him, looking at Owen and Emma.

"You have a very rude way of staring," said Emma, feeling uncomfortable, she did not quite know why.

"Oh, never mind him; let us run and tell Maurice," said Owen. "Clive would put him out, perhaps, and you know unless Maurice takes to a thing and likes it there is no fun at all."

Emma knew, but she did not run down the walk as fast as Owen. She was glad that he who was so slow to notice people's faces or take a hint should reach Maurice first, and say, as he could say, that Clive had come into the plan of his own accord, and that all was right. She had a kind of idea that Maurice would not think it all right if he knew exactly what had passed. She felt a little unhappy about it herself, but then she thought it would be such a pity to spoil the holiday—it did make everything so uncomfortable to have Maurice once thoroughly put out, and as it was settled there could be no use in saying anything more now.

Maurice's first thought when he heard Owen's news was that he would thank Clive for his good nature, and make up to him for the unkind speech he had overheard; but when he got back to the house Clive was nowhere to be found, and Maurice, thinking it would do any time, did not take much trouble to look for him. He was soon very busy, and quite in his element, running up and down stairs, telling his plan to all the servants, and making his way after his mamma into the larder and store closet, to help her to decide how much cold meat and bread and cake had better be packed in the baskets for dinner. Mrs. Lloyd entered as kindly into the spirit of the expedition as she did into all her children's pleasures, and when Mr. Lloyd came back and said that the boat would be at the landing-place in three quarters of an hour, and that they must eat their breakfast in haste, and not keep old Rollo waiting if they meant to go at all, the whole household was in such a bustle that there was every opportunity for putting aside inconvenient thoughts; and Emma and Maurice got into the boat, when the time came, with almost as light hearts and bright anticipations of pleasure as if there had been no overbearing temper and want of truth shown in their efforts to attain their wishes.

CHAPTER VII

ST. DAVID'S ISLAND

"THE SEA is far too smooth and calm for Clive even to think of being ill or afraid," said Mrs. Lloyd, smiling at him when she saw him squeeze his brother's hand tightly as the boat rocked gently up and down on the waves.

Clive had lately been learning to appreciate Mrs. Lloyd's gentle words and ways, and to brighten almost as happily as Gwen did when she spoke to him; but to-day, instead of answering, he shoved himself further back into his corner, and put up his shoulder with the little wilful grimace which had been his constant answer to kind speeches when he first came to Gorphwysfa.

Mrs. Lloyd looked surprised, and Gwen turned anxiously to Maurice, who was bustling about to find a convenient place for the baskets at the bottom of the boat.

"I do wish, Maurice," she said, "that I knew the truth about whether Clive really likes going with us or not. I cannot get any one to tell me."

"Now, Gwen," said Maurice, "you know what a bore it is to me when people *won't* like things that are done on purpose to please them. Can't you let me enjoy myself for once without troubling about the Maynes? I have made up my mind to forget them."

From his efforts to accomplish this, perhaps, Maurice was excessively noisy all the time they were going in the boat. He talked loudly and long, first about the absurd way in which the Fletchers had conducted their pic-nic, and then, when Mrs. Lloyd made a sign to him to change the subject, to old Rollo about his fishing and his way of managing his boat, which Maurice thought might be improved. He nearly upset the boat by persisting in helping Rollo to shift the sail, and he went on baling water out of the bottom, though he was told there was no necessity for doing so, till he had drenched Gwen's dress and one of the provision baskets with salt water.

When they came near the island Rollo civilly, but decidedly, begged Maurice to sit still and hold his tongue. He must mind his business now, he said, and the young gentleman had better be quiet. Maurice chose a seat at the furthest end of the boat, and was silent all at once. He found out that his face was hot, that he was tired already, and that he had not been enjoying himself particularly after all. He looked across to the other end of the boat where the Maynes were sitting. Walter was talking to Clive and Conny; Emma and Gwen were leaning forward to hear what he said; and even Mr. Lloyd had put down his book, and seemed to be listening too. It was some shipwreck story he was telling them—horrid stuff out of a book Maurice felt sure. He thought it very provoking that even on a holiday Walter must be bringing up things that no one knew but himself. Why need Gwen listen too? Maurice made a sign to her to come over to him, and when, for once in her life, she took no notice, he turned his back upon them all, and looked down into the sea with a very sulky face. By this means he lost the prettiest sight that there was to be seen during the whole day—a sight that made Conny forget to think that she had a headache, and Clive shake off his fears and his pettishness.

They were skirting the island before they put in at the little cove which made the one safe landing-place. There were tall white rocks standing round one half of the island like an army of giants facing the sea. The waves had worn them below into all manner of fantastic shapes. Every now and then you caught a glimpse of some dark cave into which the sea ran gurgling, and here and there perfect archways of white stone stood out in the water like gateways leading to some silent enchanted castle beyond. Far above the sea-birds clamoured, wheeling round and round their nests in the rocks, or dropping suddenly like snow-flakes into the water.

Walter left off talking and stood quite still, and Clive put his arm round his brother's neck, and rested his head on his shoulder with a happier expression on his little face than it had worn ever since he came to Gorphwysfa.

"How happy we should be if we could live here!" he said, after a little time.

"And make a picturesque desert island family party," said Mr. Lloyd, laughing. "I am afraid mamma will not take to the plan very readily."

"Oh! I meant Walter, and Conny, and me," said Clive, looking gloomy again.

"Did any one ever live here?" asked Walter, eagerly.

"Well, sir," said Rollo, answering from the other end of the boat, "it is an old story, but I'm as likely to know about it as any one, for I had it from my own grandfather, and he saw him his own self when he was a boy."

"Who, Rollo?" cried Maurice, forgetting his ill-temper in curiosity.

"Why, him that lived and died here all alone, they say, on St. David's Island. There was a terrible storm, I have heard my grandfather say, on the night when he was thought to have died. The wind blew from the sea, and it brought sounds of moaning and sighing into all the houses on Gorphwysfa shore. Some said that he had committed a murder in his youth, and that evil spirits were let loose upon him; but there were others who said that he had once been a great man, and that he was outlawed for taking part in some conspiracy against the king. They said that his friends sometimes came to see him from the Irish coast, and that they held their communings together in St. David's Cave, and that lights were seen moving about on the island by fishermen out at sea on still summer nights, when boats could put in at the bay as we are doing now."

"Where did he live? Had he a house?" asked Walter.

"There's a bit of an old stone wall standing still among some trees in the middle of the island, where they say his house stood, and the few yards of soil round it bear marks, I've heard, of having been dug and planted once."

"And it might be again," said Walter, thoughtfully.

"Do you believe it's true, papa?" asked Emma, who had no taste for marvels.

"There is no doubt some slight foundation for the story. I can believe easily enough that lights were seen on the island, for it was once a great resort for smugglers, and I daresay that those who did know the truth, and those who did not, were equally ready to tell mysterious stories about it."

"Well," said Rollo, "one person says one thing and another person says another thing; but I had it from my grandfather, and he saw with his own eyes."

"I believe your story exactly, Rollo," said Walter, moving nearer to the old man; "and I should like to know more particularly how your man lived, and what he ate, and everything about him."

"Well, master, I've turned that over many a time when I have been out near the island fishing. It's a wild, bleak sort of a place, and I think he must have had hungry times of it in the winter months, when no boat can come near the rocks, or put out from them to sea."

"O no, indeed, Rollo; you are mistaken," said Gwen. "You have no idea how very comfortable people always are on desert islands. They are a great deal better off than we are at home. It is the pleasantest kind of life. You would understand it if you had only read how they always manage in books."

"Very likely, miss. I am no scholar, and I know there is a great deal to be got out of books if one takes to them when one is young. It is too late for me; and now, perhaps, you'll all be kind enough to sit quite still, for the next wave will bring us close upon the beach, and I am going to run the boat aground."

The landing was very merry work. Luckily for Maurice's temper the boat could not be drawn quite close to the landing-place, and his self-complacency was restored by finding that his services were required in carrying the children and the baskets through the shallow water to the bar of smooth white sand that lay above. Walter did not offer to help; he sat still in the boat by Mrs. Lloyd, who chose to see all the party safely out before she left it. Mrs. Lloyd wondered what he could be thinking of, he looked up at the rocks with such an absorbed face. At last he turned and said, in a more confidential manner than usual with him,—

"Do you know that I wonder very much why birds and fish find it so easy to live, and can go where they like, and be happy anywhere, when it is so very difficult for people? They must stay just where they happen to be, whether they like it or not. I wish I was a sea-gull."

" 'Foxes have holes, and the birds of the air have nests; but the Son of Man had not where to lay his head.' I think you would rather be what *He* was, Walter," said Mrs. Lloyd, gently.

"Mamma," cried Maurice, who caught something of the grave tones, "we are all waiting for you and Walter, and I must say that I do think it's a pity to stand talking when there is so very much to be seen and done."

"Well, come then, Walter," said Mrs. Lloyd, smiling; "and ,suppose we try to be sea-gulls for this one day, and enjoy ourselves without taking so very much thought. Nothing would please me better than to see you and Clive able to be amused with little things. I sometimes think you are both a great deal older than I am."

Walter smiled in answer, but Mrs. Lloyd was sorry to see that he slipped away from all the others, and took a solitary stroll along the beach, while the delightful bustle of unpacking the baskets and laying out the dinner was going on. He wandered so far away that she was beginning to be uneasy about him, and was just going to despatch Maurice to look for him when he re-appeared, very eager and breathless, bringing a sprig of something green in his hand.

"What have you been about?" cried Maurice. "You have lost all the best part of the fun."

"I have been up the cliffs. I do believe I have seen the place where Rollo's man lived; and look what I have found."

"Rollo's man seems to have made a great impression on you, Walter," said Mr. Lloyd, laughing. "What proof of his existence have you discovered?"

"It is nothing but a piece of wild thyme I'm afraid," said Mrs. Lloyd, looking at the sprig Walter placed in her hand.

"Wild thyme! Oh! I thought it was mint or some garden herb. I thought it was such a proof that there had been a garden on the island once."

"Let us imagine that it is mint, pray," said Mr. Lloyd; "it must have been so useful to our islander to boil with his green peas, and make sauce for his roast lamb on Easter Sunday."

"You need not laugh, papa," said Gwen; "the islander had all that, and a great deal more. Those people with lights had grand suppers in the cave, you may depend upon it."

"Perhaps Charles Edward has been here," said Walter, looking around.

"O no, not Charles Edward," said Maurice; "he has been in so many places. We will have a person who disappeared mysteriously for our island. There was Harold, the last of the Saxon kings. You know some people say that he was not really killed at the battle of Hastings, but that he lived on for an immense time, and became a one-eyed calender— monk I mean."

"And spoke to Rollo's grandfather," said Walter.

"Well, it's not history day," said Maurice; "one can't be expected to be particular about dates; and, after all, I think the man had better be a smuggler, for if we make any more guesses from English history papa will pull Keightley out of his pocket, and we shall find ourselves in the middle of afternoon lessons before we are aware."

"And the tide will be in the caves before we have begun dinner," said Owen.

The best part of the dinner to the boys was the fun they had in running down to the sea every five minutes to wash the plates. Mrs. Lloyd had packed up one plate for each person, and Maurice was peremptory in insisting that no one should eat two different things from one plate without its being washed between. All this running backwards and forwards caused great amusement to the children, but it took up time; and when the plates had had their final washing, and were packed in the basket, Mr. Lloyd took out his watch, and found that in about two hours the state of the tide would oblige them to begin their voyage home, and that Walter's wish of exploring the island thoroughly could not be gratified. There, were, however, several curious caves not far off, which Rollo undertook to show them. The largest of these was called St. David's Cave, because there was a tradition that St. David had, on some occasion, taken refuge in it; and this, though it was rather difficult to reach, Maurice was bent on exploring.

Constance rather drew back when she saw the narrow, dark passage that led to the wider part of the cave, but Clive whispered something to her, and then she stooped down without a word, and allowed Rollo to lead her along the narrow ledge of rock. When she came out to the light, and was allowed to stand upright again, she was surprised to find herself in an immense open space, rock above and around her, and light streaming in from the arched opening that looked upon the sea. Rollo left her to guide one of the other children, but Conny was too much taken up by the beauty and wonder of what she saw to feel as much afraid as she would have done in any other strange place alone. Maurice came next, and brought plenty of noise and tumult in with him. He and Owen were soon racing through the cave, trying who could run fastest in slippery places without falling, while Walter and Conny stood still, hand in hand, talking in whispers, and feeling much as they felt when their father had taken them into a grand cathedral abroad. Clive and Gwen were soon intent upon the wonders of a shallow pool, where sea anemones and endless varieties of strange living shapes were moving about; and Mr. Lloyd had to be very peremptory, and to speak strongly about the danger of staying in the cave after the tide had turned, before he could persuade any of them to move on.

By the time he had succeeded in collecting his party at the entrance of the cave the water was just beginning to ripple in on the side where the rock jutted out furthest to the sea, and they had some difficulty in rounding the point which formed the entrance to the cavern, and coming out on to another stretch of smooth white sand that lay on the opposite side of the island to that on which they had landed. It was found impossible for Mrs. Lloyd and the children to return through the cave; but Rollo thought, as the tide was high and the sea smooth, that he could bring the boat round the peak, and take them up at the mouth of the opening. There would be about an hour to wait. Mrs. Lloyd took out her sketch-book, the younger children amused themselves by building a sand castle, and Maurice proposed to Walter to walk along the beach till they came to the next projecting point of rock. It was at some distance, and Mrs. Lloyd called after them to beg them not to be more than an hour away. Maurice set off at a great speed, for he was determined, he said, as they were on the island, to see as much as possible of it; but he could not get on quite as fast as he liked, for Clive had chosen to follow Walter, and his slow walking hindered them very much, as Maurice took care to remark frequently. Walter would not have him hurried or left behind, and during the walk he and Maurice got a good deal out of temper with each other about it. They had nearly reached the ledge of rock which must end their walk, and Walter was just beginning to propose their turning back, when a sudden sound made them all stand still and listen. It was only the noise of a gun going off, but it woke a hundred answering echoes, and the warning cry of the sea-gulls sounded from rock to rock. Walter and Clive looked at each other with a smile of pleasure.

"It is the Fletchers!" cried Maurice, eagerly. "There, now, is it not provoking that they should come here on the same day as we do? One would think they did it on purpose."

"They could not well have come by accident," said Walter, laughing; "but what is their coming to us? Let us turn round and walk back; we shall be late as it is."

"No, no," cried Maurice; "I must know whether it really is the Fletchers or not, and what they can be doing. Just you stay a minute or two where you are, while I climb up on to the rock and look over to the other side. Their boat will be just beyond the point, and I shall see quite plainly. I won't be five minutes.".

"What is the use?" said Walter.

But Maurice ran on without waiting to listen to anything more. He was a good climber, so he did not find the ascent of the rock very difficult, though it was steep and rough. Walter and Clive lost sight of him behind the ledge for a few minutes, but they soon saw him again making his way down, and running to them with a very eager face.

"It is the Fletchers," he cried, when he came near; "and what *do* you think? They have just shot a sea-gull. I saw it fall into a pool of water in a ledge half way up the rock. The poor thing is not killed; it has only got its wing hurt, and there it lies flapping in the water. I should have brought it away with me to keep the Fletchers from getting hold of it, only I thought I could not manage to get down by myself with my hands full. I want you to come with me and bring Clive's basket, and then between us we shall manage easily. Come, be quick, do!"

"You had much better let it alone," said Walter; "the Fletchers are not likely to go after it up there, and as it is not much hurt it can take better care of itself than you can take of it."

"No, it can't; besides, I tell you I want to have it," said Maurice, "and we have no time to waste in talking."

"Do you mind being left here alone for a few minutes, Clive?" asked Walter.

Clive cast a wistful glance up and down the solitary beach.

"Can't you speak?" said Maurice, sharply.

"Well, I certainly *should* mind. I don't like being left by myself, Walter knows," said the child.

"There's nothing to hurt you," said Maurice, in an impatient tone. "I want Walter to help me, and he really must. If you are frightened about such foolish things you will have to be frightened."

" 'Will have to be frightened!' No, *that* he sha'n't," said Walter, flushing up. "You may do as you like; I shall not leave *him* to please *you*."

"Well, I never heard anything like it," cried Maurice. "I declare I believe you are frightened yourself of climbing up the rocks. You would not encourage him in being such a coward if you were not one yourself."

"Oh, Walter, go!" said Clive, letting go his brother's hand; "go and show him. I don't mind being left. I forgot; I did not mean to say it. Oh, do go!"

"No," said Walter, proudly; "I don't choose to be taunted into going, or ordered either, so now at last Maurice knows. We are not *all* his servants."

"Servants! I don't know what you mean. I never heard anything so ill-natured," said Maurice, speaking very fast and stammering with anger. "I did not order you, I only asked. I never order any one."

Walter laughed, and turning away took up a stone, and told Clive to watch how far he could make it skim across the waves.

The laugh put the finishing stroke to Maurice's anger.

"You are as spiteful as Roger Fletcher," he said, stamping his foot on the sand. "I will never ask you to do anything again as long as I live. Go back to the girls if you like; I will get the sea-gull in spite of you."

Clive had put the basket down on the sand, and, without saying anything more, Maurice seized it, and ran off towards the rocks. His heart was beating very fast with anger, and when he began to climb he went stumbling on, not minding where he was going, sending showers of loose stones down on the sands, and bruising his knees against hard points in the rock. Once he thought he heard Walter calling to him to take more care, and it made him go faster and faster. He succeeded, however, without mishap, in gaining the point to which he had climbed before, but when there he found that he could not get his hand into the water, where the bird lay, without standing on tiptoe and stretching far over the ledge. Even Maurice thought this too dangerous a feat to perform without a steadying hand to help him, but he could not bear to go down without having succeeded in his purpose. Looking round, he saw a large solid-looking white stone on the other side of the ledge, which seemed to be quite safely embedded in some loose gravel that had, some time or another, slipped from above. He thought he could reach the pool easily if he stood upon that, so, with a successful stride, he swung himself over the ledge, and found even standing ground.

The bird was still in the pool, and Maurice succeeded in fishing it out and putting it into his basket. As he did so he observed a beautiful sea anemone spreading itself out at the edge of the pool. He thought he should like to get that too, and he once more stretched out his hand towards the tiny basin in the rock above. This time he found it more difficult to dip his hand into the water; he must be standing lower than before, and, as soon as the thought struck him, he felt that the stone on which he was standing was slipping down the steep rock on which it rested. It was loosening gradually under

his weight, and he knew that it would soon move faster. In an agony of fear he threw away the basket, and clung with hands and knees to the slippery side of the ledge he had quitted. A moment after he heard a loud splash in the water far below. His heart turned sick at the sound, and his head giddy: he felt as if he never could do anything but cling fast to the stones, and yet as if his trembling fingers must loose their hold. He heard the sea-gulls, disturbed by the sound, clamouring far above his head, and the sea dashing against the cliffs at his feet, and it seemed to him as if he were miles away from any possibility of help. He had just presence of mind enough left to support one foot on a projecting point in the almost perpendicular rock, but the very thought of making any movement to regain the ledge made him shudder. He tried to call out, but his voice seemed to die away, faint and low, lost in the clamour all around. He was getting quite faint, and his fingers numb, when he was roused by hearing his name called above.

"Here, leave hold of the rock, and give me one hand," some one said, quietly; and his hand was seized, before he dare lift it, in a strong, firm clasp.

"Now, then, don't pull so hard, or you'll have us both over," said another voice, rather roughly. "Help yourself; put your knee up there. Come, now, it's no such great stride. That's it; here you are, all safe enough."

At the first sound of voices and clasp of hands Maurice's nervous feelings left him; he was able to exert himself again, and in another moment he was on the safe side of the ledge, but still clinging with trembling hands to Walter Mayne and Roger Fletcher, who had pulled him over.

Roger was the first person who spoke.

"You're a nice fellow to go after other people's birds, now ain't you?" he said, the instant Maurice was safely landed. "We heard every word you said, for our boat was just round the point. 'Keep the bird out of our hands,' indeed! Next time you want our birds you'd better ask us to get them for you, for there does not seem much chance of your ever getting any for yourself."

To this speech Maurice could not answer one word. He was still stunned and trembling, and it seemed to him dreadful of Roger to begin jeering him just then, when he was just going to thank him so warmly for coming to his help. The rough speech froze up his gratitude at once, and made him feel somehow ashamed of himself. He took his hand off Roger's shoulder directly, and, when Walter offered to help him down the steep path, he said that he supposed he could get down such a place as that easily enough by himself. He did not get down easily, however, for he stumbled several times in places down which Walter and Roger bounded lightly. Walter did not offer to help him again, and Roger laughed, and cried, "Well done!" and said, "Was not he just the chap to go after sea-gulls?" When they had got down to the sands Roger said he must run back to Tom and the boat. Walter wished him good-by, and thanked him for coming to help, but Maurice stood stock still without saying a word. He knew he ought to be grateful, but what could he say to Roger Fletcher when he had just been laughing at him, and when Walter Mayne was standing by, with that provoking kind of look on his face which always had come upon it from the first time Maurice had begun to talk to him about the Fletchers?

Walter seemed to think that if there were no thanks for Roger Fletcher there should be none for him, for he took hold of Clive's hand, and set off walking briskly, without taking any further notice of Maurice. Maurice limped on behind, very much bruised and thoroughly unhappy. He made one great, and, as he thought, wonderful effort to conquer his temper.

"I say," he said to Walter, when the walk was nearly ended, "I—I really am, you know, very much obliged to you for coming to help me."

Walter turned round with an expression of surprise on his face; but it was not at all the sort of pleased surprise, ready to meet him half way, that Maurice expected; it really was a very provoking look.

"Oh, I am glad to hear it," he said. "I was beginning to think you would rather have been left on the rock all night than have had one of the Fletchers to help you down."

"It's too bad—it's a shame to talk so," cried Maurice.

"Oh, very well; I don't want to talk any more about it, nor does Clive, as you will see."

Maurice found that this was meant for a promise not to allude again to his adventure, for, when they reached the rest of the party, and found Mr. Lloyd and Rollo waiting, and Mrs. Lloyd anxious on their account, neither Walter nor Clive offered any excuse for their long absence. A very few weeks ago Maurice would have scorned the thought of hiding anything from his father and mother, but he had allowed his pride and party spirit to grow to such a height that he felt it would be almost impossible to humble himself, and acknowledge an obligation to Roger Fletcher before the whole party; he thought it would be easier to give up his long habits of perfect openness, and bear the weight of a secret.

He snubbed Gwen when she asked him questions about his walk, and during the return home sat moody and silent in the corner Clive had chosen in the morning. This day, which was to put every one in good spirits, and make the Maynes begin to feel really at home, had certainly produced very different results from those Maurice foretold. He could not help acknowledging it to himself, and feeling aggrieved that everything that he planned should go wrong. He did not, however, take much blame to himself; it was so clear to him that only such very bad behaviour as Roger Fletcher's could have produced such uncomfortable feelings, and made Walter's having saved his life a reason for his being less inclined to make a friend of him than ever.

CHAPTER VIII

A CASTLE IN THE AIR, AND WHAT IT LED TO

MAURICE WOKE the next morning with a very strong wish in his mind to hear nothing more of St. David's Island, sea-gulls, rock-climbing, or Roger Fletcher; and, to keep himself out of the way of being reminded of disagreeable subjects, he determined to go, as soon as ever school was over, to the opposite side of Gorphwysfa Hill, from which there was no sea view, and give his whole attention to a scheme for building a toolhouse in the little wood behind widow Hughes' house, which he and Griffith had planned in the beginning of the spring. He had often talked about it to Walter, and he had no doubt that he would be ready to give his help when he was wanted; for, though he had heard Clive and Conny say something at breakfast about a walk down to the shore, it never occurred to him that their plans for the playhours were to be allowed to interfere with his.

When he had collected his tools, and was ready to start, he was rather disturbed to find Walter sitting quietly by the school-room window, with a book in his hand.

"Why, Walter," he said, "I never saw such a lazy fellow as you are. I told you this morning to be looking out some nails and string, and here you are sitting still reading, as if you had nothing in the world to do. I declare I don't believe any one would ever do anything if I did not look after them."

"I don't know what you mean," said Walter, without looking up from his book; "I have nothing particular to do; there is plenty of time."

"Why, are you not going out this afternoon?"

"Presently, perhaps."

"But presently won't do. You forget where the wood is, and how much we have to do; there won't be time."

"There will be time for all I mean to do. I am going to the shore with Conny and Clive to look for shells."

"What, this afternoon?"

"Yes, this afternoon."

"But did not you hear me say that I was going to work at our toolhouse? Any day will do for Conny and Clive, or they can go by themselves; but I must have some one to help me, and you know that Griffith can't come *now* as he used to do before you all came."

Walter made no answer whatever to this speech. Any one who had known his face would have seen that there was a little angry trembling of his upper lip; but he sat quite still, and did not lift his eyes from his book.

It was all very provoking to Maurice, and the more he thought about it the more aggravating every circumstance seemed. The very book Walter was reading was one of his own, which he had put on the shelf in his room with such pleasant feelings.

Walter turned a leaf in his book, and Maurice's anger broke out in words he would not have said if he had thought a minute about them.

"How I hate to see people reading in playhours!" he exclaimed; "I never would have given you half my books if I had known that you would have read them in this way, just to spite me. I wish I had never let you have one of them."

"Was this book yours?" cried Walter, jumping up with a flushed face, and spinning it across the table; "I thought it had been Gwen's. Never mind, I will never touch another of your books. Come, Clive, you and I will go out. The shore does not belong to any one: we can do as we like *there,* I suppose."

Walter took Clive's hand as he spoke, and walked out of the room, leaving Maurice in a state of temper that could only be vented by a great deal of stamping up and down the room and throwing furniture about. Mr. Lloyd came in during this cooling process, and expressed considerable surprise at the state in which he found Maurice and the school-room.

He said something rather sharp about idleness and disorder being a very bad return for an unusual indulgence, and poor Maurice, after having been made, unwillingly, to put up the books and straighten the carpet, walked at last into the garden, feeling more thoroughly discontented and unhappy than he had ever been in his life before. Fresh disappointments awaited him there. Griffith Hughes had gone down the village on a message, and Owen had asked leave to walk with him. Emma and Gwen were helping Mrs. Lloyd to unpack parcels in the store closet, and Maurice felt that, unless he were prepared to answer questions, it would not do to take his cross face in there. The Maynes had gone down to the shore; there was no one to be seen about in the garden; and at last Maurice set off on his long walk alone, overloaded with tools, and making himself crosser and crosser as he toiled up the hill in the heat, by turning over in his own mind how it was a shame that Walter Mayne should hate him after all he had done for him, and that people were quite right when they said that there really *was* nothing but ingratitude in the world.

While Maurice was nourishing his anger by his own exaggerated thoughts, Walter was becoming confirmed in the proud reserve that was his chief fault, by the kind of conversation he was hearing from his little brother and sister. Constance had not often lately been alone with her brother, and she took this opportunity of pouring out all her real and fancied troubles into his ears. She had been used to tell her troubles to Walter all her life, and it was a consolation she thought she could not deny herself, though experience and her conscience told her it would often be better for both if she could be silent about her grievances, or, at all events, take care that they did not sound worse in the telling than they really were.

She was not exactly of a discontented temper, but she was very weak-spirited. She found it very difficult to get over a sharp look or a hasty word, and she was apt to measure such by the pain she felt, rather than by the intention of the offender. She told all this pain to Walter without feeling very angry or indignant herself, and when she saw how angry it made him she wished she could recall her words, and came back from one of these confidences more dispirited than ever.

Walter encouraged her to talk; he was not tired of hearing the same things over and over again. It suited his kind of temper to think that he was the *only* person who could take care of his brother and sister, and he liked them to depend entirely on him. He was as fond of ruling and being first as Maurice, but it was in a different and less obvious way.

Constance's complaints lasted during the long walk to the shore, and were resumed again when they sat down on the sands to rest, after Clive had collected the shells and stones he wanted. She had nothing new to tell, only what Walter had heard before about Mrs. Lloyd's extreme exactness in lesson hours, so unlike the careless teaching Constance had been used to at the little day-school she had attended in London, and about the scoldings she received from nurse for leaving her room and drawers untidy, and little unkind speeches which she had now and then to bear from Emma, who was liable to get angry when she observed a fresh scratch on the workbox, or ink stain on the desk, which, according to Maurice's rule, she and Constance shared between them.

"I wish, Oh! how I wish," said Constance, winding up with her usual chorus, "that she had never given me anything. I hate the sight of all the playthings now, they have made me unhappy so often; and yet when I don't use them Emma and Owen say I am sulky; and when I do touch them they are sure to break, and then they are angry."

"I have made up my mind from this day," said Walter, "never to touch anything that Maurice pretends to have given me, and I advise you and Clive to do the same."

"And yet some of the playthings are very pretty," said Clive; "and it is really very hard to have nothing that one may touch without being scolded."

"Oh! If I were only a man—if I could only be a man at once!" cried Walter, throwing himself impatiently down on the sands, and hiding his face with his arms.

Clive and Constance looked at each other dismayed. It always frightened them rather when Walter gave way to one of these bursts of impetuous feeling; and they had known them lead once or twice to outbreaks of self-willed conduct bad for them all.

"O dear!" said Constance, half crying, "I wish I had not said so much; it was very wrong to tell it all to you. I have so often got you into trouble by telling things."

"Now, Constance," said Walter, looking up suddenly, "the only thing that ever makes me angry with you is when you talk like that; you know I always expect you to tell everything to me."

Poor Conny's little pale face hung very low at this. No harsh words hurt her like harsh words from Walter; and this pain she could never tell any one.

"Promise me once for all," Walter went on, "that you will tell me whenever any one does or says anything to vex you;" and Walter's dark eyes grew very dark as he spoke.

"But do you think it is quite right to repeat every little unkind thing?" said Conny, hesitatingly.

"Of course it is," said Walter, "to me. You have no one else to tell things to; and I promised papa always to stand up for you and Clive."

Constance had a dim idea that Walter's way of standing up for them was not exactly what their papa meant; and she remembered something that he had said to them at the same time about One to whom they might always safely tell their wrongs and sorrows;

but she had very seldom courage to say out what she thought, so she answered, in her usual despairing way,—

"There is no use in promising, Walter, for you know I never can help telling you everything, whether I think it right or not."

"I like to know," said Walter, fixing his eyes far off on the sea, "because some day I *shall* be a man, and then I will pay back to every one all that has been done to you."

"Oh, Walter! is it right to feel like that?" said Conny, shrinking.

Walter made no answer; and Constance thought she had been very courageous in saying what she did, though in her heart she blamed herself, and wondered how it was that they dwelt so long on every little unkindness, while the great causes for gratitude were scarcely ever mentioned between them.

She had time to think a good deal about this, for Walter fell into one of his musing fits; and Clive, leaning on his knee, seemed to find amusement enough in watching the changes in his brother's face. Clive spoke first.

"Now, Walter," he said, "you must tell us the story. I have been quite still while you have been thinking it out, and I have watched it growing in your face. It is a story, I know, of what you will do when you are a man."

"Yes, do tell us a story," cried Conny, "for I have been thinking such melancholy thoughts."

Walter roused himself at the sound of their voices.

"It is not a story of what I am going to do when I am a man," he said; "it is something better than that. Conny, Clive, just suppose that we three could go and live on the island where we were yesterday, and work for ourselves, and have no one to scold us or interfere with us: should not we be happy? I would do all the work, and you should play."

"No, we would all work," cried Clive, eagerly. "I am sure I could work with you."

"And so could I," said Conny. "But you don't mean really, Walter; you only said 'suppose.' "

"Let us suppose, at all events," said Clive. "Tell us how it all might be, Walter; make a story of it."

Walter was famous for his stories. He had often told them to while away tedious hours in the old London lodgings, when his father's sleep depended on the children being perfectly quiet, or to make them forget cold and sorrow, in the dark back parlour of their aunt's dull house; but nothing he had ever thought of before pleased his hearers so much as this one. It was the best, Clive said, because it was real; they agreed to talk about it again very often; and it made the idea of going home to commonplace ways seem very flat and dull indeed.

Constance was the first to remember that Mrs. Lloyd had desired Clive not to stay too long on the hot beach, and it was not without a good deal of grumbling about having to obey unnecessary orders that Walter took up the basket of stones, and turned towards the Rectory. Clive had chosen the stones and shells without thinking much about their weight, and Walter found the basket rather a heavy burden to carry up the steep road. When he reached the top he put it down, and looked disconsolately along the winding lane that led from the cliff to the Rectory back garden.

"I have a great mind," he said at last, "to take the short cut through the Fletchers' field. I can't see what harm there could be in going that way."

"Maurice would be very angry with us if we did," said Constance, imprudently; and before the words were well out of her lips Walter had swung his basket into the field, and vaulted over the stile after it. Clive followed, as he would have done wherever Walter had led the way.

"Conny, I am waiting to help you over the stile," said Walter; and Conny felt she had no choice left but to follow too.

"I wish you would turn back, Walter," she said when they had got half way across the field; "there is Roger Fletcher standing on the gate at the other end, and Mrs. Lloyd does not like us to talk to him, and I know he will not let us pass quietly."

"We shall see about that when we get there," said Walter, hastening on, while Clive and Conny fell a little behind.

Roger was hanging on the gate, with his back to the lane, his arms resting on the top rails, and his round, red, impudent face staring down at the children. He answered Walter's civil request that he would get down and let them pass by going through a variety of grimaces, and asking after each one, "Don't you wish I would?" He had several times had the pleasure of seeing Maurice lose his temper on much smaller provocation; but Walter had attended a day-school in London, and become accustomed to teasing boys and grimaces about nothing. He neither laughed nor looked angry, and Roger, finding that no such amusement as a quarrel could be obtained from him, resolved to put up with the inferior pleasure of hearing some gossip about the Rectory.

"I say," he began in his most cordial manner, "tell us what you've got in that basket, come now, and I'll let you pass."

Walter opened the lid and let him look in.

"Stones! What a weight to carry up the hill! I know who set you to get them. What a shame!"

"I set myself," said Walter, indignantly.

Roger winked and nodded.

"Yes, yes; but you need not talk like that to me. I know them well enough. I sha'n't tell of you. Should not I be precious sorry to stand in your shoes!"

Walter's eyes fell on Roger's great feet in his clumsy, soiled shoes, and he smiled.

Fortunately for Roger's temper he was not very quick in reading looks; he thought Walter was smiling at his cleverness, and he jumped from the gate into the field in high good humour.

"I'll tell you what I'll do for you," he said; "the gate's locked, and she (looking at Conny) does not look as if she could climb it. I'll take you into our orchard and through the house, and let you out just opposite your own garden door."

Mrs. Lloyd had once desired the children not to go to the farm without leave. Constance remembered it, and gave Walter's jacket a pull, but he took no notice of her. He thanked Roger quite warmly, and, as they crossed the field together, Constance heard him asking questions about the island, and where the boat was kept. She kept as close to Walter as she could, but he was talking so eagerly that she had no opportunity of putting in a word till they reached the farm-house.

Mrs. Fletcher was in the kitchen when they entered the back door with Roger, and, as soon as she saw them, she insisted on taking them into the parlour to rest. She was very kind and friendly in her manner, and it was quite beyond Constance's courage to make any objection. Walter did not seem to think of doing so.

Mrs. Fletcher asked Constance a great many questions, when she had made her sit down, about when they got up, and when they went to bed, and what they ate, and how many times in the week they went to church, and after every answer she threw up her hands and looked at Tom, Nancy, and Roger, who had all crowded into the room. She seemed determined to find something to pity the children for in everything that they said; and when Conny, under the force of the questioning, let out one or two things that did seem hardships to her, Mrs. Fletcher's indignation grew quite loud, and she went off into a long tirade about what she called Welsh ways, so outlandish and mean, and sympathised so pathetically with the children for coming into a foreign country, without father or mother to care for them, that the ever-ready tears began to overflow Conny's eyes. At sight of them Mrs. Fletcher checked herself, and, by way of diversion, produced from a cupboard a large plate of very rich cake and a bottle of sweet wine. Walter and Conny had rather not have eaten anything, for they were not hungry; but Mrs. Fletcher would not let them go away without. Clive was pleased at the sight of the cake, for he liked sweet things, and, as his health was delicate, Mrs. Lloyd very seldom allowed him to taste them. He was easily persuaded to take a second large slice of cake, and Mrs. Fletcher overcame Walter's objection by asserting that it would do him good.

"It was her opinion," she said, and she had told it twenty times to Fletcher, "that the poor child was pined, and that what he wanted to make him strong was to get what he liked to eat."

Walter remembered that Clive had been used to eat what he liked when they lived at home; and, in spite of all the proofs he had had of Mrs. Lloyd's kindness, he allowed a feeling of distrust about her conduct to Clive to rise in his mind, and he encouraged his brother to disobey her wishes. While they were eating Roger ran out of the room and returned with a basket, in which lay a live sea-gull.

"There!" he said, putting it down before Clive, "I don't know whether it's the same bird Master Lloyd wanted to get last night, but I picked it up on the sea after you were gone. It has broken its wing. It will never fly again, but it would live in your garden. I could show you how to feed it if you liked to keep it for a pet. I'll give it to you, but I would not let Master Lloyd have it for anything."

"There's a good boy, Roger," cried good-natured Mrs. Fletcher, who saw the admiring look with which Clive shyly put his hand to stroke the purple feathers on the bird's neck. "I'll give you something else for it that you'll like a great deal better."

"Good to give what does not belong to him; I shot it," cried Tom, sulkily.

"And I found it," said Roger, very loudly.

"Come, come," said Mrs. Fletcher, uneasily, "don't quarrel before the young lady and gentlemen; you shall both have something—there now!"

The angry looks did not change, and Conny, quite frightened, pulled Walter's jacket very hard, and begged him in a whisper to come away.

Mrs. Fletcher, Tom, and Nancy followed them to the gate. Mrs. Fletcher kept them there some minutes, telling them how glad she had been to see them, and how much she hoped *they* were not above stepping in now and then in a neighbourly way, while Tom amused himself by slyly letting loose the yard dog, and encouraging him to bark at the children.

"Don't be afraid, dear," Mrs. Fletcher said to Clive, seeing him shrink; "he won't hurt you while I am here."

"He is not afraid," said Walter, proudly; and Clive got a look which made him, trembling as he was, walk straight up to the dog, and put his small hand on its head. Walter looked defiance at Tom, and Mrs. Fletcher held up her hands.

"Well," she said, "I never did see such a dear—so pretty, and with such a spirit!"

Many more flattering speeches she made, with entreaties that they would come to her whenever they were in trouble or wanted anything, and Conny thought her so kind that she was ashamed of feeling glad when they were safe through the gate into the lane.

She found that her brothers were not at all inclined to listen to scruples of hers. The flattery, the cake, and his present had put Clive into unusually high spirits, and Walter seemed full of thoughts and plans of his own. He would not hear anything about not going to the Fletchers' again, and gave all his attention to Clive, who was intent on building a stone house for his sea-gull in a sheltered place in the lane just under Maurice's wall.

Gwen heard them from the garden talking about it, and came out to help, and they were all hard at work, eager and happy, when Maurice, tired with his long walk, and out of spirits with his solitary afternoon, turned into the lane. He saw the children before they saw him, and wondered what they could all have found to do that interested them so much while he was away, and especially it puzzled him to see Walter so busy and in such good spirits. *He* had been very unhappy ever since their quarrel, and he thought it odd that Walter should not appear to care at all. It made him alter his intention of being the first to speak cordially. He thought Gwen would have run forward to meet him, but she did not happen to look round, and he stood still for some time without any one noticing him.

"What *are* you all doing?" he asked at last in a very querulous tone.

"Oh, Maurice! we are making such a beautiful stone house," cried Gwen; "and you will never guess what Clive has got in that basket."

"I don't like guessing," said Maurice, crossly; "you must tell me."

"No, no, no!" cried Clive, putting his hand over Gwen's mouth; "Maurice must not know—it's a secret."

"Always secrets," said Maurice; "I hate secrets."

"Other people's secrets you mean," said Walter, dryly; "but don't say too much about this, for perhaps it will turn out to be one of your own."

"Mine! What do you mean?" cried Maurice. "I never have a secret; *I'm not so deceitful.*"

"You may look in and see if you like," said Walter.

Maurice lifted up the lid of the basket, and quite started when he saw the sea-gull. He looked at it for a moment bewildered, and then turned to Walter with flushed cheeks and angry eyes.

"You got that gull on purpose to provoke me, I know you did," he cried. "You have been talking to the Fletchers about it; but I declare I will not bear it a moment longer. I'll show you what it is to be spiteful to me. I'll——"

"What will you do?" said Walter, standing straight before him.

Maurice did not quite know, and before he had made up his mind a loud laugh from the opposite wall made them all turn round and discover Roger Fletcher's red face, with its broadest grin on it, looking down with great delight on the scene.

"That's right," he cried; "have it out at last; let's see who's master."

Confused thoughts rushed through Maurice's mind of knocking Walter down, rolling

Clive in the dust, and throwing all the stones in the road into Roger's face; but just at this critical moment the little door in the back garden opened, and Mrs. Lloyd came out into the lane. Roger's face disappeared instantly behind the wall, Clive and Conny huddled together, and Maurice and Walter stood opposite each other looking somewhat ashamed. Mrs. Lloyd came out with a smiling face.

"The tea-bell has rung three times, children," she said. "How busy you must have been! But what is the matter?"

No one answered. Mrs. Lloyd looked at Maurice, and he saw how the pleasant, bright look changed into a very sad one. She did not ask any more questions, but led the way back into the house. The boys followed last, and scowled at each other over their unfinished quarrel.

Maurice had many uncomfortable thoughts to bear all that evening, especially when he happened to look into his mother's anxious face. He knew very well that she saw there was something amiss, and that she was hoping that he would come, as he had always been used to do till lately, to confess his faults of temper to her before he went to bed. He felt that a full talk and confession to his mother of all that he had done wrong would be the very best thing to set him right; but Maurice did not honestly wish to be set right. He excused himself by thinking that while so many other people were to blame it was impossible to tell the exact truth, and that, as his mother would certainly not approve of his confessing any one's faults but his own, there was no use in saying anything at all, for it would be only making himself out worse than he really was.

Clive had a bad headache all the evening, and could not eat his supper. Mrs. Lloyd attributed it to his having been out too long in the heat. Conny secretly thought of Mrs. Fletcher's cake; but as Clive could talk of nothing, when Wlter took him up to bed, but his sea-gull, and his anxiety lest Maurice should do anything to prevent his keeping it, Walter set down his brother's pale looks to the account of Maurice's temper, and made many fierce resolves about watching over his interests more vigorously than ever. He promised Clive over and over again that Maurice should never interfere with him, and that he should keep his new pet in spite of every one; but the promise did not give the comfort he expected—it only sent Clive off into one of his interminable fits of crying; and it was quite true, as Maurice had said, that when Clive once began to cry it was very difficult to find out what he was crying for. Remorse for having drawn his brother into a quarrel had more to do with his sorrow than he knew how to make Walter understand.

Long after Clive had cried himself to sleep Walter lay awake thinking. The vexations of the last two days had made him more dissatisfied with his present lot than ever, and in this mood the story he had planned on the shore recurred to his mind as something pleasant to think about, and he thought about it so long that at last, instead of being a castle in the air, it began to look like a possible plan for the future, which excused him from caring much what he did or left undone in the present.

Gwen, too, was awake a long time. She sat up in her little crib for more than an hour watching for Maurice, and when she saw him pass the nursery door, on his way to his own room, she begged he would come in and hear her repeat the hymn she had learned for Sunday. Maurice wondered at first why she had learned it so early in the week, and why she had chosen such a long one; but he guessed her motive when she came to the middle of the hymn, and, raising herself on her elbow in bed and looking at him, repeated earnestly:—

" 'A little child I chanced to meet
Once in a cottage bred,
Taught by his mother to repeat
What Solomon has said,—

" 'That he who ruleth well his heart
And keeps his temper down
Is greater, acts a wiser part,
Than he who takes a town.' "

Maurice listened patiently to the end of the verses, but the remark he made when he returned the book to Gwen hardly repaid her for having kept awake an hour to learn them.

"It is all very well, Gwen," he said, "for people to put such things in hymns; but I can tell you that taking a town—yes, if it were Troy or Sebastopol itself—is just a joke to keeping one's temper with Roger Fletcher next door, and Clive and Walter Mayne living in the house."

CHAPTER IX

A RAINY DAY AND TALK

"THERE, NOW," said Maurice, coming into the nursery one day after dinner, "it has begun to rain, and it will go on raining just like this all the afternoon I know."

"It is the first rainy day we have had for a whole month remember," said Gwen.

"That's just why it's so provoking that it should begin to-day," said Maurice, "when I am not at all in the humour to like being shut up in the house, and when Mr. Holdsworth has come to see papa, and we are sure of a half holiday."

"It always does rain when one wants it to be fine," said Owen, looking as if he had made a discovery.

"Nay, now, it did not rain on our island day," cried Gwen, who always thought it necessary to stand up for everything, including the weather.

"It would have been just as well for us if it had as far as any pleasure we got out of the day goes," observed Maurice, sharply. "Now, Gwen, even you must allow that they have been getting worse and worse ever since."

"Have they done any harm to-day?" asked Gwen, with a side glance towards the other end of the room, where the three Maynes were standing.

"As much as they could, considering that they have had no chance of going out again to the Fletchers'," said Maurice. "Walter asked papa questions about every line of our Virgil in this morning's lesson, and Clive stood listening to papa's explanations with his eyes wide open, as if they had been entertaining. We were kept a whole quarter of an hour longer at lessons than we need have been."

"That did not signify so much as it rained," said Gwen.

"It puts such notions into papa's head," objected Maurice. "He said to-day that he wished he could see me really *anxious* to know more Latin. Only seeing the Maynes could have made him expect such a thing. That's the sort of way they behave at lessons, and now just look at them in playhours."

It was not an encouraging sight for even such a determined looker on the bright side as Gwen. The three orphans were standing listlessly at the window looking out at the rain. Since the day of the quarrel Walter had kept his resolution of never reading any of Maurice's books, and so deprived himself of his favourite amusement; and Conny and Clive thought themselves obliged to follow his example, and refuse to touch any of the toys in the toy-cupboard, or join in any of the nursery games. It was really enough to throw a gloom over the whole party to see the three keeping together, speaking in whispers, and never attempting to do anything pleasant.

A rainy holiday afternoon, while this state of things was going on in the nursery, was not a very agreeable prospect, and for five minutes Gwen looked almost unhappy.

"Oh, Maurice!" she said at last, "I wonder whether we have tickets enough to buy one of mamma's stories. You know she often lets us have one on a rainy day, even if we don't quite deserve it."

"My ticket bag is nearly empty," said Maurice, "and has been ever since Walter came; but you can go and see."

Gwen came back triumphant. She had found Mrs. Lloyd in her own room, actually writing something in the red-backed MSS. book, which was always connected in the children's minds with a new story, and she had so readily granted the request to bring the book into the nursery, and made so little inquiry into the state of the ticket bags, that Gwen was inclined to think that mamma must have anticipated the rainy afternoon, and that she had some particular reason for being ready with a story.

The little Maynes had heard enough about Mrs. Lloyd's stories to make them press eagerly round when she came in, and take their places in the circle with almost as bright faces as the other children when she began to read.

"It is to be quite a new story I hope, mamma," said Maurice, while Mrs. Lloyd turned over the leaves of her book.

"Quite new and true," said Mrs. Lloyd; "but I am going to choose it myself, as you have none of you earned it. I have called it 'Getting out of Bed the Wrong Way.' "

"That sounds very nicely, certainly," said Gwen.

"I am not sure that it is exactly nice," said Mrs. Lloyd; "but you shall judge for yourselves."

GETTING OUT OF BED THE WRONG WAY

"Well, Master Edward," said Susan, "any one may see that *you* got out of bed the wrong way this morning. If I were you I should be ashamed of going into such passions."

Susan was brushing Edward's hair when she said this, and Edward, who hated having his hair brushed, was twisting his head crossly backwards and forwards and grumbling all the time.

He had been an hour and a quarter in dressing, and the consequence was that he was vexed with himself and inclined to quarrel with every one else. Susan's remark did not make him feel better.

"Well," he said to himself, "as you have made up your mind that I am to be naughty I won't trouble myself to try to be good; I'll be still naughtier than you expect me to be;" and he *was* still naughtier. He waited till Susan had made his hair quite smooth, and then he snatched the brush out of her hand, ruffled his hair into a terrible tangle, and tossed the brush through the night nursery door with such force that it went spinning across the play-room, and broke a pane of glass in his little sister Ellie's baby house.

"As sure as ever you were born I'll tell your papa of this, Master Edward," shouted Susan; but Edward put his hands over his ears and ran downstairs as fast as ever he could to the little school-room, where he ought to have been an hour ago learning his morning lessons.

There was a fire in the little school-room, and Ellie was sitting before it with her books in her lap.

"Good morning, brother," she said; but Edward did not answer her. He felt more angry with Ellie than with any one else; first, because she had been up in time when he had not; and, secondly, because he had just broken her baby house, and given her a reason for being angry with him.

He took up his Latin grammar, but he could not attend to a word of it. When he had looked at it for about five minutes he laid it down, and began to unbolt the window which opened on to the gravel walk.

"Please, brother, don't open the window," said Ellie; "I have a cough, and mamma says I am not to sit in a draught."

"Who said you would have to sit in a draught?" answered Edward. "Can't I shut the window from the outside, pray?"

"Oh! but I think you must not go out this damp morning," said Ellie; "you must stay in and learn your lessons."

"Must, indeed!" said Edward; "I shall do just whatever I like best;" and he flung the window wide open as he spoke, and jumped out into the garden.

It was a damp, misty morning, the gravel walk was all strewn with fallen leaves, and the dahlias in the borders hung their heads and dripped rain from all their petals like long rows of naughty crying children.

Edward kicked the damp leaves about till his slippers were quite wet and he felt as cold as possible. It was not at all pleasant being out; but he saw that Ellie was very anxious that he should come in, for she kept tapping at the window and beckoning him, and that made him feel a naughty wish to stay out as long as ever he could.

At last, when he had turned his back to the window and was amusing himself by counting the drops of dew on a cobweb, he felt somebody touch his shoulder, and looking round he saw Ellie standing behind him with his Latin grammar in her hand.

"Do learn it, brother," she said.

"You little, tiresome, interfering thing!" cried Edward; "how dare you come here? Go away directly!"

But Ellie did not go away; she came a little nearer, and tried to slip the book into her brother's hand. Then a great gust of passion rose in Edward's heart. He felt his cheeks grow very hot, and, scarcely knowing what he did, he lifted up his hand and struck a hard blow on Ellie's little white cheek.

"Oh, brother!" said Ellie.

She had not time to say more, for just then the prayer-bell rang, and the children ran as fast as they could down the gravel walk and through the school-room to the breakfast parlour.

The servants were coming in to prayers as they entered, so no one asked what they had been doing.

Edward would not kneel near Ellie at prayers. He went into a corner as far from all the others as he could, and while they were praying he was saying to himself that there never was any one who had so much reason for being out of temper as he had, and that he was certain Job himself would have been cross if he had been obliged to stand for half an hour every morning to have his hair brushed, and if little girls had come interfering, and putting *him* in mind of his lessons.

"Ellie," said their mamma while they were eating their breakfast, "what is the matter with your face? You have one white cheek and one red cheek this morning."

"Have I, mamma?" said Ellie; "how odd!"

Ellie tried to laugh as she said this, but Edward saw that her lip trembled, and that a tear hung under her long dark eyelashes.

"How tiresome it is that girls will cry for such little things!" he thought; but while he was thinking this he felt a pain in his heart, and he half wished he could tell Ellie that he was sorry.

It was only half a wish, for the next minute he had an opportunity, and he did not take it. Ellie came behind his chair, and put her piece of buttered toast on his plate. It would have been very easy to have whispered to her then, but a sullen feeling of pride rose up and stopped him. He turned his back upon her and said he hated buttered toast, and that he wished she would not bring him things she knew he did not like.

Ellie crept back to her high chair, and Edward ate large mouthsful of dry bread without quite knowing what he was doing.

"I know what I will do," he thought at last; "I will say it to her when she brings my book-bag before I go to school."

It was time to get ready for school when breakfast was over. Edward put on his coat and hat, and waited at the hall door for Ellie to bring him his book-bag as she did every morning. He waited for nearly ten minutes, and then his mamma brought the bag. She said Ellie had got such a bad cough that she dare not let her come into the cold hall, and that Edward must be sure and shut the door carefully after him.

"I need not mind," thought Edward; "there will be plenty of time to say it when I come home at night."

That day at school seemed a very long one to Edward. He was as busy about his lessons and as noisy and merry in the playground as any of his schoolfellows, and yet he felt all the time as if there was something wrong, and every now and then he said to himself, "I wish I had said that thing to Ellie before I left home."

When school was over and he set off to walk home he felt happier, and he began to plan how he would run upstairs the instant he came in, and put his arms round Ellie's neck and say, "Ellie, I am sorry," and then he knew that Ellie's face would flush with pleasure, and that she would say, "Never mind, brother; it was a great deal my fault;" for that was always the way in which their quarrels ended.

When Edward got home he did run up into the play-room, but Ellie was not there; then he went into the school-room, and the dining-room, and the drawing-room, but he found no one. The house seemed to be in a strange sort of bustle. Servants were running up and down stairs with things in their hands, and there was a gig at the door. It looked like the doctor's gig.

At last Edward went up to the room opposite his mamma's bed-room, where Ellie had slept since she had had a cough. Just as he was going to turn the handle of the door Susan caught hold of him and pulled him back.

"You must not go in there, Master Edward," she said.

"Why not?"

"Miss Ellie has gone to bed."

"Well, I only want to say one thing; I sha'n't be long. Let me go, Susan; I must, I must say one thing;" and Edward got so eager as he spoke that, if Susan had not held him very fast, he would have kicked the door.

As they were struggling the door opened, and Edward's papa and the doctor came out together. They did not see Edward, so he took the opportunity of slipping past them and standing inside the door.

Ellie was sitting on the bed. Her face was not pale now; it was redder than any scarlet rose. She was coughing in a strange way, and every now and then there came a sharp cry, and she gasped as if she could hardly breathe.

Edward saw it was no time now to say the one thing. He stood looking at her for a moment, and then he turned quickly away, and ran into the play-room, and threw himself down on the floor.

A terrible thought had come into his head—if Ellie were to die, if Ellie were to die, and never know that he was sorry?

He lay for a long time on the floor thinking of this and crying.

He thought of the numbers of plays they had had together, and how he used to say every evening, "It shall be your turn to choose the play next," and how Ellie's turn never came. He recollected that yesterday evening, when they were playing at Old Gaunt Thief Place, he had made Ellie let him choose the places they were to play in, and that he had promised she should choose to-morrow when they finished the game; and, Oh! suppose they should never finish it, and that Ellie should never have her fair share in the game!

Then he remembered how unjust he had been last Saturday about their new balls— how he had taken the prettiest himself, and said that the ugly one must be meant for Ellie.

"But it shall never be so again," he said out loud, though there was no one to hear him; "only get well and play with me again, Ellie, and you shall always choose; you shall have all the best things."

When he had said this he got up. It was almost dark—long past teatime—but no one came to him.

He went and stood at the play-room door. Now and then some one passed up the stairs and went into Ellie's room, and then, when the door was open, Edward heard the strange sharp cry and difficult breathing.

When it was quite dark Susan came with some supper for him and a candle. She told him that Ellie had got the croup, and that the doctor was coming again to see her in the middle of the night.

This comforted Edward. He knew that Ellie had had the croup before, and yet that she had been well enough to play with him the very next day, so he ate his supper quietly, and went to bed and to sleep.

When he awoke it was morning. The curtains had never been drawn, and a single ray of light stole through the night nursery window. He got up quickly and dressed himself, and stood at the play-room door.

The house was very still now. There was no one going up and down stairs, nor any sound of coughing or of difficult breathing.

"Ellie must be better," thought Edward; "I will go softly into her room before any one gets up, and say the thing that I want so very much to tell her."

He was afraid that if Susan saw him she would stop him, so he went at once, treading on tip toe along the passage.

The door of Ellie's room stood ajar—he pushed it open and went in. There was a lamp burning low on the table. Ellie lay on her back in the bed; her cheeks were as pale now as they always were; a white handkerchief was tied under her chin, and her pretty brown curls were gathered up under her cap. Edward walked across the room and sat down close to the bed.

"I will wait until she wakes," he said, "and then I will tell her."

He sat still a long time, the lamp went out, and the light in the room grew stronger; but Ellie did not awake. At last he began to be afraid that some one would come in and send him away, so he climbed into the bed and put his mouth close to Ellie's ear.

"Ellie," he said, "open your eyes, look up; I want to speak to you—I want to say just one thing."

Ellie had always been ready enough to hear all that Edward had to say; but now she did not open her eyes or look up.

"Ellie, Ellie, Ellie!" said Edward; and each time he spoke his voice grew louder and louder, till it ended in a wild scream, which brought his papa and mamma and every one in the house into the room; for now he had found out the truth—Ellie was dead, and he could never tell her that he was sorry.

Many years have passed since that sad, dark morning. Edward is now a grown-up man. He is a grave, quiet man. No one has ever known him to go into a passion, or heard him say a hasty word; but if ever he sees brothers and sisters quarrelling, or sees one child taking an unfair advantage over another, there comes a stern, sad look on his face, and his voice trembles when he speaks to them. People who do not know him are surprised that he should care so very much for the angry words of little children; but his friends are not surprised, for when that sad look comes over his face they know that he is thinking of Ellie.

"Oh, mamma!" said Emma, drawing a long breath, "did you say it was a true story?"

"I do not think I would have written it out for you if I had not known that the substance of it was true," said Mrs. Lloyd, sadly.

"Do you know him now, mamma?" said Owen.

"Yes; and so do you."

"But how can he go on living? how can he bear it?" cried Gwen.

"And yet," said Mrs. Lloyd, "boys and girls too do as bad things as he did, and they go on living, and think themselves happy; the only difference is, that in the story I have told you the punishment followed quickly on the fault, and in other cases the consequences follow more slowly, and you don't always see them or know what they are."

"But, Oh, mamma! people often have bad tempers, and say and do passionate things, and nothing happens," said Emma.

"Yes, something always, Emma; and, do you know, I am not sure that the consequences of Edward's passion, dreadful as they seemed, were the very worst that could have happened. It is almost too shocking to hear of a brother being the cause of his sister's death; but do not you know that you can do people far greater injury than killing their bodies is? You can help the devil to destroy their souls; and there are few weapons stronger than angry words to do this. Think what far more dreadful remorse must be felt if one day, when all secrets are known, one brother or companion should say to another, 'It was your temper, your angry words and overbearing ways, that first awoke hatred in my heart, and separated my soul from God.' Yes, it was happy for Edward, perhaps, that his punishment came so soon; that it was only a little, weak body that his bad temper killed, and not an immortal soul."

"Oh, mamma, mamma!" sobbed Gwen, "I wish you had not told us such a very sad story."

Mrs. Lloyd looked at Maurice's averted face as he sat on a stool at her feet, and occupied himself in twisting and untwisting the fringe of her shawl, and she almost wished the same. She saw, by the particular twitch of Maurice's mouth, that he was trying to harden himself against the effect of her words, and she was almost sorry that she had given him the opportunity of slighting another warning. "I can't think why mamma will go on talking at me as if I had a bad temper," Maurice's face said plainly enough, though his tongue was silent; and this display of his self-justifying humour made Mrs. Lloyd so hopeless of doing good by anything she might say that she relapsed into silence, and turned over the leaves of her book in a disconsolate mood. She was roused by hearing a deep sob from Constance. As is generally the case the person who wanted the story least was busiest applying it, and, anxious not to leave too sad an impression on her mind, Mrs. Lloyd felt glad when Emma and Owen broke the silence by clamorous entreaties for a story that should end well.

"And do let it be a fairy tale," pleaded Gwen; "it is so very, very long since we have had one of your own kind, and Clive and Conny would like it so very much."

"But you are too old for fairy tales, and I have left off writing them," said Mrs. Lloyd.

"Never mind, mamma," said Gwen; "you generally tell the best stories when you make them out as you go on. We will give you a few minutes to think, and I will give you a subject. Let it be about a king's son, and let there be something in it that has been enchanted; but you need not begin at the very beginning, and tell us all that old part about the fairies being invited to the christening, and the spiteful one being forgotten, and coming through the keyhole with bad gifts, for we can imagine that all that has been said. Begin when the prince is about our age, and describe what sort of enchanted castle, or garden, or brazen tower he has been shut up in."

"Well, let me think for a few minutes," said Mrs. Lloyd, good-naturedly. "Yes, I think I can recollect a story I once heard, and it is about princes, for there are two of them;

but it is not so much that they were shut up in an enchanted castle as that they were obliged to wear enchanted clothes that makes there be a story to tell about them. I will pass over the part about the christening as you desire, and begin my story when the princes were old enough to play about in their nursery, and walk where they liked in the beautiful gardens and pleasure grounds which the king had set apart for their use.

"They had all the wonderfully beautiful playthings, the talking birds, the singing fish, the picture looking-glasses, the boxes full of leaden soldiers, who could fire rifles and present arms, and march without any one touching them, such as kings' sons in fairy-land would be sure to have; but, with all these, they soon found that they were not always happy. They found that, whether their games went well or ill, whether the days were bright and pleasant or long and dreary, depended on whether they had the company of one or other of two little fairies, who, ever since they were born, had been in the habit of coming in and out of their nursery. They were very unlike each other, but they both had the same trick of creeping noiselessly in, and at some unexpected moment popping their heads between the little boys, and, by a single word or look, making them feel either happy or miserable. One was a crooked little old woman, who always leaned on a crab-stick, while she held in the other hand a black snuff-box, from which she was constantly scattering some bitter-tasting powder. The little boys never called her by any name, or, indeed, addressed her at all, for they never wished for her presence; but they knew well enough what she was called, for when the light fell on her wrinkled forehead they could read some black letters there, and they made the word Discord. The other was a gentle, beautiful, winged fairy, who was always welcome wherever she came; but she seemed to be of a timid disposition—very easily frightened away. When she had been spending an afternoon with the princes, and when the plays were all going on beautifully, some one would speak a cross word, or, perhaps, only think an unkind thought in his heart, and when he looked round the good fairy was gone, the room had become quite dull and gloomy, and there was no such thing as entering again into the spirit of the game. This fairy, too, had her name written on her forehead; it was traced in letters of gold, and they made the word Love.

"The princes always said that they very much preferred the company of the kind fairy to that of the cross old woman, but they did not always behave as if they meant what they said; for, if they had cared very much and taken notice, they would soon have found that there were certain words and ways which always brought the company of one or the other.

"Discord's favourite words were *I* and *mine*, and *It is my right*. She was always to be seen behind the speaker of one of these words, clapping him on the back with her ugly hand, and sprinkling her bitter-tasting powder into his mouth. The words Love liked to hear were *you* and *yours*, and *I will give up*. The instant they were spoken the air of the room became clearer, Discord and her powder were blown away, and Love's soft eyes were seen shining in some sunny corner."

"I would always have taken care to have her, I know," said Gwen.

"Would you? Ah, well, let us see *next* time there is a holiday in the nursery on a rainy afternoon. You can't think how fond Discord is of whole holidays and rainy afternoons. But you really must not interrupt the story. I have not told you yet the names of the two princes. The elder of the two was called Lofty. He had dark hair and eyes, and was, altogether, a handsome, well-grown boy for his age. The second was called Cherry, chiefly, I believe, on account of his rosy cheeks and lips, and the merry expression that was natural to his face.

"It happened one day that the boys had a whole holiday in honour of the king's birthday. There was to be a grand *fête* in the evening, and, as all the attendants were occupied in preparing for it, the two little princes were allowed to roam about the gardens and pleasure grounds as they pleased. After playing some little time they went into an arbour to rest, and there they found a basket of beautiful fruit, which one of the gardeners had placed there as a present for the little princes. Nothing, you will say, could be pleasanter than sitting in a shady arbour eating beautiful fruit when one is tired with playing; but unluckily Discord was perched up somewhere among the leaves of a thorn tree which formed the back of the arbour, and, as soon as Lofty sat down, she began to whisper in his ear, 'Look at Cherry; he is helping himself to all the best fruit.' Cherry had, indeed, taken up the basket, and began to divide the fruit into two equal parts. At the bottom of the basket lay a remarkably fine peach, and Discord, leaning down, dexterously scattered a handful of her powder over it. This powder had the curious property of making everything it touched look extremely nice, so that people could not help wishing for it; but when they obtained the wished-for thing it tasted bitter or looked changed, and they had no pleasure in it.

"Lofty and Cherry had proved this often enough, but they forgot their past experience now, and they both made up their minds to have that one particular peach.

" 'It's my right to have it,' said Lofty, thrusting his hand into the basket; 'for I'm the eldest.'

" 'No, no,' said Cherry; 'you always take the best things for yourself, and I will stand up for my own rights.'

" 'Well said!' cried Discord; and she went on clapping her hands and flourishing her crab-stick, while the two boys struggled together for the peach till they had overturned the table and trampled all the rest of the juicy fruit to pieces on the ground.

"Just then it happened that Love passed by on her way to visit a drooping rose that was struggling for life among the prickles of the thorn tree, and as she passed she whispered into Cherry's ear, 'Do you care more for a peach than for your brother?'

" 'I don't care at all about the peach,' said Cherry; 'I only care about having my own right.'

"At the word Love flew away, but she had left a sweet breath behind her that blew away the dust from Cherry's eyes.

" 'After all,' he thought, 'it is not worth quarrelling about;' and he turned away with not a very good grace, and threw himself on the ground of the arbour.

"Lofty ran away with the peach, and sat down under a plane tree to eat it; but at the very first mouthful he discovered the trick that Discord had played him, and was obliged to throw it away in disgust.

"In the meantime Cherry lay groaning on the floor of the arbour.

" 'This is always the way,' he said; 'all our pleasures, all our happy days, are spoilt! O Love, Love! why won't you come and live with us?'

" 'I am here,' said Love from the other side of the arbour. 'You see I always come when I am called for.'

" 'But you keep so far off,' said Cherry; 'you never come quite close to me, and stay by me a long time, as I have seen you do with other people.'

" 'That I would gladly do,' said Love; 'but unfortunately you are wearing the wrong sort of clothes. I cannot be very intimate with people who don't choose to put on my livery. You have got on Discord's clothes, and I really dare not come very near you, for the prickles hurt my soft skin and tear my delicate wings.'

" 'I don't know what you mean about clothes,' said Cherry. 'I think I am dressed in a very princely manner.'

" 'You think so because you are so blind,' said Love. 'The truth is that Discord and I engaged at your birth to supply you with enchanted clothes, but you have hitherto always perversely preferred the garments she brings you to mine. My clothes are called *Habits of Self-denial,* and it cannot be denied that they fit rather tightly, and that there is a little restraint in them when they are first put on; but their beauty and value no tongue can tell. They are marked with the word *Thou,* and I am never absent long from any one who wears them. Discord's clothes are called *Habits of Self-indulgence.* They fit easily enough, but they are sown all over with hard, prickly *I*'s, and it would be the death of me if I ventured near them.'

"As Love finished speaking Cherry looked at himself, and he perceived, for the first time, that his clothes on every side were one mass of prickles; wilful, sharp thorns were sticking up all over him; and every thorn, however crooked and crabbed, made a capital letter *I*.

" 'How horribly ugly!' said Cherry, with a sigh. 'Dear Love, help me to take off these unbecoming clothes, and give me some of yours instead.'

" 'My enchanted garments are earned, not given. Every time you give up your own way, every time you do something you dislike yourself to please another, one of Discord's clothes will slip away from you, and you will find one of mine in its place.'

" 'Unluckily I like my own way so very much the best,' said Cherry.

" 'Good-by, then, for the present,' said Love, tripping from the arbour.

"For some time Cherry lay grumbling to himself, but at last his eye was caught by a bright silver button that lay on the ground. Thinking that it was one which he had lost from his own dress when he had thrown himself on the ground, he picked it up and placed it in the sleeve of his coat. As he did so Lofty re-entered the arbour. He was tired of wandering about by himself, and he had come to ask Cherry to play with him.

" 'Come, Cherry,' he said, 'our holiday is passing away, and we are doing nothing. Let us go and row in our boat on the lake.'

"Cherry had no particular wish to row in the boat, and he was just going to say so when he was stopped by hearing several little voices, and to his surprise he found that his clothes were talking to him. Most of them said, in shrill voices, 'Do as you like yourself—that is pleasant;' but one soft, clear voice came from the little button with which he had fastened his sleeve, and it said, 'Do as your brother likes—that is right.' Cherry was pleased with the sweet tones of this voice, and he turned to follow its advice. As he was going he felt a pull from behind: Discord was dragging him back by a ribbon he wore around his neck. He resolutely took a step forward, the ribbon gave way, and Discord disappeared with it in her hand, and in its place there came a band of silver tissue, which Cherry knew at once must be one of the fairy Love's enchanted clothes.

"After this day, whenever Cherry was asked to do anything, there was sure to be a dispute among his clothes. When they had all said the same thing he had never heard them speak, but now he was almost distracted with their different voices; some saying, shrill and loud, 'Do as you like, do as you like;' and others, in gentle tones, 'Do as you ought, do as you ought.' Whenever Cherry listened to the first voices he was sure to see Discord's ugly face poked over his shoulder, and to have a shower of her blinding powder in his eyes; but if he listened to the second Love's sweet voice smiled on him, and he won another of her enchanted garments.

"As years passed on there was silence again among Cherry's clothes, they once more all said the same thing, and were in harmony together. He was clothed from head to foot in the good fairy's most splendid garments; but he had become so used to them that he had no idea himself of the grand appearance he made, or how strong, and wise, and invincible the constant wearing of such enchanted armour made him.

"He and Lofty were now young men, and accompanied the king, their father, into the camp and the council-room; and Cherry soon became renowned through the kingdom as the bravest and wisest fairy prince that had ever been seen. He had just returned from a successful campaign, in which he had vanquished a horrible two-headed ogre, who had made great ravages in his father's dominions, when he and Lofty received an invitation to attend a tournament at the court of a neighbouring king, to which all the princes and knights in fairy-land had been summoned. This king had an only and very beautiful daughter, called Blanchefleur; and it was rumoured that he invited this large assembly of princes to his court that he might judge of their merits, and choose from among them a husband worthy of the beautiful princess.

"Lofty and Cherry traveled together to the old king's court, and they were surprised to find that they were received, on their arrival, by their old friend the fairy Love. She welcomed them both to the court with equal politeness; but each saw her with different eyes, and she bestowed a different greeting on each. Lofty had seen little of her since his earliest nursery days, and he could not help thinking that the fairy had changed much since she had last noticed him; at all events she no longer had the power of driving Discord away as in former times. Though he was frequently in Love's company now, for she was a constant attendant of the Princess Blanchefleur, he could not help perceiving that Discord was never absent from his side. She was for ever whispering angry and jealous thoughts in his ear, and her hard hand lay like a heavy weight on his heart.

"Lofty, too, now for the first time began to perceive the weight and inconvenience of his clothes. He was now really anxious to distinguish himself in the trials of skill which daily took place among the princes; but his clothes were always in the way, and were constantly the cause of his being discomfited and disgraced in the eyes of the court.

"At last the day came when the choice of the king and the princess was to be made known. The princes assembled in the hall of the palace, each dressed in his most splendid robes of state; and the king and Blanchefleur sat on two thrones at the upper end. The king held a sceptre in his hand, pointed with a diamond of peculiar brightness; and he said that as he should, if he depended on his own wisdom, find it very difficult to select the worthiest among so many princes, he had determined to trust to the virtues of this talisman to help him to come to a just decision. His sceptre was a test which never failed to discover a real from a false prince.

"At these words many voices were raised in anger that the king should have any doubt of his guests being each and all real princes.

" 'A real prince,' said the king, quietly, 'is known by his clothes.'

"Lofty lifted up his head when he heard this, for he was more splendidly attired than any other prince present; but, while he was still gazing proudly round, the king waved his talisman in the air, and a strange change came over the assembly.

"All Discord's clothes were, by virtue of the talisman, changed to sordid rags, while such of the princes' clothes as had been the gift of the fairy Love shone with resplendent brightness. Lofty found himself clothed from head to foot with rags.

"Some of the princes were partly clothed like kings, and partly like beggars; others had their handsome clothes spoilt by some one bad habit that hung down and disgraced the rest. Cherry's garments alone had stood the test uninjured; he was found to be from head to foot habited like a prince. The king approached him, and took him by the hand to lead him to the foot of Blanchefleur's throne, while all the people shouted, 'Long live the true prince!' "

"I am glad this story ends happily," said Owen.

"Mamma," said Maurice, looking up briskly, "there is one part of your story that I quite understand and agree with—the part where it says that the fairy Love can't come near people who are wearing Discord's clothes. That is just what I mean about the Fletchers; there are some people that it is quite impossible to like."

"Oh, Maurice!" said Gwen, "you are putting it quite the wrong way; it is the people who wear Discord's clothes who cannot love any one. Mamma did not say that no one could love them."

"Ah," said Mrs. Lloyd, "there is one thing about the enchanted clothes that I had almost forgotten to mention. It is that, whichever suit you wear yourself, you are almost sure to fancy that you see the same upon all your neighbours."

"I wish there really were two fairies, and that one could earn enchanted clothes," said Constance, earnestly. "It always seems so much easier and nicer in allegories where there is some real thing to do, such as working in a vineyard or going on a journey. I always think when I hear it how glad I should be to set off at once."

"And so do I," said Gwen. "I feel disappointed when I recollect that it only means being good."

"Is not that because you forget that being good, as you call it, means doing the *real* things that form your daily duty in the very best way, and believing always that the unseen help is nearer and more real than anything else?"

"I think with me," said Walter, speaking slowly, "it is because I should like best to have to do one great thing."

"And because you don't know what a great thing the right doing of little things is."

"Mamma," said Maurice, "it is very easy to put things in stories; but I can't see how it is possible to like people just because one knows one ought."

"Nor do I, Maurice, and I am glad you have found that out; for there *is* one thing that can make us love people—people the most opposite to ourselves; and that is, believing in the love of Him who said, 'Ye are my friends if ye do whatsoever I command you. This is my commandment, that ye love one another as I have loved you.' He who knows what kind of hearts and tempers we have would not have told us to love one another unless He were able and willing to help us to do so. And, Maurice, *one another* does not mean a few people who agree with us and suit our tempers, but the neighbours and companions who have been placed near us, and who may or may not be exactly what we should have chosen for ourselves."

"Mamma," said Owen, "I never knew you put such a long moral to a story before; you used always to say we were to find out the moral for ourselves."

"And there is the tea-bell," said Gwen; "so if there is any more moral we must find it out. I hear papa's voice and Mr. Holdsworth's in the hall; they are going into the drawing-room, and you will have to go I suppose, mamma. Oh, what a nice short rainy afternoon this has been!"

After tea was over and the visitor had taken his departure, Gwen and Emma amused papa with a very tolerable version of mamma's story; but Mrs. Lloyd was disappointed to see that Maurice took a book, and settled himself at the further corner of the room to avoid hearing; and when Gwen appealed to his memory he told her that there was nothing he disliked more than hearing the same thing twice over.

CHAPTER X

THE CARREGLLWYD DAY

"GRIFFITH HUGHES is very careless about fastening the back garden gate," said Mr. Lloyd one morning at breakfast, about a fortnight after Walter's and Maurice's quarrel. "I have fastened it several times myself after supper, and last night it must have been left open till morning, for farmer Fletcher's pony has been trampling all over the garden."

"It is not Griffith's fault; he fastened the door last night I'm certain," cried Maurice; "he always does."

Maurice said this a great deal more quickly and eagerly than the occasion appeared to call for, and looked angrily across the table towards Walter as he spoke. Walter went on quietly pouring milk into Clive's breakfast cup, but when he had finished he turned to Mr. Lloyd.

"I believe, sir," he said, "that Griffith *did* fasten the door last night; I was in the garden, and I saw him."

"Very well," said Mr. Lloyd, "then some one must have unfastened it again. You can sit still under the supposition, cannot you, Maurice? Nothing very dreadful has happened, though the Fletchers' pony has been into the garden, only I wish that, when any of you children go to play in the lane after tea, you would fasten the gate after you when you come in. You can't expect Griffith Hughes to do it more than once."

"The gate of the Fletchers' paddock must have been left open too," observed Mrs. Lloyd. "I am surprised at that; they are generally very careful."

This remark was not seemingly a very interesting one, but it occasioned a great sensation at the breakfast table. Owen and Emma both nudged Maurice so energetically that he let his spoon fall out of his hand with a loud clatter on to his plate, and Clive gave such a start that he capsized the sugar-basin, which Mrs. Lloyd had given him to hand to Constance.

"What absurd children you are!" said Mr. Lloyd, rather sharply. "I really am tired of seeing grimaces made every time Mr. Fletcher's name is mentioned. Maurice, understand, once for all, I don't allow it. You have been talking nonsense about the Fletchers to Clive; I have seen him start before in that way at the sound of their names. I really will not have our good-natured neighbour turned into a bugbear."

Maurice's face had become redder, and redder, and redder as his father spoke, and he sat still in perfect silence, with a more sullen look on his face than it had been seen to wear since he was an unreasonable child of four years old.

"I don't think Maurice has anything to do with that," said Walter in a low voice; but the words did not reach Maurice's ears, for Clive made them still more indistinct by putting his hand over his brother's mouth, and Mr. Lloyd gave him no opportunity to repeat them. He had finished his breakfast, and, being busy, he gathered up his letters and newspaper, and left the room without asking any more questions, only turning around at the door to tell Maurice to come to the school-room in half an hour in a good humour.

The bread-and-milk basins were emptied in silence, but Mrs. Lloyd heard sounds of very loud, eager talking as soon as the children had escaped from the room and were alone in the garden. She wondered, with a sigh, how it was that there was now so much silence when the family were together, and so much loud talking or whispering in twos and threes when the children were out of sight of their elders. It had never been so till lately; but now there always appeared to be a mystery, and the children divided into parties, and were never seen playing or talking happily together. Mrs. Lloyd looked out of the window, and was sorry to observe how completely the two groups of children kept apart that morning; she would have been still more sorry if she could have joined first one party and then another, and heard what they talked about.

Maurice was, of course, the centre of one; Owen, Emma, and Gwen crowded round him; and Griffith Hughes stood at a little distance listening with his mouth open. The commencement of the conversation had been nothing but exclamations of anger from Maurice and echoes of sympathy from the others; but at last Griffith Hughes found an opportunity to strike in with a long complaint about the garden door, and he mixed up with it so many mysterious hints about Walter and Roger Fletcher that Maurice could not help questioning him, though the warnings he had received against gossiping with Griffith about the Fletchers were too numerous to reckon.

"So you have seen Walter and Clive going to the Fletchers' again, have you, Griffith?"

"Yes, that I have, Master Maurice, and I know what I know."

"What do you know, then?"

"You are so sharp upon one, Master Maurice. The other day, when I was going to tell you something, I overheard Master Mayne saying to Roger in the lane, you turned round quite sharp, and said something about a spy: that was not handsome at all, Master Maurice."

"Well, well, Griffith, but when I tell you to tell a thing, why, I've told you," cried Maurice, eagerly.

"Yes, sir, and you have," answered Griffith, looking down, and beginning to scrape one boot over the other, with a certain stupid expression that had once or twice before baffled Maurice when Griffith had chosen to stop short in the midst of a fit of talkativeness.

"So you know what Walter talks about to Roger, and why he goes so often to the Fletchers'?" asked Owen.

"I?" said Griffith, indignantly. "How should I know? I would not so much as set my foot inside their dirty house and garden."

"It is not dirty particularly," said Gwen in a remonstrating tone.

"I really think," said Emma, "that you ought to tell papa that Walter talks to Roger Fletcher and goes to the farm."

"We are not sure that he goes to the farm," said Maurice, "and we have never been forbidden to speak to Roger. There would be no use in going to papa about it. Walter really must learn to mind what *I* say to him. I am sure I warn him often enough."

"That you do, Master Maurice," interposed Griffith; "I hear you my own self the day you find him talking to that Roger at the garden gate. 'I insists,' says you, 'that you never speak to one of the Fletchers again, for if you be friends with the Fletchers you sha'n't be friends with us;' and the more you insisted the more determined Master Walter he looked. 'I wonder at you, Master Walter,' says I; and he twist up his head and he walk into the house without so much as looking twice at either of us."

"I don't suppose I said *insist*," interrupted Maurice; "you are so inaccurate, Griffith; but I know I did say that if he, and Conny, and Clive were to be always talking to and plotting with the Fletchers, they must not expect any of us to play with them or take any notice of them, and, though it is three days ago, we none of us have, except you, Gwen, and I must say I am very much surprised to find you so obstinate and disobedient to me."

"I can't help it," said Gwen, shaking her little head sadly. "Only look at them standing by themselves talking, talking, talking in such a quiet way, and never laughing, or running, or playing, or doing anything the least bit nice."

"I am sure *we* have little enough *now* of laughing, or playing, or doing anything nice," said Maurice. "Papa is angry with me already this morning, and I have got so many things on my mind that I have not been able to get my lessons perfectly. A pleasant morning I shall have! You go in directly, Gwen, and put the books out. I shall come soon; but I send you first, because I know if I don't that you will go and talk to Clive, who is standing now with the garden door open, looking into the Fletchers' lane, just on purpose, I do believe, to provoke me."

Gwen felt the difference between being asked to do things for Maurice's own pleasure and being sent out of the way to prevent her from following her own wishes; but she had been subject to a good deal of contradiction of late while she had been acting umpire between the contending parties, and she was getting used to it.

In the meantime the little Maynes were sauntering up and down the lower part of the garden, which was beginning to be called their play-place, since the other children had refused to share their amusements with them.

Clive stood on tiptoe lifting and letting fall the latch of the door, and every now and then looking listlessly into the lane; and Walter walked up and down the gravel walk talking to Constance, who listened eagerly.

"How nice it sounds," she said, when he had been holding forth for some time; "if only, if only it could all be managed without our doing anything deceitful—if only we had leave to go."

"Now, Conny," said Walter, "I have explained to you so often that it really is not deceitful, and that it is all nonsense to think of asking leave."

"Only, you see, I don't quite understand," said Constance.

"Well, there is no use in arguing then. Once let us get on our own desert island, where there will be no one to please but me, and all will be right. You can't be unhappy about being deceitful there, for we shall be our own masters and do just as we like. Roger and I will work, get fish, and eggs, and oysters, and all sorts of nice things, and dig in the garden as the Unknown Man did, and you and Clive shall play all day with shells in the nice dry cave that is to be our house. Don't you remember what Roger said it was like? Bright, white sand at the bottom, and then a rocky archway and a darker cave beyond, with a clear green pool of water in the middle. Only think how beautiful! How much better than a house with furniture in it, that one is always being scolded for spoiling!"

"Do you think they will ever find us?" said Constance.

"I am sure they will not, hidden in the cave. Besides, Oh, Conny! they don't want us; they will all be glad when we are gone. I don't think I should care so much for going if it were not for that."

"Clive does not seem quite so happy about going as he did when you talked about it first," said Conny.

"Do you think he is ill?" asked Walter, turning round anxiously to look at the little boy's slight, languid figure, as he stood by the door.

"I think it is going out late and eating things he ought not to eat at the Fletchers'," said Constance. "It makes his head ache, and he cannot understand his lessons, and Mr. Lloyd is angry, and everything goes wrong. You help him more than you ought, and Clive knows it is not right."

"Well, Conny," said Walter, brightening, "we need not mind; it will all be right soon. There will be no Mrs. Fletcher with cake on the island, and no lessons and headaches there, if only Roger would make up his mind to go at once."

"Sometimes I think he never means to make up his mind," said Constance, "and that he only likes to hear you talk."

"I wish you would not always say such discouraging things," cried Walter, rather pettishly; "I am certain Roger is in earnest, and as soon as ever lessons are over I will run down to the farm and find out."

Constance sighed; but since their first introduction to Mrs. Fletcher, Walter and Clive had got into a habit of paying almost daily visits to the farm, and she had allowed herself so often to be argued and entreated into joining them, that she felt her objections could have no influence now.

Mrs. Fletcher was always glad to see them, and always ready to console Clive and Constance, by injudicious petting, for any trouble they might be in at home; and Walter put up with a great deal of rough treatment from Roger and Tom, because he fancied that while he was helping them to work in the vegetable garden, or following them about the farm, he was gaining useful knowledge and preparing himself for the desert island life which he had planned.

One day Roger, who professed a great liking for Walter, joined him on the shore when he was talking over his plan with Conny and Clive. Roger laughed very heartily at first when he discovered what they were talking about; but just as Walter was getting angry he seemed to see the plan in a new light, and said he was so anxious to hear all about it, that Walter was tempted to open his heart and take him into their counsels.

The children soon began to think that they had fallen in with an invaluable ally; for, after Roger joined them, so many of their difficulties were smoothed away that Walter's scheme seemed much less like a story than it had done at first, and more like a thing that was really to happen. Walter was even sometimes a little startled when he remembered that since Roger had promised to row them to the island in his father's boat there really was nothing to prevent their setting off any fine morning early, or Saturday afternoon, when every one had gone out.

Roger talked quite grandly of the preparations he was making for their benefit, and the children were suprised to find how many little things they had which Roger could turn to account, and which it became necessary to trust to his hands. Walter's large clasp-knife, his father's last present, Clive's pocket-book, and even Conny's scissors, were all given up one by one, and their very small stock of pocket-money followed soon after.

With so many anxieties on their minds it was not likely that the little orphans should have much spirit or application to give to their studies. Their example had a bad effect on the other children, and school hours, which had been such a pleasant part of the day, began to be dreaded by teachers and pupils.

Mrs. Lloyd was quite tired of seeing Constance either dreaming or in tears. Clive never finished a lesson unless he had an opportunity of being helped by Walter; Maurice was careless and irritable; Walter absent; Owen more dull than usual; and Mr. Lloyd quite out of patience.

On the morning when the consultation had taken place in the garden Mr. Lloyd happened to be very busy, and, as was sometimes the case, he was obliged, after showing the boys their morning's work of sums and exercises, to leave them to finish it while he went into the village. He gave them as much, and not more than would fairly occupy them in his absence, and as he left the room, he gave very strict orders that there should be no talking or playing till twelve o'clock.

"Remember, Maurice," he said, looking back at the door, "that unless your exercises are well done when I come back I cannot take you to ride as I promised, and I shall be very sorry, for we have had very few rides together lately, and this is the last chance this week."

"Oh, papa! why?" cried Maurice, with an uncomfortable recollection of his half-prepared lessons.

"Your mamma and I find ourselves obliged to go to Carregllwyd this afternoon," answered Mr. Lloyd; "we cannot be back till late to-morrow night, and on Friday and Saturday I am always too busy to ride you know."

If Maurice wished to have his mind free for his lessons he had better not have heard this piece of news. The very mention of Carregllwyd was apt to put him out of temper; and he and Emma had lately been indulging themselves in a great deal of grumbling, and in grudging recollections of the past delightful expeditions that were never to come over again.

Maurice allowed himself now to sit for a full half hour with his dictionary upside down before him, while he magnified to himself all the pleasure they had given up for the Maynes' sake, and worked himself up into a fit of indignation about what he called their ingratitude and unkindness. When at last he roused himself to look at his lesson, it did not help him to find that Walter, having finished his own translation, was carrying on a whispered conversation with Clive in the window-seat, during which Roger Fletcher's name occurred often and loud enough to keep Maurice's curiosity constantly roused. He broke his own rule about speaking to the Maynes, to tell them that they would certainly not have their lessons done, and that papa would be angry, and got nothing by it but a recommendation from Walter to mind his own business. Even when the brothers left off talking, and resumed their lessons again, Maurice found his attention distracted; he would look off from his own work to notice how often Clive brought his exercise book to Walter, that he might correct a difficult sentence, or to count how many figures of his sum were put down at Walter's suggestion. He had to begin his own sum, which happened to be a much easier one than Clive's, three or four times over, before he could flatter himself that he was doing it right, and, every time he rubbed it out, he fancied that Walter and Clive smiled at one another.

He had just begun it the fifth time when the clock struck twelve, and Mr. Lloyd entered the room. He looked grave when he saw the empty slate, but the gravity deepened to serious displeasure when he came to look into the rest of the morning's work, and Maurice produced, first a blotted copybook, then a careless translation, and then an exercise full of faults. Mr. Lloyd tossed the offending books to the other end of the room, declaring that they were too bad to look at, and then made Maurice remark Clive's well-written exercise and correctly-worked sum, and asked him if he were not thoroughly ashamed of himself. Maurice turned over the leaves with a burning face, but there was far more anger than shame in it. The shame seemed to rest with Walter and Clive, who both looked so confused and shrinking that Mr. Lloyd thought they were more sorry for Maurice's disgrace than he was himself, and felt pleased with them accordingly.

Maurice saw at once that all chance of a ride was over for him, and with it went another secret hope. He had been half expecting that his papa and mamma would take him to Carregllwyd after all, as he was the eldest, and he felt now that, even if such a project had been entertained, he had forfeited all claim to the indulgence, and that he could not even suggest it to his mamma, as he had intended to do.

Mr. Lloyd offered to take Walter to ride instead of Maurice, and he was shocked to see how very much crosser Maurice's face grew at the proposal. Walter looked almost as much disconcerted, and Mr. Lloyd, after sending Owen and Clive to play in the garden, and desiring Maurice to pick up his disgraced book, and make up for his morning's idleness by working hard till dinner, set off on his ride with a very silent companion, and feeling more puzzled and unhappy about his children than he had ever been before. He had still some calls to make in the village, and Walter had to hold his horse several times while he went into the cottages. Once Mr. Lloyd fancied he heard some one talking to Walter outside while he was speaking to a sick person within, and, when he had mounted his horse, he felt almost sure that he caught a glimpse of Roger Fletcher's figure creeping behind a hedge; but he had always taken it so entirely for granted that the Maynes partook of the Fletcher feud with his children, that he thought it quite unnecessary to ask Walter if Roger and he had been talking together. He felt rather obliged to him for having nothing to say on the universal subject.

Griffith Hughes was waiting to take the horses when they returned from their ride,

and Mr. Lloyd recollected that he wished to speak to him, before he left home, about the back garden door.

"We must see about finding some better fastening," he said, "for I think the latch is worn, and comes open with a very slight touch. There used to be a bettter latch in the old tool-house. Come with me, Walter, to look for it, while Griffith puts up the horses."

Walter followed, rather reluctantly; the tool-house was a favourite haunt of Clive's—he kept his tame sea-gull there, and sundry desert island preparations might have been discovered, if any one had taken the trouble to look for them.

The old crazy door stood a little way open, and the sound of some one crying very bitterly reached Mr. Lloyd's ears as he came near.

"Whose voice is that?" he asked, anxiously.

"It's Clive's voice," cried Walter, pushing past to get in first, "and there's Maurice teasing him because I'm away."

Mr. Lloyd hoped it was not quite so bad as that; but when the door was pushed open the light showed Clive sitting on the floor with a dead sea-gull in his lap, crying as if his heart would break, and Maurice standing near him with a half-bewildered and half-angry expression on his face.

"What is the meaning of all this?" asked Mr. Lloyd.

"He's a little spiteful thing," cried Maurice; "he won't believe that it was an accident."

"My bird! my bird! he has killed my own dear bird!" sobbed Clive, turning to Walter with a piteous expression, which inclined Mr. Lloyd to be very angry with Maurice.

"Maurice!" he said, in a tone of extreme displeasure, "is it possible that you have done such a cruel thing?"

"He did it because Roger Fletcher gave the bird to Clive," said Walter, indignantly.

"What a cowardly fellow you are, Maurice, to come here when I was away. If I had been near you dare——"

"Hush, hush!" interrupted Mr. Lloyd. "What have you got to say, Maurice?"

Maurice spoke in a husky voice, half choked with passion.

"I've said it was an accident once, and you don't believe me. I believe they put the bird into that crazy stone house on purpose that I might kick it down. How could I tell there was anything inside? It is too bad that I am to be blamed for everything;" and hardly knowing what he was saying between shame and anger, he poured out a confused tale of Clive's and Walter's misconduct; their visits to the Fletchers'; their mysterious talks after supper in the lane with Roger; and Clive's idleness and the unfair help Walter gave him in the school-room.

Mr. Lloyd, as he listened, hardly knew whether he was most pained by the vindictive temper displayed by his own son or the want of truth discovered in the children he had been trusting so perfectly. He was really too unhappy to speak for a minute or two after Maurice ceased; and when he began his voice sounded so stern that Clive left off sobbing and clung in dismay to Walter.

"That will do, Maurice," he said, "not a word more. I'm shocked to see you in such a temper. I cannot even tell whether you are speaking the truth or not. Go into the house at once, without a word."

That his father should doubt his truth was just the crowning point of Maurice's trouble. He pushed between Walter and Clive, nearly upsetting the latter against Mr. Lloyd, and dashed out at the door in a very disrespectful manner.

Mr. Lloyd turned to Walter.

"Now, how much of all this is true?" he asked, gravely.

Walter hesitated. The visits to the Fletchers' looked very different when he thought of them with Mr. Lloyd's grave, pained face before him, from what they had done when he had considered them as proofs that he would not submit to Maurice's domineering. He could not think of any words in which to begin; and Clive was squeezing his hands in an agony of fright that made it very difficult for him to attend to anything else.

Mr. Lloyd's face grew still sterner and graver as Walter hesitated; but just as he was going to speak again the sound of the dinner-bell from the house recalled to his mind that he had no time to enter just then into a long investigation.

"There!" he said, "I cannot give any more time to you now; the carriage is to come to the door directly after dinner, and it will not do to miss the train. I am sorry to leave you in suspense, but it can't be helped. When I come back I must hear all about it; and in the meantime, to prevent any more quarrelling, I shall desire Maurice to stay in his room, and you two must not leave the garden. Your best and only way will be to tell the whole truth."

Mr. Lloyd walked into the garden as he spoke, and Walter and Clive followed at a considerable distance behind. Every one was seated at dinner in the dining-room when they entered, and they took their places in silence. It was the most silent dinner that had ever been eaten at the Rectory. There had been no time for Mrs. Lloyd to hear what had happened; but she soon saw that something was amiss, and the very sight of Maurice's stormy face took away her appetite. Gwen and Conny both cried out of sympathy; Mr. Lloyd was grave and absent; and even Emma and Owen, who were always the last to discover other people's moods, left off talking about the presents they expected from Carregllwyd when they found that no one was paying the least attention to them. The carriage came to the door before dinner was over, and there was a great bustle; but it was quite unlike the old, happy bustles when they were all going to set off together, or even when Mr. and Mrs. Lloyd had on other occasions gone from home for a day or two. Griffith Hughes had all the trouble of putting the parcels into the carriage, for Maurice ran away and shut himself up in his room, instead of being the chief person and ordering every one about as he generally did when anything was going on. No one even went out to look at the carriage but Owen, and though Emma and Gwen ran upstairs to help mamma to put her bonnet on they soon came down quite quietly, for they saw she was too unhappy to care for any of their talk.

At the very last minute she seemed half inclined to stay at home, and she had tears in her eyes when she wished the children good-bye. It disturbed Gwen so much that she could not help bursting into a fresh fit of crying when the carriage drove off, though Emma and Owen scolded her, and told her she was very silly, as she did not know in the least what there was to cry about.

In despair Gwen went upstairs to Maurice to hear his story and be comforted; but she stayed so long that Emma grew impatient, and went up to hear about it too, and by degrees it became known through the house that Master Maurice was in great disgrace, and that his papa had ordered him not to leave his room till he came back from Carregllwyd.

Griffith Hughes, who had securely counted on being sent for by Maurice to join in some pleasant scheme for the holiday afternoon, now came in dismay to the school-room to get the rights of the story from Owen. Owen only understood that Walter and Clive had hindered Maurice all the morning at his lessons, and then said or done something to put him in a passion, just on purpose that papa might punish him. Griffith pronounced it to be just like them, and his and Owen's comments on the story soon made the Maynes glad to escape into the garden, out of hearing.

Emma, in the meantime, had been into the kitchen to tell cook and nurse that there was no use in going on with certain preparations for a pic-nic dinner to-morrow on Gorphwysfa hill, which mamma had planned in the morning to console the children for not going to Carregllwyd, and entrusted to Emma's care to be kept secret till the right time. The servants were nearly as much disappointed at the interruption as Emma herself, and when, a short time after, the cook went into the garden to gather gooseberries, and saw the little Maynes walking soberly up and down the walk, she stopped them and told them her mind about mischief-making children, and new comers, who spoilt all the comfort of the house, with so much vehemence that Conny and Clive made a hasty retreat into the house, and would not be persuaded by anything Walter could say to come out again.

There was not much comfort for them in the house. Nurse, who never would believe that Master Maurice could do wrong, was crying in the nursery, and she shut the door in Clive's face when he tried to come in. The house maid happened to be cleaning the upper rooms, and at last Constance settled herself in a forlorn way on the landing-place near Maurice's door. Clive curled himself up on the rug on the top of the staircase, and Walter sat a few steps below him in a considering attitude, with his face hid in his hands.

They were all very unhappy, and Clive and Conny were thoroughly frightened and dismayed at the thought of Mr. Lloyd's displeasure, but there was no one to whom they could take their troubles; no one seemed to sympathise with them in the least. Even Gwen would not speak to them when she came running up to Maurice's room, and Clive sat up, and caught hold of her frock to stop her; she pulled it away from him, and only said, shaking her head sorrowfully, "I can't talk to you now while Maurice is unhappy;" and then, without taking any notice of Clive's reproachful looks, she ran on into Maurice's room, and did not come out again all the evening.

Gwen left the door of Maurice's room a little way open, and the Maynes, from their place on the stairs, could not help hearing part of the conversation that went on within.

A great deal of pity and sympathy from Emma and Gwen had helped Maurice out of his sullen mood into a state of temper which, with him, generally preceded perfect recovery, when he *would* talk in an exaggerated way, and insist on putting everything in the worst possible light. His sisters had seen him in despairing moods before, and knew exactly what his dismal speeches meant, but to Walter and Conny they sounded very startling indeed.

"No, Emma," they heard, in Maurice's vehement voice, "there is no use in saying anything more about it. I shall never be happy again as long as I live, never. Papa said I was vindictive. He hates me. Yes, it is just that; I don't care whether it was the Maynes' fault or not now: it is all the same. Papa will never believe me again: he as good as said so."

"Oh, Maurice!" interposed Gwen's gentle tones.

"Well, he looked as if he were going to say so—it's all the same," groaned Maurice.

"How happy we were this time last year," sighed Emma, "all on the road to Carregllwyd with papa and mamma; and, if the Maynes had never come, we should have been doing just that now."

"Oh! I wish they had never come," said Maurice, rolling himself over and over on the floor, and bestowing vigorous kicks against the wall. "We thought that it would be so nice to have them, but it's horrid. I declare they are worse than the Fletchers. Oh! I wish we had never heard of them——"

"Or that they would go quite away, and never come back again," said Emma.

"Is it quite right to wish such things?" asked Gwen's sweet voice.

"I am sure it is," said Emma, sharply, "when it comes to their making papa and mamma unhappy, as you might very well see that they do if you chose, Gwen. Mamma is quite worn out with Clive and Conny, they are so helpless and tiresome, and Walter has such a disagreeable temper. I heard Mrs. Morgan talking about it when she called last Saturday, and she said that mamma must be quite worn out. And then for them to make friends of the Fletchers!"

"I'm sure I'm quite worn out," interrupted Maurice, giving the door a kick this time which happily sent it to, and finished the conversation as far as the Maynes were concerned.

They had hardly recollected they were listening till the door shut, and then Conny got up and came down two steps to where Walter was sitting, and pulled his hands from his face.

"Walter, we won't wait any longer," she said; "we will go away to the desert island, and live by ourselves in the stone cave, and never come back again."

"Yes, we will go to-morrow," said Walter. "They wish us to go away, and we will go, and be happy in our own way. Oh, Conny! I am so glad that you have quite made up your mind for Roger said he could take us to-morrow. I will run to him at once and settle all about it, and you and Clive shall go into the tool-house, and pack up our desert island treasures in the old brown box."

"To-morrow! I don't think I quite meant to-morrow," said Conny, sitting down on the step again, rather sorry for her words.

But Walter sat down beside her, and put her in mind of all their preparations and plans, and of their favourite stories of children who had been happy in desert islands; and then he persuaded her to come down into the tool-house, and begin to work; and the business of packing up the box was so real and delightful that Conny's resolution rose high, and she let Walter slip away for one more private talk with Roger Fletcher without feeling much as if she wished to call him back. Her courage went up and down again a great many times during the evening. At teatime, when Walter did not come in till all the others had assembled round the table, Conny began to hope that Roger had thrown some difficulty in the way, as he had done once before when Walter had talked seriously about setting off; and she could not help feeling rather disappointed when Walter came in with a nod and an important look that showed her that all was right.

After tea they all walked about the garden together, and the thought that they had such a very great secret in their keeping was very pleasant. Conny wondered if nurse would have spoken differently to her if she had known what a new kind of life she was going to begin to-morrow, like what people wrote books about; and Walter and Clive busied themselves very much in collecting odds and ends of things, and found out wonderful uses for them, which they talked about to Conny till she quite longed to try them.

The being sent to bed by nurse came in very badly in the midst of this castle-building, and when it came to wishing Walter good night at his room door Conny's courage nearly went out altogether; if nurse had not looked very forbidding, and stood at the window all the time Conny was preparing for bed, without speaking a word to her, the important secret would have had little chance of being kept after all.

In the meantime Roger Fletcher was chuckling over the thought of the fright he should give Mr. Lloyd by taking the little Maynes away from him for a whole day, or even for longer, if he found the island amusing, and no one happened to think of going there to look for them. Mr. Lloyd had spoken to Mr. Fletcher about the paddock gate, and, as it was Roger's business to see that it was properly fastened, his father had been much displeased with him, and threatened him with a punishment that made him very much like the idea of getting out of the way till his father's displeasure had cooled, and perhaps putting his mother into a fright about his safety that would dispose her to receive him favourably on his return.

Mr. Fletcher and Tom were going to set off early the next morning to attend a fair at some distance. It was Mrs. Fletcher's busy day in the dairy, and she was too much accustomed to Roger's wandering habits to look for him when he was not wanted. Everything seemed to favour the expedition. Roger was accustomed to make depredations on the larder when he intended to wander far from home, and his reckless mind saw nothing in Walter's beloved scheme but an amusing way of procuring a day's idleness for himself.

CHAPTER XI

DESERT ISLAND IN REALITY

Conny woke in the morning with a strong wish in her mind that it might prove a rainy day, and that they might be prevented from going out; but the first glance from the window destroyed all hope of the kind. It was a bright, breezy morning, the reapers were going out to their early work, and dewdrops lay glittering on the grass and low shrubs of the garden. She had risen earlier than usual; but, before she was quite dressed, Walter tapped softly at her door, and came in to see if she were ready.

"So you have not changed your mind—you mean really to go?" said Conny, looking at him rather anxiously.

"Now, Conny, what are you thinking of?" said Walter. "Roger will be waiting for us. We must go."

"And we have packed up all our things so nicely," cried Clive.

"No more lessons, no more scoldings, nothing disagreeable on a *desert island*," said Walter, cheerfully.

Conny made no answer, but she put on her bonnet and cape leisurely, and spent some little time in folding down the bedclothes, and tidying and arranging the room.

"You won't have all that trouble in our house, Conny," said Walter. "There will be no nurse to scold you to-morrow morning if everything is not tidily folded."

It occurred to Conny that to-morrow morning there would be nothing to fold, and she was thinking of asking some perplexing questions about how they were to do for beds, and towels, and wash-hand-basins, when Clive exclaimed suddenly,—

"Oh! I have thought of such a capital thing—such a real desert island thing;" and then he bustled back into his own room, dived down into a drawer, and returned with a paper bag in his hand, so triumphant and bright that Conny's misgivings began to be charmed away.

They found no one up when they went downstairs but the cook. She had opened the back door, and was in the dairy setting the milkpails ready for Griffith Hughes when he should bring in the morning's milk from the cowshed. She was surprised to see the children up so early, but she did not think it necessary to prevent their going into the garden, as Emma and Maurice, when their gardening zeal happened to be strong, were accustomed to spend whole hours there before breakfast. It occurred to her, however, knowing Mrs. Lloyd's anxiety about Clive's health, to call them back as they were leaving the house, and give them each a cup of milk and a slice of bread. She watched them from the back garden door into the little tool-house, where she knew they often played for hours, and then she returned to her milkpail, and thought no more about them.

The little brown box which they had packed the evening before stood ready in a corner of the tool-house, and even Conny agreed that it looked very nice. There was, besides, a bag of seed corn, which Walter had one day begged of farmer Fletcher, and Clive begged to be allowed to carry it, as it was considered the most important of all their preparations. Walter loaded himself with a spade, rake, and hoe, and a bundle of sticks to light their first fire on the island, and made Conny observe how much better they were off at starting than Robinson Crusoe or Philip Quarle. The latch of the garden door had not been mended, so it was very easily pulled open, and the fresh breeze from the sea blew pleasantly in their faces as they came out into the lane.

Conny had no appetite for her breakfast, and was going to throw her bread away; but Walter took it from her, and put it with part of his own into a little basket she was carrying.

"You and Clive will like to eat this bread some day, perhaps," he said. "You know it will be a long time before we shall have any of our own. I shall, of course, sow this corn directly (it was oats, only Walter did not know the difference); but it will be some time before it comes up, and it will have to ripen and be cut, and all that. In the meantime we shall, of course, live on fish and eggs, and—and other things that will be growing on the island."

' "What shall we have to drink do you think?" asked Constance.

"Why, Constance, there is water all round," cried Clive.

"It is salt water."

"But, my dear Constance," said Walter, "what are you thinking of? There must be fresh water somewhere; it rains on our island as well as anywhere else."

"Oh! yes, to be sure," said Constance, brightening; "I forgot that."

"It will not be *very* nice to drink nothing but rain water, will it?" asked Clive, doubtfully.

"We shall not," said Walter; "there will be goats on the island. It is rocky, and goats live in rocky places. We shall soon have tame goats as Robinson Crusoe had, and Conny shall milk them."

"If I can," said Conny; "but I never could get the least drop of milk when cook let me try to milk the cow."

"Roger will easily teach us," said Walter.

"If there *are* any goats on the island, and if we can catch them, and if we had a pail," said Constance.

"A pail! Dear me, I wonder what Robinson Crusoe did about the pail; but never mind, we need not think of all that now," said Walter, "for here we are on the sands, and there, I declare, is Roger Fletcher beckoning to us to be quick."

It was somewhat of a surprise and disappointment to Constance; but there certainly was Roger waiting for them with his father's little boat at the landing-place.

"That's right; you are just in time," cried Roger, as they came up; "the wind and the tide are as right as possible. Come, get in before any of the village people come and stop us. Ain't we going to have a spree? Mother sent me off into the harvest field; but they'll have to whistle for me if they want me there. I helped myself to a harvester's dinner and beer, however: there they are in that basket at the bottom of the boat. Come, little miss, you sit down there. What have you got in your basket—anything to eat? Dry bread! I would not thank you for dry bread on a holiday; one might get that much at home. You shall see if I have not thought of something better."

Roger was in high good humour; he had secured a holiday, and he meant to enjoy it. On the whole he rather liked the Maynes; their talk amused him excessively—it was like a story-book without the trouble of reading, and there were even times when Walter's plans sounded so real and pleasant, that, for a few minutes, Roger found himself almost believing in them, and saying to himself, Why should not he be his own master, and have an island to himself as well as another?

There was a brisk little breeze blowing straight from the shore to the island, and more motion on the water than there had been for many days; but Roger had lived all his life near the sea (though only for the last year at Gorphwysfa), and been allowed, from very early days, to go out with the fishermen, and idle away his time on the water. He was quite able to manage the boat, and no difficulty occurred during the voyage.

The island, as they came near it, looked fair enough in the morning sun to answer to the brightest fairy-land dreams. The one spot of verdure, with its few tangled shrubs, looked so very green contrasted with the white rocks; the rocks reflected the light so dazzlingly as they rose from the clear, green sea; and there was such a sweet, gurgling sound of water echoing from all the caves, that Conny could not be surprised when the boys took off their hats and shouted with delight.

"How still it is!" said Walter, when the echoes of their shout had all died away. "It did not seem so still when we were here before. What makes the difference? Oh! where are all the sea-gulls I wonder?"

"Gone, to be sure," said Roger. "Don't you know they always leave the rocks in the autumn?"

"That's rather unfortunate," said Walter, gravely. "I expected that we should have had such quantities of sea-gulls' eggs to eat."

"You did not suppose that sea-gulls laid eggs all the year round, come now," said Roger, contemptuously.

Walter's countenance fell a little, but Roger wanted his help to get down the sail and pull the boat up to the landing-place. It was hard work; Walter's help did more harm than good; and, when Roger had done his very best, he could not get the boat by any means so near the shore as Rollo had done. It did not signify, he said; they must take off their shoes and stockings, and wade through the water. Walter promised to carry Clive and Constance on his back; but, though Conny saw Clive safely landed on the dry sand, she could not help feeling rather nervous, and she clutched Walter so tightly that she nearly choked him, and made him let her fall on her feet in the shallow water near the shore. She managed to scramble up to the dry sand, but she looked sadly dismayed at the sight of her soaked shoes and stockings and splashed frock.

"O dear! what will nurse say?" she exclaimed; "my new muslin frock and clean stockings!"

Walter clapped his hands.

"Now, Conny, only see the good of being on a desert island; there is no one to see how wet you are. Nurse will never know anything about it."

"Oh! to be sure not," said Conny; "but then—but then I can't go to nurse for dry clothes, and these are, Oh! so wet and cold."

"Now, Conny," said Walter, very gravely, "we are on a desert island, and you really must recollect that desert island people never let themselves get frightened, or make a fuss about little things. They are just a little uncomfortable at first—Philip Quarle was; but in a very short time it all comes right, and they get everything they want, and so you will see it will be with us. Only remember how wet Robinson Crusoe was when he first landed on his island, and how well he got on afterwards."

Conny went on squeezing the water out of the bottom of her frock, and pressing it

from her stockings, without looking much comforted by the example of Robinson
Crusoe. Walter could not help saying that he thought her rather unreasonable, and
Conny learned that people could look cross on desert islands as well as anywhere else.

The little cloud did not last long, however, for Roger called to Walter to help him to
lift the provision basket out of the boat, and they all grew busy and merry again. The
tide was going out rapidly, and almost every wave left a fresh strip of bright yellow sand,
rich in treasures of beautiful shells. It was not much like grave preparations for settling
for life, but Walter could not refuse Clive and Conny permission to wander about
collecting those shells, and Roger dared him to climb first one point of rock and then
another, and to try who could throw stones furthest into the sea, and so, without quite
knowing how, a great part of the morning passed. Walter was provoked with himself for
having wasted so much time when he heard Roger complain of being hungry, and say
that he was going to unpack the basket and have dinner.

"But it is not wise to eat our provisions the first day, you know," he said; "we ought to
provide ourselves with a dinner on the island, and keep what we have brought from the
wreck—from home I mean—till some time when we are more in want of it."

"We shall never be more in want of it than we are just now," said Roger. "Do you
suppose I came here to wait for my dinner? Eat or not as you like, you'll not find me
starving."

Walter thought, perhaps, he never *should* be more hungry than he was just then, and,
at any rate, the contents of Roger's basket, when unpacked, were not such as could be
resisted by children who had played all day by the seashore. There were slices of cold
meat and home-made bread, and tempting-looking apple turn-overs, which Mrs. Fletcher
had set aside to be taken into the harvest field; and this dinner, without knives, or forks,
or plates, looked really like a beginning of Robinson Crusoe life. At the bottom of the
basket was a good-sized bottle of strong beer. The little Maynes did not like the taste of
it, and only took a sip now and then for the pleasure of drinking out of a bottle. Roger,
however, was quite willing to take the lion's share, and, by the time dinner was over, he
had eaten and drunk so much that he was sleepy and stupid, and could not be roused,
by all Walter's entreaties, to begin the important business of exploring the island and
choosing a place of shelter for the night, which, according to desert island precedent,
was the only proper employment for new settlers. It was soon plain that the examples
Walter cited were lost upon Roger. He did not seem to care what the Swiss Family
Robinson, or Philip Quarle, or any one else had done. He drew his cap over his face,
stretched himself on a sheltered bank of soft sand, and in five minutes he was fast
asleep.

"I am glad he has gone to sleep," said Conny.

"So am I," said Walter; "for now we can really begin to work. I am afraid we have
wasted our time rather foolishly this morning, and left ourselves a great deal of work
for the afternoon. I have no doubt that we shall soon find something to eat, and that we
shall be cooking something very nice for our supper long before bedtime; but I think we
had better begin to explore at once. Roger showed me the way to the cave: let us go
there first."

"Up there?" cried Constance.

"To be sure," said Walter. "Give me your hand; the climbing is as easy as possible. My
dear Constance, you must not pant and tremble like that. Only consider, you will have

to climb up here every night, and come down every morning. You ought to think nothing of it."

This prospect did not make the difficult climbing pleasanter to Conny; but with a great deal of help, and by Walter's telling her where to put her feet, she managed to get up in time, and found herself in the opening of a high, wide cave. Water must have gurgled through it at some time; but now, for many years, the opening had been above the mark of the highest tide. The softest white sand strewed the bottom, and the rocky sides were smooth and dry, and reflected the afternoon's sun, which shone in at the opening in many beautiful colours.

"Oh, Conny! is not this a charming house?" cried Walter. "What could you want better? Look at all those shelves in the rock for us to put our stores on, and the soft, white carpet, and the beautiful, beautiful walls."

"There is, Oh! there is a very dark part down there," said Conny, holding her brother's hand tightly.

"It is only the opening into the other cave—the cave that has water in it. We will go and look," said Walter.

The cave narrowed very much towards the end. There was a slippery ledge of rock, and then a dark cavern. Walter leaned over and threw a stone in: far below they heard it splash in the water.

"You said the other cave was a pretty place, with a shallow pool of water where we could sail boats," said Conny.

"Well, I thought so," said Walter; "that was how I fancied it would be."

"How dark it is! How dreadful it would be to fall down there!" said Conny, shuddering.

"Come away; we are none of us going to fall down," said Walter.

Conny gladly came quite away, and stood stock still in the very middle of the cave while Walter helped Clive up the rock. Then she and Clive stood still together while Walter went to the boat and brought out the box and tools. He did not tell them, but he had great difficulty in getting into the boat; and he felt rather afraid that he had disturbed it from its fastenings in jumping out.

Clive found courage when Walter was standing by to choose a very convenient shelf for his little paper bag, which contained some biscuits Mrs. Fletcher had once given him; but both he and Conny were pleased when Walter decided that they need not stay in the cave any longer, for that there was no time to arrange their treasures just then.

When they got down to the sands again Walter was a little dismayed to find that the shadows of the rocks were growing quite long; and, by the time they had climbed up the steep path that led to the interior of the island, he was very impatient that so much time should have passed without their lighting on any of the useful discoveries that usually await desert islanders.

"I see," he said, "that it will not do for us to go on exploring in this slow way; people never do. Don't you remember that the Swiss Family separated and went different ways, and when they met again every one had found something useful? That is what we must do. Clive and I will go together, and you, Conny, shall go by yourself. Look round and choose which way you would like to go best."

If Conny had said what she really wished it would have been to sit down and rest exactly where she was, for she was very tired. She cast a frightened look all around, and what she saw was not very inviting.

The island was, in truth, a chain of rocks, which jutted out for a mile and a half into the sea. On the highest part there was a scanty deposit of poor soil, on which grew some coarse grass, a few wind-battered shrubs, and two or three stunted trees. The lower part was barren and rocky, with nothing growing on it but patches of rock-samphire and seaweed. Conny had a horror of slippery places and possible caves; but the sun was now under a cloud, the wind was making a melancholy sound among the branches of the old trees, and who could say what might be hidden among the long grass and straggling brushwood?

"Come," said Walter at last, "it won't do to stand looking all day; I will settle how it shall be. I will go up and you shall go down. I know you don't like slippery places, and you cannot possibly hurt yourself on the grass. Clive and I will explore the rocks; we shall find crabs and oysters in those pools I have no doubt; and you must give your mind to what you are about, and look carefully. You really seem to me to forget that you are on a desert island, Conny."

"O no, indeed, brother!" cried Conny, alarmed at such a serious accusation; "only I am beginning to be a little afraid that we have not come to quite the right sort of desert island. I promise to look as well as ever I can; and if I find anything I will call out, and you must come to me."

"That will depend on what I am finding myself," said Walter. "We had better not disturb each other. We shall all meet at supper-time and show what we have found. Now, that is the way you are to take."

Walter gave his hand to Clive and helped him to step over a slippery stone as he spoke; but Conny stood stock still till Walter had turned round twice and waved his hand impatiently, and then she began slowly to climb the path he had pointed out.

When she proposed calling to her brother if she found anything she meant in her heart if anything found her; and, as soon as she reached level ground and began to look carefully around her, it was not so much with any romantic hope of lighting upon a bread-fruit or a yam as in dread of having before her eyes that footprint of a savage, whose picture in "Robinson Crusoe" she always carefully avoided looking at.

The clump of shrubs, when she reached it, looked no better than a lair for all the wild beasts she had seen in the Zoological Gardens, and she walked half round it with trembling steps. At last she came to an opening that looked rather more inviting, and the sight of some long, straggling bramble shoots hanging within her reach, and tolerably laden with fruit, tempted her on. Blackberries were still a treat to the London-bred children; and, when Conny saw the abundance before her, her opinion of desert islands began to revive. She went on farther and farther, filling her basket, when, just as she was standing on tiptoe trying to catch the tip of a high branch tantalisingly full of fruit, a low growling sound reached her ears and made her start. She listened for a minute, trembling. "Oh! it must have been fancy," she said to herself as she heard nothing more; "Walter told me there were no wild beasts on our island. It was the wind among those doleful trees. I wonder which way I had better take to get out to the path again."

She looked all round, but before she had decided the sound came again, too distinct now for her to think it fancy or the wind: first a low growling, then a rustling among the branches, as if some creature were making its way towards her. Conny did not wait to see what it was; she threw away her basket, and fled wildly, without looking where she went. She took the longest way through the bushes in her haste, and only managed

to free herself from them by leaving her bonnet and part of her dress among the branches. Once clear, she got on faster, but the sounds that terrified her from behind came nearer and nearer. She called for help as loudly as her panting breath would let her, and still rushed blindly on. Her flight was ended at last by her dress being caught in a hold too strong for her to break from. She fell backwards on the ground, and, when she dared to look up, saw some shaggy hair and two bright eyes close to her face. If she had been anywhere but on a desert island she would, perhaps, have looked further, and discovered, in her enemy, farmer Fletcher's yard dog. As it was, nothing less dreadful than a wolf would come into her head, and she lay still, wondering when the first bite would come, till the sound of Walter's voice comforted her a little. A horrible growling and snarling followed, and then her frock was released, and she found that she could sit up.

"Oh, Walter!" she said, "how have you made that dreadful creature go away?"

"It is only farmer Fletcher's dog Tartar, Constance. I did not know him at first when I saw him standing over you, and I struck him and made him angry. Clive had more sense; he called him by his name, and there he is now licking Clive's hand."

Conny looked round, and saw Clive at a little distance, with the great dog standing quietly near him, and began to recover her senses a little.

"O dear! I wonder why he pulled me down?"

"Conny," said Walter, "look where you were going."

They were standing close to the edge of the rock, and Conny saw that, if she had taken one more step forward, she would have thrown herself over the precipice.

"Oh, how dreadful!" she said. "I did not see at all where I was going."

"No, I saw you did not; and, Oh! how glad I was when the dog pulled you down. If you had gone over, Conny, you would have been killed, and it would have been my fault for leaving you."

"Come further away, do," said Conny becoming more frightened as she saw how pale her brother looked.

When they had joined Clive, Walter made Conny, who was shaking all over, sit down upon a stone.

"Are you hurt anywhere?" he asked, anxiously.

"No, but you are. Oh, Walter! let me look at your hand; it is all torn and bleeding, I can see, though you are trying to hide it."

"Never mind," said Walter, putting his hand behind him.

"And Clive's knees are bleeding too. Did the dog hurt him?"

"No; he ran so fast he fell down, and cut them on the rock."

"Never mind," said Clive, trying to imitate Walter's "never mind" as bravely as he could, though his lips were quivering, and his eyes opened very wide to keep back tears.

"I have made you both get hurt," said Conny, remorsefully.

"It was my fault for leaving you," said Walter. "I ought to have remembered that Tartar was here. Roger told us this morning, only I suppose you did not hear, that Tom had been angry with Tartar for killing one of his rabbits, and had taken him to the island last night, and tied him up for a punishment. He intended Roger to bring him back this evening; but, of course, Roger will not, for you know dogs are invaluable on desert islands."

"Are they?" said Conny, doubtfully. "But, Walter, don't you think that it has got dark very suddenly? It can't be nearly night, can it? How very different the sea looks from what it did in the morning, and how very black and dark the clouds are over there!"

The children had indeed been too much absorbed during the last two hours to notice a great change that had taken place in the weather since they left the sands. The wind, which was blowing rather briskly from the land in the morning, had now veered completely round, and came in sudden, fitful gusts from the south-west; and the tide was coming in with high, white-crested waves, which broke with an angry sound over the rocks; and dark clouds were drifting up against the wind.

"It's only going to be a storm," said Walter, looking a little gravely, it must be confessed, from the sea to the sky; "one must expect storms on a desert island. But I do wish we had not wasted so much time this morning. I wish we had found something to cook for our supper, for if the waves come rolling in like that it will soon be impossible to go on the low rock again; and I do think I was just going to find some oysters when Conny called out. Where can Roger be all this time?"

"There he is," cried Clive, "coming up the road, running as fast as Conny did from the dog. What can be the matter? Do look how he is throwing his arms about. How strange he looks!"

Very wild and strange Roger certainly did look. He had lost his breath with running, and seemed to be trying to say something without having the power to make himself heard; his hair was tossed about by the wind; and when he came near they saw that he looked paler than Conny had looked when the dog was standing over her.

"What have you done with the boat?" he gasped at length, in a voice quite hoarse with agitation. "We have not a moment to lose. Where, where is the boat?"

"I am sure I don't know," said Walter, surprised; "where we left it I suppose. It was

safe this afternoon when I got into it to bring out our box and the tools. Is it not at the landing-place?"

"No," cried Roger, his voice rising almost to a scream; "you must have unfastened it. It has drifted out to sea. We are lost, we are lost! Don't you see that a storm has set in? No one can come to us from the shore till the wind changes, perhaps not for days. We shall stay here and be starved. It was all your fault, your fault. Why was I such a fool as to listen to you, and let you come?"

"I thought you intended us all to stay here," said Walter, hesitatingly, feeling a little infected by his companion's fear; "I thought we were all going to live comfortably on a desert island."

"Don't talk that nonsense to me *now!*" cried Roger, fiercely. "Come down to the sand, and try if you can see anything of the boat."

Roger led the way at a running pace; but, though he often turned back and beckoned angrily, Walter would not follow any quicker than Clive and Constance could keep up with him. The rain began to descend in torrents before they reached the sands, and in a few minutes the children were drenched to the skin. The boat was nowhere to be seen, and the increasing darkness gave them little chance of finding it till a flash of lightning revealed it to Walter, floating half a mile out at sea, with its bottom upwards.

When Roger understood this he gave way to a passion of despair that frightened Conny even more than the thunder and wind; he threw himself on the sands sobbing and screaming, and would not listen to a word Walter said to him.

Walter's desert island reading was really of some use to them all now. He had so often imagined himself in some such situation, and he had so little idea of its real danger, that he did not lose courage. He persuaded Conny and Clive to take shelter in the cave, and, dismal as it was with the rain and spray driving into it, there was a sheltered spot at the lower end, and they were at least safe from the incursions of the tide, as they would not have been if they had lingered longer on the shore. Roger was soon driven to join them, and Walter, who seemed naturally to take the place now of the elder of the two, directed him to help in piling up the bundle of sticks they had brought from home. There was paper in Roger's basket, and lucifer matches in the brown box, so that they had not much difficulty in making a fire. It did not burn long, and the smoke filled the cave, and made their eyes smart dreadfully; but it dried their clothes and warmed them a little. Walter carefully divided the pieces of bread they had saved in the morning into equal portions, and Roger brightened a little when he saw something to eat.

Clive whispered to Walter that there were biscuits in his paper bag, and seeing what a small piece of bread Walter had eaten, begged him to take one for himself; but Walter shook his head, and entreated him not to produce the biscuits before Roger to-night. Walter's ideas of the fertility of desert islands had altered very much during the last few hours, and what Roger kept saying about starving seemed much less improbable now, as he sat listening to the wind howling through the cave, than it would have done in the morning.

After a long time Roger cried himself to sleep on the softest heap of sand at the bottom of the cave, and the three little Maynes sat closely together. It was pitch dark; the storm rose higher and higher as the night fell; the waves dashed furiously against the rocks; the wind moaned among the trees; and every now and then a vivid flash of lightning showed the dark sky and the angry sea through the opening of the cave.

"Walter," said Clive, "this is really being in a desert island as we have planned so often; but, Oh! how different real things are from what one fancies."

"I should think the candles are lighted at home," said Conny. "It will be supper-time; Mr. and Mrs. Lloyd are come; they are all looking at the things from Carregllwyd; by and by they will have prayers."

CHAPTER XII

MISSING

"MAURICE, WHAT DO YOU THINK?" cried Emma, bursting into Maurice's room on Thursday morning as soon as breakfast was over; "what do you think? Neither Walter, nor Conny, nor Clive came in to breakfast. Cook says they were up ever so early this morning, and Griffith Hughes has been telling Owen that he saw them go out into the lane, and that he has no doubt they have gone into the harvest field with Roger Fletcher."

"I am very sorry," said Maurice.

Emma thought the answer would have been, "What a shame!"

"Sorry, my dear Maurice?" she cried. "Are you not very much surprised? To the harvest field with Roger Fletcher, when papa told them not on any account to leave the garden till he came back! I heard quite distinctly—*not on any account*, he said."

"Emma," interrupted Maurice, looking very solemn as he spoke, "I'll tell you something."

"Well, what?"

"I have been thinking of it ever since last night, and I see quite plainly that it is our fault, *yours and mine*, that the Maynes ever made friends with Roger Fletcher."

"But, my dear Maurice," cried Emma, throwing up her hands as she had seen Mrs. Morgan do when she talked over refractory school-children with Mrs. Lloyd; "my dear Maurice, when we have been talking and talking, and, I am sure, giving the best advice every day of our lives——"

"Well, I know all that," said Maurice; "but, Emma, do you remember what papa said on the evening when he first talked to us about their coming? He said the very worst of all would be to bring them here, and not make them feel quite at home."

"Well," said Emma, "I am sure I have been always giving things to Conny."

"Giving is not all," said Maurice; "at least, not giving things. Emma, I mean to tell papa to-night that it was not all their fault that they went so often to the Fletchers', for that we provoked them, and made them unhappy, and they could not help being glad to get away from us."

"Ah!" said Emma, "it is all the Fletchers. If it had not been for the Fletchers we should have been as happy as possible; they make everything go wrong."

"I am not quite sure about that either," said Maurice.

"Why, Maurice, it is what you have said over and over again at least a hundred times."

"I know," said Maurice, feeling as other great potentates do when their flatterers inadvertently throw past opinions in their teeth.

"Well, then?"

"I am going to do my lessons," said Maurice, shortly; "so don't come in to tell me anything more, even about the Fletchers, till dinner-time."

Emma retreated, feeling rather aggrieved. She was accustomed to follow Maurice's lead in everything like an obedient sister; but, if he meant to turn straight round about the Fletchers, it was too puzzling to be understood in one morning.

No one said or thought anything more about the Maynes till dinner-time. The servants, taking advantage of Mr. Lloyd's absence, were extremely busy turning out the study, according to long-established custom on Carregllwyd day; Gwen and Emma had to watch the baby in the nursery while nurse assisted in the business downstairs; and Griffith Hughes was kept from making any further discoveries by being employed in beating the study carpet in the back garden, with the knowledge that nurse's sharp eyes were watching him from the window.

Nurse said, when one o'clock came, that she should not wait dinner for the Maynes; if they did not choose to come in at proper times they might go without their meals; they gave trouble enough without keeping every one waiting on cleaning days. But after all, when the children had done dinner, she kept the meat and pudding on the table; and all the afternoon, in the midst of the bustle of putting down the carpet and re-arranging the books, she was running constantly to the door or the window, and calling to Griffith Hughes to know if he did not see anything of those tiresome children coming.

As it grew late she became more uneasy, and left her work altogether, and stood looking out at the front door. Griffith Hughes came up and took occasion to observe, with very wide-open eyes, that to be sure the children would never have gone out in the boat with Roger Fletcher; but nurse told him angrily to hold his tongue and go back to his work, and not invent things that were enough to frighten people out of their senses.

When he had gone, however, nurse said that she certainly did wonder, and it always would pass her comprehension altogether, how a person of cook's age could let three innocent children set off at that time in the morning without so much as taking the trouble of asking them where they were going. If any harm happened she should like to know whose fault it would be. Cook had an angry retort to make, and they talked so long and so loudly that Maurice heard a good deal of what they said from his bedroom window, out of which he was leaning, thinking what a dreadful thing it was to be shut up on a fine afternoon.

A sudden recollection of what he and Emma had been wishing yesterday afternoon, and how they had talked of the Maynes going away and never coming back again, flashed into his mind, and he felt more frightened and unhappy than there seemed to be any reason for.

Suppose the Maynes should really never come back, and that the time in the tool-house, when he had been in such a passion, should be the very last on which he should ever see them. The thought was so painful that Maurice could not sit still and bear it. He walked up and down, and opened and shut his door so furiously, that Gwen brought the baby out of the nursery, and came to his room to see what was the matter with him.

Gwen was always a very sympathising listener, and baby had to be content to lie quietly in the middle of the bed for half an hour, while Maurice went over all his fears and remorse, and talked about himself and the Maynes in a different way from what he had done yesterday afternoon. One moment Maurice was sure that the Maynes had gone off to London, and would never be heard of more, or that they were now on their way to America in farmer Fletcher's boat; and the next that all would be quite right if only he could go and speak to Walter in the harvest field, where he never would believe but that they were all the time.

Gwen at last asked timidly if it would do for her to go, and Maurice caught at the idea. Gwen was the only person except himself who had any sense, or who could be trusted with a message. He knew, he said, quite well where farmer Fletcher's harvesters had been at work yesterday, and he had no doubt they were in the same field to-day. It was not so very far off, only down the road, and over a piece of the common, and across the brook, and then you were there. Gwen could not possibly mind it.

Gwen did mind it. She thought of the black bull on the common, and the crazy state of the bridge over the brook, and the disagreeableness of coming into the field among the strange harvesters; but she said nothing of all this to Maurice; she did not even remark, as she might have done, that it looked very much like a thunder-storm; the idea of being useful—useful to Maurice—overruled all her fears; she ran upstairs for her bonnet and cape, and Maurice soon had the satisfaction of seeing her make a safe exit at the front garden gate without nurse or any one interfering to stop her. He felt in better spirits when she had gone, and he was, besides, obliged to give his whole attention to the baby, who would not be patient any longer in the middle of the bed. But by and by nurse came up very much agitated, to ask if Master Maurice could recollect at what time the pony carriage was to be sent to the station for Mr. and Mrs. Lloyd, and to pour out a long story about her having been over to the Fletchers' to seek those unlucky children, and not being able to hear any tidings of them, and about the perplexity she was in, as to whether it would be better to send Griffith out to look for them, or make him drive off at once to the station to meet the train, "such a dreadful storm as was coming on, too."

Maurice observed now, for the first time, how very dark it was, and a sudden flash of lightning and crash of thunder frightened him into confessing the errand on which he had despatched Gwen. Nurse was almost beside herself with anxiety, and the whole house was in a bustle. Griffith Hughes was despatched to look for Gwen; cook ran over to the Fletchers' to see if any disengaged person could be found to drive the carriage to the railway; and, when neither of the two came back as soon as nurse expected, she turned her gown over her head, and ran down the road as far as the turnpike, where she met Mr. and Mrs. Lloyd coming home in a carriage hired at the station, and frightened them with her wild looks and strange story.

The children never afterwards forgot that dreadful home-coming. Mr. Lloyd just brought Mrs. Lloyd into the house, desired nurse and Emma to leave off shrieking at every fresh flash of lightning, and then went out again into the storm to look for Gwen. No one felt inclined to shriek or think about his own fears when he saw Mrs. Lloyd's face. Maurice came down from his room, and they all sat in the study for what seemed to the children an immense time. The first interruption was Griffith Hughes' return, bringing the tidings that he had looked all over, and could see nothing of Miss Gwen anywhere, but that, to be sure, the brook was wonderfully swollen with the rain or something. By and by cook came in to tell how put about Mrs. Fletcher was, and to repeat what every one said of the storm. It was worse out at sea. Did they not hear how the waves were driving in against the rocks? It would be bad for any poor fishermen who happened to be out in boats that night.

Owen took this unlucky moment to repeat Griffith's suggestion that perhaps the Maynes were out in a boat with Roger Fletcher; and immediately nurse, cook, Maurice, and Griffith himself all set upon him with indignant denials that such a thought had ever entered any one's head for a moment. Mrs. Lloyd begged them, in a trembling voice, to be silent, for they did not know. The tone of her voice fell like a blow on Maurice. He said to himself that he could not bear it, but soon afterwards he would have been very glad to have had only that amount of suspense to bear.

After a time, not a longer time than might have been expected, Mr. Lloyd returned with Gwen—drenched, and cold, and pale, but quite safe—in his arms. Griffith, bewildered by nurse's directions, had taken the wrong road. Mr. Lloyd had found her sheltered in an old shed on the common, much less frightened for herself than her friends had been about her.

There was great rejoicing over her, but Maurice saw at a glance that his father's face was graver than it had been when he had gone out. He felt quite sure that he had heard bad news about the Maynes, even before he called Mrs. Lloyd back from following Gwen upstairs, and said, "I must go out again, and I may not be able to come back to-night. Don't wait tea for me."

Mrs. Lloyd became very pale; but, before she had time to say anything, Maurice rushed forward.

"Oh, papa, do tell us what you have heard! I know it is something bad, but it is far worse not to know."

"I think so too," said Mrs. Lloyd, faintly.

"It is very alarming, or I should have told you at first," said Mr. Lloyd; "still things are often exaggerated, and there may be some mistake."

"Go on," said Mrs. Lloyd.

"I have just been speaking to Rollo. He tells me that two of his children were on the beach this morning, and saw Roger Fletcher and the three little Maynes set out in farmer Fletcher's boat early this morning. No one has seen anything of them since; but there is a report that an empty boat has been driven on to the rocks—it may not be the Fletchers'. I am going down to the shore to see, and to inquire if it is possible for a boat to put out in this storm."

"Oh, papa, wait one minute!" cried Maurice; "I must tell you something before you go. It is all my fault that they went away—all my fault, and how am I ever to bear it?"

Maurice was going on, but Mrs. Lloyd put a very cold hand on his lips.

"Hush, Maurice," she said, "not now; your papa cannot stay, and it is quite bad enough for him to bear without your telling him *that* just now. I am very sorry for you, but you must try to think of other people, and not of yourself; it is all you can do now."

Maurice saw that, at all events, his mother did this. She found plenty of helpful things to do, and was busy all the evening. She went over to the farm to comfort poor Mrs. Fletcher, who was in the greatest anxiety; she made arrangements for having a message sent to hasten Mr. Fletcher's return; consulted with Rollo; and questioned the children who had seen the boat set off. Maurice, Emma, and Owen sat in the study listening to the wind, which grew louder and louder as the thunder and lightning passed off. How sad and strange it was to see the Maynes' lesson-books lying about, and the little pictures that Clive had been so fond of drawing on every spare scrap of paper!

The evening seemed so dreadfully long that they were glad to go to bed when nurse told them. Maurice, however, lay awake long, listening to every voice and step in the house. Quite late his mamma came into his room, but she had no good news to bring. The storm did not abate, and it had been ascertained that the boat drifted ashore was Mr. Fletcher's. Maurice found this out by asking questions. Mrs. Lloyd was very kind, and read him some verses in the Bible; but she said she thought it better for them both not to talk much then.

"I must say just one thing," said Maurice, before she went away. "Oh, mamma! do you remember the night when you came to my bedside before they came, and when I would not believe I was overbearing? You said I should have to learn the truth about myself, but I never thought it would be in such a dreadful way."

CHAPTER XIII

LONG DAYS

F OR TWO DAYS there was no sign of abatement in the storm; the wind blew in wild gusts from the sea; and the waves at every fresh tide were driven further and further beyond their accustomed landmarks. Griffith Hughes and Owen spent the greater part of their time in watching the tides come in, and in bringing news of how much higher the water had risen, and how one landmark after another was washed away; but Maurice, Emma, and Gwen shut themselves up in the day nursery, which faced the hill, and could not bear to look at the sea, or hear all the talk about the storm which the servants and villagers would keep bringing to the house. Mr. Lloyd was out nearly all day on the shore; but Mrs. Lloyd often found time to come and sit with her children, and then Maurice felt a little lightening of his trouble while he told his mother all the pain and remorse that burdened his conscience. He was very clear now about his own faults, and the share they had had in bringing about this dreadful punishment. His feelings towards the Fletchers and Walter Mayne sounded very strange to him as he confessed them to his mother; and numberless little overbearing words and ways, which would have seemed quite natural and right a week ago, rose up before him now in their true colours. The sight of Maurice's repentance opened Emma's eyes to her own share of blame, and helped her to find out where she had been wanting in her conduct to the orphans.

Among other things Maurice accused himself bitterly for having set the example of deceit by concealing his adventure on the island. He knew that, if he had continued his old habit of confessing all his faults to his parents, they could not have remained ignorant of what was going on in the family, and that he would have had more right to incite the Maynes to openness if he had not felt all the time that he was wanting in it himself. Emma remembered and confessed her unkindness to Clive on the morning of the pic-nic, and when she thought of never seeing Conny again she began to wonder how the workbox and the desk could ever have seemed worth quarrelling about.

"Is there any use," Owen asked once, "in going over all this just now when you are so very miserable?"

Mrs. Lloyd was sorry to see them miserable, but she could not give them comfort that was not true, or wish them to neglect the lesson that the sorrow was meant to teach.

One comfort came out of these talks. From sayings of Clive which Gwen now repeated, and conjectures conveyed through Owen from Griffith Hughes, Mrs. Lloyd made out Walter's cherished plan of living on the desert island; and it gave her a faint hope that he might have persuaded Roger to take him and his brother and sister there, and that it might be possible to bring them back before it was too late. The return of the empty boat made this conjecture seem very improbable to most people, and Mr. Lloyd had to warn the children not to cling with too much hope to it. In spite of all warning, however, they talked of it all day long as if it were certainty; but, as night and darkness came on, the thought of their companions hungry, and cold, and alone, exposed to the storm, seemed to them the most dreadful idea of all; and Gwen awoke shuddering and sobbing at every fresh burst of the wind, and half hoped she were sure that they were safe at home in heaven. Very slowly and painfully the days and nights passed.

On Sunday morning the wind had fallen, and the sun shone clear and bright, showing the wreck the three days' storm had made,—the harvest sheaves rent asunder and scattered about the fields; the trees torn up by the roots; the inroads of water on the low lands.

Maurice found Rollo and another old sailor consulting with Mr. Lloyd when he went down to breakfast. He listened to what they said; but he was too dispirited to ask any questions. He heard a great deal about a ground swell, and that no one in his senses had ever thought of coming near St. David's rocks when the sea was rough; and he augured no good from the grave shakes of the head with which every sentence came out.

Mr. Lloyd observed sadly, as he sat down to the breakfast table, that the unaccountable prejudice of the villagers against Mr. Fletcher and his family was more than ever to be regretted now. The sailors were less willing to run the risk of going to the island than they would have been if any one but Roger Fletcher had taken out the boat. They had always been sure, they said, that he could come to no good. Such storms did not come for nothing, and it was mere folly to risk more lives in looking for such as he.

Maurice thought of the old talks with Griffith on the garden wall, and sighed.

When the bells rang for church, and Mrs. Lloyd, Emma, and Gwen came down ready to set out, it seemed to Maurice just the crowning point of his despair that every one should be going to church that morning just as usual. He was half inclined to feel angry, and grumble to himself because nothing was done, and hope given up too soon; but when he knelt down in his place, and the accustomed words of prayer, in his father's earnest voice, reached his ears, better thoughts came, and he felt thankful to be where he was. A different kind of hope came into his mind, calmer and more resigned; and he was humbled to find that, even in the midst of his repentance, he had thought so little of the one way in which even he might do something. Meanings which he had never understood before came to him in the prayers; in the confessions of sin; the petitions for all who were in peril by land or by sea; and he wondered how it was that words which he had so often gabbled over without caring for them, should now be found to express what he was longing to say without knowing how.

It was a new service to Emma too. She remembered how she had wasted her time last Sunday in glancing across to the Fletchers' pew, that she might tell Maurice afterwards how badly Nancy and Roger behaved during the singing; and how she was far more occupied in regulating Clive's manner of kneeling than in listening to the prayers; and when she glanced at the empty places of those whom she had judged, and thought where they might be now, she was able to enter with all her heart into the prayer to be delivered from the envy, hatred, and uncharitableness which had made her bring such thoughts into the very presence of God.

After service was over Maurice and Emma walked slowly and thoughtfully home without speaking. Owen went on first with Gwen more quickly, and when Maurice entered the back garden he found him with Griffith Hughes, perched on the old watching-place on the wall. Owen beckoned Maurice to join them.

"Come here, Maurice," he said; "there is good news. Rollo is trying to get his boat out; they are going to the island to bring back the Maynes. Climb up and see."

Maurice climbed up, but he found that his eyes were so dim that he could hardly distinguish anything. There was a group of sailors on the shore; he could not make out what they were doing, but he heard their loud voices, and they seemed to be disputing eagerly, as if there were different opinions among them. Would the boat ever really go off?

At last Maurice saw a dancing black spot on the heaving waves, receding further and further from the shore. Some of the sailors took off their hats, and cheered the boat as it made its way bravely by the vigorous strokes of the oars against wind and tide. Owen and Griffith, though it was Sunday, took off their caps and shouted too; but Maurice jumped off the wall, and hurried in to shut himself up in his own room. Who could say what news the boat might bring back? The next few hours of suspense would be the worst of all. Maurice had learned that morning what was the best way in which to spend them.

*   *   *   *   *

It was a very strange thought to Walter and Constance, and Roger Fletcher, that it was Sunday morning. Two days of pain and cold, and hunger and thirst, and loneliness, lay like a gulf between them and their last Sunday. It seemed to them as if they had only lived those two days, and that everything else that had ever happened to them was a pleasant, distant dream. It was by slow degrees, the painful hours passing one after another, that they had been brought into this state. Clive had for some time passed beyond it. He lay with his head on Walter's lap, and his eyes shut. When they spoke to him, or tried to raise him up, he moaned a little, and then was quite quiet again.

They had suffered more from thirst than from hunger. On the first day they had had Clive's little store of biscuits, which Walter doled out as prudently as Roger would allow. Roger was very difficult to manage. He would not hear reason, he would have his share early in the day, and, when he grew savage with hunger in the evening, quarrelled with Walter for not giving him the portion he had saved for the others. Walter had a hard struggle to save the last biscuit from him, which, though it fairly belonged to his own share, he divided between Conny and Clive late on Friday night, when they could not sleep for hunger.

On Saturday they had nothing, and Clive said he was glad, because there could be no more quarrelling. He was very quiet, but now and then he talked in a strange way.

Conny could think of nothing but the ripe blackberries which she knew were growing above their heads on the top of the cliff, and she talked so wildly about going out to gather them, that, to satisfy her, Walter made several attempts to wade through the water round the rocky point, and climb up to the top of the cliff; but he was always driven back, wet, and tired, and bruised with falls on the slippery stones.

Nothing would induce Roger to leave the cave; he knew, he said, that there was nothing to be gained, even if they could reach the upper part of the island; and it was less trouble to sit still and starve in the cave than to go anywhere else.

By Saturday afternoon Walter had no other wish than to sit still. They all slept more on Saturday than they had done before; and when Conny woke up on Sunday morning, and saw the sun shining into the cave, she felt very weak and strange; but the pain from which she had been suffering the evening before had almost gone, and she thought that even if she had known that there were food and water a hundred yards off she would rather not get up to look for them.

The sun, not yet risen very high, made a road of golden light upon the sea, which seemed to stretch from the opening of the cave straight to heaven; and it came into Conny's head that it was Sunday morning, and that at Gorphwysfa people would wake up to hear the bells ringing, and to prepare for going to church.

"How strange it was, Walter," she said, "that when we used to talk and plan about our desert island we never thought about Sunday coming, and that we should have no church to go to, and no one to teach us!"

"It is all part of the same thing," said Walter, sadly; "all my fault. I wanted to have everything my own way, and to rule you all. I would not trust any one else, and it has ended, I see now, in my having made you ungrateful and disobedient, and brought you here to die. Oh! what shall I say to papa?"

"Or to God?" said Conny. "We have been disobedient children to Him too, and if He sends for us now shall not you be afraid to go?"

"I think we ought not to be," said Walter, after being silent some time. "Papa would not have liked us to be afraid to come to him if we had been ever so naughty, and God loves us even better than papa did, and He has promised to forgive us when we are sorry, for Jesus Christ's sake, who was always an obedient child."

"I will try to think about that," said Conny, "for I can't talk any more. I like to look at that light on the sea; I wish it would never be dark any more."

"Perhaps it never will to us," said Walter; and then he sat planning how some people would perhaps come some day and look into the cave, and find them sitting there quite dead, and he wondered whether they would be sorry, and what they would say, and everything seemed to him vague and dreamlike.

The road of light spread on the sea till every wave was dancing in sunshine; the shadows of the rocks grew shorter, and were beginning to lengthen again; and the children sat still, hardly speaking or moving. At last Walter found that, for a long time, he had been watching unconsciously a black spot that was rising and falling on the water. Once he thought it had disappeared, and he felt disappointed without having any clear idea why. When it caught his eye again it was much nearer, and he saw quite clearly that it was a boat with people in it approaching the island.

He watched it coming nearer and nearer; he saw the difficulty the sailors had in approaching the rocks, and how a retreating wave had nearly upset the boat; but he had not strength left to be very anxious about it.

When at last two men succeeded in wading to the shore, and Walter saw them looking round, and putting their hands to their mouths as if they were shouting, he recollected that they could not possibly see into the cave, and that, unless he could do something to attract their attention, they would return to the boat, and that he should see them sailing away. He made a desperate effort, crept to the mouth of the cave, and stood up and waved his handkerchief. The fresh air made him feel still more faint and giddy; he tried, as one tries in a dream, to call out, and felt that his voice was dying away, and that he was slipping down the steep path before him.

When he recovered his consciousness again he was being carried in the arms of one of the men through the surge to the boat. Conny and Clive had been taken there before him, and he could distinguish Roger's voice talking to the men who were carrying him. His signal had been seen from the sands, and Roger and Conny, who had not perceived the approach of the boat, were roused out of their stupor of despair to find the deliverance come.

The sound of voices round him was very pleasant to Walter in his dreamy state of half-consciousness, and his not being able to understand the words that were said saved him a great deal of pain.

The sailors hardly knew how to express sorrow enough at the sight of Clive's pale, deathlike face. "He will never open his pretty eyes again," they said; and they would have laid him softly down at the bottom of the boat, but Walter would not be easy till he saw that his brother and sister were near him, and at last they placed the child in his arms, and Walter held him, without knowing what a still, senseless burden it was.

There was almost all Gorphwysfa village assembled on the sands to watch for the boat's return. Griffith Hughes brought word to Maurice that it was coming back fuller than it went, as soon as the keenest eyes could discern the outline of the figures in the distance; and Maurice ran down to the shore as full of joy as he had been of sorrow, and eager to be the first to welcome the wanderers home. His joy was checked by the first glance he got at the faces in the boat—so changed, even Roger's.

Roger got out of the boat first, and Maurice heard his mother's cry, half of joy and half of compassion, as she ran forward to support his tottering steps. Then Walter, and Conny, and Clive were lifted out, and carried up the hill to the Rectory; and Maurice was so frightened at their looks that he could hardly find courage to follow them. Mrs. Lloyd's expressions of thankfulness, when she received the little orphans once more under her roof, revived Maurice's and Emma's hopes a little; and they had need of comfort, for they had many days of anxiety and suspense to bear yet—strange, still, breathless days, such as had never before been known at the Rectory, when the shadow of death seemed hovering over the house.

Maurice and Emma and Gwen never forgot all their lives after their wanderings up and down the garden in the early mornings, waiting for news of how the invalids had passed the night; and the watchings at the garden gate for the doctor, and the joy they felt when they crowded round him on the first day when he could pronounce Clive out of danger. On the evening of that day Maurice had leave to enter the brothers' room for the first time, and stand by Walter's bed, and say the words he had been longing to say for so many days: "It was all my fault;" but even then he had to stoop very low to catch Walter's answer, "No, it was mine;" and he was not allowed to contradict it, for Mrs. Lloyd said they had had talk enough for one day.

It was a pleasant time when the little Maynes first came down into the school-room, and were able to join again in the lessons and plays; and, Oh! how differently their companions felt about them now! Emma wondered, as she looked at Conny, how she could ever have made her unhappy about trifles, or how she could have cared more about playthings than about her companion's happiness; and, as Maurice tried to amuse away Clive's listlessness and invent pleasures for Walter, he could not understand how he could ever have indulged such angry feelings against them.

On the last bright September Sunday, Walter, Conny, and Clive were well enough to be allowed to accompany the other children to church. Maurice had expected to be quite happy on that day, but, when the time came, there was one great drawback to his rejoicing. When Mr. Lloyd returned thanks in the service for those who had been saved in great peril, Roger Fletcher was not there to join his thanksgivings with those of his fellow-sufferers. He had seemed to be the first to get well, and there had been no particular anxiety felt about him, only his mother observed that he was never quite himself.

As the Maynes grew better, however, he became worse; and the doctor, who had to be again called in, pronounced that long exposure to cold had brought an attack of rheumatic fever, which would probably make him an invalid for a long time. He was by no means a patient sufferer, and groans and cries of pain from him were heard in the Rectory garden, and disturbed the peace of the first days when Conny and Clive were brought out to enjoy the autumn sunshine. Maurice could do nothing for thinking of them. He asked leave to be the person who should always go to inquire for Roger. He was often long away, and Owen and Griffith Hughes opened their eyes widely when it came out that Maurice, with his father's permission, spent almost all his playhours in sitting by Roger's bed and trying to amuse him.

His old prejudice looked very strange to Maurice in the presence of the suffering he had now to see, and he began to be still more ashamed of it when he found that Roger looked forward to his coming more than to any other event in his day, and when he heard Mrs. Fletcher attributing the gradual improvement in Roger's temper to *his* kindness, and the interest he had awakened in new pursuits.

Neither Clive Mayne nor Roger Fletcher entirely recovered health during the winter, and it was perhaps as well for all the children that the consequences of their faults lasted long enough to keep alive the remembrance of them after the first excitement had passed away.

They wanted a continual reminder, for faults are not conquered at one blow; and the children did not become amiable and loving all at once, because they had suffered, and become convinced of their failings.

Old temptations and difficulties rose up again and again. Things did not always go on pleasantly. There were still often little misunderstandings and troubles; but they were met now in a different spirit. Each had now learnt to distrust himself, and to go for help to the One who, by the shedding of His own blood, brought help by which we may all conquer our sins.

It was a struggle that had to be renewed again and again; but at last the victory was won. Self-sacrifice instead of self-will was to each the ruling principle of action; and then, and not till then, Gorphwysfa became to all, what its name imports.

"THE HOUSE OF PEACE."

THE END

$$\boxed{6}$$

Countess Kate

By CHARLOTTE M. YONGE

IN THE PREFATORY HEADNOTES to the other Victorian children's books here reprinted, we have repeatedly referred to Charlotte M. Yonge (1823–1901) as representing enlightened judgments on the work of her Victorian predecessors and contemporaries. She herself was perhaps the most influential, versatile, widely read, and beloved of all Victorian writers for young people. She published well over one hundred fifty books, and for more than forty years (1851–1894)—the last three years with her friend Christabel R. Coleridge as co-editor—edited *The Monthly Packet*, a famous magazine read mostly by girls, published by Harriet Mozley's brother-in-law. Its full title was *The Monthly Packet of Evening Readings for Younger Members of the English Church*, a clear warning that Catholics and Dissenters would find its teachings unpalatable. Many of Yonge's books were not written primarily for children, but young people read them all. She believed in making her readers stretch a bit intellectually. But not even the most careful parent would need to fear that any of her works for adults could bring the proverbial blush to the cheek of the most sheltered proverbial Young Person. Charlotte Yonge has never been wholly forgotten and is perpetually being rediscovered. The Charlotte Yonge Society, a group of witty and serious Englishwomen, deeply learned in the sacred texts of her writings, keeps her memory green by holding regular meetings at which they give scholarly papers.

Charlotte Yonge spent her entire life in the heart of rural southern England: Hampshire. She never married. Her parents were country gentry. Her personal life was centered in her family and her church. Kind and loving, but exerting undisputed domestic authority, her father was one of the two most influential people in her life. The second was John Keble (1792–1866), priest of the Church of England, fellow of Oriel with Newman and E. B. Pusey. Keble's book, *The Christian Year* (1827), a collection of original devotional verse with a poem for every day of the year, leapt into instant popularity and retained it throughout the nineteenth century. In 1833, when Charlotte Yonge was only ten, Keble initiated the Oxford Movement by a sermon on "National Apostasy"; he later wrote seven of the *Tracts for the Times*. Whereas Newman became a Catholic and Pusey stayed in Oxford, engaged all his life in religious polemic, Keble in 1836 took a rural parish, Hursley, only a short distance from the Yonges, whose intimate family friend and counselor he became.

While Keble lived, he read each of Charlotte's books before she sent it to the publishers, often suggesting alterations, which she always adopted. Her father's rigorous training in Greek and mathematics (she knew French and Italian already), and Keble's precise ecclesiastical instruction in Tractarian ideas and practices, gave her an intellectual and spiritual grounding that lasted throughout her life. Charlotte Yonge had an excellent mind and was naturally devout. She was gladly submissive, not only for herself, but in her view of woman's proper role. She took her lead from her male heroes; the intellectual girls in her novels always give up their own education if they are needed for other duties. Yonge's life was narrowly provincial, wrapped up in the duties of family and of parish, and she was content to have it so. But she was a woman of enormous creative energy and power, with a keen ear, a warm heart, and a cool realization of the foibles of human nature.

It was entirely typical that her first book, *Le Château de Melville*, published probably in 1838, was written in French for sale at a church bazaar. Six years later came the first of her books in English, *Abbeychurch* (1844), and from then until she died no year went by without several publications. The first great success came in 1853, with one of the most famous best sellers of the century, *The Heir of Redclyffe*, written for adults but read from the first by teenagers as well, a romance imbued with Tractarian ideals, full of excellent conversation and well-realized dramatic action. All its large profits went to missionary enterprise. Yonge wrote many sound historical tales, of which the best remembered is *The Little Duke* (1854), about a young prince of the Normans. She wrote true narratives of ancient and modern history; she wrote several biographies. But most often she wrote stories of English domestic life, in which the characters were so lifelike that several generations of readers discussed their triumphs and defeats as they did the experiences of their personal friends. Perhaps the most famous of these is *The Daisy Chain* (1856), the first of a series of "linked" novels dealing with the history of several large families, related to one another, intermarrying, having children, and moving on into the next generation. These appeared at intervals until 1900, interspersed with much other fiction.

The length of *The Daisy Chain* made it impractical for inclusion here. The much shorter *Countess Kate* (1862), however, written specifically for children but much loved by adults, provides an ideal alternative. In every respect it is vintage Charlotte Yonge. Its characters make their first appearance in its pages (although she had already invented some of their ancestors in her medieval novel of 1855, *The Lances of Lynwood*), and she reintroduced them later into *The Pillars of the House* (1873) and *The Long Vacation* (1895). But the story is complete in itself; and it is widely supposed that the heroine is in many ways a self-portrait of Charlotte at thirteen, which enhances its interest. Moreover, though embodying and emphasizing her principles in their full strictness, it takes a more tolerant attitude toward rebellion and resistance than almost any other one of her novels.

Countess Kate is a "family romance" in the historical, cultural, and psychoanalytic sense of the term. No well-read and properly brought-up child of the upper middle classes in nineteenth-century England can possibly have escaped the daydream that he or she was in fact a member of the peerage. Lost heirs and unexpected successions stud the pages of Victorian fiction for adults and children alike. For Kate Umfraville, orphaned, and being kindly brought up in a simple rural parsonage by a widowed uncle (whom she calls "papa"), surrounded by a family of loving cousins, the dream is realized at ten. She is Countess of Caergwent in her own right, and must go off to London to be looked after by two maiden great-aunts. Mingled with her despair at leaving her beloved family and her chagrin at the severity of her new way of life is an exhilarating sense of her own new social importance. Charlotte Yonge manages this ambiguity beautifully.

Obedience, humility, unselfishness: these are the traits that the high-strung, intelligent, emotional little girl requires, Charlotte Yonge assures us (in accordance with Keble's teaching), to make her life happier in the new, confined, rigidly controlled household of her great-aunts. Here she may not make a noise, is severely restricted in her friendships, and is given a kind but remote and listless governess. She has few pleasures, no real companionship, little exercise, and insufficient love. Some of the commands she must obey are outrageous: in her new dignity as Countess she is not even allowed to refer to her beloved uncle as "papa," which she has done for years. But there are reasons for the harsh regime: the aunts too have suffered; the loving aunt is ill; the managing aunt has always disliked Kate's dead ancestors, for family reasons, and finds the child intolerable at times. Kate's tantrums, her near-despair, her occasional pleasures, which render her almost as hysterical with joy as her frustrations do with sorrow, her decision to run away, and the final resolution of her problems are wholly convincing.

Unlike the Evangelicals, the Tractarians did not directly preach their message in their fiction. There is very little theology in Charlotte Yonge's books, and none in *Countess Kate*. But on the very first page when Kate wishes for money so that her "papa should have a pretty parsonage, and we would make the church beautiful," she is speaking like a young Tractarian. To make the church beautiful, to build a new church: these were among the leading Tractarian impulses, which their Evangelical opponents severely criticized as emphasis on externals, as a waste of money on architecture, sculpture, stained glass, church ornament, in emulation of Rome—money that should be spent on the good causes the Evangelicals favored. At her first opportunity in her new role as Countess, Kate begs her new acquaintance, Lord de la Poer, to contribute to building a new aisle in her uncle's church.

The degeneration of Kate's character in her unhappiness is characteristically Yongeian. Obedient and wholly truthful at the beginning, Kate makes her first slip when she disobeys orders and allows a playmate to call her a nickname instead of "Lady Caergwent," and then fails to report her delinquency. Thereafter, almost as with Eric, but on a miniature scale and with all allowances made for her being a girl, it is downhill "little by little" with Kate. Soon she acts in "direct defiance" of her aunt's commands; she is deceitful, although she never tells an outright lie. Steeped in her conviction of her own guilt, and well read in children's fiction. Kate is sure she is growing wicked. Dramatically she declares, "It's the fashionable world. It's corrupting my simplicity. It always does. And I shall be lost!" With a similar comic owlish pompousness, she tells her young cousin Charlie, "You little know, in your peaceful retirement, what are the miseries of the great," to which he properly retorts, "Come, Kate, don't talk bosh out of your books." Yonge leavens the lump of her moral instruction with humor and natural youthful conversation. And, not being Evangelical, Kate need not be "converted" or have her spirit wholly broken.

In the end, despite Kate's bad behavior, she is rescued from the rigid governance of the managing great-aunt, whom Charlotte Yonge reduces to tears and even a form of apology. The ways of grown-ups are not to be questioned; Kate has been a grave offender; but an impartial judge accuses the aunt of having kept the child a "state prisoner," and of alienating her from her true friends. "There were faults on both sides, Katharine," the vanquished dragon says by way of farewell. In *Countess Kate*, written early in her career but at the height of her powers, Charlotte Yonge wrote a spirited, wholly moral, Tractarian story for children, full of exciting and laughable episodes, introducing a charming but flawed heroine in need of improvement (as who is not?), and at the end striking a balance rare for her between the need for submission by the child and the need for love and understanding from the adult. *Countess Kate* is a little gem.

The text of Countess Kate *is reprinted from an American edition (Boston: Loring, 1866).*

"But whether it were ill or well
That Katy did, not one will tell
To either me or you.
Still, Katy did, *she did*,—is yet
The only answer we can get
To—What did Katy do?
Though all who marked that hurried lay,
And querulous emphatic way
In which they say or said it,
Might think (if fame had not forbid
Such evil thought) what Katy did
Was not to Katy's credit."
                    M. HOWITT

CHAPTER I

"THERE, I'VE DONE every bit I can do! I'm going to see what o'clock it is."

"I heard it strike eleven just now."

"Sylvia, you'll tip up! what a tremendous stretch!"

"Oh dear! We shan't get one moment before dinner! Oh, horrible! oh, horrible! most horrible!"

"Sylvia, you know I hate hearing Hamlet profaned."

"You can't hate it more than having no one to hear our lessons."

"What on earth can Mary be about?"

"Some tiresome woman to speak to her, I suppose."

"I'm sure it can't be as much her business as it is to mind her poor little sisters. Oh dear! if papa could only afford us a governess!"

"I am sure I should not like it at all; besides, it is wrong to wish to be richer than we are."

"I don't wish; I am only thinking how nice it would be, if some one would give us a famous quantity of money. Then papa should have a pretty parsonage, and we would make the church beautiful, and get another pony or two, to ride with Charlie."

"Yes, and have a garden with a hothouse!"

"Oh yes; and a governess to teach us to draw. But best of all—Sylvia! would n't it be nice not to have to mind one's clothes always? Yes, you laugh; but it comes easier to you; and, oh dear, dear! it is so horrid to be always having to see one does not tear one's self."

"I don't think you do see," said Sylvia, laughing.

"My frocks always *will* get upon the thorns. It is very odd."

"Only do please, Katie dear, let me finish this sum; and then if Mary is not come, she can't scold, if we are amusing ourselves."

"I know!" cried Kate. "I'll draw such a picture, and tell you all about it when your sum is over."

Then silence ensued in the little room, half parlor, half study, nearly filled with books and piano; and the furniture, though carefully protected with brown holland, looking the worse for wear, and as if danced over by a good many young folks.

The two little girls, who sat on the opposite sides of a little square table in the bay window, were both between ten and eleven years old, but could not have been taken for twins, nor even for sisters, so unlike were their features and complexion; though their dress was exactly the same, except that Sylvia's was enlivened by scarlet braid, Kate's darkened by black,—and moreover, Kate's apron was soiled, and the frock bore traces of a great darn. In fact, new frocks for the pair were generally made necessary by Kate's tattered state, when Sylvia's garments were still available for little Lily, or for some school child.

Sylvia's brown hair was smooth as satin; Kate's net did not succeed in confining the loose rough waves of dark chestnut, on the road to blackness. Sylvia was the shorter, firmer, and stronger, with round white limbs; Kate was tall, skinny, and brown, though perfectly healthful. The face of the one was round and rosy, of the other thin and dark; and one pair of eyes were of honest gray, while the others were large and hazel with blue whites. Kate's little hand was so slight, that Sylvia's strong fingers could almost crush it together, but it was far less effective in any sort of handiwork; and her slim neatly made foot always was a reproach to her for making such boisterous steps, and wearing out her shoes so much faster than the quieter movements of her companion did,—her sister, the children would have said, for nothing but the difference of surnames reminded Katharine Umfraville that she was not the sister of Sylvia Wardour.

Her father, a young clergyman, had died before she could remember anything, and her mother had not survived him three months. Little Kate had then become the charge of her mother's sister, Mrs. Wardour, and had grown up in the little parsonage, belonging to the district church of St. James's, Oldburgh, amongst her cousins, calling Mr. and Mrs. Wardour papa and mamma, and feeling no difference between their love to their own five children and to her.

Mrs. Wardour had been dead for about four years, and the little girls were taught by the eldest sister, Mary, who had been at a boarding-school to fit her for educating them. Mr. Wardour too taught them a good deal himself, and had the more time for them since Charlie, the youngest boy, had gone every day to the grammar-school in the town.

Armyn, the eldest of the family, was with Mr. Brown, a very old solicitor, who, besides his office in Oldburgh, had a very pretty house and grounds two miles beyond St. James's, where the children were delighted to spend an afternoon now and then.

Little did they know that it was the taking the little niece as a daughter that had made it needful to make Armyn enter on a profession at once, instead of going to the university and becoming a clergyman like his father; nor how cheerfully Armyn had agreed to do whatever would best lighten his father's cares and troubles. They were a very happy family; above all, on the Saturday evenings and Sundays that the good-natured elder brother spent at home.

"There!" cried Sylvia, laying down her slate-pencil, and indulging in another tremendous yawn; "we can't do a thing more till Mary comes! What can she be about?"

"Oh, but look, Sylvia!" cried Kate, quite forgetting everything in the interest of her drawing on a large sheet of paper. "Do you see what it is?"

"I don't know," said Sylvia, "unless—let me see—That's a very rich little girl, isn't it?"

pointing to an outline of a young lady, whose wealth was denoted by the flounces on her frock, the bracelets on her arms, and the necklace on her neck.

"Yes; she is a very rich and grand—Lady Ethelinda; isn't that a pretty name? I do wish I was Lady Katharine."

"And what is she giving? I wish you would not draw men and boys, Kate; their legs always look so funny, as you do them."

"They never will come right; but never mind, I must have them. That is Lady Ethelinda's dear good cousin, Maximilian; he is a lawyer—don't you see the parchment sticking out of his pocket?"

"Just like Armyn."

"And she is giving him a box with a beautiful new microscope in it; don't you see the top of it? And there is a whole pile of books. And I would draw a pony, only I never can nicely; but look here,"—Kate went on drawing as she spoke,—"here is Lady Ethelinda with her best hat on, and a little girl coming. There is the little girl's house, burnt down; don't you see?"

Sylvia saw with the eyes of her mind the ruins, though her real eyes saw nothing but two lines, meant to be upright, joined together by a wild zig-zag, and with some peaked scrabbles and round whirls intended for smoke. Then Kate's ready pencil portrayed the family, as jagged in their drapery as the flames; and presently Lady Ethelinda appeared before a counter (such a counter!) buying very peculiar garments for the sufferers. Another scene in which she was presenting them followed, Sylvia looking on, and making suggestions; for in fact there was no quiet pastime more relished by the two cousins than drawing stories, as they called it, and most of their money went in paper for that purpose.

"Lady Ethelinda had a whole ream of paper to draw on!" were the words pronounced in Kate's shrill key of eagerness, just as the long-lost Mary and her father opened the door.

"Indeed," said Mr. Wardour, a tall grave-looking man; "and who is Lady Ethelinda?"

"O Papa, it's just a story I was drawing," said Kate, half eager, half ashamed.

"We have done all the lessons we could, indeed we have," began Sylvia; "my music and our French grammar, and—"

"Yes, I know," said Mary; and she paused, looking embarrassed and uncomfortable, so that Sylvia stood in suspense and wonder.

"And so my little Kate likes thinking of Lady—Lady Etheldredas," said Mr. Wardour, rather musingly; but Kate was too much pleased at his giving any sort of heed to her performances to note the manner, and needed no more encouragement to set her tongue off.

"Lady Ethelinda, Papa. She is a very grand rich lady, though she is a little girl; and see there, she is giving presents to all her cousins; and there she is buying new clothes for the orphans that were burnt out; and there she is building a school for them."

Kate suddenly stopped, for Mr. Wardour sat down, drew her between his knees, took both her hands into one of his, and looked earnestly into her face so gravely that she grew frightened, and looking appealingly up, cried out, "O Mary, Mary! have I been naughty?"

"No, my dear," said Mr. Wardour; "but we have heard a very strange piece of news about you, and I am very anxious as to whether it may turn out for your happiness."

Kate stood still and looked at him, wishing he would speak faster. Could her great-uncle in India be come home, and want her to make him a visit in London? How delightful! If it had been anybody but papa, she would have said, "Go on."

"My dear," said Mr. Wardour at last, "you know that your cousin, Lord Caergwent, was killed by an accident last week."

"Yes, I know," said Kate; "that was why Mary made me put this black braid on my frock."

"I did not know till this morning that his death would make any other difference to you," continued Mr. Wardour. "I thought the title went to male heirs, and that Colonel Umfraville was the present earl; but, my little Katharine, I find that it is ordained that you should have this great responsibility. As your grandfather was the elder son, the title and property come to you."

Kate did not look at him, but appeared intent on the marks of the needle on the end of her forefinger, holding down her head.

Sylvia, however, seemed to jump in her very skin, and opening her eyes, cried out, "The title! Then Kate is—is—"

"A countess," said Mr. Wardour, with a smile, "our little Kate is Countess of Caergwent."

"My dear Sylvia!" exclaimed Mary in amazement; for Sylvia, like an India-rubber ball, had bounded over the little arm-chair by which she was standing.

But there her father's look and uplifted finger kept her still and silent. He wanted to give Kate time to understand what he had said.

"Countess of Caergwent," she repeated; "that's not so pretty as if I were Lady Katharine."

"The sound does not matter much," said Mary. "You will always be Katharine to those that love you best. And oh!—" Mary stopped short, her eyes full of tears.

Kate looked up at her astonished. "Are you sorry, Mary?" she asked, a little hurt.

"We are all sorry to lose our little Kate," said Mr. Wardour.

"Lose me, Papa!" cried Kate, clinging to him, as the children scarcely ever did, for he seldom made many caresses; "O, no, never! Does n't Caergwent Castle belong to me? Then you must all come and live with me there; and you shall have lots of big books, Papa; and we will have a pony carriage for Mary, and ponies for Sylvia and Charlie and me, and—"

Kate saw that the melancholy look on Mr. Wardour's face rather deepened than lessened, and she stopped short.

"My dear," he said, "you and I have both other duties."

"Oh, but if I build a church! I dare say there are people at Caergwent as poor as they are here. Could n't we build a church, and you mind them, Papa?"

"My little Katharine, you have yet to understand that 'the heir, so long as he is a child, differeth in nothing from a servant, but is under tutors and governors.' You will not have any power over yourself or your property till you are twenty-one."

"But you are my tutor and my governor, and my spiritual pastor and master," said Kate. "I always say so whenever Mary asks us questions about our duty to our neighbor."

"I have been so hitherto," said Mr. Wardour, setting her on his knee; "but I see I must explain a good deal to you. It is the business of a court in London, that is called the Court of Chancery, to provide that proper care is taken of young heirs and heiresses and their estates, if no one has been appointed by their parents to do so; and it is this court that must settle what is to become of you."

"And why won't it settle that I may live with my own papa and brothers and sisters?"

"Because, Kate, you must be brought up in a way to fit your station: and my children must be brought up in a way to fit theirs. And besides," he added more sadly, "nobody that could help it would leave a girl to be brought up in a household without a mother."

Kate's heart said directly, that as she could never again have a mother, her dear Mary must be better than a stranger; but somehow any reference to the sorrow of the household always made her anxious to get away from the subject, so she looked at her finger again, and asked, "Then am I to live up in this Court of Chances?"

"Not exactly," said Mr. Wardour. "Your two aunts in London, Lady Barbara and Lady Jane Umfraville, are kind enough to offer to take charge of you. Here is a letter that they sent enclosed for you."

"The Countess of Caergwent," was written on the envelope; and Kate's and Sylvia's heads were together in a moment to see how it looked before opening the letter, and reading, " 'My dear Niece,'—dear me, how funny to say niece!—'I deferred writing to you upon the melancholy—' oh, what is it, Sylvia?"

"The melancholy comet!"

"No, no; nonsense."

"Melancholy event," suggested Mary.

"Yes, to be sure. I can't think why grown-up people always write on purpose for one not to read them.—'Melancholy event that has placed you in possession of the horrors of the family.' "

"Horrors—Kate, Kate!",

"Well, I am sure it *is* horrors," said the little girl rather perversely.

"This is not a time for nonsense, Kate," said Mr. Wardour; and she was subdued directly.

"Shall I read it to you?" said Mary.

"Oh, no, no!" Kate was too proud of her letter to give it up, and applied herself to it again. " 'Family honors, until I could ascertain your present address. And likewise, the shock of your poor cousin's death so seriously affected my sister's health in her delicate state, that for some days I could give my attention to nothing else.' Dear me! This is my Aunt Barbara, I see! Is Aunt Jane so ill?"

"She has had very bad health for many years," said Mr. Wardour; "and your other aunt has taken the greatest care of her."

" 'We have now, however, been able to consider what will be best for all parties; and we think nothing will be so proper as that you should reside with us for the present. We will endeavor to make a happy home for you; and will engage a lady to superintend your education, and give you all the advantages to which you are entitled. We have already had an interview with a very admirable person, who will come down to Oldburgh with our butler next Friday, and escort you to us, if Mrs. Wardour will kindly prepare you for the journey. I have written to thank her for her kindness to you.' "

`"Mrs. Wardour!" exclaimed Sylvia.

"The ladies have known and cared little about Kate or us for a good many years," said Mary, in such a hurt tone, that her father looked up with grave reproof in his eyes, as if to remind her of all he had been saying to her during the long hours that the little girls had waited.

" 'With your Aunt Jane's love, and hoping shortly to be better acquainted, I remain, my dear little niece, your affectionate aunt, Barbara Umfraville.' Then I am to go and live with them!" said Kate, drawing a long sigh. "O Papa, do let Sylvia come too, and learn of my governess with me."

"Your aunts do not exactly contemplate that," said Mr. Wardour; "but perhaps there may be visits between you."

Sylvia began to look grave. She had not understood that this great news was to lead to nothing but separation. Everything had hitherto been in common between her and Kate, and that what was good for the one should not be good for the other, was so new and strange, that she did not understand it at once.

"Oh yes! we will visit. You shall all come and see me in London, and see the Zoölogical Gardens and the British Museum; and I will send you such presents!"

"We will see," said Mr. Wardour kindly; "but just now, I think the best thing you can do is to write to your aunt, and thank her for her kind letter; and say that I will bring you up to London on the day she names, without troubling the governess and the butler."

"Oh, thank you!" said Kate; "I shan't be near so much afraid if you come with me."

Mr. Wardour left the room; and the first thing Mary did was to throw her arms round the little girl in a long embrace. "My little Kate! my little Kate! I little thought this was to be the end of it!" she cried, kissing her, while the tears dropped fast.

Kate did not like it at all. The sight of strong feeling distressed her. "Don't, Mary," she said, laughing and disengaging herself; "never mind; I shall always come and see you; and when I grow up, you shall come to live with me at Caergwent."

And that little laugh seemed to do Mary good, for she rose and began to rule the single lines for Kate's letter. Kate could write a very tidy little note; but just now she was too much elated and excited to sit down quietly, or quite to know what she was about. She went skipping about from one chair to another, chattering fast about what she would do, and wondering what the aunts would be like, and what Armyn would say, and what Charlie would say, and the watch she would buy for Charlie, and the great things she was to do for everybody—till Mary muttered something in haste, and ran out of the room.

"I wonder why Mary is so cross," said Kate.

Poor Mary! No one could be farther from being cross; but she was thoroughly upset. She was fond of Kate as of her own sisters, and was not only sorry to part with her, but was afraid that she would not be happy in the new life before her.

CHAPTER II

THE DAYS PASSED very slowly with Kate, until the moment when she was to go to London, and take her state upon her, as she thought. Till that should come to pass, she could not feel herself really a countess. She did not find herself any taller or grander; Charlie teased her rather more instead of less; and she did not think either Mr. Wardour or Mary or Armyn thought half enough of her dignity; they looked sad instead of pleased when she chattered about the fine things she should do. Mr. and Mrs. Brown, to be sure, came to wish her good-bye; but they were so respectful, and took such pains that she should walk first, that she grew shy and sheepish, and did not like it at all.

She thought ease and dignity would come by nature when she once was in London; and she was so certain of soon seeing Sylvia again, that she did not much concern herself about the parting with her; while she was rather displeased with Mary for looking grave, and not making more of her, and trying to tell her that all might not be as delightful as she expected. She little knew that Mary was grieved at her eagerness to leave her happy home, and never guessed at the kind sister's fears for her happiness. She set it all down to what she was wont to call crossness. Instead of that, Mary only thought whether Lady Barbara and Lady Jane would make her little Kate happy and good. She was sure they were proud, hard, cold people; and her father had many talks with her, to try to comfort her about them.

Mr. Wardour told her that Kate's grandfather had been such a grief and shame to the family, that it was no wonder they had not liked to be friendly with those he had left behind him. There had been help given to educate the son, and some notice had been taken of him, but always very distant; and he had been thought very foolish for marrying when he was very young, and very ill off. At the time of his death, his uncle, Colonel Umfraville, had been very kind, and had consulted earnestly with Mr. Wardour what was best for the little orphan; but had then explained that he and his wife could not take charge of her, because his regiment was going to India, and she could not go there with them; and that his sisters were prevented from undertaking the care of so young a child, by the bad health of the elder, who almost owed her life to the tender nursing of the younger. And as Mrs. Wardour was so eager to keep to herself all that was left of her only sister, it had been most natural that Kate should remain at St. James's Parsonage; and Mr. Wardour had full reason to believe that had there been any need, or if he had asked for help, the aunts would have gladly given it. He knew them to be worthy and religious women; and he told Mary that he thought it very likely that they might deal better with Kate's character than he had been able to do. Mary knew she herself had made mistakes, but she could not be humble for her father, or think any place more improving than under his roof.

And Kate meanwhile had her own views. And when all the good-bys were over, and she sat by the window of the railway-carriage, watching the fields rush by, reduced to silence, because "papa" had told her he could not hear her voice, she wove a web in her brain something like this: "I know what my aunts will be like: they will be just like ladies in a book. They will be dreadfully fashionable! Let me see,—Aunt Barbara will have a turban on her head, and a bird of paradise, like the bad old lady in Armyn's book, that Mary took away from me; and they will do nothing all day long but try on flounced gowns, and count their jewels, and go out to balls and operas,—and they will want me to do the same,—and play at cards Sunday! 'Lady Caergwent,' they will say, 'it is becoming to your position!' And then the young countess presented a remarkable contrast in her ingenuous simplicity," continued Kate, not quite knowing whether she was making a story or thinking of herself,—for indeed she did not feel as if she were herself, but somebody in a story. "Her waving hair was only confined by an azure ribbon (Kate loved a fine word when Charlie did not hear it to laugh at her); and her dress was of the simplest muslin, with one diamond aigrette of priceless value."

Kate had not the most remote notion what an aigrette might be, but she thought it would sound well for a countess; and she went on musing very pleasantly on the amiable simplicity of the countess, and the speech that was to cure the aunts of playing at cards on a Sunday, wearing turbans, and all other enormities, and lead them to live in the country, giving a continual course of school-feasts, and surprising meritorious families with gifts of cows. She only wished she had a pencil to draw it all, to show Sylvia, provided Sylvia would know her cows from her tables.

After more vain attempts at chatter, and various stops at stations, Mr. Wardour bought a story-book for her; and thus brought her to a most happy state of silent content, which lasted till the house roofs of London began to rise on either side of the railway.

Among the carriages that were waiting at the terminus was a small brougham, very neat and shiny; and a servant came up and touched his hat, opening the door for Kate, who was told to sit there while the servant and Mr. Wardour looked for the luggage. She was a little disappointed. She had once seen a carriage go by with four horses, and a single one did not seem at all worthy of her; but she had two chapters more of her story to read, and was so eager to see the end of it, that Mr. Wardour could hardly persuade her to look out and see the Thames when she passed over it, nor the Houses of Parliament, and towers of Westminster Abbey.

At last, while passing through the brighter and more crowded streets, Kate, having satisfied herself what had become of the personages of her story, looked up, and saw nothing but dull houses of blackened cream color; and presently found the carriage stopping at the door of one.

"Is it here, papa?" she said, suddenly seized with fright.

"Yes," he said, "this is Bruton Street;" and he looked at her anxiously as the door was opened and the steps were let down. She took tight hold of his hand. Whatever she had been in her day-dreams, she was only his own little frightened Kate now; and she tried to shrink behind him as the footman preceded them up the stairs, and, opening the door, announced—"Lady Caergwent and Mr. Wardour!"

Two ladies rose up, and came forward to meet her. She felt herself kissed by both, and heard greetings, but did not know what to say, and stood up by Mr. Wardour, hanging down her head, and trying to stand upon one foot with the other, as she always did when she was shy and awkward.

"Sit down, my dear," said one of the ladies, making a place for her on the sofa. But Kate only laid hold of a chair, pulled it as close to Mr. Wardour as possible, and sat down on the extreme corner of it, twining her ancles round the leg of the chair. She knew very well that this was not pretty; but she never could recollect what was pretty behavior when she was shy. She was a very different little girl in a day-dream and out of one. And when one of the aunts asked her if she were tired, all she could do was to give a foolish sort of smile, and say "N—no."

Then she had a perception that papa was looking reprovingly at her; so she wriggled her legs away from that of the chair, twisted them together in the middle, and said something meant for "No, thank you;" but of which nothing was to be heard but "q," apparently proceeding out of the brim of her broad hat, so low did the young countess, in her amiable simplicity, hold her head.

"She is shy!" said one of the ladies to the other; and they let her alone, and began to talk to Mr. Wardour about the journey, and various other things, to which Kate did not listen. She began to let her eyes come out from under her hat brim, and satisfied herself that the aunts certainly did not wear either turbans or birds of paradise, but looked quite as like other people as she felt herself, in spite of her title.

Indeed, one aunt had nothing on her head at all, but a little black velvet and lace, not much more than Mary sometimes wore, and the other only a very light cap. Kate thought great aunts must be as old at least as Mrs. Brown, and was much astonished to see that these ladies had no air of age about them. The one who sat on the sofa had a plump, smooth, pretty, pink and white face, very soft and pleasant to look at, though an older person than Kate would have perceived that the youthful delicacy of the complexion showed that she had been carefully shut up and sheltered from all exposure and exertion, and that the quiet innocent look of the small features was that of a person who had never had to use her goodness. Kate was sure that this was Aunt Jane, and that she should get on well with her, though that slow way of speaking was rather wearisome.

The other aunt, who was talking the most, was quite as slim as Mary, and had a bright dark complexion, so that if Kate had not seen some shades of gray in her black hair, it would have been hard to believe her old at all. She had a face that put Kate in mind of a picture of a beautiful lady in a book at home,—the eyes, forehead, nose, and shape of the chin were so finely made; and yet there was something in them that made the little girl afraid, and feel as if the plaster cast of Diana's head on the study mantelpiece had got a pair of dark eyes, and was looking very hard at her; and there was a sort of dry sound in her voice that was uncomfortable to hear.

Then Kate took a survey of the room, which was very prettily furnished, with quantities of beautiful work of all kinds, and little tables, and brackets covered with little devices in china and curiosities under glass, and had flowers standing in the windows; and by the time she had finished trying to make out the subject of a print on the walls, she heard some words that made her think that her aunts were talking of her new governess, and she opened her ears to hear, "So we thought it would be an excellent arrangement for her, poor thing!" and "papa" answering, "I hope Kate may try to be a kind, considerate pupil." Then seeing by Kate's eyes that her attention had been astray, or that she had not understood Lady Barbara's words, he turned to her, saying, "Did you not hear what your aunt was telling me?"

"No, papa."

"She was telling me about the lady who will teach you. She has had great afflictions. She has lost her husband, and is obliged to go out as governess, that she may be able to send her sons to school. So, Kate, you must think of this, and try to give her as little trouble as possible."

It would have been much nicer if Kate would have looked up readily, and said something kind and friendly; but the fit of awkwardness had come over her again, and with it a thought so selfish, that grown-up people in trouble were very tiresome, and never let young ones have any fun.

"Shall I take you to see Mrs. Lacy, my dear?" said Lady Barbara, rising. And as Kate took hold of Mr. Wardour's hand, she added, "You will see Mr. Wardour again after dinner. You had better dress, and have some meat for your tea with Mrs. Lacy, and then come into the drawing-room."

This was a stroke upon Kate. She who had dined with the rest ever since she could remember,—she, now that she was a countess, to be made to drink tea up-stairs, and lose all that time of papa's company! She swelled with displeasure; but Aunt Barbara did not look like a person whose orders could be questioned, and "papa" said not a word in her favor. Possibly the specimen of manners she had just given had not led either him or Lady Barbara to think her fit for a late dinner.

Lady Barbara first took her up-stairs, and showed her a little long narrow bedroom, with a pretty pink curtained bed in it. "This will be your room, my dear," she said. "I am sorry we have not a larger one to offer you; but it opens into mine, as you see, and my sister's is just beyond. Our maid will dress you for a few days, when I hope to engage one for you.

Here *was* something like promotion! Kate dearly loved to have herself taken off her own hands, and not to be reproved by Mary for untidiness, or roughly set to rights by Lily's nurse. She actually exclaimed, "Oh, thank you!" And her aunt waited till the hat and cloak had been taken off, and the chestnut hair smoothed, looked at her attentively, and said: "Yes, you are like the family."

"I'm very like my own papa," said Kate, growing a little bolder, but still speaking with her head on one side, which was her way when she said anything sentimental.

"I dare say you are," answered her aunt, with the dry sound. "Are you ready now? I will show you the way. The house is very small," continued Lady Barbara, as they went down the stairs to the ground floor; "and this must be your schoolroom for the present."

It was the room under the back drawing-room; and in it was a lady in a widow's cap, sitting at work. "Here is your little pupil,—Lady Caergwent,—Mrs. Lacy," said Lady Barbara. "I hope you will find her a good child. She will drink tea with you, and then dress, and afterwards I hope we shall see you with her in the drawing-room."

Mrs. Lacy bowed, without any answer in words, only she took Kate's hand and kissed her. Lady Barbara left them, and there was a little pause. Kate looked at her governess, and her heart sank, for it was the very saddest face she had ever seen,—the eyes looked soft and gentle, as if they had wept until they could weep no longer; and when the question was asked, "Are you tired, my dear?" it was in a tone trying to be cheerful, but the sadder for that very reason. Poor lady! it was only that morning that she had parted with her son, and had gone away from the home where she had lived with her husband and children.

Kate was distressed; yet she felt more at her ease than with her aunts, and answered, "Not at all, thank you," in her natural tone.

"Was it a long journey?"

Kate had been silent so long, that her tongue was ready for exertion; and she began to chatter forth all the events of the journey, without heeding much whether she were listened to or not, till having come to the end of her breath, she saw that Mrs. Lacy was leaning back in her chair, her eyes fixed as if her attention had gone away. Kate thereupon roamed round the room, peeped from the window, and saw that it looked into a dull, narrow garden, and then studied the things in the room. There was a piano, at which she shook her head. Mary had tried to teach her music, but after a daily fret for six weeks, Mr. Wardour had said it was waste of time and temper for both; and Kate was delighted. Then she came to a bookcase; and there the aunts had kindly placed the books of their own younger days, some of which she had never seen before. When she had once begun on the "Rival Crusoes," she gave Mrs. Lacy no more trouble, except to rouse her from it to drink her tea, and then go and be dressed.

The maid managed the white muslin so as to make her look very nice; but before she had gone half way down-stairs there was a voice behind—"My Lady! my Lady!"

She did not turn, not remembering that she herself must be meant; and the maid running after her, caught her rather sharply, and showed her her own hands, all blacked and grimed.

"How tiresome!" cried she. "Why I only just washed it!"

"Yes, my Lady; but you took hold of the balusters all the way down. And your forehead! Bless me! what would Lady Barbara say?"

For Kate had been trying to peep through the balusters into the hall below, and had, of course, painted her brow with London blacks. She made one of her little impatient gestures, and thought she was very hardly used,—dirt stuck upon her, and brambles tore her like no one else.

She got safely down this time, and went into the drawing-room with Mrs. Lacy, there taking a voyage of discovery among the pretty things, knowing that she must not touch, but asking endless questions, some of which Mrs. Lacy answered in her sad indifferent way, others she could not answer, and Kate was rather vexed at her not seeming to care to know.

The aunts came in, and with them Mr. Wardour. She was glad to run up to him, and drag him to look at a group in white Parian under a glass, that had delighted her very much. She knew it was Jupiter's Eagle; but who was feeding it? "Ganymede," said Mr. Wardour; and Kate, who always liked mythological stories, went on most eagerly talking about the legend of the youth who was borne away to be the cup-bearer of the gods. It was a thing to make her forget about the aunts and everybody else; and Mr. Wardour helped her out, as he generally did when her talk was neither foolish nor ill-timed; but he checked her when he thought she was running on too long, and went himself to talk to Mrs. Lacy, while Kate was obliged to come to her aunts, and stood nearest to Lady Jane, of whom she was least afraid.

"You seem quite at home with all the heathen gods, my dear," said Lady Jane; "how come you to know them so well?"

"In Charlie's lesson books, you know," said Kate: and seeing that her aunt did not know, she went on to say, "there are notes and explanations. And there is a Homer—an English one, you know; and we play at it."

"We seem to have quite a learned lady here!" said Aunt Barbara, in the voice Kate did not like. "Do you learn music?"

"No: I have n't got any ear; and I hate it!"

"Oh!" said Lady Barbara, drily: and Kate seeing Mr. Wardour's eyes fixed on her rather anxiously, recollected that *hate* was not a proper word, and fell into confusion.

"And drawing?" said her Aunt.

"No; but I want *to*—"

"Oh!" again said Lady Barbara, looking at Kate's fingers, which in her awkwardness she was apparently dislocating in a method peculiar to herself.

However it was soon over, for it was already later than Kate's home bedtime; she bade every one good-night, and was soon waited on by Mrs. Bartley, the maid, in her own luxurious little room.

But luxurious as it was, Kate for the first time thoroughly missed home. The boarded floor, the old crib, would have been welcome, if only Sylvia had been there. She had never gone to bed without Sylvia in her life. And now she thought with a pang that Sylvia was longing for her, and looking at her empty crib, thinking too, it might be, that Kate had cared more for her grandeur than for the parting.

Not only was it sorrowful to be lonely, but also Kate was one of the silly little girls to whom the first quarter of an hour in bed was a time of fright. Sylvia had no fears, and always accounted for the odd noises and strange sights that terrified her companion. She never believed that the house was on fire, even though the moon made very bright sparkles; she always said the sounds were the servants, the wind, or the mice; and never would allow that thieves would steal little girls, or anything belonging to themselves. Or if she were fast asleep, her very presence gave a feeling of protection.

But when the preparations were *very* nearly over, and Kate began to think of the strange room, the roar of carriages in the streets, her heart failed her, and the fear of being alone quite overpowered her dread of the staid Mrs. Bartley, far more of being thought a silly little girl.

"Please,—please, Mrs. Bartley," she said in a trembling voice, "are you going away?"

"Yes, my Lady: I am going down to supper when I have placed my Lady Jane's and my Lady Barbara's things."

"Then please,—please," said Kate in her most humble and insinuating voice, "do leave the door open while you are doing it."

"Very well, my Lady," was the answer, in a tone just like that in which Lady Barbara said "Oh!"

And the door stayed open; but Kate could not sleep. There seemed to be the rattle and bump of the train going on in her bed, the gas lights in the streets below came in unnaturally, and the noises were much more frightful and unaccountable than any she had ever heard at home. Her eyes spread with fright, instead of closing in sleep; then came the longing yearning for Sylvia, and tears grew hot in them; and by the time Mrs. Bartley had finished her preparations, and gone down, her distress had grown so unbearable, that she absolutely began sobbing aloud, and screaming, "Papa!" She knew he would be very angry, and that she should hear that such folly was shameful in a girl of her age; but any anger would be better than this dreadful loneliness. She screamed louder and louder; and she grew half frightened, half relieved, when she heard his step, and a buzz of voices on the stairs; and then there he was, standing by her, and saying gravely, "What is the matter, Kate?"

"O papa, papa, I want—I want Sylvia!—I am afraid!"

Then she held her breath, and cowered under the clothes. "Poor child!" he said quietly and sadly. "You must put away this childishness, my dear. You know that you are not really alone, even in a strange place."

"No, no, papa; but I am afraid,—I cannot bear it!"

"Have you said the verse that helps you to bear it, Katie?"

"I could not say it without Sylvia."

She heard him sigh; and then he said, "You must try another night, my Katie, and think of Sylvia saying it at home in her own room. You will meet her prayers in that way. Now let me hear you say it."

Kate repeated, but half choked with sobs, "I lay me down in peace," and the rest of the calm words, with which she had been taught to lay herself in bed; but at the end, she cried, "O papa, don't go!"

"I must go, dear: I cannot stay away from your aunts. But I will tell you what to do to-night,—and other nights when I shall be away,—say to yourself the Ninety-first Psalm. I think you know it.—"Whoso abideth under the defence of the Most High—"

"I think I do know it."

"Try to say it to yourself, and then the place will seem less dreary, because you will feel Who is with you. I will look in once more before I go away, and I think you will be asleep."

And though Kate tried to stay awake for him, asleep she was.

CHAPTER III

I N A VERY FEW DAYS, Kate had been settled into the ways of the household in Bruton Street; and found one day so like another, that she sometimes asked herself whether she had not been living there years instead of days.

She was always to be ready by half-past seven. Her French maid, Josephine, used to come in at seven, and wash and dress her quietly, for if there were any noise Aunt Barbara would knock and be displeased. Aunt Barbara rose long before that time, but she feared lest Aunt Jane should be disturbed in her morning's sleep; and Kate thought she had the ears of a dragon for the least sound of voice or laugh.

At half-past seven, Kate met Mrs. Lacy in the schoolroom, read the Psalms and Second Lesson, and learnt some answers to questions in the Catechism, to be repeated to Lady Barbara on a Sunday. For so far from playing cards in a bird of paradise turban all Sunday, the aunts were quite as particular about these things as Mr. Wardour, —more inconveniently so, the countess thought; for he always let her answer his examination out of her own head, and never gave her answers to learn by heart;

"Answers that I know before quite well," said Kate, "only not made tiresome with fine words."

"That is not a right way of talking, Lady Caergwent," gravely said Mrs. Lacy; and Kate felt cross and rebellious.

It was a trial; but if Kate had taken it humbly, she would have found that even the stiff hard words and set phrases gave accuracy to her ideas; and the learning of the texts would have been clear gain, if she had been in a meeker spirit.

This done, Mrs. Lacy gave her a music lesson. This was grievous work, for the question was not, *how* the learning should be managed, but whether the thing should be learnt at all.

Kate had struggled hard against it. She informed her aunts that Mary had tried to teach her for six weeks in vain, and that she had had a bad mark every day; that papa had said it was all nonsense, and that talents could not be forced; and that Armyn said she had no more ear than an old hen.

To which Lady Barbara had gravely answered, that Mr. Wardour could decide as he pleased while Katharine was under his charge, but that it would be highly improper that she should not learn the accomplishments of her station.

"Only I can't learn," said Kate, half desperate; "you will see that it is of no use, Aunt Barbara."

"I shall do my duty, Katharine," was all the answer she obtained.

Lady Barbara was right in saying that it was her duty to see that the child under her charge learnt what is usually expected of ladies; and though Kate could never acquire music enough to give pleasure to others, yet the training and discipline were likely not only to improve her ear and untamed voice, but to be good for her whole character, —that is, if she had made a good use of them. But in these times, being usually already out of temper with the difficult answers of the Catechism questions, and obliged to keep in her pettish feelings towards what concerned sacred things, she let all out in the music lesson, and with her murmurs and her inattention, her yawns and her blunders, rendered herself infinitely more dull and unmusical than Nature had made her, and was a grievous torment to poor Mrs. Lacy, and her patient "One, two, three,—now, my dear."

Kate thought it was Mrs. Lacy who tormented her! I wonder which was the worst to the other! At any rate, Mrs. Lacy's heavy eyes looked heavier, and she moved as though wearied out for the whole day by the time the clock struck nine, and released them; whilst her pupil, who never was cross long, took a hop, skip, and jump to the dining-room, and was as fresh as ever in the eager hope that the post would bring a letter from home.

Lady Barbara read prayers in the dining-room at nine, and there breakfasted with Kate and Mrs. Lacy, sending up a tray to Lady Jane in her bedroom. Those were apt to be grave breakfasts; not like the merry mornings at home, when chatter used to go on in half whispers between the younger ones, with laughs breaking out in sudden gusts, till a little over-loudness brought one of Mary's good-natured "Hushes," usually answered with, "O Mary, such fun!"

It was Lady Barbara's time for asking about all the lessons of the day before; and though these were usually fairly done, and Mrs. Lacy was always a kind reporter, it was rather awful; and what was worse, were the strictures on deportment. For it must be confessed, that Lady Caergwent, though neatly and prettily formed, with delicate little feet and hands, and a strong upright back, was a remarkably awkward child; and the more she was lectured, the more ungraceful she made herself, partly from thinking about it, and from fright, partly from being provoked. She had never been so ungainly at Oldburgh; she never was half so awkward in the schoolroom, as she would be while taking her cup of tea from Lady Barbara, or handing the butter to her governess. And was it not wretched to be ordered to do it again, and again, and again (each time worse than the last), when there was a letter in Sylvia's writing lying on the table unopened?

She could never be found fault with, but she answered again. She had been scarcely broken of replying and justifying herself, even to Mr. Wardour, and had often argued with Mary, till he came in and put a sudden stop to it; and now she usually defended herself with "papa says—" or "Mary says—" and though she really thought she spoke the truth, she made them say such odd things, that it was no wonder Lady Barbara thought they had very queer notions of education, and that her niece had nothing to do but to unlearn their lessons. In fact, Kate could hardly be forbidden anything without replying that papa or Mary *always* let her do it; till at last she was ordered, very decidedly, never again to quote Mr. and Miss Wardour, and especially not to call him papa.

Kate's eyes flashed at this, and she was so angry, that no words would come but a passionate stammering "I can't,—I can't leave off; I won't."

Lady Barbara looked stern and grave. "You must be taught what is suitable to your position, Lady Caergwent; and until you have learned to feel it yourself, I shall request Mrs. Lacy to give you an additional lesson every time you call Mr. Wardour by that name."

Aunt Barbara's low, slow way of speaking when in great displeasure was a terrific thing, and so was the set look of her handsome mouth and eyes. Kate burst into a violent fit of crying, and was sent away in dire disgrace. When she had spent her tears and sobs, she began to think over her aunt's cruelty and ingratitude, and the wickedness of trying to make her ungrateful too, ending with "I will call him papa, with my last breath!"

But the mere fixing of those great dark eyes was sufficient to cut off pa—at its first syllable, and turn it into a faltering "my uncle;" although Kate's heart was very sore and angry, and never except once or twice when the word slipped out by chance, did she incur the penalty, though she would have respected herself more if she had been brave enough to bear something for the sake of showing her love to Mr. Wardour.

After breakfast, she was sent out with Mrs. Lacy for a walk. If she had a letter from home, she read it while Josephine dressed her as if she had been a doll; or else she had a story-book in hand, and was usually lost in it when Mrs. Lacy looked into her room to see if she were ready.

To walk along the dull street, and pace round and round the gardens in Berkley Square, was not so entertaining as morning games in the garden with Sylvia; and these were times of feeling very like a prisoner. Other children in the gardens seemed to be friends, and played together; but this the aunts had forbidden her, and she could only look on, and think of Sylvia and Charlie, and feel as if one real game of play would do her all the good in the world.

To be sure, she could talk to Mrs. Lacy, and tell her about Sylvia, and deliver opinions upon the characters in her histories and stories; but it often happened that low, grave, "Yes, my dear," showed by the very tone that her governess had not heard a word; and at the best, it was dreary work to look up and discourse to nothing but the black crape veil that Mrs. Lacy always kept down.

"I cannot think why I should have a governess in affliction; it is very hard upon me!" said Kate to herself.

Why did she never bethink herself how hard the afflictions were upon Mrs. Lacy, and what good it would have done her if her pupil had tried to be like a gentle little daughter to her.

The lesson-time followed. Kate first repeated what she had learnt the day before; and then had a French master two days in a week; on two more, one for arithmetic and geography; and on the other two, a drawing master. She liked these lessons, and did well in all, as soon as she left off citing Mary Wardour's pronunciations, and ways of doing sums. Indeed, she had more lively conversation with her French master, who was a very good-natured old man, than with any one else, except Josephine; and she liked writing French letters for him to correct, making them be from the imaginary little girls whom she was so fond of drawing and sending them to Sylvia.

After the master was gone, Kate prepared for the next day, and did a little Italian reading with Mrs. Lacy; after which followed reading of history, and needlework. Lady Barbara was very particular that she should learn to work well, and was a good deal shocked at her very poor performances. "She had thought that plain needlework, at least, would be taught in a clergyman's family."

"Mary tried to teach me; but she says all my fingers are thumbs."

And so poor Mrs. Lacy found them.

Mrs. Lacy and her pupil dined at the ladies' luncheon; and this was pleasanter than the breakfast, from the presence of Aunt Jane, whose kiss of greeting was a comforting, cheering moment, and who always was so much distressed and hurt at the sight of her sister's displeasure, that Aunt Barbara seldom reproved before her. She always had a kind word to say; Mrs. Lacy seemed brighter and less oppressed in the sound of her voice; every one was more at ease; and when speaking to her, or waiting upon her, Lady Barbara was no longer stern in manner nor dry in voice. The meal was not lively; and though she was helped first, and ceremoniously waited on, she must not speak unless she was spoken to; and was it not very cruel, first to make everything so dull that no one could help yawning, and then to treat a yawn as a dire offence?

The length of the luncheon was a great infliction, because all the time from that to three o'clock was her own. It was a poor remnant of the entire afternoons which she and Sylvia had usually disposed of much as they pleased; and even what there was of it, was not to be spent in the way for which the young limbs longed. No one was likely to play at blindman's buff, and hare and hounds, in that house; and even her poor attempt at throwing her gloves against the wall, and catching them in the rebound, and her scampers up-stairs two steps at once, and runs down with a leap down the last four steps, were summarily stopped, as unladylike and too noisy for aunt Jane. Kate did get a private run and leap whenever she could, but never with a safe conscience, and that spoilt the pleasure, or made it guilty.

All she could do really in peace was reading, drawing, or writing letters to Sylvia. Nobody had interfered with any of these occupations, though Kate knew that none of them were perfectly agreeable to Aunt Barbara, who had been heard to speak of children's reading far too many silly story books nowadays, and had declared that the child would cramp her hand for writing or good drawing with that nonsense.

However, Lady Jane had several times submitted most complacently to have a whole long history in pictures explained to her, smiling very kindly, but not apparently much the wiser. And one, at least, of the old visions of wealth was fulfilled, for Kate's pocket-money enabled her to keep herself in story books and unlimited white paper, as well as to set up a paint-box with real good colors. But somehow, a new tale every week had not half the zest that stories had when a fresh book only came into the house by rare and much prized chances; and though the paper was smooth, and the blue and the red lovely, it was not half so nice to draw and paint as with Sylvia helping, and the remains of Mary's rubbings for making illuminations; nay, Lily spoiling everything, and Armyn and Charlie laughing at her, were now remembered as ingredients in her pleasure; and she would hardly have had the heart to go on drawing, but that she could still send her pictorial stories to Sylvia, and receive remarks on them. There were no more Lady Ethelindas in flounces in Kate's drawings now; her heroines were always clergymen's daughters, or those of colonists cutting down trees, and making the butter.

At three o'clock the carriage came to the door; and on Mondays and Thursdays took Lady Caergwent and her governess to a mistress who taught dancing and calisthenic exercises, and to whom her aunts trusted to make her a little more like a countess than she was at present. Those were poor Kate's black days of the week; when her feet were pinched, and her arms turned the wrong way, as it seemed to her; and she was in perpetual disgrace. Those wishes, that her Ladyship would assume a more aristocratic deportment were so infinitely worse than a good scolding! Nothing could make it more dreadful, except Aunt Barbara's coming in at the end to see how she was getting on.

The aunts, when Lady Jane was well enough, used to take their drive while the dancing lesson was in progress, and send the carriage afterwards to bring their niece home. On the other days of the week, when it was fine, the carriage set Mrs. Lacy and Kate down in Hyde Park for their walk, while the aunts drove about; and this, after the first novelty, was nearly as dull as the morning walk. The quiet decorous pacing along was very tiresome after skipping in the lanes at home; and once, when Mrs. Lacy had let her run freely in Kensington Gardens, Lady Barbara was much displeased with her, and said Lady Caergwent was too old for such habits.

There was no sight-seeing. Kate had told Lady Jane how much she wished to see the Zoölogical Gardens and British Museum, and had been answered that some day when she was very good Aunt Barbara would take her there; but the day never came, though, whenever Kate had been in no particular scrape for a little while, she hoped it was coming. Though certainly days without scrapes were not many: the loud tones, the scream of laughing that betrayed her undignified play with Josephine, the attitudes, the skipping and jumping like the gambols of a calf, the wonderful tendency of her clothes to get into mischief,—all were continually bringing trouble upon her. If a splash of mud was in the street, it always came on her stockings; her meals left reminiscences on all her newest dresses; her hat was always blowing off; and her skirts curiously entangled themselves in rails and balusters, caught upon nails, and tore into ribbons: and though all the repairs fell to Josephine's lot, and the purchase of new garments was no such difficulty as of old, Aunt Barbara was even more severe on such mishaps than Mary, who had all the trouble and expense of them.

After the walk, Kate had lessons to learn for the next day,—poetry, dates, grammar, and the like; and after them came her tea; and then her evening toilette, when, as the aunts were out of hearing, she refreshed herself with play and chatter with Josephine. She was supposed to talk French to her; but it was very odd sort of French, and Josephine did not insist on its being better. She was very good natured, and thought "Miladi" had a dull life; so she allowed a good many things that a more thoughtful person would have known to be inconsistent with obedience to Lady Barbara.

When dressed, Kate had to descend to the drawing-room, and there await her aunts coming up from dinner. She generally had a book of her own, or else she read bits of those lying on the tables, till Lady Barbara caught her, and in spite of her protest that at home she might always read any book on the table, ordered her never to touch any without express permission.

Sometimes the aunts worked; sometimes Lady Barbara played and sang. They wanted Kate to sit up as they did with fancy work, and she had a bunch of flowers in Berlin wool which she was supposed to be grounding; but she much disliked it, and seldom set three stitches when her aunts' eyes were not upon her. Lady Jane was a great worker, and tried to teach her some pretty stitches; but though she began by liking to sit by the soft gentle aunt, she was so clumsy a pupil, that Lady Barbara declared that her sister must not be worried, and put a stop to the lessons. So Kate sometimes read, or dawdled over her grounding; or when Aunt Barbara was singing, she would nestle up to her other aunt, and go off into some dreamy fancy of growing up, getting home to the Wardours, or having them to live with her at her own home; or even of a great revolution, in which, after the pattern of the French nobility, she should have to maintain Aunt Jane by the labor of her hands! What was to have become of Aunt Barbara was uncertain; perhaps she was to be in prison, and Kate to bring food to her in a little basket every day; or else she was to run away: but Aunt Jane was to live in a nice little lodging, with no one to wait on her but her dear little niece, who was to paint beautiful screens for her livelihood, and make her coffee with her own hands. Poor Lady Jane!

Bedtime came at last—horrible bedtime, with all its terrors! At first, Kate persuaded Josephine and her light to stay till sleep came to put an end to them; but Lady Barbara came up one evening, declared that a girl of eleven years old must not be permitted in such childish nonsense, and ordered Josephine to go down at once, and always to put out the candle as soon as Lady Caergwent was in bed.

Lady Barbara would hardly have done so if she had known how much suffering she caused; but she had always been too sensible to know what the misery of fancies could be, or how the silly little brain imagined everything possible and impossible: sometimes that thieves were breaking in,—sometimes that the house was on fire,—sometimes that she should be smothered with pillows, like the princes in the Tower, for the sake of her title.

It is true that Kate did not feel as if obedience to Lady Barbara was the same duty as obedience to "papa." Perhaps it was not in the nature of things that she should; but no one can habitually practise petty disobedience to one "placed in authority over" her, without hurting her whole disposition.

CHAPTER IV

"THURSDAY MORNING! Bother—calisthenic day,—I'll go to sleep again, to put it off as long as I can. If I was only a little countess in her own feudal keep, I would get up in the dawn, and gather flowers in the May dew,—primroses and eglantine!—Charlie says it is affected to call sweetbriar eglantine. Sylvia! Sylvia! that thorn has got hold of me; and there's Aunt Barbara coming down the lane in the baker's jiggetting cart!—O dear! was it only dreaming? I thought I was gathering dog-roses with Charlie and Sylvia in the lane; and now it is only Thursday, and horrid calisthenic day! I suppose I must wake up.

> " 'Awake, my soul, and with the sun
> Thy daily stage of duty run.'

"I'm sure it's a very tiresome sort of stage! We used to say, 'As happy as a queen:' I am sure if the Queen is as much less happy than a countess as I am than a common little girl, she must be miserable indeed! It is like a rule of three sum. Let me see,—if a common little girl has one hundred happinesses a day, and a countess only—only five,—how many has the Queen? No,—but how much higher is a queen than a countess? If I was Queen, I would put an end to aunts and to calisthenic exercises; and I would send for all my orphan nobility, and let them chose their own governesses and playfellows, and always live with country clergymen! I am sure nobody ought to be oppressed as Aunt Barbara oppresses me: it is just like James V. of Scotland when the Douglases got hold of him! I wonder what is the use of being a countess, if one never is to do anything to please one's self, and one is to live with a cross old aunt!"

Most likely every one is of Lady Caergwent's morning opinion,—that Lady Barbara Umfraville was cross, and that it was a hard lot to live in subjection to her. But there are two sides to a question; and there were other hardships in that house besides those of the Countess of Caergwent.

Forty years ago, two little sisters had been growing up together, so fond of each other that they were like one; and though the youngest, Barbara, was always brighter, stronger, braver, and cleverer, than gentle Jane, she never enjoyed what her sister could not do; and neither of them ever wanted any amusement beyond quiet play with their dolls and puzzles, contrivances in pretty fancy works, and walks with their governess in trim gravel paths. They had two elder brothers and one younger; but they had never played out of doors with them, and had not run about or romped since they were almost babies: they would not have known how; and Jane was always sickly and feeble, and would have been very unhappy with loud or active ways.

As time passed on, Jane became more weakly and delicate; while Barbara grew up very handsome, and full of life and spirit, but fonder of her sister than ever, and always coming home from her parties and gayeties, as if telling Jane about them was the best part of all.

At last, Lady Barbara was engaged to be married to a brother officer of her second brother, James; but just then poor Jane fell so ill, that the doctors said she could not live through the year. Barbara loved her sister far too well to think of marrying at such a time, and said she must attend to no one else. All that winter and spring she was nursing her sister day and night, watching over her, and quite keeping up the little spark of life, the doctors said, by her tender care. And though Lady Jane lived on day after day, she never grew so much better as to be fit to hear of the engagement, and that, if she recovered, her sister would be separated from her; and so weeks went on, and still nothing could be done about the marriage.

As it turned out, this was the best thing that could have happened to Lady Barbara; for in the course of this time, it came to her father's knowledge that her brother and her lover had both behaved disgracefully, and that if she had married, she must have led a very unhappy life. He caused the engagement to be broken off. She knew it was right, and made no complaint to anybody; but she always believed that it was her brother James who had been the tempter, who had led his friend astray; and from that time, though she was more devoted than ever to her sick sister, she was soft and bright to nobody else. She did not complain, but she thought that things had been very hard with her; and when people repine, their troubles do not make them kinder, but the brave grow stern, and the soft grow fretful.

All this had been over for nearly thirty years, and the brother and the friend had both been long dead. Lady Barbara was very anxious to do all that she thought right; and she was so wise and sensible, and so careful of her sister Jane, that all the family respected her and looked up to her. She thought she had quite forgiven all that had passed: she did not know why it was so hard to her to take any notice of her brother James's only son. Perhaps if she had, she would have forced herself to try to be more warm and kind to him, and not have inflamed Lord Caergwent's displeasure when he married imprudently. Her sister Jane had never known all that had passed: and it was not Lady Barbara's way to talk to other people of her own troubles. But Jane was always led by her sister, and never thought of people, or judged events, otherwise than as Barbara told her; so that, kind and gentle as she was by nature, she was like a double of her sister, instead of by her mildness telling on the family councils. The other brother, Giles, had been aware of all, and saw how it was; but he was so much younger than the rest, that he was looked on by them like a boy long after he was grown up, and had not felt entitled to break through his sister Barbara's reserve, so as to venture on opening out the sorrows so long past, and pleading for his brother James's family, though he had done all he could for them himself. He had indeed been almost constantly on foreign service, and had seen very little of his sisters.

Since their father's death, the two sisters had lived their quiet life together. They were just rich enough to live in the way they thought the duty of persons in their rank, keeping their carriage for Lady Jane's daily drive, and spending two months every year by the sea, and one at Caergwent Castle with their eldest brother. They always had a spare room for any old friend who wanted to come up to town; and they did many acts of kindness, and gave a great deal to be spent on the poor of their parish. They did the same quiet things every day: one liked what the other liked; and Lady Barbara thought, morning, noon, and night, what would be good for her sister's health; while Lady Jane rested on Barbara's care, and was always pleased with whatever came in her way.

And so the two sisters had gone on year after year, and were very happy in their own way, till the great grief came of losing their eldest brother; and not long after him his son, the nephew who had been their great pride and delight, and for whom they had so many plans and hopes.

And with his death, there came what they felt to be the duty and necessity of trying to fit the poor little heiress for her station. They were not fond of any children; and it upset all their ways very much to have to make room for a little girl, her maid, and her governess; but still, if she had been such a little girl as they had been, and always like the well-behaved children whom they saw in drawing-rooms, they would have known what kind of a creature had come into their hands.

But was it not very hard on them that their niece should turn out a little wild harum-scarum creature, such as they had never dreamt of,—really unable tò move without noises that startled Lady Jane's nerves, and threw Lady Barbara into despair at the harm they would do,—a child whose untutored movements were a constant eyesore and distress to them; and though she could sometimes be bright and fairy-like if unconstrained, always grew abrupt and uncouth when under restraint,—a child very far from silly, but apt to say the silliest things,—learning quickly all that was mere head-work, but hopelessly or obstinately dull at what was to be done by the fingers,—a child whose ways could not be called vulgar, but would have been completely tom-boyish, except for a certain timidity that deprived them of the one merit of courage, and a certain frightened consciousness that was in truth modesty, though it did not look like it? To have such a being to endure, and more than that, to break into the habits of civilized life, and the dignity of a lady of rank, was no small burden for them; but they thought it right, and made up their minds to bear it.

Of course it would have been better if they had taken home the little orphan when she was destitute, and an additional weight to Mr. Wardour; and had she been actually in poverty or distress, with no one to take care of her, Lady Barbara would have thought it a duty to provide for her: but knowing her to be in good hands, it had not then seemed needful to inflict the child on her sister, or to conquer her own distaste to all connected with her unhappy brother James. No one had ever thought of the little Katharine Aileve Umfraville becoming the head of the family; for then young Lord Umfraville was in his full health and strength.

And why *did* Lady Barbara only now feel the charge of the child a duty? Perhaps it was because, without knowing it, she had been brought up to make an idol of the state and consequence of the earldom, since she thought breeding up the girl for a countess incumbent on her, when she had not felt tender compassion for the brother's orphan grandchild. So somewhat of the pomps of this world may have come in to blind her eyes; but whatever she did, was because she thought it right to do, and when Kate thought of her as cross, it was a great mistake. Lady Barbara had great control of temper, and did every thing by rule, keeping herself as strictly as she did every one else except Lady Jane; and though she could not like such a troublesome little incomprehensible wildcat as Katharine, she was always trying to do her strict justice, and give her whatever in her view was good or useful.

But Kate esteemed it a great holiday when, as sometimes happened, Aunt Barbara went out to spend the evening with some friends; and she, under promise of being very good, used to be Aunt Jane's companion.

Those were the times when her tongue took a holiday, and it must be confessed, rather to the astonishment and confusion of Lady Jane.

"Aunt Jane, do tell me about yourself when you were a little girl."

"Ah! my dear, that does not seem so very long ago. Time passes very quickly. To think of such a great girl as you being poor James's grandchild."

"Was my grandpapa much older than you?"

"Only three years older, my dear."

"Then do tell me how you played with him?"

"I never did, my dear; I played with your Aunt Barbara."

"Dear me! how stupid! One can't do things without boys."

"No, my dear; boys always spoil girl's play, they are so rough."

"Oh! no, no, Aunt Jane; there's no fun unless one is rough,—I mean, not exactly; but it's no use playing unless one makes a jolly good noise."

"My dear," said Lady Jane, greatly shocked, "I can't bear to hear you talk so, nor to use such words."

"Dear me, Aunt Jane, we say jolly twenty times a day at St. James's, and nobody minds."

"Ah! yes; you see you have played with boys."

"But our boys are not rough, Aunt Jane," persisted Kate, who liked hearing herself talk much better than any one else. "Mary says Charlie is a great deal less riotous than I am, especially since he went to school; and Armyn is too big to be riotous. O dear, I wish Mr. Brown would send Armyn to London; he said he would be sure and come to see me, and he is the jolliest, most delightful fellow in the world!"

"My dear child," said Lady Jane, in her soft distressed voice, "indeed, that is not the way young ladies talk of—of—boys."

"Armyn is not a boy, Aunt Jane; he is a man. He is a clerk, you know, and will get a salary in another year."

"A clerk!"

"Yes, in Mr. Brown's office, you know. Aunt Jane, did you ever go out to tea?"

"Yes, my dear; sometimes we drank tea with our little friends in the doll's tea-cups."

"Oh! you can't think what fun we have when Mrs. Brown asks us to tea. She has got the nicest garden in the world, and a greenhouse, and a great syringe, to water it; and we always used to get it, till once, without meaning it, I squirted right through the drawing-room window, and Mrs. Brown thought it was Charlie, only I ran in and told of myself, and Mrs. Brown said it was very generous and gave me a Venetian weight with a little hermit in a snow-storm; only it is worn out now, and won't snow, so I gave it to little Lily when we had the whooping-cough."

By this time Lady Jane was utterly ignorant what the gabble was about, except that Katharine had been in very odd company, and done very strange things with those boys, and she gave a melancholy little sound in the pause; but Kate taking breath, ran on again—

"It is because Mrs. Brown is not used to educating children, you know, that she fancies one wants a reward for telling the truth; I told her so, but Mary thought it would vex her, and stopped my mouth. Well, then we young ones—that is, Charlie, and Sylvia, and Armyn, and I—drank tea out on the lawn. Mary had to sit up and be company; but we had such fun! There was a great old laurel-tree, and Armyn put Sylvia and me up into the fork; and that was our nest, and we were birds, and he fed us with strawberries; and we pretended to be learning to fly, and stood up flapping our frocks and squeaking, and Charlie came under and danced the branches about. We didn't like that, and Armyn said it was a shame, and hunted him away, racing all round the garden; and we scrambled down by ourselves, and came down on the slope. It is a long green slope, right down to the river, all smooth and turfy, you know; and I was standing at the top, when Charlie came slyly, and saying he would help the little bird to fly, gave me one push, and down I went, till Sylvia *really* thought she heard my neck crack! Was n't it fun?"

"But the river, my dear!" said Lady Jane, shuddering.

"Oh! there was a good flat place before we came to the river, and I stopped long before that! So then, as we had been the birds of the air, we thought we would be the fishes of the sea; and it was nice and shallow, with dear little caddises and river crayfish, and great pearl shells at the bottom. So we took off our shoes and stockings, and Charlie and Armyn turned up their trousers, and we had such a nice paddling. I really thought I should have got a pearl then; and you know there were some in the breastplate of Venus."

"In the river! Did your cousin allow that?"

"O yes; we had on old our blue checks; and Mary never minds anything when Armyn is there to take care of us. When they heard in the drawing-room what we had been doing, they made Mary sing Auld Lang Syne, because of "We twa hae paidlit in the burn frae morning sun till dine;" and whenever in future times I meet Armyn, I mean to say—

> " 'We twa hae paidlit in the burn
>   Frae morning sun till dine;
> We've wandered many a weary foot
>   Sin' auld lang syne.'

Or perhaps I shall be able to sing it, and that will be still prettier."

And Kate sat still, thinking of the prettiness of the scene of the stranger, alone in the midst of numbers, in the splendid drawing-rooms, hearing the sweet voice of the lovely young countess at the piano, singing this touching memorial of the simple days of childhood.

Lady Jane meanwhile worked her embroidery, and thought what wonderful disadvantages the poor child had had, and that Barbara really must not be too severe on her, after she had lived with such odd people, and that it was very fortunate that she had been taken away from them before she had grown any older, or more used to them.

Soon after, Kate gave a specimen of her manners with boys. When she went into the dining-room at luncheon-time one wet afternoon, she heard steps on the stairs behind her aunt's, and there appeared a very pleasant-looking gentleman, followed by a boy of about her own age.

"Here is our niece," said Lady Barbara. "Katharine, come and speak to Lord de la Poer."

Kate liked his looks, and the way in which he held out his hand to her; but she knew she should be scolded for her awkward greeting; so she put out her hand as if she had no use of her arm above the elbow, hung down her head, and said, "—do;" at least no more was audible.

But there was something comfortable and encouraging in the grasp of the strong large hand over the foolish little fingers; and he quite gave them to his son, whose shake was a real treat; the contact with anything young was like meeting a fellow-countryman in a foreign land, though neither as yet spoke.

She found out that the boy's name was Ernest, and that his father was taking him to school, but had come to arrange some business matters for her aunts upon the way. She listened with interest to Lord de la Poer's voice, for she liked it, and was sure he was a greater friend there than any she had before seen. He was talking about Giles,—that was her uncle, the Colonel in India; and she first gathered from what was passing that her uncle's eldest and only surviving son, an officer in his own regiment, had never recovered from a wound he had received at the relief of Lucknow, and that if he did not get better at Simlah, where his mother had just taken him, his father thought of retiring and bringing him home, though all agreed that it would be a very unfortunate thing that the colonel should be obliged to resign his command before getting promoted; but they fully thought he would do so, for this was the last of his children; another son had been killed in the Mutiny, and two or three little girls had been born and died in India.

Kate had never known this. Her aunts never told her anything, nor talked over family affairs before her; and she was opening her ears most eagerly, and turning her quick bright eyes from one speaker to the other with such earnest attention, that the guest turned kindly to her, and said, "Do you remember your uncle?"

"O dear, no! I was a little baby when he went away."

Kate never used *dear* as an adjective except at the beginning of a letter, but always, and very unnecessarily, as an interjection; and this time it was so emphatic, as to bring Lady Barbara's eyes on her.

"Did you see either Giles or poor Frank before they went out to him?"

"O dear, no!"

This time the *dear* was from the confusion that made her always do the very thing she ought not to do.

"No; my niece has been too much separated from her own relations," said Lady Barbara, putting this as an excuse for the "O dears."

"I hope Mr. Wardour is quite well," said Lord de la Poer, turning again to Kate.

"O yes, quite, thank you;" and then, with brightening eyes, she ventured on, "Do you know him?"

"I saw him two or three times," he answered with increased kindness of manner. "Will you remember me to him when you write?"

"Very well," said Kate, promptly; "but he says all those sort of things are nonsense."

The horror of the two aunts was only kept in check by the good manners that hindered a public scolding; but Lord de la Poer only laughed heartily, and said, "Indeed! What sort of things, may I ask, Lady Caergwent?"

"Why,—love and regards, and remembrances. Mary used to get letters from her school-fellows, all filled with dearest loves, and we always laughed at her; and Armyn used to say them by heart beforehand," said Kate.

"I beg to observe," was the answer, in the grave tone which, however, Kate understood as fun, "that I did not presume to send my love to Mr. Wardour. May not that make the case different?"

"Yes," said Kate, meditatively; "only I don't know that your remembrances would be of more use than your love."

"And are we never to send any messages unless they are of use?"

This was a puzzling question, and Kate did not immediately reply.

"None for pleasure,—eh?"

"Well, but I don't see what would be the pleasure."

"What, do you consider it pleasurable to be universally forgotten?"

"Nobody ever could forget pa,—my Uncle Wardour," cried Kate, with eager vehemence flashing in her eyes.

"Certainly not," said Lord de la Poer, in a voice as if he were much pleased with her; "he is not a man to be forgotten. It is a privilege to have been brought up by him. But come, Lady Caergwent, since you are so critical, will you be pleased to devise some message for me that may combine use, pleasure, and my deep respect for him:" and as she sat beside him at the table, he laid his hand on hers, so that she felt that he really meant what he said.

She sat fixed in deep thought; and her aunts, who had been miserable all through the conversation, began to speak of other things; but in the midst the shrill little voice broke in, "I know what!" and good-natured Lord de la Poer turned at once smiling, and saying, "Well, what?"

"If you would help in the new aisle! You know the church is not big enough; there are so many people come into the district, with the new iron works, you know; and we have not got half room enough, and can't make more, though we have three services; and we want to build a new aisle, and it will cost £250, but we have only got £139 15s. 6d. And if you would be so kind as to give one sovereign for it,—that would be better than remembrances and respects, and all that sort of thing."

"I rather think it would," said Lord de la Poer; and though Lady Barbara eagerly exclaimed, "Oh! do not think of it; the child does not know what she is talking of. Pray excuse her,"—he took out his purse, and from it came a crackling, smooth five-pound note, which he put into the hand, saying "There, my dear, cut that in two, and send the two halves on different days to Mr. Wardour, with my best wishes for his success in his good works. Will that do?"

Kate turned quite red, and only perpetrated a choked sound of her favourite,—"q." For the whole world she could not have said more; but though she knew perfectly well that anger and wrath were hanging over her, she felt happier than for many a long week.

Presently the aunts rose, and Lady Barbara said to her in the low ceremonious voice that was a sure sign of warning and displeasure, "You had better come up stairs with us, Katharine, and amuse Lord Ernest in the back drawing-room while his father is engaged with us."

Kate's heart leapt up at the sound "amuse." She popped her precious note into her pocket, bounded up stairs, and opened the back drawing-room door for her playfellow, as he brought up the rear of the procession.

Lord de la Poer and Lady Barbara spread the table with papers; Lady Jane sat by; the children were behind the heavy red curtains that parted off the second room. There was a great silence at first, then began a little tittering, then a little chattering, then presently a stifled explosion. Lady Barbara began to betray some restlessness; she really must see what that child was about.

"No, no," said Lord de la Poer; "leave them in peace. That poor girl will never thrive unless you let her use her voice and limbs. I shall make her come over and enjoy herself with my flock when we come up *en masse*."

The explosions were less carefully stifled, and there were some sounds of rushing about, some small shrieks, and then the door shut and there was a silence again.

By this it may be perceived that Kate and Ernest had become tolerably intimate friends. They had informed each other of what games were their favorites; Kate had told him the Wardour names and ages, and required from him in return those of his brothers and sisters. She had been greatly delighted by learning that Adelaide was no end of a hand at climbing trees; and that whenever she should come and stay at their house, Ernest would teach them to ride. And then they began to consider what play was possible under the present circumstances,—beginning they hardly knew how, by dodging one another round and round the table, making snatches at one another, gradually assuming the characters of hunter and Red Indian. Only when the hunter had snatched up Aunt Jane's tortoise-shell paper-cutter to stab with, complaining direfully that it was a stupid place, with nothing for a gun, and the Red Indian's crinoline had knocked down two chairs, she recollected the consequence in time to strangle her own war-whoop, and suggested that they should be safer on the stairs; to which Ernest readily responded, adding that there was a great gallery at home all full of pillars and statues, the jolliest place in the world for making a row.

"O dear! O dear! how I hope I shall go there," cried Kate, swinging between the rails of the landing-place. "I do want of all things to see a statue."

"A statue! why don't you see lots every day?"

"Oh! I don't mean great equestrian things like the Trafalgar Square ones,—or the Duke,—or anything big and horrid, like Achilles in the Park, holding up a shield like a green umbrella. I want to see the work of the great sculptor Julio Romano."

"He wasn't a sculptor."

"Yes he was; didn't he sculp—no, what is the word—Hermione. No; I mean they pretended he had done her."

"Hermione! What, have you seen the Winter's Tale?"

"Papa—Uncle Wardour, that is—read it to us last Christmas."

"Well, I've seen it. Alfred and I went to it last spring, with our tutor."

"O! then do, pray, let us play at it. Look there's a little stand up there, where I have always so wanted to get up and be Hermione, and descend to the sound of slow music. There's a musical box in the back drawing-room that will make the music."

"Very well; but I must be the lion and bear killing the courtier."

"O yes,—very well, and I will be courtier; only I must get a sofa cushion to be Perdita."

"And where is Bohemia."

"Oh! the hall must be Bohemia, and the stair carpet the sea, because then the aunts won't hear the lion and bear roaring."

With these precautions, the characteristic roaring and growling of lion and bear, and the shrieks of the courtier, though not absolutely unheard in the drawing-room, produced no immediate results. But in the very midst of Lady Jane's signing her name to some paper she gave a violent start and dropped the pen,—for they were no stage shrieks,—"Ah! ah! It is coming down! Help me down! Ernest, Ernest! help me down! Ah!" and then a great fall.

The little mahogany bracket on the wall had been mounted by the help of a chair, but it was only fixed into the plaster, being intended to hold a small lamp, and not for young ladies to stand on; so no sooner was the chair removed by which Kate had mounted than she felt not only giddy in her elevation, but found her pedestal loosening! There was no room to jump; and Ernest, perhaps enjoying what he regarded as a girl's foolish fright, was a good way off, endeavoring to wind up the musical-box when the bracket gave way, and Hermione descended precipitately with anything but the sound of soft music; and as the inhabitants of the drawing-room rushed out to the rescue, her legs were seen kicking in the air upon the landing-place; Ernest looking on, not knowing whether to laugh or be dismayed.

Lord de la Poer picked her up, and sat down on the stairs with her between his knees to see whether she were hurt, or what was the matter, while she stood half sobbing with the fright and shock. He asked his son, rather severely, what he had been doing to her.

"He did nothing," gasped Kate; "I was only Hermione."

"Yes, that's all, papa," repeated Ernest; "it is all the fault of the plaster."

And a sort of explanation was performed between the two children, at which Lord de la Poer could hardly keep his gravity though he was somewhat vexed at the turn affairs had taken. He was not entirely devoid of awe of the Lady Barbara, and would have liked his children to be on their best behavior before her.

"Well," he said, "I am glad there is no worse harm done. You had better defer your statue-ship till we can find you a sounder pedestal, Lady Caergwent."

"Oh! call me Kate," whispered she in his ear, turning redder than the fright had made her.

He smiled and patted her hand; then added, "We must go and beg pardon, I suppose; I should not wonder if the catastrophe had damaged Aunt Jane the most; and if so, I don't know what will be done to us!"

He was right; Lady Barbara had only satisfied herself that no bones had been broken, and then turned back to reassure her sister; but Lady Jane could not be frightened without suffering for it, and was lying back on the sofa, almost faint with palpitation, when Lord de la Poer, with Kate's hand in his, came to the door, looking much more consciously guilty than his son, who on the whole was more diverted than penitent at the commotion they had made.

Lady Barbara looked very grand and very dignified, but Lord de la Poer was so grieved for Lady Jane's indisposition, that she was somewhat softened; and then he began asking pardon, blending himself, with the children so comically, that, in all her fright and anxiety, Kate wondered how her aunt could help laughing.

It never was Lady Barbara's way to reprove before a guest; but this good gentleman was determined that she should not reserve her displeasure for his departure, and he would not go away till he had absolutely made her promise that his little friend, as he called Kate, should hear nothing more about anything that had that day taken place.

Lady Barbara kept her promise. She uttered no reproof either on her niece's awkward greeting, her abrupt conversation and its tendency to pertness, nor on the loudness of the unlucky game and the impropriety of climbing; nor even on what had greatly annoyed her, the asking for the subscription to the church. There was neither blame nor punishment, but she could not help a certain cold restraint of manner, by which Kate knew that she was greatly displeased, and regarded her as the most hopeless little saucy romp that ever maiden aunt was afflicted with.

And certainly it was hard on her. She had a great regard for Lord de la Poer, and thought his a particularly well-trained family; and she was especially desirous that her little niece should appear to advantage before him. Nothing, she was sure, but Katharine's innate naughtiness, could have made that well-behaved little Ernest break out into rudeness; and though his father had shown such good nature he must have been very much shocked. What was to be done to tame this terrible little savage, was poor Lady Barbara's haunting thought, morning, noon, and night!

And what was it that Kate did want? I believe nothing could have made her perfectly happy, or suited to her aunt; but that she would have been infinitely happier and better off, had she had the spirit of obedience, of humility, or of unselfishness.

CHAPTER V

T HE ONE HOUR of play with Ernest de la Poer had the effect of making Kate long more and more for a return of "fun," and of intercourse with beings of her own age and of high spirits.

She wove to herself dreams of possible delights with Sylvia and Charlie, if the summer visit could be paid to them; and at the other times she imagined her Uncle Giles's two daughters still alive, and sent home for education, arranging in her busy brain wonderful scenes, in which she, with their assistance, should be happy in spite of Aunt Barbara.

These fancies, however, would be checked by the recollection, that it was shocking to lower two happy spirits in heaven into playful little girls upon earth; and she took refuge in the thought of the coming chance of playfellows, when Lord de la Poer was to bring his family to London. She had learnt the names and ages of all the ten; and even had her own theories as to what her contemporaries were to be like,—Mary and Fanny, Ernest's elders, and Adelaide and Grace, who came next below him; she had a vision for each of them, and felt as if she already knew them.

Meanwhile, the want of the amount of air and running about to which she had been used, did really tell upon her; she had giddy feelings in the morning, tired limbs, and a weary listless air, and fretted over her lessons at times. So they showed her to the doctor, who came to see Lady Jane every alternate day; and when he said she wanted more exercise, her morning walk was made an hour longer, and a shuttlecock and battledores were bought, with which it was decreed that Mrs. Lacy should play with her for exactly half an hour every afternoon, or an hour when it was too wet to go out.

It must be confessed that this was a harder task to both than the music lessons. Whether it were from the difference of height, or from Kate's innate unhandiness, they never could keep that unhappy shuttlecock up more than three times; and Mrs. Lacy looked as grave and melancholy all the time, as if she played it for a punishment, making little efforts to be cheerful that were sad to see. Kate hated it, and was always cross; and willingly would they have given it up by mutual consent, but the instant the tap of the cork against the parchment ceased, if it were not half past five, down sailed. Lady Barbara to inquire after her prescription.

She had been a famous battledore player in the galleries of Caergwent Castle; and once when she took up the battledore to give a lesson, it seemed as if, between her and Mrs. Lacy, the shuttlecock would not come down,—they kept up five hundred and eighty-one, and then only stopped because it was necessary for her to go to dinner.

She could not conceive any one being unable to play at battledore, and thought Kate's failures and dislike pure perverseness. Once Kate by accident knocked her shuttlecock through the window, and hoped she had got rid of it; but she was treated as if she had done it out of naughtiness, and a new instrument of torture, as she called it, was bought for her.

It was no wonder she did not see the real care for her welfare, and thought this intensely cruel and unkind; but it was a great pity that she visited her vexation on poor Mrs. Lacy, to whom the game was even a greater penance than to herself, especially on a warm day, with a bad headache.

Even in her best days at home, Kate had resisted learning to take thought for others. She had not been considerate of Mary's toil, nor of Mr. Wardour's peace, except when Armyn or Sylvia reminded her; and now that she had neither of them to put it into her mind, she never once thought of her governess as one who ought to be spared or pitied. Yet if she had been sorry for Mrs. Lacy, and tried to spare her trouble and annoyance, how much irritability and peevishness, and sense of constant naughtiness, would have been prevented! And it was that feeling of being always naughty, had become the real dreariness of Kate's pleasant home, and was far worse than the music, the battledore, or even the absence of fun.

At last came a message that Lady Caergwent was to be dressed for going out to make a call with Lady Barbara as soon as luncheon was over.

It could be on no one but the De la Poers; and Kate was so delighted, that she executed all manner of little happy hops, skips, and fidgets, all the time of her toilette, and caused many an expostulation of *"Mais Miladi!"* from Josephine, before the pretty delicate blue and white muslin, worked white jacket, and white ribboned and feathered hat, were adjusted. Lady Barbara kept her little countess very prettily and quietly dressed; but it was at the cost of infinite worry of herself, Kate, and Josephine, for there never was a child whom it was so hard to keep in decent trim.

However, on this occasion, she did get safe down to the carriage, clothes, gloves, and all, without detriment or scolding,—and jumped in first. She was a long way yet from knowing that, though her aunts gave the first place to her rank, it would have been proper in her to yield it to their years, and make way for them.

She was too childish to have learnt this as a matter of good breeding, but she might have learnt it of a certain parable, which she could say from beginning to end, that she should "sit not down in the highest room."

Her aunt sat down beside her, and spent the first ten minutes of the drive in enjoining on her proper behavior at Lady de la Poer's. The children there were exceedingly well brought up, she said, and she was very desirous they should be her niece's friends; but she was certain that Lady de la Poer would allow no one to associate with them who did not behave properly.

"Lord de la Poer was very kind to me just as I was," said Kate, in her spirit of contradiction, which was always reckless of consequences.

"Gentlemen are no judges of what is becoming to a little girl," said Lady Barbara severely. "Unless you make a very different impression upon Lady de la Poer, she will never permit you to be the friend of her daughters."

"I wonder how I am to make an impression," meditated Kate, as they drove on; "If the horses would only upset us at the door, and Aunt Barbara be nicely insensible, and the young countess show the utmost presence of mind! But nothing nice and like a book ever does happen. And after all, I believe that it is all nonsense about making impressions. Thinking of them is all affectation; and one ought to be as simple and unconscious as one can." A conclusion which did honor to the countess's sense. In fact, she had plenty of sense, if only she had ever used it for herself, instead of for the little ladies she drew on her quires of paper.

Lady Barbara had started early, as she really wished to find her friends at home; and accordingly, when the stairs were mounted, and the aunt and niece were ushered into a pretty bright-looking drawing-room, there they found all that were not at school, enjoying their after-dinner hour of liberty with their father and mother.

Lord de la Poer himself had the youngest in his arms, and looked very much as if he had only just scrambled up from the floor; his wife was really sitting on the ground, helping two little ones to put up a puzzle of wild beasts; and there was a little herd of girls at the farther corner, all very busy over something, towards which Kate's longing eyes at once turned,—even in the midst of Lord de la Poer's very kind greeting, and his wife's no less friendly welcome.

It was true that, as Lady Barbara had said, they were all exceedingly well-bred children. Even the little fellow in his father's arms, though but eighteen months old, made no objection to hold out his fat hand graciously, and showed no shyness when Lady Barbara kissed him! and the others all waited quietly over their several occupations, neither shrinking foolishly from notice, nor putting themselves forward to claim it. Only the four sisters came up, and took their own special visitor into the midst of them as their own property; the elder of them, however, at a sign from her mamma, taking the baby in her arms, and carrying him off, followed by the other two small ones,—only pausing at the door for him to kiss his little hand, and wave it in the prettiest fashion of baby stateliness.

The other sisters drew Kate back with them into the room, where they had been busy. Generally, however much she and Sylvia might wish it, they had found acquaintance with other children absolutely impossible in the presence of grown-up people, whose eyes and voices seemed to strike all parties dumb. But these children seemed in nowise constrained; one of them said at once, "We are so glad you are come. Mamma said she thought you would before we went out, one of these days."

"Isn't it horrid going out in London?" asked Kate, at once set at ease.

"It is not so nice as it is at home," said one of the girls, laughing; "except when it is our turn to go out with mamma."

"She takes us all out in turn," explained another, "from Fanny, down to little Cecil the baby,—and that is our great time for talking to her, when one has her all alone."

"And does she never take you out in the country?"

"O yes! but there are people staying with us then, or else she goes out with papa. It is not a regular drive every day, as it is here."

Kate would not have had a drive with Aunt Barbara every day, for more than she could well say. However she was discreet enough not to say so, and asked what they did on other days.

"Oh, we walk with Miss Oswald in the park, and she tells us stories, or we make them. We don't tell stories in the country, unless we have to walk straight along the drives, that, as papa says, we may have some solace."

Then it was explained that Miss Oswald was their governess, and that they were very busy preparing for her birthday. They were making a paper-case for her, all themselves, and this hour was their only time for doing it out of her sight in secret.

"But why do you make it yourselves?" said Kate; "One can buy such beauties at the bazaars."

"Yes; but mamma says a present one has taken pains to make, is worth a great deal more than what is only bought; for trouble goes for more than money."

"But one can make nothing but tumble-to-pieces things," objected Kate.

"That depends," said Lady Mary, in a very odd merry voice; and the other two, Adelaide and Grace, who were far too much alike for Kate to guess which was which, began in a rather offended manner to assure her that *their* paper-case was to be anything but tumble-to-pieces. Fanny was to bind it, and papa had promised to paste its back and press it.

"And mamma drove with me to Richmond, on purpose to get leaves to spatter," added the other sister.

Then they showed Kate, whose eyes brightened at anything approaching to a mess, that they had a piece of colored card-board, on which leaves, chiefly fern, were pinned tightly down, and that the entire sheet was then covered with a spattering of ink from a tooth-brush drawn along the teeth of a comb. When the process was completed, the form of the leaf remained in the primitive color of the card, thrown out by the cloud of ink-spots, and only requiring a tracing of its veins by a pen.

A space had been cleared for these operations on a side-table; and in spite of the newspaper, on which the appliances were laid, and even the comb and brush, there was no look of disarrangement or untidiness.

"Oh, do,—do show me how you do it!" cried Kate, who had had nothing to do for months with the dear delight of making a mess, except what she could contrive with her paints.

And Lady Grace resumed a brown-holland apron and bib, and opening her hands with a laugh, showed their black insides, then took up her implements.

"Oh, do,—do let me try," was Kate's next cry; "one little bit to show Sylvia Wardour."

With one voice, the three sisters protested that she had better not; she was not properly equipped, and would ink herself all over. If she would pin down a leaf upon the scrap she held up, Grace should spatter it for her, and they would make it up into anything she liked.

But this did not satisfy Kate at all; the pinning out of the leaf was stupid work compared with the glory of making the ink fly. In vain did Adelaide represent that all the taste and skill was in the laying out the leaves, and pinning them down, and that any one could put on the ink; in vain did Mary represent the dirtiness of the work; this was the beauty of it in her eyes; and the sight of the black dashes spattering through the comb, filled her with emulation; so that she entreated, almost piteously, to be allowed to "do" an ivy leaf, which she had hastily, and not very carefully, pinned out with Mary's assistance,—that is, she had feebly and unsteadily stuck every pin, and Mary had steadied them.

The new friends consented, seeing how much she was set on it; but Fanny, who had returned from the nursery, insisted on precautions,—took off the jacket, turned up the frock sleeves, and tied on an apron; though Kate fidgeted all the time, as if a great injury were being inflicted on her; and really, in her little frantic spirit, thought Lady Fanny a great torment, determined to delay her delight till her aunt should go away and put a stop to it.

When once she had the brush, she was full of fun and merriment, and kept her friends much amused by her droll talk, half to them, half to her work.

"There's a portentous cloud, isn't there? An inky cloud, if ever there was one! Take care, inhabitants below; growl, growl, there's the thunder; now comes the rain; hail, hail, all hail, like the beginning of Macbeth."

"Which the Frenchman said was in compliment to the climate," said Fanny; at which the whole company fell into convulsions of laughing; and neither Kate nor Grace exactly knew what hands, or brush, or comb were about; but whereas the little De la Poers had from their infancy laughed almost noiselessly, and without making faces, Kate, for her misfortune, had never been broken of a very queer contortion of her lips, and a cackle like a bantam hen's.

When this unlucky cackle had been several times repeated, it caused Lady Barbara, who had been sitting with her back to the inner room to turn round.

Poor Lady Barbara! It would not be easy to describe her feelings when she saw the young lady, whom she had brought delicately blue and white, like a speedwell flower, nearly as black as a sweep!

Lord de la Poer broke out into an uncontrollable laugh, half at the aunt, half at the niece. "Why, she has grown a moustache!" he exclaimed; "Girls, what have you been doing to her?" and walking up to them, he turned Kate round to a mirror, where she beheld her own brown eyes looking out of a face dashed over with black specks, thicker about the mouth, giving her altogether much the coloring of a very dark man closely shaved. It was so exceedingly comical that she went off into fits of laughing, in which she was heartily joined by all the merry party.

"There," said Lord de la Poer, "do you want to know what your Uncle Giles is like? you've only to look at yourself! See, Barbara, is it not a capital likeness?"

"I never thought her like *Giles*," said her aunt gravely, with an emphasis on the name, as if she meant that the child did bear a likeness that was really painful to her.

"My dears," said the mother, "you should not have put her in such a condition; could you not have been more careful?"

Kate expected one of them to say, "She would do it in spite of us;" but instead of that Fanny only answered, "It is not so bad as it looks, mamma; I believe her frock is quite safe; and we will soon have her face and hands clean."

Whereupon Kate turned round and said, "It is all my fault, and *nobody else's*. They told me not, but it was such fun!"

And therewith she obeyed a pull from Grace, and ran up-stairs with the party to be washed; and as the door shut behind them, Lord de la Poer said, "You need not be afraid of *that* likeness, Barbara. Whatever else she may have brought from her parsonage, she has brought the spirit of truth."

Though knowing that something awful hung over her head, Kate was all the more resolved to profit by her brief minutes of enjoyment; and the little maidens all went racing and flying along the passages together; Kate feeling as if the rapid motion among the other young feet was life once more.

"Well! your frock is all right; I hope your aunt will not be very angry with you," said Adelaide. (She knew Adelaide now, for Grace was the inky one.)

"It is not a thing to be angry for," added Grace.

"No, it would not have been at my home," said Kate, with a sigh; "but, O! I hope she will not keep me from coming here again."

"She shall not," exclaimed Adelaide; "papa won't let her."

"She said your mamma would mind what your papa did not," said Kate, who was not very well informed on the nature of mammas.

"O, that's all stuff," decidedly cried Adelaide. "When papa told us about you, she said, 'poor child! I wish I had her here.'"

Prudent Fanny made an endeavor at checking her little sister; but the light in Kate's eye, and the responsive face, drew Grace on to ask, "She didn't punish you, I hope, for your tumbling off the bracket?"

"No, your papa made her promise not; but she was very cross. Did he tell you about it?"

"O yes; and what do you think Ernest wrote? You must know he had grumbled excessively at papa's having business with Lady Barbara; but his letter said, 'It wasn't at all slow at Lady Barbara's for there was the jolliest fellow there you ever knew; mind, you get her to play at acting.'"

Lady Fanny did not think this improving, and was very glad that the maid came in with hot water and towels, and put an end to it with the work of scrubbing.

Going home, Lady Barbara was as much displeased as Kate had expected, and with good reason. After all her pains, it was very strange that Katharine should be so utterly unfit to behave like a well-bred girl. There might have been excuse for her before she had been taught, but now it was mere obstinacy. She should be careful how she took her out for a long time to come!

Kate's heart swelled within her. It was not obstinacy, she knew; and that bit of injustice hindered her from seeing that it was really wilful recklessness. She was elated with Ernest's foolish schoolboy account of her, which a more maidenly little girl would not have relished; she was strengthened in her notion that she was ill-used by hearing that the De la Poers pitied her: and because she found that Aunt Barbara was considered to be a little wrong, she did not think that she herself had ever been wrong at all.

And Lady Barbara was not far from the truth when she told her sister "that Katharine was perfectly hard and reckless; there was no such thing as making her sorry!"

CHAPTER VI

AFTER THAT FIRST VISIT, Kate did see something of the De la Poers, but not more than enough to keep her in a constant ferment with the uncertain possibility, and the longing for the meetings.

The advances came from them; Lady Barbara said very truly, that she could not be responsible for making so naughty a child as her niece the companion of any well-regulated children; she was sure that their mother could not wish it, since nice and good as they naturally were, this unlucky Katharine seemed to infect them with her own spirit of riot and turbulence whenever they came near her.

There was no forwarding of the attempts to make appointments for walks in the Park, though really very little harm had ever come of them, guarded by the two governesses, and by Lady Fanny's decided ideas of propriety. That Kate embarked in long stories, and in their excitement raised her voice, was all that could be said against her on those occasions, and Mrs. Lacy forbore to say it.

Once, indeed, Kate was allowed to ask her friends to tea; but that proved a disastrous affair. Fanny was prevented from coming; and in the absence of her quiet elder sisterly care, the spirits of Grace and Adelaide were so excited by Kate's drollery, that they were past all check from Mary, and drew her along with them, into a state of frantic fun and mad pranks.

They were full of merriment all tea time, even in the presence of the two governesses; and when that was over, and Kate showed "the bracket," they began to grow almost ungovernable in their spirit of frolic and fun; they went into Kate's room, resolved upon being desert travellers, set up an umbrella hung round with cloaks for a tent, made camels of chairs, and finding these tardy, attempted riding on each other,—with what results to Aunt Jane's ears below may be imagined,—dressed up wild Arabs in bournouses of shawls, and made muskets of parasols, charging desperately, and shrieking for attack, defence, "for triumph or despair," as Kate observed, in one of her magnificent quotations. Finally, the endangered traveller, namely, Grace, rushed down the stairs headlong, with the two Arabs clattering after him, banging with their muskets, and shouting their war-cry the whole height of the house.

The ladies in the drawing-room had borne a good deal; but Aunt Jane was by this time looking meekly distracted; and Lady Barbara sallying out, met the Arab Sheikh with his white frock over his head, descending the stairs in the rear, calling to his tribe in his sweet voice, not to be so noisy,—but not seeing before him the said bournouse, he had very nearly struck Lady Barbara with his parasol before he saw her.

No one could be more courteous or full of apologies than the said Sheikh, who was in fact a good deal shocked at his unruly tribe, and quite acquiesced in the request that they would all come and sit quiet in the drawing-room, and play at some suitable game there.

It would have been a relief to Mary to have them thus disposed of safely; and Adelaide would have obeyed; but the other two had been worked up to a state of wildness, such as befalls little girls who have let themselves out of the control of their better sense.

They did not see why they should sit up stupid in the drawing-room; "Mary was as cross as Lady Barbara herself to propose it," said Grace, unfortunately just as the lady herself was on the stairs to enforce her desire, in her gravely courteous voice; whereupon Kate, half tired and wholly excited, burst out into a violent passionate fit of crying and sobbing, declaring that it was very hard, that whenever she had ever so little pleasure, Aunt Barbara always grudged it to her.

None of them had ever heard anything like it; to the little De la Poers she seemed like one beside herself, and Grace clung to Mary, and Adelaide to Miss Oswald, almost frightened at the screams and sobs, that Kate really could not have stopped if she would. Lady Jane came to the head of the stairs, pale and trembling, begging to know who was hurt; and Mrs. Lacy tried gentle reasoning and persuading, but she might as well have spoken to the storm beating against the house.

Lady Barbara sternly ordered her off to her room; but the child did not stir, indeed she could not, except that she rocked herself to and fro in her paroxysms of sobbing, which seemed to get worse and worse every moment. It was Miss Oswald at last, who being more used to little girls and their naughtiness than any of the others, saw the right moment at last, and said, as she knelt down by her, half kindly, half severely, "My dear, you had better let me take you up-stairs. I will help you: and you are only shocking every one here."

Kate did let her take her up-stairs, though at every step there was a pause, a sob, a struggle; but a gentle hand on her shoulder, and a firm persuasive voice in her ear, moved her gradually onwards, till the little pink room was gained; and there she threw herself on her bed in another agony of wild sobs, unaware of Miss Oswald's parley at the door with Lady Barbara and Mrs. Lacy, and her entreaty that the patient might be left to her, which they were nothing loth to do.

When Kate recovered her speech, she poured out a wild and very naughty torrent, about being the most unhappy little girl in the world; the aunts were always unkind to her; she never got any pleasure; she could not bear being a countess; she only wanted to go back to her old home, to papa and Mary and Sylvia; and nobody could help her.

Miss Oswald treated the poor child almost as if she had been a little out of her mind, let her say it all between her sobs, and did not try to argue with her, but waited till the talking and sobbing had fairly tired her out; and by that time the hour had come at which the little visitors were to go home. The governess rose up, and said she must go, asking in a kind quiet tone, as if all that had been said were mere mad folly, whether Lady Caergwent would come down with her, and tell her aunts she was sorry for the disturbance she had made.

Kate shrank from showing such a spectacle as her swollen, tear-stained, red-marbled visage. She was thoroughly sorry, and greatly ashamed, and she only gasped out, "I can't, I can't; don't let me see any one."

"Then I will wish Mary and her sisters good-by for you."

"Yes, please." Kate had no words for more of her sorrow and shame.

"And shall I say anything to your aunt for you?"

"I—I don't know; only don't let any one come up."

"Then shall I tell Lady Barbara you are too much tired out now for talking, but that you will tell her in the morning how sorry you are?"

"Well, yes," said Kate, rather grudgingly. "O, must you go."

"I am afraid I must, my dear. Their mamma does not like Addy and Grace to be kept up later than their usual bedtime."

"I wish you could stay. I wish you were my governess," said Kate, clinging to her, and receiving her kind, friendly, pitying kiss.

And when the door had shut upon her, Kate's tears began to drop again at the thought that it was very hard that the little De la Poers, who had father, mother, and each other, should likewise have such a nice governess, while she had only poor sad dull Mrs. Lacy.

Had Kate only known what an unselfish little girl and Mrs. Lacy might have been to each other!

However, the first thing she could now think of was to avoid being seen or spoken to by any one that night; and for this purpose she hastily undressed herself, bundled up her hair as best she might, as in former days, said her prayers, and tumbled into bed, drawing the clothes over her head, resolved to give no sign of being awake, come who might.

Her shame was real and very great. Such violent crying fits had overtaken her in past times, but had been thought to be outgrown. She well recollected the last. It was just after the death of her aunt, Mrs. Wardour, just when the strange stillness of sorrow in the house was beginning to lessen, and the children had forgotten themselves, and burst out into noise and merriment, till they grew unrestrained and quarrelsome; Charlie had offended Kate,—she had struck him, and Mary coming on them, grieved and hurt at their conduct at such a time, had punished Kate for the blow, but missed the perception of Charlie's offence; and the notion of injustice had caused the shrieking cries and violent sobs, that had brought Mr. Wardour from the study in grave, sorrowful severity.

What she had heard afterwards from him, about not making poor Mary's task harder, and what she had heard from Mary, about not paining him, had really restrained her; and she had thought such outbreaks passed by among the baby faults she had left behind, and was the more grieved and ashamed in consequence. She felt it a real exposure: she remembered her young friends' surprised and frightened eyes, and not only had no doubt their mother would really think her too naughty to be their playfellow, but almost wished that it might be so,—she could never, never bear to see them again.

She heard the street door close after them, she heard the carriage drive away; she felt half relieved: but then she hid her face in the pillow, and cried more quietly, but more bitterly.

Then some one knocked; she would not answer. Then came a voice, saying, "Katharine." It was Aunt Barbara's, but it was rather wavering. She would not answer, so the door was opened, and the steps, scarcely audible in the rustling of the silk, came in; and Kate felt that her aunt was looking at her, wondered whether she had better put out her head, ask pardon, and have it over, but was afraid; and presently heard the moire antique go sweeping away again.

And then the foolish child heartily wished she had spoken, and was seized with desperate fears of the morrow, more of the shame of hearing of her tears, than of any punishment. Why had she not been braver?

After a time came a light, and Josephine moving about quietly, and putting away the clothes that had been left on the floor. Kate was not afraid of her, but her caressing consolations and pity would have only added to the miserable sense of shame; so there was no sign, no symptom of being awake, though it was certain that before Josephine went away, the candle was held so as to cast a light over all that was visible of the face. Kate could not help hearing the low muttering of the Frenchwoman, who was always apt to talk to herself: "Asleep! Ah, yes! She sleeps profoundly. How ugly *la petite* has made herself! What cries! Ah, she is like Miladi, her aunt! a demon of a temper!"

Kate restrained herself till the door was shut again, and then rolled over and over, till she had made a strange entanglement of the bedclothes, and brought her passion to an end by making a mummy of herself, bound hand and foot, snapping with her mouth all the time, as if she longed to bite.

"Oh, you horrible Frenchwoman! You are a flatterer, a base flatterer; such as always haunt the great! I hate it all. I a demon of a temper? I like Aunt Barbara? Oh, you wretch! I'll tell Aunt Barbara to-morrow, and get you sent away!"

Those were some of Kate's fierce angry thoughts in her first vexation; but with all her faults, she was not a child who ever nourished rancor or malice; and though she had been extremely wounded at first, yet she quickly forgave.

By the time she had smoothed out her sheet, and settled matters between it and her blanket, she had begun to think more coolly. "No, no, I won't. It would be horribly dishonorable, and all that, to tell Aunt Barbara. Josephine was only thinking out loud; and she can't help what she thinks. I was very naughty; no wonder she thought so. Only next time she pets me, I will say to her, 'You cannot deceive me, Josephine; I like the plain truth better than honeyed words.' "

And now that Kate had arrived at the composition of a fine speech that would never be made, it was plain that her mind was pretty well composed. That little bit of forgiveness, though it had not even cost an effort, had been softening, soothing, refreshing; it had brought peacefulness; and Kate lay not absolutely asleep, but half dreaming in the summer twilight, in the soft undefined fancies of one tired out with agitation.

She was partly roused by the various sounds in the house, but not startled,—the light nights of summer always diminished her alarms: and she heard the clocks strike, and the bell ring for prayers, the doors open and shut, all mixed in with her hazy fancies. At last came the silken rustlings up the stairs again, and the openings of bedroom doors close to her.

Kate must have gone quite to sleep, for she did not know when the door was opened, and how the soft voices had come in that she heard over her.

"Poor little dear! How she has tossed her bed about! I wonder if we could set the clothes straight without wakening her."

How very sweet and gentle Aunt Jane's voice was in that low cautious whisper!

Some one—and Kate knew the peculiar sound of Mrs. Lacy's crape—was moving the bedclothes as gently as she could.

"Poor little dear!" again said Lady Jane; "it is very sad to see a child who has cried herself to sleep. I do wish we could manage her better. Do you think the child is happy?" she ended by asking in a wistful voice.

"She has very high spirits," was the answer.

"Ah, yes! her impetuosity; it is her misfortune, poor child! Barbara is so calm and resolute, that—that—" Was Lady Jane really going to regret anything in her sister? She did not say it, however; but Kate heard her sigh, and add, "Ah, well! if I were stronger, perhaps we could make her happier; but I am so nervous. I must try not to look distressed when her spirits do break out; for perhaps it is only natural. And I am so sorry to have brought all this on her, and spoilt those poor children's pleasure!"

Lady Jane bent over the child, and Kate reared herself up on a sudden, threw her arms round her neck, and whispered, "Aunt Jane, dear Aunt Jane, I'll try never to frighten you again! I am so sorry."

"There, there; have I waked you? Don't, my dear; your aunt will hear. Go to sleep again. Yes, do."

But Aunt Jane was kissing and fondling all the time; and the end of this sad naughty evening was, that Kate went to sleep with more softness, love, and repentance in her heart, than there had been since her coming to Bruton Street.

CHAPTER VII

Lady caergwent was thoroughly ashamed and humbled by that unhappy evening. She looked so melancholy and subdued in the morning, with her heavy eyelids and inflamed eyes, and moved so meekly and sadly, without daring to look up, that Lady Barbara quite pitied her, and said—more kindly than she had ever spoken to her before—

"I see you are sorry for the exposure last night, so we will say no more about it. I will try to forget it. I hope our friends may."

That hope sounded very much like "I do not think they will;" and truly Kate felt that it was not in the nature of things that they ever should. She should never have forgotten the sight of a little girl in that frenzy of passion! No, she was sure that their mamma and papa knew all about it, and that she should never be allowed to play with them again, and she could not even wish to meet them, she should be miserably ashamed, and would not know which way to look.

She said not one word about meeting them, and for the first day or two even begged to walk in the Square instead of the Park; and she was so good and steady with her lessons, and so quiet in her movements, that she scarcely met a word of blame for a whole week.

One morning, while she was at breakfast with Lady Barbara and Mrs. Lacy, the unwonted sound of a carriage stopping, and of a double knock, was heard. In a moment the color flushed into Lady Barbara's face, and her eyes lighted: then it passed away into a look of sadness. It had seemed to her for a moment as if the bright young nephew who had been the light and hope of her life, were going to look in on her; and it had only brought the remembrance that he was gone forever, and that in his stead there was only the poor little girl, to whom rank was a misfortune, and who seemed as if she would never wear it becomingly. Kate saw nothing of all this; she was only eager and envious for some change and variety in these long dull days. It was Lord de la Poer and his daughter Adelaide, who the next moment were in the room; and she remembered instantly that she had heard that this was to be Adelaide's birthday, and wished her many happy returns in all due form, her heart beating the while with increasing hope that the visit concerned herself.

And did it not? Her head swam round with delight and suspense, and she could hardly gather up the sense of the words in which Lord de la Poer was telling Lady Barbara that Adelaide's birthday was to be spent at the Crystal Palace at Sydenham; that the other girls were gone to the station with their mother, and that he had come round with Adelaide to carry off Kate, and meet the rest at ten o'clock. Lady de la Poer would have written, but it had only been settled that morning on finding that he could spare the day.

Kate squeezed Adelaide's hand in an agony. O! would that aunt let her go?

"You would like to come?" asked Lord de la Poer, bending his pleasant eyes on her. "Have you ever been there?"

"Never! O, thank you! I should like it so much. I never saw any exhibition at all, except once the Gigantic Cabbage! May I go, Aunt Barbara?"

"Really, you are very kind, after—"

"O, we never think of *afters* on birthdays,—do we, Addie?"

"If you are so very good, perhaps Mrs. Lacy will kindly bring her to meet you."

"I am sure," said he, turning courteously to that lady, "that we should be very sorry to give Mrs. Lacy so much trouble. If this is to be a holiday to every one, I am sure you would prefer the quiet day."

No one could look at the sad face and widow's cap without feeling that so it must be, even without the embarrassed "Thank you, my Lord, if—"

"If—if Katharine were more to be trusted," began Lady Barbara.

"Now, Barbara," he said, in a drolly serious fashion, "if you think the Court of Chancery would seriously object, say so at once."

Lady Barbara could not keep the corners of her mouth quite stiff, but she still said, "You do not know what you are undertaking."

"Do you deliberately tell me that you think myself and Fanny, to say nothing of young Fanny, who is the wisest of us all, unfit to be trusted with this one young lady?" said he, looking her full in the face, and putting on a most comical air; "it is humiliating, I own."

"Ah! if Katharine were like your own daughters, I should have no fears," said the aunt. "But—however, since you are so good,—if she will promise to be very careful—"

"O yes, yes, Aunt Barbara!"

"I make myself responsible," said Lord de la Poer. "Now, young woman, run off and get the hat; we have no time to lose."

Kate darted off, and galloped up the stairs at a furious pace, shouted "Josephine" at the top; and then, receiving no answer, pulled the bell violently; after which she turned round and obliged Adelaide with a species of dancing hug, rather to the detriment of that young lady's muslin jacket.

"I was afraid to look back before," she breathlessly said, as she released Adelaide; "I felt as if your papa was Orpheus, when—

> "Stern Proserpine relented,
> And gave him back the fair—"

and I was sure Aunt Barbara would catch me, like Eurydice, if I only looked back."

"What a funny girl you are to be thinking about Orpheus and Eurydice!" said Adelaide. "Aren't you glad?"

"Glad? Ain't I, just? as Charlie would say. O dear! your papa is a delicious man; I'd rather have him for mine than anybody, except Uncle Wardour!"

"I'd rather have him than any one," said the little daughter.

"Because he is yours," said Kate; "but somehow, though he is more funny and good-natured than Uncle Wardour, I would n't,—no, I should n't like him so well for a papa. I don't think he would punish so well."

"Punish!" cried Adelaide. "Is that what you want? Why, mamma says children ought to be always pleasure and no trouble to busy fathers. But there, Kate; you are not getting ready,—and we are to be at the station at ten."

"I am waiting for Josephine! Why does n't she come?" said Kate, ringing violently again.

"Why don't you get ready without her?"

"I don't know where anything is! It is very tiresome of her, when she knows I never dress myself," said Kate, fretfully.

"Don't you? Why, Grace and I always dress ourselves, except for the evening. Let me help you. Are not those your boots?"

Kate rushed to the bottom of the attic stairs, and shouted "Josephine," at the top of her shrill voice; then receiving no answer, she returned, condescended to put on the boots that Adelaide held up to her, and noisily pulled out some drawers; but not seeing exactly what she wanted, she again betook herself to screams of her maid's name, at the third of which out burst Mrs. Bartley in a regular state of indignation: "Lady Caergwent! Will your Ladyship hold your tongue! There's Lady Jane startled up, and it's a mercy if her nerves recover it the whole day,—making such a noise as that!"

"But Josephine won't come, and I'm going out, Bartley," said Kate, piteously. "Where is Josephine?"

"Gone out, my Lady, so it is no use making a piece of work," said Bartley, crossly, retreating to Lady Jane.

Kate was ready to cry; but behold, that handy little Adelaide had mean time picked out a nice black silk cape, with hat and feather, gloves and handkerchief, which, if not what Kate had intended, were nice enough for anything, and would have—some months ago—seemed to the orphan at the parsonage like robes of state. Kind Adelaide held them up so triumphantly that Kate could not pout at their being only every-day things; and as she began to put them on, out came Mrs. Bartley again, by Lady Jane's orders, pounced upon Lady Caergwent, and made her repent of all wishes for assistance by beginning upon her hair, and in spite of all wriggles, and remonstrances, dressing her in the peculiarly slow and precise manner by which a maid can punish a trouble-some child; until finally Kate,—far too much irritated for a word of thanks, tore herself out of her hands, caught up her gloves, and flew down-stairs, as if her life depended on her speed. She thought the delay much longer than it had really been, for she found Lord de la Poer talking so earnestly to her aunt, that he hardly looked up when she came in,—something about her Uncle Giles in India, and his coming home,—which seemed to be somehow becoming possible,—though at a great loss to himself; but there was no making it out; and in a few minutes he rose, and after some fresh charges from Lady Barbara to her niece "not to forget herself," Kate was handed into the carriage, and found herself really off.

Then the tingle of wild impatience and suspense subsided, and happiness began! It had not been a good beginning, but it was very charming now.

Adelaide and her father were full of jokes together, so quick and bright that Kate listened instead of talking. She had almost lost the habit of merry chatter, and it did not come to her quickly again; but she was greatly entertained; and thus they came to the station, where Lady de la Poer and her other three girls were awaiting them, and greeted Kate with joyful faces.

They were the more relieved at the arrival of the three, because the station was close and heated, and it was a very warm summer day, so that the air was extremely oppressive.

"It feels like thunder," said some one. And thenceforth Kate's perfect felicity was clouded. She had a great dislike to a thunder-storm, and she instantly began asking her neighbors if they *really* thought it would thunder.

"I hope it will," said Lady Fanny; "It would cool the air, and sound so grand in those domes."

Kate thought this savage, and with an imploring look asked Lady De la Poer if she thought there would be a storm.

"I can't see the least sign of one," was the answer. "See how clear the sky is!" as they steamed out of the station.

"But do you think there will be one to-day?" demanded Kate.

"I do not expect it," said Lady De la Poer, smiling: "and there is no use in expecting disagreeables."

"Disagreeables! O, mamma, it would be such fun," cried Grace, "if we had only a chance of getting wet through!"

Here Lord De la Poer adroitly called off the public attention from the perils of the clouds by declaring that he wanted to make out the fourth line of an advertisement on the banks, of which he said he had made out one line as he was whisked by on each journey he had made; and as it was four times over in four different languages, he required each damsel to undertake one; and there was a great deal of laughing over which it should be that should undertake each language. Fanny and Mary were humble, and sure they should never catch the German; and Kate, more enterprising, undertook the Italian. After all, while they were chattering about it, they went past the valuable document, and were come in sight of the "monsters" in the Gardens,—and Lord De la Poer asked Kate if she would like to catch a pretty little frog; to which Mary responded, "O what a tadpole it must have been!" and the discovery that her friends had once kept a preserve of tadpoles to watch them turn into frogs, was so delightful as entirely to dissipate all remaining thoughts of thunder, and leave Kate free for almost breathless amazement at the glittering domes of glass, looking like enormous bubbles in the sun.

What a morning that was, among the bright buds and flowers, the wonders of nature and art all together! It was to be a long day, and no hurrying; so the party went from court to court at their leisure, sat down, and studied all that they cared for, or divided according to their tastes. Fanny and Mary wanted time for the wonderful sculptures on the noble gates in the Italian court; but the younger girls preferred roaming more freely, so Lady De la Poer sat down to take care of them, while her husband undertook to guide the wanderings of the other three.

He particularly devoted himself to Kate, partly in courtesy as to the guest of the party, partly because, as he said, he felt himself responsible for her; and she was in supreme enjoyment, talking freely to one able and willing to answer her remarks and questions, and with the companionship of girls of her own age besides. She was most of all delighted with the Alhambra,—the beauty of it was to her like a fairy tale; and she had read Washington Irving's "Siege of Granada," so that she could fancy the courts filled with the knightly Moors, who were so noble that she could not think why they were not Christians; nay, the tears quite came into her eyes as she looked up in Lord de la Poer's face, and asked why nobody converted the Abencerrages instead of fighting with them.

It was a pity that Kate always grew loud when she was earnest; and Lord de la Poer's interest in the conversation was considerably lessened by the discomfort of seeing some strangers looking surprised at the five syllables in the squeaky voice coming out of the mouth of so small a lady.

"Gently, my dear," he softly said; and Kate, for a moment, felt it hard that the torment about her voice should pursue her even in such moments, and spoil the Alhambra itself.

However, her good humor recovered the next minute at the Fountain of Lions. She wanted to know how the Moors came to have lions; she thought she had heard that no Mahometans were allowed to represent any living creature for fear it should be an idol. Lord de la Poer said she was quite right, and that the Mahometans think these forms will come round their makers at the last day, demanding to have souls given to them; but that her friends, the Moors of Spain, were much less strict than any others of their faith. She could see, however, that the carving of such figures was a new art with them, since these lions were very rude and clumsy performances for people who could make such delicate tracery as they had seen within. And then, while Kate was happily looking with Adelaide at the orange-trees that completed the Spanish air of the court, and hoping to see the fountain play in the evening, he told Grace that it was worth while taking people to see sights if they had as much intelligence and observation as Kate had, and did not go gazing idly about, thinking of nothing.

He meant it to stir up his rather indolent-minded Grace,—he did not mean the Countess to hear it; but some people's eyes and ears are wonderfully quick at gathering what is to their own credit, and Kate, who had not heard a bit of commendation for a long time, was greatly elated.

Luckily for appearances, she remembered how Miss Edgeworth's Frank made himself ridiculous by showing off to Mrs. J—, and how she herself had once been overwhelmed by the laughter of the Wardour family for having rehearsed to poor Mrs. Brown all the characters of the gods of the Northmen,—Odin, Thor, and all,—when she had just learnt them. So she was more careful than before not to pour out all the little that she knew; and she was glad she had not committed herself, for she had very nearly volunteered the information that Pompeii was overwhelmed by Mount Etna, before she heard some one say Vesuvius, and perceived her mistake, feeling as if she had been rewarded for her modesty like a good child in a book.

She applauded herself much more for keeping back her knowledge till it was wanted, than for having it; but this self-satisfaction looked out in another loophole. She avoided pedantry, but she was too much elated not to let her spirits get the better of her, and when Lady de la Poer and the elder girls came up, they found her in a suppressed state of capering, more like a puppy on its hind legs, than like a countess or any other well-bred child.

The party met under the screen of kings and queens, and there had some dinner, at one of the marble tables, that just held them pleasantly. The cold chicken and tongue were wonderfully good on that hot hungry day, and still better were the strawberries that succeeded them; and oh! what mirth went on all the time! Kate was chattering fastest of all, and loudest; not to say the most nonsensically. It was not nice nonsense, —that was the worst of it,—it was pert and saucy. It was rather the family habit to laugh at Mary de la Poer, for ways that were thought a little fanciful; and Kate caught this up, and bantered without discretion, in a way not becoming towards anybody, especially one some years her elder. Mary was good-natured, but evidently did not like being asked if she had strayed in the mediæval court, because she was afraid the great bulls of Nineveh would run at her.

"She will be afraid of being teased by a little goose another time," said Lord de la Poer, intending to give his little friend a hint that she was making herself very silly; but Kate took it quite another way, and not a pretty one, for she answered, "Dear me, Mary, can't you say boo to a goose!"

"Say what?" cried Adelaide, who was always apt to be a good deal excited by Kate; and who had been going off into fits of laughter at all these foolish sallies.

"It was not a very nice thing to say," answered her mother gravely; "so there is no occasion to learn it."

Kate did take the hint this time, and colored up to the ears, partly with vexation, partly with shame. She sat silent and confused for several minutes, till her friends took pity on her, and a few good-natured words about her choice of an ice quite restored her liveliness. It is well to be good-humored; but it is unlucky, nay wrong, when a check from friends without authority to scold, does not suffice to bring soberness instead of rattling giddiness. Lady de la Poer was absolutely glad to break up the dinner, so as to work off the folly and excitement by moving about, before it should make the little girl expose herself, or infect Adelaide.

They intended to have gone into the gardens till four o'clock, when the fountains were to play; but as they moved towards the great door they perceived a dark heavy cloud was hiding the sun that had hitherto shone so dazzlingly through the crystal walls.

"That is nice," said Lady Fanny; "it will be cool and pleasant now before the rain."

"If the rain is not imminent," began her father.

"Oh! is it going to be a thunder-storm?" cried Kate. "O dear! I do so hate thunder! What shall I do?" cried she; all her excitement turning into terror.

Before any one could answer her, there was a flash of bright white light before all their eyes, and a little scream.

"She's struck! she's struck!" cried Adelaide, her hands before her eyes.

For Kate had disappeared. No, she was in the great pond, beside which they had been standing, and Mary was kneeling on the edge, holding fast by her frock. But before the deep voice of the thunder was roaring and reverberating through the vaults, Lord de la Poer had her in his grasp, and the growl had not ceased before she was on her feet again, drenched and trembling, beginning to be the centre of a crowd, who were running together to help or to see the child who had been either struck by lightning or drowned.

"Is she struck? Will she be blind?" sobbed Adelaide, still with her hands before her eyes; and the inquiry was echoed by the nearer people, while more distant ones told each other that the young lady was blind for life.

"Struck! nonsense!" said Lord le la Poer; "the lightning was twenty miles off at least. Are you hurt, my dear!"

"No," said Kate, shaking herself, and answering "No," more decidedly. "Only I am so wet, and my things stick to me."

"How did it happen?" asked Grace.

"I don't know. I wanted to get away from the thunder!" said bewildered Kate.

Meantime, an elderly lady, who had come up among the spectators, was telling Lady de la Poer that she lived close by, and insisting that the little girl should be taken at once to her house, put to bed, and her clothes dried. Lady de la Poer was thankful to accept the kind offer without loss of time; and in the fewest possible words it was settled that she would go and attend to the little drowned rat, while her girls should remain with their father at the palace till the time of going home, when they would meet at the station. They must walk to the good lady's house, be the storm what it would, as the best chance of preventing Kate from catching cold. She looked a rueful spectacle, dripping so as to make a little pool on the stone floor; her hat and feather limp and streaming; her hair in long lank rats' tails, each discharging its own waterfall; her clothes, ribbons, and all, pasted down upon her! There was no time to be lost; and the stranger took her by one hand, Lady de la Poer by the other, and, exchanging some civil speeches with one another half out of breath, they almost swung her from one step of the grand stone stairs to another, and hurried her along as fast as these beplastered garments would let her move. There was no rain as yet, but there was another clap of thunder much louder than the first; but they held Kate too fast to let her stop, or otherwise make herself more foolish.

In a very few minutes they were at the good lady's door; in another minute in her bedroom, where, while she and her maid bustled off to warm the bed, Lady de la Poer tried to get the clothes off, a service of difficulty, when every tie held fast, every button was slippery, and the tighter garments fitted like skins. Kate was subdued and frightened; she gave no trouble, but all the help she gave was to pull a string so as to make a hopeless knot of the bow that her friend had nearly undone.

However, by the time the bed was warm, the dress was off, and the child, rolled up in a great loose night-dress of the kind lady's, was installed in it, feeling—sultry day though it were—that the warm dryness was extremely comfortable to her chilled limbs. The good lady brought her some hot tea, and moved away to the window, talking in a low murmuring voice to Lady de la Poer. Presently a fresh flash of lightning made her bury her head in the pillow; and there she began thinking how hard it was that the thunder should come to spoil her one day's pleasure; but soon stopped this, remembering Who sends storm and thunder, and feeling afraid to murmur. Then she remembered that perhaps she deserved to be disappointed. She had been wild and troublesome, had spoilt Adelaide's birthday, teased Mary, and made kind Lady de la Poer grave and displeased.

She would say how sorry she was, and ask pardon. But the two ladies still stood talking. She must wait till this stranger was gone. And while she was waiting,—how it was she knew not,—but Countess Kate was fast asleep.

CHAPTER VIII

WHEN KATE opened her eyes again, and turned her face up from the pillow, she saw the drops on the window shining in the sun, and Lady de la Poer, with her bonnet off, reading under it.

All that had happened began to return on Kate's brain in a funny medley; and the first thing she exclaimed was, "O! those poor little fishes, how I must have frightened them!"

"My dear!"

"Do you think I did much mischief?" said Kate, raising herself on her arm. "I am sure the fishes must have been frightened, and the water-lilies broken! Did it hurt them much, do you think?"

"I should think the fish had recovered the shock," said Lady de la Poer, smiling; "but as to the lilies, I should be glad to be sure you had done yourself as little harm as you have to them."

"O no," said Kate, "I'm not hurt,—if Aunt Barbara won't be terribly angry. Now I would n't mind that, only that I've spoilt Addy's birthday, and all your day. Please, I'm very sorry!"

She said this so sadly and earnestly, that Lady de la Poer came and gave her a kind kiss of forgiveness, and said: "Never mind, the girls are very happy with their father, and the rest is good for me."

Kate thought this very comfortable and kind, and clung to the kind hand gratefully; but though it was a fine occasion for one of the speeches she could have composed in private, all that came out of her mouth was, "How horrid it is,—the way everything turns out with me!"

"Nay, things need not turn out horrid, if a certain little girl would keep herself from being silly."

"But I *am* a silly little girl!" cried Kate with emphasis. "Uncle Wardour says he never saw such a silly one, and so does Aunt Barbara!"

"Well, my dear," said Lady de la Poer very calmly, "when clever people take to being silly, they *can* be sillier than any one else."

"Clever people!" cried Kate half breathlessly.

"Yes," said the lady, "you are a clever child; and if you made the most of yourself, you could be very sensible, and hinder yourself from being foolish and unguarded, and getting into scrapes."

Kate gasped. It was not pleasant to be in a scrape; and yet her whole self recoiled from being guarded and watchful, even though for the first time she heard she was not absolutely foolish. She began to argue, "I was naughty, I know, to tease Mary; and Mary, at home, would not have let me; but I could not help the tumbling into the pond. I wanted to get out of the way of the lightning."

"Now, Kate, you *are* trying to show how silly you can make yourself."

"But I can't bear thunder and lightning. It frightens me so, I don't know what to do; and Aunt Jane is just as bad. She always has the shutters shut."

"Your Aunt Jane has had her nerves weakened by bad health; but you are young and strong, and you ought to fight with fanciful terrors."

"But it is not fancy about lightning. It does kill people."

"A storm is very awful, and is one of the great instances of God's power. He does sometimes allow his lightnings to fall; but I do not think it can be quite the thought of this that terrifies you, Kate, for the recollection of his hand is comforting."

"No," said Kate, honestly, "it is not thinking of that. It is that the glare,—coming no one knows when,—and the great rattling clap are so,—so frightful!"

"Then, my dear, I think all you can do is to pray not only for protection from lightning and tempest, but that you may be guarded from the fright that makes you forget to watch yourself, and so renders the danger greater! You could not well have been drowned where you fell; but if it had been a river,—"

"I know," said Kate.

"And try to get self-command. That is the great thing, after all, that would hinder things from being horrid!" said Lady de la Poer with a pleasant smile, just as a knock came to the door, and the maid announced that it was five o'clock, and Miss's things were quite ready; and in return she was thanked, and desired to bring them up.

"Miss!" said Kate, rather hurt: "don't they know who we are?"

"It is not such a creditable adventure that we should wish to make your name known," said Lady de la Poer, rather dryly; and Kate blushed, and became ashamed of herself.

She was really five minutes before she recovered the use of her tongue, and that was a long time for her. Lady de la Poer mean time was helping her to dress as readily as Josephine herself could have done, and brushing out the hair, which was still damp. Kate presently asked where the old lady was.

"She had to go back as soon as the rain was over, to look after a nephew and niece, who are spending the day with her. She said she would look for our party, and tell them how we were getting on."

"Then I have spoilt three people's pleasure more!" said Kate ruefully. "Is the niece a little girl?"

"I don't know; I fancy her grown up, or they would have offered clothes to you."

"Then I don't care!" said Kate.

"What for?"

"Why, for not telling my name. Once it would have been like a fairy tale to Sylvia and me, and have made up for anything, to see a countess,—especially a little girl. But don't you think seeing me would quite spoil that?"

Lady de la Poer was so much amused, that she could not answer at first; and Kate began to feel as if she had been talking foolishly, and turned her back to wash her hands.

"Certainly, I don't think we are quite as well worth seeing as the Crystal Palace! You put me in mind of what Madame Campan said. She had been governess to the first Napoleon's sisters; and when, in the days of their grandeur, she visited them, one of them asked her if she was not awe-struck to find herself among so much royalty. "Really," she said, "I can't be much afraid of queens whom I have whipped!""

"They were only mock queens," said Kate.

"Very true. But, little woman, it is *all* mockery, unless it is the *self* that makes the impression; and I am afraid being perched upon any kind of pedestal makes little faults and follies do more harm to others. But come, put on your hat: we must not keep papa waiting."

The hat was the worst part of the affair; the color of the blue edge of the ribbon had run into the white, and the pretty soft feather had been so draggled in the wet, that an old hen on a wet day was respectability itself compared with it, and there was nothing for it but to take it out; and even then the hat reminded Kate of a certain Amelia Matilda Bunny, whose dirty finery was a torment and a by-word in St. James's Parsonage. Her frock and white jacket had been nicely ironed out, as to show no traces of the adventure; and she disliked all the more to disfigure herself with such a thing on her head for the present, as well as to encounter Aunt Barbara by-and-by.

"There's no help for it," said Lady de la Poer, seeing her disconsolately surveying it; "perhaps it will not be bad for you to feel a few consequences from your heedlessness."

Whether it were the hat or the shock, Kate was uncommonly meek and subdued as she followed Lady de la Poer out of the room; and after giving the little maid half a sovereign and many thanks for having so nicely repaired the damage, they walked back to the palace, and up the great stone stairs, Kate hanging down her head, thinking that every one was wondering how Amelia Matilda Bunny came to be holding by the hand of a lady in a beautiful black lace bonnet and shawl, so quiet and simple, and yet such a lady.

She hardly even looked up when the glad exclamations of the four girls and their father sounded around her, and she could not bear their inquiries whether she felt well again. She knew that she owed thanks to Mary and her father, and apologies to them all; but she had not manner enough to utter them, and only made a queer scrape with her foot, hung her head, and answered "Yes."

They saw she was very much ashamed, and they were in a hurry besides; so when Lord de la Poer had said he had given all manner of thanks to the good old lady, he took hold of Kate's hand, as if he hardly ventured to let go of her again, and they all made the best of their way to the station, and were soon in full career along the line, Kate's heart sinking as she thought of Aunt Barbara. Fanny tried kindly to talk to her; but she was too anxious to listen, made a short answer, and kept her eyes fixed on the two heads of the party, who were in close consultation, rendered private by the noise of the train.

"If ever I answer for any one again!" said Lord de la Poer. "And now for facing Barbara!"

"You had better let me do that."

"What! do you think I am afraid?" and Kate thought the smile on his lip very cruel, as she could not hear his words.

"I don't do you much injustice in thinking so," as he shrugged up his shoulders like a boy going to be punished; "but I think Barbara considers you as an accomplice in mischief, and will have more mercy if I speak."

"Very well! I'm not the man to prevent you. Tell Barbara I'll undergo whatever she pleases, for having ever let go the young lady's hand! She may have me up to the Lord Chancellor if she pleases!"

A little relaxation in the noise made these words audible; and Kate, who knew the Lord Chancellor had some power over her, and had formed her notions of him from a picture, in a history book at home, of Judge Jeffries holding the Bloody Assize, began to get very much frightened; and her friends saw her eyes growing round with alarm, and not knowing the exact cause, pitied her; Lord de la Poer seated her upon his knee, and told her that mamma would take her home, and take care Aunt Barbara did not punish her.

"I don't think she will punish me," said Kate: "she does not often! But pray come home with me!" she added getting hold of the lady's hand.

"What would she do to you then?"

"She would—only—be dreadful!" said Kate. Lord de la Poer laughed; but observed, "Well, is it not enough to make one dreadful to have little girls taking unexpected baths in public? Now Kate please inform me, in confidence, what was the occasion of that remarkable somerset."

"Only the lightning," muttered Kate.

"O! I was not certain whether your intention might not have been to make that polite address to an aquatic bird, for which you pronounced Mary not to have sufficient courage!"

Lady de la Poer, thinking this a hard trial of the poor child's temper, was just going to ask him not to tease her; but Kate was really candid and good-tempered, and she said; "I was wrong to say that! It was Mary that had presence of mind, and I had not."

"Then the fruit of the adventure is to be, I hope, Look before you Leap!—Eh, Lady Caergwent?"

And at the same time the train stopped, and among kisses and farewells, Kate and kind Lady de la Poer left the carriage, and entering a brougham that was waiting for them, drove to Bruton Street; Kate very grave and silent all the way, and shrinking behind her friend in hopes that the servant who opened the door would not observe her plight,—indeed, she took her hat off on the stairs, and laid it on the table in the landing.

To her surprise, the beginning of what Lady de la Poer said, was chiefly apology for not having taken better care of her. It was all quite true: there was no false excuse made for her, she felt, when Aunt Barbara looked ashamed and annoyed, and said how concerned she was that her niece should be so unmanageable, and her protector answered—

"Not that, I assure you! She was a very nice little companion, and we quite enjoyed her readiness and intelligent interest; but she was a little too much excited to remember what she was about when she was startled."

"And no wonder," said Lady Jane. "It was a most tremendous storm, and I feel quite shaken by it still. You can't be angry with her for being terrified by it, Barbara dear, or I shall know what you think of me;—half drowned too, poor child!"

And Aunt Jane put her soft arm round Kate, and put her cheek to hers. Perhaps the night of Kate's tears had really made Jane resolve to try to soften even Barbara's displeasure; and the little girl felt it very kind, though her love of truth made her cry out roughly, "Not half drowned! Mary held me fast, and Lord de la Poer pulled me out!"

"I am sure you ought to be extremely thankful to them," said Lady Barbara, "and overcome with shame at all the trouble and annoyance you have given!"

Lady de la Poer quite understood what the little girl meant by her aunt being dreadful. She would gladly have protected her; but it was not what could be begged off like punishment, nor would truth allow her to say there had been no trouble nor annoyance. So what she did say was: "When one has ten children, one reckons upon such things!" and smiled as if they were quite pleasant changes to her.

"Not, I am sure, with your particularly quiet little girls," said Aunt Barbara. "I am always hoping that Katharine may take example by them."

"Take care what you hope, Barbara," said Lady de la Poer, smiling; "and at any rate forgive this poor little maiden for our disaster, or my husband will be in despair."

"I have nothing to forgive," said Lady Barbara, gravely. "Katharine cannot have seriously expected punishment for what is not a moral fault. The only difference will be the natural consequences to herself of her folly. You had better go down to the schoolroom, Katharine, have your tea, and then go to bed; it is nearly your usual time."

Lady de la Poer warmly kissed the child, and then remained a little while with the aunts, trying to remove what she saw was the impression, that Kate had been complaining of severe treatment, and taking the opportunity of telling them what she herself thought of the little girl. But though Aunt Barbara listened politely, she could not think that Lady de la Poer knew anything about the perverseness, heedlessness, ill-temper, disobedience, and rude ungainly ways, that were so tormenting. She said no word about them herself, because she would not expose her niece's faults; but when her friend talked of Kate's bright, candid, conscientious character, her readiness, sense and intelligence, she said to herself, and perhaps justly, that here was all the difference between at home and abroad, an authority and a stranger.

Meantime, Kate wondered what would be the natural consequences of her folly. Would she have a rheumatic fever or a consumption, like a child in a book?—and she tried breathing deep, and getting up a little cough, to see if it was coming! Or would the Lord Chancellor hear of it? He was a new bugbear recently set up. What did he do with the seals? Did he seal up mischievous heiresses in closets, as she had seen a door fastened by two seals and a bit of string? Perhaps the Court of Chancery was full of such prisons!

It must be owned that it was only half asleep at night that Kate was so absurd. By day she knew very well that the Lord Chancellor was only a great lawyer; but she also knew that whenever there was any puzzle or difficulty about her or her affairs, she always heard something mysteriously said about applying to the Lord Chancellor, till she began to really suspect that it was by his commands that Aunt Barbara was so stern with her; and that if he knew of her fall into the pond, something terrible would come of it. Perhaps that was why the De la Poers kept her name so secret!

She trembled as she thought of it; and here was another added to her many terrors. Poor little girl! If she had rightly feared and loved One, she would have had no room for the many alarms that kept her heart fluttering!

CHAPTER IX

IT MAY BE DOUBTED whether Countess Kate ever did in her childhood discover what her Aunt Barbara meant by the natural consequences of her folly, but she suffered under them, nevertheless. When the summer was getting past its height of beauty, and the streets were all sun and misty heat, and the grass in the parks looked brown, and the rooms were so close that even Aunt Jane had one window open, Kate grew giddy in the head almost every morning, and so weary and dull all day that she had hardly spirit to do anything but read story-books. And Mrs. Lacy was quite poorly too, though not saying much about it; was never quite without a headache, and was several times obliged to send Kate out for her evening walk with Josephine. It was high time to be going out of town, and Mrs. Lacy was to go and be with her son in his vacation.

This was the time when Kate and the Wardours had hoped to be together. But "the natural consequence," of the nonsense Kate had talked, about being "always allowed" to do rude and careless things, and her wild romping games with the boys, had persuaded her aunts that they were very improper people for her to be with, and that it would be wrong to consent to her going to Oldburgh.

That was one natural consequence of her folly. Another was, that when the De la Poers begged that she might spend the holidays with them, and from father and mother downwards were full of kind schemes for her happiness and good, Lady Barbara said to her sister that it was quite impossible; these good friends did not know what they were asking, and that the child would again expose herself in some way that would never be forgotten, unless she were kept in their own sight till she had been properly tamed and reduced to order.

It was self-denying in Lady Barbara to refuse that invitation, for she and her sister would have been infinitely more comfortable together without their troublesome countess, above all when they had no governess to relieve them of her. The going out of town was sad enough to them, for they had always paid a long visit at Caergwent Castle, which had felt like their home through the lifetime of their brother and nephew, but now it was shut up, and their grief for their young nephew came back all the more freshly at the time of year when they were used to be kindly entertained by him in their native home.

But as they could not go there, they went to Bourne Mouth; and the first run Kate took upon the sands took away all the giddiness from her head, and put an end to the tired feeling in her limbs! It really was a run! Aunt Barbara gave her leave to go out with Josephine; and though Josephine said it was very sombre and savage, between the pine woods and the sea, Kate had not felt her heart leap with such fulness of enjoyment since she had made snow-balls last winter at home. She ran down to the waves and watched them sweep in and curl over and break as if she could never have enough of them, and she gazed at the gray outline of the Isle of Wight opposite, feeling as if there was something very great in really seeing an island.

When she came in, there was so much glow on her brown cheeks, and her eyelids looked so much less heavy, that both the aunts gazed at her with pleasure, smiled to one another, and Lady Jane kissed her, while Lady Barbara said, "This was the right thing."

She was to be out as much as possible, so her aunt made a new set of rules for the day. There was to be a walk before breakfast, then breakfast; then Lady Barbara heard her read her chapter in the Bible, and go through her music. And really the music was not half as bad as might be expected with Aunt Barbara. Kate was too much afraid of her to give the half attention she had paid to poor Mrs. Lacy, fright and her aunt's decision of manner forced her to mind what she was about; and though Aunt Barbara found her really very dull and unmusical, she did get on better than before, and learnt something, though more like a machine than a musician.

Then she went out again till the hottest part of the day, during which a bit of French and of English reading was expected from her, and half an hour of needlework; then her dinner, and then out again,—with her aunts this time, Aunt Jane in a wheeled-chair, and Aunt Barbara walking with her,—this was rather dreary,—but when they went in she was allowed to stay out with Josephine, with only one interval in the house for tea, till it grew dark, and she was so sleepy with the salt wind, that she was ready for bed, and had no time to think of the Lord Chancellor.

At first, watching those wonderful and beautiful waves was pleasure enough, and then she was allowed, to her wonder and delight, to have a holland dress and dig in the sand, making castles and motes, or rocks and shipwrecks, with beautiful stories about them; and sometimes she hunted for the few shells and sea-weeds there, or she sat down and read some of her favorite books, especially poetry,—it suited the sea so well; and she was trying to make Ellen's Isle and all the places of the Lady of the Lake in sand, only she never had time to finish them, and they always were either thrown down or washed away before she could return to them.

But among all these amusements, she was watching the families of children who played together, happy creatures. The little sturdy boys that dabbled about so merrily, and minded so little the "Now Masters" of their indignant nurses; the little girls in brown hats with their baskets full; the big boys that even took off shoes, and dabbled in the shallow water; the great sieges of large castles where whole parties attacked and defended,—it was a sort of melancholy glimpse of fairy land to her, for she had only been allowed to walk on the beach with Josephine on condition she never spoke to the other children. Would the Lord Chancellor be after her if she did? Her heart quite yearned for those games, or even to be able to talk to one of those little damsels; and one day when a bright-faced girl ran after her with a piece of weed that she had dropped, she could hardly say "thank you" for her longing to say more; and many were the harrangues she composed within herself to warn the others not to wish to change places with her, for to be a countess was very poor fun indeed.

However, one morning at the end of the first week, Kate looked up from a letter from Sylvia, and said with great glee, "Aunt Barbara! O Aunt Barbara! Alice and the other Sylvia,—Sylvia Joanna,—are coming! I may play with them, mayn't I?"

"Who are they?" said her aunt, gravely.

"Uncle Wardour's nieces," said Kate; "Sylvia's cousins, you know, only we never saw them, but they are just my age; and it will be such fun; only Alice is ill, I believe. Pray, please let me play with them!" and Kate had tears in her eyes.

·"I shall see about it when they come."

"Oh but,—but I can't have them there, Sylvia's own cousins, and not play with them. Please, Aunt Barbara!"

"You ought to know that this impetuosity never disposes me favorably, Katharine; I will inquire and consider."

Kate had learnt wisdom enough not to say any more just then, but the thought of sociability, the notion of chattering freely to young companions, and of a real game at play, and the terror of having all this withheld, and of being thought too proud and haughty for the Wardours, put her into such an agony, that she did not know what she was about, made mistakes even in reading, and blundered her music more than she had ever done under Lady Barbara's teaching; and then, when her aunt reproved her, she could not help laying down her head and bursting into a fit of crying. However, she had not forgotten the terrible tea-drinking, and was resolved not to be as bad as at that time, and she tried to stop herself, exclaiming between her sobs, "O, Aunt Bar—bar—a—I—can—not—help—it."

And Lady Barbara did not scold or look stern. Perhaps she saw that the little girl was really trying to check herself, for she said quite kindly, "Don't, my dear."

And just then, to Kate's great wonder, in came Lady Jane, though it was full half an hour earlier than she usually left her room; and Lady Barbara looked up to her, and said quite as if excusing herself, "Indeed, Jane, I have not been angry with her."

And Kate, somehow understanding that she might, flung herself down by Aunt Jane, and hid her face in her lap, not crying any more, though the sobs were not over, and feeling the fondling hands on her hair very tender and comforting, though she wondered to hear them talk as if she were asleep or deaf,—or perhaps they thought their voices too low, or their words too long and fine for her to understand; nor perhaps did she, though she gathered their drift well enough, and that kind Aunt Jane was quite pleading for herself in having come to the rescue.

"I could not help it, indeed,—you remember Lady de la Poer,—Dr. Woodman both,—excitable nervous temperament,—almost hysterical."

"This unfortunate intelligence,—untoward coincidence—" said Lady Barbara. "But I have been trying to make her feel I am not in anger, and I hope there really was a struggle for self-control."

Kate took her head up again at this, a little encouraged; and Lady Jane kissed her forehead and repeated, "Aunt Barbara was not angry with you, my dear."

"No, for I think you have tried to conquer yourself," said Lady Barbara. She did not think it wise to tell Kate that she thought she could not help it, though, oddly enough, the very thing had just been said over the child's head, and Kate ventured on it to get up and say quietly, "Yes, it was not Aunt Barbara's speaking to me that made me cry, but I am so unhappy about Alice and Sylvia Joanna;" and a soft caress from Aunt Jane made her venture to go on, "It is not only the playing with them, though I *do* wish for that very, very much indeed, but it would be so unkind, and so proud and ungrateful, to despise my own cousin's cousins!"

This was more like the speeches Kate made in her own head than anything she had ever said to her aunts; and it was quite just besides, and not spoken in naughtiness, and Lady Barbara did not think it wrong to show that she attended to it. "You are right, Katharine," she said; "no one wishes you to be either proud or ungrateful. I would not wish entirely to prevent you from seeing the children of the family, but it must not be till there is some acquaintance between myself and their mother, and I cannot tell whether you can be intimate with them, till I know what sort of children they are. Much too must depend on yourself, and whether you will behave well with them."

Kate gave a long sigh and looked up relieved; and for some time she and her aunt were not nearly so much at war as hitherto, but seemed to be coming to a somewhat better understanding.

Yet it rather puzzled Kate. She seemed to herself to have got this favor for crying for it; and it was a belief at home, not only that nothing was got by crying, but that, if by some strange chance it were, it never came to good; and she began the more to fear some disappointment about the expected Wardours.

For two or three days she was scanning every group on the sands with all her might, in hopes of some likeness to Sylvia, but at last she was taken by surprise; just as she was dressed, and Aunt Barbara was waiting in the drawing-room for Aunt Jane, there came a knock to the door, and "Mrs. Wardour" was announced.

In came a small quiet-looking lady in mourning, and with her a girl of about Kate's own age; there was some curtseying and greeting between the two ladies, and her aunt said, "Here is my niece. Come and speak to Mrs. Wardour, my dear," and motioned her forwards.

Now to be motioned forward by Aunt Barbara always made Kate shrink back into herself, and the presence of a little girl before elders likewise rendered her shy and bashful, so she came forth as if intensely disgusted, put out her hand as if she were going to poke, and muttered her favorite "do" so awkwardly and coldly, that Lady Barbara felt how proud and ungracious it looked, and to make up said, "My niece has been very eager for your coming." And then the two little girls drew off into the window and looked at each other under their eyelashes in silence.

Sylvia Joanna Wardour was not like her namesake at home, Sylvia Katharine. She was a thin slight, quiet-looking child, and so little to note about her face, that Kate was soon wondering at her dress being so much smarter than her own was at present. She herself had on a holland suit with a deep cape, which except that they were adorned with labyrinths of white braid, were much what she had worn at home, also a round brown hat, shading her face from the sun; whereas Sylvia's face was exposed by a little turban hat so deeply edged with blue velvet, that the white straw was hardly seen; also she had a little watered silk jacket, and a little flounced frock of a dark silk figured with blue, that looked slightly fuzzed out, and perhaps she was not at ease in this fine dress, for she stood with her head down, and one hand on the window-sill, pretending to look out of the window, but really looking at Kate.

Meanwhile the two grown-up ladies were almost as stiff and shy, though they could not keep dead silence like the children. Mrs. Wardour had heard before that Lady Barbara Umfraville was a formidable person, and was very much afraid of her; and Lady Barbara was not a person to set any one at ease.

So there was a little said about taking the liberty of calling, for her brother-in-law was so anxious to hear of Lady Caergwent; and Lady Barbara said her niece was very well and healthy, and had only needed change of air.

And then came something in return about Mrs. Wardour's other little girl, a sad invalid, she said, on whose account they were come to Bourne Mouth; and there was a little more said of bathing, and walking, and whether the place was full, and then Mrs. Wardour jumped up and said she was detaining Lady Barbara, and took leave; Kate, though she had not spoken a word to Sylvia Wardour, looking at her wishfully with all her eyes, and feeling more than usually silly.

And when the guests were gone, her aunt told her how foolish her want of manner was, and how she had taken the very means to make them think she was not glad to see them. She hung down her head, and pinched the ends of her gloves; she knew it very well, but that did not make it a bit more possible to find a word to say to a stranger before the elders, unless the beginning were made for her as by the De la Poers.

However, she knew it would be very different out of doors, and her heart bounded when her aunt added, "They seem to be quiet lady-like inoffensive people, and I have no objections to your associating with the little girl in our walks, as long as I do not see that it makes you thoughtless and ungovernable."

"O, thank you, thank you, Aunt Barbara," cried Kate, with a bouncing bound that did not promise much for her thought or her governableness; but perhaps Lady Barbara recollected what her own childhood would have been without Jane, for she was not much discomposed, only she said—

"It is very odd you should be so uncivil to the child in her presence, and so ecstatic now! However, take care you do not get too familiar. Remember, these Wardours are no relations, and I will not have you letting them call you by your Christian name."

Kate's bright looks sank. That old married woman sound, Lady Caergwent, seemed as if it would be a bar between her and the free childish fun she hoped for. Yet when so much had been granted, she must not call her aunt cross and unkind, though she did think it hard and proud.

Perhaps she was partly right; but after all, little people cannot judge what is right in matters of familiarity. They have only to do as they are told, and they may be sure of this, that friendship and respect depend much more on what people are in themselves, than on what they call one another.

This lady was the widow of Mr. Wardour's brother, and lived among a great clan of his family in a distant country, where Mary and her father had sometimes made visits; but the younger ones never. Kate was not likely to have been asked there, for it was thought very hard that she should be left on the hands of her aunt's husband; and much had been said of the duty of making her grand relations provide for her, or of putting her into the "Clergy Orphan Asylum." And there had been much displeasure when Mr. Wardour answered that he did not think it right that a child who had friends should live on the charity intended for those who had none able to help them; and soon after this decision he had placed his son Armyn in Mr. Brown's office, instead of sending him to the University. All the Wardours were much vexed then, but they were not much better pleased when the little orphan had come to her preferment, and he made no attempt to keep her in his hands, and obtain the large sum allowed for her board,—only saying that his motherless household was no place for her, and that he could not at once do his duty by her and by his parish. They could not understand the real love and uprightness that made him prefer her advantage to his own,—what was right to what was convenient.

Mrs. George Wardour had not scolded her brother-in-law for his want of prudence and care for his own children's interests; but she had agreed with those who did; and this, perhaps, made her feel all the more awkward and shy when she was told that she *must* go and call upon the Lady Umfravilles, whom the whole family regarded as first so neglectful and then so ungrateful, and make acquaintance with the little girl who had once been held so cheap. She was a kind gentle person, and a careful anxious mother, but not wishing to make great acquaintance, nor used to fine people, large or small, and above all, wrapped up in her poor little delicate Alice.

The next time Kate saw her, she was walking by the side of Alice's wheeled-chair, and Sylvia by her side, in a more plain and suitable dress. Kate set off running to greet them; but at a few paces from them was seized by a shy fit, and stood looking and feeling like a goose, drawing great C's with the point of her parasol in the sand, Josephine looking on, and thinking how "*bête*" English children were. Mrs. Wardour was not much less shy; but she knew she must make a beginning, and so spoke in the middle of Kate's second C: and there was a shaking of hands, and walking together.

They did not get on very well: nobody talked but Mrs. Wardour, and she asked little frightened questions about the Oldburgh party, as she called them, which Kate answered as shortly and shyly,—the more so from the uncomfortable recollection that her aunt had told her that this was the very way to seem proud and unkind; but what could she do?—she felt as if she were frozen up stiff, and could neither move nor look up like herself. At last Mrs. Wardour said that Alice would be tired, and must go in; and then Kate managed to blurt out a request that Sylvia might stay with her. Poor Sylvia looked a good deal scared, and as if she longed to follow her mamma and sister; but the door was shut upon her, and she was left alone with these two strange people,—the Countess and the French woman!

However, Kate recovered the use of her limbs and tongue in a moment, and instantly took her prisoner's hand, and ran off with her to the corner where the scenery of Loch Katrine had so often been begun, and began with great animation to explain. This—a hole that looked as if an old hen had been grubbing in it—was Loch Katrine!

"Loch Katharine, that's yours! And which is to be Loch Sylvia?" said the child recovering, as she began to feel by touch, motion, and voice, that she had only to do with a little girl after all.

"Loch nonsense!" said Kate, rather bluntly. "Did you never hear of the Lochs, the Lakes, in Scotland?"

"Loch Lomond, Loch Katrine, Loch Awe, Loch Ness?—But I don't do my geography out of doors!"

" 'Tisn't geography; 'tis 'The Lady of the Lake.' "

"Is that a new game?"

"Dear me! did you never read 'The Lady of the Lake?'—Sir Walter Scott's poem—

" 'The summer dawn's reflected hue—' "

"O! I've learnt that in my extracts; but I never did my poetry task out of doors!"

" 'Tisn't a task—'tis beautiful poetry! Don't you like poetry better than anything?"

"I like it better than all my other lessons, when it is not very long and hard."

Kate felt that her last speech would have brought Armyn and Charlie down on her for affectation, and that it was not strictly true that she liked poetry better than anything, for a game at romps, and a very amusing story, were still better things; so she did not exclaim at the other Sylvia's misunderstanding, but only said, " 'The Lady of the Lake,' is story and poetry too, and we will play at it."

"And how?"

"I'll tell you as we go on. I'm the King,—that is, the Knight of Snowdon,—James Fitzjames, for I'm in disguise, you know; and you're Ellen."

"Must I be Ellen? We had a horrid nurse once, who used to strike us, and was called Ellen."

"But it was her name. She was Ellen Douglas, and was in banishment on an island with her father. You are Ellen, and Josephine is your old harper,—Allen Bane; she talks French, you know, and that will do for Highland: Gallic and Gaelic sound alike, you know. There! Then I'm going out hunting, and my dear gallant grey will drop down dead with fatigue, and I shall lose my way; and when you hear me wind my horn, too-too, you get upon your hoop,—that will be your boat, you know,—and answer 'Father!' and when I, too-too, again, answer 'Malcolm!' and then put up your hand behind your ear, and stand listening,—

> " 'With locks thrown back and lips apart,
> Like monument of Grecian art;'

and then I'll tell you what to do."

Away scudded the delighted Kate; and after having lamented her gallant grey, and admired the Trosachs, came up too-tooing through her hand with all her might, but found poor Ellen, very unlike a monument of Grecian art, absolutely crying, and Allan Bane using his best English and kindest tones to console her.

"Miladi l' a stupéfaite,—la pauvre petite!" began Josephine; and Kate in consternation asking what was the matter, and Josephine encouraging her, it was all sobbed out. She did not like to be called Ellen,—and she thought it unkind to send her into banishment, —and she had fancied she was to get astride on her hoop, which she justly thought highly improper,—and above all, she could not bear to say "Father—" because—

"I never thought you would mind that," said Kate, rather abashed. "I never did; and I never saw my papa or mamma either."

"No,—so you did n't care."

"Well then," said Kate gravely, "we won't play at that. Let's have 'Marmion,' instead; and I'll be killed."

"But I don't like you to be killed."

"It is only in play."

"Please—please, let us have a nice play!"

"Well, what do you call a nice play?"

"Alice and I used to drive hoops."

"That's tiresome! My hoop always tumbles down: think of something else."

"Alice and I used to play at ball; but there's no ball here."

"Then I'll stuff my pocket-handkerchief with sea-weed, and make one;" and Kate spread out her delicate cambric one,—not quite so fit for such a purpose as the little cheap cotton ones at home, that Mary tried in vain to save from cruel misuse.

"Here's a famous piece! Look, it is all wriggled: it is a mermaid's old stay-lace that she has used and thrown away! Perhaps she broke it in a passion, because her grandmother made her wear so many oyster-shells on her tail!"

"There are no such creatures as mermaids," said Sylvia, looking at her solemnly.

This was not a promising beginning: Sylvia Joanna was not a bit like Sylvia Katharine, nor like Adelaide and Grace de la Poer; yet by seeing each other every day, she and Kate began to shake together, and become friends.

There was no fear of her exciting Kate to run wild: she was a little pussy-cat in her dread of wet, and guarded her clothes as if they could feel,—indeed, her happiest moments were spent in the public walks by Alice's chair, studying how the people were dressed; but still she thought it a fine thing to be the only child in Bourne Mouth who might play with the little Countess, and was so silly as to think the others envied her, when she was dragged and ordered about, bewildered by Kate's loud rapid talk about all kinds of odd things in books, and distressed at being called on to tear through the pine-woods, or grub in wet sand. But it was not all silly vanity: she was a gentle, loving little girl, very good-natured, and sure to get fond of all who were kind to her; and she liked Kate's bright ways and amusing manner,—perhaps really liking her more than if she had understood her better; and Kate liked her, and rushed after her on every occasion, as the one creature with whom it was possible to play and to chatter.

No, not quite the *one;* for poor sick Alice was better for talk and quiet play than her sister. She read a great deal; and there was an exchange of story books, and much conversation over them, between her and Kate,—indeed, the spirit and animation of this new friend quite made her light up, and brighten out of her languor, whenever the shrill laughing voice came near. And Kate, after having got over her first awe at coming near a child so unlike herself, grew very fond of her, and felt how good and sweet and patient she was. She never ran off to play till Alice was taken in-doors; and spent all her spare time in-doors in drawing picture stories, which were daily explained to the two sisters at some seat in the pine-woods.

There was one very grand one, that lasted all the latter part of the stay at Bourne Mouth,—as the evenings grew longer, and Kate had more time for preparing it, at the rate of four or five scenes a day, drawn and painted,—being the career of a very good little girl, whose parents were killed in a railway accident (a most fearful picture was that,—all blunders being filled up by spots of vermilion blood and orange-colored flame!) and then came all the wonderful exertions by which she maintained her broth- ers and sisters, taught them, and kept them in order. They all had names; and there was a naughty little Alexander, whose monkey tricks made even Sylvia laugh. Sylvia was very anxious that the admirable heroine, Hilda, should be rewarded by turning into a countess; and could not enter into Kate's first objection,—founded on fact,—that it could not be without killing all the brothers. "Why could n't it be done in play, like so many other things?" To which Kate answered: "There is a sort of true in play;" but as Sylvia could not understand her, nor she herself get at her own idea, she went on to her other objection, a still more startling one,—that "She could n't wish Hilda anything so dreadful!"

Thus the time at the sea-side was very happy,—quite the happiest since Kate's change of fortune. The one flaw in these times on the sands, was when she was alone with Sylvia and Josephine: not in Sylvia's dulness,—that she had ceased to care about,—but in a little want of plain dealing. Sylvia was never wild or rude, but she was not strictly obedient when out of sight; and when Kate was shocked, would call it very unkind, and caress and beseech her not to tell.

They were such tiny things, that they would hardly bear mention; but one will do as a specimen. Sylvia was one of those very caressing children who can never be happy without clinging to their friends, kissing them constantly, and always calling them dear, love, and darling.

Now Mrs. Wardour knew it was not becoming to see all this embracing in public, and was sure besides, that Lady Barbara would not like to see the Countess hung upon in Sylvia's favorite way; so she forbade all such demonstrations, except the parting and meeting kiss. It was a terrible grievance to Sylvia,—it seemed as if her heart could not love without her touch; but instead of training herself in a little self-control and obedience, she thought it "cross;" and mamma was no sooner out of sight, than her arm was round Kate's waist. Kate struggled at first,—it did not suit her honorable conscientiousness; but then Sylvia would begin to cry at the unkindness, say Kate did not love her, that she would not be proud if she was a countess; and Kate gave in, liked the love,—of which, poor child! she got so little,—and let Sylvia do as she pleased, but never without a sense of disobedience and dread of being caught.

So, too, about her title. Sylvia called her darling, duck, and love; and she called Sylvia by plenty of such names; but she had been obliged to tell of her aunt's desire, that Katharine and Kate should never be used.

Sylvia's ready tears fell; but the next day she came back cheerful, with the great discovery that darling Lady Caergwent might be called K, her initial, and the first syllable of her title. It was the cleverest invention Sylvia had ever made; and she was vexed when Kate demurred, honestly thinking that her aunts would like it worse than even Kate, and that therefore she ought not to consent.

But when Sylvia coaxingly uttered, "My own dear duck of a K," and the soft warm arm squeezed her, and the eyes would have been weeping and the tongue reproaching in another moment, she allowed it to go on,—it was so precious and sweet to be loved; and she told Sylvia she was a star in the dark night.

No one ever found out these and one or two other instances of small disobedience. They were not mischievous. Josephine willingly overlooked them, and there was nothing to bring them to light. It would have been better for Sylvia if her faults had been of a sort that brought attention on them more easily.

Meanwhile, Lady Barbara had almost found in her a model child,—except for her foolish shy silence before her elders, before whom she always whispered,—and freely let the girls be constantly together. The aunt little knew that this meek well-behaved maiden was giving the first warp to that upright truth that had been the one sterling point of Kate's character!

CHAPTER X

IT HAD BEEN INTENDED that Mrs. Lacy should rejoin her pupil at Bourne Mouth at the end of six weeks; but in her stead came a letter saying that she was unwell, and begging for a fortnight's grace. At the fortnight's end came another letter; to which Lady Barbara answered that all was going on so well, that there was no need to think of returning till they should all meet in London on the 1st of October.

But before that 1st, poor Mrs. Lacy wrote again with great regret and many excuses for the inconvenience she was causing. Her son and her doctor had insisted on her resigning her situation at once; and they would not even allow her to go back until her place could be supplied.

"Poor thing!" said Lady Jane. "I always thought it was too much for her. I wish we could have made her more comfortable; it would have been such a thing for her!"

"So it would," answered Lady Barbara, "if she had had to do with any other child. A little consideration or discretion, such as might have been expected from a girl of eleven years old towards a person in her circumstances, would have made her happy, and enabled her to assist her son. But I have given up expecting feeling from Katharine."

That speech made Kate swell with anger at her aunt's tone; and in her anger she forgot to repent of having been really thoughtless and almost unkind, or to recollect how differently her own gentle Sylvia at home would have behaved to the poor lady. She liked the notion of novelty, and hoped for a new governess as kind and bright as Miss Oswald.

Moreover, she was delighted to find that Mrs. George Wardour was going to live in London for the present, that Alice might be under doctors, and Sylvia under masters. Kate cared little for the why, but was excessively delighted with plans for meetings, hopes of walks, talks, and tea-drinkings together; promises that the other dear Sylvia should come to meet her; and above all, an invitation to spend Sylvia Joanna's birthday with her on the 21st of October, and go all together either to the Zoölogical Gardens or to the British Museum, according to the weather.

With these hopes, Kate was only moderately sorry to leave the sea and pine trees behind her, and find herself once more steaming back to London, carrying in her hand a fine blue and white travelling bag, worked for her by her two little friends, but at which Lady Barbara had coughed rather drily. In the bag were a great many small white shells done up in twists of paper, that pretty story "The Blue Ribbons," and a small blank book, in which, whenever the train stopped, Kate wrote with all her might. For Kate had a desire to convince Sylvia Joanna that one was much happier without being a countess, and she thought this could be done very touchingly and poetically by a fable in verse: so she thought she had a very good idea by changing the old daisy that pined for transplantation and found it very unpleasant, into a harebell.

> A harebell blue on a tuft of moss
> In the wind her bells did toss.

That was her beginning; and the poor harebell was to get into a hothouse, where they wanted to turn her into a tall stately campanula, and she went through a great deal from the gardeners. There was to be a pretty fairy picture to every verse; and it would make a charming birthday present, much nicer than anything that could be bought; and Kate kept on smiling to herself as the drawings came before her mind's eye, and the rhymes to her mind's ear.

So they came home; but it was odd, the old temper of the former months seemed to lay hold of Kate as soon as she set foot in the house in Bruton Street, as if the cross feelings were lurking in the old corners.

She began by missing Mrs. Lacy very much. The kind soft governess had made herself more loved than the wayward child knew; and when Kate had run into the schoolroom and found nobody sitting by the fire, no sad sweet smile to greet her, no one to hear her adventures, and remembered that she had worried the poor widow and that she would never come back again, she could have cried, and really had a great mind to write to her, ask her pardon, and say she was sorry. It would perhaps have been the beginning of better things if she had; but of all things in the world, what prevented her? Just this,—that she had an idea that her aunt expected it of her! O Kate! Kate!

So she went back to the harebell, and presently began rummaging among her books for a picture of one to copy; and just then Lady Barbara came in, found half a dozen strewn on the floor, and ordered her to put them tidy, and then be dressed. That put her out, and after her old bouncing fashion she flew up-stairs, caught her frock in the old hitch at the turn, and half tore off a flounce.

No wonder Lady Barbara was displeased, and that was the beginning of things going wrong; nay, worse than before the going to Bourne Mouth.

Lady Barbara was seeking for a governess, but such a lady as she wished for was not to be found in a day; and in the mean time she was resolved to do her duty by her niece, and watched over her behavior, and gave her all the lessons that she did not have from masters.

Whether it was that Lady Barbara did not know exactly what was to be expected of a little girl, or whether Kate was more fond of praise than was good for her, those daily lessons were more trying than ever they had been. Generally she had liked them; but with Aunt Barbara, the being told to sit upright, hold her book straight, or pronounce her words rightly, always teased her, and put her out of humor at the beginning. Or she was reminded of some failure of yesterday, and it always seemed to her unjust that by-gones should not be by-gones; or even when she knew she had been doing her best, her aunt always thought she could have done better, so that she had no heart or spirit to try another time, but went on in a dull save-trouble way, hardly caring to exert herself to avoid a scolding, it was so certain to come.

It was not right,—a really diligent girl would have won for herself the peaceful sense of having done her best, and her aunt would have owned it in time; whereas poor Kate's resistance only made herself and her aunt worse to each other every day, and destroyed her sense of duty and obedience more and more.

Lady Barbara could not be always with her, and when once out of sight there was a change. If she were doing a lesson with one of her masters, she fell into a careless attitude in an instant, and would often chatter so that there was no calling her to order, except by showing great determination to tell her aunt. It made her feel both sly and guilty to behave so differently out of sight, and yet now that she had once begun, she seemed unable to help going on; and she was sure, foolish child, that Aunt Barbara's strictness made her naughty!

Then there were her walks. She was sent out with Jospehine in the morning, and desired to walk nowhere but in the Square; and in the afternoon she and Josephine were usually set down by the carriage together in one of the parks, and appointed where to meet it again after Lady Jane had taken her airing when she was well enough, for she soon became more ailing than usual. They were to keep in the quiet paths, and not speak to any one.

But neither Josephine nor her young lady had any turn for what was "triste." One morning, when Kate was in great want of a bit of India rubber, and had been sighing because of the displeasure she should meet for having lost her own through using it in play hours, Josephine offered to take her—only a little out of her way—to buy a new piece.

Kate knew this was not plain dealing, and hated herself for it, but she was tired of being scolded, and consented! And then how miserable she was; how afraid of being asked where she had been; how terrified lest her aunt should observe that it was a new, not an old, piece; how humiliated by knowing she was acting untruth!

And then Josephine took more liberties. When Kate was walking along the path, thinking how to rhyme to "pride," she saw Josephine talking over the iron rail to a man with a beard; and she told her maid afterwards that it was wrong; but Josephine said, "Miladi had too good a heart to betray her," and the man came again and again, and once even walked home part of the way with Josephine, a little behind the young lady.

Kate was desperately affronted, and had a great mind to complain to her aunts. But then Josephine could have told that they had not been in the Square garden at all that morning, but in much more entertaining streets! Poor Kate, these daily disobediences did not weigh on her nearly as much as the first one did; it was all one general sense of naughtiness!

Working at her harebell was the pleasantest thing she did, but her eagerness about it often made her neglectful and brought her into scrapes. She had filled one blank book with her verses and pictures, some rather good, some very bad; and for want of help and correction she was greatly delighted with her own performance, and thought it quite worthy of a little ornamental album, where she could write out the verses and gum in the drawings.

"Please, Aunt Barbara, let me go to the Soho Bazaar to-day."

"I cannot take you there, I have an engagement."

"But may I not go with Josephine?"

"Certainly not. I would not trust you there with her. Besides, you spend too much upon trumpery, as it is."

"I don't want it for myself; I want something to get ready for Sylvia's birthday,—the Sylvia that is come to London, I mean."

"I do not approve of a habit of making presents."

"Oh! but, Aunt Barbara, I am to drink tea with her on her birthday, and spend the day, and go to the Zoölogical Gardens, and I have all ready but my present! and it will not be in time if you won't let me go to-day."

"I never grant anything to pertinacity," answered Lady Barbara. "I have told you that I cannot go with you to-day, and you ought to submit."

"But the birthday, Aunt Barbara!"

"I have answered you once, Katharine; you ought to know better than to persist."

Kate pouted, and the tears swelled in her eyes at the cruelty of depriving her of the pleasure of making her purchase, and at having her beautiful fanciful production thus ruined by her aunt's unkindness. As she sat over her geography lesson, out of sight of her own bad writing, her broken-backed illuminated capitals, her lumpy campanulas, crooked-winged fairies, queer perspective, and daubs of blue paint, she saw her performance not as it was, but as it was meant to be, heard her own lines without their awkward rhymes and bits like prose, and thought of the wonder and admiration of all the Wardour family, and of the charms of having it secretly lent about as a dear simple sweet effusion of the talented young countess, who longed for rural retirement. And down came a great tear into the red trimming of British North America, and Kate unadvisedly trying to wipe it up with her handkerchief, made a red smear all across to Cape Verde! Formerly, she would have exclaimed at once; now she only held up the other side of the book that her aunt might not see, and felt very shabby all the time. But

Lady Barbara was reading over a letter, and did not look. If Kate had not been wrapt up in herself, she would have seen that anxious distressed face.

There came a knock to the schoolroom door. It was Mr. Mercer, the doctor, who always came to see Lady Jane twice a week; and, startled and alarmed, Lady Barbara sprang up. "Do you want me, Mr. Mercer? I'll come."

"No, thank you," said the doctor, coming in. "It was only that I promised I would look at this little lady, just to satisfy Lady Jane, who does not think her quite well."

Kate's love of being important always made her ready to be looked at by Mr. Mercer, who was a kind fatherly old gentleman, not greatly apt to give physic, very good-natured, and from his long attendance more intimate with the two sisters than perhaps any other person was. Lady Barbara gave an odd sort of smile, and said, "Oh! very well!" and the old gentleman laughed as the two bright clear eyes met his, and said, "No great weight there, I think! Only a geography fever, eh! Any more giddy heads lately, eh? Or only when you make cheeses!"

"I can't make cheeses now, my frocks are so short," said Kate, whose spirits always recovered with the least change.

"No more dreams?"

"Not since I went to Bourne Mouth."

"Your tongue." And as Kate, who had a certain queer pleasure in the operation, put out the long pinky member with its ruddier tip, quivering like an animal, he laughed again, and said, "Thank you, Lady Caergwent; it is a satisfaction once in a way to see something perfectly healthy! You would not particularly wish for a spoonful of cod-liver oil, would you?"

Kate laughed, made a face, and shook her head.

"Well," said the doctor as he released her, "I may set Lady Jane's mind at rest. Nothing the matter there with the health."

"Nothing the matter but perverseness, I am afraid," said Lady Barbara, as Kate stole back to her place, and shut her face in with the board of her atlas. "It is my sister who is the victim, and I cannot have it go on. She is so dreadfully distressed whenever the child is in disgrace, that it is doing her serious injury. Do you not see it, Mr. Mercer?"

"She is very fond of the child," said Mr. Mercer.

"That is the very thing! She is constantly worrying herself about her, takes all her naughtiness for illness, and then cannot bear to see her reproved. I assure you I am forced for my sister's sake to overlook many things which I know I ought not to pass by (Kate shuddered.) But the very anxiety about her is doing great harm."

"I thought Lady Jane nervous and excited this morning," said Mr. Mercer; "but that seemed to me to be chiefly about the Colonel's return."

"Yes," said Lady Barbara, "of course in some ways it will be a great pleasure; but it is very unlucky, after staying till the war was over, that he has had to sell out without getting his promotion. It will make a great difference!"

"On account of his son's health, is it not?"

"Yes; of course everything must give way to that, but it is most unfortunate. The boy has never recovered from his wound at Lucknow, and they could not bear to part, or they ought to have sent him home with his mother long ago; and now my brother has remained at his post till he thought he could be spared; but he has not got his promotion, which he *must* have had in a few months."

"When do you expect him?"

"They were to set off in a fortnight from the time he wrote, but it all depended on how Giles might be. I wish we knew; I wish there could be any certainty, this is so bad for my sister. And just at this very time, without a governess, when some children would be especially thoughtful and considerate, that we should have this strange fit of idleness and perverseness! It is very trying; I feel quite hopeless sometimes!"

Some children, as Lady Barbara said, would have been rendered thoughtful and considerate by hearing such a conversation as this, and have tried to make themselves as little troublesome to their elders as possible; but there are others who, unless they are directly addressed, only take in, in a strange dreamy way, that which belongs to the grown-up world, though quick enough to catch what concerns themselves. Thus Kate, though aware that Aunt Barbara thought her naughtiness made Aunt Jane ill, and that there was a fresh threat of the Lord Chancellor upon the return of her great-uncle from India, did not in the least perceive that her Aunt Barbara was greatly perplexed and harassed, divided between her care for her sister and for her niece, grieved for her brother's anxiety, and disappointed that he had been obliged to leave the army, instead of being made a General. The upshot of all that she carried away with her was, that it was very cross of Aunt Barbara to think she made Aunt Jane ill, and very very hard that she could not go to the bazaar.

Lady Jane did not go out that afternoon, and Lady Barbara set her niece and Josephine down in the Park, saying, that she was going into Belgravia, and desiring them to meet her near Apsley House. They began to walk, and Kate began to lament. "If she could only have gone to the bazaar for her album! It was very hard!"

"Eh," Josephine said, "why should they not go? There was plenty of time. Miladi Barbe had given them till four. She would take la petite."

Kate hung back. She knew it was wrong. She should never dare produce the book if she had it.

But Josephine did not attend to the faltered English words, or disposed of them with a "Bah! Miladi will guess nothing!" and she had turned decidedly out of the Park, and was making a sign to a cab. Kate was greatly frightened, but was more afraid of checking Josephine in the open street, and making her dismiss the cab, than of getting into it. Besides, there was a very strong desire in her for the red and gold square book that had imprinted itself on her imagination. She could not but be glad to do something in spite of Aunt Barbara. So they were shut in, and went off along Piccadilly, Kate's feelings in a strange whirl of fright and triumph, amid the clattering of the glasses. Just suppose she saw any one she knew!

But they got to Soho Square at last; and through the glass doors, in among the stalls,—that fairyland in general to Kate; but now she was too much frightened and bewildered to do more than hurry along the passages, staring so wildly for her albums, that Josephine touched her, and said, "Tenez, Miladi, they will think you farouche. Ah, see the beautiful wreaths!"

"Come on, Josephine," said Kate, impatiently.

But it was not so easy to get the French maid on. A bazaar was felicity to her, and she had her little lady in her power; she stood and gazed, and admired, and criticised, at every stall that afforded ornamental wearing apparel or work patterns; and Kate, making little excursions, and coming back again to her side, could not get her on three yards in a quarter of an hour, and was too shy and afraid of being lost, to wander away and transact her own business. At last they did come to a counter with ornamental stationery; and after looking at four or five books, Kate bought a purple embossed one; not at all what she had had in her mind's eye, just because she was in too great a fright to look further; and then step by step, very nearly crying at last, so as to alarm Josephine lest she should really cry, she got her out finally. It was a quarter to four, and Josephine was in vain sure that Miladi Barbe would never be at the place in time; Kate's heart was sick with fright at the thought of the shame of detection.

She begged to get out at the Marble Arch, and not risk driving along Park Lane; but Josephine was triumphant in her certainty that there was time; and on they went, Kate fancying every bay nose that passed the window, would turn out to have the brougham, the man-servant, and Aunt Barbara behind it.

At length they were set down at what the French woman thought a safe distance, and paying the cabman, set out along the side path, Josephine admonishing her lady that it was best not to walk so swiftly, or to look guilty.

But just then, Kate really saw the carriage drawn up where there was an opening in the railings, and the servant holding open the door for them. Had they been seen? There was no knowing! Lady Barbara did not say one single word: but that need not have been surprising,—only how very straight her back was, how fixed her marble mouth and chin! It was more like Diana's head than ever,—Diana, when she was shooting all Niobe's daughters, thought Kate in her dreamy vague alarm. Then she looked at Josephine, on the back seat, to see what she thought of it; but the brown sallow face in the little bonnet was quite still and like itself,—beyond Kate's power to read.

The stillness, doubt, and suspense were almost unbearable. She longed to speak, but had no courage, and could almost have screamed with desire to have it over, end as it would. Yet at last, when the carriage did turn into Bruton Street, fright and shame had so entirely the upper hand, that she read the numbers on every door, wishing the carriage would only stand still at each, or go slower, that she might put off the moment of knowing whether she was found out.

They stopped; the few seconds of ringing, of opening the doors, of getting out, were over. She knew how it would be when, instead of going up-stairs, her aunt opened the schoolroom door, beckoned her in, and said gravely, "Lady Caergwent, while you are under my charge, it is my duty to make you obey me. Tell me where you have been."

There was something in the sternness of that low lady-like voice, and of that dark deep eye, that terrified Kate more than the brightest flash of lightning; and it was well for her that the habit of truth was too much fixed for falsehood or shuffling even to occur to her. She did not dare to do more than utter in a faint voice, scarcely audible, "To the bazaar."

"In direct defiance of my commands?"

But the sound of her own confession, the relief of having told, gave Kate spirit to speak; "I know it was naughty," she said, looking up; "I ought not. Aunt Barbara, I have been very naughty. I've been often where you did n't know."

"Tell me the whole truth, Katharine;" and Lady Barbara's look relaxed, and the infinite relief of putting an end to a miserable concealment was felt by the little girl; so she told of the shops she had been at, and of her walks in frequented streets, adding that indeed she would not have gone, but that Josephine took her. "I did like it," she added, candidly; "but I know I ought not."

"Yes, Katharine," said Lady Barbara, almost as sternly as ever; "I had thought that, with all your faults, you were to be trusted."

"I have told you the truth!" cried Kate.

"*Now* you have; but you have been deceiving me all this time; you, who ought to set an example of upright and honorable conduct."

"No, no, Aunt!" exclaimed Kate, her eyes flashing. "I never spoke one untrue word to you; and I have not now,—nor ever. I never deceived."

"I do not say that you have *told* untruths. It is deceiving, to betray the confidence placed in you."

Kate knew it was; yet she had never so felt that her aunt trusted her as to have the sense of being on honor; and she felt terribly wounded and grieved, but not so touched as to make her cry or ask pardon. She knew she had been audaciously disobedient; but it was hard to be accused of betraying trust when she had never felt that it was placed in her; and yet the conviction of deceit took from her the last ground she had of peace with herself.

Drooping and angry, she stood without a word; and her aunt presently said, "I do not punish you. The consequences of your actions are punishment enough in themselves, and I hope they may warn you, or I cannot tell what is to become of you in your future life, and of all that will depend on you. You must soon be under more strict and watchful care than mine, and I hope the effect may be good. Meantime, I desire that your Aunt Jane may be spared hearing of this affair, little as you seem to care for her peace of mind."

And away went Lady Barbara; while Kate, flinging herself upon the sofa, sobbed out, "I do care for Aunt Jane! I love Aunt Jane! I love her ten hundred times more than you! you horrid cross old Diana! But I have deceived! O, I am getting to be a wicked little girl! I never did such things at home. Nobody made me naughty there. But it's the fashionable world. It is corrupting my simplicity. It always does. And I shall be lost! O Mary, Mary! O papa, papa! O, come and take me home!" And for a little while Kate gasped out these calls, as if she had really thought they would break the spell, and bring her back to Oldburgh.

She ceased crying at last, and slowly crept up-stairs, glad to meet no one; and that not even Josephine was there to see her red eyes. Her muslin frock was on the bed, and she managed to dress herself, and run down again unseen; she stood over the fire, so that the housemaid, who brought in her tea, should not see her face; and by the time she had to go to the drawing-room, the mottling of her face had abated under the influence of a story book, which always drove troubles away for the time.

It was a very quiet evening. Aunt Barbara read bits out of the newspaper, and there was a little talk over them; and Kate read on in her book, to hinder herself from feeling uncomfortable. Now and then Aunt Jane said a few soft words about "Giles and Emily;" but her sister always led away from the subject, afraid of her exciting herself, and getting anxious.

And if Kate had been observing, she would have heard in the weary sound of Aunt Barbara's voice, and seen in those heavy eyelids, that the troubles of the day had brought on a severe headache, and that there was at least one person suffering more than even the young ill-used countess.

And when bedtime came, she learnt more of the "consequences of her actions." Stiff Mrs. Bartley stood there with her candle.

"Where is Josephine?"

"She is gone away, my Lady."

Kate asked no more, but shivered and trembled all over. She recollected that in telling the truth she had justified herself, and at Josephine's expense. She knew Josephine would call it a blackness—a treason. What would become of the poor bright merry Frenchwoman? Should she never see her again? And all because she had not had the firmness to be obedient! Oh, how wicked this place made her! and would there be any end to it?

And all night she was haunted through her dreams with the Lord Chancellor in his wig, trying to catch her, and stuff her into the woolsack, and Uncle Wardour's voice always just out of reach. If she could only get to him!

CHAPTER XI

T HE YOUNG COUNTESS was not easily broken down. If she was ever so miserable for one hour, she was ready to be amused the next; and though when left to herself she felt very desolate in the present, and much afraid of the future, the least enlivenment brightened her up again into more than her usual spirits. Even an entertaining bit in the history that she was reading would give her so much amusement, that she would forget her disgrace in making remarks and asking questions, till Lady Barbara gravely bade her not waste time, and decided that she had no feeling.

It was not more easy to find a maid than a governess to Lady Barbara's mind, nor did she exert herself much in the matter, for as Kate heard her tell Mr. Mercer, she had decided that the present arrangement could not last; and then something was asked about Colonel and Mrs. Umfraville; to which the answer was, "O no, quite impossible; she could never be in a house with an invalid;" and then ensued something about the Chancellor and an establishment, which, as usual, terrified Kate's imagination.

Indeed, that night terrors were at their height, for Mrs. Bartley never allowed dawdling, and with a severely respectful silence made the undressing as brief an affair as possible, brushing her hair till her head tingled all over, putting away the clothes with the utmost speed, and carrying off the candle as soon as she had uttered her grim "Good night, my Lady," leaving Kate to choose between her pet terrors,—either of the Lord Chancellor, or of the house on fire, or a very fine new one,—that some one would make away with her to make way for her Uncle Giles, and his son to come to her title. Somehow Lady Barbara had contrived to make her exceedingly in awe of her Uncle Giles, the strict stern soldier who was always implicitly obeyed, and who would be so shocked at her. She wished she could hide somewhere when he was coming! But there was one real good bright pleasure near, that would come before her misfortunes; and that was the birthday to be spent at the Wardours. As to the present, Josephine had had the album in her pocket, and had never restored it, and Kate had begun to feel a distaste to the whole performance, to recollect its faults, and to be ashamed of the entire affair; but that was no reason she should not be very happy with her friends, who had promised to take her to the Zoölogical Gardens.

She had not seen them since her return to London; they were at Westbourne Road, too far off for her to walk thither even if she had had any one to go with her, and though they had called, no one had seen them; but she had had two or three notes, and had sent some "Story pictures" by the post. And the thoughts of that day of freedom and enjoyment, of talking to Alice, being petted by Mrs. Wardour and caressed by Sylvia, seemed to bear her through all the dull morning walks, in which she was not only attended by Bartley, but by the man-servant; all the lessons with her aunt, and the still more dreary exercise which Lady Barbara took with her in some of the parks in the afternoon. She counted the days to the 21st, whenever she woke in the morning; and at last Saturday was come, and it would be Monday.

"Katharine," said Lady Barbara at breakfast, "you had better finish your drawing to-day; here is a note from Madame to say it will suit her best to come on Monday instead of Tuesday."

"O! but, Aunt Barbara, I am going to Westbourne Road on Monday."

"Indeed! I was not aware of it."

"O, it is Sylvia's birthday! and I am going to the Zoölogical Gardens with them."

"And pray, how came you to make this engagement without consulting me?"

"It was all settled at Bourne Mouth. I thought you knew! Did not Mrs. Wardour ask your leave for me?"

"Mrs. Wardour said something about hoping to see you in London, but I made no decided answer. I should not have allowed the intimacy there if I had expected that the family would be living in London; and there is no reason that it should continue. Constant intercourse would not be at all desirable."

"But may I not go on Monday?" said Kate, her eyes opening wide with consternation.

"No, certainly not. You have not deserved that I should trust you; I do not know who you might meet there; and I cannot have you going about with any chance person."

"O, Aunt Barbara! Aunt Barbara, I have promised!"

"Your promise can be of no effect without my consent."

"But they will expect me. They will be so disappointed!"

"I cannot help that. They ought to have applied to me for my consent."

"Perhaps," said Kate, hopefully, "Mrs. Wardour will write to-day. If she does, will you let me go?"

"No, Katharine. While you are under my charge, I am accountable for you, and I will not send you into society I know nothing about. Let me hear no more of this, but write a note excusing yourself, and we will let the coachman take it to the post."

Kate was thoroughly enraged, and forgot even her fears. "I shan't excuse myself," she said; "I shall say you will not let me go."

"You will write a proper and gentlewoman-like note," said Lady Barbara, quietly, "so as not to give needless offence."

"I shall say," exclaimed Kate more loudly, "that I can't go, because you won't let me go near old friends."

"Go into the schoolroom, and write a proper note, Katharine; I shall come presently, and see what you have said," repeated Lady Barbara, commanding her own temper with some difficulty.

Kate flung away into the schoolroom, muttering, and in a tumult of exceeding disappointment, anger, and despair, too furious even to cry, and dashing about the room calling Aunt Barbara after every horrible heroine she could think of, and pitying herself and her friends, till the thought of Sylvia's disappointment stung her beyond all bearing. She was still rushing hither and thither, inflaming her passion, when her aunt opened the door.

"Where is the note?" she said quietly.

"I have not done it."

"Sit down then this instant, and write," said Lady Barbara, with her Diana face and cool way, the most terrible of all.

Kate sulkily obeyed, but, as she seated herself, muttered—

"I shall say you won't let me go near them."

"Write as I tell you.—My dear Mrs. Wardour—"

"There."

"I fear you may be expecting to see me on Monday—"

"I don't fear; I know she is."

"Write—I fear you may be expecting me on Monday, as something passed on the subject at Bourne Mouth; and in order to prevent inconvenience, I write to say that it will not be in my power to call on that day, as my aunt had made a previous engagement for me."

"I am sure I shan't say that!" cried Kate, breaking out of all bounds in her indignation.

"Recollect yourself, Lady Caergwent," said Lady Barbara, calmly.

"It is not true!" cried Kate passionately, jumping up from her seat. "You had not made an engagement for me! I won't write it! I won't write lies, and you shan't make me."

"I do not allow such words or such a manner in speaking to me," said Lady Barbara, not in the least above her usual low voice; and her calmness made Kate the more furious, and jump and dance round with passion, repeating, "I'll never write lies, nor tell lies, for you or any one; you may kill me, but I won't!"

"That is enough exposure of yourself, Lady Caergwent," said her aunt. "When you have come to your senses, and choose to apologize for insulting me, and show me the letter written as I desire, you may come to me."

And away walked Lady Barbara, as cool and unmoved apparently as if she had been made of cast iron; though within she was as sorry, and hardly less angry, than the poor frantic child she left.

Kate did not fly about now. She was very indignant, but she was proud of herself too; she had spoken as if she had been in a book, and she believed herself persecuted for adhering to old friends, and refusing to adopt fashionable falsehoods, such as she had read of. She was a heroine in her own eyes, and that made her inclined to magnify all the persecution and cruelty. They wanted to shut her up from the friends of her childhood, to force her to be false and fashionable; they had made her naughtier and naughtier ever since she came there; they were teaching her to tell falsehoods now, and to give up the Wardours. She would never, never do it! Helpless girl as she was, she would be as brave as the knights and earls,—her ancestors, and stand up for the truth. But what would they do at her! Oh! could she bear Aunt Barbara's dreadful set Diana face again, and not write as she was told!

The poor weak little heart shrank with terror as she only looked at Aunt Barbara's chair,—not much like the Sir Giles de Umfraville she had thought of just now. "And I'm naughty now; I did betray my trust; I'm much naughtier than I was. Oh, if papa was but here!" And then a light darted into Kate's eye, and a smile came on her lip. "Why should not I go home? Papa would have me again; I know he would! He would die rather than leave his child Kate to be made wicked, and forced to tell lies! Perhaps he'll hide me! Oh, if I could go to school with the children at home in disguise, and let Uncle Giles be Earl of Caergwent if he likes! I've had enough of grandeur! I'll come as Cardinal Wolsey did, when he said he was come to lay his bones among them,—and Sylvia and Mary, and Charlie and Armyn,—oh, I must go where some one will be kind to me again! Can I really, though? Why not?" and her heart beat violently. "Yes, yes; nothing would happen to me; I know how to manage! If I can only get there, they will hide me from Aunt Barbara and the Lord Chancellor; and even if I had to go back, I should have had one kiss of them all. Perhaps if I don't go now I shall never see them again!"

With thoughts like these, Kate, moving dreamily, as if she were not sure that it was herself or not, opened her little writing-case, took out her purse, and counted the money. There was a sovereign and some silver; more than enough, as she well knew. Then she took out her worked travelling-bag, and threw in a few favorite books; then stood and gasped, and opened the door to peep out. The coachman was waiting at the bottom of the stairs for orders, so she drew in her head, looked at her watch, and considered whether her room would be clear of the housemaids. If she could once get safely out of the house she would not be missed till her dinner-time, and perhaps then might be supposed sullen, and left alone. She was in a state of great fright, starting violently at every sound; but the scheme having once occurred to her, it seemed as if St. James's Parsonage was pulling her harder and harder every minute; she wondered if there were really such things as heart-strings; if there were, hers must be fastened very tight round Sylvia.

At last she ventured out, and flew up to her own room more swiftly than ever she had darted before! She moved about quietly, and perceived by the sounds in the next room that Mrs. Bartley was dressing Aunt Jane, and Aunt Barbara reading a letter to her. This was surely a good moment; but she knew she must dress herself neatly, and not look scared, if she did not mean to be suspected and stopped, and she managed to get quietly into her little shaggy coat, her black hat and feather, and warm gloves,—even her boots were remembered,—and then whispering to herself, "It can't be wrong to get away from being made to tell stories! I'm going to papa!" she softly opened the door, went on tip-toe past Lady Jane's door; then after the first flight of stairs, rushed like the wind, unseen by any one, got the street door open, pulled it by its outside handle, and heard it shut!

It was done now! She was on the wide world, in the street! She could not have got in again without knocking, ringing, and making her attempt known; and she was far more terrified at the thought of Lady Barbara's stern face and horror at her proceedings, than even at the long journey alone.

Every step was a little bit nearer Sylvia, Mary, and papa,—it made her heart bound in the midst of its frightened throbs,—every step was farther away from Aunt Barbara, and she could hardly help setting off in a run. It was a foggy day, when it was not easy to see far, but she longed to be out of Bruton Street, where she might be known; yet when beyond the quiet familiar houses, the sense of being alone, left to herself, began to get very alarming, and she could hardly control herself to walk like a rational person to the cab-stand in Davies Street.

Nobody remarked her; she was a tall girl for her age, and in her sober dark dress, with her little bag, might be taken for a tradesman's daughter going to school, even if any one had been out who had time to look at her. Trembling, she saw a cabman make a sign to her, and stood waiting for him, jumped in as he opened his door, and felt as if she had found a refuge for the time upon the dirty red plush cushions and the straw. "To the Waterloo Station," said she, with as much indifference and self-possession as she could manage. The man touched his hat, and rattled off: he perhaps wondering if this were a young runaway, and if he should get anything by telling where she was gone; she working herself into a terrible fright for fear he should be going to drive round and round London, get her into some horrible den and murder her for the sake of her money, her watch, and her clothes. Did not cabmen always do such things? She had quite decided how she would call a policeman, and either die like an Umfraville or offer a ransom of "untold gold," and had gone through all possible catastrophes long before she found herself really safe at the railway station, and the man letting her out, and looking for his money.

The knowledge that all depended on herself, and that any signs of alarm would bring on inquiry made her able to speak and act so reasonably, that she felt like one in a dream. With better fortune than she could have hoped for, a train was going to start in a quarter of an hour; and the station clerk was much too busy and too much hurried to remark how scared were her eyes, and how trembling her voice, as she asked at his pigeon-hole for "A first-class ticket to Oldburgh, if you please," offered the sovereign in payment, swept up the change, and crept out to the platform.

A carriage had "Oldburgh" marked on it; she tried to open the door, but could not reach the handle; then fancied a stout porter, who came up with his key, must be some messenger of the Lord Chancellor come to catch her, and was very much relieved when he only said, "Where for, Miss?" and on her answer, "Oldburgh," opened the door for her, and held her bag while she tripped up the steps. "Any luggage, miss?" "No, thank you." He shot one inquiring glance after her, but hastened away; and she settled herself in the very farthest corner of the carriage, and lived in an agony for the train to set off before her flight should be detected.

Once off, she did not care; she should be sure of at least seeing Sylvia, and telling her uncle her troubles. She had one great start, when the door was opened, and a gentleman peered in; but it was merely to see if there were room, for she heard him say "Only a child," and then came a lady and two gentlemen, who at least filled up the window so that nobody could see her, while they talked a great deal to some one on the platform. And then after some bell-ringing, whistling, sailing backwards and forewards, and stopping, they were fairly off,—getting away from the roofs of London,—seeing the sky clear of smoke and fog,—getting nearer home every moment; and Countess Kate relaxed her shy, frightened, drawn-up attitude, gave a long breath, felt that the deed was done, and began to dwell on the delight with which she should be greeted at home, and think how to surprise them all!

There was plenty of time for thinking and planning and dreaming, some few possible things, but a great many more most impossible ones. Perhaps the queerest notion of all was her plan for being disguised like a school-child all day, and always noticed for her distinguished appearance by ladies who came to see the school, or overheard talking French to Sylvia; and then, in the midst of her exceeding anxiety not to be detected, she could not help looking at her travelling companions, and wondering if they guessed with what a grand personage they had the honor to be travelling! Only a child, indeed! What would they think if they knew? And the little goose held her pocket-handkerchief in her hand, feeling as if it would be like a story if they happened to wonder at the coronet embroidered in the corner; and when she took out a story-book, she would have liked that the fly-leaf should just carelessly reveal the Caergwent written upon it. She did not know that selfishness had thrown out a branch of self-consequence.

However, nothing came of it; they had a great deal too much to say to each other to notice the little figure in the corner; and she had time to read a good deal, settle a great many fine speeches, get into many a fright lest there should be an accident, and finally grow very impatient, alarmed, and agitated, before the last station but one was passed, and she began to know the cut of the hedgerow trees, and the shape of the hills,—to feel as if the cattle and sheep in the fields were old friends, and to feel herself at home.

Oldburgh Station! They were stopping at last, and she was on her feet, pressing to the window between the strangers. One of the gentlemen kindly made signs to the porter to let her out, and asked if she had any baggage, or any one to meet her. She thanked him by a smile and shake of the head; she could not speak for the beating of her heart; she felt almost as much upon the world as when the door in Bruton Street had shut behind her; and besides, a terrible wild fancy had seized her,—suppose, just suppose, they were all gone away, or ill, or some one dead! Perhaps she felt it would serve her right, and that was the reason she was in such terror.

CHAPTER XII

W HEN KATE had left the train, she was still two miles from St. James's; and it was half past three o'clock, so that she began to feel that she had run away without her dinner, and that the beatings of her heart made her knees ache, so that she had no strength to walk.

She thought her best measure would be to make her way to a pastry-cook's shop that looked straight down the street to the Grammar School, and where it was rather a habit of the family to meet Charlie, when they had gone into the town on business, and wanted to walk out with him. He would be out at four o'clock, and there would not be long to wait. So, feeling shy, and even more guilty and frightened than on her first start, Kate threaded the streets she knew so well, and almost gasping with nervous alarm, popped up the steps into the shop, and began instantly eating a bun, and gazing along the street. She really could not speak till she had swallowed a few mouthfuls; and then she looked up to the woman, and took courage to ask if the boys were out of school yet.

"O no, Miss; not for a quarter of an hour yet."

"Do you know if—if Master Charles Wardour is there to-day?" added Kate, with a gulp.

"I don't Miss." And the woman looked hard at her.

"Do you know if any of them—any of them from St. James's are in to-day?"

"No, Miss; I have not seen any of them, but very likely they may be. I saw Mr. Wardour go by yesterday morning."

So far they were all well, then; and Kate made her mind easier, and went on eating like a hungry child till the great clock struck four; when she hastily paid for her cakes and tarts, put on her gloves, and stood on the step, half in and half out of the shop, staring down the street. Out came the boys in a rush, some making straight for the shop, and brushing past Kate; she, half alarmed, half affronted, descended from her post, still looking intently. Half a dozen more big fellows, eagerly talking, almost tumbled over her, and looked as if she had no business there; she seemed to be quite swept off the pavement into the street, and to be helpless in the midst of a mob, dashing around her. They might begin to tease her in a minute; and more terrified than at any moment of her journey, she was almost ready to cry, when the tones of a well-known voice came on her ear close to her,—"I say, Will, you come and see my new terrier;" and before the words were uttered, with a cry of "Charlie, Charlie!" she was clinging to a stout boy, who had been passing without looking at her.

"Let go, I say. Who are you?" was the first rough greeting.

"O Charlie, Charlie!" almost sobbing, and still grasping his arm tight.

"Oh, I say!" and he stood with open mouth staring at her.

"O Charlie! take me home!"

"Yes, yes; come along! Get off with you, fellows!" he added, turning round upon the other boys, who were beginning to stare and exclaim; "it's nothing but our Kate!"

Oh! what a thrill there was in hearing those words; and the boys, who were well-behaved and gentlemanly, were not inclined to molest her. So she hurried on, holding Charles's arm for several steps, till they were out of the hubbub, when he turned again and stared, and again exclaimed, "I say!" all that he could at present utter; and Kate looked at his ruddy face and curly head, and dusty coat and inky collar, as if she would eat him for very joy.

"I say!" and this time he did really say, "Where are the rest of them?"

"At home, are n't they?"

"What, did n't they bring you?"

"O no!"

"Come, don't make a tomfoolery of it; that's enough. I shall have all the fellows at me for your coming up in that way, you know. Why could n't you shake hands like any one else?"

"O Charlie, I could n't help it. Please let us go home!"

"Do you mean that you are n't come from there?"

"No," said Kate, half ashamed, but far more exultant, and hanging down her head; "I came from London—I came by myself. My aunt wanted me to tell a story, and—and I have run away. O Charlie! take me home!" and with a fresh access of alarm, she again threw her arms round him, as if to gain his protection from some enemy.

"Oh, I say!" again he cried, looking up the empty street and down again, partly for the enemy, partly to avoid eyes; but he only beheld three dirty children and an old woman, so he did not throw her off roughly. "Ran away!" and he gave a great whistle.

"Yes, yes. My aunt shut me up because I would not tell a story," said Kate, really believing it herself. "Oh, let us get home, Charlie, do."

"Very well, if you won't throttle a fellow; and let me get Tony in here," he added, going on a little way towards a small stable-yard.

"Oh, don't go," cried Kate, who, once more protected, could not bear to be left alone a moment; but Charlie plunged into the yard, and came back not only with the pony, but with a plaid, and presently managed to mount Kate upon the saddle, throwing the plaid round so as to hide the short garments and long scarlet stockings, that were not adapted for riding, all with a boy's rough but tender care for the propriety of his sister's appearance.

"There, that will do," said he, holding the bridle. "So you found it poor fun being my lady, and all that."

"Oh! it was awful, Charlie! You little know, in your peaceful retirement, what are the miseries of the great."

"Come, Kate, don't talk bosh out of your books. What did they do to you? They did n't strike you, did they?"

"No, no; nonsense," said Kate, rather affronted; "but they wanted to make me forget all that I cared for, and they really did shut me up because I said I would not write a falsehood to please them! They did, Charlie!" and her eyes shone.

"Well, I always knew they must be a couple of horrid old owls," began Charlie.

"Oh! I did n't mean Aunt Jane," said Kate, feeling a little compunction. "Ah!" with a start and scream, "who is coming?" as she heard steps behind them.

"You little donkey, you'll be off. Who should it be but Armyn?"

For Armyn generally overtook his brother on a Saturday, and walked home with him for the Sunday.

Charles hailed him with a loud "Hollo, Armyn! What d'ye think I've got here?"

"Kate! Why, how d'ye do? Why, they never told me you were coming to see us."

"They did n't know," whispered Kate.

"She's run away, like a jolly brick!" said Charlie, patting the pony vehemently as he made this most inappropriate comparison.

"Run away! You don't mean it!" cried Armyn, standing still and aghast, so much shocked that her elevation turned into shame, and Charles answered for her.

"Yes, to be sure she did, when they locked her up, because she wouldn't tell lies to please them. How did you get out, Kittens? What jolly good fun it must have been!"

"Is this so, Kate?" said Armyn, laying his hand on the bridle; and his displeasure roused her spirit of self-defence, and likewise a sense of ill-usage.

"To be sure it is," she said, raising her head indignantly. "I would not be made to tell fashionable falsehoods: and so—and so I came home, for papa to protect me;" and if she had not had to take care to steady herself on her saddle, she would have burst out sobbing with vexation at Armyn's manner.

"And no one knew you were coming?" said he.

"No, of course not; I slipped out while they were all in Aunt Jane's room, and they were sure not to find me gone till dinner-time; and if they are very cross, not then."

"You go on, Charlie," said Armyn, restoring the bridle to his brother; "I'll overtake you by the time you get home."

"What are you going to do?" cried boy and girl with one voice.

"Well, I suppose it is fair to tell you," said Armyn. "I must go and telegraph what is become of you."

There was a shriek at this. They would come after her and take her away, when she only wanted to be hid and kept safe; it was a cruel shame, and Charles was ready to fly at his brother and pommel him; indeed, Armyn had to hold him by one shoulder, and say in the voice that meant that he would be minded, "Steady, boy!—I'm very sorry, my little Katie; it's a melancholy matter, but you must have left those poor ladies in a dreadful state of alarm about you, and they ought not to be kept in it!"

"O! but Armyn, Armyn, do only get home, and see what papa says."

"I am certain what he will say, and it would only be the trouble of sending some one in, and keeping the poor women in a fright all the longer. Besides, depend on it, the way to have them sending down after you would be to say nothing. Now, if they hear you are safe, you are pretty secure of spending to-morrow at least with us. Let me go, Kate; it must be done. I cannot help it."

Even while he spoke, the kind way of crossing her will was so like home, that it gave a sort of happiness, and she felt she could not resist; so she gave a sigh, and he turned back.

How much of the joy and hope of her journey had he carried away with him! His manner of treating her exploit made her even doubt how his father might receive it; and yet the sight of old scenes, and the presence of Charlie, was such exceeding delight, that it seemed to kill off all unpleasant fears or anticipations; and all the way home it was one happy chatter of inquiries for every one, of bits of home news, and exclamations at the sight of some well-known tree, or the outline of a house remembered for some adventure; the darker the twilight, the happier her tongue. The dull suburb, all little pert square red brick houses, with slated roofs and fine names, was dear to Kate; every little shop window with the light streaming out, was like a friend, and she anxiously gazed into the rough parties out for their Saturday purchases, intending to nod to any one she might know, but it was too dark for recognitions; and when at length they passed the dark outline of the church, she was silent, her heart again bouncing as if it would beat away her breath and senses. The windows were dark; it was a sign that evening service was just over. The children turned in at the gate, just as Armyn overtook them. He lifted Kate off her pony. She could not have stood, but she could run, and she flew to the drawing-room. No one was there; perhaps she was glad. She knew the cousins would be dressing for tea, and in another moment she had torn open Sylvia's door.

Sylvia, who was brushing her hair, turned round. She stared as if she had seen a ghost. Then the two children held out their arms, and rushed together with a wild scream that echoed through the house, and brought Mary flying out of her room to see who was hurt! and to find rolling on her sister's bed, a thing that seemed to have two bodies and two faces glued together, its arms and hands wound round and round.

"Sylvia! What is it? Who is it? What is she doing to you?" began Mary; but before the words were out of her mouth, the thing had flown at her neck, and pulled her down too; and the grasp and the clinging and the kisses told her long before she had room or eyes or voice to know the creature by. A sort of sobbing out of each name between them was all that was heard at first.

At last, just as Mary was beginning to say, "My own, own Katie; how did you come,—" Mr. Wardour's voice on the stairs called "Mary!"

"Have you seen him, my dear?"

"No;" but Kate was afraid, now she had heard his voice, for it was grave.

"Mary!" And Mary went. Kate sat up, holding Sylvia's hand.

They heard him ask, "Is Kate there?"

"Yes." And then there were lower voices that Kate could not hear, and which therefore alarmed her; and Sylvia, puzzled and frightened, sat holding her hand, listening silently.

Presently Mr. Wardour came in; and his look was graver than his tone, but it was so pitying, that in a moment Kate flew to his breast, and as he held her in his arms she cried, "O papa! papa! I have found you again! you will not turn me away."

"I must do whatever may be right, my dear child," said Mr. Wardour, holding her close, so that she felt his deep love, though it was not an undoubting welcome. "I will hear all about it when you have rested, and then I may know what is best to be done."

"Oh! keep me, keep me, papa."

"You will be here to-morrow at least," he said, disengaging himself from her. "This is a terrible proceeding of yours, Kate, but it is no time for talking of it; and as your aunts know where you are, nothing more can be done at present; so we will wait to understand it till you are rested and composed."

He went away; and Kate remained sobered and confused, and Mary stood looking at her, sad and perplexed.

"O Kate! Kate!" she said, "what have you been doing?"

"What is the matter? Are not you glad?" cried Sylvia; and the squeeze of her hand restored Kate's spirit so much, that she broke forth with her story, told in her own way, of persecution and escape, as she had wrought herself up to believe in it; and Sylvia clung to her, with flushed cheeks and ardent eyes, resenting every injury that her darling detailed, triumphing in her resistance, and undoubting that here she would be received and sheltered from all; while Mary, distressed and grieved, and cautioned by her father to take care not to show sympathy that might be mischievous, was carried along in spite of herself to admire and pity her child, and burn with indignation at such ill treatment, almost in despair at the idea that the child must be sent back again, yet still not discarding that trust common to all Mr. Wardour's children, that "Papa would do *anything* to hinder a temptation."

And so, with eager words and tender hands, Kate was made ready for the evening meal, and went down, clinging on one side to Mary, on the other to Sylvia; a matter of no small difficulty on the narrow staircase, and almost leading to a general avalanche of young ladies, all upon the head of little Lily, who was running up to greet and be greeted, and was almost devoured by Kate when at length they did get safe down stairs.

It was a quiet, grave meal: Mr. Wardour looked so sad and serious, that all felt that it would not do to indulge in joyous chatter, and the little girls especially were awed; though through all there was a tender kindness in his voice and look, whenever he did but offer a slice of bread to his little guest, such as made her feel what was home and what was love,—"like a shower of rain after a parched desert," as she said to herself; and she squeezed Sylvia's hand under the table whenever she could.

Mr. Wardour spoke to her very little. He said he had seen Colonel Umfraville's name in the Gazette, and asked about his coming home; and when she had answered that the time and speed of the journey was to depend on Giles's health, he turned from her to Armyn, and began talking to him about some public matters that seemed very dull to Kate; and one little foolish voice within her said, "He is not like Mrs. George Wardour, he forgets what I am;" but there was a wiser, more loving, voice to answer, "Dear papa, he thinks of me as myself; he is no respecter of persons. Oh, I hope he is not angry with me!"

When tea was over, Mr. Wardour stood up, and said, "I shall wish you children good-night now; I have to read with John Bailey for his Confirmation, and to prepare for to-morrow; and you, Kate, must go to bed early. Mary, she had better sleep with you."

This was rather a blank, for sleeping with Sylvia again had been Kate's dream of felicity; yet this was almost lost in the sweetness of once more coming in turn for the precious kiss and good-night, in the midst of which she faltered, "O papa, don't be angry with me!"

"I am not angry, Katie," he said, gently; "I am very sorry. You have done a thing that nothing can justify, and that may do you much future harm; and I cannot receive you as if you had come properly. I do not know what excuse there was for you, and I cannot attend to you to-night; indeed, I do not think you could tell me rightly; but another time we will talk it all over, and I will try to help you. Now good-night, my dear child."

Those words of his, "I will try to help you," were to Kate like a promise of certain rescue from all her troubles; and, elastic ball that her nature was, no sooner was his anxious face out of sight, and she secure that he was not angry, than up bounded her spirits again. She began wondering why papa thought she could not tell him properly, and forthwith began to give what she intended for a full and particular history of all that she had gone through.

It was a happy party round the fire; Kate and Sylvia both together in the large arm-chair, and Lily upon one of its arms; Charles in various odd attitudes before the fire; Armyn at the table with his book, half reading, half listening; Mary with her work; and Kate pouring out her story, making herself her own heroine, and describing her adventures, her way of life, and all her varieties of miseries, in the most glowing colors. How she did rattle on! It would be a great deal too much to tell.

Sylvia and Charlie took it all in, pitied, wondered, and were indignant, with all their hearts; indeed, Charlie was once heard to wish he could only get that horrid old witch near the horsepond; and when Kate talked of her Diana face, he declared that he should get the old brute of a cast into the field, and set all the boys to stone her!

Little Lily listened, not sure whether it was not all what she called "A made-up story only for prettiness;" and Mary, sitting over her work, was puzzled, and saw that her father was right in saying that Kate could not at present give an accurate account of herself. Mary knew her truthfulness, and that she would not have said what she knew to be invention; but those black eyes, glowing like little hot coals, and those burning cheeks, as well as the loud squeaky key of the voice, all showed that she had worked herself up into a state of excitement, such as not to know what was invented by an exaggerating memory. Besides, it could not be all true; it did not agree; the ill-treatment was not consistent with the grandeur. For Kate had taken to talking very big, as if she was an immensely important personage, receiving much respect wherever she went; and though Armyn once or twice tried putting in a sober matter-of-fact question for the fun of disconcerting her, she was too excited to care or understand what he said.

O no! she never was allowed to do anything for herself. That was quite a rule, and it was very tiresome.

"Like the King of Spain, you can't move your chair away from the fire without the proper attendant."

"I never do put on coals or wood there."

"There may be several reasons for that," said Armyn, recollecting how nearly Kate had once burnt the house down.

"Oh, I assure you it would not do for me," said Kate. "If it were not so inconvenient in that little house, I should have my own man-servant to attend to my fire, and walk out behind me. Indeed, now Perkins always does walk behind me, and it is such a bore."

And what was the consequence of all this wild chatter? When Mary had seen the hot-faced eager child into bed, she came down to her brother in the drawing-room with her eyes brimful of tears, saying, "Poor, dear child! I am afraid she is very much spoilt!"

"Don't make up your mind to-night," said Armyn, "she is slightly insane as yet! Never mind, Mary; her heart is in the right place, if her head is turned a little."

"It is very much turned indeed," said Mary. "How wise it was of papa not to let Sylvia sleep with her! What will he do with her? O dear!"

CHAPTER XIII

T HE SUNDAY at Oldburgh was not spent as Kate would have had it. It dawned upon her in the midst of horrid dreams, ending by wakening to an overpowering sick headache, the consequence of the agitations and alarms of the previous day, and the long fast, appeased by the contents of the pastry-cook's shop, with the journey and the excitement of the meeting,—altogether quite sufficient to produce such a miserable feeling of indisposition, that if Kate could have thought at all of anything but present wretchedness, she would have feared that she was really carrying out the likeness to Cardinal Wolsey by laying her bones among them.

That it was not quite so bad as that, might be inferred from her having no doctor but Mary Wardour, who attended to her most assiduously from her first moans at four o'clock in the morning, till her dropping off to sleep about noon; when the valiant

Mary, in the absence of every one at church, took upon herself to pen a note, to catch the early Sunday post, on her own responsibility, to Lady Barbara Umfraville, to say that her little cousin was so unwell that it would be impossible to carry out the promise of bringing her home on Monday, which Mr. Wardour had written on Saturday night.

Sleep considerably repaired her little ladyship, and when she had awakened, and supped up a bowl of beef tea, toast and all, with considerable appetite, she was so much herself again that there was no reason that any one should be kept at home to attend to her. Mary's absence was extremely inconvenient, as she was organist and leader of the choir.

"So, Katie dear," she said, when she saw her patient on her feet again, making friends with the last new kitten of the old cat, "you will not mind being left alone, will you? It is only for the Litany and catechizing, you know."

Kate looked blank, and longed to ask that Sylvia might stay with her, but did not venture; knowing that she was not ill enough for it to be a necessity, and that no one was ever kept from church, except for some real and sufficient cause.

But silly thoughts passed through the little head in the hour of solitude. In the first place, she was affronted. They made very little of her, considering who she was, and how she had come to see them at all risks, and how ill she had been! They would hardly have treated a little village child so negligently as their visitor, the Countess,—

Then her heart smote her. She remembered Mary's tender and assiduous nursing all the morning, and how she had already stayed from service and Sunday school; and she recollected her honor for her friends for not valuing her for her rank; and in that mood she looked out the psalms and lessons, which she had not been able to read in the morning, and when she had finished them, began to examine the bookcase in search of a new, or else a very dear old, Sunday book.

But then something went "crack,"—or else it was Kate's fancy,—for she started as if it had been a cannon ball; and though she sat with her book in her lap by the fire in Mary's room, all the dear old furniture and pictures round her, her head was weaving an unheard-of imagination, about robbers coming in rifling everything,—coming up the stairs, seizing her for the sake of her watch! What an article there would be in the paper,—"Melancholy disappearance of the youthful Countess of Caergwent." Then Aunt Barbara would be sorry she had treated her so cruelly; then Mary would know she ought not to have abandoned the child who had thrown herself on her protection.

That was the way Lady Caergwent spent her hour. She had been kidnapped and murdered a good many times, before there was a buzz in the street, her senses came back, and she sprang out on the stairs to meet her cousins, calling herself quite well again. And then they had a very pleasant peaceful time; she was one of them again, when, as of old, Mr. Wardour came into the drawing-room, and she stood up with Charles, Sylvia, and little Lily, who was now old enough for the Catechism, and then the Collect, and a hymn. Yes, she had Collect and hymn ready too, and some of the Gospel; Aunt Barbara always heard her say them on Sunday, besides some very difficult questions, not at all like what Mr. Wardour asked out of his own head.

Kate was a little afraid he would make his teaching turn on submitting to rulers; it was an Epistle that would have given him a good opportunity. If he made his teaching personal, something within her wondered if she could bear it, and was ready to turn angry and defiant. But no such thing; what he talked to them about was the gentle

Presence that hushed the waves and winds in outward nature, and calmed the wild spiritual torments of the possessed; and how all fears and terrors, all foolish fancies and passionate tempers, will be softened into peace, when the thought of Him rises in the heart.

Kate wondered if she should be able to think of that next time.

But at present all was like a precious dream, to be enjoyed as slowly as the moments could be persuaded to pass. Out came the dear old Bible history, with pictures of everything,—pictures that they had looked at every Sunday since they could walk, and could have described with their eyes shut; and now Kate was to feast her eyes once again upon them, and hear how many little Lily knew; and a pretty sight it was, that tiny child, with her fat hands clasped behind her so as not to be tempted to put a finger on the print, going so happily and thoroughly through all the creatures that came to Adam to be named, and showing the whole procession into the Ark, and, her favorite of all, the Angels coming down to Jacob.

Then came tea; and then Kate was pronounced, to her great delight, well enough for evening service. The evening service she always thought a treat, with the lighted church, and the choicest singing,—the only singing that had ever taken hold of Kate's ear, and that seemed to come home to her. At least to-night it came home as it had never done before; it seemed to touch some tender spot in her heart, and when she thought how dear it was, and how little she had cared about it, and how glad she had been to go away, she found the candles dancing in a green mist, and great drops came down upon the Prayer Book in her hand.

Then it could not be true that she had no feeling. She was crying, the first time she had ever known herself cry except for pain or at reproof, and she was really so far pleased that she made no attempt to stop the great tears that came trickling down at each familiar note, at each thought how long it had been since she had heard them. She cried all church time; for whenever she tried to attend to the prayers, the very sound of the voice she loved so well set her off again; and Sylvia, tenderly laying a hand on her by way of sympathy, made her weep the more, though still so softly and gently that it was like a strange sort of happiness,—almost better than joy and merriment. And then the sermon,—upon the text, "Peace, be still,"—was on the same thought on which her uncle had talked to the children; not that she followed it much; the very words, "peace," and "be still," seemed to be enough to touch, soften, and dissolve her into those sweet comfortable tears.

Perhaps they partly came from the weakening of the morning's indisposition; at any rate, when she moved, after the Blessing, holding the pitying Sylvia's hand, she found that she was very much tired, her eyelids were swollen and aching, and in fact she was fit for nothing but bed, where Mary and Sylvia laid her; and she slept, and slept in dreamless soundness, till she was waked by Mary's getting up in the morning, and found herself perfectly well.

"And now, Sylvia," she said, as they went down stairs hand-in-hand, "let us put it all out of our heads, and try and think all day that it is just one of our old times, and that I am your old Kate. Let me do my lessons and go into school, and have some fun, and quite forget all that is horrid."

But there was something to come before this happy return to old times. As soon as breakfast was over, Mr. Wardour said, "Now, Kate I want you." And then she knew what was coming; and somehow, she did not feel exactly the same about her exploit and its causes by broad daylight, now that she was cool. Perhaps she would have been glad to hang back; yet on the whole, she had a great deal to say to "papa," and it was a relief, though rather terrific, to find herself alone with him in the study.

"Now, Kate," said he again, with his arm round her, as she stood by him, "will you tell me what led you to this very sad and strange proceeding?"

Kate hung her head, and ran her fingers along the mouldings of his chair.

"Why was it, my dear!" asked Mr. Wardour.

"It was,—" and she grew bolder at the sound of her own voice, and more confident in the goodness of her cause, "it was because Aunt Barbara said I must write what was not true, and,—and I'll never tell a falsehood,—never, for no one!" and her eyes flashed.

"Gently, Kate," he said, laying his hand upon her; "I don't want to know what you never *will* do, only what you have done. What was this falsehood?"

"Why, papa, the other Sylvia—Sylvia Joanna, you know—has her birthday to-day, and we settled at Bourne Mouth that I should spend the day with her; and on Saturday, when Aunt Barbara heard of it, she said she did not want me to be intimate there, and that I must not go, and told me to write a note to say she had made a previous engagement for me."

"And do you know that she had not done so?"

"O papa! she could not; for when I said I would not write a lie, she never said it was true."

"Was that what you said to your aunt?"

"Yes"—and Kate hung her head—"I was in a passion."

"Then, Kate, I do not wonder that Lady Barbara insisted on obedience, instead of condescending to argue with a child who could be so insolent."

"But, papa," said Kate, abashed for a moment, then getting eager, "she does tell fashionable falsehoods; she says she is not at home when she is, and—"

"Stay, Kate; it is not for you to judge of grown people's doings. Neither I nor Mary would like to use that form of denying ourselves; but it is usually understood to mean only not ready to receive visitors. In the same way, this previous engagement was evidently meant to make the refusal less discourteous, and you were not even certain it did not exist."

"My Italian mistress did want to come on Monday," faltered Kate, "but it was not 'previous.' "

"Then, Kate, who was it that went beside the mark in letting us believe that Lady Barbara locked you up to make you tell falsehoods?"

"Indeed, papa, I did not say *locked*,—Charlie and Sylvia said that."

"But did you correct them?"

"O papa, I did not mean it! But I am naughty now! I always am naughty, so much worse than I used to be at home. Indeed I am, and I never do get into a good vein now. O papa, papa, can't you get me out of it all? If you could only take me home again! I don't think my aunts want to keep me,—they say I am so bad and horrid, and that I make Aunt Jane ill. Oh, take me back, papa!"

He did take her on his knee, and held her close to him. "I wish I could, my dear," he said; "I should like to have you again! but it cannot be. It is a different state of life that has been appointed for you, and you would not be allowed to make your home with me, with no older person than Mary to manage for you. If your aunt had not been taken from us, then;"—and Kate ventured to put her arm round his neck,—"then this would have been your natural home; but as things are with us, I could not make my house such as would suit the requirements of those who arrange for you. And, my poor child, I fear we let the very faults spring up that are your sorrow now."

"O no, no, papa, you helped me! Aunt Barbara only makes me—oh! may I say—hate her? for indeed there is no helping it? I can't be good there."

"What is it? what do you mean, my dear? What is your difficulty? and I will try to help you."

Poor Kate found it not at all easy to explain when she came to particulars. "Always cross," was the clearest idea in her mind; "never pleased with her, never liking anything she did,—not punishing,—but much worse." She had not made out her case, she knew; but she could only murmur again, "It all went wrong, and she was very unhappy."

Mr. Wardour sighed from the bottom of his heart; he was very sorrowful too for the child that was as his own. And then he went back and thought of his early college friend, and of his own wife who had so fondled the little orphan,—all that was left of her sister. It was grievous to him to put that child away from him when she came clinging to him and saying she was unhappy, and led into faults.

"It will be better when your uncle comes home," he began.

"O no, papa, indeed it will not. Uncle Giles is more stern than Aunt Barbara. Aunt Jane says it used to make her quite unhappy to see how sharp he was with poor Giles and Frank."

"I never saw him in his own family," said Mr. Wardour, thoughtfully; "but this I know, Kate, that your father looked up to him, young as he then was, more than to any one; that he was the only person among them all who ever concerned himself about you or your mother; and that on the two occasions when I saw him, I thought him very like your father."

"I had rather he was like you, papa," sighed Kate. "Oh, if I was but your child!" she added, led on by a little involuntary pressure of his encircling arm.

"Don't let us talk of what is not, but of what is," said Mr. Wardour; "let us try to look on things in their right light. It has been the will of Heaven to call you, my little girl, to a station where you will, if you live, have many people's welfare depending on you, and your example will be of weight with many. You must go through training for it, and strict training may be the best for you. Indeed, it must be the best, or it would not have been permitted to befall you."

"But it does not make me good, it makes me naughty."

"No, Kate; nothing, nobody, can make you naughty; nothing is strong enough to do that."

Kate knew what he meant, and hung her head.

"My dear, I do believe that you feel forlorn and dreary, and miss the affection you have had among us; but have you ever thought of the Friend who is closest of all to us, and who is especially kind to a fatherless child?"

"I can't,—I can't feel it,—papa, I can't. And then why was it made so that I must go away from you and all?"

"You will see some day, though you cannot see now, my dear. If you use it rightly, you will feel the benefit. Meantime you must take it on trust, just as you do my love for you, though I am going to carry you back."

"Yes; but I can feel you loving me."

"My dear child, it only depends on yourself to feel your Heavenly Father loving you. If you will set yourself to pray with your heart, and think of his goodness to you, and ask him for help and solace in all your present vexations and difficulties, never mind how small, you *will* become conscious of his tender pity and love to you."

"Ah! but I am not good!"

"But he can make you so, Kate. You have been wearied by religious teaching hitherto, have you not?"

"Except when it was pretty and like poetry," whispered Kate.

"Put your heart to your prayers now, Kate. Look in the Psalms for verses to suit your loneliness; recollect that you meet us in spirit when you use the same prayers, read the same Lessons, and think of each other. Or, better still, carry your troubles to Him, and when you *have* felt His help, you will know what that is far better than I can tell you."

Kate only answered with a long breath; not feeling as if she could understand such comfort, but with a resolve to try.

"And now," said Mr. Wardour, "I must take you home to-morrow, and I will speak for you to Lady Barbara, and try to obtain her forgiveness; but, Kate, I do not think you quite understand what a shocking proceeding this was of yours."

"I know it was wrong to fancy *that*, and say *that* about Aunt Barbara. I'll tell her so," said Kate, with a trembling voice.

"Yes, that will be right; but it was this,—this expedition that I meant."

"It was coming to you, papa!"

"Yes, Kate; but did you think what an outrageous act it was? There is something particularly grievous in a little girl, or a woman of any age, casting off restraint, and setting out in the world unprotected and contrary to authority. Do you know, it frightened me so much that till I˙saw more of you, I did not like you to be left alone with Sylvia."

The deep red color flushed all over Kate's face and neck in her angry shame and confusion, burning darker and more crimson, so that Mr. Wardour was very sorry for her, and added, "I am obliged to say this because you ought to know that it is both very wrong in itself, and will be regarded by other people as more terrible than what you are repenting of more. So, if you do find yourself distrusted and in disgrace, you must not think it unjust and cruel, but try to submit patiently, and learn not to be reckless and imprudent. My poor child, I wish you could have so come to us that we might have been happier together. Perhaps you will some day; and in the mean time, if you have any troubles, or want to know anything, you may always write to me."

"Writing is not speaking," said Kate, ruefully.

"No; but it comes nearer to it as people get older. Now go, my dear; I am busy, and you had better make the most of your time with your cousins."

Kate's heart was unburthened now; and though there was much alarm, pain, and grief, in anticipation, yet she felt more comfortable in herself than she had done for months. "Papa" had never been so tender with her, and she knew that he had forgiven her. She stepped back to the drawing-room, very gentle and subdued, and tried to carry out her plans of living one of her old days, by beginning with sharing the lessons as usual, and then going out with her cousins to visit the school, and see some of the parishioners. It was very nice and pleasant; she was as quiet and loving as possible, and threw herself into all the dear old home matters. It was as if for a little while Katharine was driven out of Katharine, and a very sweet little maiden left instead,—thinking about other things and people instead of herself, and full of affection and warmth. The improvement that the half year's discipline had made in her bearing and manners was visible now; her uncouth abrupt ways were softened, though still she felt that the naturally gentle and graceful Sylvia would have made a better countess than she did.

They spent the evening in little tastes of all their favorite drawing-room games, just for the sake of having tried them once more; and papa himself came in and took a share,—a very rare treat;—and he always thought of such admirable things in "Twenty questions," and made "What's my thought like?" more full of fun than any one.

It was a very happy evening,—one of the happiest that Kate had ever passed. She knew *how* to enjoy her friends now, and how precious they were to her; and she was just so much tamed by the morning's conversation, and by the dread of the future, as not to be betrayed into dangerously high spirits. That loving, pitying way of Mary's, and her own Sylvia's exceeding pleasure in having her, were delightful; and all through she felt the difference between the real genuine love that she could rest on, and the mere habit of fondling of the other Sylvia.

"O Sylvia," she said as they walked up-stairs hand-in-hand, pausing on every step to make it longer, "how could I be so glad to go away before?"

"We did n't know," said Sylvia.

"No," as they crept up another step; "Sylvia, will you always think of me just here on this step as you go up to bed?"

"Yes," said Sylvia, "that I will. And, Katie, would it be wrong just to whisper a little prayer then that you might be good and happy?"

"It could n't be wrong, Sylvia, only could n't you just ask, too, for me to come home?"

"I don't know," said Sylvia, thoughtfully, pausing a long time on the step. "You see we know it is sure to be God's will that you should be good and happy; but if it was not for you to come home, if we asked it too much, it might come about in some terrible way."

"I did n't think of that," said Kate. And the two little girls parted gravely and peacefully; Kate somehow feeling, as if though grievous things were before her, that the good little kind Sylvia's hearty prayers must obtain some good for her.

There is no use in telling how sad the parting was when Mr. Wardour and the little countess set out for London again. Mary had begged hard to go too, thinking that she could plead for Kate better than any one else; but Mr. Wardour thought Lady Barbara more likely to be angered than softened by their clinging to their former charge; and besides, it was too great an expense.

He had no doubt of Lady Barbara's displeasure from the tone of the note that morning received, coldly thanking him and Miss Wardour for their intelligence, and his promise to restore Lady Caergwent on Tuesday. She was sorry to trouble him to bring the child back; she would have come herself, but that her sister was exceedingly unwell from the alarm coming at a time of great family affliction. If Lady Caergwent were not able to return on Tuesday, she would send down her own maid to bring her home on Wednesday. The letter was civility itself; but it was plain that Lady Barbara thought

Kate's illness no better than the "previous engagement," in the note that never was written.

What was the family affliction? Kate could not guess; but was inclined to imagine privately that Aunt Barbara was magnifying Uncle Giles's return without being a General, into a family affliction, on purpose to aggravate her offence. However, in the train, Mr. Wardour, who had been looking at the supplement of the Times, lent to him by a fellow traveller, touched her and made her read—

"On the 11th, at Alexandria, in his 23d year, Lieutenant Giles de la Poer Umfraville, of the 109th regiment; eldest and last survivor, of the children of the Honorable Giles Umfraville, late Lieutenant-Colonel of the 109th regiment."

Kate knew she ought to be very sorry, and greatly pity the bereaved father and mother; but, somehow, she could not help dwelling most upon the certainty that every one would be much more hard upon her, and cast up this trouble to her, as if she had known of it, and run away on purpose to make it worse. It must have been this that they were talking about in Aunt Jane's room, and this must have made them so slow to detect her flight.

In due time the train arrived, a cab was taken, and Kate, beginning to tremble with fright, sat by Mr. Wardour, and held his coat, as if clinging to him as long as she could was a comfort. Sometimes she wished the cab would go faster, so that it might be over; sometimes,—especially when the streets became only too well known to her,—she wished they would stretch out and out forever, that she might still be sitting by papa, holding his coat. It seemed as if that would be happiness enough for life!

Here was Bruton Street; here the door that on Saturday had shut behind her! It was only too soon open, and Kate kept her eyes on the ground, ashamed that even the butler should see her. She hung back, waiting till Mr. Wardour had paid the cabman; but there was no spinning it out, she had to walk up-stairs, her only comfort being that her hand was in his.

No one was in the drawing-room; but before long Lady Barbara came in. Kate durst not look up at her, but was sure, from the tone of her voice, that she must have her very sternest face; and there was something to make one shiver in the rustle of her silk dress as she courtesied to Mr. Wardour.

"I have brought home my little niece," he said, drawing Kate forward; "and I think I may truly say, that she is very sorry for what has passed."

There was a pause; Kate knew the terrible black eyes were upon her, but she felt besides, the longing to speak out the truth, and a sense that with papa by her side, she had courage to do so.

"I am sorry, Aunt Barbara," she said; "I was very self-willed, I ought not to have fancied things, nor said you used me ill, and wanted me to tell stories."

Kate's heart was lighter; though it beat so terribly as she said those words. She knew that they pleased *one* of the two who were present, and she knew they were right.

"It is well you should be so far sensible of your misconduct," said Lady Barbara; but her voice was as dry and hard as ever; and Mr. Wardour added, "She is sincerely sorry; it is from her voluntary confession that I know how much trouble she has given you; and I think, if you will kindly forgive her, that you will find her less self-willed in future."

And he shoved Kate a little forward, squeezing her hand, and trying to withdraw his own. She perceived that he meant that she ought to ask pardon; and though it went against her more than her first speech had done, she contrived to say, "I do beg pardon, Aunt Barbara; I will try to do better."

"My pardon is one thing, Katharine," said Lady Barbara. "If your sorrow is real, of course I forgive you," and she took Kate's right hand,—the left was still holding by the fingers' ends to Mr. Wardour. "But the consequences of such behavior are another consideration. My personal pardon cannot, and ought not, to avert them, as I am sure you must perceive, Mr. Wardour," she added, as the frightened child retreated upon him. Those consequences of Aunt Barbara's were fearful things! Mr. Wardour said something, to which Kate scarcely attended in her alarm, and her aunt went on—

"For Lady Caergwent's own sake, I shall endeavor to keep this most unfortunate step as much a secret as possible. I believe that scarcely any one beyond this house is aware of it; and I hope that your family will perceive the necessity of being equally cautious."

Mr. Wardour bowed, and assented.

"But," added Lady Barbara, "it has made it quite impossible for my sister and myself to continue to take the charge of her. My sister's health has suffered from the constant noise and restlessness of a child in the house: the anxiety and responsibility are far too much for her; and, in addition to this, she has had such severe nervous seizures from the alarm of my niece's elopement, that nothing would induce me to subject her to a recurrence of such agitation. We must receive the child for the present, of course; but as soon as my brother returns, and can attend to business, the matter must be referred to the Lord Chancellor, and an establishment formed, with a lady at the head, who may have authority and experience to deal with such an ungovernable nature."

"Perhaps," said Mr. Wardour, "under these circumstances, it might be convenient for me to take her home again for the present."

Kate quivered with hope; but that was far too good to be true; Lady Barbara gave a horrid little cough, and there was a sound almost of offence in her,—"Thank you, you are very kind, but that would be quite out of the question. I am at present responsible for my niece."

"I thought, perhaps," said Mr. Wardour, as in excuse for the offer, "that as Lady Jane is so unwell, and Colonel Umfraville in so much affliction, it might be a relief to part with her at present."

"Thank you," again said Lady Barbara, as stiffly as if her throat were lined with whalebone; "no inconvenience can interfere with my duty."

Mr. Wardour knew there was no use in saying any more, and inquired after Lady Jane. She had, it appeared, been very ill on Saturday evening, and had not since left her room. Mr. Wardour then said that Kate had not been aware, till a few hours ago, of the death of her cousin, and inquired anxiously after the father and mother; but Lady Barbara would not do more than answer direct questions, and only said that her nephew had been too much weakened to bear the journey, and had sunk suddenly at Alexandria, and that his father was, she feared, very unwell. She could not tell how soon he was likely to be in England. Then she thanked Mr. Wardour for having brought Lady Caergwent home, and offered him some luncheon; but in such a grave grand way, that it was plain that she did not want him to eat it; and, feeling that he could do no more good, he kissed poor Kate, and wished Lady Barbara good-bye.

Poor Kate stood drooping, too much constrained by dismay even to try to cling to him, or run after him to the foot of the stairs.

"Now, Katharine," said her aunt, "come up with me to your Aunt Jane's room. She has been so much distressed about you, that she will not be easy till she has seen you."

Kate followed meekly; and found Aunt Jane sitting by the fire in her own room, looking flushed, hot, and trembling. She held out her arms, and Kate ran into them, but neither of them dared to speak, and Lady Barbara stood up, saying, "She says she is very sorry, and thus we may forgive her; as I know you do all the suffering you have undergone on her account."

Lady Jane held the child tighter, and Kate returned her kisses with all her might; but the other aunt said, "That will do. She must not be too much for you again." And they let go as if a cold wind had blown between them.

"Did Mr. Wardour bring her home?" asked Lady Jane.

"Yes; and was kind enough to propose taking her back again," was the answer, with a sneer, that made Kate feel desperately angry, though she did not understand it.

In truth, Lady Barbara was greatly displeased with the Wardours. She had always been led to think her niece's faults the effect of their management; and she now imagined that there had been some encouragement of the child's discontent to make her run away: and that if they had been sufficiently shocked and concerned, the truant would have been brought home much sooner. It all came of her having allowed her niece to associate with those children at Bourne Mouth. She would be more careful for the future.

Careful, indeed, she was! She had come to think of her niece as a sort of a small wild beast that must never be let out of sight of some trustworthy person, lest she should fly away again.

A daily governess, an elderly person, very grave and silent, came in directly after breakfast, walked with the countess, and heard the lessons; and after her departure, Kate, was always to be in the room with her aunts, and never was allowed to sit in the schoolroom, and amuse herself alone, but her tea was brought into the dining-room while her aunts were at dinner; and morning, noon and night, she knew that she was being watched.

It was very bitter to her. It seemed to take all the spirit away from her, as if she did not care for books, lessons or anything else. Sometimes her heart burnt with hot indignation, and she would squeeze her hands together, or wring round her handkerchief in a sort of misery; but it never got beyond that; she never broke out, for she was depressed by what was still worse, the sense of shame. Lady Barbara had not said many words, but had made her feel, in spite of having forgiven her, that she had done a thing that would be a disgrace to her forever; a thing that would make people think twice before they allowed their children to associate with her; and that put her below the level of other girls. The very pains that Lady Barbara took to hush it up, her fears lest it should come to the ears of the De la Poers, her hopes that it *might* not be necessary to reveal it to her brother, assisted to weigh down Kate with a sense of the heinousness of what she had done, and sunk her so that she had no inclination to complain of the watchfulness around her. And Aunt Jane's sorrowful kindness went to her heart.

"How *could* you do it, my dear?" she said, in such a wondering wistful tone, when Kate was alone with her.

Kate hung her head. She could not think now.

"It is so sad," added Lady Jane; "I hoped we might have gone on so nicely together. And now I hope your uncle Giles will not hear of it. He would be so shocked, and never trust you again."

"*You* will trust me, when I have been good a long time, Aunt Jane?"

"My dear, I would trust you any time, you know; but then that's no use. I can't judge; and your Aunt Barbara says, after such lawlessness, you need very experienced training to root out old associations."

Perhaps the aunts were more shocked than was quite needful, and treated Kate as if she had been older and known better what she was doing; but they were sincere in their horror at her offence, and once she even heard Lady Barbara saying to Mr. Mercer that there seemed to be a doom on the family,—in the loss of the promising young man,—and—

The words were not spoken, but Kate knew that she was this greatest of all misfortunes to the family.

Poor child! In the midst of all this, there was one comfort. She had not put aside what Mr. Wardour had told her about the Comforter she could always have. She *did* say her prayers as she had never said them before, and she looked out in the Psalms and Lessons for comforting verses. She knew she had done very wrong, and she asked with all the strength of her heart to be forgiven, and made less unhappy; and that people might be kinder to her. Sometimes she thought no help was coming, and that her prayers did no good, but she went on; and then, perhaps, she got a kind little caress from Lady Jane, or Mr. Mercer spoke good-naturedly to her, or Lady Barbara granted her some little favor, and she felt as if there was hope, and things were getting better; and she took courage all the more to pray that Uncle Giles might not be very hard upon her, nor the Lord Chancellor very cruel.

CHAPTER XIV

A FORTNIGHT had passed, and had seemed nearly as long as a year, since Kate's return from Oldburgh, when one afternoon, when she was lazily turning over the leaves of a story book that she knew so well by heart that she could go over it in the twilight, she began to gather from her aunt's words that somebody was coming.

They never told her anything direct; but by listening a little more attentively to what they were saying, she found out that a letter,—no, a telegram,—had come while she was at her lessons; that Aunt Barbara had been taking rooms at a hotel; that she was insisting that Jane should not imagine they would come to-night,—they would not come till the last train, and then neither of them would be equal—

"Poor dear Emily! But could we not just drive to the hotel and meet them? It will be so dreary for them."

"You go out at night! and for such a meeting! when you ought to be keeping yourself as quiet as possible! No, depend upon it, they will prefer getting in quietly, and resting to-night; and Giles, perhaps, will step in to breakfast in the morning."

"And then you will bring him up to me at once! I wonder if the boy is much altered!"

Throb! throb! throb! went Kate's heart! So the terrible stern uncle was in England, and this was the time for her to be given up to the Lord Chancellor. She had never loved Aunt Jane so well; she almost loved Aunt Barbara, and began to think of clinging to her with an eloquent speech, pleading to be spared from the Lord Chancellor!

To-morrow morning,—that was a respite!

There was a sound of wheels. Lady Jane started.

"They are giving a party next door," said Lady Barbara.

But the bell rang.

"Only a parcel coming home," said Lady Barbara. "Pray do not be nervous, Jane."

But the red color was higher in Barbara's own cheeks as there were steps on the stairs; and in quite a triumphant voice the butler announced, as he opened the door, "Colonel and Mrs. Umfraville!"

Kate stood up, and looked. It was Aunt Barbara's straight, handsome, terrible face, and with a great black moustache to make it worse. She saw that, and it was all she feared! She was glad the sofa was between them!

There was a lady besides, all black bonnet and cloak; and there was a confusion of sounds, a little half sobbing of Aunt Jane's; but the other sister and the brother were quite steady and grave. It was his keen dark eye, sparkling like some wild animal's in the fire-light, as Kate thought, which spied her out; and his deep grave voice said, "My little niece," as he held out his hand.

"Come and speak to your uncle, Katharine," said Lady Barbara; and not only had she to put her hand into that great firm one, but her forehead was scrubbed by his moustache. She had never been kissed by a moustache before, and she shuddered as if it had been on a panther's lip.

But then he said, "There, Emily;" and she found herself folded up in such arms as had never been round her before, with the very sweetest of kisses on her cheeks, the very kindest of eyes, full of moisture, gazing at her as if they had been hungry for her. Even when the embrace was over, the hand still held hers, and as she stood by the new aunt, a thought crossed her that had never come before, "I wonder if my mamma was like this!"

There was some explanation of how the travellers had come on, &c., and it was settled that they were to stay to dinner; after which Mrs. Umfraville went away with Lady Barbara to take off her bonnet.

Colonel Umfraville came and sat down by his sister on the sofa, and said, "Well, Jane, how have you been?"

"Oh! much as usual;" and then there was a silence, till she moved a little nearer to him, put her hand on his arm, looked up in his face with swimming eyes, and said, "O Giles! Giles!"

He took her hand, and bent over her, saying, in the same grave steady voice, "Do not grieve for us, Jane. We have a great deal to be thankful for, and we shall do very well."

It made that loving tender-hearted Aunt Jane break quite down, cling to him, and sob, "O Giles,—those dear noble boys—how little we thought,—and dear Caergwent too,—and you away from home."

She was crying quite violently, so as to be shaken by the sobs; and her brother stood over her, saying a kind word or two now and then, to try to soothe her; while Kate remained a little way off, with her black eyes wide open, thinking her uncle's face was almost displeased,—at any rate, very rigid. He looked up at Kate, and signed towards a scent-bottle on the table. Kate gave it; and then, as if the movement had filled her with a panic, she darted out of the room, and flew up to the bedrooms, crying out, "Aunt Barbara, Aunt Jane is crying so terribly!"

"She will have one of her attacks! Oh!" began Lady Barbara, catching up a bottle of sal volatile.

"Had we not better leave her and Giles to one another?" said the tones that Kate liked so much.

"Oh! my dear, you don't know what these attacks are!" and away hurried Lady Barbara.

The bonnet was off now, leaving only a little plain net cap under it, round the calm gentle face. There was a great look of sadness, and the eyelids were heavy and drooping; but there was something that put Kate in mind of a mother dove in the softness of the large tender embrace, and the full sweet caressing tone. What a pity that such an aunt must know that she was an ill-behaved child, a misfortune to her lineage! She stood leaning against the door, very awkward and conscious. Mrs. Umfraville turned round, after smoothing her hair at the glass, smiled, and said, "I thought I should find you here, my little niece. You are Kate, I think."

"I used to be, but my aunts here call me Katharine."

"Is this your little room?" said Mrs. Umfraville, as they came out. The fact was, that she thought the sisters might be happier with their brother if she delayed a little; so she came into Kate's room, and was beginning to look at her books, when Lady Barbara came hurrying up again.

"She is composed now, Emily. Oh! it is all right; I did not know where Katharine might be."

Kate's color glowed. She could not bear that this sweet Aunt Emily should guess that she was a state prisoner, kept in constant view.

Lady Jane was quiet again, and nothing more that could overthrow her spirits passed all the evening; there was only a little murmur of talk, generally going on chiefly between Lady Barbara and Mrs. Umfraville, though occasionally the others put in a word. The Colonel sat most of the time with his set serious face, and his eyes fixed as if he was not attending, though sometimes Kate found the quick keen brilliance of his look bent full upon her, so as to terrify her by its suddenness, and make her hardly know what she was saying or doing.

The worst moments were at dinner. She was, in the first place, sure that those dark questioning eyes had decided that there must be some sad cause for her not being trusted to drink her tea elsewhere; and then, in the pause after the first course, the eyes came again, and he said, and to her, "I hope your good relations, the Wardours, are well."

"Quite well,—thank you," faltered Kate.

"When did you see them last?"

"A—a fortnight ago—" began Kate.

"Mr. Wardour came up to London for a few hours," said Lady Barbara, looking at Kate as if she meant to plunge her below the floor; at least, so the child imagined.

The sense that this was not the whole truth made her especially miserable; and all the rest of the evening was one misery of embarrassment, when her limbs did not seem to be her own, but as if somebody else was sitting at her little table, walking up stairs, and doing her work. Even Mrs. Umfraville's kind ways could not restore her; she only hung her head and mumbled when she was asked to show her work, and did not so much as know what was to become of her piece of cross-stitch when it was finished.

There was some inquiry after the De la Poers, and Mrs. Umfraville asked if she had found some play-fellows among their daughters.

"Yes," faintly said Kate; and with another flush of color, thought of having been told, that if Lady de la Poer knew what she had done, she would never be allowed to play with them again, and therefore that she never durst attempt it!

"They were very nice children," said Mrs. Umfraville.

"Remarkably nice children," returned Lady Barbara, in a tone that again cut Kate to the heart.

Bedtime came; and she would have been glad of it, but that all the time she was going to sleep there was the Lord Chancellor to think of, and the uncle and aunt with the statue faces, dragging her before him.

Sunday was the next day, and the uncle and aunt were not seen till after the afternoon service, when they came to dinner, and much such an evening as the former one passed; but towards the end of it, Mrs. Umfraville said, "Now, Barbara, I have a favor to ask. Will you let this child spend the day with me to-morrow? Giles will be out, and I shall be very glad to have her for my companion."

Kate's eyes glistened, and she thought of stern Proserpine.

"My dear Emily, you do not know what you ask. She will be far too much for you."

"I'll take care of that," said Mrs. Umfraville, smiling.

"And I don't know about trusting her. I cannot go out, and Jane cannot spare Bartley so early."

"I will come and fetch her," said the Colonel.

"And bring her back too. I will send the carriage in the evening, but do not let her come without you," said Lady Barbara, earnestly.

Had they told, or would they tell after she was gone to bed? Kate thought Aunt Barbara was a woman of her word, but did not quite trust her. Consent was given; but would not that stern soldier destroy all the pleasure? And people in sorrow too! Kate thought of Mrs. Lacy, and had no very bright anticipations of her day; yet a holiday was something, and to be out of Aunt Barbara's way a great deal more.

She had not been long dressed when there was a ring at the bell, and, before she had begun to expect him, the tall man with the dark lip and gray hair stood in her schoolroom. She gave such a start, that he asked, "Did you not expect me so soon?"

"I did not think you would come till after breakfast; but—"

And with an impulse of running away from his dread presence, she darted off to put on her hat, but was arrested on the way by Lady Barbara at her bedroom door.

"Uncle Giles is come for me," she said, and would have rushed on, but her aunt detained her to say, "Recollect, Katharine, that wildness and impetuosity, at all times unbecoming, are particularly so where there is affliction. If consideration for others will not influence you, bear in mind that on the impression you make on your uncle and aunt, it depends whether I shall be obliged to tell all that I would willingly forget."

Kate's heart swelled, and without speaking, she entered her own room, thinking how hard it was to have even the pleasure of hoping for ease and enjoyment taken away.

When she came down, she found her aunt—as she believed—warning her uncle against her being left to herself; and then came, "If she should be too much for Emily, only send a note, and Bartley or I will come to fetch her home."

"She wants him to think me a little wild beast!" thought Kate; but her uncle answered, "Emily always knows how to deal with children. Good-by."

"To deal with children! What did that mean?" thought the countess, as she stepped along by the side of her uncle, not venturing to speak, and feeling almost as shy and bewildered as when she was on the world alone.

He did not speak, but when they came to a crossing of a main street, he took her by the hand; and there was something protecting and comfortable in the feel, so that she did not let go; and presently, as she walked on, she felt the fingers close on hers with such a quick tight squeeze, that she looked up in a fright, and met the dark eye turned on her quite soft and glistening. She did not guess how he was thinking of little clasping hands that had held there before; and he only said something rather hurriedly about avoiding some coals that were being taken in through a round hole in the pavement.

Soon they were at the hotel, and Mrs. Umfraville came out of her room with that greeting which Kate liked so much, helped her to take off her cloak, and smooth her hair, and then sat her down to breakfast.

It was a silent meal to Kate. Her uncle and aunt had letters to read, and things to consult about that she did not understand; but all the time there was a kind watch kept up that she had what she liked; and Aunt Emily's voice was so much like the deep notes of the wood-pigeons round Oldburgh, that she did not care how long she listened to it, even if it had been talking Hindostanee!

As soon as breakfast was over, the Colonel took up his hat, and went out; and Mrs. Umfraville said, turning to Kate, "Now, my dear, I have something for you to help me in; I want to unpack some things that I have brought home."

"Oh, I shall like that!" said Kate, feeling as if a weight was gone with the grave uncle.

Mrs. Umfraville rang, and asked to have a certain box brought in. Such a box, all smelling of choice Indian wood; the very shavings that stuffed it were delightful! And what an unpacking! It was like nothing but the Indian stall at the Baker Street Bazaar! There were two beautiful large ivory work-boxes, inlaid with stripes and circles of tiny mosaic; and there were even more delicious little boxes of soft fragrant sandal wood, and a set of chessmen in ivory. The kings were riding on elephants with canopies over their heads, and ladders to climb up by; and each elephant had a tiger in his trunk. Then the queens were not queens, but grand viziers, because the queen is nobody in the East; and each had a lesser elephant; the bishops were men riding on still smaller elephants; the castles had camels, the knights horses, and the pawns were little foot soldiers, the white ones with guns, as being European troops, the red ones with bows and arrows. Kate was perfectly delighted with these men, and looked at and admired them one by one, longing to play a game with them. Then there was one of those wonderful clusters of Chinese ivory balls, all loose, one within the other, carved in different patterns of network; and there were shells spotted and pink-mouthed, card cases, red shining boxes, queer Indian dolls; figures in all manner of costumes, in gorgeous colors, painted upon shining transparent talc or on soft rice paper. There was no describing how charming the sight was, nor how Kate dwelt upon each article; and how pleasantly her aunt explained what it was intended for, and where it came from, answering all questions in the nicest, kindest way. When all the wool and shavings had been pinched, and the curled up toes of the slippers explored, so as to make sure that no tiny shell or ivory carving lurked unseen, the room looked like a museum; and Mrs. Umfraville said, "Most of these things were meant for our home friends: there is an Indian scarf and a Cashmere shawl for your two aunts, and I believe the chessmen are for Lord de la Poer."

"O, Aunt Emily, I should so like to play one game with them before they go."

"I will have one with you, if you can be very careful of their tender points," said Mrs. Umfraville, without one of the objections that Kate had expected; "but first, I want you to help me about some of the other things. Your uncle meant one of the work-boxes for you!"

"O, Aunt Emily, how delightful! I really will work with such a dear, beautiful box," cried Kate, opening it, and again peeping into all its little holes and contrivances. "Here's the very place for a dormouse to sleep in! And who is the other for?"

"For Fanny de la Poer, who is his god-child."

"Oh, I am so glad! Fanny always has such nice pretty work about!"

"And now I want you to help me choose the other presents. There, these," pointing to a scarf and a muslin dress adorned with the wings of diamond beetles, "are for some young cousins of my own; but you will be able to choose what the other De la Poers and your cousins at Oldburgh would like best."

"My cousins at Oldburgh!" cried Kate. "May they have some of these pretty things?" and as her aunt answered, "We hope they will," Kate flew at her, and hugged her quite tight round the throat; then, when Mrs. Umfraville undid the clasp, and returned the kiss, she went like an India-rubber ball, with a backward bound, put her hands together over her head, and gasped out, "Oh, thank you, thank you."

"My dear, don't go quite mad. You will jump into that calabash, and then it won't be fit for anybody. Are you so very glad?"

"Oh! so glad! Pretty things do come so seldom to Oldburgh!"

"Well, we thought you might like to send Miss Wardour this shawl."

It was a beautiful heavy shawl of the soft wool of the Cashmere goats; really of every kind of brilliant hue, but so dextrously blended together, that the whole looked dark and sober. But Kate did not look with favor on the shawl.

"A shawl is so stupid," she said. "If you please, I had rather Mary had the workbox."

"But the workbox is for Lady Fanny."

"Oh! but I meant my own," said Kate, earnestly. "If you only knew what a pity it is to give nice things to me; they always get into such a mess. Now, Mary always has her things so nice; and she works so beautifully; she has never let Lily wear a stitch but of her setting; and she always wished for a box like this. One of her friends at school had a little one; and she used to say, when we played at roc's egg, that she wanted nothing but an ivory work-box; and she has nothing but an old blue one, with the steel turned black!"

"We must hear what your uncle says, for you know that he meant the box for you."

"It isn't that I don't care for it," said Kate, with a sudden glistening in her eyes; "it is because I do care for it so very much, that I want Mary to have it."

"I know it is, my dear;" and her aunt kissed her; "but we must think about it a little. Perhaps Mary would not think an Indian shawl quite so stupid as you do."

"Mary isn't a vain conceited girl," cried Kate, indignantly. "She always looks nice; but I heard papa say her dress did not cost much more than Sylvia's and mine, because she never tore anything, and took such care!"

"Well, we will see," said Mrs. Umfraville, perhaps not entirely convinced that the shawl would not be a greater prize to the thrifty girl than Kate perceived.

Kate meanwhile had sprung unmolested on a beautiful sandal-wood case for Sylvia, and a set of rice-paper pictures for Lily; and the appropriating other treasures to the De la Poers, packing them up, and directing them, accompanied with explanations of their habits and tastes, lasted till so late, that, after the litter was cleared away, there was only time for one game at chess with the grand pieces; and in truth the honor of using them was greater than the pleasure. They covered up the board, so that there was no seeing the squares, and it was necessary to be most inconveniently cautious in lifting them. They were made to be looked at, not played with; and yet, wonderful to relate, Kate did not do one of the delicate things a mischief.

Was it that she was really grown more handy, or was it that with this gentle aunt she was quite at her ease, yet too much subdued to be careless and rough?

The luncheon came; and after it, she drove with her aunt first to a few shops, and then to take up the Colonel, who had been with his lawyer. Kate quaked a little inwardly, lest it should be about the Lord Chancellor, and tried to frame a question on the subject to her aunt; but even the most chattering little girls know what it is to have their lips sealed by an odd sort of reserve upon the very matters that make them most uneasy; and just because her wild imagination had been thinking that perhaps this was all a plot to waylay her into the Lord Chancellor's clutches, she could not utter a word on the matter, while they drove through the quiet squares where lawyers live.

Mrs. Umfraville, however, soon put that out of her head by talking to her about the Wardours, and setting open the flood-gates of her eloquence about Sylvia. So delightful was it to have a listener, that Kate did not grow impatient, long as they waited at the lawyer's door in the dull Square, and indeed was sorry when the Colonel made his appearance. He just said to her that he hoped she was not tired of waiting, and as she replied with a frightened little "No, thank you," began telling his wife something that Kate soon perceived belonged to his own concerns, not to hers; so she left off trying to gather the meaning in the rumble of the wheels, and looked out of the window, for she could never be quite at ease when she felt that those eyes might be upon her.

On coming back to the hotel, Mrs. Umfraville found a note on the table for her: she read it, gave it to her husband, and said, "I had better go directly."

"Will it not be too much? Can you?" he said very low; and there was the same repressed twitching of the muscles of his face as Kate had seen when he was left with his sister Jane.

"O yes!" she said, fervently; "I shall like it. And it is her only chance; you see she goes to-morrow."

The carriage was ordered again, and Mrs. Umfraville explained to Kate that the note was from a poor invalid lady, whose son was in their own regiment in India, that she was longing to hear about him, and was going out of town the next day.

"And what shall I give you to amuse yourself with, my dear?" asked Mrs. Umfraville. "I am afraid we have hardly a book that will suit you."

Kate had a great mind to ask to go and sit in the carriage, rather than remain alone with the terrible black moustache, but she was afraid of the Colonel's mentioning Aunt Barbara's orders that she was not to be let out of sight. "If you please," she said, "If I might write to Sylvia."

Her aunt kindly established her at a little table, with a leathern writing-case, and her uncle mended a pen for her. Then her aunt went away, and he sat down to his own letters. Kate durst not speak to him, but she watched him under her eyelashes, and noticed how he presently laid down his pen, and gave a long heavy sad sigh, such as she had never heard when his wife was present; then sat musing, looking fixedly at the gray window; till, rousing himself with another such sigh, he seemed to force himself to go on writing, but paused again, as if he were so wearied and oppressed that he could hardly bear it.

It gave Kate a great awe of him, partly because a little girl in a book would have gone up, slid her hand into his, and kissed him; but she could nearly as soon have slid her hand into a lion's; and she was right, it would have been very obtrusive.

Some little time had passed before there was an opening of the door, and the announcement, "Lord de la Poer."

Up started Kate, but she was quite lost in the greeting of the two friends; Lord de la Poer, with his eyes full of tears, wringing his friend's hand, hardly able to speak, but just saying, "Dear Giles, I am glad to have you at home! How is she?"

"Wonderfully well," said the Colonel, with the calm voice but the twitching face. "She is gone to see Mrs. Ducie; the mother of a lad in my regiment, who was wounded at the same time as Giles, and whom she nursed with him."

"Is not it very trying?"

"Nothing that is a kindness ever is trying to Emily," he said, and his voice did tremble this time.

Kate had quietly reseated herself in her chair. She felt that it was no moment to thrust herself in; nor did she feel herself aggrieved even though unnoticed by such a favorite friend. Something in the whole spirit of the day had made her only sensible that she was a little girl, and quite forget that she was a countess.

The friends were much too intent on one another to think of her, as she sat in the recess of the window, their backs to her. They drew their chairs close to the fire, and began to talk, bending down together; and Kate felt sure, that as her uncle at least knew she was there, she need not interrupt. Besides, what they spoke of was what she had longed to hear, and would never have dared to ask. Lord de la Poer had been like a father to his friend's two sons when they were left in England; and now the Colonel was telling him,—as, perhaps, he could have told no one else,—about their brave spirit, and especially of Giles's patience and resolution through his lingering illness; how he had been entirely unselfish in entreating that anything might happen rather than that his father should resign his post; but though longing to be with his parents, and desponding as to his chance of recovery, had resigned himself in patience to whatever might be thought right; and how through the last sudden accession of illness brought on by the journey, his sole thought had been for his parents.

"And she has borne up!" said Lord de la Poer.

"As *he* truly said, 'As long as she has any one to care for, she will never break down.' Luckily, I was entirely used up for a few days just at first; and coming home, we had a poor young woman on board very ill, and Emily nursed her day and night."

"And now you will bring her to Fanny and me to take care of."

"Thank you,—another time. But, old fellow, I don't know whether we either of us could stand your house full of children yet. Emily would be always among them, and think she liked it; but I know how it would be. It was just so when I took her to a kind friend of ours after the little girls were taken; she had the children constantly with her, but I never saw her so ill as she was afterwards."

"Reaction! Well, whenever you please; you shall have your rooms to yourselves, and only see us when you like. But I don't mean to press you; only, what are you going to do next?"

"I can hardly tell. There are business matters of our own, and about poor James's little girl, to keep us here a little while." ("Who is that?" thought Kate.)

"Then you must go into our house. I was in hopes it might be so, and told the housekeeper to make ready."

"Thank you; if Emily,—we will see when she comes in. I want to make up my mind about that child. Have you seen much of her?"

Kate began to think honor required her to come forward, but her heart throbbed with fright.

"Not as much as I could wish. It is an intelligent little monkey, and our girls were delighted with her; but I believe Barbara thinks me a corrupter of youth, for she discountenances us."

"Ah! one of the last times I was alone with Giles, he said, smiling, 'That little girl in Bruton Street will be just what mamma wants;' and I know Emily has never ceased to want to get hold of the motherless thing ever since Mrs. Wardour's death. I know it would be the greatest comfort to Emily, but I only doubted taking the child away from my sisters. I thought it would be such a happy thing to have Jane's kind heart drawn out; and if Barbara had forgiven the old sore, and used her real admirable good sense affectionately, it would have been like new life to them. Besides, it must make a great difference to their income. But is it possible that it can be the old prejudice, De la Poer? Barbara evidently dislikes the poor child, and treats her like a state prisoner!"

Honor prevailed entirely above fear and curiosity. Out flew Kate to the exceeding amaze and discomfiture of the two gentlemen. "No, no, Uncle Giles; it is,—it is because I ran away! Aunt Barbara said she would not tell, for if you knew it, you would,—you would despise me;—and you," looking at Lord de la Poer, "would never let me play with Grace and Addy again!"

She covered her face with her hands,—it was all burning red; and she was nearly rushing off, but she felt herself lifted tenderly upon a knee, and an arm round her. She thought it her old friend; but behold, it was her uncle's voice that said, in the softest gentlest way, "My dear, I never despise where I meet with truth. Tell me how it was; or had you rather tell your Aunt Emily?"

"I'll tell you," said Kate, all her fears softened by his touch. "Oh, no! please don't go,

Lord de la Poer; I do want you to know, for I could n't have played with Grace and Adelaide on false pretenses!" And encouraged by her uncle's tender pressure, she murmured out, "I ran away,—I did,—I went home!"

"To Oldburgh?"

"Yes,—yes! It was very wrong; papa,—Uncle Wardour, I mean—made me see it was."

"And what made you do it?" said her uncle, kindly. "Do not be afraid to tell me."

"It was because I was angry. Aunt Barbara would not let me go to the other Wardours, and wanted me to write a—what I thought—a fashionable falsehood; and when I said it was a lie," (if possible Kate here became a deeper crimson than it was before,) "she sent me to my room till I would beg her pardon, and write the note. So,—so,—I got out of the house, and took a cab, and went home by the train. I did n't know it was so very dreadful a thing, or indeed I would not."

And Kate hid her burning face on her uncle's breast, and was considerably startled by what she heard next from the marquis.

"Hm! All I have to say is, that if Barbara had the keeping of me, I should run away at the end of a week."

"Probably;" and Lord de la Poer saw what Kate did not, the first shadow of a smile on the face of his friend, as he pressed his arm round the still trembling girl; "but you see, Barbara justly thinks you corrupt youth. My little girl, you must not let *him* make you think lightly of this"—

"O no, I never could! Papa was so shocked!" and she was again covered with confusion at the thought.

"But," added her uncle, "it is not as if you had not gone to older and better friends than any you have ever had, my poor child. I am afraid you have been much tried, and have not had a happy life since you left Oldburgh."

"I have always been naughty," said Kate.

"Then we must try if your Aunt Emily can help you to be good. Will you try to be as like her own child to her as you can, Katharine?"

"And to you," actually whispered Kate; for somehow at that moment she cared much more for the stern uncle than the gentle aunt.

He lifted her up and kissed her, but set her down again with a sigh, that told how little she could make up to him for the son he had left in Egypt. Yet, perhaps, that sigh made Kate long with more fervent love for some way of being so very good and affectionate as quite to make him happy, than if he had received her demonstration as if satisfied by it.

CHAPTER XV

Nothing of note passed during the rest of the evening. Mrs. Umfraville came home; but Kate had fallen back into the shy fit that rendered her unwilling to begin on what was personal, and the Colonel waited to talk it over with his wife alone before saying any more.

Besides, there were things far more near to them than their little great niece, and Mrs. Umfraville could not see Lord de la Poer without having her heart very full of the sons to whom he had been so kind. Again they sat round the fire, and this time in the dark, while once more Giles and Frank and all their ways were talked over and over, and Kate was forgotten; but she was not sitting alone in the dark window,—no, she had a footstool close to her uncle, and sat resting her head upon his knee, her eyes seeking red caverns in the coals, her heart in a strange peaceful rest, her ears listening to the mother's subdued tender tones in speaking of her boys, and the friend's voice of sympathy and affection. Her uncle leant back and did not speak at all; but the other two went on and on, and Mrs. Umfraville seemed to be drinking in every little trait of her boys' English life, not weeping over it, but absolutely smiling when it was something droll or characteristic.

Kate felt subdued and reverent, and loved her new relations more and more for their sorrows; and she begun to dream out castles of the wonderful goodness by which she would comfort them; then she looked for her uncle's hand, to see if she could dare to stroke it, but one was over his brow, the other out of reach, and she was shy of doing anything.

The dinner interrupted them; and Kate had the pleasure of dining late, and sitting opposite to Lord de la Poer, who talked now and then to her, and told her what Adelaide and Grace were doing; but he was grave and sad, out of sympathy with his friends, and Kate was by no means tempted to be foolish.

Indeed, she began to feel that she might hope to be always good with her uncle and aunt, and that they would never make her naughty. Only too soon came the announcement of the carriage for Lady Caergwent; and when Aunt Emily took her into the bedroom to dress, she clung to that kind hand and fondled it.

"My dear little girl!" and Aunt Emily held her in her arms, "I am so glad! Kate, I do think your dear uncle is a little cheered to-night! If having you about him does him any good, how I shall love you, Katie!" and she hugged her closer. "And it is so kind in Lord de la Poer to have come! Oh, now he will be better! I am so thankful he is in England again! You must be with us whenever Barbara can spare you, Kate dear, for I am sure he likes it."

"Each wants me to do the other good," thought Kate; and she was so much touched and pleased that she did not know what to do, and looked foolish.

Uncle Giles took her down stairs; and when they were in the carriage, in the dark, he seemed to be less shy; he lifted her on his knee and said, "I will talk to your aunt, and we will see how soon you can come to see us, my dear."

"Oh, do let it be soon," said Kate.

"That must depend upon your Aunt Barbara," he answered, "and upon law matters perhaps. And you must not be troublesome to her; she has suffered very much, and will not think of herself, so you must think for her."

"I don't know how, Uncle Giles," said poor sincere Kate. "At home, they always said I had no consideration."

"You must learn," he said, gravely. "She is not to be harassed."

Kate was rather frightened; but he spoke in a kinder voice. "At home, you say. Do you mean with my sisters, or at Oldburgh?"

"Oh, at Oldburgh, Uncle Giles!"

"You are older now," he answered, "and need not be so childish."

"And please one thing,—"

"Well,—"

There came a great choking in her throat, but she did get it out. "Please, please, don't think all I do wrong is the Wardours' fault! I know I am naughty and horrid and unladylike, but it is my own fault, indeed it is, and *nobody's else's!* Mary and Uncle Wardour would have made me good,—and it was all my fault."

"My dear," and he put the other hand so that he completely encircled the little slim waist, "I do quite believe that Mr. Wardour taught you all the good you have. There is nothing I am so glad of as that you love and reverence him as he deserves,—as far as such a child can do. I hope you always will, and that your gratitude will increase with your knowledge of the sacrifices that he made for you."

It was too much of a speech for Kate to answer; but she nestled up to him, and felt as if she loved him more than ever. He added, "I should like to see Mr. Wardour, but I can hardly leave your aunt yet. Would he come to London?"

Kate gave a gasp. "O dear! Sylvia said he would have no money for journeys now! It cost so much his coming in a first-class carriage with me."

"You see how necessary it is to learn consideration," said the Colonel; "I must run down to see him and come back at night."

By this time they were at the aunt's door, and both entered the drawing-room together.

Lady Barbara anxiously hoped that Katharine had behaved well.

"Perfectly well," he answered; and his face was really brighter and tenderer.

It was Kate's bedtime, and she was dismissed at once. She felt that the kiss and momentary touch of the hand, with the "Bless you," were far more earnest than the mere greeting kiss. She did not know that it had been his wonted good-night to his own children.

When she was gone, he took a chair, and explained that he could remain for a little while, as Lord de la Poer would bear his wife company. Lady Jane made room for him on the sofa, and Lady Barbara looked pleased.

"I wished to talk to you about that child," he said.

"I have been wishing it for some time," said Lady Barbara: "waiting, in fact, to make arrangements till your return."

"What arrangements?"

"For forming an establishment for her."

"The child's natural home is with you or with me."

There was a silence; then Lady Jane nervously caught her brother's hand, saying, "O Giles, Giles, you must not be severe with her, poor little thing!"

"Why should I be severe, Jane?" he said. "What has the child done to deserve it?"

"I do not wish to enter into particulars," said Lady Barbara. "But she is a child who has been so unfortunately brought up as to require constant watching, and to have her in the house does so much harm to Jane's health, that I strongly advise you not to attempt it in Emily's state of spirits."

"It would little benefit Emily's spirits to transfer a duty to a stranger," said the Colonel. "But I wish to know why you evidently think so ill of this girl, Barbara?"

"Her entire behavior since she has been with us—" began Lady Barbara.

"Generalities only do mischief, Barbara. If I have any control over this child, I must know facts."

"The truth is, Giles," said his sister, distressed and confused, "that I promised the child not to tell you of her chief piece of misconduct, unless I was compelled by some fresh fault."

"An injudicious promise, Barbara. You do the child more harm by implying such an opinion of her than you could do by letting me hear what she has actually done. But you are absolved from the promise, for she has herself told me."

"Told you! That girl has no sense of shame! After all the pains I took to conceal it!"

"No, Barbara, it was with the utmost shame that she told me. It was unguarded of me, I own; but De la Poer and I had entirely forgotten that she was present, and I asked him if he could account for your evident dislike and distrust of her. The child's honorable feelings would not allow her to listen, and she came forward, and accused herself, not you!"

"Before Lord de la Poer! Giles, how could you allow it;" cried Lady Barbara, confounded. "That whole family will tell the story, and she will be marked forever!"

"De la Poer has some knowledge of child nature," said the Colonel, slightly smiling.

"A gentleman often encourages that sort of child, but condemns her the more. She will be a by-word in that family! I always knew she would be our disgrace!"

"O Giles, do tell Barbara it cannot be so very bad!" entreated Lady Jane. "She is such a child,—poor little dear!—and so little used to control!"

"I have only as yet heard her own confused account."

Lady Barbara gave her own.

"I see," said the Colonel, "the child was both accurate and candid. You should be thankful that your system has not destroyed her sincerity."

"But, indeed, dear Giles," pleaded Lady Jane, "you know Barbara did not want her to say what was false."

"No," said the Colonel: "that was a mere misunderstanding. It is the spirit of distrust that,—assuming that a child will act dishonorably,—is likely to drive her to do so."

"I never distrusted Katharine till she drove me to do so," said Lady Barbara, with cold, stern composure.

"I would never bring an accusation of breach of trust, where I had not made it evident that I reposed confidence," said the Colonel.

"I see how it is," said Lady Barbara; "you have heard one side. I do not contradict. I know the girl would not wilfully deceive by word; and I am willing to confess that I am not capable of dealing with her. Only from a sense of duty did I ever undertake it."

"Of duty, Barbara?" he asked.

"Yes,—of duty to the family."

"We do not see those things in the same light," he said quietly. "I thought, as you know, that the duty was more incumbent when the child was left an orphan,—a burthen on relatives who could ill afford to be charged with her. Perhaps, Barbara, if you had noticed her *then,* instead of waiting till circumstances made her the head of our family, you might have been able to give her that which has been wanting in your otherwise conscientious training,—affection."

Lady Barbara held up her head stiffly; but she was very near tears, of pain and wounded pride, but she would not defend herself; and she saw that even her faithful Jane did not feel with her.

"I came home, Barbara," continued the Colonel, "resolving that,—much as I wished for Emily's sake that this little girl should need a home with us,—if you had found in her a new interest and delight, and were in her,—let me say it, Barbara, healing old sores,—and giving her your own good sense and high principle, I would not say one word to disturb so happy a state of things. I come and find the child a state prisoner, whom you are endeavoring to alienate from the friends to whom she owes a daughter's gratitude; I find her not complaining of you, but answering me with the saddest account a child can give of herself,—she is always naughty. After this, Barbara, I can be doing you no injury in asking you to concur with me in arrangements for putting the child under my wife's care as soon as possible."

"To-morrow, if you like," said Lady Barbara. "I took her only from a sense of duty; and it has half killed Jane. I would not keep her upon any consideration!"

"O Barbara, it has not hurt me. O Giles, she will always be so anxious about me, it is all my fault for being nervous and foolish," cried Lady Jane, with quivering voice, and tears in her eyes. "If it had not been for that, we could have made her so happy, dear little spirited thing. But dear Barbara spoils me, and I know I give way too much."

"This will keep you awake all night!" said Barbara, as the Colonel's tender gesture agitated Jane more. "Indeed, Giles, you should have chosen a better moment for this conversation,—on almost your first arrival too! But the very existence of this child is a misfortune!"

"Let us trust that in a few years she may give you reason to think otherwise," said the Colonel. "Did you mean what you said,—that you wished us to take her to-morrow?"

"Not to incommode Emily. She can go on as she has done till your plans are made. You do not know what a child she is."

"Emily shall come and settle with you to-morrow," said Colonel Umfraville. "I have not yet spoken to her, but I think she will wish to have the child with her."

"And you will be patient with her. You will make her happy," said Lady Jane, holding his hand.

"Everything is made happy by Emily," he answered.

"But has she spirits for the charge?"

"She has always spirits enough to give happiness to others," he answered; and the dew was on his dark lashes.

"And you, Giles? You will not be severe even if the poor child is a little wild?"

"I know what you are thinking of, Jane," he said kindly. "But indeed, my dear, such a wife as mine, and such sorrows as she has helped me to bear, would have been wasted indeed, if by God's grace, they had not made me less exacting and impatient than I used to be. Barbara," he added after a pause, "I beg your pardon if I have spoken hastily, or done you injustice. All you have done has been conscientious; and if I spoke in displeasure—you know how one's spirit is moved by seeing a child unhappy,—and my training in gentleness is not as complete as it ought to be, I am sorry for the pain I gave you."

Lady Barbara was struggling with tears she could not repress; and at last she broke quite down, and wept so that Lady Jane moved about in alarm and distress, and her brother waited in some anxiety. But when she spoke it was humbly.

"You were right, Giles. It was not in me to love that child. It was wrong in me. Perhaps if I had overcome the feeling when you first told me of it, when her mother died, it would have been better for us all. Now it is too late. Our habits have formed themselves, and I can neither manage the child nor make her happy. It is better that she should go to you and Emily. And, Giles, if you still bring her to us sometimes, I will try—"

The last words were lost.

"You will," he said, affectionately, "when there are no more daily collisions. Dear Barbara, if I am particularly anxious to train this poor girl up at once in affection and in self-restraint, it is because my whole life,—ever since I grew up,—has taught me what a grievous task is left us, after we are our own masters, if our childish faults—such as impetuosity and sullenness,—are not corrected on principle, not for convenience, while we are children."

After this conversation every one will be sure that Mrs. Umfraville came next day, and after many arrangements with Lady Barbara, carried off the little countess with her to the house that Lord de la Poer had lent them.

Kate was subdued and quiet. She felt that she had made a very unhappy business of her life with her aunts, and that she should never see Bruton Street without a sense of shame. Lady Barbara, too, was more soft and kind than she had ever seen her; and Aunt Jane was very fond of her, and grieved over her not having been happier.

"Oh, never mind, Aunt Jane, it was all my naughtiness. I know Aunt Emily will make me good; and nobody could behave ill in the house with Uncle Giles, could they now? So I shall be sure to be happy. And I'll tell you what, Aunt Jane; some day you shall come to stay with us and then I'll drive you out in a dear delicious open carriage with two prancing ponies!"

And when she wished her other aunt good-by, she eased her mind by saying, "Aunt Barbara, I am very sorry I was such a horrid plague."

"There were faults on both sides, Katharine," her aunt answered, with dignity. "Perhaps in time we may understand one another better."

The first thing Katharine heard when she had left the house with Mrs. Umfraville was, that her uncle had gone down to Oldburgh by an early train, and that both box and shawl had gone with him.

But when he came back late to Lord de la Poer's house, whom had he brought with him?

Mary! Mary Wardour herself! He had, as a great favor, begged to have her for a fortnight in London to take care of her little cousin, till further arrangements could be made; and to talk over with Mrs. Umfraville the child's character, and what would be good for her.

If there was one shy person in the house that night, there was another happier than words could tell!

Moreover, before very long, the Countess of Caergwent had really seen the Lord Chancellor, and found him not so very unlike other people after all; indeed, unless Uncle Giles had told her, she never would have found out who he was! And when he asked her whether she would wish to live with Colonel Umfraville or with Lady Barbara and Lady Jane, it may be very easily guessed what answer she made!

So it was fixed that she should live at Caergwent Castle, with her uncle and aunt, and be brought up to the care of her own village and poor people, and to learn the duties of her station under their care.

And before they left London, Mrs. Umfraville had chosen a very bright pleasant young governess, to be a friend and companion, as well as an instructress. Further, it was settled that as soon as Christmas was over, Sylvia should come for a long visit, and learn of the governess with Kate.

Those who have learned to know Countess Kate can perhaps guess whether she found herself right in thinking it impossible to be naughty near Uncle Giles or Aunt Emily. But of one thing they may be sure, that Uncle Giles never failed to make her truly sorry for her naughtiness, and increasingly earnest in the struggle to leave it off.

And as time went on, and occupations and interests grew up round Colonel and Mrs. Umfraville, and their niece lost her childish wildness, and loved them more and more, they felt their grievous loss less and less, and did not so miss the vanished earthly hope. Their own children had so lived that they could feel them safe; and they attached themselves to the child in their charge till she was really like their own.

Yet, all the time, Kate still calls Mr. Wardour "papa;" and Sylvia spends half her time with her. Some people still say that in manners, looks, and ways, Sylvia would make a better countess than Lady Caergwent; but there are things that both are learning together, which alone can make them fit for any lot upon earth, or for the better inheritance in heaven.

$$\boxed{7}$$

Jessica's First Prayer

By "HESBA STRETTON"

JESSICA'S

FIRST PRAYER.

BY THE AUTHOR OF
"FERN'S HOLLOW," "FISHERS OF DERBY HAVEN,"
"PILGRIM STREET," "MAX KRÖMER." ETC.

LONDON

SARAH SMITH (1832–1911), daughter of a bookseller in Shropshire, as a child read her father's stock of literature (mostly edifying, we may be sure) and began to write in the late 1850s. Dickens enthusiastically published her early stories in his periodicals, *Household Words* and its successor, *All the Year Round.* She took the pseudonym Hesba Stretton, the surname from the Shropshire village of All Stretton, and the forename from the initials of her brothers and sisters. Like Catherine Sinclair, the author of *Holiday House,* she was a practicing philanthropist as well as a writer, taking an active part in the founding of the London Society for the Prevention of Cruelty to Children. And like Catherine Sinclair, she was a dedicated Evangelical churchwoman. Early in her career she wrote several novels for adults, which appeared in the conventional three volumes, but her best work and her most successful was her writing for children, short tales published in the sixties and early seventies by the Religious Tract Society.

The early sixties saw the revival of dramatic novels of mystery and crime for adults, beginning with Wilkie Collins's *The Woman in White* (1860), Mrs. Henry Wood's *East Lynne* (1861), and Mary Elizabeth Braddon's *Lady Audley's Secret* (1862), whose success precipitated a flood of other novels of the same type. Quickly christened "sensation-novels," they were condemned as immoral by many critics. So when Annie Keary's sister Eliza scornfully denounced the Religious Tract Society's publications for children as "sensational stories of ragged London depravity," she was tarring them with the brush of disapproval so widely applied to adult "sensation-novels." Miss Keary, we may be sure, was particularly troubled by the new appeal that Hesba Stretton and others were making to the middle and upper classes.

In earlier decades such Evangelical fiction ("Tract-books"), often distributed free, had been aimed at "cottage" families: the rural poor. Designed to make them content with their lot, the stories gave practical advice to poor country children destined to go into domestic service in the homes of the rich; they consoled the poor with the thought that no matter how poor they were, there were others still poorer, and often suggested that the purity of a child might reform even a hardened, unbelieving grown-up. A large stream of temperance literature, in which angelic children eventually rescued their drunken and abusive fathers from grog shops, flowed into this river of uplifting cheap fiction, all piously designed to justify the social structure of the world as it was. So long as the rich were sometimes kindhearted, all that the poor needed to do was tug their forelocks respectfully, and soberly and piously enjoy life in the station to which it had pleased Providence to assign them.

Other stories, of which Maria Louisa Charlesworth's *Ministering Children* (1854) was the most successful, worked the other side of the street, teaching rich children their duties to their less fortunate neighbors. *Ministering Children* shows little change in attitudes toward the poor over the fifteen years since 1839, when *Holiday House* appeared. It still prescribes the same extreme caution in helping the wretched that Major Graham and Lady Harriet practiced and taught to Harry and Laura. Each time the benevolent rich "ministering" children help a member of the deserving "Poor" (always capitalized), they are agreeably conscious that they have done the right thing, and glow with gratified self-approval. Presents of coal, warm clothes or blankets, nourishing food, and small amounts of money are the ordinary forms of charity: the condition of the poor as such is never presented as remediable. Nobody considers raising wages; nobody discusses or proposes long-range measures. The poor are there in their squalid rural cottages to be helped by the rich; the rich attain merit by helping the poor.

However deplorable, hypocritical, self-serving, or inadequate such an attitude might have been with respect to the English countryside in the earlier decades of the century—and some novelists, notably Charles Kingsley in *Yeast* (1851), expressed their indignation in novels for adults—it was wholly untenable when applied to the poor of the great industrial cities, such as Manchester or London itself. With their problems too, and with the evils of the factory system, novelists for adults (Mrs. Trollope, Mrs. Gaskell, Kingsley, Dickens, and others) had been struggling in fiction since the 1840s. But it was not until the sixties that the "ragged London depravity" that Eliza Keary disliked to see in "Sunday" literature was brought home to the children of the middle and upper classes by the new Evangelical writers, of whom Hesba Stretton was the most prominent. Later classified as "Street Arab" tales, their writings were viewed with some distaste by Charlotte Yonge. She could never come to grips with the city or with any but the rural poor, and she made a sharp distinction in her own mind and in her writing style between the stories she wrote for members of her own class and those she wrote for the lower classes. But even Charlotte Yonge selected Hesba Stretton's *Little Meg's Children* (1868) as one of the two best "Street Arab" stories.

It is a grim tale indeed. Only one hundred forty-four small pages of large print in a small, almost square little volume bound in bright green cloth and illustrated with affecting woodcuts, it tells of a little girl of ten, whose father has gone to sea, and whose mother dies, leaving her in a wretched London slum attic to care single-handedly for a brother of five and a baby sister until their father comes home. Meg must never let anybody enter their room, for under the bed, in a large box among the family clothes, is a sack containing forty gold sovereigns, which her father (a brute when drunk) has promised to keep intact for one of his shipmates. Stark hardship follows: Meg must pawn the family clothes, and eventually go to work for threepence a day in the house of a benevolent woman, in order to feed the younger ones. In her absence at work, she has no choice but to entrust them to Kitty, a kindhearted but irresponsible girl, a drunkard and a prostitute. When sober, Kitty bemoans her fallen state; but when drunk, she allows one of her men companions to quiet Meg's crying baby sister by giving the child so much alcohol that it dies. Starvation is looming when father's ship arrives at last. The untouched hoard of gold proves to be his own: he had lied about it only to force his wife to keep it intact. And he has found religion, and is prepared to give his surviving children a happy new life. Shamelessly tear-jerking, *Little Meg's Children* is still enormously readable. If we scoff at it or reject it, we shall be turning our backs upon essential aspects of the Victorian age, and will never understand Victorian children.

Above all, *Little Meg's Children* is a devoutly Evangelical story. Throughout, Meg clings to her belief that all is in the hands of a good God. Her conviction that "if people do grow up bad . . . God can make 'em good again, if they'd only ask him" eventually brings about the repentance of Kitty, who, under Meg's direction, asks God to have mercy on her and make her a good girl again. This is all that is necessary, as the kind woman who has given Meg a job is Kitty's estranged mother, and welcomes her back with open arms. And Meg's father, who in the past had never beaten the children *much* when drunk, has, while ill abroad, come to realize that Christ died to save him. "I'd nobody to fly to but Jesus if I wanted to be aught else but a poor, wicked, lost rascal, as got drunk and was no better than a brute. And so I turned it over and over in my mind, lying abed; and now, please God, I'm a bit more like a Christian than I was. I reckon that's what bless means, little Meg." So, like Eric, Meg's father has undergone the necessary conversion. Even the deaths of Meg's mother and the baby girl were God's doing, and signs of His kindness.

Alone in London (1869), another of Hesba Stretton's best stories, tells of a poverty-stricken but noble elderly newspaper vendor who shelters not only his little granddaughter, Dolly, but a virtuous street-urchin. This boy has never previously heard of Christ but is receptive to the divine message, and by sheer hard work lifts himself from penury to the proprietorship of a muddy street-crossing for sweeping, and then to a pleasant outdoor job in the country. Because every bed in the Children's Hospital is full, little Dolly dies. But, as often with Hesba Stretton, the lost child is replaced: her parents, back from India, have another daughter, and Dolly, after all, has only "gone home to the father's house, and was waiting" for them there. So the Evangelicals sought to have it both ways: to extract the maximum of pathos from children's deathbeds, but to reassure the weeping reader at the same time that there was nothing tragic about the deaths: rather, they were triumphs. *Pilgrim Street* (1872), a vivid story of poverty in Manchester—where Hesba Stretton lived for some time—may be the most fully developed of all her children's stories. But the one that first made her famous and that gives the flavor of her writing most characteristically and fairly is *Jessica's First Prayer*, published in *Sunday at Home* in 1866, and shortly afterwards as a small book. It sold more than a million and a half copies, and was translated into all the languages of Europe, and into many Asian and African languages as well.

Here Hesba Stretton for the first time explored London poverty and the sufferings of a mistreated child. Neglected and abused by her drunken mother, Jessica is befriended by Daniel, the kind proprietor of a coffee stall, who is also caretaker of a large church. When she follows him there, she is told that the church is "for ladies and gentlemen" and that she must go away. Learning that the rich pray there, and that prayer means asking God for what they want, she is astonished that the rich should want anything, and inquires what God is. She hides in the church to hear the service, and is discovered by the minister's children, who want to invite her into their pew but realize that she is too ragged and dirty. They know that the Bible commands that "a poor man in vile raiment" be treated the same as one "in goodly apparel." But the church itself seems to be flouting Scripture. Here is a deep dilemma. The minister himself deals with it in part by inviting Jessica to sit at the steps of his pulpit, and assures her that God will let her speak to Him as readily as He would a well-dressed child. It is then that Jessica offers up her first prayer: "O God! I want to know about you. And please pay Mr. Dan'el for all the warm coffee he's give me." Jessica is a born Evangelical, calling at once with confidence upon a personal God who intervenes as a father when summoned.

Of course, her prayer is answered. She becomes the instrument for truly converting Daniel. And Daniel, at last regenerate, harshly blames the minister, to whom he has listened in vain, Sunday after Sunday, without his heart being touched. Not until Jessica had asked him questions that went deep into his heart had he been a "saved man." So, not only by implication but explicitly—as she and the other authors of Evangelical fiction, whether "Street Arab" tales or not, so seldom did—Hesba Stretton came to grips with the real problem: the inadequacy of the church, and the self-conscious pride of purse of its members. Even the kind minister tells Jessica that if she were to come and live in his house, she would have to "be washed and clothed in new clothing to make you fit for it." Although the words are spoken with reference to spiritual improvement, and to the putting on of new spiritual garments, they have an important double meaning, for they must also be taken literally. Ragged dirty Jessica cannot be taken into the minister's proper middle-class household as she is: the words of Scripture are violated every day in practice by those most committed to living up to them. Society equates poverty with sinfulness, and in her way, in *Jessica's First Prayer*, Hesba Stretton—herself secure in the Evangelical middle class—was effectively protesting. It is this that makes *Jessica's First Prayer* so important a document of Victorian children's fiction.

The text of Jessica's First Prayer *is reprinted from the first edition (London: The Religious Tract Society, 1867).*

CHAPTER I

THE COFFEE-STALL AND ITS KEEPER

In a screened and secluded corner of one of the many railway-bridges which span the streets of London, there could be seen, a few years ago, from five o'clock every morning until half-past eight, a tidily set out coffee-stall, consisting of a trestle and board, upon which stood two large tin cans, with a small fire of charcoal burning under each, so as to keep the coffee boiling during the early hours of the morning when the work-people were thronging into the city, on their way to their daily toil. The coffee-stall was a favourite one, for besides being under shelter, which was of great consequence upon rainy mornings, it was also in so private a niche that the customers taking their out-of-door breakfast were not too much exposed to notice; and moreover, the coffee-stall keeper was a quiet man, who cared only to serve the busy workmen, without hindering them by any gossip. He was a tall, spare, elderly man, with a singularly solemn face, and a manner which was grave and secret. Nobody knew either his name or dwelling-place; unless it might be the policeman who strode past the coffee-stall every half-hour, and nodded familiarly to the solemn man behind it. There were very few who cared to make any enquiries about him; but those who did could only discover that he kept the furniture of his stall at a neighbouring coffee-house, whither he wheeled his trestle and board and crockery every day, not later than half-past eight in the morning; after which he was wont to glide away with a soft footstep, and a mysterious and fugitive air, with many backward and sidelong glances, as if he dreaded observation, until he was lost among the crowds which thronged the streets. No one had ever had the persevering curiosity to track him all the way to his house, or to find out his other means of gaining a livelihood; but in general his stall was surrounded by customers, whom he served with silent seriousness, and who did not grudge to pay him his charge for the refreshing coffee he supplied to them.

For several years the crowd of work-people had paused by the coffee-stall under the railway-arch, when one morning, in a partial lull of his business, the owner became suddenly aware of a pair of very bright dark eyes being fastened upon him and the slices of bread and butter on his board, with a gaze as hungry as that of a mouse which has been driven by famine into a trap. A thin and meagre face belonged to the eyes, which was half hidden by a mass of matted hair hanging over the forehead, and down the neck; the only covering which the head or neck had, for a tattered frock, scarcely fastened together with broken strings, was slipping down over the shivering shoulders of the little girl. Stooping down to a basket behind his stall, he caught sight of two bare little feet curling up from the damp pavement, as the child lifted up first one and then the other, and laid them one over another to gain a momentary feeling of warmth. Whoever the wretched child was, she did not speak; only at every steaming cupful which he poured out of his can, her dark eyes gleamed hungrily, and he could hear her smack her thin lips, as if in fancy she was tasting the warm and fragrant coffee.

"Oh, come now!" he said at last, when only one boy was left taking his breakfast leisurely, and he leaned over his stall to speak in a low and quiet tone: "why don't you go away, little girl? Come, come; you're staying too long, you know."

"I'm just going, sir," she answered, shrugging her small shoulders to draw her frock up higher about her neck; "only it's raining cats and dogs outside; and mother's been away all night, and she took the key with her; and it's so nice to smell the coffee; and the police has left off worriting me while I've been here. He thinks I'm a customer taking my breakfast." And the child laughed a shrill little laugh of mockery at herself and the policeman.

"You've had no breakfast, I suppose," said the coffee-stall keeper, in the same low and confidential voice, and leaning over his stall till his face nearly touched the thin, sharp features of the child.

"No," she replied, coolly, "and I shall want my dinner dreadful bad afore I get it, I know. You don't often feel dreadful hungry, do you sir? I'm not griped yet, you know; but afore I taste my dinner it'll be pretty bad, I tell you. Ah! very bad indeed!"

She turned away with a knowing nod, as much as to say she had one experience in life to which he was quite a stranger; but before she had gone half a dozen steps, she heard the quiet voice calling to her in rather louder tones, and in an instant she was back at the stall.

"Slip in here," said the owner, in a cautious whisper; "here's a little coffee left and a few crusts. There, you must never come again, you know. I never give to beggars; and if you'd begged, I'd have called the police. There; put your poor feet towards the fire. Now, aren't you comfortable?"

The child looked up with a face of intense satisfaction. She was seated upon an empty basket, with her feet near the pan of charcoal, and a cup of steaming coffee on her lap; but her mouth was too full for her to reply, except by a very deep nod, which expressed unbounded delight. The man was busy for a while packing up his crockery; but every now and then he stopped to look down upon her, and to shake his head gravely.

"What's your name?" he asked, at length; "but there, never mind! I don't care what it is. What's your name to do with me, I wonder?"

"It's Jessica," said the girl: "but mother and everybody calls me Jess. You'd be tired of being called Jess, if you was me. It's Jess here, and Jess there; and everybody wanting me to go errands. And they think nothing of giving me smacks, and kicks, and pinches. Look here!"

Whether her arms were black and blue from the cold, or from ill-usage, he could not tell; but he shook his head again seriously, and the child felt encouraged to go on.

"I wish I could stay here for ever and ever, just as I am!" she cried. "But you're going away, now; and I'm never to come again, or you'll set the police on me!"

"Yes," said the coffee-stall keeper, very softly, and looking round to see if there were any other ragged children within sight; "if you'll promise not to come again for a whole week, and not to tell anybody else, you may come once more. I'll give you one other treat. But you must be off now."

"I'm off, sir," she said, sharply; "but if you've a errand I could go on, I'd do it all right, I would. Let me carry some of your things."

"No, no," cried the man; "you run away, like a good girl; and mind! I'm not to see you again for a whole week."

"All right!" answered Jess, setting off down the rainy street at a quick run, as if to show her willing agreement to the bargain; while the coffee-stall keeper, with many a cautious glance around him, removed his stock-in-trade to the coffee-house near at hand, and was seen no more for the rest of the day in the neighbourhood of the railway-bridge.

CHAPTER II

JESSICA'S TEMPTATION

JESSICA KEPT her part of the bargain faithfully; and though the solemn and silent man under the dark shadow of the bridge looked out for her every morning as he served his customers, he caught no glimpse of her wan face and thin little frame. But when the appointed time was finished, she presented herself at the stall, with her hungry eyes fastened again upon the piles of buns and bread and butter, which were fast disappearing before the demands of the buyers. The business was at its height, and the famished child stood quietly on one side watching for the throng to melt away. But as soon as the nearest church clock had chimed eight, she drew a little nearer to the stall, and at a signal from its owner she slipped between the trestles of his stand, and took up her former position on the empty basket. To his eyes she seemed even a little thinner, and certainly more ragged, than before; and he laid a whole bun, a stale one which was left from yesterday's stock, upon her lap, as she lifted the cup of coffee to her lips with both her benumbed hands.

"What's your name?" she asked, looking up to him with her keen eyes.

"Why?" he answered, hesitatingly, as if he was reluctant to tell so much of himself; "my christened name is Daniel."

"And where do you live, Mr. Dan'el?" she enquired.

"Oh, come now!" he exclaimed, "if you're going to be impudent, you'd better march off. What business is it of yours where I live? I don't want to know where you live, I can tell you."

"I didn't mean no offence," said Jess, humbly, "only I thought I'd like to know where a good man like you lived. You're a very good man, aren't you, Mr. Dan'el?"

"I don't know," he answered, uneasily; "I'm afraid I'm not."

"Oh, but you are, you know," continued Jess. "You make good coffee; prime! And buns too! And I've been watching you hundreds of times afore you saw me, and the police leaves you alone, and never tells you to move on. Oh, yes! you must be a very good man."

Daniel sighed, and fidgeted about his crockery with a grave and occupied air, as if he were pondering over the child's notion of goodness. He made good coffee, and the police left him alone! It was quite true; yet still as he counted up the store of pence which had accumulated in his strong canvas bag, he sighed again still more heavily. He purposely let one of his pennies fall upon the muddy pavement, and went on counting the rest busily, while he furtively watched the little girl sitting at his feet. Without a shade of change upon her small face, she covered the penny with her foot, and drew it in carefully towards her, while she continued to chatter fluently to him. For a moment a feeling of pain shot a pang through Daniel's heart; and then he congratulated himself on having entrapped the young thief. It was time to be leaving now; but before he went he would make her move her bare foot, and disclose the penny concealed beneath it, and then he would warn her never to venture near his stall again. This was her gratitude, he thought; he had given her two breakfasts and more kindness than he had shown to any fellow-creature for many a long year; and at the first chance, the young jade turned upon him, and robbed him! He was brooding over it painfully in his mind, when Jessica's uplifted face changed suddenly, and a dark flush crept over her pale cheeks, and the tears started to her eyes. She stooped down, and picking up the coin from amongst the mud, she rubbed it bright and clean upon her rags, and laid it upon the stall close to his hand, but without speaking a word. Daniel looked down upon her solemnly and searchingly.

"What's this?" he asked.

"Please, Mr. Daniel," she answered, "it dropped, and you didn't hear it."

"Jess," he said, sternly, "tell me all about it."

"Oh, please," she sobbed, "I never had a penny of my very own but once; and it rolled close to my foot; and you didn't see it; and I hid it up sharp; and then I thought how kind you'd been, and how good the coffee and buns are, and how you let me warm myself at your fire; and please, I couldn't keep the penny any longer. You'll never let me come again, I guess."

Daniel turned away for a minute, busying himself with putting his cups and saucers into the basket, while Jessica stood by trembling, with the large tears rolling slowly down her cheeks. The snug, dark corner, with its warm fire of charcoal, and its fragrant smell of coffee, had been a paradise to her for these two brief spans of time; but she had been guilty of the sin which would drive her from it. All beyond the railway arch the streets stretched away, cold and dreary, with no friendly faces to meet hers, and no warm cups of coffee to refresh her; yet she was only lingering sorrowfully to hear the words spoken which should forbid her to return to this pleasant spot. Mr. Daniel turned round at last, and met her tearful gaze, with a look of strange emotion upon his own solemn face.

"Jess," he said, "I could never have done it myself. But you may come here every Wednesday morning, as this is a Wednesday, and there'll always be a cup of coffee for you."

She thought he meant that he could not have hidden the penny under his foot, and she went away a little saddened and subdued, notwithstanding her great delight in the expectation of such a treat every week; while Daniel, pondering over the struggle that must have passed through her childish mind, went on his way, from time to time shaking his head, and muttering to himself, "I couldn't have done it myself: I never could have done it myself."

CHAPTER III

AN OLD FRIEND IN A NEW DRESS

Week after week, through the three last months of the year, Jessica appeared every Wednesday at the coffee-stall, and after waiting patiently till the close of the breakfast-ing business, received her pittance from the charity of her new friend. After a while Daniel allowed her to carry some of his load to the coffee-house, but he never suffered her to follow him farther, and he was always particular to watch her out of sight before he turned off through the intricate mazes of the streets in the direction of his own home. Neither did he encourage her to ask him any more questions: and often but very few words passed between them during Jessica's breakfast time.

As to Jessica's home, she made no secret of it, and Daniel might have followed her any time he pleased. It was a single room, which had once been a hayloft over the stable of an old inn, now in use for two or three donkeys, the property of costermongers dwelling in the court about it. The mode of entrance was by a wooden ladder, whose rungs were crazy and broken, and which led up through a trap-door in the floor of the loft. The interior of the home was as desolate and comfortless as that of the stable below, with only a litter of straw for the bedding, and a few bricks and boards for the furniture. Everything that could be pawned had disappeared long ago, and Jessica's mother often lamented that she could not thus dispose of her child. Yet Jessica was hardly a burden to her. It was a long time since she had taken any care to provide her with food or

clothing, and the girl had to earn or beg for herself the meat which kept a scanty life within her. Jess was the drudge and errand-girl of the court; and what with being cuffed and beaten by her mother, and over-worked and ill-used by her numerous employers, her life was a hard one. But now there was always Wednesday morning to count upon and look forward to; and by and by a second scene of amazed delight opened upon her.

Jessica had wandered far away from home in the early darkness of a winter's evening, after a violent outbreak of her drunken mother, and she was still sobbing now and then with long-drawn sobs of pain and weariness, when she saw, a little way before her, the tall, well-known figure of her friend Mr. Daniel. He was dressed in a suit of black, with a white neckcloth, and he was pacing with brisk yet measured steps along the lighted streets. Jessica felt afraid of speaking to him, but she followed at a little distance, until presently he stopped before the iron gates of a large building, and, unlocking them, passed on to the arched doorway, and with a heavy key opened the folding-doors and entered in. The child stole after him, but paused for a few minutes, trembling upon the threshold, until the gleam of a light lit up within tempted her to venture a few steps forward, and to push a little way open an inner door, covered with crimson baize, only so far as to enable her to peep through at the inside. Then, growing bolder by degrees, she crept through herself, drawing the door to noiselessly behind her. The place was in partial gloom, but Daniel was kindling every gaslight, and each minute lit it up in more striking grandeur. She stood in a carpeted aisle, with high oaken pews on each side, almost as black as ebony. A gallery of the same dark old oak ran round the walls, resting upon massive pillars, behind one of which she was partly concealed, gazing with eager eyes at Daniel, as he mounted the pulpit steps and kindled the lights there, disclosing to her curious delight the glittering pipes of an organ behind it. Before long the slow and soft-footed chapel-keeper disappeared for a minute or two into a vestry; and Jessica, availing herself of his short absence, stole silently up under the shelter of the dark pews until she reached the steps of the organ loft, with its golden show. But at this moment Mr. Daniel appeared again, arrayed in a long gown of black serge; and as she stood spell-bound gazing at the strange appearance of her patron, his eyes fell upon her, and he also was struck speechless for a minute, with an air of amazement and dismay upon his grave face.

"Come, now," he exclaimed, harshly, as soon as he could recover his presence of mind, "you must take yourself out of this. This isn't any place for such as you. It's for ladies and gentlemen; so you must run away sharp before anybody comes. How ever did you find your way here?"

He had come very close to her, and bent down to whisper in her ear, looking nervously round to the entrance all the time. Jessica's eager tongue was loosened.

"Mother beat me," she said, "and turned me into the streets, and I see you there, so I followed you up. I'll run away this minute, Mr. Daniel; but it's a nice place. What do the ladies and gentlemen do when they come here? Tell me, and I'll be off sharp."

"They come here to pray," whispered Daniel.

"What is pray?" asked Jessica.

"Bless the child!" cried Daniel, in perplexity. "Why, they kneel down in those pews; most of them sit, though; and the minister up in the pulpit tells God what they want."

Jessica gazed into his face with such an air of bewilderment that a faint smile crept over the sedate features of the pew-opener.

"What is a minister and God?" she said; "and do ladies and gentlemen want anything? I thought they'd everything they wanted, Mr. Daniel."

"Oh!" cried Daniel, "you must be off, you know. They'll be coming in a minute, and they'd be shocked to see a ragged little heathen like you. This is the pulpit where the minister stands and preaches to 'em; and there are the pews, where they sit to listen to him, or to go to sleep, may be; and that's the organ to play music to their singing. There, I've told you everything, and you must never come again, never."

"Mr. Daniel," said Jessica, "I don't know nothing about it. Isn't there a dark little corner somewhere that I could hide in?"

"No, no," interrupted Daniel, impatiently; "we couldn't do with such a little heathen, with no shoes or bonnet on. Come now, it's only a quarter to the time, and somebody will be here in a minute. Run away, do!"

Jessica retraced her steps slowly to the crimson door, casting many a longing look backwards; but Mr. Daniel stood at the end of the aisle, frowning upon her whenever she glanced behind. She gained the lobby at last, but already some one was approaching the chapel door, and beneath the lamp at the gate stood one of her natural enemies, a policeman. Her heart beat fast, but she was quickwitted, and in another instant she spied a place of concealment behind one of the doors, into which she crept for safety until the path should be clear, and the policeman passed on upon his beat.

The congregation began to arrive quickly. She heard the rustling of silk dresses, and she could see the gentlemen and ladies pass by the niche between the door and the post.

Once she ventured to stretch out a thin little finger and touch a velvet mantle as the wearer of it swept by, but no one caught her in the act, or suspected her presence behind the door. Mr. Daniel, she could see, was very busy ushering the people to their seats; but there was a startled look lingering upon his face, and every now and then he peered anxiously into the outer gloom and darkness, and even once called to the policeman to ask if he had seen a ragged child hanging about. After a while the organ began to sound, and Jessica, crouching down in her hiding-place, listened entranced to the sweet music. She could not tell what made her cry, but the tears came so rapidly that it was of no use to rub the corners of her eyes with her hard knuckles; so she lay down upon the ground, and buried her face in her hands, and wept without restraint. When the singing was over, she could only catch a confused sound of a voice speaking. The lobby was empty now, and the crimson doors closed. The policeman, also, had walked on. This was the moment to escape. She raised herself from the ground with a feeling of weariness and sorrow; and thinking sadly of the light, and warmth, and music that were within the closed doors, she stepped out into the cold and darkness of the streets, and loitered homewards with a heavy heart.

CHAPTER IV

PEEPS INTO FAIRY LAND

I T WAS NOT the last time that Jessica concealed herself behind the baize-covered door. She could not overcome the urgent desire to enjoy again and again the secret and perilous pleasure; and Sunday after Sunday she watched in the dark streets for the moment when she could slip in unseen. She soon learned the exact time when Daniel would be occupied in lighting up, before the policeman would take up his station at the entrance, and again, the very minute at which it would be wise and safe to take her departure. Sometimes the child laughed noiselessly to herself, until she shook with suppressed merriment, as she saw Daniel standing unconsciously in the lobby, with his solemn face and grave air, to receive the congregation, much as he faced his customers at the coffee-stall. She learned to know the minister by sight, the tall, thin, pale gentleman, who passed through a side door, with his head bent as if in deep thought, while two little girls, about her own age, followed him with sedate yet pleasant faces. Jessica took a great interest in the minister's children. The younger one was fair, and the elder was about as tall as herself, and had eyes and hair as dark; but oh, how cared for, how plainly waited on by tender hands! Sometimes, when they were gone by, she would close her eyes, and wonder what they would do in one of the high black pews inside, where there was no place for a ragged, barefooted girl like her; and now and then her wonderings almost ended in a sob, which she was compelled to stifle.

It was an untold relief to Daniel that Jessica did not ply him with questions, as he feared when she came for breakfast every Wednesday morning; but she was too shrewd and cunning for that. She wished him to forget that she had ever been there, and by and by her wish was accomplished, and Daniel was no longer uneasy, while he was lighting the lamps, with the dread of seeing the child's wild face starting up before him.

But the light evenings of summer-time were drawing near apace, and Jessica foresaw with dismay that her Sunday treats would soon be over. The risk of discovery increased every week, for the sun was later and later in setting and there would be no chance of creeping in and out unseen in the broad daylight. Already it needed both watchfulness and alertness to dart in at the right moment in the grey twilight; but still she could not give it up; and if it had not been for the fear of offending Mr. Daniel, she would have resolved upon going until she was found out. They could not punish her very much for standing in the lobby of a chapel.

Jessica was found out, however, before the dusky evenings were quite gone. It happened one night that the minister's children, coming early to the chapel, saw a small tattered figure, bareheaded and barefooted, dart swiftly up the steps before them and disappear within the lobby. They paused and looked at one another, and then, hand in hand, their hearts beating quickly, and the colour coming and going on their faces, they followed this strange new member of their father's congregation. The pew-opener was nowhere to be seen, but their quick eyes detected the prints of the wet little feet which had trodden the clean pavement before them, and in an instant they discovered Jessica crouching behind the door.

"Let us call Daniel Standring," said Winny, the younger child, clinging to her sister; but she had spoken aloud, and Jessica overheard her, and before they could stir a step she stood before them with an earnest and imploring face.

"Oh, don't have me drove away," she cried; "I'm a very poor little girl, and it's all the pleasure I've got. I've seen you lots of times, with that tall gentleman as stoops, and I didn't think you'd have me drove away. I don't do any harm behind the door, and if Mr. Daniel finds me out, he won't give me any more coffee."

"Little girl," said the elder child, in a composed and demure voice, "we don't mean to be unkind to you; but what do you come here for, and why do you hide yourself behind the door?"

"I like to hear the music," answered Jessica, "and I want to find out what pray is, and the minister, and God. I know it's only for ladies and gentlemen, and fine children like you; but I'd like to go inside just for once, and see what you do."

"You shall come with us into our pew," cried Winny, in an eager and impulsive tone; but Jane laid her hand upon her outstretched arm, with a glance at Jessica's ragged clothes and matted hair. It was a question difficult enough to perplex them. The little outcast was plainly too dirty and neglected for them to invite her to sit side by side with them in their crimson-lined pew, and no poor people attended the chapel with whom she could have a seat. But Winny, with flushed cheeks and indignant eyes, looked reproachfully at her elder sister.

"Jane," she said, opening her Testament, and turning over the leaves hurriedly, "this was papa's text a little while ago:—'For if there come into your assembly a man with a gold ring, in goodly apparel, and there come in also a poor man in vile raiment; and ye have respect to him that weareth the gay clothing, and say unto him, Sit thou here in a good place; and say to the poor, Stand thou there, or sit here under my footstool; are ye not then partial in yourselves, and are become judges of evil thoughts?' If we don't take this little girl into our pew, we 'have the faith of our Lord Jesus Christ, the Lord of glory, with respect of persons.' "

"I don't know what to do," answered Jane, sighing; "the Bible seems plain; but I'm sure papa would not like it. Let us ask the chapel-keeper."

"Oh, no, no!" cried Jessica; "don't let Mr. Daniel catch me here. I won't come again, indeed; and I'll promise not to try to find out about God and the minister, if you'll only let me go."

"But, little girl," said Jane, in a sweet but grave manner, "we ought to teach you about

God, if you don't know him. Our papa is the minister, and if you'll come with us, we'll ask him what we must do."

"Will Mr. Daniel see me?" asked Jessica.

"Nobody but papa is in the vestry," answered Jane, "and he'll tell us all, you and us, what we ought to do. You'll not be afraid of him, will you?"

"No," said Jessica, cheerfully, following the minister's children as they led her along the side of the chapel towards the vestry.

"He is not such a terrible personage," said Winny, looking round encouragingly, as Jane tapped softly at the door, and they heard a voice saying "Come in."

CHAPTER V

A NEW WORLD OPENS

THE MINISTER was sitting in an easy chair before a comfortable fire, with a hymn-book in his hand, which he closed as the three children appeared in the open doorway. Jessica had seen his pale and thoughtful face many a time from her hiding-place, but she had never met the keen, earnest, searching gaze of his eyes, which seemed to pierce through all her wretchedness and misery, and to read at once the whole history of her desolate life. But before her eyelids could droop, or she could drop a reverential curtsey, the minister's face kindled with such a glow of pitying tenderness and compassion, as fastened her eyes upon him, and gave her new heart and courage. His children ran to him, leaving Jessica upon the mat at the door, and with eager voices and gestures told him the difficulty they were in.

"Come here, little girl," he said; and Jessica walked across the carpeted floor till she stood right before him, with folded hands, and eyes that looked frankly into his.

"What is your name, my child?" he asked.

"Jessica," she answered.

"Jessica," he repeated, with a smile; "that is a strange name."

"Mother used to play 'Jessica' at the theatre, sir," she said, "and I used to be a fairy in the pantomime, till I grew too tall and ugly. If I'm pretty when I grow up, mother says I shall play too; but I've a long time to wait. Are you the minister, sir?"

"Yes," he answered, smiling again.

"What is a minister?" she enquired.

"A servant!" he replied, looking away thoughtfully into the red embers of the fire.

"Papa!" cried Jane and Winny, in tones of astonishment; but Jessica gazed steadily at the minister, who was now looking back again into her bright eyes.

"Please, sir, whose servant are you?" she asked.

"The servant of God and of man," he answered, solemnly. "Jessica, I am your servant."

The child shook her head, and laughed shrilly as she gazed round the room, and at the handsome clothing of the minister's daughters, while she drew her rags closer about her, and shivered a little, as if she felt a sting of the east wind, which was blowing keenly through the streets. The sound of her shrill, childish laugh made the minister's heart ache, and the tears burn under his eyelids.

"Who is God?" asked the child. "When mother's in a good temper, sometimes she says 'God bless me!' Do you know him, please, minister?"

But before there was time to answer, the door into the chapel was opened, and Daniel stood upon the threshold. At first he stared blandly forwards, but then his grave face grew ghastly pale, and he laid his hand upon the door to support himself until he could recover his speech and senses. Jessica also looked about her, scared and irresolute, as if anxious to run away or to hide herself. The minister was the first to speak.

"Jessica," he said, "there is a place close under my pulpit where you shall sit, and where I can see you all the time. Be a good girl and listen, and you will hear something about God. Standring, put this little one in front of the pews by the pulpit steps."

But before she could believe it for very gladness, Jessica found herself inside the chapel, facing the glittering organ, from which a sweet strain of music was sounding. Not far from her Jane and Winny were peeping over the front of their pew, with friendly smiles and glances. It was evident that the minister's elder daughter was anxious about her behaviour, and she made energetic signs to her when to stand up and when to kneel; but Winny was content with smiling at her, whenever her head rose above the top of the pew. Jessica was happy, but not in the least abashed. The ladies and gentlemen were not at all unlike those whom she had often seen when she was a fairy at the theatre; and very soon her attention was engrossed by the minister, whose eyes often fell upon her, as she gazed eagerly, with uplifted face, upon him. She could scarcely understand a word of what he said, but she liked the tones of his voice, and the tender pity of his face as he looked down upon her. Daniel hovered about a good deal, with an air of uneasiness and displeasure, but she was unconscious of his presence. Jessica was intent upon finding out what a minister and God were.

CHAPTER VI

THE FIRST PRAYER

W HEN THE SERVICE was ended, the minister descended the pulpit steps, just as Daniel was about to hurry Jessica away, and taking her by the hand in the face of all the congregation, he led her into the vestry, whither Jane and Winny quickly followed them. He was fatigued with the services of the day, and his pale face was paler than ever, as he placed Jessica before his chair, into which he threw himself with an air of exhaustion; but bowing his head upon his hands, he said in a low but clear tone, "Lord, these are the lambs of Thy flock. Help me to feed Thy lambs!"

"Children," he said, with a smile upon his weary face, "it is no easy thing to know God. But this one thing we know, that he is our Father—my Father and your Father, Jessica. He loves you, and cares for you more than I do for my little girls here."

He smiled at them and they at him, with an expression which Jessica felt and understood, though it made her sad. She trembled a little, and the minister's ear caught the sound of a faint though bitter sob.

"I never had any father," she said, sorrowfully.

"God is your Father," he answered, very gently; "he knows all about you, because he is present everywhere. We cannot see him, but we have only to speak, and he hears us, and we may ask him for whatever we want."

"Will he let me speak to him as well as these fine children that are clean and have got nice clothes?" asked Jessica, glancing anxiously at her muddy feet and her soiled and tattered frock.

"Yes," said the minister, smiling, yet sighing at the same time; "you may ask him this moment for what you want."

Jessica gazed round the room with large, wide-open eyes, as if she were seeking to see God; but then she shut her eyelids tightly, and bending her head upon her hands, as she had seen the minister do, she said, "O God! I want to know about you. And please pay Mr. Dan'el for all the warm coffee he's give me."

Jane and Winny listened with faces of unutterable amazement; but the tears stood in the minister's eyes, and he added "Amen" to Jessica's first prayer.

CHAPTER VII

HARD QUESTIONS

Daniel had no opportunity for speaking to Jessica; for, after waiting until the minister left the vestry, he found that she had gone away by the side entrance. He had to wait, therefore, until Wednesday morning, and the sight of her pinched little face was welcome to him, when he saw it looking wistfully over the coffee-stall. Yet he had made up his mind to forbid her to come again, and to threaten her with the policeman if he ever caught her at the chapel, where for the future he intended to keep a sharper look-out. But before he could speak, Jess had slipped under the stall, and taken her old seat upon the up-turned basket.

"Mr. Dan'el," she said, "has God paid you for my sups of coffee yet?"

"Paid me?" he repeated; "God? No."

"Well, he will," she answered, nodding her head sagely; "don't you be afraid for your money, Mr. Dan'el; I've asked him a many times, and the minister says he's sure to do it."

"Jess," said Daniel, sternly, "have you been and told the minister about my coffee-stall?"

"No," she answered, with a beaming smile, "but I've told God lots and lots of times since Sunday, and he's sure to pay in a day or two."

"Jess," continued Daniel, more gently, "you're a sharp little girl, I see; and now mind, I'm going to trust you. You're never to say a word about me or my coffee-stall; because the folks at our chapel are very grand, and might think it low and mean of me to keep a coffee-stall. Very likely they'd say I mustn't be chapel-keeper any longer, and I should lose a deal of money."

"Why do you keep the stall, then?" asked Jessica.

"Don't you see what a many pennies I get every morning?" he said, shaking his canvas bag. "I get a good deal of money that way in a year."

"What do you want such a deal of money for?" she enquired; "do you give it to God?"

Daniel did not answer, but the question went to his heart like a sword-thrust. What did he want so much money for? He thought of his one bare and solitary room, where he lodged alone, a good way from the railway-bridge, with very few comforts in it, but containing a desk, strongly and securely fastened, in which was his savings-bank book and his receipts for money put out at interest, and a bag of sovereigns, for which he had been toiling and slaving both on Sundays and week-days. He could not remember giving anything away, except the dregs of the coffee and the stale buns, for which Jessica was asking God to pay him. He coughed, and cleared his throat, and rubbed his eyes; and then, with nervous and hesitating fingers, he took a penny from his bag, and slipped it into Jessica's hand.

"No, no, Mr. Dan'el," she said; "I don't want you to give me any of your pennies. I want God to pay you."

"Ay, he'll pay me," muttered Daniel; "there'll be a day of reckoning by and by."

"Does God have reckoning days?" asked Jessica. "I used to like reckoning days when I was a fairy."

"Ay, ay," he answered; "but there's few folks like God's reckoning days."

"But you'll be glad, won't you?" she said.

Daniel bade her get on with her breakfast, and then he turned over in his mind the thoughts which her questions had awakened. Conscience told him he would not be glad to meet God's reckoning day.

"Mr. Dan'el," said Jessica, when they were about to separate, and he would not take back his gift of a penny, "if you wouldn't mind, I'd like to come and buy a cup of coffee to-morrow, like a customer, you know: and I won't let out a word about the stall to the minister next Sunday, don't you be afraid."

She tied the penny carefully into a corner of her rags, and with a cheerful smile upon her thin face, she glided from under the shadow of the bridge, and was soon lost to Daniel's sight.

CHAPTER VIII

AN UNEXPECTED VISITOR

WHEN JESSICA came to the street into which the court where she lived opened, she saw an unusual degree of excitement among the inhabitants, a group of whom were gathered about a tall gentleman, whom she recognised in an instant to be the minister. She elbowed her way through the midst of them, and the minister's face brightened as she presented herself before him. He followed her up to the low entry, across the squalid court, through the stable, empty of the donkeys just then, up the creaking rounds of the ladder, and into the miserable loft, where the tiles were falling in, and the broken window-panes were stuffed with rags and paper. Near to the old rusty stove, which served as a grate when there was any fire, there was a short board laid across some bricks, and upon this the minister took his seat, while Jessica sat upon the floor before him.

"Jessica," he said, sadly, "is this where you live?"

"Yes," she answered, "but we'd a nicer room than this when I was a fairy, and mother played at the theatre; we shall be better off when I'm grown up, if I'm pretty enough to play like her."

"My child," he said, "I'm come to ask your mother to let you go to school in a pleasant place down in the country. Will she let you go?"

"No," answered Jessica; "mother says she'll never let me learn to read, or go to church; she says it would make me good for nothing. But please, sir, she doesn't know anything about your church, it's such a long way off, and she hasn't found me out yet. She always gets very drunk of a Sunday."

The child spoke simply, and as if all she said was a matter of course; but the minister shuddered, and he looked through the broken window to the little patch of gloomy sky overhead.

"What can I do?" he cried mournfully, as though speaking to himself.

"Nothing, please, sir," said Jessica; "only let me come to hear you of a Sunday, and tell me about God. If you was to give me fine clothes like your little girls, mother 'ud only pawn them for gin. You can't do anything more for me."

"Where is your mother?" he asked.

"Out on a spree," said Jessica, "and she won't be home for a day or two. She'd not hearken to you, sir. There's the missionary came, and she pushed him down the ladder, till he was nearly killed. They used to call mother the Vixen at the theatre, and nobody durst say a word to her."

The minister was silent for some minutes, thinking painful thoughts, for his eyes seemed to darken as he looked round the miserable room, and his face wore an air of sorrow and disappointment. At last he spoke again.

"Who is Mr. Daniel, Jessica?" he enquired.

"Oh," she said cunningly, "he's only a friend of mine as gives me sups of coffee. You don't know all the folks in London, sir!"

"No," he answered, smiling; "but does he keep a coffee-stall?"

Jessica nodded her head, but did not trust herself to speak.

"How much does a cup of coffee cost?" asked the minister.

"A full cup's a penny," she answered, promptly; "but you can have half a cup; and there are halfpenny and penny buns."

"Good coffee and buns?" he said, with another smile.

"Prime," replied Jessica, smacking her lips.

"Well," continued the minister, "tell your friend to give you a full cup of coffee and a penny bun every morning, and I'll pay for them as often as he chooses to come to me for the money."

Jessica's face beamed with delight, but in an instant it clouded over as she recollected Daniel's secret, and her lips quivered as she spoke her disappointed reply,

"Please, sir," she said, "I'm sure he couldn't come; oh! he couldn't. It's such a long way, and Mr. Daniel has plenty of customers. No, he never would come to you for the money."

"Jessica," he answered, "I will tell you what I will do. I will trust you with a shilling every Sunday, if you'll promise to give it to your friend the very first time you see him. I shall be sure to know if you cheat me." And the keen, piercing eyes of the minister looked down into Jessica's, and once more the tender and pitying smile returned to his face.

"I can do nothing else for you?" he said, in a tone of mingled sorrow and questioning.

"No, minister," answered Jessica; "only tell me about God."

"I will tell you one thing about him now," he replied. "If I took you to live in my house with my little daughters, you would have to be washed and clothed in new clothing to make you fit for it. God wanted us to go and live at home with him in heaven, but we were so sinful that we could never have been fit for it. So he sent his own Son to live amongst us, and die for us, to wash us from our sins, and to give us new clothing, and to make us ready to live in God's house. When you ask God for anything, you must say 'For Jesus Christ's sake.' Jesus Christ is the Son of God."

After these words the minister carefully descended the ladder, followed by Jessica's bare and nimble feet, and she led him by the nearest way into one of the great thoroughfares of the city, where he said good-bye to her, adding "God bless you, my child," in a tone which sank into Jessica's heart. He had put a silver sixpence into her hand to provide for her breakfast the next three mornings, and, with a feeling of being very rich, she returned to her miserable home.

The next morning Jessica presented herself proudly as a customer at Daniel's stall, and paid over the sixpence in advance. He felt a little troubled as he heard her story, lest the minister should endeavour to find him out; but he could not refuse to let the child come daily for her comfortable breakfast. If he was detected, he would promise to give up his coffee-stall rather than offend the great people of the chapel; but unless he was, it would be foolish of him to lose the money it brought in week after week.

CHAPTER IX

JESSICA'S FIRST PRAYER ANSWERED

EVERY SUNDAY evening the barefooted and bareheaded child might be seen advancing confidently up to the chapel where rich and fashionable people worshipped God; but before taking her place she arrayed herself in a little cloak and bonnet, which had once belonged to the minister's elder daughter, and which was kept with Daniel's serge gown, so that she presented a somewhat more respectable appearance in the eyes of the congregation. The minister had no listener more attentive, and he would have missed the pinched, earnest little face if it were not to be seen in the seat just under the pulpit. At the close of each service he spoke to her for a minute or two in his vestry, often saying no more than a single sentence, for the day's labour had wearied him. The shilling, which was always lying upon the chimney-piece, placed there by Jane and Winny in turns, was immediately handed over, according to promise, to Daniel as she left the chapel, and so Jessica's breakfast was provided for her week after week.

But at last there came a Sunday evening when the minister, going up into his pulpit, did miss the wistful, hungry face, and the shilling lay unclaimed upon the vestry chimney-piece. Daniel looked out for her anxiously every morning, but no Jessica glided into his secluded corner, to sit beside him with her breakfast on her lap, and with a number of strange questions to ask. He felt her absence more keenly than he could have expected. The child was nothing to him, he kept saying to himself; and yet he felt that she was something, and that he could not help being uneasy and anxious about her. Why had he never enquired where she lived? The minister knew, and for a minute Daniel thought he would go and ask him, but that might awaken suspicion. How could he account for so much anxiety, when he was supposed only to know of her absence from chapel one Sunday evening? It would be running a risk, and, after all, Jessica was nothing to him. So he went home and looked over his savings-bank book, and counted his money, and he found to his satisfaction that he had gathered together nearly four hundred pounds, and was adding more every week.

But when upon the next Sunday Jessica's seat was again empty, the anxiety of the solemn chapel-keeper overcame his prudence and his fears. The minister had retired to his vestry, and was standing with his arm resting upon the chimney-piece, with his eyes fixed upon the unclaimed shilling, which Winny had laid there before the service, when there was a tap at the door, and Daniel entered with a respectful but hesitating air.

"Well, Standring?" said the minister, questioningly.

"Sir," he said, "I'm uncomfortable about that little girl, and I know you've been once to see after her; she told me about it; and so I make bold to ask you where she lives, and I'll see what's become of her."

"Right, Standring," answered the minister; "I am troubled about the child, and so are my little girls. I thought of going myself, but my time is very much occupied just now."

"I'll go, sir," replied Daniel, promptly; and, after receiving the necessary information about Jessica's home, he put out the lights, locked the door, and turned towards his lonely lodgings.

But though it was getting late upon Sunday evening, and Jessica's home was a long way distant, Daniel found that his anxiety would not suffer him to return to his solitary room. It was of no use to reason with himself, as he stood at the corner of the street, feeling perplexed and troubled, and promising his conscience that he would go the very first thing in the morning after he shut up his coffee-stall. In the dim, dusky light, as the summer evening drew to a close, he fancied he could see Jessica's thin figure and wan face gliding on before him, and turning round from time to time to see if he were following. It was only fancy, and he laughed a little at himself; but the laugh was husky,

and there was a choking sensation in his throat, so he buttoned his Sunday coat over his breast, where his silver watch and chain hung temptingly, and started off at a rapid pace for the centre of the city.

It was not quite dark when he reached the court, and stumbled up the narrow entry leading to it; but Daniel did hesitate when he opened the stable door, and looked into a blank, black space, in which he could discern nothing. He thought he had better retreat while he could do so safely; but as he still stood with his hand upon the rusty latch, he heard a faint, small voice through the nicks of the unceiled boarding above his head.

"Our Father," said the little voice, "please to send somebody to me, for Jesus Christ's sake, Amen."

"I'm here, Jess," cried Daniel, with a sudden bound of his heart, such as he had not felt for years, and which almost took away his breath as he peered into the darkness, until at last he discerned dimly the ladder which led up into the loft.

Very cautiously, but with an eagerness which surprised himself, he climbed up the creaking rounds of the ladder and entered the dismal room, where the child was lying in desolate darkness. Fortunately he had put his box of matches into his pocket, and the end of a wax candle, with which he kindled the lamps, and in another minute a gleam of light shone upon Jessica's white features. She was stretched upon a scanty litter of straw under the slanting roof where the tiles had not fallen off, with her poor rags for her only covering; but as her eyes looked up into Daniel's face bending over her, a bright smile of joy sparkled in them.

"Oh!" she cried, gladly, but in a feeble voice, "it's Mr. Dan'el! Has God told you to come here, Mr. Dan'el?"

"Yes," said Daniel, kneeling beside her, taking her wasted hand in his, and parting the matted hair upon her damp forehead.

"What did he say to you, Mr. Dan'el?" said Jessica.

"He told me I was a great sinner," replied Daniel. "He told me I loved a little bit of dirty money better than a poor, friendless, helpless child, whom he had sent to me to see if I would do her a little good for his sake. He looked at me, or the minister did, through and through, and he said, 'Thou fool, this night thy soul shall be required of thee: then whose shall those things be which thou hast provided?' And I could answer him nothing, Jess. He was come to a reckoning with me, and I could not say a word to him."

"Aren't you a good man, Mr. Dan'el?" whispered Jessica.

"No, I'm a wicked sinner," he cried, while the tears rolled down his solemn face. "I've been constant at God's house, but only to get money; I've been steady and industrious, but only to get money; and now God looks at me, and he says, 'Thou fool!' Oh, Jess, Jess! you're more fit for heaven than I ever was in my life."

"Why don't you ask him to make you good for Jesus Christ's sake?" asked the child.

"I can't," he said. "I've been kneeling down Sunday after Sunday when the minister's been praying, but all the time I was thinking how rich some of the carriage people were. I've been loving money and worshipping money all along, and I've nearly let you die rather than run the risk of losing part of my earnings. I'm a very sinful man."

"But you know what the minister often says," murmured Jessica. " 'Herein is love, not that we loved God, but that he loved us, and sent his Son to be the propitiation for our sins.' "

"I've heard it so often that I don't feel it," said Daniel. "I used to like to hear the minister say it, but now it goes in at one ear and out at the other. My heart is very hard, Jessica."

By the feeble glimmer of the candle Daniel saw Jessica's wistful eyes fixed upon him with a sad and loving glance; and then she lifted up her weak hand to her face, and laid it over her closed eyelids, and her feverish lips moved slowly.

"God," she said, "please to make Mr. Dan'el's heart soft, for Jesus Christ's sake, Amen."

She did not speak again, nor Daniel, for some time. He took off his Sunday coat and laid it over the tiny, shivering frame, which was shaking with cold even in the summer evening; and as he did so he remembered the words which the Lord says he will pronounce at the last day of reckoning, "Forasmuch as ye have done it unto one of the least of these my brethren, ye have done it unto me." Daniel Standring felt his heart turning with love to the Saviour, and he bowed his head upon his hands, and cried in the depths of his contrite spirit, "God be merciful to me, a sinner."

CHAPTER X

THE SHADOW OF DEATH

THERE WAS NO coffee-stall opened under the railway arch the following morning, and Daniel's regular customers stood amazed as they drew near the empty corner, where they were accustomed to get their early breakfast. It would have astonished them still more if they could have seen how he was occupied in the miserable loft. He had intrusted a friendly woman out of the court to buy food and fuel, and all night long he had watched beside Jessica, who was light-headed and delirious, but in the wanderings of her thoughts and words often spoke of God, and prayed for her Mr. Dan'el. The neighbour informed him that the child's mother had gone off some days before, fearing that she was ill of some infectious fever, and that she, alone, had taken a little care of her from time to time. As soon as the morning came he sent for a doctor, and, after receiving permission from him, he wrapped the poor deserted Jessica in his coat, and bearing her tenderly in his arms down the ladder, he carried her to a cab, which the neighbour brought to the entrance of the court. It was to no other than his own solitary home that he had resolved to take her; and when the mistress of the lodgings stood at her door with her arms a-kimbo, to forbid the admission of the wretched and neglected child, her tongue was silenced by the gleam of a half-sovereign, which Daniel slipped into the palm of her hard hand.

By that afternoon's post the minister received the following letter:—

"REVEREND SIR,

"If you will condescend to enter under my humble roof, you will have the pleasure of seeing little Jessica, who is at the point of death, unless God in his mercy restores her. Hoping you will excuse this liberty, as I cannot leave the child, I remain with duty,

"Your respectful Servant,

"D. STANDRING.

"P.S. Jessica desires her best love and duty to Miss Jane and Winny."

The minister laid aside the book he was reading, and without any delay started off for his chapel-keeper's dwelling. There was Jessica lying restfully upon Daniel's bed, but the pinched features were deadly pale, and the sunken eyes shone with a waning light. She was too feeble to turn her head when the door opened, and he paused for a minute, looking at her and at Daniel, who, seated at the head of the bed, was turning over the papers in his desk, and reckoning up once more the savings of his lifetime. But when the minister advanced into the middle of the room, Jessica's white cheeks flushed into a deep red.

"Oh, minister!" she cried, "God has given me everything I wanted except paying Mr. Dan'el for the coffee he used to give me."

"Ah! but God had paid me over and over again," said Daniel, rising to receive the minister. "He's given me my own soul in exchange for it. Let me make bold to speak to you this once, sir. You're a very learned man, and a great preacher, and many people flock to hear you till I'm hard put to it to find seats for them at times; but all the while, hearkening to you every blessed Sabbath, I was losing my soul, and you never once said to me, though you saw me scores and scores of times, 'Standring, are you a saved man?'"

"Standring," said the minister, in a tone of great distress and regret, "I always took it for granted that you were a Christian."

"Ah," continued Daniel, thoughtfully, "but God wanted somebody to ask me that question, and he did not find anybody in the congregation, so he sent this poor little lass to me. Well, I don't mind telling now, even if I lose the place; but for a long time, nigh upon ten years, I've kept a coffee-stall on week-days in the city, and cleared, one week

with another, about ten shillings: but I was afraid the chapel-wardens wouldn't approve of the coffee business, as low, so I kept it a close secret, and always shut up early of a morning. It's me that sold Jessica her cup of coffee, which you paid for, sir."

"There's no harm in it, my good fellow," said the minister, kindly; "you need make no secret of it."

"Well," resumed Daniel, "the questions this poor little creature has asked me have gone quicker and deeper down to my conscience than all your sermons, if I may make so free as to say it. She's come often and often of a morning, and looked into my face with those dear eyes of hers, and said, 'Don't you love Jesus Christ, Mr. Dan'el?' 'Doesn't it make you very glad that God is your Father, Mr. Dan'el?' 'Are we getting nearer heaven every day, Mr. Dan'el?' And one day, says she, 'Are you going to give all your money to God, Mr. Dan'el?' Ah, that question made me think indeed, and it's never been answered till this day. While I've been sitting beside the bed here, I've counted up all my savings: 397l. 17s. it is; and I've said, 'Lord, it's all thine; and I'd give every penny of it rather than lose the child, if it be thy blessed will to spare her life.' "

Daniel's voice quavered at the last words, and his face sank upon the pillow where Jessica's feeble and motionless head lay. There was a very sweet yet surprised smile upon her face, and she lifted her wasted fingers to rest upon the bowed head beside her, while she shut her eyes and shaded them with her other weak hand.

"Our Father," she said, in a faint whisper which still reached the ears of the minister and the beadle, "I asked you to let me come home to heaven; but if Mr. Dan'el wants me, please to let me stay a little longer, for Jesus Christ's sake, Amen."

For some minutes after Jessica's prayer there was a deep and unbroken silence in the room, Daniel still hiding his face upon the pillow, and the minister standing beside them with bowed head and closed eyes, as if he also were praying. When he looked up again at the forsaken and desolate child, he saw that her feeble hand had fallen from her face, which looked full of rest and peace, while her breath came faintly but regularly through her parted lips. He took her little hand into his own with a pang of fear and grief; but instead of the mortal chillness of death, he felt the pleasant warmth and moisture of life. He touched Daniel's shoulder, and as he lifted up his head in sudden alarm, he whispered to him, "The child is not dead, but is only asleep."

Before Jessica was fully recovered, Daniel rented a little house for himself and his adopted daughter to dwell in. He made many enquiries after her mother, but she never appeared again in her old haunts, and he was well pleased that there was nobody to interfere with his charge of Jessica. When Jessica grew strong enough, many a cheerful walk had they together, in the early mornings, as they wended their way to the railway bridge, where the little girl took her place behind the stall, and soon learned to serve the daily customers; and many a happy day was spent in helping to sweep and dust the chapel, into which she had crept so secretly at first, her great delight being to attend to the pulpit and the vestry, and the pew where the minister's children sat, while Daniel and the woman he employed cleaned the rest of the building. Many a Sunday also the minister in his pulpit, and his little daughters in their pew, and Daniel treading softly about the aisles, as their glance fell upon Jessica's eager, earnest, happy face, thought of the first time they saw her sitting amongst the congregation, and of Jessica's first prayer.

8

Castle Blair

A Story of Youthful Days

By FLORA L. SHAW

I_N *Castle Blair*, five children inhabit a world wholly their own on an Irish estate. They create their own society, make their own rules, manage their own lives, adopt the cause of the Irish tenantry, and develop a running feud with their uncle's land agent, which steadily mounts in intensity until human lives are at stake. They revel in their freedom out of doors, manage intrigue cleverly and enterprisingly, work themselves up to a savage pitch of hatred, and display a ruthless inability to consider any interests but their own. Their young cousin is the sole intermediary between them and the adult world. Of the books selected here only Annie Keary's *Rival Kings* even hinted that children could be such creatures; and even her Maurice Lloyd was hedged about by parental and social restrictions that in *Castle Blair* have disappeared.

No other nineteenth-century author seems to have asked the questions about children that Flora Shaw asked, or to have reached the same conclusions as to their capabilities. To meet children with the same terrifying single-mindedness and independence of the adult world, one must turn to Richard Hughes's *High Wind in Jamaica* (1929) and William Golding's *Lord of the Flies* (1950), and neither of these was written primarily for children. Not until well along in the twentieth century, then, did young Murtagh, the ringleader of the *Castle Blair* children, find a fellow spirit. In all three books, an island provides a major feature of the setting. *Castle Blair*'s brilliant re-creation of the Irish scene, its swift, easy, compelling style, make it as distinguished artistically as it is in theme. Yet the known circumstances of the author's life still leave her admirers without satisfactory answers to the question: how was it possible for her to write such a book?

Flora Shaw (1852–1939) was the third of fourteen children born to a general of Irish Protestant ancestry, who, when stationed on the Indian Ocean island of Mauritius, married the beautiful daughter of the French Catholic governor. All the children were brought up as Protestants. They spent the summers on their grandfather's estate, Kimmage, not far from Dublin. Here Flora and her brothers and sisters lived a life almost as free as the life she portrayed in *Castle Blair*. The stream, the island, the hut, the village, and the relationship between the villagers and the children—all came from her own experience. But the harsh agent was an invention of her own, created to provide a whetstone on which the brilliant, proud, and ruthless Murtagh might sharpen his wits.

Beautiful, intelligent, and vivacious, Flora Shaw was the brightest star in a bright family constellation. In her teens, heavy responsibilities fell upon her when her mother became an invalid. Flora bore much of the burden of the upbringing and education of her eleven younger brothers and sisters; after her mother died in 1870, the task became hers alone for three years until her father remarried. Financial worries and ill health added to her anxieties. Although she was extremely attractive to young men, and had at least one proposal from an ardent suitor, she preferred not to marry. She had a series of friendships with older men. At seventeen, she became a confidante of John Ruskin (then in his fifties) during his anguished courtship of the fragile and beautiful Rose La Touche, no older than Flora Shaw, which ended in disaster when Rose died in 1875. Ruskin even discussed with Flora the details of his bouts of madness. George Meredith, Admiral Maxse, and Charles Eliot Norton were only three among the distinguished men far older than she who sought her company and made her their friend.

In the late seventies, she took complete charge of another family of children, and later of the aging parents of her girlhood admirer. She did much social work in the London slums, especially among prostitutes, and was deeply shocked at the horrors of child prostitution. Like so many of her generation, she was torn by religious doubts, and especially by the apparently insoluble contradiction in the notion of an ostensibly all-loving God who at the same time had decreed eternal punishment for the unregenerate. So until her early thirties, her life was much like that of Annie Keary, largely one of self-denial. It was during this period that she wrote *Castle Blair* and her two other books for children.

In 1886, while on a trip to Gibraltar, Flora Shaw obtained an interview with a Sudanese Pasha exiled to the Rock by the British authorities. Its success led to an entirely new career. Flora Shaw became an influential newspaper correspondent and an expert on colonial problems. She visited South Africa, Australia, Canada, making friends everywhere, regarded as an authority on her subject by officials as well as journalists. At fifty, in 1902, she married Sir Frederick Lugard, later Lord Lugard, soldier and colonial governor with long experience in Africa. During the last twenty-seven years of her life, Flora Shaw, as Lady Lugard, accompanied him to his posts as governor of Northern Nigeria and of Hong Kong before retiring to England. Of a later generation than Annie Keary and from a different social background, Flora Shaw escaped from the confined Victorian spinster's life of surrogate motherhood, religious conflict, and writing for children, into an active world.

The mystery of *Castle Blair* can best be approached by comparing it with her other children's books. In *Hector* (1881) a young French-speaking boy comes to live with French relatives, and his little cousin, Zélie, falls in love with him. Independent and vigorous, scornful of learning, Hector is much like Murtagh in *Castle Blair,* and his relationship to Zélie parallels Murtagh's to his loving cousin, Nessa. In *Hector,* the setting—in the region of the Landes, in the foothills of the Pyrenees—was remembered from Flora Shaw's visits to a beloved French aunt, and the episode of the billeting of French troops on the household and their excellent behavior (and the incompetence of the officers) were actual experiences.

In *Phyllis Browne* (1883), the scene is an Essex village, site of a large gunpowder factory. Between Phyllis, the brave and beautiful fourteen-year-old daughter of the commanding officer of the "Works," and her slightly younger cousin Lal (Ladislas, refugee son of a Polish nobleman), there exists an even more intimate friendship than that between Nessa and Murtagh. There is much kissing; they are in and out of one another's bedrooms, and Phyllis "tucks Lal up" at night. What is clearly passion is sublimated by innocence. As in *Castle Blair*, the children sympathize with the village poor in their squalid hovels.

So the reader comes away with the impression that together with her romantic memories of childhood adventure at Kimmage, Flora Shaw cherished in her imagination—and perhaps in her own memory—a dream of idyllic friendship between boy and girl cousins: Murtagh and Nessa, Hector and Zélie, Lal and Phyllis. We are free to conjecture (but no more) that Flora Shaw's reluctance to marry until she was fifty, and some of the genius of *Castle Blair*, may derive from this dream.

She knew both from memory and from observation how older children might, for example, allow a younger child to struggle vainly in an ice-cold stream while trying to wade as fast as her elders, until she was almost frozen and sure she was being abandoned. Flora Shaw knew how a child could love a dog and would mourn his loss. The children's scheme to help the wretched Theresa and the villagers resembles nothing so much as

Tom Sawyer's fantastic plan to set Jim free from the cabin at Aunt Sally's and Uncle Silas's. Ruskin, who encouraged Flora Shaw to write *Castle Blair,* called it "good and lovely and true," and said that the description of Winnie was the best description of a noble child he had ever read. At the distance of almost a century, we may agree with him. But, as with many artistic miracles, efforts to explain and account for *Castle Blair* only enhance the mysteries of its creation.

The text of Castle Blair *is reprinted from an American edition (Boston: Roberts Brothers, 1878).*

CHAPTER I

I T WAS RAINING HARD. Night had closed in already round Castle Blair. In the park the great trees, like giant ghosts, loomed gloomily indistinct through the dim atmosphere. Not a sound was to be heard but the steady down-pour of descending rain, and, from time to time, a long, low shudder of trees as the night wind swept over the park.

The darkness and the rain had it all their own way outside, but there was one spot of light in the landscape. The hall door of the castle stood open, and behind it, in hospitable Irish fashion, there blazed a fire from which the warm rays streamed out and illumined the very rain itself; for the dampness outside caught the pleasant glow and reflected it back again, till all round about the doorway there was, as it were, a halo of golden mist. The stone arch of the door was hidden by it, but it formed in itself an arch above the shining granite steps,—a beautiful framework of light for certain little figures, who, dark and ruddy against the glowing back-ground of the hall, were to be seen dancing backwards and forwards as though impatiently waiting for something. They were only children, and impatiently waiting for something they certainly were. There were three of them, two fair-haired girls, and a boy.

"When will she come, I wonder?" said the elder of the girls, looking anxiously through the darkness in the direction of the avenue. "I'm sure the train must have been ever so late."

"Of course it was!" replied the boy; "it always is, and besides it would take half the day to get from Ballyboden in this weather. We ought to have sent a sailing vessel for her instead of the carriage."

"I say, Murtagh, I wonder what she *will* be like. Uncle Blair's never seen her. Donnie doesn't know anything about her. It's very funny having French cousins one doesn't know anything about."

"Oh, she's sure to be all right; Uncle Harry was papa's favorite brother! But I wish Bobbo and Winnie had got in in time. Hark! what's that?"

"That" was the sound of carriage wheels, the sound the little listeners expected. It drew nearer and nearer, approaching slowly along the winding avenue; the wet gravel crunched under the wheels, and at last out of the darkness emerged a heavy old carriage drawn by a pair of heavy old horses.

"I say, David, look sharp!" called Murtagh from the doorway. The horses were startled into activity by an unexpected touch of the whip, and the next instant the carriage stopped at the bottom of the steps.

The boy who had spoken dashed down to open the door, but a sudden shyness seemed to fall upon his two companions, and they shrank back into the hall. There was, however, little to be afraid of in the girl who in another moment stood upon the threshold. She seemed to be about eighteen or nineteen. Tired and travel-stained though she looked, there was a quiet grace in the slight figure; and the face in its setting of ruffled gold hair was as soft as it was sparkling. Her most remarkable feature was a pair of large, dark gray eyes which were looking out just now with a half-interested, half-wistful expression, that seemed to say this was no common arriving.

And indeed for her it was not. An absolute stranger, she was arriving for the first time at Castle Blair, to make a new home in a new country amongst relations she did not know. She had been told she was to live with an old bachelor uncle, and that was literally all the information she possessed. If the children, as their words had indicated, knew little about her, she knew still less of them, for she was not even aware of their existence.

Notwithstanding the first movement of hesitation the elder little girl seemed quite to understand that upon her devolved the duties of hostess, for she came forward now, and holding out her hand said shyly, "How do you do?"

The new comer felt shy too perhaps, but she took the hand and kept it in hers, drawing the child nearer to her as she answered in a sweet, clear voice: "I am very well, thank you, only a little tired with traveling. A long journey is very tiring."

"Yes, very," said the little girl, blushing again; and there the conversation would have been likely to stop, but the boy who had opened the carriage door, having taken the stranger's wraps from her, had now followed her into the hall and exclaimed heartily:

"Awfully tiring, and that drive from Ballyboden is so long. You must be very cold; come over to the fire."

As he spoke he dropped her rug and bag on the floor, and ran and pulled forward one of the wooden armchairs that were ranged along the wall on either side of the fire-place. "Did you see the fire as you came up?" he added; "the door had got shut somehow, but we opened it on purpose."

"Yes, I saw it, just now," she replied, as after a minute's hesitation she seated herself in the chair. "It looked so pleasant and cheerful through the rain, it made me wish to get to it."

"A fire's rather a jolly thing to see after a long drive in the dark," said the boy; "and we do know how to make fires here if we don't know anything else."

The children evidently expected their guest to stay in the hall, so she unfastened her gloves, and drawing them off held out two white hands to the blaze in quiet enjoyment of the warmth. Then after a pause, during which the children were studying her appearance, and she was wondering who her little companions might be, she turned again to the boy and said:

"We have not any one to introduce us to each other so we must introduce ourselves; I daresay you know my name is Adrienne. Will you tell me your name, and the names of your sisters?"

The two girls blushed again, the little one shrinking behind the elder, but the boy replied at once:

"I'm Murtagh. That tallest one is Rosamond Mary; Rosie we call her. She's twelve years old."

"No, Murtagh, you always make mistakes; I'm thirteen very nearly !" exclaimed Rosie, suddenly forgetting her shyness.

"Oh well! it's all the same. Of course, girls always like to be thought old," he explained, with a funny little chuckle, to Adrienne. "Besides, you won't be thirteen till the winter."

"And that little thing is Eleanor Grace," he continued, addressing himself to his duty as master of the ceremonies; "Ellie, she's called. She's only three. Winnie's the best of them; she's worth two of Rosie; but she and Bobbo are out in the garden."

"Out! In this pouring rain?" said Adrienne, looking towards the open door.

"What does that matter?" returned Murtagh. "We don't mind rain. We're hardy little barbarians; you needn't expect to find us like dandy French children."

The boy spoke flippantly; he was evidently in a state of excited high spirits.

A merry twinkle woke in Adrienne's eyes. Already she was forgetting the fear of strange bachelor uncles.

"No," she replied, with a significant glance at the dishevelled state of the children's toilettes. "I did not think you were dandy."

Murtagh blushed in spite of himself, and looked deprecatingly at the knees of his somewhat worn nickerbockers, while his sister hastened to excuse herself.

"It really is impossible to keep tidy with the boys," she explained; "they do pull one about so."

"Come now, the boys didn't tear that dress; you tore it yourself on Tuesday, coming down a nut tree," said Murtagh.

A contemptuous reply from Rosie seemed likely to lead to a sharp answer, but Adrienne interposed a question. She felt quite at home with the children now, and she wanted to find out something about them.

"Do you always live here?" she asked.

"Of course we do!" answered both the children at once. "There's nowhere else where we could live since we came back from India."

"Are there any more of you besides Winnie and Bobbo?"

"No," said Murtagh, "that's all. And quite enough, I expect you'll think before long," he added, looking thoughtfully into the fire, and suddenly ceasing from his former flippant manner.

Still Adrienne looked as though she would like to know more, and after hesitating for a moment she continued: "Who else is there in the house? Who takes care of you?"

"Oh!" said Rosie, "there's Mrs. Donegan. She takes care of everything you know, and cooks the dinner and all that. Then there's Peggy Murphy. She does the schoolroom, and mends our clothes; and there is Kate Murphy; and then there's the new housemaid, and Uncle Blair's man, Brown; and that's all except Mr. Plunkett."

"Mr. Plunkett!" repeated Murtagh in a tone of disgust.

"Oh he is so horrible," continued Rosie, who seemed prepared for any amount of chatter now she had thrown away her shyness. "He settles all about everything, and gives us our pocket-money on Saturdays, and gives Mrs. Donegan money to buy our clothes, and orders everybody about, and interferes. Mrs. Plunkett says his mother was a second cousin of Uncle Blair's mother, but I don't believe she was. He's quite vulgar; he doesn't have later dinner or anything. But he doesn't live in this house, you know; he lives in a house in the park."

"He's dot such a nice ickle baby," put in Ellie, who had come close to Adrienne, and had been following the conversation with wide-open eyes and ears.

"Has he?" said Adrienne, encircling the child with her arm. "What is it like?"

"It's dot two dreat big eyes and—"

"It's got a nose, Ellie, don't forget that," interrupted Murtgah mockingly.

Little Ellie was silenced; she flushed up, and tears came into her eyes. But without paying any attention to her Rosie continued:

"And that's all the people there are in the house."

"Except—Monsieur Blair," suggested Adrienne, comforting Ellie as she spoke by hanging her watch round the child's neck.

"Oh! Uncle Blair! Yes, of course he's here, only I forgot all about him."

"You don't see much of him?"

"No," said Murtagh, with a chuckle; "he thinks we're perfect little savages. He has breakfast with us every morning, because, you know, he thinks he ought to; but you should see how funny he looks. I believe he's always expecting us to set upon him and eat him, or do something of that kind."

"Hullo, Mrs. Donegan!" he called out suddenly, recovering his excited spirits as a good-humored, shrewd-looking woman entered the hall. "There you are! and it's high time you came, too. Here's a poor lady sitting freezing in the hall just for want of some one to show her to her room. Allow me to introduce Mrs. Bridget Donegan Esquire of Tipperary."

Adrienne acknowledged the introduction with a smile, and Mrs. Donegan, curtseying, began at once to apologise for not having met her at the door.

"It's very sorry I am, Ma'am, that you should have been kept sitting out here. I've been waiting this last half-hour to hear the bell go," she began with much respectful dignity. And then suddenly turning round upon the children: "It's you, Master Murtagh, might ha' thought to ring it; and where's your manners, Miss Rose, to keep Miss Blair sitting out here in the cold instead of taking her into the drawing-room."

"It's not very cold," said Adrienne, with a smiling glance at the fire. But she rose as she spoke, and Mrs. Donegan continued: "Mr. Blair desired his compliments, Ma'am, and he was sorry he was engaged to dine out the evening you arrived, but he hoped the young ladies and gentlemen would make you comfortable. And, if you please, Ma'am, I've boiled a couple of fowls for you, and there's a nice little drop o' soup; and will you have dinner served in the dining-room, or wouldn't it be more comfortable like, if I sent it up with the children's tea into the school-room."

"Oh, I should like that much the best, please," said Adrienne. And the expression of relief that lighted up her countenance was perhaps hardly complimentary to Mr. Blair.

"Then it's no use going to that smelly old drawing-room!" exclaimed Murtagh. "Come along to the school-room!"

He turned round as he spoke, and led the way across the hall, treating with silent contempt the expostulations of Rose and Mrs. Donegan, who were evidently of opinion that Adrienne ought first to be conducted to the drawing-room. He told Ellie to run on and open the door, so that there might be some light in the passage; but her little fingers not proving strong enough to turn the handle, the whole party had to grope their way in the dark. At the end of a long passage Rosie threw open a door, saying, "Here's the school-room! It's not particularly tidy. We did make it neat this morning, but somehow it always gets wrong again."

If it had been made neat that morning, it certainly had got considerably wrong again. It was a good-sized room, with a large window at one end and another smaller one at the side. But the curtains were not drawn before either of them, and one was open, letting the rain beat in upon the carpet. The fire had burnt low, and the fender was full of ashes and chestnut-husks. The rest of the room was so strewn with toys, books, cooking-utensils, and miscellaneous rubbish of every description, that there was some difficulty in distinguishing any article of furniture: only the tea-table, clean and white in the midst, stood out against the general disorder like an ark in a second deluge.

"Deed faith, it's time ye had some one to see after yez," muttered Mrs. Donegan to herself. "Where's Miss Winnie and Master Bobbo?" she added aloud.

"Gone to the garden to get some apples," answered Murtagh. "I wish they'd look sharp in."

"Well, when they do come in there isn't a dress for Miss Winnie to put on. All the print dresses are gone to the wash-tub, and she soaked her old black one through and through this morning."

"Oh well, she can dry herself all right. Don't you bother her about it and she won't bother you," replied Murtagh, good-humoredly, sitting down to the piano as he spoke, and beginning to play "St. Patrick's Day in the Morning."

"That's just the way it is with them all; there's no getting them to listen to reason; an' it isn't that they don't have frocks enough," explained poor Mrs. Donegan in despair, "but you might just every bit as well try to keep clean pinafores on the ducks and chickens out in the yard as try to keep them tidy."

Murtagh's only answer was to crow like a cock, and then he fell into the more meditative quacking of ducks as he began an elaborate variation upon his air.

Their guest began to look just a little forlorn. She might have been amused at first, and perhaps relieved too by the children's want of ceremony, but after traveling for three or four days people are apt to be tired, and it did not seem to occur to any one that she might like to be shown to a room where she could rest a little and wash away the dust of her long journey. There was apparently no chair disengaged either, upon which she might sit down, so she stood leaning against the chimney-piece, while Rosie tried hurriedly to make the room a little tidier, and Ellie sat down upon the floor, delighted with the treasure that had been left hanging round her neck.

But Rosie had some idea of the duties of a hostess, and she soon noticed how white the girl looked.

"You look dreadfully tired," she said in a voice so gentle that Adrienne was quite surprised. "Wait a minute, here's a comfortable chair; I'll clear the music out of it." As she spoke she tipped up an arm-chair, so as to empty what was in it on the floor, and wheeled it to the fire-place.

"Thank you," said Adrienne; "but if you would show me where my room is: I should like to take off these," indicating with a little gesture her bonnet and cloak; "I am so tired." She meant to smile, but she really was so tired that she was much more near having tears in her eyes.

"Oh, yes," said Rosie; "and I'll get you some—" but the end of her sentence was lost as she ran out of the room.

The variation of "St. Patrick's Day" was growing so intricate that Murtagh was completely absorbed by it. Mrs. Donegan was engaged in picking up books and toys from the floor; there was nothing for Adrienne to do but to sit down and wait.

"You do look tired, Ma'am," said Mrs. Donegan presently, pausing with a broken Noah's ark in her hand. "I think, Master Murtagh, I'll go and send the tea in at once. There's no use waitin' for Miss Winnie and Master Bobbo."

"Fire away," grunted Murtagh from the piano, executing some difficult chords with his left hand. His music was very good, quite unlike the playing of most children, and Adrienne began to think it pleasant to listen to as she lay back in the big chair Rosie had prepared for her.

But in another moment the music was interrupted by a rushing sound, a collision of some kind, and then a confusion of voices in the hall.

"Whatever are you thinking of, Master Bobbo?" came out clearly in Donnie's energetic tones.

"I do wish you'd look where you're going, Donnie; you've nearly knocked me into the middle of next week!" retorted a hearty boy's voice.

"Hurrah! here they are," cried Murtagh, and forgetting the interest of his music he started up and dashed into the hall. There was some whispering outside the door; Adrienne heard plainly, "What's she like?" and then Bobbo and Murtagh entered the room, followed by Winnie.

Bobbo was a pleasant strong-looking boy, with clear eyes, rosy cheeks, and a turned-up nose, a contrast to Murtagh's sallow face and dark deep-set eyes.

Winnie was a little elf-like thing, and as she came in at the door, her scarlet cloak twisted all crooked with the wind, the skirt of her brown dress gathered up in both hands to hold the apples they had been to fetch, her hair beaten down over her forehead by the rain, her great dark eyes dancing, her cheeks glowing, the merry mouth ready to break into smiles, she seemed the very incarnation of life and brightness.

"The Queen of robin redbreasts!" was the idea that flashed through Adrienne's mind, and she sat up with revived animation to greet the new comers.

Bobbo walked up to her and said, "How do you do?" with a decidedly Irish intonation, retiring then behind her chair and entering into a whispered conversation with little Ellie.

Winnie advanced to the hearth-rug and dropped all her apples upon it, saying as she did so: "Fetch the dishes, Bobbo, from the pantry." Then she shook hands with Adrienne, looking at her with clear, intelligent eyes.

"You have got your apples," said Adrienne. "Your brother told me you were gone for them. He said you did not mind being wet."

"Mind being wet!" said Winnie, with a bright look of amusement; "of course we don't. Are you fond of apples?" she continued, looking down at the rosy fruit and wet leaves scattered on the hearth-rug. "We thought we'd have some for tea as you were coming, so Bobbo and I went to fetch them. We meant to have been in by the time you came, only it was so dark it made us longer. See, here's a beauty!" she added, kneeling down upon the rug and picking out a specially fine Ribstone Pippin. "Do try this; I'm sure it's good."

She held it up towards Adrienne as she spoke, large and rich-colored, still wet with rain, the cluster of leaves under which it had ripened yet crisp upon its stalk, and she looked so thoroughly persuaded of its deliciousness that Adrienne could not help taking it, and answered smilingly—

"I will have it for dessert after the chickens."

But with a sudden change of expression, forgetting all about Adrienne, Winnie turned to Murtagh, and exclaimed eagerly—

"Oh, it has been such fun getting these; wasn't it, Bobbo? I *must* tell you all about it. Well, we got past Bland's cottage all safe enough; the rain and the wind were making such a jolly row there wasn't a chance of our being heard."

"Bland's the gardener," explained Murtagh to Adrienne, "and he always tries to catch us when we bag the fruit."

"But just as we were nearly in the garden," continued Winnie,—"Bobbo was on the top of the gate, and I'd got up as far as the lock,—what should we hear but Bland coming, tramp, tramp, along the gravel; and Bobbo was such an awful little muff, he called out: 'I say, he's got a lantern, an' he's sure to see us.' And, of course, don't you see that made him hear us, and it would be all up if we couldn't get hid quick enough; so I jumped down and squeezed in under a bush, but when Bobbo tried to get down, one of the spikes of the gate went through his knickerbockers, and there he stuck. On came Bland, and called out: 'Ha! ye good-for-nothing vagabones; it's caught ye are this time!' and, lo and behold! it wasn't Bland at all, but a great big policeman. He pulled Bobbo down off the gate, and didn't he tear a fine hole in the back of his knickerbockers, just? Poor Bobbo got in such a fright he couldn't say a word, so I jumped out from under the bush, and I said: 'We're not stealing! we're only going to take some apples for tea. We're ladies and gentlemen.' So he looked at the hole in Bobbo's clothes as if he wasn't quite sure, so I said: 'You tore that, taking him off the gate!' Bobbo did look awfully untidy though, with the light of the lantern shining full on the raggy part of him. Then he turned the lantern on to my face, and then he laughed, and said: 'I'm sure I beg your pardon, Miss; I hadn't an idea it would be any one but ragamuffins out o' the village about this wild night.'

"So I said, very politely, you know: 'Please *would* you just help us over the gate? It's so very high to climb when the bars are slippery with rain.' So he helped us both over, and then I said: 'Would you mind just standing about here till we come back? And if you hear Bland coming give a good loud whistle, will you?' So he said he would, and we ran off and got the apples, and then he helped us back over the gate again, and we gave him some apples, and here we are. By the by, Bobbo, I've left my hat up in that first apple tree. But wasn't it jolly fun making the policeman keep watch for us?"

"Awfully jolly!" said Murtagh. "What's his number? we'll make him do it to-morrow night, too. No, no, Winnie; that's not the way to settle those apples. Put the streaked one next the rosy one. So. Now put a yellow one, and a Virginian creeper leaf. There; that's it! You've no more eye for color than a steam-engine."

Tired though she was, Adrienne's face had glistened with responsive fun as Winnie, with expressive gestures, described their little adventure. She had not the least idea who these children were, but they were merry and charming, and their manners put her at ease.

Just as Winnie stopped speaking the schoolroom door was pushed slowly open, and Rosie entered, carefully holding in both hands a salver upon which was a glass of wine. "You look so tired," she said to Adrienne, "that I thought you'd better have this without waiting for tea."

"Thank you," said Adrienne. The wine was just what she needed, and as she put the glass back upon the salver she added gratefully: "You are accustomed to be mistress of a house I see."

Rosie flushed with pleasure, and replied: "There's nobody but me except when Cousin Jane's here. I'll go and see now about hurrying tea: I can't think what they're taking such a time for."

"But my room," suggested Adrienne again; "if I might go to it first, I am so dusty."

"Oh yes!" said Rosie, "I'll be back in a minute;" and she departed on her errand to the kitchen.

"I'll show you your room if you like," said Winnie, jumping up from the floor. "Come along!"

But the fire was drawing clouds of steam from the child's wet clothes, and as Adrienne looked towards her she perceived it.

"Do you know," she exclaimed in dismay, "your dress must be quite wet through? Please do not mind about my room, but go and change it quickly."

"Oh, it doesn't hurt me being wet," laughed Winnie.

"Besides," said Murtagh, "she hasn't got anything to change into. Didn't you hear Donnie say all her clothes were in the wash-tub?"

Adrienne hesitated. She did not like to insist. At the same time she had already made such friends with these children that she felt as though it were somehow her business to prevent them catching cold.

"Haven't you a dressing-gown?" she asked at length. "I think it must be very bad to stay so wet as that."

"Oh yes!" said Winnie, "I'll go and undress and put on my dressing-gown, then I'll be ready to jump into bed without any more trouble; that'll be rather fun. Do you know where my dressing-gown is, Murtagh?" she added, as she danced off towards the door. "You had it last, the day we were dressing up, don't you remember?"

"I'm sure I don't know where we left it," replied Murtagh, pausing to contemplate the dishes with his head on one side and an apple in each hand. "It's somewhere about, I suppose."

"Oh, well, never mind. I'll get Rosie's. Don't finish settling those apples till I come down;" and she vanished into the passage.

Murtagh dropped the apples which he held, and jumped up.

"Shall I show you your room?" he asked, taking a candle from the chimney-piece and turning with sudden politeness to Adrienne. "You really must want to get your things off. Let me carry your umbrella. And you would like to have your bag. We left it in the hall, I think."

He led the way, as he spoke, out again into the hall, and crossing over to the other end began to mount a broad oak staircase.

It was dark with age, and the light of the candle which Murtagh carried sufficed to show that in places bits of carving had dropped or been broken from the high wainscot and massive balustrade: doors were let into the wainscoting, and two of them stood open, but they only disclosed dark distances that seemed to tell of long passages or descending flights of steps.

Murtagh was quite silent at first, preceding Adrienne by a few steps, but when they reached the corridor above he fell back so as to walk beside her.

She said something about the house being very large.

"Yes, and it seems beastly lonely to you now; doesn't it?" he said in a tone different from any he had used before. "I did feel so nasty at first when we came from India. But you must cheer up, you know; you won't think us so bad, I expect, when you get accustomed to us, and it's a dear old place. There's a beautiful river full of rocks, and real wild mountains with heather on them."

"I'm sure I shall like everything," she replied warmly.

"Well, you know," said Murtagh, thoughtfully, "we're awfully rampageous and everything. That's why people don't like us. You see we can't help it exactly, we're always that way." There was a half-sad undertone in the boy's voice, and his companion turned her sweet eyes kindly upon him as she answered, "You've been very kind to me."

He looked gratified, but he put an end to the conversation by throwing open a door and exclaiming, "This is your room."

It was a large, comfortable room with old-fashioned, faded furniture, and a great four-post bed; the big fire that blazed cheerily at one end filling it all with warm light and dancing shadows.

"Have you got water, and all that kind of thing?" he inquired with a look round the room.

"Yes, thank you. Will you unfasten that little box for me?"

Murtagh, having unfastened the box and poked the fire, retired, saying that he would come and fetch her as soon as tea was ready; and the girl was left alone to realize that her new life had actually begun.

She was an orphan. Her mother had been French, her father was the Uncle Harry of whom the children spoke. But both had died while she was yet a baby, and her father had particularly desired that after being brought up by her mother's relations in France she should, as soon as she was old enough, go to live with his brother John.

From her babyhood she had known that she was to come to Ireland when she was eighteen. Though she had never seen her Uncle John, nor even heard from him directly, his arrangements for her had been always so kindly and generous that she had been taught to think of him with both affection and respect. With her French blood she had inherited, too, French adaptability. No one could like having to come to live with strangers, but it was not so bad as having to do as many of her companions had done—marry a perfect stranger; it had to be borne, and she was fully prepared to make the best of it. She was quite ready to be interested in the place and its inhabitants. This rambling house with its dark corridors, its old staircase and endless doors, telling of unoccupied rooms, was unlike anything she had ever seen in France; the idea of living in it pleased her. Irish ways certainly seemed different from any that she knew; but she had expected that they would be different, and the children had received her with such quaint familiarity that already, to an extent she could hardly have believed possible, she felt at home.

CHAPTER II

A‌T EIGHT O'CLOCK next morning, as a great bell ringing through the house announced that breakfast was ready, Murtagh and Rosie set off together from the school-room to fetch their guest, both of them anxious for the glory of introducing her to their uncle.

By the time they got up-stairs Adrienne had already left her room, and was standing in the strip of sunlight that streamed through her open door, looking doubtfully down the corridor. She wore a rough gray woolen dress, fastened at the throat with a knot of bright blue ribbon, and in her belt she had put two or three red leaves from the Virginian creeper that clustered round her window. The sunlight, shining full upon her golden hair, made of the whole a picture that was extremely satisfactory to Murtagh's eye.

"I say, Rosie!" he exclaimed, standing still in the dark end of the corridor, "doesn't she look jolly like that."

"Yes, isn't she pretty? I expect she's had all her clothes made in Paris too," Rosie replied in an enthusiastic whisper, which betrayed that however much the young lady's education had been neglected in other respects, there were some things she did reverence.

"Paris!" retorted Murtagh, contemptuously. But at that moment Adrienne perceived them, and came forward with a bright "Good morning."

"I guessed that the bell meant breakfast," she continued, "and I was wondering how I should find my way to the dining-room."

"That's why we came," said Rosie; "and then there's Uncle Blair, you know, you haven't seen him yet."

"No," said Adrienne. "And the others?" she continued after a little pause, "where are they? Are they in the dining-room?"

"Oh, Bobbo's in bed, I think," replied Rosie, "but he'll be down in a minute or two; and Winnie's—out," she added, letting her voice drop mysteriously at the last word.

"Then she did go?" asked Murtagh eagerly.

"Yes, quite early, while it was dark, about three o'clock, I think; the stable clock struck, but I was so sleepy I couldn't count."

"Is it a secret?" asked Adrienne.

"Well, it's not exactly—at least it's a sort of a secret," replied Rose, doubtfully. She looked at Murtagh as she spoke, to see what he thought; but he was looking at Adrienne, and she had to decide for herself.

"I think you might know," she continued. "She's gone to the Liss of Voura to see if she can see the—Fairies." The last word came out with a vivid blush.

"They say they dance there every morning when the sun rises. But I daresay it's not true," she added in a would-be careless tone, her skepticism arising not from any doubt in the fairies' existence, but from a sudden fear that Adrienne might think such idea ridiculous.

"Why shouldn't it be true I should like to know?" asked Murtagh, with a somewhat fierce ring of championship in his tone. But they had reached the dining-room, and Rosie gladly avoided the necessity for answering by throwing open the door and ushering Adrienne into the presence of Mr. Blair.

He had been sitting reading the newspaper, but as they entered he rose and stretched out both hands to Adrienne, saying in a warm gentle voice: "My dear child, you are very welcome."

As Adrienne advanced, blushing a little, to lay her hands in his, he gazed at her with something of surprised tenderness in his face, and murmured, "Rénée!" Then he added aloud: "What is your name, my dear?"

"Adrienne," she answered.

"Ah, yes, yes. That was her name too," he said dreamily to himself. Then drawing out a chair from the table he continued: "Sit down, and make the tea; I shan't have to do it for myself, any more now."

She sat down as she was told, and began to busy herself with the tea-making. Her uncle stood beside her some little time in silence watching her movements.

"Why didn't they tell me you were so like your mother?" he asked presently.

"My mother!" exclaimed Adrienne. "Am I like her? She died so long ago I don't remember her at all," she added sadly.

"Yes, yes; only two years after she married him. It's a long time ago now. How old are you, my dear?"

"I was eighteen my last birthday," replied Adrienne; but her uncle did not seem to hear. He walked away to his place at the bottom of the table, and his next remark was to ask Rosie where the other children were. Rosie answered sedately that she thought they were coming presently, all except Winnie; and breakfast proceeded in silence till Bobbo came tumbling into the room with little Ellie following upon his heels.

He did not speak to any one, and would have taken his place at once at the breakfast table; but as Adrienne naturally held out her hand and said "Good morning," he came around and shook hands with her, asking with a hearty look out of his frank blue eyes, whether she had got rested yet. Then, though the children kept up a half-whispered conversation between themselves at their end of the table, they did not speak either to their uncle or to Adrienne. Mr. Blair maintained complete silence, and Adrienne devoted herself to Ellie, whose high chair was placed beside her.

The little thing was too shy to speak much, but she looked her surprise and delight at the nicely cut fingers of bread and butter which Adrienne built up into castles on her blue plate, and watched with almost solemn interest the important, and, to her, altogether novel operation of sifting sugary snow upon the roofs of them. Then, as she grew bolder, a little rosy finger was put out, and when some of the snow fell upon it there came such a merry peal of baby laughter that Adrienne laughed too, and Mr. Blair looked up in benign astonishment.

The other children regarded with some surprise the consideration with which the wants of their small sister were supplied, but their chief attention was devoted to their breakfast.

They ate continuously till their hunger was appeased; then Murtagh pushed out his chair, and they all went away, not having been more than a quarter of an hour in the room.

Mr. Blair had finished his breakfast, and apparently was absorbed again in the reading of his newspaper, so Adrienne quietly prepared to follow the children. But as she moved across the room her uncle looked up.

"You have had a sorry welcome, I am afraid, my dear," he said; "but I hope you will be able soon to feel that, for all that, we are none the less glad to have you amongst us." He rose, as he spoke, and walked slowly towards the fire-place where Adrienne stood. "You understand, of course," he continued, "that so long as you live with me you are mistress here. Donegan is very anxious to make you comfortable, but I daresay she may not know everything you require. So you must just make yourself as much at home as you can from the very first, and order anything you want. May I trust you to do this?"

"You are very kind," Adrienne replied gratefully. Then as she looked up at the kind, dreamy face that was turned towards her she was encouraged to add: "But I had a very kind welcome; the children were watching for me, and they took charge of me."

"Ah yes, the children," replied her uncle. "You must try and put up with them as well as you can. Mr. Plunkett tells me that they are very unruly; but they are the children of my brother Launcelot, and till he sends for them they will remain here. Who knows," he added in the tone of one struck by a sudden idea; "perhaps you will not mind having them: they may serve as a sort of companion for you, my poor child. I am afraid you will be very lonely here."

"Do you mean," said Adrienne, puzzled, "you thought I would not like to have the children? Oh, but I am so glad!" And there was no questioning the sudden lighting up of her face. "I was so afraid," she continued; then a vivid blush interrupted the new sentence, and she ended in some confusion—"I love children very much."

"They are very lucky," said her uncle, with a glance of admiration at the pretty confused figure that stood before him on the hearthrug.

"I did not mean,"—she began, responding half-laughingly to the amused look in his face, and at the same time coloring more deeply as she saw that he had divined the end of her sentence.

"My dear child," he interrupted, "you did not mean anything but what was perfectly natural,—that you dreaded the dullness of living alone with a worn-out old man. And I am right glad to find that the children are likely to be a pleasure to you instead of a worry; indeed, I wonder I did not think of that before, for there is only just enough difference of age between you," he added, smiling, "to make *you* delightful to me; while the others!—" An expression of comic despair finished the sentence.

"But now," he continued, "you will be a Godsend to all of us. Since you care about children you will look after them a little for me. And as for them; well, even I will credit them with good taste enough to appreciate in some measure at least the privilege of having such a little guardian. And now, my dear, I will not keep you any longer."

He bent forward, as he spoke, and touched her forehead with his lips. Then with a kindly pressure of the hand he walked to the door, and held it open while she passed out. His rooms lay in the opposite direction to those occupied by the children, so outside the dining-room he turned away; and Adrienne, after crossing the hall and wandering about a little among smaller passages, was guided by the sound of voices to a door which she recognized at once, thanks to a crooked brass handle and the letters "L. B." cut with a penknife in the brown wood above the lock.

She opened it, and found herself straightway in the presence of all the children. The large window at the end of the room was open wide, and Winnie seated sideways on the window-sill, with her head resting against the gray stone frame-work, was eating a large hunch of bread. A flock of pigeons and white ducks clamored for scraps on the terrace outside; curled up in her lap lay four small kittens, and the big mother cat sat sunning herself upon the window-sill; but Winnie seemed to be paying only a mechanical attention to her pets. She was white from want of food, and there was a general air of pre-occupation and disappointment in her attitude,—disappointment which seemed to have communicated itself in a measure to the other children, who stood grouped around her.

"No," she was saying as Adrienne entered; "it's just Peggy's rubbish, and there's an end of it."

"Well, but," said Murtagh doubtfully, "they might be there another day and not be there to-day."

"No," returned Winnie decidedly; "I don't believe they're ever there. It was quite dark when I got up on the Liss, and I hid under a bush and watched with my eyes wide open till it was blazing light all over everywhere, and I didn't see a single thing, and there—there's an end of it. It's just rubbish!" She flung a piece of crust out on the grass as she spoke, so that the poor ill-used ducks had to turn round and waddle quite a journey before they got it. But perhaps even ducks can look reproachful, for she broke almost immediately another bit from her hunch of bread, and threw it to a fat laggard, with a compassionate—"There, poor old Senior, that's for you." And then, turning more gently to Murtagh, she said: "Never mind, Myrrh, you know it wasn't any use believing it if it wasn't true."

Murtagh did not answer. But suddenly an idea crossed Bobbo's mind, and he exclaimed, half-doubtfully: "Win, do you think—they might have known you were coming, and perhaps they didn't choose for you to see them?"

The notion seemed to find some favor with the other children. Winnie glanced at Murtagh to see what he thought; but Murtagh, who had been aware of Adrienne's entrance, was looking to her, so Winnie's eyes followed his.

"No, I do not think that exactly," said Adrienne slowly, finding that she was expected to speak. She seated herself on the window-sill opposite Winnie, and began to stroke the old cat. Then she continued in the same slow, thoughtful tone: "Once I used to believe in fairies as you do, and I used to want to see them, but I never did. I used to think I did sometimes, but I never did. Then I began to think they could not be true, and that made me very unhappy, for I loved them so. I don't think you can love them as much as I did. Everything that happened to me I used to think the fairies were there; you see, I wasn't like you; I was all alone, and hadn't anybody but the fairies. When it was fine I thought the fairies were in the sun; when it rained I thought they were in the rain. I thought they were in the flowers, in the moon,—everywhere, in everything. But still I began to be afraid they could not be true.

"I do not know how long that lasted, but I remember quite, quite well the day when it was all finished—the very last day when I ever believed in them.

"It was when I was eight years old. It was one wet winter afternoon. I had been alone nearly all day, and I had been standing a long time by the window watching the rain beat down upon the pavement. It was growing dark, but still I did not go away; for I always used to think the little splashes were water-fairies dancing, and I liked to watch them. I was thinking about them, and half-dreaming, I think, when suddenly, quite suddenly, I seemed to know that they were not fairies at all—nothing but water-splashes. I felt almost frightened, and I went away from the window and sat down on the hearthrug in front of the fire. But then the sight of the fire reminded me that there were no fire-fairies either; no fairies anywhere all over the world. It seemed such a dreadful thing to know; and I couldn't help it,—I just hid my face in the hearthrug, and cried like a little baby."

The children had fixed their eyes with interest and sympathy on Adrienne, but her attention was apparently concentrated on stroking old Griffin, who purred in the sunshine.

"I never shall forget that afternoon," she continued, "I was so very unhappy; and it wasn't only that afternoon; for months afterwards I couldn't bear to think of a fairy. But the reason I tell you about it," she added, raising her eyes and looking towards the children, "is because afterwards it went away. One of my uncles came to live with us, and he told me about the true fairies; I mean the angels; and I have believed them ever since. And so you need not be disappointed because the fairies do not really dance where Winnie went to look, because the angels are better, and they are true. Some people don't think the angels are all round us everywhere as the fairies were, but I do. I think it is so beautiful to believe that they are everywhere, in everything; sent down from heaven to make the flowers sweet, and the fruit ripe, and to put good into us."

She looked out, as she finished speaking, to the sunny park, where the great trees stood in all their autumn glory. The children looked out too and were silent. Just for the moment they were all feeling, as it were, the presence of angels.

But suddenly Bobbo was struck by another idea. "Why you're talking English!" he exclaimed. "But you know you're French! I'd forgotten all about it!" He seemed quite excited by his discovery, and Adrienne began to laugh.

"Oh yes!" cried Winnie, "of course you are, and Murtagh and I had got some things ready to say. Hadn't we, Murtagh? 'Comment vous portez vous,' and 'Parlez vous Anglais.' "

"I am very well, thank you,' said Adrienne, with a little mock bow. "And I speak English just as easily as I do French. We lived for years in England, you know, and then I always had English governesses. Grand'mère knew, of course, that I was coming here, so she paid particular attention to my English."

"Oh!" said all the children in chorus; and then Rosie, coloring violently, asked a question which it had evidently been agreed beforehand that she should ask.

"What did you say your name was? Murtagh says it's *Adrenne;* but *that* isn't a name exactly at all, is it?"

"Yes," said Adrienne, smiling. "He is quite right; Adrienne Marie Véronique Erstein Blair!"

"Good Lord!" exclaimed Bobbo, doubling himself up as though the very sound gave him a pain. "What a name to go to bed with! Do you expect us to say all that every time we want the door shut?"

The faces of the other children were so full of genuine dismay that Adrienne laughed outright.

"Grand'mere used to call me Reine," she said; "that's a little shorter, isn't it?"

"Yes, but," said Murtagh doubtfully, " 'Rain!' It's not pretty, or anything. You're not a bit rainy-looking."

"Pitter, patter! Drip, drop, dropsy!" exclaimed Bobbo, his blue eyes lighting up impudently.

"Hush, Bobbo, be quiet; you're behaving very rudely," said Rosie, with a little anxious glance at Adrienne. "We can't call you by any of those names," she added in her pleasantest voice, "they are not pretty enough."

"Would you mind saying your name again, please," said Murtagh, looking puzzled; "the first one, I mean, that we'll have to call you by?"

Adrienne repeated it slowly once or twice, and the children said it after her. But they didn't seem satisfied with their own pronunciation.

"It will never be the same as yours," exclaimed Bobbo, after two ineffectual attempts. "I'll call you Topsy; it's much easier!"

"I'll tell you what," said Winnie, who had been silently finishing her piece of bread. "Suppose we call her Nessa, after poor Nessa that died." She spoke slowly as children do speak when their words are full of sad memories; and she looked doubtfully at the others, not sure what they would think of her proposition. They hesitated, and a grave silence fell for a moment on the little group. Adrienne regretted that she had been the means of saddening them.

"Who was Nessa?" she asked at length gently.

"She was so pretty," said Winnie, "with long soft brown hair and beautiful big eyes."

"I think she *was* a little bit like you," said Murtagh; "only her hair was browner than yours."

"Oh, Murtagh!" exclaimed Rosie.

"Was she as old as me?" asked Adrienne.

"Oh, no," said Murtagh, "she was quite young; but she did bark so beautifully."

"She did *what!*" exclaimed Adrienne.

"Bark! bark at all the strangers that came near the place."

"Oh!" said Adrienne, completely taken aback. "Then—then—she must have been a dog!"

"Yes," said Rosie, hurriedly. "It's ridiculous Murtagh saying she was like you; she was only a little dog that we found in the road."

"Why, what else did you suppose she was?" asked Murtagh in surprise.

"I—I thought," said Adrienne, blushing, and then brimming over with laughter,—"I thought she was your elder sister."

The children greeted her speech with such peals of laughter that the sadness connected with Nessa was effectually dispersed, and no further hesitation was entertained as to Adrienne's name. Nothing could she be now but "Nessa;"—"Our elder sister Nessa," as Murtagh half-impudently, half-admiringly called her.

"And it's perfect nonsense, Rosie," said Murtagh, "to say that the other Nessa wasn't like her. Her hair was darker, and so were her eyes; but there was a sort of likeness about them all the same,—a sort of golden look in their faces; wasn't there, Winnie?"

"How silly you are, Murtagh!" replied Rosie contemptuously, "just as if a dog could be like a real grown-up person."

"Yes, they can," replied Murtagh; "and I heard papa saying one day to a gentleman who had a blue ribbon on his coat, at one of the big dinner-parties, that everybody has a sort of a likeness to some animal. There!"

"Then if they have, you're like a little black monkey," replied Rosie, hotly and inconsequently; "but it's nonsense all the same, silly nonsense, to say that a little brown dog out on the road is like this Nessa!"

"But it isn't nonsense, Rosie, when I see—" began Murtagh.

Rosie contemptuously turned her back upon him, and Winnie remarked quietly:

"It's no use arguing with Rosie, you know, Myrrh."

"The only chance with her is to knock her down and sit upon her," said Bobbo, good humoredly indifferent.

Murtagh paid no attention to either of them, but followed Rosie, exclaiming eagerly: "Can't you understand if I see a likeness—" Rosie never listened to what her opponent said, and perhaps she thought he was going to follow Bobbo's advice, for she pushed him away so violently that he lost his balance and fell over little Ellie, who was, as usual, sitting upon the floor. The child began to scream; Adrienne sprang forward to pick her up; and in the midst of the confusion the door opened, and Peggy's voice made itself heard, saying: "Whisht, Miss Ellie; get up, Mr. Murtagh, dear; here's Mr. Plunkett."

"Hang Mr. Plunkett!" muttered Murtagh, getting up slowly, and pulling his jacket straight. Adrienne had already picked up Ellie, and carried her in her arms back to the window-sill, but the child had been hurt; and, nothing abashed by the sight of the correct-looking person who appeared in the doorway, she continued to roar with all her might, her little red face puckered up, and bright salt tears dropping on Adrienne's shoulder.

Mr. Plunkett stood in the doorway surveying the scene.

"Is this the best specimen, sir, that you can give Miss Blair of your behavior?" he inquired sternly, addressing Murtagh.

Murtagh made no answer.

"And you are not content," continued Mr. Plunkett, looking at Rosie's hot, angry face, "with displaying such unruliness yourself, but you draw all your brothers and sisters after you."

Murtagh walked over to the piano and began to arrange the music, humming, "There was an old woman who lived in a shoe."

"Incorrigible boy!" said Mr. Plunkett in an undertone. Then turning to Adrienne he saluted her with a bow and a respectfully polite, "Miss Blair, I presume."

Notwithstanding the first movement of hostility that his manner was likely to excite, there was a certain severe dignity in his bearing that commanded respect. He wished to be courteous to Adrienne, and though his piercing eyes did not soften in the least while he spoke with her, he said well and politely all that was natural for him to say to a newly-arrived inmate of Castle Blair.

Yet it was certainly not even his politest manner that commanded respect. It was something deeper—something that seemed indeed almost hidden by his manner; a strength of some kind, the presence of which was felt at once through all the superficial accidents of his nature.

Adrienne, engaged in soothing Ellie, replied to his remarks with a certain gracious gentleness peculiar to her. Presently the child forgot her grief in a sudden curiosity as to the method of buttoning and unbuttoning Adrienne's dress, and with the tears still glistening on her cheeks she began to smile with pleasure as she poked her little fingers through the button-holes. Then Adrienne wiped away the tears, and the conversation with Mr. Plunkett grew into a more animated discussion of the beauties of the surrounding country.

"I hope," said Mr. Plunkett at length, "that you will be kind enough to let me know if there is anything you desire. It is Mr. Blair's wish that I should do everything in my power to make you comfortable. As for the children, when they trouble you, pray have no hesitation in applying to me for assistance. And I hope," he added, raising his voice a little, and addressing the children without looking at them, "that common hospitality will induce you to inflict as little as possible of your wildness upon your cousin."

Adrienne thanked him, but looking across at the children, she said: "I think we are going to be friends; aren't we?"

The children's faces, more or less expressive, showed their acceptance of the treaty. Mr. Plunkett looked as though he felt somehow vaguely disapprobatory; and then, turning round to Murtagh, he changed the subject by saying severely:

"I hear, sir, that you have been at your old tricks again, stealing fruit from the garden."

"You heard wrong, then," returned Murtagh, his brow lowering.

"Don't add untruth to your other misdeeds; you were seen by one of the policemen. It is useless to deny it."

"*Gentlemen* don't tell lies," returned Murtagh, with a sneering accentuation of the words that made them nothing less than insulting. Adrienne was shocked and astonished at the scene. From where she sat on the window-sill, behind Mr. Plunkett, she looked across at Murtagh, while Mr. Plunkett answered angrily:

"What do you mean by speaking to me in such a manner?"

Murtagh's eyes met Adrienne's, and perhaps the expression that he found there made some impression on him. His features relaxed a little, and he remained silent.

Mr. Plunkett continued: "I am tired of speaking of this robbing of the garden. I see nothing but strong measures are of any use, and I give you fair warning that the next time any of you are caught in the garden you shall be severely punished." Mr. Plunkett evidently intended his words to end the conversation, but Murtagh looked blacker than ever, and some answer as bitter as the last trembled on his lips. Before he had time to speak, however, Adrienne exclaimed innocently:

"Why, how the time is going! Don't let me keep you all in-doors. I must unpack a little, and write a letter; but if you will go out now I will join you as soon as I am ready."

Murtagh looked perversely inclined to stay where he was, but an appealing glance from Adrienne persuaded him to follow the others, who rushed at once into the passage.

"Those children are running perfectly wild," said Mr. Plunkett; "they make their own laws, and are the annoyance of every one in the place. It is little short of madness to keep them here under the present conditions; but Winnie and Murtagh suffered severely from fever in India, and Mr. Launcelot Blair refuses to send them to school. It is mistaken treatment. The discipline of school would be far better for them than the riotous life they lead. But it is, of course, for their parents to decide."

"Do they do no lessons at all?" asked Adrienne.

"They do nothing useful, Miss Blair," said Mr. Plunkett severely. Then changing the subject with a decision that showed he wished to say no more upon the matter, he returned to his former measured courteous manner; and after a little further conversation, he wished Adrienne "Good morning," and left her to write her letters.

Whatever Mr. Plunkett might think of the children, they had, as has been seen, no high opinion of him. On this occasion they were no sooner well outside the school-room than Bobbo relieved his feelings by exclaiming:

"Oh, that brute Plunkett! wouldn't I like to punch his head!"

"It's no good thinking about him, Myrrh," said Winnie, seeing that the black look had not faded from Murtagh's face. "Let's do something. Shall we go and steal some more apples? I am awfully hungry."

"Oh, no!" said Rosie, "don't let us do that; but I'll tell you what'll be fun. Let's get some brown cake from Donnie, and go and boil potatoes on one of the islands."

Winnie agreeing, the little girls ran off to the kitchen; and Bobbo, left alone with Murtagh, returned to his subject.

"I say, Murtagh," he continued, "we must just do something to that old Plunkett. He's getting worse and worse."

"I think I'll kill him some day!" burst out Murtagh, with such concentrated passion in his voice that Bobbo looked at him, quite startled, and paused for a minute before he answered:

"I don't vote for killing, exactly. But I'd like to dip him in the river, or do something or other that would just take him down a peg."

But Murtagh did not seem disposed to talk any more about it at that moment. He thrust his hands deep into his pockets and slowly followed the others to the kitchen, where Mrs. Donegan was buttering slices of brown cake, and at the same time declaring that "she wasn't going to be getting them into bad habits of eating between their meals."

CHAPTER III

ADRIENNE'S LETTERS were very quickly written. She was anxious to go out to the children, and to make acquaintance with the place. But when she went to look for them they were nowhere to be found.

Enchanted with the place, which, neglected as it was, seemed to her very beautiful, she wandered about for a time in the pleasure ground and shrubberies that lay at the back of the house; and then, tempted by the lovely brightness of the morning, she set off to make further discoveries.

Land seemed to be no consideration in that part of the world; a wide park, dotted with trees and clustering bushes, lay stretched out on three sides of the house. The grass was too wet to cross after yesterday's rain, but a sunny avenue, winding away between old thorns and oaks, offered a charming walk, and as Adrienne went along she looked around her in delight.

On the left the ground sloped down to the bed of a broad rocky stream, which wound about and flowed, as she knew, past that end of the house in which was the big window of the school-room. To the right, undulating park-land stretched for some distance, and, beyond the park, trees and fields and hedges seemed to grow closer and closer together, till out of the indistinctness rose suddenly a bold line of purple hills. In the park, soft-eyed cows were cropping the autumn grass. Thrushes were singing in the thorns. Red haws lay scattered in profusion under the trees. The air was pure, and the earth smelt sweet after the rain.

Adrienne was so glad the place was pretty that for more than half a mile she walked along, just enjoying it and thinking of nothing else. She had for the moment forgotten the children, when, enticed by a little side path, she turned off the avenue and came suddenly upon a child standing on tiptoe in the wet grass, and stretching up in a vain endeavor to reach a branch of roseberries that hung temptingly out from a clump of bushes. She was not the least like the children Adrienne had seen hitherto. A sylph-like, tender little thing, she looked as though a sudden gust of wind would blow her right away. And then she was carefully dressed; the golden hair that hung down to her waist was neatly brushed, and the hand stretched up to the roseberries was cased in a warm cloth glove.

Adrienne stepped on to the grass and succeeded in reaching the branch. Blushing and surprised the little girl thanked her with a sweet smile. At the same moment a voice exclaimed, "Marion, Marion, for goodness sake come off that sopping grass!" and looking up, Adrienne perceived a lady, in a shiny black silk gown, who with an anxious face was hurrying down the path.

"Let me see your feet," she continued, coming up to them and taking Marion's hand as the child stepped obediently on to the path. "Yes, they're soaking wet! You must come back and change them at once! I beg your pardon, Miss Blair," she added, looking up at Adrienne. "I know I ought to have spoken to you first, but this child is so delicate she keeps me in a perpetual fright. How could you think of going on the grass, Marion?"

"I'm so sorry, mother," replied the child in her sweet little voice, "I quite forgot."

"Well, well, come back and change as quickly as you can, and perhaps there'll be no harm done. And you, Miss Blair, I am sure your feet must be wet too! Will you come in, and let me have your boots dried in the kitchen? The house is quite close. I am Mrs. Plunkett."

The last piece of information came out with an odd little confused jerk. It was an after-thought for which Adrienne was grateful; she had not the slightest idea who her newly-made acquaintance might be.

"Thank you," she said; "I don't think my feet are at all wet. I was only on the grass for a moment."

"Ah! but you don't know this climate; it is most treacherous; you have no idea how the wet penetrates. Marion, don't bring that litter into the house, there's a good child." As she spoke she pulled the branch of roseberries out of Marion's hand and threw it away, continuing in the meantime without a single full stop between her sentences: "There's nothing more dangerous than wet feet, I can assure you—I lost my poor sister through nothing in the world but that,—and Mr. Plunkett's mother often said, 'anything else you please, James, but no wet feet, I beg.' "

It was difficult to find suitable answers to such remarks, but Mrs. Plunkett did not require answers; she was like a cuckoo clock, once pull the weight down and she went perfectly by herself.

Marion looked regretfully after her pretty red branch, but she said nothing, and Mrs. Plunkett continued to relate anecdotes of people who had died from the consequences of wet feet, till a few more turns in the path brought them to the back of a neat-looking house and garden.

"Pray walk in," said Mrs. Plunkett, throwing open the gate. And in a minute or two more, Adrienne, good-humoredly helpless in the hands of the fussy little woman, found herself sitting without her boots in a wicker arm-chair beside the nursery fire. A beautiful nursery it was—a real honest nursery, where it would seem impossible for children to be anything but healthy and happy; beautiful, not from any special luxury of furniture, but by its exquisite cleanliness. The white boarded floor was as spotless as scrubbing could make it; the brass knobs of the fireplace glittered in the sunlight; the window-panes could not have been more brilliantly transparent.

Two little children in white pinafores were playing with wooden bricks on the floor. Marion, perched on a chair on the other side of the fireplace, stretched out two little blue-stockinged feet to the blaze; and while Nurse took the boots down stairs, the clean fat baby was transferred to Adrienne's lap.

Finding that Adrienne was fond of children, Mrs. Plunkett grew confidential over the sayings and doings of her own four; and then suddenly interrupting herself in the midst of a description of little Johnnie's appearance when he had the measles, she exclaimed in a tone half-curious, half-confidential:

"But your cousins, Miss Blair! Have they left you alone already? I *should* have thought they would have liked to show you the place. Ah, it's very sad to see children lead such lives."

"Yes," said Adrienne, trying to disengage her hair from the convulsive grasp with which Master Baby had seized upon one of the coils, "it is almost the same as though they had neither father nor mother, poor little things."

"It is their own fault, I assure you; entirely their own fault. For shame, baby! is that the way you treat ladies who are kind enough to nurse you, sir? Mr. Plunkett and I were prepared to take every interest in them," she continued, bending over Adrienne, and helping to extricate her hair from baby's fat, rosy fingers. "We were away for our summer trip when Murtagh and Winnie first arrived. Poor little Marion was the only one we had then, and we were very near losing her that same summer. You would never suppose, would you, that she's nearly four years older than any of these; she's such a little mite to look at. When we came back, we found that that poor foolish Mrs. Donegan had already done a great deal of harm. There now, Master Baby, keep your hands to yourself, sir.

"The two children were making themselves ill with pining, and she encouraging them, and letting them do every mortal thing they liked, under the pretence that they must be amused. My husband saw at once that it was his duty to remonstrate; he was quite shocked to see the way things were going. And I'm sure it was enough to shock any one to see those two children, with their heads cropped after the fever, and their wizened yellow faces, and their little sticks of arms; they were enough to frighten one. I assure you I scarcely liked to look much at them just at that time.

"They had suffered so terribly from fever that Mr. Launcelot insisted upon their having what he called perfect rest. He would not even allow them to have a governess. He said that their brains were too active, and that the thing he most desired to hear of them was that they were growing as ignorant as the village children. Some people certainly have queer fancies, and he, of all people in the world, so clever as he is! Well, I hope he's satisfied now.

"But my husband was determined to do his duty by them. He spoke sharply to Mrs. Donegan about her behavior, and there were most unpleasant scenes between them. She came down here one evening and said the most dreadful things. She told me myself, Miss Blair, that he ought to be ashamed to be so hard on poor little fatherless, motherless children, who were pining for a bit of love. I remember her expression quite well; I was quite upset after she went away. But my husband never minds those things. He does his duty, and he doesn't mind what anybody says. He spoke to Murtagh himself next day, and told him how sinful it was to give way like that to every fanciful feeling that came over him,—one minute pining and miserable, and the next rampaging like wild animals all about everywhere, not minding a word anybody said to them. But it was all no use: Murtagh wouldn't answer a word, and from that day to this they've just gone on growing worse and worse.

"My husband has tried severity with them; but Mr. Blair doesn't like to hear of their being punished, and James hesitates to take the responsibility entirely upon himself. If they were his own children he'd soon bring them to order. But why should he hesitate to take the responsibility? that is what I ask him. He manages all Mr. Launcelot's business matters the same as he does Mr. Blair's. Mr. Launcelot trusts him just as much as Mr. Blair does, and he gave him full authority to do whatever he thought needful for them.

"He worries himself about those children ten times as much as he's ever had occasion to worry about his own. Why, their governesses alone have given him more trouble than all his own servants put together, and it isn't a bit of use, as I'm always telling him. What's the good of worrying about other people's children? They are not one bit grateful. I really believe, Miss Blair, that they hate him; I believe those children hate every one; there's never been one day's peace since they've been here."

Exhausted by her own vehemence, Mrs. Plunkett paused to take breath, and Marion, profiting by the opportunity, said in a slow gentle way that seemed years older than her little self: "I don't think they hate me, mother."

"What do you know about it, child?" asked Mrs. Plunkett.

"Because," said Marion, raising her eyes from the fire to her mother's face, "I looked at them in church, and a butterfly flew in, and went on the side of Murtagh's nose, and I laughed, and he laughed too, quite kind."

Adrienne could not help smiling at the earnest, half-pleading tone in which the child spoke, but Mrs. Plunkett said; "Nonsense, Maimy, you don't know anything about it! No; I don't believe there's any one in this world they care one bit about, except it is little Frankie."

As Mrs. Plunkett enunciated for the second time her disbelief in the children's powers of affection, some one called from down-stairs, "Marion, Maimy!"

"It's father!" exclaimed the child, springing off her chair. "Back already! Yes, father, I'm coming. Nurse, my slippers please, quick!"

But nurse had gone down-stairs to fetch the dried boots, and while Marion went to the cupboard to find her own slippers, a firm regular step quickly ascended the staircase, and Mr. Plunkett entered the nursery, holding in his hand the very branch of roseberries which had brought about all the wet feet.

Adrienne had been surprised at the voice in which Marion's name had been called; it was scarcely to be recognized as belonging to the stern man she had seen that morning. But she was still more surprised to see the soft beaming welcome that broke out over little Marion's face as her father entered the room.

She was sitting on the floor, putting on her slippers, one little blue leg stretched out, the other doubled up to enable her to button her shoe-strap. She did not jump up to kiss her father, but she turned her face up towards him, with a sweet glad look in her eyes.

"Are you going to have dinner with us after all, Fardie?" she asked.

"Yes," he replied, looking down with a smile at the upturned face. "I'm going to dine here to-day. I shall go to the farms to-morrow instead. See," he continued, holding out towards her the branch of roseberries, "I've brought you something pretty. It was lying in the middle of the path, and I thought it would please you."

"Why, it's my own branch! How could you know it was just what I wanted?"

The shoe was fastened by this time, so she got up from the floor, holding the branch of roseberries in one hand, and slipped the other hand into her father's. Then he perceived Adrienne. A few polite sentences were interchanged; the boots were brought; baby was given into Nurse's arms; and Adrienne, wishing them all "Good morning," walked back along the avenue, her pretty golden head as full as it would hold of thoughts about all these new people.

She was destined to have further lights on the subject of her little cousins' behavior, however, that morning.

As she approached the house she found that the hall-door was shut, and passing round to the back in order to find another entrance, she ventured to open what seemed to her like a kitchen door. It was not the door of the kitchen. She found herself on the threshold of a large, airy room, littered all over with clothes in various stages of washing, drying, and ironing. Mrs. Donegan, with her sleeves tucked up, was busy ironing print frocks at a large table near the fire, and at the sound of the door opening she exclaimed:

"Do, for goodness' sake, shut that door, Kate. Why ever don't you stop in the kitchen and attend to your dinner?"

"It's not Kate," said Adrienne; "I came round this way because the hall-door was shut. May I come in?"

Mrs. Donegan looked up, and grew quite red with confusion as she discerned her mistake.

"Oh, Ma'am, I beg your pardon!" she exclaimed, setting down her iron and coming forward to meet Adrienne. "I'm sure I never thought to see you here, and the laundry in such a mess too; of a Friday there is so much to do. Walk in, Ma'am, if you please."

"Please don't let me disturb you," said Adrienne, as she shut the door. "Can I get through to the house this way?"

"Yes, Ma'am," replied Mrs. Donegan, taking up her iron again, "it's always through here or through the kitchen the children come."

"Have they come back yet?" asked Adrienne.

"Lord, no, Ma'am! they were in the kitchen with me this morning, getting some bits of griddle-cake to go off with somewhere, an' if they're back to dinner it's as much as they'll be."

"You can't tell me where to find them, can you?" suggested Adrienne.

"Tell you where to find them!" exclaimed Mrs. Donegan, pushing her spectacles up on her forehead, and pausing in her work to look at Adrienne. "It's plain you don't know much about their ways yet, Ma'am. Maybe it's up the mountains they are, or maybe up the river, or maybe across the fields, five miles away by this time. But wherever it is, ye might look for them a month o' Sundays, and never find them if ye're wanting them; and so sure as ye're not wanting them they'll turn up fast enough, bless their hearts!"

"They live out of doors a great deal, don't they?" asked Adrienne, smiling at Mrs. Donegan's description of their proceedings.

"God bless you, yes, Ma'am. They'd never be confined with stoppin' in a house, but out and about, no matter what weather it is. They're a bit wild like, but they're the best-hearted children ever lived. But won't you sit down, Ma'am," added Mrs. Donegan, interrupting herself to set a chair near the table.

"If I stay may I help you?" asked Adrienne, attracted to the free-spoken old woman, and very willing to stay and talk to her. "I can *tuyauter* these frills. I don't know what that word is in English."

She took up a pair of gaufreing tongs as she spoke, and Mrs. Donegan looked amused at the notion of her help.

"Sure you don't know anything about such work, an' it's not so easy as it looks. But you may try if you like, Miss," she added good-humoredly, dropping the more formal "Ma'am," and from that time forth adopting Adrienne as one of the children of the house.

Adrienne, all unconscious of the greatness of the concession Mrs. Donegan had made in allowing her to touch her linen, laid her hat on one side, and in another minute was sitting gaufreing pillow-case frills in so business-like a manner that Mrs. Donegan, looking on critically, exclaimed after a minute or two:

"Upon my word, Miss, you do it better than I do it myself."

Adrienne laughed, and Mrs. Donegan, going back to her work, returned to the current of her thoughts.

"I could tell you more about those children than anybody else that's here," she continued. "But whatever you do, Miss, don't you go to believe anything Mr. Plunkett says about them. It's not the like of him can understand these children. Wasn't I here in the nursery in old Mrs. Blair's time, and nursemaid to Mr. Launcelot himself? I know what Master Launce was when his mother died, and I know what sort his children's come of. And they're Mr. Launcelot's children to the very backbone; that they are, Miss, as you'll see when you come to know them better. Master Harry was always quieter, but you're not much like him, Miss, except when you laugh you have a look of him about the eyes, I think."

Mrs. Donegan liked to talk, but she liked to talk after her own fashion, so before Adrienne could hear anything about the children she had to listen to a panegyric upon their father, which wound up with an account of how he married Mrs. Launcelot, who was "very nice for the matter of that; a Catholic too she is, just like your own mother, Miss, and a perfect lady, Mr. Launcelot wouldn't have married none other, but a little, gentle, delicate bit of a thing, who had a French maid to look after her, and let the children do whatever they pleased."

Then, and not till then, Adrienne was told that Mr. and Mrs. Launcelot had been in India now nearly seven years, and how Winnie and Murtagh had been sent home four years ago. "And Mr. Launcelot wrote me a letter with his own hand," added Donnie, "asking me to take care of his two little orphans till he came himself to fetch them; and he told me to 'mother them, when they were lonely, the way I'd mothered him long ago when he needed it.' Those were his very words. Many an' many a time I've read the letter. And when I saw the poor little things drooping and pining, I used to think o' the night, thirty-two years ago now come Michaelmas, when the poor missis died, an' I crep' into the nursery after the old nurse was asleep, an' Master Launce was sobbing in his bed; and when I tried to comfort him like, he knelt up in his little nightgown an' put his two arms round about my neck,—and, 'Oh, Biddy,' says he, 'what *shall* I do now?' "
Donnie's tears were running down at the remembrance.

"And he laid his head upon my shoulder, and he was that tired out with crying that after a bit he fell asleep kneeling up against me there; an' I carried him away into my own bed, and kept him warm till the morning. And then," she continued, indignantly sniffing away her tears, "tell me I don't know what I'm doing with his children. Deed, faith, I know a deal better than them as tells me such nonsense."

"They were very lonely when they first came. were they not?" said Adrienne, remembering Murtagh's words of the evening before.

"Deed they were! poor little lambs, sick and lonely enough; they scarce cared to do anything like, and I never could get them off my mind. Then after a bit, when the summer came, they used to go off whole days up the mountains; and when I saw that pleased them I used to give them their dinner to take with them, and then they took to rampaging about, and I began to grow easier, bless their hearts! For there's nothing like it, take my word for it, Miss.

"When Miss Rose and Master Bobbo were sent over after with the baby—Miss Ellie that is—they were every bit as yellow and skinny like as Master Murtagh and Miss Winnie; and where would you see finer, heartier-looking children now than the four of them? I'm not for cossetting children too much. Give 'em plenty of good fresh air, and plenty o' good food, and let 'em alone, that's what I say. Stuff o' rubbish, confining them an' regulatin' 'em! Time enough for that by-an'-by when they go to school."

"But don't you think," said Adrienne, looking up with a smile, "that now they have had the fresh air and the food they might have just a little learning too, without doing them any harm?"

"Well," replied Donnie, with the air of one willing to make concessions, "I don't say but what they might have a governess, and let them do a bit of learning every day. But when they first came Mr. Launcelot said they wasn't to be allowed to see a book at all, but running about wild in the good mountain air; and quite right he was too. And since then they begged so hard not to have a governess in the house, that Mr. Blair giv' in to them, and got them governesses from Ballyboden.

"But what with one thing and another they never stay. One says it's too far to come every day, and another says she can't manage the children, an' the last went away close upon three months ago because Mr. Murtagh slipped a handful of hailstones down her back. But, Lord! it doesn't signify; they weren't any good, when they did come; they hadn't got the wit to teach these children.

"They tell me there'll be a real clever German governess got next year, when the young gentlemen go to school. But it don't make much matter one way or the other. If they never got a governess at all, there's no fear but what Mr. Launcelot's children would be plenty clever enough. They may be a bit wild-like, but if they've got the good blood in them, they'll never go far wrong. I'm old, and I've seen a lot o' people one way or another, backwards and forwards in the world, an' I tell you, Miss, you may always let the good blood have its way; it's only the half-an'-half folks take such a deal o' looking after.

"Then, it isn't every one can understand that, and that's where the trouble is. With these children, now, ye can manage them with a crick o' your little finger, if you take them the right way. They'd give you the coats off o' their backs and the bit out o' their mouths if they thought you wanted it. But they won't be driven; it isn't a bit of use talking about it. There's nothing but gentleness is a bit o' good with them, and that's where it is them and Mr. Plunkett is such enemies."

Such were Donnie's opinions, and she descanted upon them at length, till Kate came to say that she thought it was no use waiting any longer for the children, and she had sent up Miss Blair's luncheon to the dining-room.

Mr. Blair did not take luncheon, so Adrienne sat alone at the head of the big table. She spent her afternoon alone, too, and had plenty of leisure to decide that Murtagh was right; the drawing-room was a musty-smelling old room. She opened the windows wide, and filled the old china bowls and vases with flowers, and pushed the furniture about till the room looked more habitable. Then she unpacked her needlework and her music, and tried to occupy herself; but finally, she was very glad when at half-past five Brown came to inform her that six o'clock was the dinner hour—an intimation which she took as a respectful hint that in Brown's opinion it was now time for her to dress.

CHAPTER IV

THE CHILDREN MEANWHILE had completely forgotten the existence of their new cousin. After leaving the kitchen they raced along with their spoil towards the river. The morning was deliciously bright; there was a fresh scent in the air that made them all feel inclined to caper about without exactly knowing why. Even Murtagh forgot his troubles with Mr. Plunkett, and raced and shouted with the others.

Their river was a branch of a broad mountain stream, but now at the end of the dry season the water did not come down with a steady rolling current as in the winter. It came trickling, sparkling, dancing between the great bits of moss-grown rock that strewed its course, finding for itself thousands of little channels, tumbling unexpectedly from time to time head over heels down the side of a big stone, and then lying still and clear in pools sheltered by the rocks. Only in the very middle was there anything like a real current, and there the water flowed swiftly along in uneven ripples, slapping up against obtrusive rocks with a ruffle of white spray that made the delight of the children.

But what was not a delight in that river? There was simply no end to its resources. There was the water to splash and paddle in, with stones for those who liked to practice hardening their feet, and patches of sand where one could enjoy that delicious half-tickling sensation of feet sinking and sand oozing up between all one's toes; then there were the pools for sailing boats; and the current in the middle for floating hats, with all the fun of not being quite sure whether they could be caught in time.

And the rocks covered over with thick sunny moss that seemed to grow on purpose for warming cold feet, and all the wonderful things that were to be found in the river,—things that came floating down, things that grew, and things that had got there somehow. Then there were the islands; the river's course was dotted with them. And then there were the trout and the minnows.

It was to one of the islands that the children were going now. Notwithstanding the heavy rain of the preceding afternoon the night had been fine, and when the children got down upon the beach they found their beloved river a little fuller perhaps and rather more energetic in its twirls and dashes, but just as bright and as tempting as it always was on these lovely autumn mornings. The water looked like clear brown crystal in the sunlight, and soon everything was forgotten in the excitement of looking for trout. It was one of their favorite occupations; but not a fish did they see this morning, till, just as they were crossing the stepping-stones to a little island, Winnie pulled Murtagh's jacket, and pointed silently to where a great fellow lay under a rock, the sun shining on his spotted side.

"Golly loo!" whispered Murtagh, "isn't he a beauty?"

They stood a minute watching, but the trout scarcely moved.

"I say, how still he keeps," whispered Winnie: "I believe I could catch him in my hands."

In a minute she had set her saucepan down on the stone, had pulled off her shoes and stockings, and was cautiously stepping into the water. The icy cold of it made her screw up her eyes, but on she went trying to make as little splash as possible. Still the trout never moved. Murtagh's interest was intense; he could scarcely refrain from giving vent to his excitement in a shout. Winnie could hardly believe her own good fortune. She got close up behind the trout; she bent down; her hands were just closing on it, when,—there was a tremendous splash behind her, and in an instant the trout had whisked far away out of sight. She closed her hands with a convulsive grasp at its tail, but it was no use,—it was clean gone.

Even Winnie's equanimity was upset by such a disappointment.

"You little idiot, Murtagh! you *might* have waited till I'd caught him," she said, angrily.

"I beg your pardon awfully, Winnie," said Murtagh, who with both legs up to the knees in water was sitting upon the rock a picture of abject penitence; "I'm dreadfully sorry. I didn't do it on purpose. I was watching you, and I didn't see I was come to the edge of the stone."

"Who said you did it on purpose?" replied Winnie unappeased. "You might have looked where you were going."

"I'm awfully sorry," repeated Murtagh.

But Winnie didn't feel as if she could forgive him yet. She turned away in silence, and occupied herself with rescuing from the water her boots and stockings, which had of course been kicked off the stone when Murtagh slipped.

By the time she had done that, she had recovered herself a little; and presently, having fished out the garters, she turned round again and said with something very like a twinkle in her eye:

"As you threw it in you may fetch it out."

She pointed as she spoke to where the saucepan lay on the bottom of the pool. Murtagh having employed himself in taking off his wet boots and stockings, hooked it out cleverly with his foot; then Winnie slung boots and stockings and saucepan all on a garter round her neck, and tucking up her frock said quite cheerily:

"Never mind; come along, and let's see if we can't catch him somewhere else."

Just at that moment a shout arose from the other side of the island, and Bobbo, bursting through the bushes, exclaimed in breathless delight that Rosie had caught a trout "in her hands in the water." Winnie told her of her disappointment.

"What's up with the trout, I wonder?" said Bobbo. "Generally they're off like lightning if you so much as look at them. By the Holy Poker, there's another!" he added, suddenly beginning to strip off his shoes and stockings, while Murtagh practically suggested that some one had been throwing lime into the water.

But Winnie's sharp eyes saw the trout as soon as Bobbo, and she had the start of him, being already in the water; so, signing to the others to be quiet, she advanced cautiously up stream till she got close behind it, Bobbo pausing meanwhile with one boot in his hand to watch her success. Then, bending down, she quickly clasped her little brown hands under the trout, and with a successful jerk threw it high and dry on to a sunny bit of rock.

"Hurrah!" shouted Murtagh. "She's got it. Come along, Bobbo; off with your other boot, and let's go up the river and try for some more."

"What shall we do with Ellie?" asked Rose. "There's no beach a little higher up where the river gets narrower, and she'll never be able to jump from one rock to another."

The children were far too much excited to pay great attention to such a trifle.

"Oh, she must manage somehow!" said Winnie. "Come along. Pull off your boots and socks, Ellie, there's a good child, and don't be afraid of the water, it won't hurt you."

Ellie looked very doubtfully at her feet, and then at the water, as if she did not at all like the prospect; however, Rosie didn't wait for her to make objections, but, pulling off the little boots, lifted her down into the stream, and then waded off herself after the others.

Ellie had her own ideas of duty, and knew what was expected of her when she was out with people bigger and stronger than herself; so after one shuddering exclamation of dismay as her feet first touched the water, she tried bravely to do as the others did.

But she found it very hard work. The water was bitterly cold, and where it was only deep enough to come a few inches above the other children's ankles it was already nearly up to her knees. She saw that the others twisted up their frocks, so she tried to twist hers up too, but she could only get up one little bit at a time, and the rest dabbled against her legs. Soon the hem was all wet, and her petticoats were wet, and the frills of her little white knickerbockers were wet. She was cold all over. The pebbles at the bottom hurt her feet. And then she didn't seem to get along one bit.

For a while she held tight on to the bit of frock that she was lifting up so boldly in front, and tried to encourage herself from time to time by saying half-aloud, "Ellie can walk in the river too, Ellie can;" but the big blue eyes often filled with tears, and her little stock of heroism began soon to melt away.

At last there came a bend in the river; the water grew deeper; and Ellie, getting into a place where there was a slight current, was very nearly taken off her legs. She saved herself by catching at a rock, but when she looked up to call one of the others to help her she found that they were out of sight.

That was more than she could bear. She was all lost now, and she never would be able to get out of the river any more, and it was no good trying to be brave, so she gave it all up, and sobbing out, "Oh, me is so told! me is so told!" she laid her head down on the rock and began to cry at the very tip top of her voice.

The others meanwhile had completely forgotten her. The fish were, as Murtagh thought, stupefied with lime, but not so stupefied as to be incapable of trying to save themselves from pursuing hands. The chase after them raised the children's spirits to the highest pitch. The banks of the river were wild and more or less wooded. All civilization might have been miles away.

Not a soul did the children pass, except one disconsolate-looking little girl sitting upon the bank. But, bare-legged and bare-armed, their hats hanging down upon their backs, their hair blown wildly about, with sparkling eyes and laughing faces, they splashed along in the bright cold water, or jumped from rock to rock to warm their feet, oblivious of everything in this world save the speckled trout for which they looked so eagerly in the clear brown pools by the rocks. Fortunately for Ellie, however, the thought of her flashed at last through Murtagh's mind.

"Why, Rosie," he exclaimed, "what's become of Ellie? she's not in sight."

The reflection caused some dismay for a moment among the children; but Bobbo volunteered to go back and fetch her, so they comfortably concluded that it was all right, and troubled themselves no further. Back he went accordingly, and Ellie's loud-voiced grief soon guided him to the spot where she stood. But when he had got there, and comforted her, and rubbed her chilled legs warm again, and wrung the water out of her skirt, and rolled up her damp knickerbockers, he found that it was all very well, but she had had enough of trying to be heroic, and nothing would induce her to enter the water again.

It was a difficulty that he had not counted upon, but there was no getting over it,—coaxing and scolding were alike in vain. Good-natured as he was, he was not going to lose his share in the fishing; and moreover. he was accustomed to solve all difficulties in the readiest manner that came to hand; so, putting her on his back, he just waded to shore, and trotted along the bank till he overtook the other children. They could settle together what was to be done with her.

He found them in a state of wild excitement. Winnie had that instant caught another fish, and Rosie, opening the skirt of her dress which she had gathered up as a bag, displayed three shining trout caught by herself and Murtagh.

"That's five altogether!" shouted Murtagh. "And we're going up to Long Island, and we'll light a fire there and cook them. Rosie's got the cake and things tied up in her hat, so it's not a bit wet, and that'll be loads for our dinner."

"Oh, that will be glorious!" cried Bobbo. "But look here, I say, Myrrh, what'll we do with Ellie? she can't get along a bit in the water."

"Couldn't you take her through the woods?" suggested Rosie.

"And miss all the fishing on the way up!" replied Bobbo. "Thank you, I've missed enough of the fun already. I think it's your turn now."

"Oh, no, indeed it isn't," replied Rosie. "I have her all day long. It's only fair that you boys should have the trouble of her sometimes."

"It's always women who look after the babies," said Murtagh.

"Well, I'm not going to this time," said Rosie decidedly. "It really is too bad that our pleasure is always spoilt with having to think about that tiresome child."

Little Ellie's head began to droop on to Bobbo's shoulder, as she looked anxiously at the children's faces. She was somewhat oppressed by a sense of her own wickedness in refusing to go into the water again, and she felt that Rosie's reproach was not altogether undeserved. Still, though she was accustomed to be called tiresome, she did not like it;

and besides, a terrible fear was arising in her mind that Rosie would make them leave her alone. The question was perplexing. Whatever Ellie might think, the children knew that they couldn't leave her there alone; but then they really could not give up their delightful expedition, and they were none of them at all inclined to start off alone with her through the woods. What was to be done?

Suddenly a brilliant idea struck Winnie.

"That girl we saw sitting on the bank!" she exclaimed. "I think I know her; I think she comes out of one of our cottages. Let's get her to take Ellie through the woods. We'll give her some of our dinner when we get up to the island, and it'll be great fun for her."

No sooner suggested than agreed to, and springing lightly from rock to rock Winnie quickly disappeared in the direction she had pointed out.

CHAPTER V

WITHOUT BEING put in the least out of breath by her rapid course she reached the spot, and finding the girl still sitting there plunged at once into conversation by saying: "I think you live in one of our cottages, don't you? What's your name, please?"

But the answer, "Theresa Curran," was given in such a miserable voice that Winnie paused and looked at her with some attention.

The girl did not look up, but remained sitting with her elbows on her knees, and her face supported on her hands, staring in front of her as though Winnie were not there. Her face was tear-stained, her eyelids swollen with crying, and there was a look of despairing wretchedness in her face which made Winnie feel that she could not go on with her message. So after standing beside her for a moment or two in silence she said: "Is there anything the matter?"

The girl did not answer; and Winnie repeated: "What's the matter?"

"I dunno what to do at all at all," replied the child drearily.

"Why?" said Winnie, "what has happened?"

Then, as though she couldn't keep it to herself any longer, the girl's grief burst forth in a passionate wail, and she sobbed out: "Oh, whatever will I do, whatever will I do? He'll kill me if I go home again."

"What is it?" said Winnie, somewhat awe-stricken. "What have you done? Who is it will kill you?"

"Oh, it's the rent!" sobbed the child, "and mother so sick and all, and he so savage at givin' it. He'll kill me; I know he will. He said he would;" and between fear and grief her words became too incoherent for Winnie to be able to understand.

"Have you lost it?" asked Winnie.

But the child's grief seemed too overpowering for her to give any answer; she only rocked herself backwards and forwards, sobbing as if her heart would break.

Winnie stood looking at her for a moment, not quite knowing what to do; then to her great relief Murtagh appeared at her side.

"What's the matter?" he whispered.

"I don't exactly know; somebody's going to kill her," returned Winnie. But Murtagh's presence made her feel as if she knew better what to do; so she climbed up the bank, and knelt down beside the girl, saying:

"Look here, don't cry like that. Here's my brother, and there are some more of us down there, and we won't let anybody kill you. Besides, he wouldn't kill you really I don't expect."

"Yes, he will," replied the girl. "He always does what he says."

"But he can't," said Murtagh. "He'll be put in prison, and hanged himself if he does." The child sobbed on, giving no heed to Murtagh's words.

"What's he going to kill you for?" asked Murtagh, climbing up after Winnie.

"When I lost the goat he said he'd kill me next time," replied the child. "Look, here," she continued, rapidly unfastening her frock, and displaying her bare neck and shoulder. "That's what he did to me yesterday." Then burying her face in her hands she burst into tears again.

The little thin shoulder was covered with a great bruise all blue and red. Down the centre of it the skin was broken in a long zigzag crack; the rapid movement of throwing off her dress had caused the blood to ooze out, and Winnie and Murtagh stood transfixed with pity and horror as they saw the dark red drops trickle slowly down.

"Oh, Win," said Murtagh, "what can we do?"

Winnie, after standing perfectly still for a moment looking at the bruise, went to the bank, and leaning over tried to scoop up some water in her hat.

Rosie and Bobbo, seeing that something was the matter, came up.

"Just give me my hat full of water, will you?" said Winnie, "and have either of you got a pocket-handkerchief?"

"What's the matter?" inquired Rosie, filling Winnie's hat for her, and handing it up as she spoke.

Winnie didn't trouble herself to answer; and Rosie and Bobbo, climbing up the bank, stood silent when they saw the wound on Theresa's shoulder.

Winnie dipped the handkerchief in water and gently bathed the bruise.

"How horrible!" said Rosie, presently.

"Great, cowardly scoundrel," ejaculated Murtagh.

"That's nothing," said the girl, her grief beginning to subside a little under the influence of the children's earnest sympathy. "He nearly broke me all to pieces entirely, the day I lost the goat, and he said he'd kill me downright next time. Oh! and then there's mother!" she added, her tears bursting forth again. "Whatever will she do? and I daren't go back. I know it's with that great stick he'll kill me, and I can't bear to be killed; I can't bear it."

"Don't cry," said Murtagh. "You shan't be killed. We'll protect her; won't we?" he added, turning confidently to the others.

"That we will," said Winnie. "Why, ye live on our land, don't you? So we're bound to protect you even if we didn't want to."

"Yez won't be able," replied the girl. "Ye don't know what he is at all when he's angry. He'd kill every one of you if ye came between us."

"What an awful man!" ejaculated Rosie, in a tone of horror.

"I don't care if he does," said Murtagh, "you'll just see if we can't prevent him touching you."

"Because you don't know," said Winnie eagerly. "We're bound up in a tribe, and we always settled we'd protect everybody against people who wanted to prevent them being free; and then, you live on our land; that makes you one of the followers of our tribe, and you'll just see if we let him touch you."

"How can yez help it?" said the girl, half-incredulous, but in spite of herself half convinced.

"Oh!" began Winnie, confidently. And there she stopped, not having as yet the slightest idea of how they were going to "help it." She consulted the others with her eyes, but confronted with the practical difficulty, no one was able immediately to propose a plan.

"Ye don't know what he's like," said Theresa, the momentary flash of hope dying out of her white face.

"Who is he?" asked Rose. "Is he your father?"

"It's my step-father, and mother had such work to get the rent from him. And now we'll be turned out all the same, an' he'll be that mad he won't know what he's doing. And it'll just break mother's heart, an' finish her off altogether, so it will! Oh dear, oh dear, oh dear! whatever will I do?"

The children looked at her in silence for a little while, then Rosie asked: "Have you lost the rent?"

"Yes, down there," she answered raising her head. "I was jumpin' over the stones goin' across to the little house to pay it, an' I'd got the two sovereigns in my hand when my foot slipped, and they flew out of my hand into the water before ever I knew they were gone at all. Just in the very middle, where the water's runnin' fast, and it swept them clean away."

"I'll tell you what!" exclaimed Murtagh, who had been thinking deeply, "we'll take her up to the island and hide her there; then afterwards we'll manage."

"Yes! yes!" cried Winnie; "of course, that's the plan. How stupid of me not to think of that! Come along; let's go up at once for fear he might come and catch her here. No one'll be able to touch you there," she added, turning to Theresa; "it's beautifully hidden, you'll see. And we can take you up provisions every day, and keep you as long as ever we like. Oh, Murtagh, what a splendid idea!"

"Spiffing!" exclaimed Bobbo. "Come along; let us be moving up. We've got a jolly lot of fish here," he explained to Theresa, "and we'll all have dinner together."

The children were so charmed with the notion that Theresa could not help being cheered. She still demurred, wondering what would become of her sick mother; but the children overbore her objections, and in a few minutes they were all going up the river's bank together.

The fish which had before been so absorbing were now completely forgotten in the interest of hearing about Theresa's life. Questions innumerable did the children ask; and Theresa, unused to sympathy, poured out willingly all her woes. It was a common enough story, but to the children it seemed almost too terrible to be true; her mother too sick to work, her step-father drinking nearly all he earned, and leaving them often for days at a time without food or money. To be hungry, cold, and beaten, such was her daily life. "And there's mother just dying away," she added; "I heard Mrs. O'Toole saying she'd never last out the winter."

But the kindness and the confident promises of help with which the children heard her story so cheered Theresa, that before long she began almost to enjoy talking over her troubles, and was even ready to laugh at one or two sallies of Murtagh's wit.

After a time the immediate bank of the river became impassable. Theresa and Ellie then struck across the woods together, Ellie prattling about everything she saw, and Theresa quite absorbed by her little charge. The others returned to the bed of the river. Bobbo, who had had scarcely any fishing, suddenly caught sight of another trout; the interest in the day's amusement was renewed; and so it came about that by the time they all met together again at Long Island not one of the whole party gave a thought to anything in the world but the fun of being on a desert island, and of getting their own dinner ready.

CHAPTER VI

Long island was one of the largest of the little islands round which the river flowed. The river at this part was more considerable. In the winter-time it was too deep to be crossed except in a boat, and even now, at the end of the dry season, it required some care and no little agility to ford it on foot. The island was so thickly overgrown with trees and bushes that from the river banks it seemed to be only an impenetrable mass of foliage. But the children knew better. In the centre of the trees and evergreens was a little cleared spot, and on that little clearance their father had, many years ago, built a hut.

The difficulty of approach, and the delightful loneliness of the place, formed a great attraction for the children; but the charm of charms was this hut. Completely hidden as it was, approachable only by two little narrow openings in the bushes, never entered by a creature except the children themselves, there was a delicious mystery about it that heightened the pleasures of possession; and then, it was their very own, built by their father when he was a child like them, and begged for them by him from their uncle, who was scarcely even aware of its existence. It was their castle, their territory, to do with absolutely as they pleased.

To grown-up eyes their castle was one of the very queerest, most tumble-down little huts that ever was built, but there was no place in the world where the children more enjoyed playing. There was only one room. Its walls were built of stones of all shapes and sizes, more or less firmly cemented together with mud; a square opening on one side served as a window; but in the doorway there were still the remains of a door, which Murtagh and Bobbo had mended so that it could shut and be fastened on the inside.

On the side opposite to the window there was a chimney, and in one of the walls there was a kind of cupboard where Rosie and Winnie kept a wooden bowl, four or five broken plates, two cups, and an old knife. Besides these things they had a good-sized empty box, that they used as a table, and five flower-pots that served as chairs; also a piece of soap, an old scrubbing-brush, a lot of raw potatoes, and a broom which they had made for themselves.

The only drawback of it all was that this island was too far off. There was a shorter way by the road, but the children always came along the river-bed, and though the distance was really far less than they imagined, the high wooded banks, the desolate fields through which the river wound, made the course of it so lonely that they always felt as if they were on an expedition into the depths of a wild country.

This very seclusion, however, made it all the more suitable to their present purpose, and to-day their sense of proprietorship was perhaps more delightful than it had ever been before.

For the moment, however, the grand and important matter was to get dinner ready, and without delay they set to work to collect wood for the fire.

Then the hut had to be cleaned, for it was more than a month since they had last been here, and cobwebs and dust abounded; so while Rosie prepared to light the fire the boys went with the bowl and saucepan to bring up water from the river, Winnie swept out the hut, and to Theresa was entrusted the business of getting the fish ready for cooking. Ellie was sent to pick laurel leaves to strew the floor. "For," remarked Murtagh, "to-day's a grand festival day, and our floor must be strewed with rushes like the ancient Britons. I'll be lord of the castle, and, Winnie, you shall be lady."

"I don't know what to do with this fire, Murtagh!" exclaimed Rose. "The three matches we had left are every one of them damp; I can't strike them."

"What a sell if we can't have a fire at all!" ejaculated Bobbo. "What's to be done?"

"Go down to the mill, of course, and get some matches from one of the men," dictated Winnie, in her bright decided way.

"Well done, my Lady Winifreda! right as usual," exclaimed Murtagh. "Be off, you varlet!" he continued in a grandiloquent tone of voice, turning to Bobbo, "and——" He paused a moment to find proper words, but fine language running short, the end of his sentence collapsed miserably into: "Look sharp back again."

"Bring a dictionary next time," laughed Bobbo, as he started off to fetch the matches.

"I say, Win, supposing we were to be Lord and Lady Macbeth," suggested Murtagh, "and the others might be ancient Britons we've taken prisoners."

"Thank you!" retorted Winnie indignantly. "I'd rather not. And besides, Myrrh," —this more doubtfully—"I don't *think* Macbeth was alive when the ancient Britons were."

"Yes, he was, somewhere about that time," replied Murtagh, decidedly. "Don't you remember in the theatre all the people called each other 'thou' and 'thy;' and besides, of course, I know he was. Don't you remember Bruce and Wallace, and King Alfred the Great, and Hengist and Horsa, and all those chaps?"

"Yes," said Winnie, "so I do, of course. Oh, well, I suppose it's all right; anyhow, it doesn't matter."

"I don't believe it's right," said Rosie, "because Macbeth was a Scotchman, and the ancient Britons were ancient Britons, so they couldn't have lived together."

"That's rubbish!" decided Murtagh; "because how do you know Macbeth wasn't a Scot and Pict? and every one knows they were with the ancient Britons."

"I don't think we'd better play games like that," replied Rosie, who had no answer ready, "because, you see, we have to do all the cooking and cleaning ourselves. We'd better be poor people living in a hut."

Rosie's plan was decided to be as good as another, and then scrubbing, sweeping, and dusting went on vigorously, till Bobbo came back from the mill bringing with him not only a whole box of matches but also a can of buttermilk, which the good-natured miller's wife had given him.

How the children enjoyed that cleaning! How they rubbed, and scrubbed, and splashed the water about! They forgot all about being hungry in the interest of sweeping, and dusting, and arranging. Any one might have supposed that they were the most orderly little mortals in existence.

Even Ellie had her share. With the skirt of her frock pinned back, and her little sleeves rolled up, she knelt upon the floor arranging laurel leaves, with the shiny sides uppermost, as though her very life depended on the completeness of the operation.

At last all began to look a little more clean and tidy, as Rose and Winnie observed with pride. The fire was lighted, the potatoes were boiling, the fish ready to cook, and now arose the great question: "How were the fish to be cooked?" The children had often seen Donnie cooking fish, but then it was always in a frying-pan, and they had no frying-pan. Murtagh was equal to the occasion. He thought he had heard somewhere that down at Killarney trout used to be grilled over a wood fire on a kind of gridiron of arbutus twigs; and there was a splendid arbutus tree on the island.

"All right," said Winnie; "I daresay it's as good a plan as another; anyhow, let's try."

The boys went out to cut the twigs, and she prepared a little wall of stones on either side of the fire, so that the sticks might be laid across from one to the other, and support the fish nicely over the red mass of glowing wood, without letting them get burned. Rosie and Theresa laid out upon the table the cracked cups and plates, the brown cake Donnie had given them, and Bobbo's can of buttermilk. Everything was ready except the trout. The children began to realize how hungry they were; and the boys coming quickly back with their bundles of rods, every one gathered round the fire, absorbed in the interest of watching the experiment of fish grilling

Winnie's plan for making the gridiron answered perfectly, and in a minute or two six trout lay sputtering and fizzing side by side upon it.

"My golly goskins! doesn't it make one hungry to look at them?" cried Bobbo in delight.

Rosie looked almost solemn; she appealed anxiously to Winnie to know how long she thought they ought to take cooking.

"I don't know exactly," said Winnie. "We must just guess!" And so well did they guess that when, after what seemed a very long time, the six trout were all served up together in the flat wooden bowl, decorated by Murtagh with sprays of arbutus leaves and berries, the children decided that they had never in all their lives sat down to such a jolly dinner.

They were as hungry as hungry could be, and tired enough to be glad to sit down. The fish and brown cake were delicious; the hut was most cosy with its carpet of green leaves and its blazing fire, and even Theresa could not help being gay and light-hearted

By the time dinner was over, however, the short October afternoon was beginning to grow dark, reminding them that, even taking the shortest way home by the road, they had some little distance to go, and nothing had yet been quite settled about Theresa.

"Now, listen, and I'll tell you what my plan is" said Murtagh, in answer to a question from Rosie. "This hut is a very nice place to live, and I vote Theresa stays here. There are three fish left, and a bit of cake. That'll do for her supper and breakfast. We can collect a lot of wood now before we go; then she can fasten the door inside and keep herself warm with having a jolly big fire all night; not a soul will ever know she's here, and to-morrow—"

"Well, but, Murtagh," interrupted Rosie, "we can't—!"

"Stop a minute, till you hear the end," said Murtagh, "I thought all about it on the way up here. Tomorrow we must just make up our minds to ask old Plunkett something. It's not very nice," he added, deprecatingly, turning to Winnie, "but then, you know, it's not the same as if it was for ourselves. We'll just tell him all about it; how the rent was lost, and all; and then, though he is such a—what he is,—of course he'll let them off paying after an accident like that. And then, Theresa, we'll all go home with you when you go, and your mother'll be so awfully glad to see you, after thinking you're lost, that she won't think a word about anything except kissing and that sort of thing; and of course when the rent's all right your step-father won't touch you."

"What a splendid plan!" cried Winnie and Bobbo together, as Murtagh, proud of the completeness of his project, looked round for admiration. There was a reality and importance in the idea of keeping her all night that pleased them greatly.

The notion was by no means so agreeable to Theresa; but at the thought of going home the terror of her step-father came over her again. She dared not face him without the rent, the remembrance of her last beating was too fresh in her mind.

"I think I'd better drown myself and have done with it!" she exclaimed, relapsing into her former state of despair.

"What in the world should you drown yourself for?" asked Winnie. "You have nothing to do except to stay here quite quietly and comfortably till to-morrow morning: then we'll come up with the rent, and we'll all go home to your house together: the night goes quite quickly, you know, when you're asleep."

Winnie's words made the affair seem certainly much simpler. It was an easy way of getting the rent, and Theresa felt ashamed of her ingratitude.

"I'm sure I ask yer pardon, every one of ye. It's much too good ye are to me," she replied warmly. Then with a sudden doubt: "Ye're sure ye'll bring it up in the morning?"

"Oh, yes!" cried Bobbo and Winnie together, "of course we'll come up the very first thing after we've got it," said Murtagh. "You know he won't actually give us two sovereigns, but he'll say you needn't pay your rent; that's just the same thing, you understand."

"But," suggested Rosie, who understood better what Theresa meant, "supposing he won't let them off paying."

"Oh, of course he'll let them off!" returned the others confidently.

"Why," said Winnie, "just think, what's two sovereigns in all the hundreds and hundreds of pounds of rent he has paid to him!"

"Why," added Murtagh, "he has more hundreds of pounds every year, I expect, than we have halfpennies, all five of us put together."

"So it would be just the same," continued Winnie, "as if some one asked us to give two halfpennies between us, and we would have to be pretty mean if we wouldn't do that."

"Yes," said Rosie, who never could understand anything the least bit like a sum, "then I think it'll be all right. He couldn't possibly refuse that."

"I should rather think not!" answered Bobbo, while Winnie, jumping up, said they must set to work at once to collect firewood.

"There's only one thing more," said Murtagh, whose first satisfaction with his own plan was a little bit damped by seeing that Theresa was not so enchanted as he had expected. "About your mother, Theresa, is that what you're thinking about? Are you afraid she'll be frightened at your not going home?"

"Oh, Murtagh, we can't help that!" said Winnie. "We must keep it all secret, or half the fun will be gone!"

Theresa replied dolefully that "She didn't know what her mother would do at all at all. She thought maybe it would kill her, she was that weak."

"I'm sure it won't kill her," said Bobbo, "and just think how jolly it'll be to see her face when we take you back to-morrow."

"If once we let out the secret of the hut we'll never have any peace here again," urged Winnie.

"Now do just listen to me," said Murtagh, suddenly illuminated by another brilliant idea. "Nobody's going to let out the secret of the hut. This is what I vote. Of course we can't tell your mother all about you, Theresa, because it would never do to let anybody know where you are; but we might write something on a piece of paper, just to let her know you're safe, and poke it under the cottage door the way the Fenians do their warnings about shooting people. We can do it on the way home, when it's too dark for any one to see us."

"Oh, Murtagh!" cried Bobbo in delight. "How ever do things get into your head?"

Murtagh tried not to look too proud of himself, but he began to feel really elated at his own genius for arranging details.

"Who's got a pencil?" he continued, producing a bit of dirty paper from his pocket.

None of them possessed such a thing; but a stick blackened in the fire and then dipped in buttermilk answered fairly well for a pen. It was found dreadfully difficult to write with; so Rose, who was the best scribe of the party, was directed to write only these words: "Theresa is safe,"—that being the very shortest message they could think of. Then Murtagh put the letter in his pocket, and they all set to work to collect firewood.

Poor Theresa was secretly terrified at the prospect of spending the night alone upon that out-of-the-way little island but she dared not speak. The only alternative was to go home, and she was still more terrified when she thought of what awaited her there. There was nothing for it but to bear her miserable fortune as best she could. While the children made their preparations for departure she sat cowering by the fire, and to tell the truth, her unhappy face tried their patience not a little. They had no conception of the nervous terrors she was undergoing, and they thought that she really might look a little happier when they had arranged such a beautiful plan for setting everything right.

Before they went, however, Murtagh asked her good-naturedly what was the matter, so she had at least the satisfaction of expressing her fears. The children tried to console and reassure her, but they could not succeed; and at last, feeling that they were only wasting words, they bade her "Good night," and picked their way across the river.

Left alone, Theresa dared not move even to bolt the door which the children had closed behind them, but turning the skirt of her dress over her head, she sank down in the corner of the hut with her face to the wall, and quivering with fear lay still and listened.

Nothing came. Not a sound was to be heard but the murmuring of the water as it rippled swiftly over the stones, and before long the perfect stillness of her position produced its own effect; she fell into a short troubled sleep. But her dreams were of terrible things, and she awoke suddenly a few hours later convinced that she had heard something, she was too agitated to attempt to define what. She gave one scream, and then sitting up she held her breath and listened. A gentle wind had arisen, the branches of the trees were swaying backwards and forwards, and she imagined she heard a sound as of ghostly footsteps. The sound continued, but nothing approached: and at last, a desperate kind of curiosity overmastering every other emotion, Theresa determined to go to the window-opening and peep out.

Trembling greatly she crept across the hut. The moon was up now, and the first object that met her eyes was a great white shimmering thing that seemed to be coming towards her, waving its arms as it approached. She stood still a moment transfixed with fright; then a gust of wind rushed through the trees; the whole island seemed to shiver; two long white arms were raised as if to seize her, and she could bear it no longer. Shrieking at the top of her voice she fled blindly, she scarcely knew where, out of the hut down to the river's edge. The sight of the shining water recalled her just sufficiently to her senses to prevent her from attempting to cross the river; but still screaming she turned and rushed—right into the arms of the ghost itself, where she fell exhausted and terrified among the straggling branches of a tall laurel.

For a moment she lay shuddering with closed eyes; but presently, venturing to look around her, she found that the ghost had vanished; that the moon was shining peaceably on the white backs of the laurel leaves as they fluttered on the swaying branches; and after the first moment of astonishment, she began to understand that all her fright had been caused by nothing more nor less than a big bush.

Poor little Theresa! She had sense enough left to feel very small and very much ashamed of herself, so picking herself up from the ground she went quietly into the hut. This time she barricaded the window and bolted the door, then blowing the fire into a blaze she ate some supper, and lying down once more fell soon into a peaceable slumber.

The children meanwhile, on leaving her, had trotted in the deepening gloom along the road till they came to the Dalys' cottage, a mere mud cabin standing back in a little garden from the roadside. But alas for Murtagh's plan of poking his bit of paper under the door! The door was wide open, and opposite to it, near the fire, a man stood smoking.

"What's to be done now?" whispered Rose. "We'd better go away; he'll see us."

"Hold your tongue," returned Murtagh. "He can't see us because we're out in the dark, but he'll hear us if you don't mind."

Rose was silenced, and Murtagh stood a minute thinking what was best to do.

"We'll hide in the ditch," whispered Winnie. "You wrap it round a stone, then shy it straight in and hide; don't run away."

Murtagh nodded in sign of approval; and while he looked for a stone the four others concealed themselves in the ditch. Standing a little on one side of the door he flung in his note. The children saw the little white thing fall at the man's feet. He started, looked round, then stooped and picked it up. As he opened it, they heard him say something in a low thick voice. Then there was a shrill cry of "Peter, what is it?" He seemed to answer; took a great stick from the chimney corner, came to the door, and looked out. They heard the woman's voice say, "Oh, Peter, catch the villains!" and their hearts began to beat a little faster as they looked at his great stick.

To their intense relief, however, after a moment of apparent irresolution, he exclaimed with a drunken laugh, "May old Nick fly away with 'em. I'm well rid of her." Then the door was shut to with a bang, and they all crept out of their hiding-places and scampered away home as fast as their legs would carry them, not feeling quite sure he wasn't after them till they were safe inside the house.

They rushed helter-skelter along the passages like a whirlwind, setting the doors banging behind them, till at the drawing-room door they were brought to a full stop by Adrienne, who hearing the noise came out to meet them.

"How late you are!" she said. "Are you not very cold? Come in here and warm yourselves while they are getting your tea ready."

The drawing-room behind was bright with lamp and firelight. In her white dress, her face a little flushed with bending over the fire, she seemed to the children almost like a being descended from some other world. Murtagh looked doubtfully at his muddy boots before he followed her into the drawing-room. The room smelt of flowers, a low chair was drawn up to the fire, and on a small table beside it was a bit of needlework and a china bowl full of ivy and late roses. The "mustiness" of the old drawing-room had somehow disappeared, as if by enchantment.

Adrienne knelt down upon the hearth-rug, and taking Ellie's two little hands in hers she rubbed them up and down to bring back the heat.

"Where have you been?" she asked. "It's very late; you must be tired and hungry."

"Don't!" burst out Murtagh, who was apparently fascinated by the contrast between Ellie's dirty little fingers and the hands in which they lay. "They are so beastly fishy; you'd better let them alone. Ellie can warm them herself at the fire."

"Ellie is so tired," said Ellie plaintively, leaning her little body against Adrienne. Adrienne sat down on the floor and took the child into her lap.

"Poor little thing!" she said, looking up at the others. "Have you been fishing? I think you have been rather too far for her."

"I should rather think we have been fishing," replied Bobbo, enthusiastically. "And we found something else besides fish; didn't we, Myrrh?"

An admonitory kick from Winnie, accompanied by a *sotto voce* "Hold your tongue, little donkey," warned him to be quiet, and Rosie hastily covered his abrupt silence by remarking: "We caught nine trout, and four of them were the very biggest I have ever seen."

Adrienne was all attention and interest, and without mentioning Theresa the children had plenty to tell. It was new to them to have a kind and intelligent listener waiting at home when they came in full of their adventures, and they thoroughly appreciated the advantage. Lolling in easy chairs by the fire, they were so warm and comfortable that they paid no attention to Peggy's announcement that tea was ready, and presently Mr.

Blair's step was heard coming along the hall. Then Adrienne looked up quickly, and said with a little hesitation:

"Hadn't you better go and take your tea now? I think that is Uncle Blair, and you are so—— You are not quite dressed for the drawing-room."

The children started out of their chairs. Murtagh contented himself with one of his queer, significant glances, embracing the whole group that stood upon the hearth-rug. Rosie blushed, and explained that, "When we were with mamma we always dressed for the evening."

Adrienne, without answering, led sleepy little Ellie to the door. She was simply anxious to get them out of the room, judging rightly that their uncle would not be at all enchanted to find such a dirty little tribe in possession of all the easy-chairs. The children were quick to understand, and they did not require to be told twice. They vanished promptly through one door as their uncle entered by the other.

The school-room was cold, and as untidy as usual. The door was standing open, and the flame of the candle which lighted the tea-table flickered in the draught. As they surveyed it, and heard in the distance the drawing-room door shut behind them, the children had a vague shut-out sort of feeling.

"What a set of dirty vagabonds we do look," said Murtagh, shivering. "Shut the door, Bobbo; the candle's running down one side on to the table-cloth."

CHAPTER VII

Next morning breakfast was half-finished when Brown entered the dining room, and said that Mr. Plunkett was in the study, and wished to know if he could see Mr. Blair.

"Ask him to come in here, Brown," said Mr. Blair.

"Take a cup of tea, and tell me your business now, Plunkett," he said, as Mr. Plunkett was ushered in. "I have promised Mr. Dalrymple to be with him at ten to look at his moss agates, so I have not a moment to give you after breakfast."

"And I shall be gone to the outlying farms by the time you come back," returned Mr. Plunkett, without seating himself. "Well, sir, a most unpleasant event has occurred, and as I think you will be called upon to institute some inquiry, I consider it my duty to inform you of it without delay. Peter Daly has just been with me."

The children were suddenly startled into attention, and made violent attempts to look as though they didn't care.

"And it appears, from his confused account, that yesterday morning his step-daughter, Theresa Curran, aged thirteen, was sent to my house with the amount due for half a year's rent, two sovereigns, which she was to pay me. The money was not paid yesterday, and the girl, it seems, has disappeared. Her mother became anxious yesterday afternoon, and despatched a little boy to make inquiries in the village. The girl had not been seen, and what gives the affair a serious aspect is this."

Here Mr. Plunkett, tucking his umbrella under his arm, drew out a pocket-book, and began to search among the papers contained in it. Then selecting one he laid it before Mr. Blair, and continued:

"Yesterday evening, after dark, this paper was mysteriously thrown into the cottage, and though, as you perceive, it is meant to be of a reassuring character, it points in my opinion to the conclusion that the girl has been forcibly abducted for the sake of the money in her possession."

Murtagh held his breath, and sat most unnaturally still for fear of betraying himself as he recognized his piece of paper. What in the world, he wondered, was the meaning of a "reassuring character?" Rosie blushed so violently that it was lucky for them no one was paying attention to their movements.

"You will observe," Mr. Plunkett went on, "that the writer is evidently a person of very little education: out of those three words two are wrongly spelt." Winnie's eyes sparkled with suppressed laughter, and she glanced at Rose as Mr. Plunkett made this remark.

"And," said Adrienne, who had risen, and was looking over her uncle's shoulder, "it has not even been written with a pen and ink."

The children began to lose all command of their countenances. They longed to be out of the room, but a sort of fascination kept them silent in their chairs. It did not occur to one of them that the simplest thing to do was to tell their story, and ask for the rent then and there.

"Everything, in fact," replied Mr. Plunkett, "tends to demonstrate that the offence has been perpetrated by members of the lowest class of society, and this invests the affair with a certain gravity. But I permit myself to hope that it may yet prove less serious than at first sight it appears."

"Go down to the cottage, Plunkett, if you have the time before starting for the farms, and I should not be at all surprised if you find her sitting quietly by the fire," said Mr. Blair. "My countrymen have a wonderful aptitude for all that savors of romance."

"I have been down, sir," said Mr. Plunkett, with something that was almost a smile, "and I fear the fact is incontestable that the girl and the rent have disappeared. The romance is not wanting. Mrs. Daly has got it into her head that a man, Patrick Foy by name, who has a grudge againt her for marrying Daly, has killed the girl, and sent this letter in order to hinder any search being made till he has had time to leave the country."

Adrienne's eyes opened wide with mixed astonishment and incredulity.

"It is quite possible, Miss Blair," said Mr. Plunkett. "The folly and passion of these people is beyond all reasonable comprehension. I do not say that in this case I consider such a solution to be probable. But you perceive," he continued, turning to Mr. Blair, "that since the woman expresses such an opinion it complicates the affair, and renders it doubly advisable to put the matter at once into the hands of the police."

A sort of gasp from Bobbo made Mr. Plunkett turn his head; but Mr. Blair, suddenly remembering the moss agates, pushed out his chair at the moment, and recalled Mr. Plunkett's attention by saying with a smile:

"Well, well, Plunkett, you know I am one with you in your crusade against these barbarians; do whatever is necessary. And if it turns out to be serious," he added more gravely, "don't let any question of expense weigh with you. The poor girl must be found."

"I shall institute proceedings at once," replied Mr. Plunkett, as he walked with Mr. Blair to the door; "and if there is evidence to confirm the mother's notion we will, of course, have Pat Foy taken up."

The two gentlemen walked away down the passage, and the children were at last able to escape.

"I say," exclaimed Bobbo, "here's a pretty go!"

"Hadn't we better say where she is at once?" said Rose anxiously; "somehow policemen—"

"You'd better look out, Rose," said Murtagh mockingly; "you'll be taken up before you know where you are and clapped into prison. You're the eldest of us, you know."

But though Murtagh could not resist the temptation to laugh at Rose, he was serious enough when he turned to Winnie and asked:

"What's to be done now? How shall we ask him for the rent?"

Winnie thought deeply for a minute or two; then she burst out ecstatically with: "Oh, Murtagh, wouldn't it be fun to keep her hidden, and have all the policemen and people searching, and Mr. Plunkett fidgeting and worrying, and taking ever so much trouble! It would pay him out so jolly, and pay out that policeman too for telling about me and Bobbo."

"No, no, Murtagh!" cried Rosie, "that would never do. We'll be getting into an awful scrape."

"I don't think Theresa would think it much fun, Win," said Murtagh, shaking his head. "No; I think we'd better get the rent. The thing is—I say!" he exclaimed, suddenly breaking off in the middle of his sentence, "isn't that old Plunkett himself on Black Shandy?"

He pointed as he spoke to the avenue, where some one on a black horse was trotting away from the house.

"It is so," replied Bobbo. "He's off to the farms now, and the Lord knows when he'll be back!"

It was useless to run after him, he was already much too far off; what was to be done? The children looked blankly at one another. Then Rose exclaimed vehemently: "Why didn't you ask him before he went, Murtagh? It was all your plan, and now what shall we do?"

"Ask him this evening instead," replied Winnie coolly, while Murtagh looked troubled. "Never mind, Myrrh, it'll all come right in the end, because things always do. As we can't ask him now the first thing we had better do is just to get something from Donnie that will do for Theresa's dinner, and then go up and tell her."

"Poor Theresa!" said Murtagh, "she'll be awfully disappointed."

Still Winnie was right. It was evidently the first thing to do; and having provided themselves with various scraps from the larder they started for the island. They went by the road; they had no heart to go up the river; and as they walked along they earnestly discussed the possibilities and probabilities of the police finding out all about it before to-morrow; for it had become evident that they must keep Theresa another night. It was more than ever impossible now for her to go home without the rent, and there was no knowing at what time Mr. Plunkett would return from the farms.

They decided that they would wait about in the avenue to waylay him as he came back, and thus lose no time in making their request; but he was not likely to return till eight or nine o'clock, and it would be too late then to go up to Theresa. If it had not been for the police they would have thought very little of keeping her a night longer, but their notions about what policemen might know and do were very vague, and they had in their secret hearts hazy visions of prison and a court of justice, which were too unpleasant to be talked about even to one another.

"I wish we'd never had anything to do with her," sighed Rose.

"No," said Murtagh; "because you know, if she hadn't met us perhaps she'd have gone home and been killed; so, of course, it's better this way."

"Yes, but supposing we don't get the rent!" suggested Rose, dolefully.

"Oh, we must get that. Nobody could refuse it after thinking she's dead and everything. If they don't find out before to-morrow it will be all right."

"I wish to goodness to-morrow was come then!" ejaculated Bobbo, who remembered how very unpleasant the policeman's hand had felt on his shoulder that evening on the garden-gate.

In this gloomy frame of mind they reached the island. Theresa had recovered from her terrors of the night before, and now feared only her step-father.

When she heard the children's account of all that had happened she very nearly relapsed into the state of despair in which they had found her the day before. Rosie had secretly hoped that she would insist upon going home, but no such thought entered her mind. She only implored Murtagh to be sure and get the rent soon. "For, you know, sir, he'll be madder than ever now after having all this botheration, and he wouldn't mind what he did."

It was impossible to comfort her, and notwithstanding Winnie's and Murtagh's confident assurances that everything would be settled on the morrow, the little party that dined on the island that day was very dreary and dismal.

The children stayed as long as they could to keep poor Theresa company, but towards four o'clock they thought it best to go and begin their watch for Mr. Plunkett; it was just possible that he might come home early.

"You mustn't expect us early to-morrow, Theresa," said Winnie; "on Sunday morning we can't get out before breakfast, because Donnie always comes and pomatums all our heads. Then we're dressed for church; then there's church; then there's dinner—oh dear! I wish Sunday didn't come so often; we shan't be able to get up till the afternoon."

"Mornin' or evenin' it don't matter; I don't believe yez'll ever be able to get the rent," replied Theresa, disconsolately; and in that desponding condition they were obliged to leave her.

They wandered about down in the park, listening anxiously for the sound of Black Shandy's hoofs. The wind was very cold, and towards six o'clock the evening closed in dark and wet. Their teeth chattered and their clothes were soon soaked with rain. Still it was no use going home till they had seen Mr. Plunkett. Theresa must not be disappointed a second time; so they marched patiently backwards and forwards to keep themselves as warm as might be, and held on bravely to their purpose.

At last there was a sound of footsteps. The children ran eagerly forward in the hope that it might be Mr. Plunkett for some reason returning on foot, but it turned out to be a laborer going home from his work.

"Whatever are ye doing out here in the rain?" he exclaimed in surprise.

"We're waiting for Mr. Plunkett," replied Murtagh; "we want to speak to him."

"Ye won't speak to him to-night then," returned the man. "He came home in the doctor's trap hours ago. Haven't ye heard the news?"

"What news?" exclaimed Murtagh.

"The news o' the shooting. He was shot at from out o' the little wood across at the back o' Dolan's fields, an' he never was touched at all; only Black Shandy killed dead as a stone,—worse luck!"

The "worse luck" may have been meant as a lamentation for Black Shandy, but the tone in which it was uttered gave it an uncommonly different signification.

"Shot at!" exclaimed the children excitedly.

"What an awful lot of funny things are happening!" said Murtagh. "Who shot at him?"

"Them as thought we've had enough o' him and his ways, I s'pose," replied the man. "And that's not a few. Good-evening to yez; ye'd better be runnin' in out o' the rain."

"Yes, but look here," said Winnie. "Did they want to shoot him dead?"

"What d'ye suppose I know about it? Maybe it was only a bit o' fun, just to see whether they could hit a man or no when they tried," he replied, with a curious kind of laugh.

"Was he hurt? Were they caught?" inquired Bobbo.

"I don't know the rights of it, but there's nothing serious. Old Nick'll always take care of his own. He fell down with the horse, and they took him up, an' carried him into the farm; then the doctor was sent for, and after a bit the two o' them drove back here together. That's all I know about it. It's up at the house ye'll hear the whole story. But my old woman'll be looking out for me. Good-night to yez." And this time he moved off quickly.

"Isn't it lucky he wasn't killed!" said Rosie. "We'd never have been able to get the rent then."

"I wonder why they always shoot people," said Winnie. "Last year when Mr. Dalrymple was in Italy they shot Mr. Williams, and now they've tried to shoot old Plunkett."

"Because they're agents," replied Murtagh promptly. "And I don't exactly know what agents are, but it's something very bad. They're tyrants, and they oppress everybody. That man that was fishing with me and Pat O'Toole said Ireland would never be free till all the agents were killed."

"Are you quite *sure* old Plunkett's an agent?" asked Bobbo with interest.

"Quite sure," replied Murtagh, "because they said so; and besides, can't we see he is ourselves? Isn't he always oppressing people?"

"Why doesn't the Queen banish them all out of Ireland?" said Winnie. "That's what I'd do if I were her."

"Oh, I say!" exclaimed Bobbo, laughing, "wouldn't it be a jolly lark if she banished old Plunkett?"

"Yes; but, Murtagh," said Rosie, who generally kept one idea at a time steadily before her mind, "how are we going to get the rent? It's all very fine talking, but we never seem to get one bit nearer to it."

"And we're not likely to get a bit nearer to it to-night," said Murtagh with a sigh. "We've just got to wait till to-morrow morning. It's no use thinking about it. Here goes, Winnie; I'll race you to the house."

But though he made the best of it he was greatly disheartened, and so too was Winnie. The plan had seemed so splendid at first, and now that it was to be carried out everything went wrong. They might pretend not to think of it; in reality it occupied all their thoughts, and when the house was reached they went very silently off to their own rooms. Bobbo and Rosie soon followed with Ellie, and while they groped their way into drier clothes the remarks exchanged across the little landing that separated the two rooms were of a decidedly doleful description.

They had some idea of staying up in their rooms till the dinner-bell rang; they did not feel in the mood to meet people and be asked questions about what they had been doing. But they had neither fires nor candles; they were cold and uncomfortable; and Murtagh soon remarked that he thought it was awful stuff staying up there in the cold.

"What's the good of it? We've often been in a row before, and, after all, people can't guess just by looking at us that we know where Theresa is."

"All right then," said Rosie; "Let's go down. But don't let us seem to be cold or anything. Let's look quite jolly, as if nothing had happened." And she ran down-stairs as she spoke, gaily talking and laughing.

The other two children admired her plan but they did not second it, and it was a very cold, hungry, dispirited-looking set of little people, who in another minute stood outside the school-room door.

"I hope to goodness the fire's not out," said Murtagh, as he groped for the handle.

He opened the door as he spoke, and disclosed to the children's somewhat astonished eyes a school-room looking so different from their ordinary place of refuge that it was hardly to be recognized. Not only was a bright fire blazing in the grate, but the whole room was in perfect order. The crimson window-curtains were drawn; the tea-table was decorated with a bouquet of fresh flowers; the books had got into the bookcases; the music into the music-stand; the more comfortable and respectable of the arm-chairs were disposed within reach of the fire; the brown moreen sofa had been dragged from its corner to occupy the place of honor at one end of the hearth-rug; and Nessa herself, in her pretty evening dress, was sitting on the sofa reading.

An undefined sensation of comfort crept over the children, but with it the elder ones had an unpleasant consciousness that somehow their wildness seemed suddenly out of place. They didn't feel quite as if they were in their own school-room, and they hesitated an instant in the doorway, wondering half-uncomfortably what Nessa would say to them. They were very quickly at their ease, however, for she looked up brightly as they entered, and exclaimed:

"Oh, there you are! I am so glad. I was expecting the dinner-bell to ring every minute, and I wanted to be here when you arrived. What do you think of it?" She looked round the room as she spoke. "Peggy and I have been working the whole afternoon."

"Awfully jolly!" said Murtagh, taking up a position on the hearth-rug, and surveying the room with a satisfied expression.

"How pretty you have made it look!" said Rosie. "What did you do to it?"

"What did we not do?" said Nessa. "Peggy scrubbed and brushed and polished, and I dusted and arranged, and pushed the furniture about. First I was going to settle it a little by myself, and then Mrs. Donegan came up and she sent Peggy to help me."

"Well, I call this very jolly," said Winnie, who had thrown herself into a chair, and was looking round with a beaming countenance. "Doesn't it seem to you just a little bit like when we were at home, Murtagh?"

"Yes," said Murtagh, slowly. "Only it isn't papa, you know."

"That reminds me," said Nessa, as she rang the bell for tea. "Who are Cousin Jane and Emma, or Emily and Frankie? because I saw Uncle Blair for a minute at lunch time, and he said they were coming to stay here."

"Frankie coming!" exclaimed the children in delight.

"Oh, I am so glad!" continued Winnie. "He is such a dear little fellow, only he is so delicate; he is as old as Murtagh, really, but you wouldn't think he is more than seven or eight years old, and he's not a bit strong. Often we have to carry him just like Ellie; two of us put our hands together, you know."

"He's just the very best little fellow that ever was born," said Murtagh, warmly. "Now he really is good, if you like. I don't know how he manages; he never even wants to do anything—I mean things he oughtn't to. I suppose he was just born so."

"I wish he was coming alone," said Bobbo.

"Why?" asked Nessa.

"Oh!" replied Murtagh, "because Emma's a prig, and Cousin Jane—well, Cousin Jane *is* a nuisance. Isn't she now, Rosie?"

"Oh, yes," replied Rosie. "You know she laughs at us; and then about our clothes too, she always teases us because we're so funnily dressed, and that isn't our fault. Donnie and Mrs. Plunkett settle all about that, and I'm sure I don't like being dressed as we are one bit; I often feel ashamed to go into church with all the funny colors we have to wear; and there's another thing, Emma hasn't half such pretty things as we used to have when we were with mamma!"

Rosie grew quite pink with indignation at the remembrance of what she had suffered by reason of Donnie's uneducated taste; and Nessa agreed that it was aggravating to have to wear clothes that one didn't like, and then be made fun of into the bargain.

"But tell me something," she continued; "are they all my cousins too?"

"Oh, yes," cried Winnie, "so they are! *Our* cousins; doesn't that sound nice?"

"What's funny," said Murtagh, "is about Cousin Jane. She's our cousin, and Emma and Frankie are our cousins too, because—Uncle William had a son. Oh, I never can remember that rigmarole; Rosie knows. Explain all about it, Rosie."

"You always begin wrong, Murtagh. That's why you can't remember," replied Rosie. "Uncle William was Uncle Blair's twin brother, and he's very, very old, you know. Then Uncle William died and had a son."

"Had a son and died, you mean," cried Murtagh, "and the son married cousin Jane, and had another son called 'little Frankie,' and then he died too, and——"

"That means Frankie died," interrupted Winnie; "you're as bad as Rosie, Murtagh!"

"Well, but I couldn't say it any other way," replied Murtagh. "If I said, then he died too and had a son called Frankie, that would mean he had Frankie after he died. Perhaps he did; I'm sure I don't know; he's been dead a very long time, that's all I know about it, and Frankie's the very jolliest little son any one could ever have! When's he coming?"

"I don't know," said Nessa; "not for some time I think. Uncle Blair said——" The dinner-bell ringing loudly, interrupted her sentence. "Uncle Blair said," she continued, rising, "that they were making a little sort of driving tour through the hills, and that they would end here."

"What a pity you have to go," said Rosie; "it is so nice talking."

"Would you like to come to the drawing-room after dinner?" said Nessa. "Uncle Blair does not come till nine o'clock."

"Don't you mind us coming?" asked Murtagh. "Emma always said we're such a nuisance!"

"Oh, no; indeed you are not to me!" replied Nessa, with an earnest warmth that made the children look up at her with pleased faces.

"When we've finished tea," said Rosie, as the door closed behind Nessa, "we might get some hot water and wash our hands and faces, don't you think, Murtagh?"

"All right!" said Murtagh, nodding his head.

And the result of their resolution was that when Nessa came out from dinner she found in the drawing-room four shiny little faces reflecting the lamplight, four tightly brushed heads, and four pairs of hands as beautifully clean as such weather-beaten little hands could be.

The children had, in fact, made themselves so clean that they felt half-ashamed, but Nessa appreciated their little attention.

"How nice you all look!" she said kindly, and then she sat down amongst them, and they spent a very happy hour chatting round the fire. They discussed their cousins' visit, and Mr. Plunkett's escape, and the children had lots to tell about the place and the people. It was so nice talking, as Rosie said, and they were very happy to be thus possessed of Nessa's undivided attention. So when bed-time came they ran gaily enough up their little staircase, and as they separated on the landing Murtagh exclaimed:

"You were quite right, Win, things always do come right in the end; only to-morrow morning and all our troubles'll be over!"

CHAPTER VIII

MURTAGH WOKE NEXT DAY with a glad feeling that something pleasant was to happen; and then, remembering what it was, he sprang out of bed with a shout of—"Hurrah, Bobbo, to-morrow has come, and we'll be all right now!" Careering across the landing in his night-shirt, he woke Rosie and Winnie in order to remind them of the same fact, and they all rejoiced together, planning what they would say to Theresa's mother, and anticipating with delight how "awfully" pleased she would look when she knew that Theresa wasn't dead, and that the money was all right.

"I'm very glad we met her, after all," reflected Murtagh, as he returned to his own room to put on some garments more suitable to the breakfast table. "Even if the police had got hold of us, it would have been something to have saved her, and this way it's jolly."

Little Ellie understood enough of what was going on to know that the others were glad about something, so she looked happy and important when they met Nessa in the dining-room. Altogether they were as bright as they could be, and capered about, forgetting even to groan at the thought of being shut up in church for two whole hours.

They expected to see Mr. Plunkett at ten o'clock. It was his custom to walk through the greenhouses at that hour on Sunday mornings. But alas for their joyful expectations! Ten o'clock struck, and eleven too, and no Mr. Plunkett made his appearance.

Ballyboden fashion was to begin morning service at twelve o'clock, and at half-past eleven the carriage came to the door. Clearly, all hope of seeing Mr. Plunkett before church must be given up, and the mood in which the children started was anything but devotional.

It must be confessed that they were not agreeable companions in church that day. Never had the service seemed so long to them, and doubly long did they make it seem to Nessa. In vain she buried her face in her hands and tried to forget them. The proximity of four sturdy children, confined against their will, is not easily to be forgotten.

They meant to be quiet, but they yawned till the tears ran down their cheeks, and not only did they change their position every five minutes, but by a painful fatality they rarely succeeded in effecting the change without administering an unintentional but resounding kick to the woodwork of the old pew. At last came the final prayer, and Winnie went down on her knees with such alacrity that more than one respectable old lady turned her head, and seemed reproachfully to ask an explanation from Nessa. Oh! why are old pews constructed on the principles of a sounding-board?

But it was over; service and sermon had come to an end; and the small congregation poured out into the churchyard.

There the children learnt that Mr. Plunkett, more shaken than he had at first thought by the fall with Black Shandy, had been, this morning, unable to leave his bed. "It was likely," said the young doctor, who gave them the news, "that he would be confined to the house for several days."

Nessa was astonished at the faces of dismay with which the children received the information.

"Are you sure?" Rosie ventured to ask. "Are you sure he won't be able to get out for several days?"

"Well, I really can't tell you that, Miss Rose," replied the doctor. "But he's not very bad,—not very bad."

The doctor had a habit of laughing when he was nervous, and it made him very nervous to stand in the middle of the churchyard talking to Nessa, so he laughed a great deal as he answered Rosie.

"Giggling idiot!" muttered Murtagh, as he thrust his hands into his pockets and walked gloomily towards the carriage.

"Why can't he say something in earnest?" he added, turning, as he thought, to Winnie. But it was not Winnie; it was Nessa who was close behind him.

"Would you like to go round by the Red House, and inquire there how he is?" she suggested, feeling quite sorry for the children's needless anxiety.

Murtagh felt doubtful of the utility of that proceeding, but a nudge from Winnie, and an expressive glance from Rosie, made him accept the proposal. Winnie had conceived the bold design of seeing Mr. Plunkett in his own house, and of asking him without more delay; but, arrived at the Red House, she found that her hopes were vain.

"Mr. Plunkett was in his own room," Mrs. Plunkett said, "and did not know when he expected to leave it."

"Mightn't we go up and see him?" suggested Winnie undauntedly, but Mrs. Plunkett answered in horror: "My dear Winnie, I wouldn't let one of you inside his room for anything in the world. Why, he won't even have one of his own children in except Marion, and she's more like a mouse than a child."

So the notion had to be given up, and they drove away feeling more than ever puzzled as to what was to be done. Poor Theresa! They scarcely dared to think of going up to her with the news that she must wait again, and this time wait till they did not know when.

Their heads were so full of Theresa's troubles that dinner was little short of torment to them. They could not eat; they were longing only for the meal to be finished in order that they might get away and consult together. What, therefore, was their confusion, when towards the end of the second course Nessa innocently suggested that they should go together and pay a visit to the poor woman whose little girl had been lost.

"Uncle Blair said it would be kind of us," she said.

The children at first were so taken aback they scarcely knew what to say.

"We—we can't," replied Murtagh. "We have to go— I mean," he said, recovering himself, "we have something else to do."

"Look here, Murtagh, I don't see a bit of use all of us going," exclaimed Rosie, gaining a sort of desperate courage from Nessa's presence; "and I'm not, for one."

"Do you mean," exclaimed Murtagh, astonished, "that you're not coming up to—" He stopped short just in time, growing scarlet at the thought of how nearly he had betrayed himself.

Nessa looked at him in surprise, while Rosie answered stoutly: "No, I'm not."

"Couldn't your business wait till to-morrow?" Nessa asked gently.

"No," said Murtagh, with a sort of shutting of himself up that made further questions impossible.

There was a minute's silence; then Nessa turned to Rosie and asked whether she knew the way to Mrs. Daly's cottage, and whether it would be too far for Ellie to walk.

"I tell you what," said Winnie presently, a vague idea that perhaps "something might turn up" at Mrs. Daly's, prompting her suggestion, "if you'll wait for us at the cottage we'll come thereafter, because anyhow that's the way we'll come home. Rosie can go with you if she likes," she added, contemptuously.

So it was arranged; and dinner over, the children went away to their own rooms to prepare for their walk.

"What is to be done, Murtagh?" asked Rosie, as they mounted the little staircase. "Goodness knows when that stupid Mr. Plunkett will get well again! I think much the best plan is to give up the whole thing, and tell Mrs. Daly now all about Theresa. We can't possibly keep her there for ever and ever, and we shall be getting into an awful row, for the police always find things out."

"What is the good of talking like that, Rosie?" interrupted Winnie impatiently. "Just as if we didn't know as well as you that we're getting into an awful row. You keep on telling us the same thing over and over again, as if that would help us out of it."

"Well, but I do tell you a way out of it," replied Rose.

"Yes, just like a sneaking woman's way," said Murtagh. "Of course, you're never to stick to any one when it gets to be any trouble sticking to them."

"Well, I'm sure I don't see much good sticking to people when you can't do any good by it," returned Rose, reddening; "and besides, you're sure to let it all out before long, with the kind of things you say before other people."

"Come now, Rosie, you're a great deal worse than Murtagh," remarked Bobbo, and a pitched battle of tongues was imminent, when Winnie again interrupted:

"Do hold your tongues, and let's settle what's to be done."

But talking about it was very little use, and soon Nessa's voice was heard at the bottom of the stairs calling out to know if Rosie and Ellie were ready.

Great indeed, as the children expected, was poor Theresa's trouble when she heard the news they brought; it was impossible to console her. Nothing but the terror of going home, which grew in proportion with the efforts made to save her from that dreaded contingency, kept her upon the island. She suffered, really, infinitely more from the fears and loneliness of her captivity than she would have suffered even from her step-father's anger. Her position on the island was indeed almost insupportable; but a sort of unreasoning shrinking from any new action, and, in spite of her desponding assurances to the contrary, a blind faith that somehow the children would make things all right in the end, kept her where she was. The first night had been the great difficulty, and that over she would now stay as long as the children could keep her.

In answer to her tears the children could say nothing but promise more confidently than ever to make it all right somehow, if only she would wait patiently; and after they had done their little best to comfort her they went away promising to come up the very first thing before breakfast and bring with them news of her mother.

The thought that they were going to see her mother reconciled her somewhat to their departure, but the hour they had spent with her had made them more than ever downspirited. They had exhausted all their courage in trying to comfort her, and the three little hearts were very heavy as they walked along the road that led to the cottage. It was Winnie as usual who brightened up a little at last.

"Never mind, Myrrh," she said, as they reached the cottage-door. "We'll do it somehow, you know, if we hold out long enough." And she seemed so sure that the boys felt surer too.

They stopped on the threshold, hesitating to enter; but Nessa's voice within, speaking to Rose, emboldened them to lift the latch. The cottage was much like many another, but bare and neglected-looking. It felt cold, like an uninhabited place. A mud floor; at one end a cupboard; at the other a bed; a table, a couple of broken chairs; and in the smoke-stained fireplace a newly-lit fire trying to burn; that was what the children saw. Rose, at the fire, was stirring something in a saucepan; Nessa was sitting beside the bed with her back turned to the door. There seemed at first to be no one else in the cottage except little Ellie, who was leaning against Nessa's knees; but as the children's eyes became used to the obscurity they distinguished on the pillow the white, wasted face of a sick woman.

Rosie looked up full of importance as they entered.

"There you are!" she exclaimed in a half-whisper. "Oh, it was such a good thing we came. Do you know she had nothing to eat, and there was no fire, and the door was open, and the pig had got in, and the chickens were pecking her oatmeal, and oh! everything was so miserably uncomfortable; but we've settled her bed, and now we're making some gruel."

Nessa looked round at the sound of their entry. Her face wore a saddened expression not usual to it.

"These are my little cousins," she said to Mrs. Daly; "but we did not know how ill you were when we agreed to come all together."

"They're very welcome, Ma'am," replied the poor woman with a trace of cordial hospitality still left in her faint voice. "Ye're kindly welcome, my dears; will yez please to sit down?"

"Thank you," said Murtagh, and they sat down at once round the fire. At home as they generally were in the cottages, they scarcely knew what to do with themselves in this one, and were glad to subside into silence. Nessa was hearing an account of the poor woman's illness, and from time to time the low indistinct sentences, interrupted by a constant cough, reached their ears.

"Isn't there anything we can do?" whispered Murtagh after a time.

"Oh, no," replied Rose. "We've done everything. We made the room tidy, and we lit the fire and everything, and there was scarcely any wood, and she has hardly any covering on her bed, and there isn't a single thing to eat except a little oatmeal and some scraps of hard bread."

"What's in the saucepan?" asked Winnie.

"Gruel," replied Rosie. "Nessa settled it. It's got to be stirred all the time, and then she's going to toast the scraps of bread when the fire gets a little brighter."

After that the children said very little; but, sitting round the fire, they employed themselves with poking bits of wood into the blaze, and listened at first almost mechanically to what Mrs. Daly was saying.

She was speaking of her husband now, telling how he was very good to her when he was sober, but that when he got a sup of drink, it was like mad it made him. "He was as kind as a body could want yesterday morning," she said, "and went up to Mr. Plunkett's to tell about the child being gone an' all; but now I suppose it's in with some of his bad companions he is, for he's never been back since. And then, you see, Ma'am, it's not like as if Theresa was his own child. Of course, he hasn't the feelings like for her that a father might have, an' she makes him mad with her flighty ways, till what with the drink an' the anger he beats her sometimes till she can scarce stan' up on her legs.

"She lost the goat up on the mountains two months ago come Wednesday, an' deed he nearly murthered her entirely. She lay moanin' there on the the straw all night fit to make your heart bleed. But for all that he's a very kind man; by nature I mean, Ma'am, you couldn't find a kinder. It's all for her good he thinks he's doing it, and with the drink—"

All this was said in detached sentences, interrupted often by a cough, or a few words from Nessa.

The children scarcely dared even to look at one another. They strained their ears to catch every word. Poor Theresa! it seemed to them that she might almost as well live with a wild beast as with such a step-father. No wonder she was afraid to come home.

But talking exhausted Mrs. Daly, and Nessa came soon to the fire to see if the gruel were ready. Then the bread had to be toasted, and a cup and plate and spoon had to be found and washed. But Nessa might have done nothing all her life except prepare gruel and toast, so quickly and deftly was it all made ready, and in a very few minutes Mrs.

Daly, propped up in her bed, was partaking of the most comfortable meal she had tasted for days.

Nessa would not let her speak any more, but in order that she might not feel hurried over her gruel began to talk herself, and amuse the children as much as Mrs. Daly by an account of her journey from Brittany to Ballyboden.

She had such a perfectly simple way of talking, that, notwithstanding a certain Parisian bonnet which had been the object of Rosie's admiration all church time, she seemed no more out of place sitting on a broken chair, making conversation in poor Mrs. Daly's cabin, than she would have been in the most elegant of drawing rooms. Mrs. Daly was cheered by the pleasant chatter, and the children were quite sorry when the gruel was finished. But it was time to go home, and after asking if Mrs. Daly would like her to come again to-morrow, Nessa took her leave.

As they passed out of the gate a man evidently the worse for drink rolled in, and staggering up the little path noisily entered the cottage.

Nessa turned quite white.

"Are you afraid?" asked Bobbo.

"I—I can't bear people who drink," she replied, recovering herself.

"Mustn't it be dreadful to live with him?" said Rosie, as they walked on.

No one answered her. The children were inclined to be very silent. This life of Theresa's seemed to them something that could not be true. They had often been in and out of cottages; they had often seen men tipsy in the village; but they had never realized before what it meant; and it came upon them to-day like a dreadful new thing they had just discovered.

"How kind you are!" said Rosie gently, coming close to Nessa, after they had walked about half a mile. "Mustn't Mrs. Daly be very glad we went?"

"Poor woman!" said Nessa, her eyes filling suddenly with tears. "She is very good. I wonder why God made us so happy."

"Yes," said Murtagh, who had been considering Rosie's words. "I think you're very kind; I think you like helping people."

"When I was little," replied Nessa, turning to him with a smile, and falling into the children's train of thought, "I had a nurse called Aimée. She used to be very unhappy because I could not go to her church, and on Sunday afternoons she always took me to try and help some one. She used to tell me that that was my way to heaven. Wasn't it a pretty thought?"

"I think you must have been quite a different little sort of girl from us," said Winnie. "We never thought about helping people, and those kind of things."

CHAPTER IX

Nessa next morning expressed her wish to go and see Mrs. Daly again, and Rosie again volunteered to accompany her.

"What's the use of my going to the island?" she said in answer to the other children's reproaches afterwards. "I can't do Theresa a bit of good, and I hate going there. I hate to think of it. It makes me miserable. Soon the police'll find out all about it; I know they will, and we'll just be put in prison."

She went away as she spoke; she didn't want to talk about the affair. She would like to have forgotten it if she could, and she kept close to Nessa all day in order to prevent the others from having an opportunity of reminding her of it.

Her gloomy view depressed the other children not a little. They were already inclined to be low-spirited enough, and Rosie's conviction that the police would interfere before long affected them in spite of themselves, adding all the trouble of vague anxiety to their practical difficulties.

Winnie said, "she didn't believe ladies and gentlemen were ever put in prison, but she was not at all sure."

"Isn't it dreadful?" she said, waking up in the morning and thinking of it first thing. She meant by "it" all their troubles.

"Yes," said Murtagh; "and all day long too; I can't manage to forget it at all, but we've just got to hold on, you know. We must be able to see old Plunkett soon now, and as for feeding her we can always manage that somehow. It's no use thinking about the police. If they're going to come why they'll have to come, that's all."

So they cheered each other as best they could till Winnie, suddenly brightening up, exclaimed: "Oh yes, Myrrh, and I'd nearly forgotten. I thought of such a good plan last night in bed; something for Theresa to do while she has to stay there. You know her mother's ill with compunction, or some name like that, and she ought to be kept very warm; so I thought supposing Theresa made her some flannel jackets while she's up there. I know how to cut one out, and we can get the needles and thread and things out of Donnie's basket."

"Where are you going to get the flannel?" asked Murtagh laughing. "Because they'll be rather queer jackets if they're made of needles and thread."

"I've thought of that too," replied Winnie triumphantly. "Come along;" and she jumped up from the staircase where she was sitting and danced into the boys' room.

"We'll have two of your flannel shirts," she explained, as she went down on her knees before a great chest of drawers and began to pull at the handles of the linen drawer.

"Well done, Winnie, you are a brick; I never knew any one like you for thinking of things," exclaimed Murtagh heartily, helping her to get the drawer open. "Here, take these two new scarlet ones; they're the biggest; and besides, all the others are in rags. Now for the needles; you fetch them, and I'll run out with these for fear Donnie catches us. Won't she be in a jolly wax when she finds out they're gone?"

"Oh, she'll never miss them," replied Winnie; "and besides, we're only taking them for a poor person, so of course it's all right."

Right or wrong the shirts were speedily conveyed to the hut; and, busy with her work,

Theresa was happier when the children left her for the night than she had been since the day of their meeting.

Thus another day went by. In vain the children hung round the Red House; Mr. Plunkett did not appear. The end of their adventures began to seem very indistinct. Supposing that Mr. Plunkett would not give them the rent when they did ask him? What was to be done then? It was a thought they refused to entertain, but in spite of themselves it crept from time to time into their minds, and it helped, with everything else, to make them unhappy. Sometimes they felt half-tempted to confide their trouble to Nessa, whose gentle ways were winning for her a warm place in their hearts, but there was a something of untamed shyness in their nature that made them shrink from exposing their secrets to any one. So they kept their perplexities to themselves, bearing them as best they could, and clinging still to the hope of getting the rent from Mr. Plunkett.

But the end of their adventure came upon them more suddenly than they expected.

On Wednesday morning they had for very idleness sauntered into the drawing-room where Nessa was engaged in rearranging the flowers, and, congregated round a little table by the window, they were watching her operations, when Donnie appeared in the doorway.

"I've brought you up the drop of soup I promised you, Miss Nessa, and a beautiful jelly it is," she exclaimed. "Ye might cut it with a knife. But the poor woman won't care much about jelly or soup this day, for it's all out about the child. The police have gone up now to search the place."

The words fell like a bomb among the children.

"What!" exclaimed Murtagh. Rosie flushed to the roots of her hair, and stooped to pick up some fallen leaves. Winnie, with two bright red spots in her cheeks, started from her seat, while Donnie, without waiting for any questions, continued:

"I sent Peggy to the village this morning, and she's just come running back an' told me all about it. The miller from the mill up there by Armaghbaeg came down this mornin', and he'd never heard a word about it before at all. But directly he heard what all the people are saying he went straight off and gave his evidence at the police-office; how, last Friday night—the very day she was missing—he heard a most awful shrieking and screaming coming from somewhere about the island up there in the river. He and his wife heard it together. Most awful he says it was, an' made their blood run cold in the bed; and he said to his wife, 'Kitty,' says he, 'I'd better be going to see what it is;' and she laid her hand on him, an' says she, ' 'Deed an' ye will not. If there's base people about you'd better stop an' take care o' them that belong to you.' So he stopped with her, and sure enough it must have been Theresa they heard. So one lot of the police are going to take up Pat Foy, and there's more going up to search in the island and there abouts. Anyways, that's the story Peggy's brought back with her."

"But they haven't found Theresa, then!" exclaimed Winnie, catching at the hope.

"Found her!" echoed Mrs. Donegan, shaking her head. "Poor child, it's little they'll ever find of her again! That's my belief."

"Oh, we must go out!" exclaimed Winnie, unable any longer to hide her excitement. "Come along." And before either Nessa or Donnie could ask them a question they were gone.

Too much excited to speak, they set off running quickly across the lawn and down the avenue. Once pausing for breath, Winnie said: "We shall get there first if they didn't start till Donnie told us!" But no one answered; they wanted all their breath for running.

They went down through the village, for the road was the shortest way. People were standing about in knots talking, but the children did not dare to ask if the police had started yet. As they passed the police-station they glanced hastily in, but naturally they saw nothing that could tell them whether they were or were not in time.

Bobbo felt his legs tremble as he thought that perhaps before evening he would be locked up there. He did not exactly know why it was such a dreadful thing to have hidden Theresa, but only felt that if the police found her something awful would happen to them. Without being the least bit cowardly the prospect seemed to him very unpleasant.

"Oh, Murtagh!" he exclaimed, with tears starting to his eyes, but Murtagh answered without looking round: "Come on; let's keep together," and quickened his own pace as he spoke.

Bobbo swallowed his tears, and after that the four pairs of legs went steadily, patter, patter, along the road and not another word was spoken.

At each turning they expected to see the police in front of them. They strained their eyes to catch the first glimpse through the hedges of those dreaded dark coats, imagining from Donnie's account that at least a regiment would be employed in the search. Every tree-trunk indistinctly seen made their hearts beat faster, but on they went— running when they could; sometimes forced to walk for want of breath.

Turn after turn was passed. No police yet. At last the island was in sight, and the ground lay clear between them and it.

"In time!" exclaimed Murtagh.

But they were not sure yet; they might be altogether too late, and find the island empty. The thought lent wings to their feet. They dashed through the little wood that separated the river from the road, scrambled down the bank, crossed the river, and stood at last before the door of the hut. Theresa was there, sitting quietly working at the flannel jacket.

"Holy Virgin! what has happened?" she exclaimed at the sight of their excited faces. "Mr. Murtagh, Miss Winnie? What is it? Is me mother dead? Ah, tell me; will one of you tell me?"

But the relief of finding her safe was too great for words to be possible. Murtagh and Winnie stood trembling, while Rosie fairly burst into tears.

"Ah, what is it? Will one of you tell me?" implored Theresa, wringing her hands. "It's me mother; I know it is! Oh, whatever did I ever come up here for? Let me go to her!" And she started up to go.

Murtagh shook his head, and stretched out his hand to prevent her.

"Good God!" cried Theresa, passionately. "Can't one of ye speak? Miss Rose, tell me; what is it?" And Rose thus appealed to dried her tears, and found words to tell that the police would be up there in a few minutes.

Winnie recovered herself, and added: "So we mustn't stay here. Now then, Murtagh, wake up, and think what we are to do next."

Murtagh took up the wooden bowl that stood half-full of water upon the table and drank; then quite himself again, he said:

"Yes, the first thing to be done is to get away from here, down the river and through the woods into one of the shrubberies; we shan't meet any one that way."

On hearing that her mother was as well as usual, Theresa was so relieved that she did not seem to think of anything else; but gathering up her work, she followed Murtagh and Winnie without question or objection.

Though Murtagh had said they would meet no one this way they did not feel safe, and hurried along in silence. Murtagh and Winnie were turning over plans in their heads of what was next to be done.

Bobbo, ashamed of his momentary weakness, began to recover his usual faith in Murtagh. But Rosie could find no comfort anywhere. Tears rolled over her cheeks as she followed the others, and she could think of nothing but the court-house as she had once seen it, with a grave-looking judge on the bench, policemen standing about, women crying, people staring and whispering. Only instead of the prisoner she had seen at the bar she imagined herself, and Murtagh, and Winnie, and Bobbo crowded in together, and her uncle and Nessa looking shocked, and Donnie talking about them. Then Mr. Plunkett would look so disagreeable, and Mrs. Plunkett too, and Cousin Jane would laugh at them, and perhaps they would be shut up in prison all their lives. One thing after another crowded into her mind, and the more she thought the more she cried. They must be found out some day soon.

"After all," said Bobbo, trying to feel brave in order to console her, "perhaps it isn't so bad. I expect Winnie and Murtagh will get us out of it somehow."

"They can't prevent the policemen taking us," returned Rose, dolefully. "I wish to goodness we'd never had anything to do with it."

"Even if we did get put in prison I believe Murtagh would get us out somehow," said Bobbo, trying hard to feel really sure of it in his heart.

"Don't talk such nonsense!" replied Rose crossly, "Murtagh's only a little boy." But she was somewhat consoled nevertheless, and by degrees stopped crying.

In the mean time they had left the river, and passing through a wood came now to the shrubbery where Winnie and Murtagh had arranged together that they might hide, and talk over plans, in a great Portuguese laurel.

The laurel was a very big one, trained into the shape of a pyramid, and there was plenty of room for the children to sit in the centre among the interlacing branches, completely hidden from outside by the close clustering leaves.

"Now," said Winnie, when they were all safely in, "have you thought of anything, Murtagh?"

"I don't exactly know," replied Murtagh slowly. "There's the mountains, but it would be awfully difficult to manage about her food. I don't see quite how we're to do it. Do you?"

"I won't do another single thing," interrupted Rose. "I told you long ago you ought to have told Mrs. Daly on Sunday. Then we'd never have got into all this dreadful scrape."

"Well, but, Rose," said Murtagh in a supernaturally gentle voice that he sometimes used when Rosie seemed to him quite unreasonable, "you know we couldn't tell on Sunday when we hadn't got the rent. How could we? It would have been worse to let her go home then than on Friday when we found her first."

"I don't know anything about the rent," returned Rose. "All I know is, it would have been much better if you'd done what I said; then we'd never have been so miserable."

"Don't talk like a fool!" ejaculated Winnie impatiently, while Murtagh said:

"But don't you see, Rose, that would have been as bad as murder, if we'd let her be killed."

"I don't see anything," answered Rose. "I only think this is the most dreadful thing we ever had, and I wish to goodness *anything* would happen, I'm so wretched. And I think it's very silly of you and Winnie ever doing it. You're only little children, and if people are going to be killed children can't prevent it."

Here Rose began to cry again, and Murtagh turned to Winnie with a despairing— "What shall we do? It's so awfully difficult to settle. I keep on thinking of plans, but—— Oh, dear! when will that tiresome Mr. Plunkett get well! Bobbo, did you go and ask about him this morning?"

"Yes; they said he was coming down-stairs this afternoon, but I asked when we'd be able to see him again, and Biddy only grinned, and said, 'Maybe a month o' Sundays, and maybe next week.' "

"Oh dear!" sighed Winnie again, really for once in her life at her wit's end. "What can we do? Can you say any plan, Murtagh?"

"The only thing we can do," said Rose, suddenly stopping her tears, "is just to take Theresa back to Mrs. Daly's now, and tell her all about it. I'm sure it's much the best plan. We haven't got anywhere to put Theresa. She can't stay here in the laurel all night. Soon Donnie'll be asking what we do with all the scraps she gives us, and I don't believe if we keep her here till doomsday that we'll ever get the money from Mr. Plunkett."

"Oh, Mr. Murtagh!" exclaimed Theresa piteously, "ye won't be sending me home now without the rent."

Murtagh gave no answer but a puzzled sigh, while Rose continued: "It's just every bit as unkind to Theresa keeping her here as it is to us. You can't do her one scrap of good. You'll only make her step-father angrier and angrier when she goes home for every day you keep her here—and there isn't a bit of sense keeping her here ever so long when there's nothing to keep her for."

While Rose was speaking, Winnie, sitting on a low branch, stared up through the net-work of twigs at a bird's nest in the top of the trees, her whole attention seemingly absorbed by trying to throw laurel-berries into it. Only the impatient swinging move-ment of her feet told that she heard what Rose was saying.

As Murtagh was still silent Rose thought he was beginning to be convinced, and she continued in a gentler tone of voice:

"Don't you see, it really would be awfully silly of us if we went on keeping her here any more? It would take us years and years before we saved up two pounds out of our Saturday money, and we couldn't possibly hide her for years and years; now, could we? So, what is the good of keeping her any longer? If her step-father is really going to beat her so dreadfully he'll only do it worse for her staying away. He daren't kill her. If he does we'll tell the police about him; besides, I'm quite sure he won't. And then it is so dreadful hiding her. I'm quite certain the police will find out about it soon, and they'll come and take us and put us into prison, and perhaps it will be us will be killed." At the thought Rosie's tears began to flow again. "It is so dreadful going to prison. I can't bear it; and if we could get her back to Mrs. Daly's now, before the police find out anything, then it would be all right."

Theresa had listened intently to every word, and now with a white face, and a wild, resolute look in her eyes, she stood up and said:

"I'm going home. Will ye let me pass, if ye please, Miss Rose?"

Rose eagerly stood on one side and held back the branches, but Winnie sprang from the seat and caught Theresa's dress, while Murtagh exclaimed:

"What do you mean?"

"I mean," said Theresa, "I'd rather go home. It don't matter what happens to the likes of me."

"It does matter," returned Murtagh vehemently. "It matters very, very much; you shan't go home."

"I don't want to be havin' yez taken to prison for a poor omadhaun like me," repeated Theresa, trying to tear her dress away from Winnie's firm hold.

"I don't care what you want; you shall stay where you are till we can do something to help you," returned Murtagh, pulling her into the centre of the bush again, while Winnie, turning to Rose, said with flashing eyes:

"I think you're a selfish coward, with your sneaking plans, and I wish with all my heart that you weren't my sister, so I do."

"I don't believe you are our sister," added Murtagh, passionately. "If papa heard you he'd never speak to you again all the days of your life. And look here—if you do turn traitor, and let out one single word of what we do, I'll——" He stopped himself suddenly, and Theresa, frightened at the storm she seemed to have raised, put her hand on his arm with an imploring, "Mr. Murtagh, dear."

Rosie burst into tears again, and sobbed out that they were very unkind. After that no one spoke. For some minutes Rosie's stifled sobs were the only sound. Then Winnie said: "I have a plan, Murtagh. How do you think this would do?"

Murtagh looked up with a start. He had not been thinking of plans. He had been thinking what a little coward Rosie was, and that perhaps, after all, she couldn't help it. All girls were, except Winnie.

"Supposing," continued Winnie, "we were to hide her in one of the empty rooms of the house just for the present, and then go this afternoon and get to see Mr. Plunkett somehow, and get the rent?"

"Yes, that's the best," said Murtagh, heartily glad to seize any chance of bringing the affair to an end without deserting Theresa.

"Come then," said Winnie, making her way out of the bush. "Run on in front, Bobbo, and see if the road's clear."

"There now," said Bobbo, turning to Rose, "I think that's a good plan; don't you? It'll soon be all over now."

"It would be much better if they took her to Mrs. Daly," replied Rose sulkily, turning her back upon them all, and beginning to move slowly towards the house.

They managed, without meeting any one, to smuggle poor Theresa into an empty room, close to their own bed-rooms, and having done that they had next to summon up all their courage for the meeting with Mr. Plunkett. They could not think why they should feel so cowardly about it. Often and often before they had been called up after some scrape to receive a rebuke, which, from Mr. Plunkett's lips, was sure to be sharp and galling. Sometimes he made them very angry, but they had never before felt nervous and trembled at the thought of an interview. Generally they went to him in a defiant, impudent mood, and talked as much as he did, but to-day matters were changed. They had to ask him for a favor. And, besides, those dreadful police seemed to make everything so different.

"What shall we say to him, Win?" asked Murtagh, sitting on the banisters of the stairs leading down from their rooms.

"I don't know exactly," said Winnie; "Rosie always talks to him best."

"I hate talking civilly to him," remarked Murtagh meditatively.

"Let Rosie do it," suggested Bobbo.

"I don't suppose she will," returned Murtagh, with a glance towards the girls' room where Rosie had remained. "Besides——"

"She may just as well be of some use," said Winnie. "It's all because of her that we have to do it in such a hurry." Then raising her voice, she called—"Rosie!"

"Well?" returned Rosie from the bed-room.

Winnie waited for Rosie to come, but seeing that she did not, she called again—"Look here!"

"Well, what do you want?" returned Rosie, without moving.

"Come out here. We can't go shouting secrets all over the house."

"I don't want to have any secrets," replied Rosie.

"All right; don't then," answered Winnie.

Murtagh muttered—"Little brute," adding after a pause: "Which of us two is the best for talking?"

"I will, if you like," said Winnie. "After all, I don't care. He's an old nuisance, and it's no use bothering our heads what to say to him. Let's say whatever comes to our tongues."

"It would be a queer saying I'd say if I did that," returned Murtagh. "However, let's go and do whatever we're going to do."

But Bobbo never could make up his mind to feel quite comfortable while a quarrel was going on between Rosie and Murtagh and Winnie.

"I'll just see again if Rosie won't come," he said. "We had much better keep together."

So the others waited while he went back to Rosie's room.

In the mean time, though Rosie pretended not to care what Winnie and Murtagh thought of her, she really cared a great deal, and she was standing by the bedroom window crying, wishing she had never said anything about taking Theresa home. However, when Bobbo put his head in at the door and began—"I say, Rosie—" she hastily dried her eyes, and her answer "Well?" was as grumpy as ever. She didn't want to make them dislike her more, but she could not help feeling sulky the minute any one spoke to her. Bobbo did not pay any attention to that, but came into the room, and continued:

"I say, Ro, I wish you'd come too; you blarney old Plunkett much better than any of us. You might just as well come."

"I don't want to go anywhere where I'm not wanted," returned Rosie. "Murtagh and Winnie don't like me helping, so I'd rather stay here."

To all Bobbo's persuasions she continued to give the same answer, till at last, thinking it was no use to stay any longer, he took hold of the handle of the door, saying:—"Don't be a donkey, Ro: Murtagh and Winnie are different, you know. They don't understand about people being afraid, and things. They think it's so awfully sneaky to be afraid. You'd much better come."

The door-handle had more effect than all Bobbo's eloquence, and Rosie moved away from the window as she answered again: "I don't want to go anywhere where I'm not wanted."

"Don't be a duffer. Come along: you'll get round old Plunkett better than any of us," replied Bobbo, seeing that he had gained his point, and turning round began to walk away.

"I'm sure I want to help Theresa just as much as any one," said Rosie, as she followed him, "but Winnie and Murtagh don't like me interfering."

"I hope to goodness there will be no women in heaven," ejaculated Murtagh.

"Except me, Myrrh," said Winnie, and then they all went clattering down the staircase.

CHAPTER X

Bᴜᴛ ᴀs ᴛʜᴇʏ ʀᴇᴀᴄʜᴇᴅ *terra firma*—for taking into consideration the manner in which they habitually descended it that was scarcely a fit name for the staircase—the first bell rang for dinner, reminding them that it would be useless to go yet to the Red House. Mr. Plunkett would not be down-stairs till the afternoon.

They had nothing to give Theresa to eat, so Winnie and Bobbo went off to the garden to get her some apples, while Murtagh and Rosie returned to the school-room. There they found Nessa waiting anxiously for news.

During their absence the wildest reports had come up from the village.

Mrs. Donegan's story, though exaggerated of course in its details by the time it reached the children, was in part true. The miller had really given evidence which caused some policemen to be sent to search the island and the woods that fringed that part of the river. The child's disappearance had naturally caused a great sensation in the little place. It had been the topic of all conversation for several days. In many minds it had been vaguely connected with the attempt upon Mr. Plunkett's life, and if some of the inhabitants of the village were better informed as to the latter event, there was a very general impression that "there were terrible things going about."

The village mind was prepared for a tragic ending of the mystery, and now that it seemed on the point of being explained the excitement was considerable. A small crowd of women and boys trooped off in the same direction as the police, in order to have the first news of that "poor, blessed child," as Theresa was generally called, and those who remained behind would have thought it a sign of "rale want o' feelin'" to do any work.

Cabins were left unswept, dinners uncooked, pigs unfed. The whole population of the little village turned out into the street, and wondered, and conjectured, and shook their heads, and had a little drink at the shop at the corner just to keep up their spirits; till from one cause or another they had worked themselves into a state of mind in which accuracy was far from being one of the predominant qualities.

No wonder then that the most extraordinary stories were brought to Mrs. Donegan and Nessa. The discovery of the fire lighted in the island hut was to the police of little importance, since it was well known that the children spent much of their time there; but in the village it was speedily transformed into circumstantial evidence of the crime which every one had long ago decided to have been committed. Rumors and conjectures spread like wild-fire. In vain Mrs. Donegan and Nessa tried to find out the truth. Some said one thing and some another, and poor old Donnie so implicitly believed always the worst account, that Nessa grew thoroughly confused, and felt half-terrified at the barbarism of a place where every one seemed to think it quite natural and probable that a little girl should be carried off and murdered in order to annoy her mother.

"Oh, I am so glad you have come back!" she exclaimed, as Murtagh and Rosie entered the school-room. "Tell me what is true about Mrs. Daly's little girl. Your countrymen talk so wildly I really cannot understand them."

There was nothing wanting but this to complete the children's distress. They had come to the school-room thoroughly wearied out, and they really could not talk over the subject of all their troubles.

"If you can't understand Irishmen you can't understand me," replied Murtagh, throwing himself into an arm-chair.

His tone was almost rude. Nessa flushed a little, and turning to Rosie she continued:

"They told us such dreadful stories. They said—they said—the floor of the hut was covered with blood; but one said one thing and one another till it was not possible to understand. It is not true, is it? It cannot be true."

It was too much; Rosie could not bear it. Her only answer was a burst of tears.

"Oh, *Mon Dieu!*" said Nessa. "Her poor mother! Is it so bad as that? Is she really dead?"

"No more dead than I am," exclaimed Murtagh, springing from the chair and walking impatiently to the window.

Rosie sobbed on, and Nessa now utterly bewildered put her arms round her and asked soothingly: "What is it that makes you cry?"

Rosie twisted herself out of Nessa's arms and made no answer. Nessa looked inquiringly towards Murtagh, but he was standing with his back turned to her staring out of the window, and almost counting every sob of Rosie's.

At last he turned and said quietly: "Don't you think you had better go up-stairs, Rose?"

Without stopping her tears Rosie went slowly out of the room, and they heard her sobs growing fainter and fainter as she walked away down the long passage.

"What is it?" asked Nessa half-timidly, as the sound of the last sob died away. "Is it something about the little girl, or have you—" She stopped, fearing to offend Murtagh by suggesting that they might have quarreled.

Poor Murtagh was at his wit's end. It was all bad enough as it was without these questions. He did not know what to do. To answer one was only to open the way to more. He felt that his secret was on the point of slipping from him, and he did not know how to keep it.

In despair he turned round to his cousin with a mute pleading look that said more than words. There were no tears in his eyes. They were like the eyes of some dumb animal in pain; they did not ask for help—they seemed only to implore a little patience.

Nessa had never seen a child look like that; she felt as though she were in the presence of a real trouble.

"Oh, I beg your pardon," she exclaimed almost involuntarily, and then remembering that Murtagh was only a little fellow she put her arms round his neck and kissed him.

"Don't be so sad," she said.

Murtagh's heart bounded at her kindness. It was nearly five years since any one had caressed him so. He kissed her warmly back again, tears that had not been there before springing to his eyes. Then little Ellie ran into the school-room, and bounding into Nessa's arms imperiously commanded her to "tum to dinner, tum to dinner, betoz I is so hungry."

The luncheon-bell ringing loudly seconded her request, and they all moved away together to the dining-room.

Ellie was in high spirits, and Murtagh and Nessa devoted themselves to the little lady, till towards the middle of the dinner Winnie and Bobbo came in from the garden.

"You are rather late," said Nessa.

"Yes," replied Winnie; "we were getting apples, and Bland nearly caught us, so we had to run round the long way. He did catch me, but I wriggled away from him. We brought the apples all safe," she added, turning to Murtagh.

"All right," said Murtagh shortly.

Winnie glanced quickly from him to Nessa, and then subsided into silence.

"I thought you ought not to take the apples," said Nessa.

"No," replied Bobbo, "but we had to; we wanted them."

The children were bad actors. Nessa wondered what was the matter, and wondered why none of them made the slightest allusion to the event which had apparently been so deeply interesting to them in the morning. It flashed across her that they were in some way connected with the disappearance of the little girl, but the idea seemed so improbable that she could scarcely accept it. She would not try to guess their secret; so she did for them what they could not do for themselves—she made conversation, and almost succeeded in covering their embarrassment.

After luncheon she was standing before the drawing-room fire, when the door opened and Murtagh ran in. To her surprise he threw his arms round her and kissed her. Then, blushing a little at what he had done, he said earnestly:

"You're awfully kind. I'll tell you about everything this evening," and without waiting for her to answer he ran away again.

His heart had been deeply touched by her sympathy in the morning, and when they had all started to go to the Red House he felt a sudden impulse to rush into the drawing-room and thank her. It was so quickly done that the others did not miss him. He joined them before they reached the door, and they slowly proceeded together across the park.

Rosie was with them, and having completely recovered from her fit of crying she was very anxious now to regain her place in Winnie's and Murtagh's esteem.

All the time that the others had been at dinner she had spent in thinking. She felt really sorry for having broken down and cried before Nessa. If Murtagh and Winnie had been angry with her for that, she could have understood them much better. That did deserve their contempt. "It was very hard too," she thought, "just at the end, when they were going to get the rent and have all the happy part of taking Theresa home, that she should be separated from them, as it were, and lose her share in the pleasure." Above all, she could not bear to be thought cowardly and stupid. She liked people to be fond of her. The result of her thinking was that she determined to do her best to coax Mr. Plunkett to give them the rent. "For if I get the rent for them," she thought, "then they can't say I didn't do as much for Theresa as any one."

Consequently she was in one of her very pleasantest humors as she walked across the park, and Winnie and Murtagh wondered at her as she talked brightly about what she was going to say to Mr. Plunkett, sketched little scenes of Mrs. Daly's delight when Theresa was given back to her, and dwelt pleasantly upon how "jolly" they would all feel afterwards for having saved Theresa.

But though they wondered, they were certainly cheered, and felt far bolder when they arrived at the Red House than they had done for some time past.

Bland was coming out as they passed in at the garden gate. He scowled at Winnie and Bobbo, but Winnie shrugged her shoulders and looked up at him with such a bright laugh that he could scarcely help smiling as he hurried away, and growled out in a would-be surly voice:

"Ye'll no do well to go in there."

Without heeding the warning they went round to the back-yard.

"We want to see Mr. Plunkett, please, Biddy," said Rose to the servant, who was hanging out clothes to dry.

"Faix it's roses at Christmas-time we'll be havin' soon," returned Biddy with a good-natured laugh. But the children were in no mood for joking, even at Mr. Plunkett's expense, so they walked soberly up to the door, while Rose asked what room he was in.

"Ye're joking, Miss Rose," replied Biddy. "You wouldn't be goin' in to him in rale earnest. Why it's like a mad bull in a china shop he is to-day, with the polis comin' in an' out, and one thing an' another."

"But we must go in," said Murtagh. "We have some business that we must speak to him about."

"Sure, Mr. Murtagh, honey, is it going to be married ye are, and come for him to draw out the dockiments?" answered Biddy, laughing outright.

"Stop being a donkey, Biddy," said Winnie decidedly, "and tell us where he is."

"Where is he? By St. Patrick, if he was where I'd like him to be, it's the fardest end o' the pole from Biddy Connolly."

"Shut up your tomfoolery," said Bobbo impatiently, while Winnie exclaimed:

"Come along; let us go in without her."

But at that Biddy dropped the wet clothes she held into the basket, and ran to the doorway.

"Is it mad ye are, Miss Rose? Ye can't go in there. The missus 'd be out upon me in a minnit if I let yez in. Poor Missus, God bless her! the way she do slave after that old skinflint!"

"Do let us in," said Rose, coaxingly. "We've got business."

"I can't, Miss Rose. 'Deed I can not. You don't know the bother he'd kick up!"

"Oh, nonsense!" exclaimed Winnie, pushing past; "we can't help it; perhaps it'll bother him well again."

And so with a little more insistance, and more expostulations from Biddy, they made their way to the parlor and knocked at the door.

"Come in," called Mr. Plunkett.

"If ye will, ye will, an' I can't help yez," remarked Biddy, shaking her head compassionately as the children went into the room.

Mr. Plunkett was sitting in an arm-chair next the window, with his back turned to the door. There was no one else in the room, and having entered, the children stood hesitating for a moment near the door where he could not see them. Now that they were actually in his room their courage seemed all to have vanished. Their hearts were beating fast, they had a queer sensation in their throats, and not one of them could have spoken a word just then.

"Is that you, Marion?" inquired Mr. Plunkett, in a voice so gentle that the children could scarcely believe it was Mr. Plunkett who was speaking.

"No," faltered Rosie. Then plucking up courage she advanced towards his chair, and said in her most winning manner: "I hope you're feeling better now. It was so unlucky, wasn't it, that you fell under poor Black Shandy?"

"Thank you; I am somewhat recovered," replied Mr. Plunkett in his usual severe voice, and the children no longer doubted their ears.

"Did it hurt you very much?" inquired Rosie.

"I suffered considerably."

"I'm so sorry," said Rosie. "I do hate being hurt so." After a little pause she continued, the color mounting to her cheeks: "We have come to ask you a favor, and we do hope you'll grant it." Here she paused again, blushing violently, and not quite knowing how to proceed. Murtagh, Winnie, and Bobbo came slowly into view, and Mr. Plunkett's face on seeing them did not look as though he were going to grant a favor.

"By what door did you come in?" he inquired sharply.

"We came in together by the back door," answered Winnie.

"I should like to know where Bridget was. These Irish servants are all alike careless and gossiping. I suppose her mind is too much taken up by the village mystery to allow her to pay attention to work."

'I'd rather have one Irish than——" began Murtagh indignantly, his temper rising as usual in Mr. Plunkett's presence, but Winnie trod on his foot and reduced him to silence.

"We all know, sir, that you would rather anything which gives you an opportunity for contradiction," returned Mr. Plunkett severely. "Perhaps if you had had as much trouble as I have had about the disappearance of this girl, you would prefer not to have the additional one of seeing your servants abandon their work and leave your house open to whoever chooses to enter."

Winnie nudged Murtagh again as a hint to remain silent, but a sense of justice to Biddy made him answer:

"Biddy didn't run away from her work. She didn't want us to come in."

"And I suppose you thought my house was like your uncle's garden, to be broken into at pleasure when you want something out of it. Bland has just been with me, and he tells me you have been taking apples again. If it were not for this unfortunate accident, I can assure you you should be punished as you deserve."

Murtagh made no answer. After a short silence Mr. Plunkett turned to Rosie and said: "Well, and what is the favor I am expected to grant?"

Poor Rosie felt that it was almost impossible now to ask it. She blushed and stammered: "I—I—at least—we—I mean—"

"Be so kind as to speak plainly. I do not understand what you are asking," said Mr. Plunkett.

Rosie looked as if she were going to cry, but Winnie in her clear voice said:

"We want you, please, to let Mrs. Daly off paying the two sovereigns she owes for her rent."

Now that it was out the children all breathed more freely. Rose recovered herself, and they stood waiting anxiously for Mr. Plunkett's reply.

He was surprised. He had expected them to ask something for themselves, and he was fully prepared to refuse, but this request astonished him so much that he paused. Though a hard man he was not at heart so disagreeable as the children imagined. To them he could not speak kindly, for he honestly believed them to be bad, but he spoke kindly to his own well-brought-up children, and he had in his way felt sorry for poor Mrs. Daly in her trouble.

For a moment he felt almost inclined to say yes. But then he considered that when the moment came for arranging such matters with Peter Daly there would be no necessity for the interference of the children, and he felt in no way disposed to give them a gratification.

The children stood like little statues while he thought. It seemed a good sign that he should take so long about it. At last the answer came:

"The paying of rent is a business transaction which does not in any way concern you. You may be quite sure that as your uncle's representative I will do whatever is right in the matter. And now, will you allow me to beg that at another time you will not force your way into my house when my servants tell you that it is contrary to my orders for any one to be admitted." And Mr. Plunkett taking up a newspaper began to read.

"But are you going to let her off paying?" inquired Winnie, standing on one foot and scratching up and down the stocking with the point of the other boot. "We want to know awfully badly."

"I shall do what I consider right after consulting with your uncle."

"Oh, I know Uncle Blair will say 'Give it to her,'" said Rosie; "and if you would say 'Yes' now, we would be so very much obliged. We have a most particular reason for wanting it."

"It will be quite time enough to consider such matters when something more certain is known of the fate of the poor woman's daughter," returned Mr. Plunkett.

"Oh, but," said Rose, not feeling quite sure how much to tell, "perhaps if it was quite certain about the money then there would be some more known about Theresa. You know," she added coaxingly, "there are such wonderful little fairies in the world that know all about everything."

"What do you mean?" exclaimed Mr. Plunkett sitting up straight in his chair. "You can't mean to say!——" But there his feelings seemed to become too strong for words, and he paused, looking at Murtagh.

"We mean to say," said Rose, in a pleasant voice, rapidly determining that whatever happened she would not go away without letting him know that they had Theresa, "that if you'll give us the rent for Mrs. Daly perhaps we'll find Theresa and bring her back all safe and sound. Don't we, Murtagh?"

"But we mean to say, too," said Murtagh grimly, looking at Rose, "that we can't possibly find out anything about her, nor say a single word more, unless we do get the rent."

"This is too much!" exclaimed Mr. Plunkett. "Do you mean to tell me, you graceless young scoundrel, that your pranks are at the bottom of all the trouble and worry we have had? Do you mean to say that for your own amusement you have given me all this trouble with the police, turned a whole village upside down for a week, and nearly killed a poor suffering woman with anxiety for her lost child! I have no language to express my opinion of you, sir."

"My dear James!" exclaimed Mrs. Plunkett, coming into the room at that moment. "What is the matter? Rosie! Bobbo! Winnie! *and* Murtagh!" she added in astonishment. "How in the world did you get into this room? Did you send for them, James? What have they been doing? You know, dear, the doctors said you were not to be excited."

"It is of little use for doctors or for any one to lay down rules while such children as these are allowed to run wild," replied Mr. Plunkett.

"Though you have confessed it yourselves," he continued, turning to Murtagh, "I can scarcely believe that you can have behaved in a manner so totally devoid of all Christian feeling. But it is the old story: mischief is your god. So long as you can have the excitement of a bit of mischief you care nothing at all for the feelings of others; and I have no doubt it seems to you an excellent joke to persuade a dying woman's child to run away, and to embitter the last days of a poor mother's life.

"I suppose that between you, you have lost, or perhaps spent, the money entrusted to the child, and now you think that to take it out of your uncle's pocket will be an easy way of paying it back. It does not surprise me in you, Murtagh; but was there not one among you," he added, looking at the other three, "who could have remembered that you hold the position of young ladies and gentlemen?"

"You see you set us such a good example of forgetting what a gentleman is like, that we really couldn't be expected to remember," replied Murtagh, coolly.

"When you come to my house I must beg that you will not be insolent, sir," replied Mr. Plunkett angrily.

"Come along, Myrrh; don't be silly," said Winnie, moving towards the door. "How could he know why gentlemen do things?"

"Winnie," exclaimed Mrs. Plunkett, "how can you talk in such a way?"

"Mr. Plunkett shouldn't be so impertinent to Murtagh," returned Winnie, who had two hot red spots in her cheeks.

"I never saw such children in my life. I'm sure I pity that poor young girl who has to live amongst you," said Mrs. Plunkett, half crying. "To speak of my husband in such a manner!"

"Serve him right!" ejaculated Bobbo.

"You deserve, every one of you, to have your ears boxed," exclaimed Mrs. Plunkett, who was at no time famous for self-control.

"Catch us first," laughed Winnie. "Come along, Bobbo." She led the way down the passage as she spoke, and in another minute they were far on their way across the park, their cause hopelessly and irretrievably lost.

CHAPTER XI

"**I**'LL TELL YOU WHAT," said Murtagh, when they were once more at home, and had fully realized that Mr. Plunkett had not only refused them the rent but what was more he knew that they were hiding Theresa, "I told Nessa I'd tell her everything this evening. You see, I thought it would be all right by then; and supposing we went down and told her now, and got her to help us."

The others were silent; it was rather a bold proposal.

"She's like us, you know," suggested Murtagh. "I think she'd understand about things."

Rosie looked anxiously towards Winnie, hoping she would say yes, but not venturing herself to give an opinion.

"All right," said Winnie, after considering a minute. "I think that's best. She might know of some plan."

"Let us go then," said Murtagh. "Whatever we do we ought to be quick about."

It was easy to be quick about getting to the drawing-room door, but there they paused. When they came to think about it, Theresa really was an awkward subject of conversation; and after the experience they had just had with Mr. Plunkett they began to feel doubtful as to what view Nessa might take of the matter.

However, something had to be done; so taking their courage in their two hands they somewhat shamefacedly entered the room. Nessa, with a big dictionary in her lap, was sitting reading Italian by the fire, and she paid little attention to their entry.

They none of them knew how to begin, but stood upon the hearth-rug alternately looking at her and glancing inquiringly at each other. The longer the silence lasted the more impossible did it seem to break it. At last Winnie began to poke the fire, and that gave Murtagh courage.

"I say," he began. But then Winnie stopped poking to listen to him, and the dead silence was too disconcerting; he stopped short as suddenly as he had begun.

"What were you going to say?" asked Nessa, raising her eyes from her book. And then in sudden surprise at the perturbed countenances of the children, she exclaimed, "Why, what is the matter?"

"Well," said Murtagh, plunging without further hesitation into his subject, "we don't know what to do, and we want to talk to you. We've been thinking about you, and we thought, you know, that you're different somehow. I mean we thought you'd think true about things instead of only about 'Christian' and 'mischief,' and 'young ladies and gentlemen.' I mean," he continued, contracting his forehead as he puzzled himself with his own attempt to explain, "it's so queer the way people are. If things are kind, or brave, or anything, then they talk about young ladies and gentlemen; and the things seem all wrong, somehow—but they aren't really wrong, you know, all the time; only it makes me get in such a rage."

"I—I don't think I quite understand," said Nessa, fairly bewildered in her attempt to follow the meaning of his somewhat complicated preamble.

"Well, I mean—" said Murtagh. "We've got Theresa, you know."

"You have what?" exclaimed Nessa, more puzzled than ever. His last words were plain enough, certainly, but they could not possibly mean what they seemed to mean. In vain she tried to see the smallest connection between them and the foregoing sentences.

"I beg your pardon. It's very stupid of me," she said, apologetically; "but I really don't understand. It must be some English I don't know."

"No, no," said Murtagh. "You'll be able to understand quite well. We'll tell you how it happened, and then you'll see. It was the day after you came. We were going up the river fishing; and Ellie couldn't—Win, you tell it; you'll tell it better than me."

The children's embarrassment was completely gone now. They were only eager for Nessa to know all about it; and beginning at the beginning Winnie, with various interruptions from the others, told the whole story to the end.

Nessa's amazement, when she began to understand the drift of what they had to tell her, was unbounded. She did not know children ever did things like that. But before the end of the story her warmest sympathies were enlisted in their cause.

"You see," said Murtagh, when Winnie had described the way in which Mr. Plunkett had received their request, "we never thought about anything except that horrible step-father, and how nice it would be taking her back with the rent and all. And you remember the way Mrs. Daly talked about her husband on Sunday. Well, of course, that only made us think of it more. But Mr. Plunkett always manages to make everything seem wicked, and he makes me wicked in reality. The very feel of him in the air makes me angry before he speaks a word. I do hate him so!"

"Yes," said Nessa, looking troubled. "It is wicked to hate. I wish you would not feel like that, because then you are wrong too. And listen," she continued, turning her face toward Murtagh, who had thrown himself on the floor beside her; "I am sure the reason why he is so disagreeable is just only because he does not understand."

"He never does understand," returned Murtagh vehemently. "He doesn't choose to understand; he likes to be unjust!"

With a sudden impulsive movement she threw her arms round his neck. "Don't be like that," she said in her sweet pleading voice; "please don't. It is such a pity."

Murtagh had drawn himself up in his anger. At Nessa's caress his muscles relaxed, his face lightened with a slow trembling. Then, possessing himself of one of her hands, he kissed it without a word.

It was not in the least like a child's answer. For the second time that day Nessa felt as though Murtagh were somehow older than she. She looked at him with a sort of surprise, but the strange expression was already gone, and the face he turned up to her was full of affectionate gratitude.

"And now," she said, "let us count our resources."

She drew a little green leather purse from her pocket as she spoke, and emptied its contents on to the open dictionary. "But I have not enough," she added, looking up almost apologetically. "How much money have you?"

"I've got a shilling," said Rosie.

"I've only twopence," said Winnie; "Bobbo, and I have been saving up. He has a penny half-penny."

"I haven't any," said Murtagh, shaking his head.

Little Ellie, who had been sitting on the rug looking exceedingly solemn while the children talked, gazed attentively at Nessa, and the money, and then got up and trotted silently out of the room.

"Well, that is all," said Nessa, after searching in each compartment of her purse; "we must do the best we can with it."

"Yes, but," said Murtagh, "We don't want to take your money. It isn't right you should give it. We couldn't promise your money. We meant to get it."

"You see it is a good thing to have an elder sister," replied Nessa, glancing up from her occupation of counting the coins spread out upon the pages of the dictionary.

"And besides, Murtagh," said Rosie, who felt that Murtagh was not to be trusted, "if you won't take Theresa home without the rent it really is the only way. I don't like taking your money either," she added, coloring and turning toward Nessa, "but what can we do? We haven't got any except one and twopence halfpenny."

"I should think you very unkind," said Nessa seriously, speaking to Murtagh, "if you did not take what I have. But," she added, "even with your money we have not enough."

"Well, then," exclaimed Murtagh decidedly, "it is no use for us to take yours. We can't take her back without the whole rent. We must just hide her up in the mountains, and I expect Uncle Blair will make Mr. Plunkett let them off the rent when he knows that will bring Theresa back. We can hide her in some safe place, and nobody on earth can make us say where she is if we don't choose."

"Oh, Murtagh!" exclaimed Nessa, "you don't know what you are saying. It would be enough to kill Mrs. Daly. Even if you had not a sou you must take Theresa back at once. You don't know—you don't know—" Nessa's voice was choked, she could not finish her sentence. She had witnessed the grief of the patient desolate mother. Only yesterday the poor woman had said to her with quiet hopelessness: "Yes, Ma'am, I'm dying—thank God."

And they could talk of prolonging the pain.

"You don't know," she said, raising her head and drying the tears that had suddenly overflowed. "You meant to be kind, and you did do all you could. But—Mrs. Daly loves Theresa."

Her voice was trembling again, and she did not trust herself to say any more. Murtagh was looking at her in consternation. Then all they had done had been a mistake; there was no doubting the meaning of those last few words. His eyes sought Winnie's. Poor children, they were sorely disappointed!

But Nessa had hardly finished speaking when the door was pushed open, and little Ellie rushed into the room shaking a tin money-box up and down.

"Ellie's dold money! Ellie's dold money!" she exclaimed triumphantly. Her little face was beaming with excitement, and running up to Murtagh she thrust the money-box into his hands.

"Ellie'll dive the money; det it out with the scissors," she said. Then ecstatically squeezing herself together she rubbed her hands up and down her cheeks till her face was burning red.

"Dear little Ellie!" exclaimed Nessa, astonished at the sudden outburst of excitement and taking the child in her arms, while Murtagh tried with a pair of scissors to extract the money from the box.

"It's her half-sovereign that Cousin Jane gave her last Christmas," exclaimed Winnie. "So it is; Donnie's kept it for her all this time."

"It's Ellie's own dold money," said Ellie, with her arms tight round Nessa's neck.

In the pleasure of seeing the rent completed, Murtagh forgot his scruples about Nessa's money.

"Three cheers for Ellie," he cried, tossing the money-box up to the ceiling as a glittering half-sovereign fell out upon the table. "It's just right now."

"We want one halfpenny more," said practical Winnie.

"Ellie's dot a ha'penny too," exclaimed the child in delight, wriggling herself down on the floor, "out in the darden."

"That's a rum place for halfpennies," remarked Bobbo.

"It's planted," said Ellie. "For seed," she added gravely, seeing the others inclined to smile.

The children all began to laugh, and Rosie exclaimed: "You little silly! you don't suppose money grows from seed, do you?"

Instantly Ellie was transformed back again into her usual quiet little self.

"Me thought ha'pennies might," she murmured, and hid away behind Nessa.

"I think it is true," said Nessa. "I think we do plant money for seed, sometimes. Only not exactly in the garden," she added, smiling as she kissed little Ellie.

And now, there lay the much-wished-for two pounds on the table, and the children were free to take Theresa home that minute. A load was off their minds, and the relief was so great that at first they could hardly realize it, but they did not feel happy as they had expected to feel.

There was no pleasure in looking forward to the meeting with Mrs. Daly. Murtagh felt rather ashamed than otherwise, and wished it was over. Everything had happened so differently from their plans. They did not know how it was; it did not seem to be their fault; but glad as they were to be so near the end of their troubles, it was without any feeling of pleasurable excitement that they gathered the money and went to set Theresa free.

Theresa, however, felt nothing but the wildest delight. Bobbo first announced to her the good news. He burst into the room where she was hidden, exclaiming, "We've got it, Theresa; we've got it." Then Rose followed rattling the money in her hands, and Theresa, who could hardly believe the news at first, saw that it was really true.

"Ah, Mr. Murtagh, Miss Winnie dear, God bless ye, God bless yez all!" she exclaimed, springing from the corner where she had been sitting, and seizing hold of Murtagh's hands. Half-laughing, half-crying with excitement, she tried to get out some more words of thanks, but could say nothing. Then exclaiming, "Glory be to God," she suddenly sank down upon her knees and burst into tears.

But they were tears of gladness and were over quickly. Drying her eyes with her apron she sprang up again and ran towards the door, saying delightedly, "My mother! Let's run down to her quick. Ah sure, won't she be glad to see us!"

The children followed with pleased faces, and as they trooped down the stairs Theresa poured out expressions of her thanks and of her delight at getting home.

"Ah, I'll never be able to thank yez right. Let us go on a bit quicker," she was exclaiming, when they rushed round a corner of the passage and nearly knocked Mrs. Donegan off her legs as she was coming slowly along, carrying a cup of tea for Nessa.

"By all the blessed saints and martyrs, and is that you, Theresa Curran?" she exclaimed, fixing her eyes upon Theresa, and forgetting in her astonishment to pick up the teacup, which had been dashed to pieces on the floor. "Riz up from the dead, with the police after you, and the master himself payin' your expenses, an' all."

"Take a good look at her, Donnie, while you're about it. It'll be a long time before you see any one else risen up from the dead, with the police after them, and the master paying their expenses," laughed Murtagh, whose spirits were rapidly rising under the influence of Theresa's joy.

Theresa, blushing and trying not to laugh, curtsied at Mrs. Donegan's notice of her, and the children, without waiting for more, carried her off like a whirlwind towards the drawing-room.

Donnie followed as close upon their heels as she could. "Miss Nessa, did ye ever hear of such a thing?" she exclaimed, as the children rushing in presented Theresa with an unceremonious "Here she is."

Theresa stood blushing with such a supremely happy face, and the children around her were all so radiant, that the infection spread to Nessa, who laughed like a child as she answered in the words Donnie was so fond of using, "They're wonderful children."

"What is it at all?" inquired Mrs. Donegan. "Did they find her when the police couldn't?"

"That's it exactly, Donnie," laughed Winnie. "Come along, Nessa. Where's your hat? Don't stand palavering with Donnie or we shan't get to Mrs. Daly's till midnight."

"Tum 'long," urged Ellie, pulling Nessa's hand.

"It's wonderful we are *entirely*," said Murtagh, turning round for a last mock at Donnie as they went out of the room.

"Mr. Launcelot's to the backbone," muttered Donnie, lifting up her hands. She stood a minute or two after she was left alone, murmuring, "Well, it's wonderful to think of," and then hurried away to the kitchen to tell the great piece of news that Theresa was found, that the children were cleverer than all the police, and found her themselves in no time when once they went to look for her.

CHAPTER XII

THERESA AND MRS. DONEGAN had between them put the children into the brightest of moods, and as they danced across the lawn they completely forgot all the wrong side of their adventure and their misgivings about meeting Mrs. Daly.

At the gates some of the lodge-keeper's children were playing. The instant they saw Theresa, one ran in shouting the news to his mother, and the others set off like deer to the village calling out to every one they met that the young ladies and gentlemen were coming down the road bringing Theresa along with them.

"What a nuisance!" said Rosie. "Now we shan't be the first to tell Mrs. Daly."

"Pat! Mick! Biddy!" shouted Bobbo. "Come back, will you!" But it was no use; they were too far down the road to pay any attention.

"Perhaps that is better," said Nessa. "She is too weak for a great surprise."

But Nessa was not prepared for the other effect of having the news spread before them.

Every one, man, woman, and child, who heard it, first refused to believe, and then were told to go and see for themselves; so by the time Theresa and her escort reached the village they were surrounded by a miscellaneous crowd, the members of which were not all quite sober, were all wanting to get near Theresa to see if she were there in "real earnest," and were all asking questions as to how she was found, and where she was found, and "what happened her."

With each addition to their party the children's spirits rose higher and higher. They were determined not to satisfy any one's curiosity, and to every question they responded with some bit of nonsense. They knew every one's private history, and bandied jokes with each new comer till their progress along the road was accompanied by continuous roars of laughter interspersed with a sort of hail of questions.

"Ah, now tell us! How was it ye outwitted the polis an' found her when they couldn't?" called one.

"Outwitted the police," returned Winnie. "Have you come to your age, Kitty, and don't know yet that the police have got no wits to put out?"

"Thrue for ye, Miss Winnie, asthore; it's me own wits are out to ask such a question!"

"But where did yez find her?" asked another, pushing Kitty aside.

"Why where the police didn't find her, of course!" laughed Murtagh.

"Then it's plenty o' places ye had to choose from; but tell us now, Mr. Murtagh, honey, how did yez find her? Was she half-dead or how was she?"

"Not half-dead at all, but dead and a half, and pining for a sight of you, Mrs. Malachy," replied Murtagh, turning to the village schoolmistress.

"Sure, Theresa! Is it yer ownself come back?" cried a woman from the edge of the crowd. "Tell out now; who was it spirited ye away?"

"The fairies—the good people," cried Rose and Winnie together, while Theresa blushed and laughed.

"Ah, Mr. Murtagh, my jewel, give over jokin' and tell us where ye found her," called Kitty again, having elbowed her way back close to them.

"Wouldn't any one know you're a woman, Kitty?" began Murtagh, when a man on the other side of him interrupted in a heavy voice:

"Don't tell her a word, Mr. Murtagh; she's the curiousest woman in the place."

"And you'd like me to tell you instead," said Murtagh, looking up with a merry twinkle at the light blue stupid eyes. "Ah, well, if you want to know, it was Miss Winnie's bright eyes did the business."

"But however was it she did it?" asked the man.

"For shame, Phelim. Were you born on April fool's day not to know that?" laughed Murtagh. "You'd better go home and find out."

"Go to Shuna Toolin an' get her to teach ye," called out several voices amid fresh derisive laughter.

"Tell us round here, Master Bobbo, honey, that niver asked a question," cried a woman persuasively, divining justly that she would get most out of Bobbo.

"Well, it was up there by the river, if you want to know so badly," returned Bobbo.

"Up by the river! Why sure that's where the police looked and niver found a bit of her!" cried several voices together.

"Don't be insulting us comparing us to those omadhauns of police, that don't know a whisky press when they see one," called Murtagh.

Roars of laughter interspersed with "Arrah whisht, Mr. Murtagh," greeted that remark. Then some one cried out, "Three cheers for the young ladies and gentlemen," and Nessa's bewildered ears were deafened with three loud "Hurrahs."

"Three groans for the polis!" called another.

In the midst of the hearty groan with which he responded to the invitation, Murtagh caught sight of Nessa trying to lift little Ellie out of the crush.

"Carry Miss Ellie, will you, Pat Molony?" he called out, laughing as he spoke, at the quaint expression of Nessa's face. Thrusting out two dirty kindly arms from behind her, Pat Molony lifted Ellie over Nessa's head, saying gallantly: "It's not fit for the likes o' you, Miss, to be carrying childer. It's more like a white lily ye are;" and when Nessa looked round to thank him she saw Ellie contentedly sitting on his shoulder, with one arm round his dirty neck.

In this fashion, joking and laughing, they passed through the village and out on the road close to Mrs. Daly's cabin. Then some ran on to tell her they were coming, and Theresa and the children, refusing to answer any more questions, made their way through the crowd, and hurried forward. At the garden-gate Theresa passed them all, and rushed into the cottage alone.

Murtagh and Winnie were close behind her. They overheard a smothered cry, then—"Oh, my darlint! my darlint! is it you yourself?" and there was something in the intensity of the voice that made them suddenly stop short. The laughter died from their faces, and they stood looking at each other. A strange awe had fallen upon them. The noisy laughing crowd seemed far away; they heard only the kisses that were being exchanged in the dark cottage, and children as they were, they understood suddenly something of what the mother had suffered.

Through all their adventure they had never given one thought to her, till Nessa's emotion this afternoon had first opened their eyes. They had forgotten so many things, and now as they stood looking wistfully into each other's faces they were filled with remorse. What was it that had been wrong in all this? Something had they felt, and yet it had seemed right. Neither of them spoke, they only looked at one another, but they knew that the same thought filled both their minds.

They did not think of entering the cottage, and the crowd seeing them stand still, stood still too. A fear ran through it that they were too late,—that Mrs. Daly had died without seeing her daughter. The noise and laughter were suddenly hushed. Some one said, "What's happened?" Faces were turned anxiously towards the door. It was as though a spell had fallen upon them, and for a minute, while Winnie and Murtagh stood gazing into each other's eyes, there was a dead silence. They neither of them ever forgot that strange hush and the bewildering thoughts that filled it.

The silence was broken by Mrs. Daly's voice in the cottage saying: "An' where are they till I thank them?"

Then Theresa ran to the door to call them in, and the crowd seeing that all was right, broke into speech again and trooped into the cottage after the children.

Mrs. Daly was sitting up in the bed; Theresa knelt beside her with her arms around her neck.

"I'll never be able to thank yez right," said Mrs. Daly, stretching out two thin hands towards the children; "but if ye care for a poor woman's blessing may it follow ye to the end of your days. And may none of ye ever feel the hundredth part of the sorra' I've had since she's been gone from me."

"True for ye, Mrs. Daly. May they have peace and happiness all the days of their life for the good turn they've done to the poor this day," cried some from behind with a ring of feeling in their voices.

The children stood by the bedside blushing.

"But we didn't," said Murtagh to Mrs. Daly—"we didn't do what you think; I mean, we didn't find her to-day. We knew where she was; we helped her to hide from her step-father when she lost the rent; but she's got it now." He spoke with difficulty, and he was glad to have got it all out.

Mrs. Daly hardly seemed to pay attention to the sense of the words. She had got her arms round Theresa and was thinking only of her.

"It's all one," she answered. "Ye've brought her back alive, an' I thought she was dead."

A few minutes more and the children had left the cottage. The crowd stayed behind anxious to hear at last Theresa's story, and they walked soberly along the road with Nessa.

"Isn't it delightful," said Rosie, "to think that it's all so well over?"

"Berry belightful," returned Ellie so emphatically that she made them all laugh. But then she wanted to know—"What for all the people were laughin'?" and while Rose explained, the other children walked on silently. They were not inclined to talk about it yet.

CHAPTER XIII

IN THE MEAN TIME Mr. Blair had heard from Mr. Plunkett an account of the children's behavior which was certainly not flattering to them, and at dinner that evening he spoke about it to Nessa.

"Mr. Plunkett does not know how to manage people," she said, after she had explained the story from the children's point of view. "It is a pity."

"Ah!" said her uncle, amused at the quaint gravity with which she announced her opinion.

"I do not like him," she continued. "He is hard. He is bad for the children."

"What! have you been thinking about it?" said her uncle, smiling. "If you have I suppose you must be right, but you astonish me. I thought he was wonderfully good for the children."

"No," said Nessa, "because he does not understand them, and he does not like them. He makes them angry. Listen," she continued; "I think it would be very difficult for these children to be good. They have but two things. Mr. Plunkett thinks that all they do is wrong, and the others—the other people—think that all is right. It is very bad for them. It is bad for them to be so much scolded, and it is bad for them to be so much flattered."

"So Plunkett thinks all is wrong, does he?" asked Mr. Blair.

"Yes," said Nessa; "he does not see anything but the wrong, and he scolds the children, oh, in such a very disagreeable way. He stirs up all their wicked thoughts; he makes them proud and angry; and then I think they *like* to do what he does not want."

"But, my dear child, that is the only rule I have ever been able to discover for children's behavior. They always like to do what I don't want," said her uncle. "Why do they always bang the doors? Why do they always shout under my windows? Why do they get up at six o'clock in the morning and clatter up and down the passage when I am enjoying my soundest sleep? Answer me all these questions if you can, little advocate."

"They bang the doors because they are always in a hurry," said Nessa, smiling. "And they shout because they are happy. And they get up early——Well, the birds get up early too."

"Well, well, well," replied her uncle, laughing, "if you will have it your own way I suppose you must. But you must learn to appreciate Plunkett's other qualities. He is a splendid fellow; he saves me more trouble than twenty other men would do in his place."

"Perhaps he is very useful," said Nessa, willing always to be polite. "But he is not interesting," she added decidedly.

"He is most interesting to me," returned Mr. Blair, still laughing. "I have twenty pounds now for every ten I used to have, and he has succeeded in making the cottagers round about keep roofs on their houses, and conform to a few other customs of civilization, unpicturesque perhaps, but very desirable. He has done it at the risk of his life too," he continued, in a more serious tone. "More than one of the men about here would think it a praiseworthy action to shoot him from behind a hedge some dark night. Plunkett knows it, and after all, little lady, your martyrs of the middle ages did not do so very much more than persevere in their duty when they knew it might cost them their life."

"Yes, that is brave," said Nessa, looking up.

Her uncle's words made Mr. Plunkett's character appear to her in a new light, but they gave her an unpleasant creeping sensation. She was beginning to think that Ireland was a very unsafe place to live in.

"Well," said her uncle, as they rose to leave the dining room, "are you convinced now of Plunkett's excellent qualities?"

"Yes," replied Nessa, coming back to her former train of thought, "but——"

"But what?"

"I do not think I could like him; he is not kind."

"Ah, you true woman!" replied Mr. Blair, as he held the door open for her. "You won't acknowledge yourself beaten; but ask his little daughter Marion if he is not kind."

Instead of going to the drawing-room Nessa went straight to the school-room to join the children, but she found it empty; the children were out, Peggy told her. Intending to wait for them a little while she went to the window and threw it open to see what the night was like. The air was warm for an autumn evening, and very still. No sound to be heard but the rippling of the river. In the dark blue sky above shone the full moon; and the park, gently undulating, lay gleaming in its silvery light. Deep black shadows from the trees fell here and there, but not a breath stirred the branches. It seemed as though the world were all asleep, and the river singing a lullaby.

Nessa rested her arms on the window-sill, and stayed there looking out. The events of the day had made her wonderfully thoughtful, and this moonlit park was more in keeping with her mood than the warm, bright drawing-room. After a while, however, her thoughts slid gradually into fancies, and she found herself dreamingly gazing out, imagining how fairies might haunt those shadowy hollows and come out from among the trees to dance on the silvered slopes.

The flowing of the streams seemed to interweave itself with her fancies, and make music for mystic dancing. She was not thinking; the beauty of the night, the stillness, the soft cadence of the water, played upon her mind and made sweet dreamy pictures there, till at last with the fairy music mixed something more tangible—sounds that seemed to be actually coming nearer.

Surely those last notes were real. They swelled by degrees into a plaintive melody that floated for a moment on the still air, then sunk again. The water rippled on over its stony bed, and Nessa looking at the dark trees and moonlit grass, half-wondered if the music had really been or if she had only imagined it.

Presently the sweet notes rose again, clearer this time and fuller, gaining strength as they went on. Then a fresh young voice began to sing strange words that Nessa did not understand, but that seemed to blend in harmony with the stream, and the night, and her fancies. The music came nearer and nearer; another voice joined the first, but after a while both music and voices died away. A faint reflection, as it were, of the sounds lingered in the air; and Nessa, listening for more, heard them soon again coming from a different direction. They seemed in some mysterious way to be behind her. She wondered how that could be, and then became aware that they were in the house, crossing the hall and coming down the passage. The music was plain enough now,—a violin; and a girl's and a boy's voice together were singing a wild Irish song.

"Can it be the children?" thought Nessa, as she turned away from the window to listen. Soon her doubt was set at rest; the door of the school-room slowly opened, and Winnie entered singing, followed by Murtagh, who was playing the violin and singing too.

They did not see Nessa, who had withdrawn into the shadow of the curtain, but stood still together in a broad strip of moonlight near the table singing as though their whole souls were in the song. Winnie's head was a little thrown back, her face looked white, her eyes unnaturally large and dark in the strange light. Murtagh had bent his head to one side over the violin, and his face was in shadow.

Nessa stood entranced watching the weird little figures. But as their voices rose to a sort of strange sweet wail that formed the refrain of their song, Murtagh's hand slipped. A sudden shriek of wrong notes was the result; both the children stopped singing, and he impatiently flung the violin on the table, exclaiming: "That's always the way when I'm just getting it best."

"There's a string gone, and that'll be sixpence to save up before we can have another singing night," remarked Winnie, ruefully, as a slight snap from the violin announced the mischief that had been done.

Nessa advanced from the window, and suggested that perhaps the string would be long enough to be used again.

"Are you there?" exclaimed Winnie, taking up the violin. "No; it's the same string that broke last time. Myrrh," she continued, "I do wish you wouldn't pitch the violin about so; couldn't you remember to give it to me every time instead of throwing it down?"

"Especially," remarked Rosie, who had come in with Bobbo, "when it's all your fault. If you practised every day the way you promised mamma, you'd never make those horrid squeaks."

"Shut up!" said Murtagh, flinging himself down on the hearth-rug beside the chair on which Nessa had seated herself. .

Winnie hovered about watching Nessa's useless endeavors to make a short string long enough, and finally settled down also upon the hearth-rug; while Rosie, after surveying them for a moment, remarked that she was going to bed, and went away up-stairs.

"You'll be throwing it in the river by mistake some of these nights, Murtagh," said Bobbo, drawing near to inspect the violin, "and that'll be an awful nuisance."

"Don't bother him!" said Winnie. "We are so tired."

Bobbo made no answer, but sat down on the floor beside her.

"I'm sick and tired of everything," exclaimed Murtagh presently. "Everything's wrong and wrong and wrong whatever you do; I think I'd like to be nice and quietly dead, then things wouldn't be all so puzzling."

"I'm so tired now," said Winnie, wearily laying her head on a footstool, "that I think I'd like to be dead or anything where you don't feel."

"Poor children!" said Nessa, "you are tired out."

"It isn't being tired I mind," said Murtagh, wearily; "but it's so dreadfully difficult all about what's right and what's wrong. I cannot understand about it, and I wish—yes, I really do wish I was dead."

"But that is not brave," said Nessa gently. "I do not think we need be afraid of our lives," she continued, after a moment's silence, "because there is always so much good that we don't know of. I felt afraid when I had to come here, and now I am very happy after all."

"Yes, but," said Murtagh, "it isn't like that; only it does puzzle me so about the wrong sides of things. We were so wretched all the week trying to keep Theresa, and we couldn't laugh at anything, and when we woke up in the morning we thought about her the first thing. But then we thought we ought to keep her; we thought Rosie was talking nonsense. Well, afterwards, all of a sudden, we find out we were all wrong somehow!"

"Oh no," said Nessa, "you were not all wrong. How can you say that when you were so kind and so brave?"

Murtagh's face brightened for a moment, but then he said: "Yes; but Winnie and I have been thinking, and it came right in the end because you helped us; but we didn't bring it right. We only made Mrs. Daly miserable, and Theresa miserable, and ourselves miserable. We wouldn't desert her because we always thought it was beastly mean deserting people, and all the time Rosie was right; and it is very funny, being brave is worse than being cowardly."

"Ah," said Nessa, "but you are mistaking the part that was wrong. If you had been older you would not have hidden Theresa in the island at all, because you would have known all the trouble it would bring; you would have come at once to Uncle Blair. But then you couldn't help not being older, and when you had hidden her there, much the best thing you could do was to be brave. If you had taken her back at first you would never have got the money."

The explanation satisfied Murtagh for a moment, but then he said: "It wasn't our keeping her that got the money. If you hadn't been here we could never have got it. And supposing it had done what Mr. Plunkett said; supposing it had killed Mrs. Daly?"

But Nessa was not accustomed to explain things, and she felt that she was growing puzzled. She was not puzzled a bit by the fact—of course she knew that it was better to be brave than to be cowardly, better to try to help people when they are in trouble than to leave them to take care of themselves—but by the difficulty of putting her conviction into words.

"I don't know how to explain," she said at last; "but I know I love you for doing as you did."

Bobbo sitting nearest her gave her hand a fervent squeeze. It was new and pleasant to them to be loved.

"And wait one moment," she continued; "I think now I can explain a little too. You know we are not perfect, and the thing we have to do is to try and be as good as we can. We are quite sure to make mistakes, but I think we ought to be brave enough to go on trying and trying to the end; and then God *is* kind; he will let us have done most good by the time we have to stop. Don't you think so?"

"I think if you were always there we should always do most good," said Murtagh warmly, kneeling beside her.

And Nessa, changing her manner, laughed and kissed his forehead, saying: "Ah, you mad fellow, if I were always with you I would not let you do so many foolish things, and you would wish me very far away."

CHAPTER XIV

T HE CHILDREN'S WAKING on the following day was a very happy one. For the last week the remembrance of Theresa had fallen like a cloud upon them the instant they opened their eyes, but this morning they sprang with light hearts from their beds. That trouble was over and gone, and all the world looked bright in consequence. It was the day for Indian letters too, the day that they all loved best in the fortnight, for there were generally two good letters, one from papa and one from mamma, and papa's letters especially were almost like stories, only better. Out of doors the sun shone, the wind was warm, birds were singing among the reddening leaves, the river sparkled and flashed invitingly. It was more like a day in August than October, and the children resolved to enjoy it.

They danced with joyous faces into the dining-room to breakfast; they seemed created to be happy. Their uncle was not there, and the post-bag lying by his plate was locked. Murtagh might smell it, shake it, try to lift up the flap and peep as much as he pleased, his anxiety for a letter had to remain unsatisfied till Mr. Blair made his appearance. But then, could anything be more delightful?—a nice fat letter from papa for Murtagh, and one from mamma for Rosie.

No sooner was Murtagh's handed to him than he bounded with it out of the window. There Nessa saw him kiss it, turn head over heels three or four times on the grass, and then tear away at full speed round the corner of the house. Breakfast was nearly over when he returned, with a radiant face, and handed the letter to Winnie to read, remarking, "It's awfully nice."

"Yes; and isn't it nice that you are to have half a sovereign for your birthday?" said Rosie, giving him her letter.

"Oh, yes, awfully jolly. Papa says I am to have one from Mr. Plunkett," he added, turning to his uncle. "Does he tell you? he says he will."

"Yes," said Mr. Blair. "When is your birthday?"

"Wednesday week," replied Murtagh. "Come along out," he exclaimed, after devoting himself during an interval of about three minutes to his breakfast, "and let us read what the pretty mother says. You come too, Nessa, and you shall hear papa's letter also. We'll go to the big chestnut-tree; that's where we always read their letters aloud." And taking a bit of bread to supplement his hasty meal, he rose from the table and led the way out.

"We get up in the branches," said Rosie, when a few minutes later they were walking along out of doors, "and sometimes we pretend it's a sort of church."

"Only, last letter day," said Winnie, "we pretended we were a family of squirrels, and mamma's letter was a dear little white dove flown over the seas to tell us not to steal nuts and apples from the other squirrels. Of course, you know, she didn't say anything about them really, but she often does tell us to be good, and that's the same as not stealing is for squirrels. It's such fun pretending, and then we put little pieces in the letters."

"And then we went off to Nut Wood to get ourselves some instead of stealing," said Bobbo, "and when Winnie was up in the very top branch of the bull's-eye tree, Mr. Plunkett came past and saw her, and called out, 'What are you stealing those nuts for?' "

"And I thought about him being a squirrel, and running up and down the trees whisking his tail," interrupted Winnie, "and I laughed so much I tumbled off the tree, and gave myself such a whack I haven't quite got well yet."

"And another day we were just Irish kings and queens, the way we generally are, and papa's letter was some river fairies come down to warn us about some scoundrelly English taking our chief palace—that's the island, you know. We rushed up there at once, and lo and behold! when we got there what do you think we found? That old piggamy, Mr. Plunkett, had chopped down our watch-tower, a splendid old oak-tree that had its branches blasted with lightning, the only one on the island. So the English had been there true enough."

They chattered on in this fashion till the big chestnut-tree was reached,—a splendid old tree, with gnarled trunk and spreading branches. In a moment the children were in it, looking indeed not unlike a family of squirrels as they scrambled about and peeped at Nessa through the clusters of pointed leaves.

Nessa had never been in a tree in her life, but the children seemed to look upon it as so easy and natural a place of habitation, that she merrily accepted their invitation to mount.

"Will it be difficult to get up there?" she asked, indicating a place about four or five feet from the ground where the trunk spread out into three great branches.

"Oh no, no," exclaimed the children, "as easy as possible. Here, take hold of our hands, and set your foot on that sort of bump lower down, then you can walk up like going up stairs."

They stretched out their hands and in a moment Nessa was seated in the tree.

"Shamrocks and Shillelaghs! There's Mr. Plunkett out again, and he's seen you, Nessa," cried Winnie in delight, "and oh, he does look so jolly shocked!"

Nessa was enchanted with her novel position. "Never mind Mr. Plunkett," she said gaily. "Let us read the letters now."

"What shall we be to-day?" said Winnie. "Nessa couldn't be a squirrel exactly, you know."

"We'll be Irish kings and queens," said Murtagh, "and Nessa will be a stranger who has brought us these letters from a far-away king."

"Oh yes," said Winnie. "And you'll live with us for a while, and afterwards we'll discover you're an Irish princess who was stolen away when she was a baby. Now then, Myrrh!"

Nessa settled herself into her place with a little pleased laugh. It was much pleasanter to be out of doors this morning than in the drawing-room. Murtagh read the letters aloud. The children had read them five or six times already, but they listened with the greatest delight, laughing again at the little jokes, and telling Nessa to "just listen to this!" when any particularly nice part was coming.

"Now," said Murtagh, when the letters were quite finished, "come along with us, and we'll show you our dominions."

"Yes," said Rosie. "It's too bad; she's been here a whole week, and we've never shown her our islands, nor nut-wood, nor the mushroom-field, nor the mountains."

"I'll tell you what, Myrrh," exclaimed Winnie, struck by a sudden inspiration, "we'll have a picnic up the mountains on your birthday. What do you think of that?"

"Yes," said Murtagh, "and oh, Win, a plan has just come into my head. Such a beauty! I'll tell you presently."

"Is it a secret?" asked Rosie.

"Yes. But I'll tell you too, by-and-by. Oh, it is so jolly; you'll go cracky when you hear it." And being unable to turn head over heels Murtagh relieved his feelings by springing to the ground.

Having once got into the tree Nessa would gladly have spent the morning there. But the children had no notion of allowing the appreciation of their roost to take that form, and for the next two or three hours she was trotted backwards and forwards from one favorite place to another, till when twelve o'clock came she was glad to go with the children to the back-door and receive at Donnie's hands a glass of milk and a slice of brown cake.

The children would not have left her then but for their anxiety to talk over Murtagh's plan. He had already in whispers confided to them the rough sketch of it, and it promised indeed to be so delightful that after disposing of their cake and milk in the yard they could restrain themselves no longer; and, leaving Nessa to enter the house alone, they merrily scampered back to the chestnut-tree to hold their consultation.

Their wonderful plan was simply this: that they were to discover Nessa to be the real princess of their tribe, and on Murtagh's birthday they were to have on the mountains the grand ceremony of crowning and receiving her into the tribe. It was the details of the plan that were so specially delightful, Murtagh said; particularly one.

"Now then, listen," he said, when they had all got back to the chestnut-tree, and he had settled himself comfortably astride a thick branch; "it's all been floating into my head the whole of this morning, and I'll tell you just how I've planned it. We'll have a regular grand—what d' ye call it? like when the Lord Lieutenant was made Knight of St. Patrick, up——"

"Ceremony," interpolated Winnie.

"Yes, ceremony, up in the ruins. We'll make a throne of stones in the middle of the court-yard, and we'll decorate it with green branches. Then we'll have garlands of evergreens and hollyhocks, and loop them up on the walls all round, and we'll have a green ribbon and a wreath of shamrocks. And I'll be sitting on the throne, and all the followers standing round. Then you four will bring her up the mountain, and as soon as she comes near, the followers will run forward and scatter shamrocks on the ground for her to walk over, and she'll be led up to the throne. Then I'll get down off the throne, and I'll say, 'Will you reign over us, our princess? and will you promise to be true to our tribe?' or something like that, and she'll say, 'Yes,' and I'll tie the green ribbon round her arm. Then comes the beautiful part of the plan! I'll make her promise to hate Mr. Plunkett, and to defend us against him."

"Oh, Murtagh!" exclaimed Rosie. "You won't be able to do that. You know she's grown up and she would never promise that."

"Yes, but you don't know how I'm going to do it," returned Murtagh triumphantly. "Just wait till you hear. After I've put on the ribbon I'll take up the shamrock wreath, and I'll say: 'Kneel down, and promise to hate the Agents, and to defend your tribe against them.' And she won't know, you see, about Mr. Plunkett being an Agent; she'll only know about them being something very bad, and so she'll say 'Yes.' "

"Then she'll be bound to help us when we get into scrapes with him; won't she?" asked Bobbo.

"Of course she will," returned Murtagh. "She'll be as much one of the tribe as you are, then."

"Oh, I say, Myrrh," cried Winnie, clapping her hands, "it's perfectly delicious. What a sell for old Plunkett!"

"What an awful lark!" said Bobbo. "It will serve him out so jolly right!"

"And look here, Myrrh," said Winnie, whose head was already full of minor details; "you must get a string for the violin with sixpence of your birthday money, and we'll teach all the children to sing some songs—'The Wearing of the Green,' and 'the Shan Van Vaugh,' and——"

"Yes," said Murtagh, "but I haven't told you yet what we're going to do with the rest of the money. You only know half the plan. With all the rest of the money we'll buy buns and things for the followers to eat, and Donnie'll give us a lot of tea, so they'll have a kind of school-feast after the ceremony; because, you know, they'll be awfully hungry, and they will be so pleased."

Never had any one imagined a more delightful birthday plan, and the children proceeded eagerly to discuss every possible detail. The number of buns and barmbracks had to be calculated, the "followers'" appetites guessed at; their voices, their appearance, the songs to be chosen, the decorations, the order of the ceremony,—all were subjects of the warmest interest.

"Isn't papa a dear old blessing of a father, remembering about my birthday all that way off, and sending me half a sovereign?" exclaimed Murtagh, gratefully pulling his letter out of his pocket and looking at it. "I never knew any one like him in all my life, he does think about things so. I wonder if he knew what a lot of fun we should have with it!"

"Oh, and I'll tell you what we must do, Myrrh!" exclaimed Winnie, completely engrossed by the matter in hand. "Every one of the followers must have a large green branch in his hand, like Birnam wood in the theatre. It'll make them look more. You remember about Macbeth in the theatre," she explained, seeing Rosie looked puzzled.

"Oh yes, of course," replied Rosie, who didn't remember a bit. "And I'll tell you, too, we'll get a lot of apples for the feast. They'll be nearly as great a treat as cakes for the followers, because they never have any."

"Yes, yes," cried Bobbo. But Murtagh objected.

"No," he said decidedly, poking his letter into his pocket again. "We won't."

"Hullo!" remarked Bobbo. "Why not?"

"Well," said Murtagh, looking at Winnie in hopes of support, "I don't want to have anything wrong at all in this plan. It's just to be a bit of fun, and so I think we had better keep clear of old Plunkett."

"Oh, stuff!" said Rosie. "Apples are nothing. He's used to us taking them."

"Yes, but," replied Murtagh, "papa gave us the money, and the grown-up people would all say we oughtn't to take them, so I vote we leave the beastly things alone. He's sure to make it an excuse for talking to us."

It was Murtagh's plan, and Murtagh's birthday, so he had a right to decide. But when the question of the apples was settled a thousand other questions arose, and they were far from being all decided when the second dinner-bell summoned the children to the house.

But the village children had to be made acquainted as soon as possible with the fact that their services would be required, and as the tribe that the children were so fond of talking about consisted exclusively of their five selves, they felt that there was some difficulty about calling together the honorary members upon whom they had so recently conferred the rank and title of followers.

However there was Pat O'Toole, a young friend and favorite of Murtagh's, to whom they had once confided their notion of enrolling themselves into a tribe, and there was Theresa Curran, who might fairly now be said to belong to it, and with these two to help they would easily be able to organize their festival.

A proposal from Nessa to go and visit Mrs. Daly after lunch was therefore accepted with delight, and while she sat and chatted with Mrs. Daly the children carried off Theresa for a consultation. Pat O'Toole also was summoned, and the wonderful plan was unfolded. It was received with enthusiasm. Anything the young ladies and gentlemen wanted was sure to be found charming, and this manner of doing honor to Nessa was just after the hearts of the people, with whom she was already in highest favor.

It was all even more easy to arrange than the children had expected. Pat and Theresa charged themselves with collecting the "followers," and Murtagh gleefully gave orders that they were to assemble that very afternoon for a first singing practice on one of the little islands.

The children came dancing home, elated and happy. What a pity all days were not like this day! Everything went well, and they felt so good and bright as they raced and capered about the lawns.

Nessa went in-doors on her return from the village, but they never went in till evening, and to-day of all days it was impossible to sit still.

Alas! their little active feet were always tripping into mischief. After a time they took it into their heads to go and prepare the island for the singing meeting. To reach it they had to cross a little bridge quite close to the garden-gate, and unfortunately, as they were racing back after having completed their preparations, they came upon Bland driving a horse and cart through the river. The horse had refused to cross the bridge, which was without a parapet; and as the children came up they found that Bland had by precaution taken out the lading of the cart before driving through the water. Large baskets of apples stood ranged side by side upon the bridge.

"Ha, ha!" cried Bland, seeing the children as he landed the cart safely and began to load it again. "We've conquered you at last, my young gentlemen. You'll have to do without apples now whether you like it or not. Every one in the garden was picked this morning by Mr. Plunkett's orders."

"I'm sure I don't care," replied Murtagh, feeling too good-humored to be annoyed. "I don't want the beastly things."

"Sour grapes, young gentleman, sour grapes!" replied Bland, chuckling. "I daresay you were on your way to the garden now, if the truth were known."

"We weren't anything of the sort, as it happens," said Bobbo.

"We'd made up our minds just this very morning not to take any," added Rosie.

"Easy talking. Words don't cost much; but I'd have been sorry to trust you under a tree of ripe apples," returned Bland, wiping his face after the exertion of getting one of the baskets into the cart.

"Shut up your impudence," said Murtagh, "or I'll just turn one of these baskets into the river, to show you how little we care for your stupid old garden stuff."

"Oh, ay. It's not so pleasant being circumvented. I don't wonder you don't like it. But here's an end of your apple-eating for this winter. In another hour every apple that was in the garden this morning will be safe in the apple-room, and the key in Mr. Plunkett's pocket."

"Here, Myrrh," said Winnie laughing, and pushing one of the heavy baskets as she spoke, "help me to give it a shove, and we'll teach them not to crow before they're out of the bush. Hurrah, there it goes! What do you think of that, Mr. Bland?" she cried triumphantly, as with the help of a hearty push from Bobbo and Murtagh the basket toppled over into the river, and a bushel of rosy-cheeked apples bobbed up and down in the rapid current. Then, without waiting for any answer from indignant Bland, the children all ran away laughing, leaving him to finish loading his cart, and to go to Mr. Plunkett with another complaint of their unruliness.

"What a pity I did it though, Myrrh! I'm very sorry," said Winnie, with a queer twinkle in her eyes, as they stopped on the hall-door steps. "But I forgot all about meaning not to take any more apples. It was such a jolly sell for Bland, just when he thought he'd got them so safe; and he didn't think we'd do it really."

"I'd like to see Mr. Plunkett's face when Bland tells him," said Bobbo laughing. "Why, we took more apples that way than we'd have taken in two months just for eating! It'll teach him to try and circumvent us."

"I'm sorry all the same," returned Winnie, laughing in spite of herself. "I am really, Myrrh."

"You don't look very bad," answered Murtagh. "Still if you want to cry I'll run and get you a pocket-handkerchief."

Just then they overheard Nessa's voice through the open drawing-room door, saying: "Have you asked Master Murtagh? He might possibly know what has become of them."

"Master Murtagh! Master Murtagh's not far off, and if it's anything important I've no objection to go and ask his opinion," exclaimed Murtagh, taking a flying leap over one of the hall-chairs, and confronting Mrs. Donegan as she made her appearance through a doorway.

" 'Deed, Master Murtagh," returned Donnie, "it's no matter for joking. The only two decent shirts you have in the world have gone clean out of your linen drawer. I've hunted for them high and low, and you'll have to go to church to-morrow without a rag to your back. It's too bad the way the things is spirited here and spirited there. You can't lay a thing out of your hand but it's gone before you turn round."

Murtagh and Winnie being in an excitable state of high spirits, both burst out laughing, and Bobbo called out: "It wasn't your shirts she had, was it?"

"Yes," ejaculated Winnie through her laughter. "Oh, Donnie, for goodness' sake, don't look so funny; you'll kill me with laughing. Look here," she continued, holding her sides and trying to control her mirth, "you needn't look so astonished; she wanted them a great deal worse than Murtagh, and she hadn't got any money to buy some."

"Miss Winnie, how can you talk in such a way! Do you suppose, I'd like to know, that I hemmed and stitched at them shirts for you to give 'em away?" returned Mrs. Donegan indignantly. "You ought to be ashamed of yourself, Miss, to go and leave your brother without a thing to go to church in of a Sunday morning."

"I have a splendid new flannel petticoat," laughed Winnie, "and I'll lend it to him with all the pleasure in life."

"It's time such doings were put a stop to," returned Mrs. Donegan. "Mr. Murtagh, how could ye think of doing such a thing?"

"I've been to Mr. Murtagh," returned Murtagh gravely, "and he says he can't give any opinion on the matter."

"Then you may tell him from me he ought to be ashamed of himself, an' it would be a good thing if he'd given his opinion before now. I'm sure I have more bother than enough with him," returned Mrs. Donegan, for once quite out of temper; "and now I'll have to stand and argufy half an hour with Mr. Plunkett before I get the money for some new ones."

"Did you know where they were, Murtagh?" asked Nessa, coming to the drawing-room door.

"Yes," replied Murtagh, not quite certain whether he felt inclined to laugh or to blush. And then Winnie explained how they had gone.

"Ye'd make a mighty generous churchwarden," remarked Donnie, as she walked off in high dudgeon to the kitchen.

The children troubled themselves very little about Donnie's scolding. But Nessa told them that she did not think they ought to give away their clothes; it was not right to be troublesome. And her little exercise of elder-sisterly rights awoke sundry uncomfortable scruples in their minds connected with their late destruction of their uncle's fruit. By tacit consent, however, the untimely fate of the apples was not alluded to in Nessa's presence, and next morning the children themselves had forgotten it.

Not so Mr. Plunkett. The incident irritated him; he saw in it a fresh defiance from the children, and when next day it was followed by Mrs. Donegan's request for new flannel shirts for Murtagh, he resolved that they should be made for once to feel his authority.

CHAPTER XV

"I NEVER HEARD of such a shame in my life. It's my own money, and I don't care what you say. I *will* have it. It's downright cheating."

Murtagh's white face and angry flashing eyes added vehemence to his words. He was standing opposite Mr. Plunkett, his little figure drawn up to its full height, one foot slightly advanced, one hand resting on a corner of the table, his hair tossed, his clothes untidy as usual, his whole attitude breathing indignation and defiance.

The other children stood in a group behind him casting hot indignant glances at Mr. Plunkett, who seemed quite unmoved. He was standing near the fire with his hat on and an umbrella in his hand. He was determined not to let himself be provoked into losing his temper, and now replied to Murtagh's words:

"To take new clothes for which your father had paid, and give them away without his permission, resembles stealing. You chose to do it when you thought it would cost you nothing, and it is perfectly just that you should bear the consequences."

"It is not right. It is not just," returned Murtagh. "Papa said I was to have that half-sovereign as a birthday present, and nobody in the world has a right to keep it from me."

"Besides," burst out Winnie, "Murtagh didn't take the shirts; I took them. I threw the apples in the river too, only you always like to fix everything on him."

"It was just the same thing," replied Mr. Plunkett. "Murtagh should not have allowed them to be taken. You don't seem to understand," he continued, addressing Murtagh, and speaking as though Winnie's remark had not been made, "that in this world if you take what does not belong to you you must pay for it. I am the steward of your father's money in all that concerns you, and in his interest I intend that you shall pay him back for the shirts you chose to give away. Had your general conduct been such as to justify me in overlooking this offence I should have taken upon myself the responsibility of paying for your new shirts with his money; but it is not so, and I am in no way disposed to shield you from the just consequences of your actions."

"It's not in papa's interest, you know it isn't. Just as if he would care for two beastly shirts. You're just doing it because you like to plague us, and oppress us, and drive us into being wicked," replied Murtagh passionately.

"I tell you what, young gentleman, if you were my son for just ten minutes I would teach you not to use such impertinent language to your elders," returned Mr. Plunkett, whose temper was not enduring.

"If you don't want me to talk to you like that you shouldn't behave so. It's my own money, that papa gave me to enjoy ourselves with, and I can't help talking to you in that way when you keep it from me. You have no right to."

"I thought you might have listened to reason," replied Mr. Plunkett coldly, "but since you choose to behave like an infant you shall be treated like an infant. I have the money and I shall keep it. If there is any over when your shirts have been paid for, it shall be returned to you." So saying he moved away towards the door.

"I *will* have it all," said Murtagh. "I don't care so much about the money, but you have no right to keep it when it's my own that papa gave me."

Mr. Plunkett left the room without making any answer. But Winnie's indignation now burst beyond all bounds, and dashing to the door she called after him: "He shall have every penny of it. It's his very own, and if you steal it I'll steal some of yours. So there now. You have fair warning."

Nessa happened to be coming down the passage just at that moment, and she overheard the speech.

"What is the matter?" she asked, looking round at the angry faces.

"Oh, it's too bad," said Winnie; "he's going to steal Murtagh's half-sovereign that papa gave him. It's just like him; he's always perfectly delighted to get a chance of plaguing us, and he thinks just because he's the strongest and has got the money, that he'll conquer this time, but he shan't, I can tell him."

"What do you mean?" said Nessa. "Steal Murtagh's half-sovereign! I don't understand."

"He says he won't give it to him," replied Winnie, calming down a little. "He's going to keep it to pay for the shirts we gave Theresa, and it was my plan about cutting them up, and I took them out of the drawer. He has no right to take Murtagh's money to pay for what I did."

"And now we can't have the feast, nor the expedition, nor anything," said Rosie, "and we've asked all the children. What shall we do? We can't tell them not to come."

Murtagh was too angry to speak a word. He stood where Mr. Plunkett had left him, kicking the leg of the table, and looking as though at that moment he would have cut Mr. Plunkett's throat with pleasure.

Nessa looked at him regretfully; and then she asked Winnie in a tone almost as disappointed as Rosie's: "How is it that you did not know till now?"

"I don't know," said Winnie. "He never said a single word till just now he came in here, and we asked him to give us the money to-day instead of the day after to-morrow, and he said: 'I have no money to give you.' First we thought he had forgotten, and we reminded him about the half-sovereign. Then he said: 'You spent that some time ago;' and he told us we were not to have it because of the shirts. And it isn't only that he won't give us our money," she continued, trying to keep down her rising anger, "but oh! he does do things in such a dreadfully disagreeable way. You don't know what he's like."

"I am so sorry," said Nessa, full of unlawful sympathy. "What can we do?"

"We can't do anything," replied Rosie. "We'll just have to disappoint everybody and do without our feast, and it was such a beautiful plan. You didn't know half of it."

"He has no right to Murtagh's money, and he shan't keep it," said Bobbo, marching indignantly out of the room as he spoke. The other children followed him away out of doors; and whatever she might feel for their disappointment, Nessa had no further opportunity of trying to console them, for she saw no more of them all day.

No further opportunity of trying to console them with words, that is to say; but what would Mr. Plunkett have thought had he seen her a little later that afternoon?

She was thoroughly vexed at the notion of the birthday being spoilt. The children had confided to her all their joy in the prospect of feasting the followers; they had told her how they were determined to have no wrong side to this "adventure;" and they had been so happy in the anticipation of this perfect birthday that it seemed really cruel to deprive them of their innocent pleasure.

The affair with Theresa had been a mistake from beginning to end. What was the use of raking up the consequences of it? Yes; the more Nessa thought, the more provoked she felt. Mr. Plunkett did not understand the children at all.

But suddenly a brilliant idea crossed her mind. She laughed aloud a merry little laugh; then jumping up she marched straightway to the kitchen. There dear old Donnie was taken into counsel, and with small regard for principles of justice they hatched between them a plot—well, a plot for which the best excuse they could find was, that, as Nessa said, "It was such a pity not to be happy on a birthday."

"Never you fear, Miss Nessa," replied Mrs. Donegan. "It's me is housekeeper here, thank the Lord, and not Mr. Plunkett; and the children shall have a far better feast than ever they'd buy with their poor little bit of money. Bless their hearts! they don't know the value of things. Whatever does he want, plaguing and worritting them for a couple o' little shirts, as if children won't be children all the world over!"

Nessa discreetly "supposed that Mr. Plunkett had his reasons;" but her eyes sparkled merrily as she added that she thought there could be no harm in giving the children a picnic to celebrate the birthday.

" 'Deed and, Miss Nessa, if you want to know the truth of it, shadow a bit I care whether it's harm or no," replied old Donnie, laughing outright. "If the children have the fancy to feast all them dirty little vagabones out of the village, why they shall feast them for all the Mr. Plunketts ever lived between this and Limerick. An' it's a pleasure to me to have the crossing of him for once, so it is."

"Well, don't tell that to the children, you wicked old thing," replied Nessa, laughing; and away she went singing along the passages without one pang of conscience for what she had done.

That evening she gleefully recounted her misdoings to her uncle, but the children gave her no opportunity of announcing to them the plan that had been arranged during their absence; they did not return to the house during the afternoon, and in the evening when Nessa went to look for them they were not in the school-room.

After she was in bed the idea occurred to her that perhaps they had not come in. It would be just like them to start away up the mountains after tea and not come home till the servants were in bed. Nothing would have surprised her in them; and she believed them quite capable of spending the night on the wet grass under the chestnut-tree if they happened to find the doors locked.

She told herself that the idea was foolish, but having once got it into her head she could not get it out again. And so, after turning and twisting two or three times upon her pillow, she decided that the best thing she could do was to go and see for herself if they were really and truly in their beds.

Slipping on her warm white dressing-gown she set off on her journey across the house; and great was her satisfaction as she softly opened the door of the little girls' bedroom, to hear through the darkness a sound of regular breathing which announced that its rightful inhabitants were not only in possession but were sound asleep.

Her mind was relieved, and she thought herself very foolish for her pains as she crossed the passage and looked also into the boys' room. Two little beds gleamed white in the far corners, but the lights and shadows were so disposed that Nessa was doubtful for a moment whether they were occupied. She advanced to the side of one of them, and while she stood contemplating Master Bobbo, whom she found safely enough tucked up in the bedclothes, a low "Nessa, is that you?" came from the other corner of the room.

She turned and saw Murtagh's dark eyes fixed upon her. "Yes," she replied, moving to his side of the room. "I hope I did not wake you?"

He looked at her for a moment without raising his head from the pillow; then he said in the same low voice: "We've got the money. Bobbo got it, and I can't go to sleep, I don't know what to do."

"How did you get it?" asked Nessa, kneeling down on the floor beside the low bed in order to speak without waking Bobbo. "What made Mr. Plunkett change his mind?"

"Mr. Plunkett didn't change his mind; Bobbo got it the way Winnie said, while Mr. Plunkett was down at supper."

"Do you mean he *stole* it?" asked Nessa in dismay.

"Yes," replied Murtagh. "At least I mean, you know, it isn't stealing really. Bobbo and Rosie say they're quite certain it couldn't be stealing because it's only our own money; papa said we were to have it, and Winnie says she thinks so too." Murtagh was evidently not quite convinced of the truth of his arguments, for he spoke in a persuasive tone of voice.

"Oh, Murtagh, I am so sorry you have done that!" said Nessa, greatly troubled. "It *is* stealing."

"It's our own money though," said Murtagh. "Papa said we were to have one half-sovereign from Mr. Plunkett, and this will be only one; only Winnie and I thought we didn't care about spending it now any more; we thought we'd like to bury it in the island or somewhere. Then we wouldn't have submitted to him tyrannizing; but nobody could say we'd regularly—— You don't think it could be *real* stealing, do you?" he asked, breaking off the other sentence, as though he shrank from saying the ugly-sounding word.

"Yes, I do," said Nessa. "But you will give it back, because, listen, Murtagh—"

"There's Winnie," said Murtagh, who was lying with his face turned to the door.

Nessa turned and saw a little barefooted white figure standing in the middle of the room. It was Winnie, who had overheard Nessa's last words.

"It can't be stealing," she said, coming up to the bedside. "I've been thinking about it ever since we went to bed, and it's our own."

"No," replied Nessa, lifting up one side of her dressing-gown for the little shivering figure to creep under. "It's not your own. You are mistaking. You are doing something that will not be honorable. Listen, I can explain it to you quite plainly. Two new shirts will cost about seven shillings and sixpence, so you gave seven and sixpence to Theresa. That is, you spent seven and sixpence, and now you have only half-a-crown. You have not got a whole half-sovereign; it would be just common stealing to take it. And then, another thing," she continued warmly, "even if it was your own I don't think it is honorable to creep into a person's house to take something when his back is turned; it would be better to lose twenty half-sovereigns. It does not matter if a gentleman loses his rights, but it does matter very much if he stoops to get them back by deceit."

This view was new to the children. They were too firmly entrenched in their own opinion to be convinced in a moment, but their rights began somehow to seem to them small things after all. They tried to reproduce the arguments with which they had convinced themselves; but reasons, excellent before, sounded weak and empty now, and after a faint attempt to defend themselves they accepted Nessa's view.

"Well, we'll give it back to him to-morrow morning," said Murtagh finally. "But if I live to be a hundred years old," he added, "I shall always hate him. He's spoiled every bit of our pleasure; it may be just, but he wouldn't have done it if he hadn't wanted to spite us for throwing the apples in the river."

"Did you throw apples in the river?" asked Nessa. "You see it is such a pity you are naughty. You vex Mr. Plunkett and he vexes you. Couldn't you try to be good?"

"No," said Murtagh, "I can't be good, because as soon as I try he does something that makes us bad again, worse than ever."

"There's one good thing," remarked Winnie, pursuing her own train of thought. "He'll know now that we could have had the money if we had chosen to keep it."

Nessa did not know what to say to them. She only gave a little sigh and said that she thought it was a great pity not to be friends with people. Then she said "Good night" to Murtagh, and under the shelter of her dressing-gown conveyed Winnie back to her little bed.

Murtagh and Winnie apparently broke to the others early next morning the news of the intended restitution, for when Nessa met them at the breakfast-table, Bobbo said to her good-humoredly, in a half-confidential whisper:

"All right; I don't mind; I only said he shouldn't keep it, so I just took it to show him he shouldn't; this way will do just as well."

Rosie was the one who disapproved most highly, for she very much disliked the prospect of giving up their delightful birthday-plan. Her anger was all directed against Mr. Plunkett. Since Nessa said it would be real stealing to keep the half-sovereign, she was willing that it should be given back. She had taken a great fancy to Nessa, and was anxious to stand well in her esteem. But as for Mr. Plunkett, no words could be bad enough for him, she thought. It was all humbug and nonsense about it being just; he didn't care a bit whether it was just or not. He was doing it to spite them and nothing else. So Rosie said to Mrs. Donegan, as the children dawdled through the kitchen after breakfast:

"And how can we manage about the feast?" she lamented. "It's so dreadful to ask people to come, and then tell them they mustn't because we haven't got any money."

" 'Deed if Mr. Plunkett thinks I'm going to stand by quiet and see such a slight put on Mr. Launcelot's children he's mighty mistaken," returned Donnie, her indignation flaming out all anew. "Never you fear, honeys, but ye shall have a feast right enough, and a better one than ever came out of a confectioner's shop, I'll warrant. If that's all ye were going to spend your money on ye shall have ye're money's worth. 'Deed, for the matter o' that, it was Miss Nessa herself came to the kitchen and settled it wid me yesterday. And as for Mr. Plunkett, I don't know where his heart is at all or if he has one, to see yez exposed like that before a parcel of ignorant gossoons that would know no better than to laugh at ye."

"Oh, Donnie!" exclaimed the children in delight, "do you mean you'll give us the things we'll want for them to eat?"

"Just settle amongst yourselves what yez want, and let me know by dinner time. I'll hurry through with my work this morning, and all ye need trouble yourselves is to bring the cart round to-morrow to the kitchen-door."

"You darling old Honey-donnie! Won't it be a sell for Mr. Plunkett?" exclaimed Bobbo, while Murtagh's face lit up joyously, and the little girls began to arrange what they would want.

"Apple-pie and custards I vote for!" exclaimed Murtagh, breaking in upon their discussion; "only let's look sharp about arranging, because Nessa has sent to ask Mr. Plunkett to come to the drawing-room."

"Ye won't let on a word to Mr. Plunkett," said Donnie, who in her secret heart was as much afraid of him as anybody. "The hen that lays the eggs is the best to hatch them."

"You needn't be afraid. We're not likely to have much conversation with him," returned Murtagh with a scornful intonation. "But did Nessa really think about that yesterday?"

"She did so," replied Donnie. "She came in there at the door, and I was whipping the cream here by the table, and 'Donnie,' says she with her sweet-looking way, 'the poor children have got into a great scrape;' and then she told me all about it, and we put our heads together. And if two women can't circumvent Mr. Plunkett," added Donnie laughing, "good Lord! he's sharper than I take him for!"

"How awfully jolly of her!" exclaimed Murtagh; "come along off to the drawing-room, and let's thank her before old Plunkett arrives."

"Oh, ay!" said Donnie, "that's it, and never a word o' thanks for me that'll have all the bother!"

But the children were already rushing off to the drawing-room, and paid not the smallest attention to her complaint.

They were in full flow of enthusiastic thanks and merry plan-making when Mr. Plunkett's step was heard crossing the hall.

"Whisht!" cried Murtagh. "Here comes the man-eater! where's his pill?" Bobbo exploded with laughter, and Murtagh desperately hunting in all his pockets had but just time to find the half-sovereign before Mr. Plunkett entered the room. Nessa feared for a moment that the children were going to turn the whole affair into a joke, but at sight of Mr. Plunkett every sign of laughter vanished from their faces.

Mr. Plunkett turned to Nessa and inquired politely what she wished to speak to him about.

"It is Murtagh who wishes to speak to you," she replied, glancing toward Murtagh to see whether he wished her to explain further. But Murtagh, without any apparent bashfulness, advanced and said with a grave dignity of manner that astonished Nessa:

"I wanted to give you back this. We took it yesterday because we thought you had no right to keep it from us; but now we have been thinking, and you are just, though you needn't have done it." As he spoke he handed the half-sovereign to Mr. Plunkett, and then, determined to say nothing more on the subject, he turned away and left the room.

"I do not understand," said Mr. Plunkett, looking at the coin lying in the palm of his hand. "I never heard of such a thing! What does the boy mean? Did he steal it?"

"No," said Bobbo, turning very red and stammering, for he never could help feeling a little frightened when he was actually in Mr. Plunkett's presence; "I took it because it was Murtagh's own, and it's a horrid shame the way you plague him!"

"Bobbo," said Nessa reproachfully, "you are not polite!"

"Polite! Miss Blair," said Mr. Plunkett, "neither he nor his brother ever are polite. But this," he continued, looking down again at the half-sovereign, "this is more than I expected even from them! I did think they would have hesitated before taking money that does not belong to them. Since it is not so, why I shall for the future be careful to lock up my purse. They are certainly charming young gentlemen!"

The scornful accentuation of the last word flushed the children's cheeks with anger, but for once they controlled themselves, and without speaking went out to rejoin Murtagh.

"Do not be too hard on them," pleaded Nessa, turning to Mr. Plunkett as the door closed behind them. "They thought they had a right to take it. You see how they give it back to you now."

"I do not pretend to be acquainted with their thoughts, Miss Blair, but in my eyes nothing can excuse a downright theft," replied Mr. Plunkett, and he bowed and left the room.

"Ah!" sighed Murtagh on the terrace as the children, joining him, repeated Mr. Plunkett's every word and gesture. "It is too bad the way every plan we have gets spoilt; I did think this one was going to be all right!"

"Well, you know there's one thing," said Winnie, "it has been all right really. About the shirts was our last plan; and we gave back the money when we thought that part wasn't right."

"Yes; but it's all the same, the way things get mixed up. You do one little thing, and then that makes you have to do a lot more. First we took Theresa, that made us want the money; then wanting the money made us give Theresa the shirts to make her happy. Then giving her the shirts made old Plunkett take our money, and that made us take his, and that made us all in a rage, and I don't care about the ceremony or anything now."

"Never mind, Myrrh," exclaimed Winnie. "It's no good making ourselves miserable now. Put it out of your head. That's what I do. I always keep some awfully jolly thing in my mind for thinking about, and then when I have any troubles I think of it instead. My thing now is what the followers will look like when they see the feast spread out. Can't you imagine?—their eyes will get so big, and their faces will get red all over."

"Oh, yes," said Murtagh, "and we must lay it out on the other side of the courtyard wall, so that they mayn't see it at first, because they will be so surprised."

And then forgetting their anger the children talked merrily on, till twelve o'clock ringing out from the stables reminded them that they were hungry.

With the half-crown that remained from Murtagh's money they bought that afternoon the green ribbon which they considered indispensable to the proper celebration of the ceremony; and having employed every spare minute of the day in making evergreen wreaths, they had a last grand singing practice on the island, and went to bed early, so as to make the morrow come quicker.

CHAPTER XVI

"I SAY, WINNIE," called Murtagh dolefully at the door of the little girls' bed-room next morning, "it's an awfully bad day, quite dull and dark, and preciously cold, too. What is to be done?"

"Oh, Myrrh, what a pity!" returned Winnie, getting out of bed and rubbing her sleepy eyes. "Yes," she continued, coming into the passage and climbing on to the high window-sill to look out, "so it is; quite cloudy-looking all over the sky. Well, we had better not stand here in our night-gowns. Let us get dressed quickly; perhaps it will look better out of doors. My teeth are chattering." With a little shiver she vanished into her bed-room, but putting her head out again to exclaim: "Many happy returns of the day! Mind, I was first!" and the next minute an "Ugh! How cold it is!" accompanied by a sound of vigorous splashing, announced that she was in her bath.

In another quarter of an hour all four children were coming down the stairs, their footsteps echoing through the stillness of the house in a ghostly fashion that harmonized with the lingering darkness.

"What a lazy pig that Peggy is!" exclaimed Murtagh, as he opened the door of the school-room and found the shutters still closed. "Not a single one of the down-stair windows open yet, and no fire. Let us go and warm ourselves in the kitchen."

"I wonder what time it is," said Rosie, with a yawn. It was too dark to see the clock as they crossed the hall, but in the kitchen they found the smoldering embers of yesterday's fire, and with the aid of a log of wood and the bellows they soon had a roaring blaze. Then Rosie spied the coffee-pot with some remains of coffee; and Bobbo, who had been to the servants' hall to see if Donnie were there, returned without Donnie, but with a loaf of bread and some butter. Winnie climbed on the dresser and peeped into jugs and bowls till she found milk and sugar, and then they all sat round the fire and made toast and sipped hot coffee till they felt thoroughly warm and comfortable.

"There," said Winnie, putting her last mouthful into her mouth. "Now let us go out and get our wreaths packed in the cart ready for starting. We've got a tremendous lot to do."

"All right," said Bobbo. "I feel very jolly now; only, do you know, when first I got up I did feel so queer and sickish. I thought I was going to be ill."

"So did I," replied Winnie. "How funny! I wonder what it was! Did you feel anything queer, Rosie?"

But Rosie had laid her head down on a log of wood and was sound asleep.

"I say, Rosie! Wake up; what in the world are you going to sleep for? We must set to work if we want to be ready in time," exclaimed Murtagh, and with a push and a little shake Rosie was wakened up again.

Crossing the kitchen the children unbarred the door and went out into the yard. The cold gray light was barely sufficient to enable them to see their way, and the air was very keen.

Murtagh sniffing it said: "I suppose it's pretty early. How nice and fresh everything always smells at this time of the day." But the others seemed to think it more fresh than nice, and shivered as they went along.

There was no one in the haggart where the cart-shed was, so they took out the cart and loaded it with their evergreen wreaths and sheaves of hollyhocks. The wreaths had been soaking in a sheltered little harbor of the river all night, and now, fresh and glistening, they looked so pretty that though the cart was almost full the children unanimously decided to make some more.

"Only let us do it indoors," said Rosie, "I am dreadfully cold." So with many laments over the dreary weather, they carried bundles of flowers and evergreens into the kitchen. Donnie was not there, the fire was blazing up splendidly as when they left it, and they sat themselves down upon the hearth to work in the pleasant warmth. At first the garlands got on fast, but soon Rosie's head went down again on the log of wood, and the flowers dropped out of her hands. Then Bobbo thought he could work much more comfortably lying down; presently his heavy eyelids drooped over his eyes, and though one hand kept tight hold of his wreath the other got somehow under his head for a pillow.

"Never mind," said Murtagh, "let them sleep; you and I must work double."

"What's that striking?" asked Winnie as a stroke rang out from the hall clock.

"One, two, three, four," counted Murtagh. "Oh! we are in very good time; still it's not too early, we have plenty to do."

But notwithstanding all there was to be done Winnie's head began to droop, and she woke herself up with a start presently, only to see that Murtagh was curled up in a ball sound asleep. She made an effort to rouse herself thoroughly, and continued to tie pink and white hollyhocks in among the laurel leaves, proud and delighted to be the only one awake. Soon, however, one of the hollyhock blossoms began to grow larger and larger till it turned into a fairy palace built of rainbows and precious stones, where extraordinary things began to happen; and the end of it all was that when Mrs. Donegan came down at six o'clock she found four children sound asleep among the evergreens.

"Bless their dear little hearts!" she murmured, standing and looking down at them. "May your sleep always be as light-hearted, ye little innocent lambs!" And then for fear they might be disturbed she would not let the maids into the kitchen, but moved about on tiptoe doing herself whatever was to be done.

Theresa came a great many times to the back door to know if the children were coming, but Mrs. Donegan told her to go about her business, she wasn't going to have them awakened; and not till eight o'clock did they stir.

Murtagh woke first; he sat up and rubbed his eyes. The kitchen was an airy south room, and the bright morning sun was pouring in at the big windows. At first he could not understand how he came down there; but then, recollecting, he sprang to his feet with a joyous bound, exclaiming:

"Wake up! Hurrah! it's a glorious day after all!"

"How jolly!" returned Winnie, waking at once but dazzled with the glare of light.

"Why," said Bobbo, sitting up in his turn and rubbing his eyes, "however did it get so sunny?"

"The sun has been lighting the lamps while you were asleep, Master Bobbo, honey," replied Donnie.

"But I've only just been asleep a minute; I just shut my eyes because—" The others began to laugh; but Bobbo insisted, and was getting into hot argument, when the ringing of the breakfast bell announced that any how it was eight o'clock now.

"Never mind, Bobbo, you've only been asleep two minutes if you like!" exclaimed Murtagh racing off. "I feel a great deal too jolly to care twopence;" and the next minute they were all entering the dining-room; where, finding it empty, Murtagh entertained them with an impromptu farce, entitled—"The benefits of early rising."

They did not dawdle long over breakfast that day, but were soon out on their way to the haggart. The followers were eagerly expecting them, and they were received with a shout of welcome.

"Long life to you, Master Murtagh!" burst from about twenty lusty throats. "May ye live to see many another birthday, and each one be happier than the last!" The last part of the speech came from Pat O'Toole. He was a black-haired, blue-eyed boy, older than Murtagh by some three or four years. But perhaps by reason of his small stature—perhaps because of a certain capacity for admiration which he possessed, he always seemed to the children younger than Murtagh, and far from attempting to lead, he was one of their most devoted servitors.

"Thank you!" returned Murtagh heartily, remembering for the first time that he was the hero of the day. "But I don't think any birthday could be happier than this. Did you ever see such a glorious day?"

"It's not likely the sun'd be behindhand in wishin' you good luck," returned Pat O'Toole.

But time was too precious to be wasted in compliments.

"We're all here, aren't we?" said Murtagh. "So now let us get the horse into the cart and be off; oh Gollyloo, to think it's come at last!"

Very soon the horse was harnessed to the cart. Pat Molony, who generally drove it, informed them that he was under orders to bring down a lot of fresh-cut grass from a certain meadow; but he was very good-natured, and when he saw it already loaded with flowers, and was told that they couldn't get on at all without it, he said he supposed they must have it, and he would manage somehow to make excuses to Bland.

"Now then," said Murtagh. "In you get as many as will fit without squashing the evergreens, and let us be off. Gee up, Tommie. Those who can't get in must run behind." And with a crack of the whip and a shake of the reins they started.

Tommie was a good horse, accustomed to heavy loads, so though the ground was rough they jogged away at a very fair pace. And as for there being no spring to the cart, who minded that? The sun was shining over the fields, and, perched as they were for the most part on the high sides of the cart, the children could see for miles around.

Golden stubble, dark hedges crossing and recrossing each other, patches of nut-trees here and there, low stone walls overgrown with moss and fern, and tufts of foxglove; all were equally delightful to them. They passed through picturesque tumbledown villages, where ragged babies were playing among the pigs and donkeys on the strip of grass by the roadside; and people came out of the cabins and wished them good luck, and gave them many a "God bless ye."

Not very many of the children could fit into the cart because of the flowers; but they perched upon the shafts, upon the plank that served for box-seat, upon the sides, where at the corners the position was tenable; and those who could not get a seat at all ran alongside. They jumped up and down by turns, so that none were tired; and though the feet of the runners were bare and dusty their faces were as happy as child-faces can be. Altogether it was a bright cavalcade, that red and blue painted cart full of children, with the strong brown horse trotting along, and the ragged happy escort panting, laughing, and turning somersaults around.

Jokes, laughter, cheers, and nonsense abounded. Before they had gone far Winnie and Rosie had both been presented with bouquets of wild flowers; dirty hands had robbed the hedges of rich clusters of blackberries, dirty lips were smeared with the crimson juice. But no king ever felt more proud of his dominion than Murtagh of his tribe; and truly if loving devotion is to be gloried in, Murtagh was right.

The air was exhilarating, and as they went higher they got among the heathery tops of the hills. Then looking back they could see the sea eight or nine miles off, with a silver mist upon it that gleamed freshly in the morning sun.

"Look back, Winnie! Look back now!" cried Murtagh, as they reached a hill-top from which the view was specially clear. "Did you ever see anything so lovely? See all this purple and gold at our feet, and the sparkling silver away there."

"Yes," said Winnie, turning round and taking a long look. "And to think," she added, with a little sigh, "that papa and mamma are really and truly away over there if only we could see far enough."

"Don't you feel as if you smell the sea?" said Murtagh, throwing his head back to draw in the air better.

"Yes, and the heather," said Winnie, "doesn't it get into you, and make you feel free? Oh, wouldn't it be glorious," she continued, her eyes sparkling and her face lighting up with animation, "if we could live up here really with our tribe, and race over the mountains all day, and live on blackberries, and fraughans, and nuts? To be perfectly free! Oh, Murtagh, just think what a life it would be! We'd have ponies, and ride about for weeks at a time among the hills, and we'd have a secret hiding-place, and be like good fairies to all the villages round. If any one was in trouble we would carry them off and hide them and feed them till the trouble was over, and some day when we got older we would rise and set Ireland free. Oh, I would like to be queen of a tribe, and I'd lead them into battle, and shout 'For Ireland and Liberty!' "

At first no one had paid attention to what Winnie and Murtagh were saying, but as Winnie grew excited she spoke louder, and her last words were received with a general cheer. The children's spirits were rising to such a pitch that they were glad of any excuse for making a noise.

"And we'd follow you to the death, Miss Winnie," cried Pat O'Toole.

"That would we," exclaimed the others enthusiastically. But at this moment their excitement was turned into another channel by an exclamation of "Hurrah, there's our tower!" which came from Bobbo, who was sitting on the shaft driving.

"Our tower" was a very old gray ruin of which scarcely anything remained. There was an enormously thick wall with an archway in it, and a worn flight of steps leading up through the thickness of the wall to a little room above the archway; and that, with the crumbling remains of walls which had once enclosed courtyards, on either side of the archway, formed the whole tower.

"Hurrah!" echoed the others as the cart stopped at the bottom of the slope. "Now then, out with us and to work as fast as we can."

"You dear, dear old mountains, how I do love you!" cried Winnie, throwing herself flat upon the heather, whilst the others were descending from the cart. In another minute the cart was unyoked. Tommie was tethered to a tree, and the children, with their arms full of evergreens, swarmed up the slope and into the tower.

One wild scamper over the heather, a few rolls down the tower slope into the mossy ditch that divided it from the road, a thorough inspection of the tower to see that all was right, and then they set to work in earnest.

Many hands make light work, and soon the old gray walls began to smile under the garlands of pink, and white, and green, with which the children decorated them. Rosie was most useful. She had helped Cousin Jane last Christmas to decorate the parish church, and she had besides a natural gift for such work. She was a capital manager, and anything approaching to a party made her so happy that she was sure to be in the best of humors.

No one could be more charming than Rosie when she tried. She knew by instinct how to please everybody and keep everybody busy. She never told a small child to hang a wreath on a place too high for him to reach. She never wasted the height of tall children by letting them decorate the lower walls. She showed every one how to do things her way, but somehow managed with her pretty thanks to make them feel as though they had done entirely according to their own ideas. She asked every one's opinion, and though she took nobody's unless it was just the same as her own, each was left with a pleasant impression that their plan was certainly the nicest.

It was impossible that any one should be cross under the influence of such a sunny good temper, and the work went on merrily until the last garland was arranged upon the throne they had erected in the centre of the courtyard. Then Murtagh drew Rosie aside to inquire if she didn't think it was time now "to go back to fetch Nessa and the feastables." Rosie thought it was. Everything was ready except the feast, and so with many rejoicings over this most delightful of birthdays, they got into the cart again and rattled home to fetch Nessa. The followers of course stayed behind, and with a light load going down-hill Tommie would take less than no time to get back. Then they would see what Donnie had got for them, and after that there would be only the drive back again between them and the ceremony.

"Three cheers!" cried Murtagh, tossing his hat into the air. "I can hardly believe the time is really come. It seems too good to be true. I don't know which I like best, the ceremony or the feast."

"One's as good as the other, and they're both the most deliciousest plans that ever were invented," said Winnie in ecstasy. "And such a glorious day as we've got. Hurrah for the sun! Hurrah for the mountains! and hurrah for being happy and free!"

"And just think of that old brute, Mr. Plunkett, wanting to prevent us having it," chimed in Bobbo. "What harm does it do him I'd like to know?"

Murtagh's face clouded suddenly, and he muttered something between his teeth. But

Rosie hated to think of disagreeable subjects when she was happy, so she said brightly: "Doesn't the tower look lovely? I never thought we should be able to make it so nice." The conversation went back to its happy strain, and Mr. Plunkett was forgotten.

They drove straight to the kitchen-door and entered, calling out: "Here we are, Donnie; out with the goodies, and let us be off again."

The goodies, as they called them, were out already; and indeed Donnie had fulfilled her promise of giving them enough and to spare. Luckily for them she had more substantial notions than Murtagh of children's appetites, and in addition to the apple-pie and custards there were meat-pies and puddings, cakes, and tarts, and everything else that children were likely to enjoy. Donnie herself was bending over a saucepan at the fire, but she did not look round or make any answer to the children's salutation.

"Donnie, you are a brick!" exclaimed Winnie and Murtagh simultaneously, at sight of the well-covered kitchen-table.

"But how in the world are we going to get all those things packed to take with us?" added Murtagh. "It would be an awful pity to spoil them after you've made them look so nice."

"If you can't pack 'em ye'd better leave them," returned Donnie crossly. "But whatever ye're going to do ye'd better make haste and be out o' this. I can't be having the place overrun with children from mornin' to night."

"Haillo! Below! What's the matter?" inquired Bobbo.

"Matter! Don't be bothering me asking questions about everything. A body can't so much as sneeze but ye'll be asking why she did it. Here, put them in there," she added, coming over to the table and pulling out from under it a large white wicker hamper.

The children knew better than to say much to Donnie when she was in one of her present moods, so Rosie and Winnie began in silence to put some of the dishes into the hamper. However, they had not gone far in their packing before Mrs. Donegan burst out again:

"My good Lord, Miss Rosie! where do you suppose that pie-crust'll be by the time you get up the mountains if you go putting the things one on top of another in that fashion? Here, get out o' this wid yez! I'd rather do it myself." And down she went on her knees beside the hamper.

"Well, I don't know anything about packing. How could I?" replied Rosie rather aggrieved. But Winnie was in too high spirits to stay quiet long. Suddenly snatching off Donnie's cap she transferred it to her own head, and began with a broad imitation of Donnie's brogue to scold the children all round and tell them to "get out o' this."

"Give me back my cap this minute, Miss Winnie! How dare ye behave in such a way?" exclaimed Mrs. Donegan. But Winnie detected a twinkle in her eye that showed she was near laughing, and returned audaciously:

"Well, you just stop being so grumpy, and tell us what's the matter. Here you are!" handing her back her cap. "Cover up your poor old head, and tell us now, what made you turn so sour?"

"Sour indeed! Ye'd be sour enough yerself too if you were worried and bothered the way I am with people writing and sayin' 'We'll be with you to-night,' as if the place was an hotel and a body hadn't enough to do without gettin' dinners and beds ready for all the rabble o' maids and fallalls they'll be bringing along with 'em. Why can't they give proper notice?"

"Cousin Jane!" exclaimed the children in voices of consternation. "It can't be any one else, because you always get in this kind of a temper when she's coming."

"Yes; it is your cousin Jane, and poor little Master Frankie, and Miss Emma, and the Lord knows how many ladies' maids, and governesses, and sich like after them. And they can't give a word of notice; but they're driven across through the mountains for Miss Emma and the governess to be sketching; and they'll be with us to-night. 'Deed they might ha' stopped without us and there'd ha' been no tears spilled."

"Oh, but Frankie!" cried Winnie in delight. "How jolly! Why yes, of course, Nessa told us ever so long ago that they were coming."

"Poor little Master Frankie! He's the only one o' the lot that's worth burying," replied Donnie, softening a little.

"He'll be here to-night, did you say?" said Winnie. "What a pity he didn't come yesterday. He *would* have enjoyed seeing the ceremony. Wouldn't he, Myrrh?"

"Yes," said Murtagh. "And isn't it a pity he can't ever come alone? As for the others—" An expressive shake of the head finished his sentence.

A few more hasty questions as to how and when the new comers were to arrive, and then the children's minds returned to the matter in hand.

"Never mind them now," cried Rosie; "let us get Nessa and Ellie, and be off."

"You are a jolly old Donnie!" said Murtagh; "and we're having such fun! Won't they all open their eyes just when they see what we've got for them!"

"It's lucky you've got the things, I can tell you, for of course Mr. Plunkett must walk in to tell me about this nice little treat of Mrs. William coming, and he couldn't choose any minute of the day but just when I'd got them all laid out here on the table. However, ye've got 'em now, so be off with you," she added laughing. "Here, Peggy, give me a hand with the hampers."

The hampers were heavy, but with assistance from Peggy and the children they were got safely into the cart. A chair was put in for Nessa to sit upon, then the cart was taken round in state to the hall door. Nessa and Ellie were handed in, and away Tommie started once more.

Nessa had not yet been among the hills, so she enjoyed the drive immensely, laughing like a child at the queer equipage and the jolts that threatened at every instant to upset both her and her chair. She was not prepared either for a sight of the sea, and Murtagh delighted in her admiration of it. As they drew nearer to the last turn in the road which hid the tower from their sight, the children's excitement became almost uncontrollable. They had invented an ingenious reason for leaving Nessa at a pretty little spot they knew of, just out of sight of the tower, in order that all might burst upon her as a surprise when they led her up to be crowned; but when they reached the place all their reasons went out of their heads, and they landed her and her chair with no further explanation than an imperious command to "stay here till we come, and be sure not to stir."

Nessa, who had long ago guessed that some wonderful mystery was on foot, merrily consented to stay just so long as it would take to make into bouquets all the flowers she could reach without going round the corner. "After that," she said, "if you keep me waiting I shall come and peep."

"No, no! Whatever you do you mustn't peep!" said the children. "We'll be as quick as *ever* we can." And with happy, excited faces they ran forward, patient Tommie trotting after them.

CHAPTER XVII

AT THE TOWER the followers were eagerly expecting the return of their little chiefs. While the children had been away they had rambled about under Pat O'Toole's direction, and had each brought a beautiful branch of mountain-ash, loaded with scarlet berries, to hold in their hands, and had gathered bunches of white heather. They had added, too, to the decorations by fixing branches of mountain-ash wherever one of the festoons was looped, and they were most anxious to know whether Rosie would approve their taste. She did heartily, and the broad, good-humored faces beamed with delight at her thanks.

Plenty of hands were ready to carry the hampers from the cart to the other side of the archway, but every one was too much excited just now about the ceremony to be able to think of anything else.

A white table-cloth was hastily thrown over the hampers, and the followers were told to wash their feet and hurry on their clean pinafores, which latter had been wisely put on one side in the early part of the day. Then Rosie said, with the branches in their hands they would all look "beautifully alike." But Ellie was to be the messenger who was to summon Nessa, and her shabby little dark green frock was far from suitable to such an occasion. Rosie looked at her in despair for a moment, but only for a moment.

"Quick, quick, Winnie, the needles and thread," she said; and then, while the followers assumed their primitive uniform, she and Winnie tacked a garland of white heather round the hem of the little frock, looped it up shepherdess fashion over the short scarlet linsey petticoat, and placed bunches of white heather on the breast and shoulders with such effect that when Murtagh crowned the child's golden head with a wreath of the same white flowers, Winnie cried in delight: "Oh, Ellie, you do look like a little fairy, so you do."

"All but the boots and stockings," returned Murtagh, surveying her with more critical eyes.

"Tate 'em off," said Ellie, eagerly holding up one foot. "Ellie want to be a fairy."

"The grass'll prick," said Winnie. But Ellie, who had stood like a little statue while they decorated her dress, replied: "Me don't mind. Ellie be a fairy then, and look *so* pretty."

So they pulled off the clumsy boots, and she danced gleefully over the grass, her golden curls falling over her dimpled shoulders, her little white feet and legs twinkling in the sunlight.

" 'Deed it's like an angel right down from heaven she is!" exclaimed more than one of the followers, while Rose, with all the anxiety of a manager, said: "Take care, Ellie; don't shake off your wreath. Now you're to come with us down to there, you see where Nessa is behind the rock, and you're to tell her— What shall we say, Murtagh?"

"Tell her to come and be one of us," replied Murtagh grandiloquently, seating himself upon the throne as he spoke, and taking up his violin.

"You lead Ellie down, Rosie. All you followers follow, and as soon as Miss Nessa comes round the rock, form into two lines for her to pass through, and scatter your flowers. Now begin to sing."

He touched his violin. Winnie's clear voice rose first, then all the others joined in, and the music swelled in harmony as the little procession moved down the slope.

Notwithstanding the sunlight, the flowers, and the gay dresses of the children, there was a something almost solemn in their voices; and little Ellie looked up into Rosie's face with wide-open wondering eyes, as though not at all sure what all this meant.

"Now go," said Rosie, loosing the child's hand as the singing began gently to die away.

With flushed cheeks and the same wondering look still in her eyes Ellie sprang round the rock, and holding out her hand to Nessa she cried earnestly:

"Oor to tum and be a fairy." Then quivering all over with excitement, she added in a tone meant to be reassuring: "Ellie's not frightened. It doesn' hurt."

"No, dear," replied Nessa, taking hold of the little hot hand and keeping it firmly in her own cool fingers. "Only fun for Nessa and Ellie together."

"Yes, *only* fun," said Ellie looking up at Nessa with a sigh of relief. But she clung very closely to Nessa's hand as they came out from behind the rock and were received with a cheer ending in a burst of music.

"How very, very pretty!" exclaimed Nessa, taking in the whole scene at a glance and standing still in admiration.

Almost opposite to them rose the grassy slope with the irregular double file of followers winding down its side. Through their ranks Nessa could see Murtagh sitting, playing his violin on the rough throne they had made. Behind rose the gray ruin wreathed in flowers, and above and beyond all, clear blue sky flecked with sunny clouds spread over the purple hill-tops as far as the eye could reach.

"Tum," said Ellie, pulling her hand; and through the singing children Nessa walked slowly towards the throne. But now little Ellie was not the only one who felt solemnity underlying the play. The children as they sang could not have told how much they were in earnest; their hearts were beating fast, they scarcely knew why, and there was a tone in their voices that filled Nessa with emotion as she passed between them. No one had intended the ceremony to be solemn; it became so without their will.

When Nessa was quite close the music ceased. Murtagh descended from his seat, and with the followers pressing eagerly round to see, Nessa was with due form received into the tribe, and the green ribbon was tied about her arm. Then came the moment for her to promise to hate the "Agents." It was the interesting point, the crisis as it were of the whole ceremony; and there was an almost breathless silence while Murtagh, his voice shaking a little with excitement, said to her: "Will you promise faithfully to hate the 'Agents,' and to defend your tribe against them?"

There was something so curious in this request, made as it was in the midst of those intensely eager faces, that Nessa felt not the slightest inclination to laugh. She looked round the listening circle with a sort of troubled astonishment, and then turning to Murtagh she answered quite gravely:

"No. I do not like hating."

A burst of expressive lament escaped from the crowd. Murtagh looked puzzled and disappointed. He could not make up his mind.

"What shall we do?" he asked at length, turning to the followers.

"Make her princess over us anyhow, Mr. Murtagh. It can't be helped," cried Pat O'Toole magnanimously, and the other followers by their acclamations seconded his request.

"Yes, do! yes, do!" cried Winnie, Bobbo, and Rosie.

Murtagh took the wreath of shamrocks and would have placed it on Nessa's head; but she drew back and said: "No; I do not think I can be your princess."

Murtagh paused with the wreath in his hands too much astonished to speak. Consternation became visible in every face; their ceremony was taking a most unexpected turn.

"Have you promised what you wanted me to promise?" asked Nessa.

"That we have; *sworn* it!" cried the children eagerly, regaining their voices.

"That was what I thought," said Nessa, beginning to unfasten the ribbon from her arm. "That is why I cannot be one of your tribe."

"Oh, stop a minute! stop a minute!" cried Rosie and the children, while Murtagh asked: "What do you want us to do?"

"I want you to undo the promise you have made, and to try never to hate any one," said Nessa resolutely, her cheeks flushing a little, and her eyes dark and bright. "Do you not feel wicked when you hate?"

There was a pause. This was very different from what they had intended, but for the moment Nessa had the little crowd in her power. Pat O'Toole was the first to speak.

" 'Deed and she's right," he exclaimed. "When my paddy's up it's little I care what I do."

"Faix, and it's little good we get by hating them," remarked another of the elder followers.

But to Murtagh himself the question was a more personal one. He was thinking deeply, and seemed at first quite undecided. Then, his whole countenance opening out into a sunny smile, he turned to Nessa and said, "I'll try."

That was all that was needed.

"So will I," said Winnie; and more or less earnestly the promise was echoed by the crowd.

"Then I will be your princess if you will have me," said Nessa. "And shall I give you a *device*,—a motto for the tribe?" she added, hesitating.

"Yes, yes," cried Murtagh. "What is it?"

" 'Peace on earth, goodwill towards men.' Will you have that?"

She looked round with a gentle pleading in her eyes, and then taking off her hat she knelt down on the grass before Murtagh.

"God bless her! God bless her!" cried the followers, and Murtagh's face was white, and his hands trembling a little, as he laid the wreath upon her head.

A chorus of cheers rose from the followers' lusty throats, and in the midst of the echoing hurrahs Murtagh led her up the steps of the throne. The excitement of the children had been growing greater and greater from the moment that Ellie first led Nessa round the rock. During the ceremony they had been obliged to keep it down, but now it burst forth without restraint.

They danced and shouted round the throne like mad creatures, and the more they danced the wilder they grew; each seemed to try and outrival the others in the noise. At last Murtagh, remembering his violin, struck the first notes of the "Shan van Vaugh," and every one found relief in spending upon that the force of their lungs. How they did sing! Their voices rang through the mountain-rocks and were echoed back again. The excitement was infectious; even little Ellie, standing on the throne beside Nessa, sang diligently all the time the only words she knew: "Says de Shan van Vaugh; says de Shan van Vaugh;" and when with a last triumphant burst came the ending lines:

> "We'll pluck the laurel tree,
> And we'll call it Liberty,
> For our country *shall* be free,
> Says the Shan van Vaugh"—

Nessa clapped her hands and cried in delight: "Oh, how pretty it is out of doors! How pretty it all is!"

Almost as she did so a strange voice exclaimed: "Well, children, are you holding a Fenian meeting?" The words were accompanied by a little laugh, but they had the effect of putting a sudden and complete stop to the children's mirth.

Nessa looked round, and standing by the low wall she perceived a lady, who at the moment was engaged in disentangling a floating gauze veil from among the bows and flowers that adorned her bonnet. By her side stood a fashionably-dressed girl of sixteen, whose face wore an expression of amused contempt far from attractive. She did not seem to be aware of the elder lady's difficulties with the veil, and Nessa advanced at once to offer her assistance.

"Or have you quite given up civilized life," continued the lady, with a series of little laughs, "and resolved to live up here with your select circle of friends? I thought you were to have some one to take care of you. How do you get on with the new cousin; eh, Murtagh? Oh, I'm sure I beg your pardon," she added, suddenly perceiving Nessa, and making up for her first oversight by a fixed and deliberate stare.

The color deepened in Nessa's cheeks as she bowed and asked whether she could not help to disengage the veil. But the new-comer continued none the less for that as she bent her head to Nessa's ministrations:

"So you have a new playfellow, children. That must be very nice for you. You have good strong nerves I suppose, and don't mind noise," she added, addressing Nessa. "Well, you are quite right; it's no good having delicate ways and ideas when you have to live with a big family. Those things do well enough where there's only one or two."

At this point Murtagh seemed to think that she had monopolized the conversation long enough, for he now walked up to her, and holding out his hand said gravely:

"How do you do, Cousin Jane? How do you do, Emma?"

The three other children followed his example with automatic regularity, and no social extinguisher could have been more effective. Cousin Jane was completely silenced.

"It is no use our staying here any longer, mamma," exclaimed Emma. "We shall see them all when they are quiet and tidy in the house this evening. We could not imagine," she said, turning politely to Nessa, "what all the noise was. That is why we came up; we left the carriage in the road."

"It is a birthday," said Nessa, smiling as she glanced at the groups of followers, "and we are *en grande fête.*"

"We've got a jolly good feast for them too," said Bobbo confidentially.

"A feast, have you?" exclaimed Cousin Jane. "Oh well, there's a lot of fruit and some lollypops and cakes in the carriage. You'd like them now I daresay as well as any other time; you can make a division. Here, you little fellow," she continued, turning to one of the followers; "do you know how to eat sweeties?"

The little girl addressed put her finger sheepishly in her mouth, and Cousin Jane pulled out of her pocket a large paper of sweeties, which she proceeded good-humoredly to distribute, while Emma turning to Nessa asked if such a noise did not make her head ache?

"No!" said Nessa, "it amused me very much."

"And I daresay you've been accustomed to it," added Cousin Jane. "But I wonder what Ma'mselle would say to such lessons; eh, Emma?"

Emma laughed contemptuously, and Cousin Jane dropping her voice to a confidential tone continued: "You know I'm the only lady they have to look after them at all, so we must have some talks about them. It is quite terrible the way poor Mr. Blair forgets his responsibility. It always has been the way with him; the idea of allowing them to come up here with that pack of dirty children. Nobody in the world but John would do such a thing. And just fancy not having got another governess for them yet, when their last went away more than three months ago. But he's so wrapped up in books, and stones, and pictures, he puts all his duties on one side. If it wasn't for Mr. Plunkett I don't know what would become of the place; that man is the salvation of the estate."

This seemed a fruitful subject to Cousin Jane, for she continued to talk without interruption till the carriage was reached.

Nessa, quite taken aback by the sudden confidence, found nothing to say, and was only glad that the children had careered on in front. Frankie was not in the carriage; he had preferred to drive in the dog-cart with a servant; so it was the affair of a few minutes only to find the basket Cousin Jane destined for the children; and then, somewhat it must be confessed to the relief of every one, the carriage drove on towards Castle Blair.

"Wait till you see Frankie," said Murtagh, turning towards Nessa as the carriage disappeared round the corner. "*He's* not a bit like that."

"I say, Murtagh," called Bobbo from the stream at the other side of the slope where he and Winnie were already disporting themselves, "come and wash your hands, and let us see about unpacking the grub." A hatful of water flung after the invitation proved irresistible; in another minute Murtagh was taking his revenge, and water was flying in every direction.

Suddenly in the midst of the fun a splendid Newfoundland dog bounded through the hedge and over the little stream, fairly upsetting Winnie, and splashing the water over them all.

"In the name of all that's wonderful where do you come from?" exclaimed Murtagh, as Winnie, picking herself up, rushed after the dog, crying: "Oh, you beauty! come here."

A low rippling laugh made both Nessa and Murtagh look round, and in a dog-cart on the other side of the hedge they saw a delicate-looking little boy sitting watching Winnie with delight.

"Frankie!" exclaimed Murtagh springing forward.

"Yes," said Frankie. "How do you do? What are you doing? Was it you making that jolly noise? Have you heard why we've come here? There is such a splendid plan. The doctors say I am to go to the seaside somewhere in the south, and some of you are to come."

Murtagh was busy climbing through the hedge and into the dog-cart, so he scarcely heard what Frankie was saying, but now took his place beside him exclaiming: "How are you, old fellow? Are you any better? Where did you get him? He is such a beauty!" The last words referred, of course, to the dog, whom Winnie had caught, and was now leading back to the stream.

The flush of excitement faded from Frankie's cheek, and he seemed to have some difficulty in getting his breath after the volley of questions he had poured out. In reply to the first part of Murtagh's inquiries he only seemed to shrink into himself, and shook his head. The servant who accompanied him began to assure Murtagh that Mr. Frank was much better, and would soon be quite well now; but Frankie seemed to wish to change the subject, and said hurriedly: "Yes, isn't he splendid! He was given to me, but I've been training him for Winnie. He's no good to me, you know; if he knocks me over I don't get my breath back for a week. But I thought she'd like him. He's as quiet as a lamb unless you set him at anybody, and then he goes at them like—"

"Like an Irishman," suggested Murtagh; but though his words were meant for a joke he looked wistfully at his cousin, wishing to ask more questions about his health. He was very fond of Frankie, and it made him sorry to see the sunken cheeks and wasted hands that told even to childish eyes how ill the boy was.

Frankie nodded and sat silently looking at Winnie and the dog with a pleased smile playing round his mouth.

Winnie had not yet perceived him, and her attention was entirely absorbed by the dog. Both her arms were round its neck, and as she walked along by its side, bending down, she showered upon it every endearing epithet she could think of.

"Perhaps you're lost, and perhaps we won't be able to find your master, however hard we look, and then you'll stay with us; won't you, my beauty?" she was saying when she glanced up and saw Frankie.

Instantly the dog was forgotten, and she flew towards the road, exclaiming: "Frankie! How jolly!"

Frankie laughed again his low, pleased laugh; but having suffered for the rapid questions with which he had saluted Murtagh, he did not attempt to say more than, "Yes; here I am," as Winnie climbed up on the wheel of the dog-cart and pulled down his face to be kissed.

"We're having such fun!" she continued; "get down, and come up to the tower with us." She jumped down herself as she spoke, and threw her arms round the dog, who stood wagging his tail.

"No, I mustn't do that," replied Frankie, looking wistfully at the tower and then smiling again as his eyes fell to the dog standing by Winnie's side. "I only stopped to see what you'd think of Royal."

"You don't mean to say that this beautiful dog is yours!" exclaimed Winnie. "Oh, Frankie, you are a lucky boy!"

"Yes it is," said Murtagh.

"Your very, very own; not your mother's or anybody's?" inquired Winnie, doubtful whether it were possible for any child to possess such a treasure.

"No," said Frankie: "he isn't mine, he is yours."

"Wha—what do you mean?" asked Winnie astonished, the color deepening a little in her cheeks as the dream-like possibility flashed across her mind.

"I mean what I say," repeated Frankie, his face beaming. "He is your very own dog; I have been training him for you, and I've brought him here for you!"

Winnie did not seem able to take it in. The color spread over her cheeks and mounted to her forehead. Her big eyes grew round and bigger, but she did not dare to believe such a thing could be till Murtagh exclaimed:

"Frankie's given him to you. He's your very own, as own as own can be!"

Then a light broke over her face, and tightening the grasp of her arms round Royal's neck she half-strangled him in an embrace, while all she could say was, "Oh, Frankie!"

Frankie seemed well satisfied with her thanks.

Murtagh laughed and said: "She doesn't believe it now."

"Yes, I do," said Winnie, "only it's too good! I can't seem to know it. Oh, Frankie, I think I shall go cracky with gladness!" Suddenly finding the power of expressing her delight she tore up the hill, calling to Royal to follow, and burst upon the assembled children, exclaiming: "He's mine! He's my very own! Frankie's just given him to me!" Then she raced down again like some mad thing, and ran away at full speed over the heather with Royal at her heels. She came back in about five minutes panting and rosy, with her hand upon the dog's collar, declaring that now she could stay quiet; and her brilliant face would have been reward enough for a more selfish person than Frankie.

Frankie stayed only to display some of Royal's accomplishments and to show Winnie's name engraved upon the collar. Then he drove away, leaving their new treasure with the children.

But it was getting to be quite afternoon by this time, and nobody had had any dinner yet, so Murtagh careered up the hill, crying: "Come along now, and let's have scene number two in the entertainment. I feel as if I was quite ready for scene number two. How are you, Winnie?"

Winnie's answer was more expressive than elegant, and then they set to work to unpack the hampers. In a very few moments the white cloth was spread upon the ground and covered with Mrs. Donegan's dainties. The children were in no way disappointed in the pleasure of watching the queer expressions of the followers' faces as dish after dish came out of the hampers. Poor hungry followers! they had had nothing to eat since an early hour that morning, and few of them had ever even seen such things as Mrs. Donegan had prepared. So it is not to be wondered at, that when they found themselves sitting on the grass round that wonderful feast, with free leave to eat whatever they pleased, the event seemed to them really too good to be true.

Winnie was in ecstacy over their pleasure. At first they were too shy to help themselves to anything, but she jumped up and had soon piled some of their plates. Rosie and the boys did the same, and the followers quickly recovered themselves sufficiently to talk, and eat, and laugh.

"Now, whatever more you want you must really help yourselves," cried Murtagh, returning to his place after having gone once round. "I'm so starving that if I don't get something soon I shall eat one of you."

Royal had waited like a perfect gentleman, as he was, till all were helped; but now he gravely poked his black muzzle into Winnie's hand in a manner that said as plainly as any words, "Give me a little cold pie, if you please." He had not to ask twice. Winnie gave him a great plateful of miscellaneous food, and as on the fast emptying plates there began to appear all manner of suitable scraps, a constant cry of, "Here, Royal! Royal!"

kept him racing round the tablecloth. One little girl wished to be very polite, and as he was Winnie's dog thought it better to call him Master Royal. That made the others ashamed of their bad manners, but they soon corrected themselves, and from that day forth he was Master Royal to the followers.

At first there was not very much talking, for all were so hungry they were glad to eat. But when once the edge was taken off their appetites the Irish tongues got loose; and then they chattered, they laughed, they sang snatches of songs, they drank healths in water, and made mock speeches each more ludicrous than the last, till everybody was half-incapacitated with laughter. Murtagh was the soul of the party. Nessa wondered where his words and ideas came from, they flowed out so fast. Seated in state at the head of the table she was very gay and happy. She was unusually amused by this wild, merry crew, and such spirits as theirs were infectious.

The feast over, Royal was with much mock solemnity received into the tribe; a ceremony which he disrespectfully brought to an abrupt ending by knocking over four or five of his sponsors. They then divided into parties, and played robber games among the hills, till the fading light warned them that even the pleasantest of days *will* come to an end. The remains of the feast were divided between the followers. Tommie was yoked into the cart again, and at last to his satisfaction, if to nobody else's, his willing head was turned homewards.

But even then the children were not tired. It was wonderful to see how they caracoled round the cart, and sang and laughed the whole way home; and when, finally, they drove up in state and deposited Nessa upon the hall-door steps, the last cheer they gave her was as hearty as any they had uttered that day.

CHAPTER XVIII

W HILE THE "TRIBE" trotted off in just the same wild spirits to return the cart and horse, Nessa entered the house with a sudden and not pleasant recollection that Cousin Jane was there, and would have to be talked to all the evening.

There was scarcely time to do more than dress for dinner, but she went to the school-room as usual before going up stairs to see if the curtains were drawn and the fire bright for the children. To her dismay she found it full of people. Cousin Jane was sitting by the fire talking to Mr. Plunkett. Emma had taken down some of the lesson-books from the bookcase, and was showing them to Mademoiselle; Frankie, looking tired and excited, was curled in an arm-chair by the window.

"Well, you see we have lost no time," exclaimed Cousin Jane as Nessa entered. "I found Mr. Plunkett, and I have just been talking to him about those children. For poor Launcelot's sake it really goes to my heart to see the state they are in. To think of children of their family and position being allowed to run wild with little beggars and vagabonds! It is quite unheard-of. I have been telling Mr. Plunkett he should keep them a little more strictly. If it were known what associates they have it would be very unpleasant for Emma. But it's always the way when there's no lady in the house to look after things. Don't be offended, my dear," she added, with a little laugh. "You are young, you know; and besides, of course, it doesn't concern you."

Nessa felt very sorry for the children. What Cousin Jane said was perfectly true, it was time for some one to look after them; but instinctively Nessa felt that Cousin Jane and Mr. Plunkett together were likely to prove worse than no one.

"Have they returned from their expedition?" inquired Mr. Plunkett.

"Yes; they have gone to take back the horse and the cart to the stable," replied Nessa innocently.

"I will go to them at once," said Mr. Plunkett, turning to Cousin Jane, "and hear what they mean by taking the horse and cart without my permission; and I will make that ragamuffin crew of theirs clearly understand for the future that if they are found trespassing on these grounds they will be taken up. That will, I think, be the best means of carrying out your wishes. And, indeed, believe me, you cannot feel more strongly than I do the necessity of breaking off the undesirable friendships that exist between these children and the little vagabonds of the village. Something should be done. I feel unfortunately my personal authority to be so vague that I hesitate to act alone, but armed with your permission there are several steps which I should like to take."

Mr. Plunkett had evidently had a long talk with Cousin Jane, and seemed to have thawed a little under the influence of her sympathy.

"We must talk it all over," replied Cousin Jane. "If they are to spend months at the sea with Frankie they must mend their ways. They will find they can't have twenty or thirty dirty followers hanging about my house."

"I feel assured," said Mr. Plunkett, "that stricter measures are necessary, and separated from their disreputable associates you will find that much can be effected."

"I'm sure I don't know what is to be done," said Cousin Jane, with a helpless sort of expression. "All I know is that I should be ashamed for any of our friends to know that there are such children in the family."

"Well, I will go now and have an explanation of their present conduct," returned Mr. Plunkett, moving towards the door.

"Oh, Mr. Plunkett, not now!" exclaimed Nessa, who did not like to interfere, but who pictured to herself only too clearly the kind of scene likely to ensue were he to meet the children in their present state of wild spirits. "They are all so excited now," she added, turning to Cousin Jane, "and when they are excited they say—they do not know what they say—Will you not wait till to-morrow?"

"I'm sure I don't know, my dear; I never had to do with children like these. Let Mr. Plunkett do as he likes."

Mr. Plunkett had stood with his hand on the door while Nessa spoke, but as Cousin Jane answered for him he merely bowed, said a general "Good-evening" and left the room.

He knew the children would be in the haggart, and he walked briskly in that direction. For a minute or two he had debated in his mind whether perhaps it would not be better to leave the matter, as Nessa suggested, till the next day. But he had quickly decided to keep to his own plan. Murtagh's spirit required to be broken. He ought to be humiliated, to be shown that his independent ways could not be tolerated. Nothing short of that would reduce him to submission, and how would he ever learn to bear the discipline of life if he were not taught now to obey? "I am the only person who is in any sort of authority over him," thought Mr. Plunkett, "and if the boy will defy me in this open manner I must show him openly that I am stronger than he."

No better opportunity than this would be likely to present itself for a long time. Murtagh had doubtless boasted before all those children how little he cared whether they took the cart with or without leave, and had probably told how nearly they had been prevented from holding their festival. Mr. Plunkett imagined him laughing over his victory, and that thought decided the matter. He would speak to Murtagh before the whole crew, and he would make the village children understand for their part that he would not have them hanging about the place. His position in the village as well as in the immediate household was affected; and in defence of his own authority it was absolutely necessary for him to speak at once, and show that he was not to be trifled with.

In this frame of mind he arrived within earshot of the haggart. Scraps of song, shouts, and laughter, reached him from time to time; some piece of fun was evidently going on.

The sound of the merriment only strengthened his resolution, and his anger was in no way abated when he stood at the gate of the haggart by seeing Murtagh and Winnie with stable lanterns in their hands standing up together on Tommie's back. They were performing some kind of circus entertainment for the amusement of the assembled crowd; and Royal, as much excited as the children, was apparently endeavoring to leap on the horse's back.

They had collected a quantity of straw lying about the haggart, and had spread it upon the ground in order that they might "fall soft," but at the first glance Mr. Plunkett imagined that they had knocked down part of a corn-rick for the purpose, and he advanced at once toward Murtagh, saying sternly:

"Stop this tomfoolery, sir, and tell me what you mean by destroying your uncle's property in this wanton manner!"

"Destroy my uncle's granny fiddlesticks!" retorted Winnie with a merry peal of laughter. "We're not destroying anything except our own bones. Look out, Murtagh, I'm slipping again." As she spoke she slipped to a sitting position, but Murtagh remained standing, and steadied himself against her shoulder while a smothered laugh burst from the crowd, and one incautious—"It's like his impudence," was distinctly heard.

"I tell you what it is, young gentleman," returned Mr. Plunkett, now thoroughly angry, "your disobedience and impertinence have gone on too long. I am tired of bearing with you, and I will do it no longer. It is time such behavior was stopped, and stopped it shall be in one way or another. Were you aware when you took that horse and the cart to-day that I had given orders for them to be employed elsewhere?"

Murtagh surveyed Mr. Plunkett for a minute from his vantage ground on the back of the horse, and then replied coolly:

"Perfectly aware."

Again an irritating titter ran through the crowd, and Mr. Plunkett answered hotly:

"Let me tell you, then, that for the future when you are aware of my commands you will be wise if you obey them. I have forgiven you often enough, and henceforth every disobedience shall be punished as it deserves. Little boys seldom gain much by setting themselves up in rebellion against their elders."

He paused. Murtagh's face had grown blacker, but he only twirled a straw between his lips, and without speaking looked straight at Mr. Plunkett.

Dead silence reigned for a minute, then Winnie gave a provoking little laugh. Her face was as distinctly visible as Murtagh's, for her lantern rested upon her knee; her eyes were sparkling, her mouth ready to break again into laughter; and as she sat there upon the horse's back, swinging her legs, she seemed to be thoroughly enjoying the scene. She was too much excited to be angry.

At the sound of her laughter Mr. Plunkett continued:

"But I should have thought that even you would have known better than to drag your sisters into such companionship as this."

He pointed as he spoke to the crowd of followers. "If you choose to pick your own companions from among the rabble of the village, you might at least have sufficient gentlemanly feeling to induce you to shield your sisters from the like associates."

"Well, you are polite," laughed Winnie, while Murtagh replied with an angry tone in his voice:

"Don't talk about my friends at all, if you please, unless you can talk more civilly."

"Friends!" returned Mr. Plunkett. "They are certainly charming friends for a young gentleman of your position! But till you learn to choose your society from a different rank you must hold your entertainments somewhere else. For I give you all fair warning," he continued, turning to the troop of children, "that the next time I catch one of you hanging about here I send you off to prison for trespassing."

"You shall do nothing of the sort," retorted Murtagh. "They *are* my friends; real, true friends, who love me, and who would do anything I told them to. Aren't you?" he added, appealing to the followers.

"That are we so!" they cried with one voice, while Murtagh continued:

"I am proud of them; they are honest and real. They love me, and I love them. What do we care about positions? They shall come here when they please, and you are not to insult them."

He drew his figure up to its full height, and delivered the last words with authority. They were received with a hearty shout by the excited followers; and as soon as Mr. Plunkett's voice could be heard above the noise, he replied with some irritation:

"Don't talk to me in such a ridiculous manner, sir. I shall do whatever seems to me to be proper; and I am not joking about this matter. If I ever again find such a dirty, disreputable crowd assembled on your uncle's premises, every member of it shall be taken up for trespassing. Whether you are invited by Mr. Murtagh, or whether you are not," he added, turning again to the crowd. "And further, unless you wish me to call a policeman now, you had better go away to your homes as fast as you can."

The followers huddled silently together not knowing what to do, but Murtagh burst out angrily:

"How dare you? Do you know what you are doing? Do you know that if I chose to tell them they would take you and duck you in the stable pond."

At the words there ran through the crowd an eager movement which made Mr. Plunkett remember thankfully that he had on one of his oldest coats. Twenty to one were unfair odds, and some of the twenty were strongly-built boys; however, he answered coldly:

"When you speak to me in such a manner I think you forget the difference of age between us, and the position in which I stand towards you. Such unseemly outbursts only serve to prove that the society you have chosen is not likely to fit you for the career of a gentleman, and leave me no alternative but to take by force the obedience you will not render willingly. I give you two minutes to clear this haggart. If it is not empty at the end of that time you and your sisters shall be taken home, and I will settle the matter my own way with this rabble."

As it happened two of the night police walked up to the gate while he was speaking and looked into the yard. Mr. Plunkett signed to them to enter, and continued significantly: "You see my words are not vain. I mean what I say. Choose your own course."

Murtagh saw that he was overpowered; he had no choice but to obey. The sense of being baffled and defeated by mere armed force was very bitter, and all the roused passion within him burst forth as he answered:

"Yes; you have conquered this time because you have got grown-up men to help you, and they are stronger than us. But you shall see I *will* be free. If you fight with me you will get the worst of it. I will receive my friends wherever I please, and you had better not dare to interfere with me again. I tell you when you do it it makes me feel as if I could kill you."

"That's right, Mr. Murtagh; an' it would be a good riddance to the country the day ye did it," shouted hot-headed Pat O'Toole, who could no longer contain his indignation.

Almost before the words were out of the boy's mouth Mr. Plunkett's hand was on his collar, and some sharp blows from Mr. Plunkett's cane repaid the speech. An angry murmur ran through the crowd. Murtagh sprang from the horse's back and threw himself between them, receiving upon his face and head a part of the swiftly-descending shower of blows. For a moment there was a confused struggle. Bobbo tried to make his way to the rescue. Winnie had risen to her feet, and with flashing eyes she called: "At him, Royal; at him!"

The great dog bounded forward, seized Mr. Plunkett's coat-sleeve in his teeth, and the next minute Murtagh and Pat were standing side by side defiantly facing Mr. Plunkett.

Murtagh's face was even whiter than usual, and across one cheek a dark red stripe showed where the cane had struck him.

"Come," he said, turning to the tribe. He led the way to the gate, and they followed him slowly, the dog holding Mr. Plunkett immovable the while.

Only Pat O'Toole did not stir. He stood facing Mr. Plunkett. From the gate Murtagh called to him. Then he turned and followed the others, but before leaving the yard he stopped, and shaking his fist at Mr. Plunkett, he exclaimed passionately:

"You shall repent this evening's work; ye haven't struck Pat O'Toole for nothing."

"Come, Royal; loose him, good dog!" cried Winnie. The dog trotted after them, and the whole troop of children disappeared into the darkness.

CHAPTER XIX

THAT EVENING Cousin Jane's proposal to take Winnie and Murtagh with her to the south of England was discussed, and of course accepted. She intended to spend a few days at Castle Blair, and to start on the first of November.

Frankie was in a state of exceeding delight at the prospect, and was eager to talk over the plan with his little cousins. But the bright red spots upon his cheeks and the feverish brilliancy of his eyes, drew many anxious glances from his mother, and she coaxed him not to wait up for them. "Every one was tired with traveling," she said; so the drawing-room party dispersed at an early hour.

Nessa was glad to be free, for though every one else had completely forgotten the children's immediate concerns, she was anxiously wondering what had been the result of their interview with Mr. Plunkett. She went at once to the school-room and found that the children had come in. They had had their tea. Rosie and Bobbo were lolling by the fire discussing the events of the day. Royal was lying curled up on the hearth-rug, and Winnie had made a pillow of his body, but she was silent. Murtagh was at the piano composing a battle piece.

He ceased as Nessa entered, and threw himself into his favorite position on the floor near her chair.

"Have you seen Mr. Plunkett?" she asked.

"Yes," said Murtagh in a tone that meant he was not going to say any more.

"And he was just as impudent as usual," added Winnie, sitting up as she spoke, and pushing back her hair. "But he got the worst of it this time, thanks to Royal."

"Oh, Winnie, what have you done?" asked Nessa.

"Well, we were only amusing ourselves and not hurting anybody, and he came up and began worrying as usual," returned Winnie, somewhat defiantly answering the tone of Nessa's voice. "And besides, he had no business to talk like that before all the followers."

Murtagh's face softened a little as he looked at Nessa's. "Tell her just what we did if she wants to know," he said.

"Oh, dear!" sighed Winnie. "What *is* the good of going all over it again? I'm sure he's bad enough when he's here without bothering about him when he's not here."

"Well, but it served him right," said Bobbo; "I only just wish Royal had given him a good bite." And beginning at the beginning Winnie told the whole story as nearly as possible as it happened, neither exaggerating nor omitting anything. Murtagh watched Nessa's face in the mean while to see what she thought of it. She did not look at him, and she listened in perfect silence till Winnie ended her recital.

"Oh, I am so sorry," she said; then looking round to Murtagh, "so very, very sorry. How could you do it?"

"Why shouldn't we do it?" asked Winnie. "He had no business to talk to us like that."

"You will only make him more and more angry with you now," said Nessa regretfully. "And then," she added, "it is wrong; it is very wrong; you must not be angry with me for telling you so, for it is only true, and makes me so sorry."

The children were silent for a moment, and then Murtagh said:

"But I can't help it. He puts me in such a rage."

"Yes," said Nessa, "but I will tell you honestly what I think. I think you ought not to let yourself be put so easily in a rage. It is not worthy of you; you could do better than that. Listen, what you have done to-day. When we were on the mountain you promised to try to be gentle and kind. You promised all together—the whole tribe—but you were the chief. And the chief ought to watch over his followers, oughtn't he? He ought to see that they keep their promises, and he ought to try to keep them out of trouble. But you did not do that; you came down from the mountain where you promised, and you broke the promise yourself, and you made all the others break it too. Now Mr. Plunkett will be angry with them all, and Pat O'Toole will be in trouble."

The defiant look faded out of Winnie's face, and Murtagh looked abashed as for the first time he remembered the promise he had made that morning.

"I quite forgot," he murmured.

"I did not think you would have forgotten so soon," said Nessa.

That quiet reproach was more bitter to Murtagh than any scolding.

"I did not mean to," he said; "I did mean to remember it always; always. But he makes me forget everything. Oh, how I hate him!"

The last words burst out passionately, and he knelt upon the hearth-rug with flashing eyes.

"I don't think that's having 'Peace and goodwill,' " remarked Rosie.

"I *can't* help it," said Murtagh in despair, looking up at Nessa; "that's just how it always comes. But I will do anything you tell me. I will—beg his pardon if you like, because I was in earnest. I did mean to remember."

"Oh, Myrrh!" remonstrated Winnie, who thought that his repentance was really carrying him beyond all reasonable bounds.

Nessa looked at him compassionately. She had never hated any one in her life, but she had often loved, and she felt as if she loved Murtagh very much just then in spite of all his faults.

"Poor Murtagh!" she said. "Perhaps it will not always be so difficult."

Murtagh looked at her with a sad wistful expression for a moment, and then he quietly dropped back again into the dark corner beside her chair.

No one spoke for a minute or two. Then Winnie returned to the subject that seemed to have disturbed her. "But you don't want Murtagh to beg his pardon, do you?" she said. "Because you know he couldn't really, of course."

"Yes, I can," came in a low resolute voice from Murtagh's corner.

"Can you? Can you really?" asked Nessa. To tell the truth she would not have liked to do it herself.

Bobbo and Rosie looked with eager curiosity towards Murtagh. They could not believe he was in earnest. But Winnie burst out again before he had time to answer: "Myrrh, you can't! You don't know what you're saying. Go and beg his pardon! That old scurmudgeon, who has always worried us from the very first day we came here!"

No words can convey the opprobrium that Winnie contrived to throw into her pronunciation of curmudgeon; the one letter she added to it expressed more than a whole volume of epithets. Murtagh's answer did not come at once, but after a moment's silence he said steadily: "Yes, I am almost sure I can."

"If you can," said Nessa, "it is the very best thing you could do. Because," she continued, seeing Winnie ready to burst out again, "it is not only for you, it is for your friend Pat. Uncle Blair has told me such dreadful things of the people about here. And perhaps it is very foolish of me, but Pat is a big boy, and if he does not forgive Mr. Plunkett he might really try to be revenged; and then if—if anything dreadful happened, it would be your fault too."

That was the first idea that had occurred to Nessa on hearing of Pat's threat. She had been so much impressed by all that she had seen and heard since her arrival that she could not help feeling as though they were living in the midst of barbarians, and she constantly dreaded some fresh disaster.

"If Murtagh does it I'll do it too," said Winnie, reflectively. "I'm not going to let him do it alone. But I don't think we can, all the same."

The next morning, however, just as Nessa had finished dressing, there came a knock at her door, and Murtagh and Winnie entered.

"We've come to tell you," said Murtagh, "that we will do what we said."

"Oh! I am so glad!" she cried joyfully. Then as she kissed them, she added, "Good morning; I think it is very good of you."

"Then after, I'll go and find Pat and make him apologize too," said Murtagh.

"Yes do," said Nessa, greatly relieved, for her night's reflection had not in the least diminished her nervous fears. At that moment the breakfast-bell ringing loudly summoned them to the dining-room, and in the corridor they were met by Cousin Jane. Her arms were full of presents that she had brought for them all, and while she was displaying them Frankie came out of his room. He began eagerly to tell of the seaside plan; the children were perfectly delighted at the prospect, Cousin Jane was pleased with their pleasure, and they were all entering the dining-room in a merry mood, when Brown, with a solemn face, informed Murtagh that Mr. Blair desired he would step into the study.

"What's up? What's the matter?" cried Murtagh and Frankie together, and Cousin Jane also asked, "Has anything happened, Brown?"

"Yes, Madam," returned Brown, who evidently desired nothing better than to tell the news. "The Red House was set fire to last night, and one of the children, they say, nearly killed. The flames were put out quickly, and this is the first we've heard of it up at the house. But it was no accident, Ma'am. It began in the hay-yard, and when the flames burst out Mrs. Plunkett jumped out of bed to see what it was, and there was a boy"—here Brown hesitated a little and glanced at Murtagh—"about as big as Master Murtagh, standing in the road, but the minute she came to the window he turned and ran."

A smothered exclamation from Murtagh caused them all to glance at him. He and Winnie were looking at each other in dismay; the same thought was in both their minds. "Had Pat already taken his revenge? If he had it was all their fault." For the first moment they were too much startled to think of anything else; the next, they had remembered that if it were one of their followers they must at least do their best to prevent suspicion falling upon him. Murtagh tried to recover himself; Winnie slipped her hand into his, and endeavored also to look unconcerned. But Mr. Plunkett could not have chosen a worse moment to make his appearance.

Before any one else could speak his voice was heard, strangely hollow, and yet more stern than usual, saying: "Be so kind as to come this way at once, sir."

Winnie did not let go Murtagh's hand as he entered the study. Cousin Jane's curiosity was aroused, and she made no scruple of pressing in with Frankie, so Nessa entered with the rest.

Mrs. Plunkett was there. Mr. Blair was sitting by the writing-table, looking graver than Nessa had ever seen him. He seemed not to see any one but Murtagh and Winnie. As they approached his chair he fixed his eyes upon Murtagh, and said:

"Tell me, Murtagh, all that you know about the burning of the Red House."

Murtagh was still very white, but he answered straightforwardly:

"I do not know anything at all except what Brown has just told us."

"What did he tell you?" inquired Mr. Blair.

"That Mr. Plunkett's haggart was burnt, and the fire spread to the house, and one of the children was hurt, and—" But here Murtagh's voice faltered and he stopped.

Cousin Jane began to have an inkling of what was the matter.

"Tell the truth, Murtagh," she exclaimed. "What else did he tell you?"

Murtagh glanced at Mr. Blair in hopes that he was satisfied, but his face wore an expression of stern expectancy that compelled Murtagh to continue. "And," he said, "that when Mrs. Plunkett looked out of the window she saw a boy standing in the road."

"And did he tell you nothing else?" inquired Mr. Blair.

"No," said Murtagh, beginning to feel really puzzled at his uncle's strange manner.

"He did not tell you who that boy was," continued Mr. Blair.

"No," exclaimed Murtagh with eager interest. Perhaps it was not one of his followers; perhaps he had been frightening himself without a cause after all.

His uncle looked at him for a moment, and then answered:

"Murtagh, it is useless to keep up this deception any longer. Mrs. Plunkett says *you* are the boy she saw."

Murtagh's nerves were already strained, and for one instant he was completely overcome by so unexpected an accusation. The color rushed to his cheeks, and his eyes filled with tears; but in a moment he was himself again, and raising his head proudly, he replied:

"Mrs. Plunkett is mistaken. I was not there, and I know nothing whatever about the fire."

Then he turned and would have left the room as was his fashion when offended with Mr. Plunkett. But his uncle said: "Stay, Murtagh, this is a very serious matter, and it is better for you to hear all the evidence against you." There was a kinder tone now, however, in Mr. Blair's voice, and the proud look died a little out of Murtagh's face as he again took up his place by the corner of his uncle's table.

Mr. Blair paused, and while the silence lasted Murtagh's eyes sought Nessa's. She had been watching him during the whole scene, and now such a look of trust and encouragement beamed upon him that for a moment he almost forgot his trouble in the pleasure of receiving it.

"Mrs. Plunkett," said Mr. Blair at length, "will you be so kind as to tell us now exactly what you saw when the flames first wakened you?"

"I saw just what I told you," began Mrs. Plunkett in her nervous hurried manner; "the haggart all in flames, and on the road where the flames were, Murtagh was standing. You know you were, Murtagh. It's no use denying it; you had on that very gray jacket you have on now, and when you saw me you turned and ran away as fast as you could. And then I woke Mr. Plunkett," she continued, turning to Mr. Blair; "and all the servants, and he went down to see what could be done, and out on the road he found this; but perhaps Murtagh will deny that this is his name." As she spoke she took up a dirty pocket-handkerchief which lay on the table beside Mr. Blair, and showed "Murtagh Blair" written in clear letters in one of its corners.

At Mrs. Plunkett's mention of the gray jacket Winnie and Murtagh mechanically turned their eyes to Murtagh's coat, and as they did so a remembrance suddenly flashed across them that yesterday Pat O'Toole had worn a gray jacket which was not at all unlike Murtagh's. Each looked at the other; the truth was becoming too clear to be doubted any longer; and the sight of the handkerchief only confirmed their fears. It had been used as a towel yesterday by the followers, and had probably remained in Pat's pocket. Murtagh saw that Winnie had no longer any doubt, and the knowledge of her conviction made his own only the more certain.

What was to be done? It was all his temper that had brought Pat into this scrape, and now every word he said in his own defence would be a means of preventing the boy from escaping the consequences. Escape he should, Murtagh was resolved upon that. He did not know the exact punishment for the burning of hay-ricks, but he had heard such accidents talked of often enough to know that they meant at the very least prison and disgrace for the offender. To shield Pat now was all that he could do. And yet he had to fight hard with the proud indignation stirred up in him by being falsely accused. It was not pleasant to let Mr. Plunkett triumph.

He stood in silence struggling with his thoughts, till his uncle asked: "What have you to say in answer to Mrs. Plunkett?"

Then a rush of anger almost overwhelmed every other feeling, and though he squeezed Winnie's hand as a signal to her not to speak he answered with sullen pride: "I said before I was not there."

His evident perplexity, his glances at Winnie, his anger, were all against him, and Mr. Blair replied coldly: "I shall be very glad, more glad than I can tell you, if you can clear yourself from this charge. But if you cannot, at least make a manly confession; this flat denial is childish."

Murtagh remained silent. Winnie's cheeks flushed, and words trembled on her lips. She could not bear Murtagh to be treated in this manner. But again the warning hand squeezed hers; she looked at Murtagh and was silent. If only she had had nothing to do with exciting Pat then she might have spoken. As it was she felt that she had no more right than Murtagh to say a word, and though she could have cried with perplexity and vexation she was forced to be silent.

Her uncle saw her half-movement, and said sadly, as though not liking to abandon his hope of drawing a confession from Murtagh himself: "Can you tell us anything of this matter, Winnie?"

Winnie bit her lips, and looked straight in front of her, with her eyes open to their very widest; it was her way of keeping back tears, but she only shook her head.

Cousin Jane's patience could bear no more.

"Really, John," she exclaimed. "I don't know how you can go on bearing with those children's sulkiness. Make them tell out what they know. It's plain to everybody in the room that they are guilty, and if they have anything to say for themselves let them say it out."

An expression of annoyance passed quickly over Mr. Blair's countenance, but he replied very gently:

"You must let me manage this matter in my own way, Jane."

"Mr. Plunkett," he continued, as Cousin Jane relapsed into indignant silence, "tell us now, if you please, before Murtagh, what you have already told me of his behavior yesterday evening."

Mr. Plunkett gave a short, business-like account of what had happened in the haggart the evening before. It was perfectly accurate; he did not try to slur over the fact that he had struck Murtagh. He said that he regretted the blows which had been meant more for one of the ragamuffins than for Murtagh: and somehow even that, which every one felt Mr. Plunkett had no right to inflict, told against Murtagh, for it furnished an additional motive for his revenge. The dark red mark was plainly visible across his cheek, and it seemed, indeed, a blow which a high-spirited boy was not likely to have received quietly. Only one thing in the story was omitted. Mr. Plunkett had forgotten Pat O'Toole's threat.

"Can you deny any of this?" asked Mr. Blair, as Mr. Plunkett ceased.

"No," replied Murtagh, "it is all quite true."

"But," said Winnie eagerly, "it shows Murtagh couldn't have set fire to the place, because we were very sorry after, and Murtagh was going to have told Mr. Plunkett so this morning."

"Were you, Murtagh?" said Mr. Blair.

"Yes," said Murtagh shortly.

Mr. Blair looked toward Mr. Plunkett to see what he thought of that, and Mr. Plunkett replied drily:

"Murtagh has never done such a thing in his life. I must be excused if I do not believe him."

The angry black look that Nessa had so often seen, spread over Murtagh's countenance. He made no answer, but Nessa said at once: "I know he was going to do that."

Her words seemed to strengthen a pleasant conviction that was growing in Mr. Blair's mind, for though he did not look at her the sound of her voice brought a quiet little smile to his lips which did not altogether die away again.

Mr. Plunkett replied in the same dry tones: "The main point of evidence against Murtagh is contained in the fact that Mrs. Plunkett saw him close to the burning haggart at the time of the fire."

"You are quite sure that it was Murtagh?" asked Mr. Blair, turning to Mrs. Plunkett.

"Oh, I'm quite sure," she replied. "I saw his black hair and his gray jacket as plain as I do now."

"But not his face," suggested Mr. Blair. "If he turned and ran away so quickly you could hardly have had time in that uncertain light to make sure of the face."

"If I was on my dying bed I'd swear it was Murtagh," returned Mrs. Plunkett almost in tears.

"And this handkerchief," said Mr. Plunkett, "how did it come in such a place?"

"Yes, Murtagh," said Mr. Blair. "How do you account for this?"

Again Winnie found the temptation to speak almost too strong for her, but Murtagh's hand was holding hers like a vice. Her own sense of right told her she must not, and she only looked more blankly than ever in front of her as Murtagh answered: "I don't know."

His uncle looked puzzled and displeased. Cousin Jane exclaimed: "I told you so; the truth's plain enough to any one who chooses to see it."

Mr. Plunkett felt quietly triumphant. He was fully persuaded that Murtagh had done this, and he was determined to bring it home to him.

But Nessa had guessed the truth from the beginning, and it was now her turn to speak.

"Uncle Blair," she said, earnestly, "I am quite sure Murtagh has not done this. I think it is another person."

Her uncle looked towards her with surprise. An expression of impatience, instantly repressed, crossed Mr. Plunkett's countenance.

"Why, my child?" said Mr. Blair, "what can you know about it?"

"Do you not remember," she said, turning to Mr. Plunkett, "at the end, before they went away, Pat O'Toole said he would be revenged because you struck him?"

"Pat O'Toole!" exclaimed Mr. Blair. "Why, Plunkett, you forgot to mention this."

"I am sorry," replied Mr. Plunkett, feeling annoyed with himself for not having been strictly business-like. "I mentioned that I thrashed a boy, but I did not know his name, and I paid little attention to the threat he uttered at the gate. The incident seemed to me to have no importance."

"But," said Nessa, a little disappointed to hear by Mr. Plunkett's voice that his conviction was unshaken, "this boy does not look much bigger than Murtagh; he has black hair too, and I think he had a gray jacket yesterday. Mrs. Plunkett might easily have been mistaken. She saw him only for one moment. And, besides," she continued, turning towards her uncle, and suddenly lighting up as she sometimes did, "Murtagh could not have done it. He would not have done it. Only one of those people would have done a thing so cowardly and so cruel."

"I think you are right, my dear," said her uncle gravely. "Plunkett, this alters the affair," he said, turning to Mr. Plunkett. "I can do no more till I see this boy. Will you send for him? I should like to speak to him immediately after breakfast. You may go now," he added, speaking to Murtagh. "I shall want you again by-and-by. You are of my opinion, are you not, Plunkett?"

"No, sir," replied Mr. Plunkett firmly. "I cannot say that my opinion is in any way altered. But it is advisable to leave no point disregarded."

Murtagh was in despair at the new turn affairs were taking. In his simplicity he had never thought of Nessa guessing too who was really guilty, and now he did not know how to prevent Pat from being found out.

"But Pat's four years older than me," he stammered, "and he's not a bit like me; is he, Winnie?"

His defence was weak and hesitating, and he scarcely dared to look up.

Mr. Plunkett was looking at him coldly. "I quite agree with you," he said.

As they left the room Frankie hurried to seize Murtagh's arm, exclaiming: "I say, Myrrh, old fellow, what a shame!" But his mother, contrary to her wont, contradicted him flatly.

"You don't know anything about the matter, Frankie," she said. "I'm sure if you were as naughty as your cousins it would break my heart. But, indeed, it is no wonder," she continued, addressing the society in general, "considering the way that Mr. Blair treats them. A thorough good whipping would do them all the good in the world."

The remark was uttered on the threshold of the study, so Mr. Blair heard it, of course; but he only looked at Nessa with one of his quaint smiles, and asked her to come to him after breakfast.

CHAPTER XX

T HE NEWS OF THE FIRE had by this time spread all over the house, and Rosie and Bobbo were waiting in the passage eager to know what was happening in the study. They seized upon Murtagh the instant the door was shut and inquired what was the matter, but while Frankie answered them Murtagh whispered something to Winnie.

"I'll come too!" she exclaimed in answer, and pushing the others on one side they ran away together.

"It will all come out now," said Murtagh despondingly, as soon as they were out of hearing; "and the only thing to be done is just to let him know what's coming."

"Yes," said Winnie with a sigh, and then they ran alongside of each other in silence till the O'Tooles' cabin came in sight.

"I say, Win, what do you think they'll do to him?" asked Murtagh, stopping to take breath, and feeling, now that he was so close, as if he would rather do anything than tell Pat he was discovered.

"I don't know," replied Winnie; "something dreadful I expect, because you see the fire spread to the house and it's burnt too. And, Myrrh, I wonder which of the children it is that's hurt. Supposing it was to die!"

"And it is all our fault!" said Murtagh.

They looked at each other for a moment in silence, but the thought was too dreadful; they could not face it. Quickening their footsteps they soon stood within the cottage.

Mrs. O'Toole was crouching over the fire, but she started up on their entrance, and they asked at once for Pat.

"What is it ye want with Pat?" she inquired, by way of answer.

"We want to talk to him about something; there's no time to lose!" replied Murtagh.

"Sure ye can leave your message with me. Is it about them night-lines he was settlin' for yez?" suggested Mrs. O'Toole.

"No, no," returned Murtagh impatiently; "I must see himself. Is he inside?"

"Sit down, yer honor, and have a bit of griddle cake," said Mrs. O'Toole, wiping a stool with her apron; "maybe he'd be in in a minnit. It's the whitest flour I've had this long time."

"No, thanks," replied Murtagh, "we can't wait; we must go and try to find him."

Out they went accordingly to the village, where he was generally to be found lolling on the grass by the roadside, minding the goat and playing marbles. They searched a long time in the village and up and down the road but they could not find him, and one of his usual playmates at last volunteered the information that Pat had not been out this morning. Mrs. O'Toole had been down herself to milk the goat, and she had told them that Pat was ill in bed.

"Ill in bed!" exclaimed Murtagh. "Then perhaps—Oh, Winnie, come along; we'd better go back."

"Mrs. O'Toole!" he exclaimed, as they once more entered the cottage. "What made you tell us Pat was out, when he's ill in bed?"

"Sure, Mr. Murtagh, honey, I never said he was out; heaven forbid! I only said maybe he'd be in in a minnit."

While he was speaking Murtagh crossed over without ceremony to the door of the little inner room. But Mrs. O'Toole started up and threw herself between him and it, exclaiming:

"Ye can't go in there, Mr. Murtagh! The place is not cleaned up at all. It's not fit for a gentleman like ye!"

"I tell you I must speak to Pat!" persisted Murtagh with his hand on the latch.

"But ye mustn't, Mr. Murtagh, dear!" cried Mrs. O'Toole, her voice growing strangely eager and imploring. "I tell ye ye mustn't. It's the infection he's got; he's down with the small-pox!"

"As if I cared twopence for the small-pox," replied Murtagh, impetuously bursting open the door as he spoke, and springing towards the press bed where Pat generally slept.

But the room was empty! and the bed had not been slept in that night.

Murtagh turned to Mrs. O'Toole more for a confirmation of his worst fears than for an explanation. But she, poor woman, seeing that no concealment was possible, had thrown her apron over her head and was rocking herself backwards and forwards in an agony of tears.

Tears came to Winnie's eyes too, as she stood and looked at her. There was no need to ask any question; but after a minute Murtagh said, half-reproachfully: "You needn't have told any lies to *me*, Mrs. O'Toole."

"Oh, Mr. Murtagh, asthore, don't betray us!" was her only answer. "It's my only son; the only one ever I had!"

"Where is he?" asked Murtagh, in a choked voice.

"He's gone away! He's gone away!" replied Mrs. O'Toole, drawing a bit of paper from her breast. "Oh, Pat, my darlint, whatever made you do it?"

Neither Murtagh nor Winnie dared to say a word. Murtagh took the bit of paper in silence, and Winnie looking over his shoulder read: "Mother, I've done it, and I'm gone away for ever! Good-by; God bless ye!"

"For ever! for ever! an' he was the only one I had," repeated the poor woman. "Oh," she cried, "may the curse of heaven and hell rest upon him that provoked him to it! They say he bate the boy last night. He's been a blight an' a curse upon the country since the day he first set foot in it; but I pray to God Almighty above us it may come back upon his own head."

"Oh, don't," said Murtagh: "it was all us. And do you know," he added, as the consequences of his temper pushed themselves one after the other upon his mind, "one of Mr. Plunkett's children was hurt in the fire too?"

"Know, ay I know," she replied fiercely. "It's his eldest too; the one they say he do care for a bit; and I've been prayin' ever since it may die, an' let him feel what it is to be robbed o' your child. Oh, my Pat! my Pat!" she sobbed out, suddenly bursting again into tears and forgetting all her fierceness.

"Listen," said Murtagh, in the greatest distress. "Let us think what we are to do. He's going to be sent for in a minute to be examined. That's what we came down to tell him."

"Is it discovered already he is?" she cried, full of a new fear. "Oh, if they catch him and bring him back to prison! Mr. Murtagh, ye won't betray us; Miss Winnie, asthore? Ye're only children, but ye won't say a word?"

"You needn't be afraid," cried Winnie and Murtagh together. "They won't get a word out of us."

"But," continued Murtagh, "how will you manage?"

"God bless yez, God bless yez," she answered warmly. And then in a different tone: "Let me alone for bamboozling the polis if they come here after him. All he'll want will be a couple of hours. If he gets till this evening never a man o' the polis will lay a hand on him."

The words were scarcely out of her mouth when a shaking of the rickety garden-gate told that some one was coming. There were only five or six steps from the gate to the cottage, and the next instant Mr. Plunkett himself stood upon the threshold.

The children glanced in despair round the room, thinking that the confusion which prevailed would surely betray something. But as if by magic everything had returned to its usual condition, the bedroom door was shut, Mrs. O'Toole's cap put straight, and she was bending over the fire stirring something in a saucepan. The children alone were confused, for while they started and blushed Mrs. O'Toole said calmly, as though in continuation of a sentence:

"I tell you, Mr. Murtagh, honey, he went out early to the bog with his father to cut peat, an' the father said maybe they'd be in to dinner and maybe they wouldn't."

"Are you speaking of your son?" inquired Mr. Plunkett, looking with suspicion at Murtagh and Winnie.

Mrs. O'Toole turned round in well-feigned astonishment at the new voice. She could not altogether repress the scowl that gathered upon her face, but she dropped a respectful curtsy as she answered:

"I am, yer honor."

She had said truly enough, that they might let her alone for bamboozling whoever came after Pat. She had been off her guard when the children came; but now Pat was out with his father sure enough, and she had such a bad recollection for names, she could not rightly call to mind whether it was out Ballybrae way he was, or up past Armaghbaeg, or maybe it wasn't there at all but up over the hills. But anyway he'd very likely be in to dinner, so it wouldn't be worth sending for him yet awhile till they saw whether he'd be coming.

Mr. Plunkett felt so convinced that his wife was not mistaken in thinking she had seen Murtagh at the fire that he never for a moment supposed Pat guilty, but placed ready faith in Mrs. O'Toole's apparent nonchalance. At the same time, however, he considered it his duty to take Pat to Mr. Blair without delay; so he said the boy must be sent for at once.

Mrs. O'Toole was quite equal to the emergency. "There were plenty of idle gossoons in the village," she said, "who would be glad of a run;" and two or three lads were sent in different directions with orders from Mr. Plunkett to bring Pat home directly.

They received private instruction from Mrs. O'Toole to wink both eyes if they saw Pat, and if they met O'Toole to tell him to keep himself out of the way; and it is needless to say whose orders they obeyed. Murtagh added that they might take as long as they liked to look for him; and before the afternoon the whole village knew that some mystery was on foot. It was the general opinion that Murtagh and Pat had between them burnt down the contents of Mr. Plunkett's haggart, and that anyhow no one was to know a word about Pat O'Toole. Sympathy was all on the boys' side. And though in the course of the morning several of the villagers were examined by Mr. Plunkett, nothing could be drawn from them.

Till Pat was found no further examination of the children would take place, but in the mean time Murtagh and Winnie were very miserable. They hung round the house watching the entrances in nervous dread lest Pat might after all be caught and brought before their uncle.

Cousin Jane forbade Frankie to speak to them till they chose to confess their guilt, and Rosie and Bobbo tried in vain to think of comforting things to say.

The instant they heard the story, Pat's guilt was as clear to them as to the other two, but since Murtagh and Winnie said the only thing to be done was to hold their tongues, the idea of attempting to clear Murtagh did not come into any of their minds. Bobbo said it was a beastly shame, but Murtagh and Winnie replied disconsolately that it was really just the same as if they had done it themselves; and as the others always accepted their morals from Murtagh and Winnie, the whole school-room took this view.

At Murtagh's suggestion Winnie went, after a time, to try and get Nessa by herself to warn her against betraying Pat. But first Nessa was in the study with Mr. Blair, and then just as Winnie was going to catch her in the passage, Cousin Jane came to the drawing-room door with a face full of dismay and beckoned. Winnie caught the words, "doctor," "terrible," "send at once." Nessa's face became very grave; then the door shut upon them both, and the child was left outside full of wondering trouble.

Finding it was useless to wait for Nessa, she returned to the others and told what she had heard. The words filled them all with vague fear. They did not quite know what they dreaded, but they were in a state of nervous depression in which everything suggested painful possibilities.

Their apprehensions were soon increased by seeing one of the men ride fast from the stable down the avenue. The stable was at some distance from the house, and before they could reach him to ask what was the matter he was out of sight.

"He's gone for the doctor, I suppose," said Winnie, but they did not dare to go in and ask any questions; somehow they felt afraid of everybody to-day.

At last Nessa came out of the house and began to walk across the park. The children hailed her appearance with relief; at least they were not afraid of her; and running up to her they asked what was the matter; was Frankie ill?

"Frankie is ill," replied Nessa; "Cousin Jane says excitement always makes him ill. But we have sent for the doctor for Mr. Plunkett's child; they say she is dying. That pretty golden-haired little girl—the eldest of them." Nessa's voice was trembling; she remembered so well the transparent beauty of the child, and the loving looks of both father and mother. "It seems a piece of wood fell upon her head when they were taking her out of the burning nursery," she continued. "First she fainted, then she seemed quite, quite well, and now the servant who came to find Mr. Plunkett says she is dying."

A sudden awe fell upon the children. "Dying!" They could scarcely believe it. No one had ever died in their experience.

"Oh, Nessa!" exclaimed Rosie, but the others were all silent.

"Will you come with me?" said Nessa, looking at their white shocked faces. "You need not come into the house, but you will know. And perhaps you may be of use if there are messages."

Most gratefully, though silently, the children accepted her invitation. At least they would know what was happening, and if they were really able to be of use that would be something. Anything was better than being shut out forgotten in the park.

At a short distance from the Red House they were overtaken by Mr. Plunkett, who with an anxious face was walking up swiftly from the village.

"David himself has gone for the doctor," said Nessa, "and if he does not find yours he will ride on at once to Ballyboden; he will not come back without one." Her voice conveyed all the sympathy that she felt. It was not a moment to put it into words.

But evidently Mr. Plunkett did not yet know of his child's danger.

"What?" he said hoarsely, trying to seem unmoved.

"You have not heard—that she is rather worse?" asked Nessa, steadying her voice in order to break the news as gently as possible.

But Mr. Plunkett was not a man to have news broken to him. Nessa's voice, when she first addressed him, had told that the doctor had not been lightly sent for, and he preferred to know the worst at once. A sort of gray color spread over his face. Standing quite still before Nessa he seemed to pierce her through with his eyes.

"Is she dying?" he asked. He stood erect as usual. He tried to keep his face in the same unrelaxed mold. For all his pain he could not bear that these strangers should see him suffer. But the cold stern voice was strangely broken; in spite of himself such a dumb agony of suspense was in his eyes that Nessa, not daring to speak untruly, was moved with sudden sympathy to put her hand in his. The touch of her fingers, the sorrow in her face, conveyed the answer she could not have framed in words.

"Not dead?" he forced his lips to say, while almost unconsciously his hand closed tightly upon hers.

"No; oh no," she answered quickly, "and the doctor will soon be here, perhaps—"

But he waited for no more. With a few rapid strides he was in the house, and Nessa not liking just then to enter, remained with the children where he had left her.

No one spoke; the children with white awe-stricken faces stood looking towards the window, as though they expected in that way to find out something of what was passing inside. Nessa tried to think if nothing could be done to help. Must they wait passively till the doctor came?

A sudden sound of one of the little Plunketts crying helped her to collect her thoughts. Telling the children to wait, she went quietly through the blackened doorway, and found, as she had expected, the three Plunkett babies alone. Their nursery had been burnt, and they were drearily trying to play in an empty kitchen. They were so hungry, the eldest said, and nobody came with their dinner.

After a few words with the nurse, who passed up the stairs and gave her some details of Marion's condition, Nessa took the children out, and told Rosie and Winnie to take them home with them for dinner, and to try and amuse them for the rest of the day. So at least the house would be quiet, and the poor parents have less to think of. Then she told the boys they must get some ice. "I am sure when the doctor comes he will order ice for her head," she said, "and it will be good to have it here."

Humbly thankful they were to have something to do. Murtagh was too miserable now for words, for he had had time to remember that this also was his fault. They found out from Donnie where they were to go for the ice, and then they went to the haggart to get the horse and cart. The straw was lying about just as they left it. Their hands had pushed the cart into its shed the evening before, but Murtagh could hardly believe, as they pulled it out, that it was only yesterday they had been so happy. Oh, why couldn't he be good?

The way was long; and it was getting late in the afternoon when the boys returned to the Little House with the ice. They had had no dinner, but they cared little for that, and only asked with anxious faces if there was nothing else they could do. Nessa understood well enough, and she set them to work at once in the garden to pound the ice as nearly as possible into powder.

It was greatly wanted. The doctor had not yet arrived, and during the early part of the afternoon little Marion had got worse and worse. Mrs. Plunkett was able to do nothing, but stood at the bottom of the bed and wept, while Mr. Plunkett sat with a face of unnatural calm, and tried to soothe the poor child's ravings with tender words. But at last Nessa had gone up and had succeeded in quieting her a little by laying wet cloths upon her head. So now with new hope they were waiting for the ice.

Long after it grew dark, though the wind was bitterly cold, the two boys still sat in the garden pounding the ice, and Nessa came backwards and forwards from the house to fetch a bowlful of it as it was wanted, comforting their hearts from time to time with an account of how little Marion grew quieter and quieter as each cloth full of the cold powder was laid upon her head.

They could not go into the house, for the sound of the pounding would have echoed through all the rooms, but they worked on, never thinking of the cold or the darkness. They felt able to do anything now they had a spark of hope.

After a time Winnie joined them with Royal. Mrs. Donegan had put the little Plunketts to bed at the house, she said, and she didn't know where Murtagh was or what he was doing, so she had come out to look for him. She seemed very disconsolate, but the boys were cheered now with their work and the better accounts of Marion; so they told what they were doing, and Bobbo groped about till he found a big stone for her to pound with too. Then she knelt down beside them and worked away, while Royal, with some wonderful instinct of their trouble, stretched himself out upon the ground and lay patiently watching the three children.

In the house, too, hope was beginning to revive. Mrs. Plunkett had been persuaded to lie down, and worn out with weeping she had fallen asleep, while Mr. Plunkett, seeing that Nessa's simple remedy had some effect, concentrated himself upon applying it. No one else touched Marion. His hardness had completely vanished, and tenderly as a woman he did for her everything that she needed. Nessa, seeing how he liked to do it, kept in the background, only preparing what was needful, and bringing it to him in order that he might remain always by the child's bedside.

So the evening wore away, till at last the rumble of wheels announced that the doctor was coming. Royal was the first to hear the welcome sound, and a low growl from him announced it to the children.

"Now we shall know," said Murtagh; and with eager expectation they watched the doctor walk up the path. Winnie ran to the door and begged Nessa to let them know quickly what he said, but it seemed to them a long, long time before any one came.

They could see three dark shadows sometimes on the blind of the room where Marion lay, and though they tried to go on with their work the ice often numbed their fingers as they absently held a lump in their hands and gazed up for some sign of Nessa coming. After one of those long looks Murtagh had just begun pounding again, when suddenly the door opened, and the doctor's voice called cheerily from the blaze of light that streamed out over the steps: "Where are you, my young workers? Your ice has saved her life."

Till those words lifted the load off their hearts, the children scarcely knew how heavy it had been.

"She won't die?" said Murtagh, eagerly springing to the bottom of the steps.

"No, no," replied the doctor; "not now if she has the same nursing through the night."

"I thought somehow she couldn't die," said Bobbo, standing up and rubbing his cramped legs. Winnie expressed her feelings by flinging her arms round Royal's neck, and giving him an ecstatic squeeze. Then Nessa appeared behind the doctor, and joined her assurance to his.

She was to stay and spend the night with Marion, but the doctor insisted on driving the children home in his gig. He was a tender-hearted man, who had a lot of merry little brothers and sisters at home, and the idea of children being so troubled as these was to him unnatural. It would have disturbed him to think of them after he got home, so as they drove along he made light of Marion's danger, and talked and laughed with them, till by the time they reached the house they were in quite a bright mood.

After the doctor left them they stopped on the steps to bid Royal good-night, and kneeling down beside him Winnie said:

"We've been very miserable to-day, Royal; very miserable; but it is wonderful how things always come right after. They always do, Royal; so if ever you're miserable you can remember that."

Royal looked solemnly at her as though he understood every word, but as she finished he put a paw upon each of her shoulders and by way of answer gravely licked her face.

Bobbo burst out laughing, and the others followed his example.

"Oh, Royal dear, you are a darling!" cried Winnie. And Cousin Jane, passing through the hall to bed, overheard them, and remarked to Emma that she never would have believed children could be so heartless as to be laughing and playing with the dog when that poor little girl might be lying dead through their wickedness.

CHAPTER XXI

URTAGH SLEPT LATE next morning, and he was wakened by Winnie who wanted him to get up and come and inquire about Pat. Anxiety about Marion had made him completely forget Pat, but now that trouble returned upon him in full force. He got up and went with Winnie to see Mrs. O'Toole. But nothing had been heard of Pat, and between her longing to see the boy and dread lest the police should find him Mrs. O'Toole was in terrible grief. The children could give her no comfort, and they wandered sadly back to the house.

Frankie was in bed, but Cousin Jane came and told them they might go in and see him. He had set his heart upon seeing them, and she could not refuse when he was ill. She begged they would not put any of their hardened notions into his head, but they were too glad of being able to see Frankie to care for anything Cousin Jane said.

He welcomed them delightedly, eager to know what they had done yesterday. Anything that concerned them was always of the deepest interest to him. He was too delicate ever to have any adventures of his own. His mother and Emma were his only companions, and all the romance of his life was centred in Murtagh and Winnie.

There was something very touching in the almost worshipful admiration with which he regarded them. He thought them nearly perfect, and if he had ever had a dream for himself it would have been to be like Murtagh, and to do the things Murtagh did. Only he never dreamt anything for himself; perhaps, poor little fellow, it did not seem to him worth while. And if he had no visions for his own future he made up for it by the fertility of imagination with which he planned out Murtagh's. Everything that most boys determine to do, when they are grown up, he used to lay plans for Murtagh to do. He would often lie for hours upon the sofa, picturing to himself Murtagh walking up before assembled rows of school-boys to receive impossible numbers of first prizes; Murtagh winning cricket-matches, or Murtagh leading troops to battle. There was no wonderful feat in history that Murtagh had not outdone many a time in Frankie's ambitious imagination.

Sometimes in his pictures he saw Winnie walking or riding by Murtagh's side; but himself never. He forgot his life in theirs. Visits to Castle Blair constituted the happiest part of his existence. So it was no wonder that he was full of eager sympathy for his two cousins in their present trouble.

Troubled as Murtagh and Winnie were at their share in this misfortune, it was very soothing to their sore consciences to talk with Frankie. His ideas of right and wrong used to become very confused where Winnie and Murtagh were concerned. All he thought about was how best to comfort them, and in the end he invariably succeeded in proving, to his own satisfaction at least, that they had been perfectly right.

They used to talk more of what they really thought with Frankie than children generally do together; more indeed than they did even to one another; and they confided to him now, in their own odd scrappy fashion, the sore regrets by which they were assailed.

With all his goodwill, even Frankie was puzzled to reconcile their resolutions on the mountain with the scene in the haggart that so closely followed them. But then he said that Mr. Plunkett was so nasty nobody could help being rude to him (Frankie had never been rude to any one in his life); and, of course, they couldn't possibly know that one of the followers would go and set fire to his haystacks. The whole misfortune, he finally declared, was as much owing to Mr. Plunkett as to them. He would go out and be disagreeable when Nessa told him they were excited. It was all his own fault; and then he could not be contented without making false accusations, and trying to get Murtagh into trouble.

But Murtagh was not easily to be comforted, and perhaps Frankie had himself some misgivings as to the strength of his arguments, for he exerted himself to divert Murtagh's thoughts into another channel.

"Never mind, Myrrh, dear," he said, "Marion will soon be well now, and I daresay they'll never find out which of your followers did it. Next week we shall all three be down at the seaside, far away, where you'll never see Mr. Plunkett nor be worried with his rules. There will be nobody to order you about there. We will all do just whatever we please, and this whole affair will be forgotten by the time you come back."

Then he launched out into enthusiastic descriptions of the place to which they were going; and in the interest of planning how they would spend the days when they got there the children were by degrees drawn into forgetting Pat, Marion, Mr. Plunkett, and everything connected with the fire. After a time they called in Royal, and Frankie made him display his various accomplishments. Bobbo and Rosie joined them later in the day, and so they forgot to be unhappy for nearly the whole afternoon.

Nessa, in the mean time, had spent her day at the Red House, but Marion was now quite out of danger, and towards four o'clock she prepared to return home.

Mr. Plunkett would not let her walk alone, and as they went together across the park he took the opportunity of thanking her warmly for all that she had done. The doctor had told him that without her timely help Marion might have died, and he was not a man to be ungrateful for any real obligation.

It was one of those moments of unreserve that come sometimes after a heavy strain.

"You may think me hard and cold," he said, "but Marion is to me more—" Then strong as he was his voice faltered. He seemed for one moment to realize all that he had so nearly lost, and instead of words there came only an inarticulate choking sound. He recovered himself immediately, but he did not try to finish his sentence. Then he allowed himself to be drawn on by Nessa's genuine admiration of his child to talk of her, and to describe some of her pretty ways: till Nessa, talking with him freely and pleasantly as she would have talked with any one else, found herself wondering how she could ever have thought him so very disagreeable.

But as they emerged from under the trees and came in sight of the house his voice suddenly changed, and he exclaimed:

"Can you wonder then that I am determined to punish to the uttermost the heartles spite that in revenge for a just rebuke could imperil such innocent lives? You, Miss Blair, a stranger, can have little conception of all that we have been forced to suffer from Murtagh and his brother and sisters, but now it passes a matter of inconvenience. Impertinence and annoyance I could and would have endured, but to have my child hurt, to have her life, her reason endangered, to gratify the caprice of an insolent boy—" Mr. Plunkett's words were coming out fiercely, and he stopped suddenly as though not trusting himself to finish his sentence.

He was transformed; he was no longer the correct Mr. Plunkett that Nessa knew. His face was pale, his eyes full of a strange light; he was a man,—a man struggling with a violent emotion.

"But you cannot, you do not think still that Murtagh set fire to your house?" she exclaimed, standing still and looking up anxiously into his face. "It was not Murtagh; I know it was not."

"You think you know, Miss Blair, but you are mistaken. I have known the boy longer than you, and I tell you he is guilty."

"You did not see him on Wednesday evening after that scene with you," said Nessa, "and you did not see him yesterday, or you could not think that. He was so sorry for you yesterday, and so anxious to help. If you had seen his white sad face you could not think it was a pretence. Examine that other boy, and you will see that Murtagh is not guilty."

Mr. Plunkett had recovered now his usual demeanor. He replied quietly: "I cannot agree with you, Miss Blair; I am perfectly willing that young O'Toole should be examined, but you have only to count up the evidences of Murtagh's guilt to be yourself convinced of the uselessness of the proceeding; his presence at the fire; his confusion on finding himself discovered; his inability to answer any of the charges made against him."

As they walked on again towards the house, he continued in a calm dispassionate voice: "Directly he left his uncle's presence he rushed off to O'Toole's cottage. What could he have wanted there if not to beg Pat to keep his secret safe? His very anxiety about my poor child is only another reason for believing him guilty. He dislikes me; he has no affection for her; and I cannot believe he would have displayed such excessive anxiety had he not been smitten with remorse and terror at the consequences of his act. If he had come forward and confessed openly, instead of allowing the blame to be half-shifted on to another, I might have entertained some softer feeling towards him, but as it is I feel nothing but a just anger and contempt. He has shown himself not only revengeful but cowardly and dishonorable."

Mr. Plunkett had only seen one side, and that the worst, of Murtagh's character. Upon that he based his judgment, and it was perfectly impossible to him to enter into the very different view which Nessa took of the same facts. In vain she pleaded Murtagh's cause. Mr. Plunkett had covered himself again with his usual shell, and words had no effect.

At last almost indignant she appealed to justice. "You ought to believe he is speaking the truth till you are quite sure he is not," she said. "You have not yet made any search among the people in the country."

But that was as useless as the rest. "It is impossible for me to believe he is speaking the truth," he answered shortly. "I am willing that every inquiry should be made, but I am perfectly convinced of his guilt, and so long as he remains hardened in denial he must expect nothing but the utmost severity from me."

Those were his parting words. They had reached the gravel sweep that divided the park from the house, and he bowed and left her.

As she entered the hall she met Murtagh, who had been watching her from Frankie's window, and who now came running down to know how little Marion was.

"Better," said Nessa, "much better;" but she was thinking of her conversation with Mr. Plunkett, and her voice was not in accordance with her news.

"You're dreadfully tired, aren't you?" said Murtagh.

"Yes," said Winnie, who had followed him down; "of course she must be after being up all night. Come along, Myrrh, we'll get her some tea. And you go and lie down in your room," she added, holding one of Nessa's hands for a moment in both of hers, and laying her cheek against it.

"Thank you," said Nessa, stooping to kiss the little brown forehead. "Yes, I should like some tea." And as the two children ran away to the kitchen she passed up the stairs.

A few minutes later they appeared in her room with their little tray. They had arranged it after their own fashion, with a white napkin and a tiny blue vase full of flowers. Winnie's cheeks were rosy with the making of toast, and while Nessa drank her tea and admired the flowers the two children watched her radiantly.

"We made it all ourselves," exclaimed Winnie when the first cup was nearly finished. "Donnie wasn't there, but we knew the water was boiling, because the top of the kettle was bobbing up and down." Nessa asked for a second cup, and the delighted children were as happy as little kings because she found their tea so good.

CHAPTER XXII

MR. PLUNKETT meant what he had said to Nessa. Convinced of Murtagh's guilt he was resolved to bring him to just punishment, and that without delay. Next day, therefore, he begged Mr. Blair to continue his investigation. Poor Mr. Blair, who had completely accepted Nessa's view, took no longer the slightest interest in the affair. Provided it was not Murtagh he did not care in the very least who was guilty. All he desired was to be left in peace.

However, since Mr. Plunkett was not satisfied, and since Mr. Plunkett had a strong will to which Mr. Blair was accustomed to yield, there was nothing for it but to send for Pat O'Toole and sift the matter to the bottom. Marion's illness had diverted all attention from Pat, and his absence was as yet undiscovered. Mr. Plunkett sent a message to him to appear; Mrs. O'Toole put off the inevitable announcement of his flight to the last moment; and it was not till every one else was assembled in the study that it became known that he was gone.

The news was received by Mr. Blair and Nessa as a simple proof of Murtagh's innocence. In their eyes nothing more was needed, and they expected that Mr. Plunkett would now be convinced of his mistake. But Mr. Plunkett held his own opinion much too firmly to be easily shaken in it.

He believed that his wife had seen Murtagh at the fire, and he said, naturally, that Pat's flight did not actually prove him guilty, and that even had it done so, Murtagh's innocence was not thereby established. The two boys were known to be friends, and what was more likely than that Murtagh should have chosen Pat as an accomplice? It was evident that they had some secret together, since Murtagh's first action after the news of the fire had been made known was to run away to the O'Tooles' cottage.

"He will hardly venture to deny this," added Mr. Plunkett, "for I saw him there myself with Winnie. And young O'Toole had not gone then, for I overheard the mother telling Murtagh that her son was on the bog with his father."

When the news of Pat's flight had arrived Murtagh had felt a grim satisfaction at the prospect of Mr. Plunkett's discomfiture, thinking like Nessa that his own innocence was now fully established. It seemed to him so plain that he could not imagine how different the case might seem to Mr. Plunkett; and now as he stood listening to the array of evidence brought forward to prove his guilt, a turmoil of bitter indignation raged within him.

All that Frankie had said the day before came back to his mind, and every bit of sorrow for his own fault was swallowed up in angry rebellion against what seemed to him wilful injustice. He could not believe that Mr. Plunkett did not in his heart know that he was innocent. Stung to the quick, he took a proud, unreasoning determination to say not one word in his own defence, and after the first stormy flash that overspread his countenance, he stood with eyes cast down and a white obdurate face that defied all questioning.

It was not so with Winnie. Through her indignation and disgust a dim suspicion, which she had herself rejected before, flashed suddenly into belief. Mr. Plunkett was doing it on purpose. He did not really believe Murtagh guilty, but he had a spite against him for what had happened in the haggart, and this was his mean way of revenging himself.

Her cheeks flamed, and her eyes flashed with indignation; but it was not her way to speak in passionate gusts as Murtagh did, so she clasped her hands on the back of her head, and waited till Mr. Plunkett wound up a somewhat elaborate argument by asking every one in the room to decide whether he had not good grounds for believing Murtagh to be guilty.

Then before any one could answer, she said in a cool aggravating voice:

"Yes, I daresay, if we didn't all know you're doing this just because you have a spite against Murtagh."

"Well!" exclaimed Cousin Jane, "these children are allowed to talk in the funniest way I ever heard."

"I don't see why things shouldn't be fair," returned Winnie. "Mr. Plunkett keeps on telling us we are telling lies, and why mayn't we tell him the same? If you won't believe what Murtagh says I don't see why you should believe what Mr. Plunkett says. Mr. Plunkett says Murtagh did this because of what happened in the haggart, but it's a *great deal* more likely Mr. Plunkett's trying to get Murtagh into a scrape to revenge himself for what happened. Just as if Murtagh would ever bother his head to be revenged on anybody like him!"

The supreme scorn of the last words was unmistakable, and Mr. Blair, in some astonishment, said with quiet dignity: "Winnie, that seems a strange way to speak to Mr. Plunkett. Every one who knows him knows that nothing could be more impossible to him."

"The idea of children talking like that to a grown-up person!" remarked Cousin Jane.

"That's always the way," cried Winnie, her pent-up wrath bursting forth at last. "Just because we are children we're to hold our tongues and let people say what they like to us, and tell all sorts of lies about our doing things we didn't do; and then if we say a word about them doing a thousand times worse things we're told to be quiet. But I don't care what five hundred million grown-up people say, Murtagh didn't do this, and Mr. Plunkett knows he didn't just as well as I do."

Mr. Blair looked at her in still greater surprise. He thought little girls were quiet and obedient. He had not the slightest idea what to do or say in reply; but at last, with a sort of instinct that it would be safest to have her near Nessa, he said:

"You may go and sit down now, my dear; Nessa will make room for you I daresay on the sofa beside her."

He glanced over at Nessa as he spoke with such a comical expression of despair that they both nearly laughed, to Cousin Jane's intense indignation.

Mr. Blair, however, became grave again at once, and turned to Mr. Plunkett to listen to all the reasons he was urging in favor of some serious punishment being inflicted upon Murtagh. Mr. Plunkett was very much in earnest upon this matter. He had thought of it a great deal, and he was determined to make an example of Murtagh which none of the other children should forget. His manner was perhaps more than usually cold and business-like, but his ordinary brevity was laid aside, and he spoke at some length. Too courteous to interrupt, Mr. Blair listened patiently till he had ceased speaking. But then instead of at once answering Mr. Plunkett, he turned to Murtagh and said:

"Murtagh, will you give me your word of honor that you were not at this fire, and that you did not in any way wilfully cause it?"

Murtagh had stood immovable while Mr. Plunkett was speaking; but his anger was at all times easy to melt, and there was a ring of trust and friendliness in his uncle's tone which made him look up straight into Mr. Blair's face with bright fearless eyes and answer at once:

"Yes; I give you my word of honor."

"I believe you, my boy!" replied Mr. Blair.

The clouds vanished from Murtagh's face, and with a clear sunny smile he looked across to Nessa for her congratulations.

Winnie and Bobbo started up and clapped their hands, while Bobbo with a beaming countenance said: "I knew it would all come right in the end."

"Plunkett," said Mr. Blair. "I feel how much truth there is in all you say, and if I could for a moment believe Murtagh guilty I would leave it to you to decide his punishment. But though you have certainly evidence enough to justify an opinion, you do not prove his guilt, and I cannot help thinking that the presumptive evidence on the other side is strong enough to make it only just to Murtagh that we should believe him when he assures us on his word of honor that he is innocent." With his mind's eye Mr. Blair saw his study already empty and himself at leisure to return to his books, and his voice was cheerful in proportion. Mr. Plunkett was too much annoyed to be able altogether to retain his calm demeanor.

"Well," he replied, "I have nothing more to say. If you are content upon such an investigation to declare Murtagh innocent the household will, of course, consider him so; but for my part I state openly here that I believe him to be guilty, and that I shall continue so to do till some other person confesses to having committed the crime without his help or instigation."

"Believe away!" retorted Winnie. "Nobody cares in the least what you think!"

"Winnie," said her uncle, "Mr. Plunkett is an old and respected friend of mine."

Mr. Blair so seldom spoke to one of the children that even Winnie's audacious tongue was silenced by the reproof.

"I am very sorry, Plunkett," continued Mr. Blair, "that we cannot persuade you, but still I can't help hoping that when you think the matter over you will come round to our opinion."

"Nothing ever will persuade me," returned Mr. Plunkett, "and Murtagh's guilty conscience can best tell him the reason why."

With those words he took up his hat and left the room.

The children were very little disturbed by his opinion. Murtagh's innocence was established, and that was all they cared about. They flocked round Murtagh, and carried him off with many expressions of pleasure.

But Cousin Jane was no better satisfied than Mr. Plunkett. She was at all times ready to find fault with these children.

She had established a sort of rivalry in her mind between them and Frankie. Frankie's delicacy was a hard trial to her. She watched over him with a faithful solicitude equalled by few mothers; but she could not hide from herself that he grew no stronger, rather weaker. He was not like other boys; he could not run and jump; he could not even laugh much without being very tired; and Cousin Jane felt in some way aggrieved at every sign of Murtagh's overflowing health and spirits. Frankie was the natural heir to all his uncle's estates; the dream of his mother's life since he had been born was to see him master of Castle Blair; and the thought that perhaps he might die and Murtagh inherit in his stead haunted her continually, till at times she almost hated Murtagh.

Then she disapproved very much of Mr. Blair. He was to her quite incomprehensible. Never opening a book herself, she could not understand the magnetic attraction of book-shelves for Mr. Blair. According to her views of human responsibility it was perfectly sinful of him to shut himself up in the library with musty old parchments and rubbishing stones, and leave his beautiful place to take care of itself. If he pretended to despise such things for his own sake he ought to think of his heirs; it was not just to them.

So Cousin Jane reasoned, and when she disliked any one she disliked everything they did. She had disapproved in the beginning of Launcelot's children coming to live with their uncle at all, and now they were here she disapproved as highly of the way they were treated. Mr. Plunkett was the only person on the estate who had any idea how things should be managed, or who in any way looked after Frankie's interests, and to him Cousin Jane used to pour out all her grievances.

It was not surprising, therefore, that in this instance she was ready to accept Mr. Plunkett's opinion of Murtagh's guilt. She had said from the first that she was sure the boy was guilty, and when once an idea got firmly fixed in her head no power of argument or demonstration could move it. Nessa soon discovered this, and after politely trying for some time to persuade her to see that Murtagh was practically proved to be innocent, she left her to her own opinion and escaped gladly to the children.

Nessa and Royal and the children spent a happy afternoon together. Frankie was better again that day, and was able to be out with them; all their troubles were over and gone—gone so completely that they even seemed not to remember them as they raced and romped upon the grass with Royal. He was a splendid dog,—big and broad-chested, but agile as Winnie herself. And he enjoyed the fun of playing. When he rolled the children over on the grass, and their peals of happy laughter shook the air, you could almost fancy he was laughing too. He sprang backwards and forwards from one child to another, his great black tail whisking about in the air; but though he rolled them over without ceremony he was thoroughly gentle; he would not have hurt them for all the world. Even little Ellie, after a first terrified rush into Nessa's arms, soon discovered that "she wasn't afraid."

She demonstrated the fact by clutching the big black head and trying to poke her little fingers into his eyes every time he gave her the opportunity. But he perhaps understood that she was a baby, for he submitted with perfect good humor, only springing away from her when he had had enough, with a suddenness that sent her sitting down plump upon the moss each time. The first time it happened she looked around with comic surprise, not quite sure whether to laugh or to cry. Then she picked herself up and ran after him, screaming out in delight when the operation was repeated: "Oh, it is such fun! Oh, Ellie do tink it is such fun!"

Then when they grew tired of romping they came and sat on Nessa's rug under the chestnut-tree, and Royal, curled up near Winnie, laid his great muzzle on his forepaws and went to sleep. The white ducks came waddling one by one from the terrace, and Winnie insisted upon introducing them each by name to Nessa as she fed them with scraps of hard bread from her pocket.

Nessa was not skilled in the varieties of form and complexion that distinguish white ducks, and though the children all laughed incredulously at her blindness she was forced to declare that she could see no difference between King, and Senior, and Ruffle, and Nigger. Her education was evidently defective, and they set to work to complete it without delay.

"Do you mean to say now, for instance," asked Winnie, with the compassionate air of one who puts an easy question to a beginner, "that you could mistake that poor sniffling little Snatch for Senior?"

But Nessa was hopelessly ignorant.

"Which is Snatch?" she asked, stretching out her hand to the one who stood nearest to her. "Is it this one?"

"Why, that's King," said Murtagh, "the very head of them all. "And all the children laughed; it seemed to them really funny that any one should know so little about white ducks.

Nessa laughed too, and Winnie said: "That's Snatch with the pale pink bill,—the one that looks as if he was always blowing his nose. We call him Snatch because he never snatches anything."

An excellent reason, no doubt, but Nessa laughed again.

"And then he's always in every one's way," added Winnie.

"Or at least he's always being pushed out of every one's way," said Murtagh. "I suppose it's the same thing." And Murtagh took a bit of bread from Winnie and threw it across her to poor Snatch. But Royal, the rogue, whom every one thought asleep, suddenly lifted his head and—Snap! Gulp! he had caught the bread, swallowed it, and settled to sleep again, while Snatch looked stupidly round to see where it had gone. How the children laughed, and Royal all the time peeped slily through his eyelashes to watch for another bit coming his way.

So they chattered and laughed all the afternoon, and fed Royal, and the ducks, and the pigeons too, who came cooing and pluming themselves and walked about in such a dignified fuss, picking all manner of scraps out of the grass. And when, for Frankie's sake, they had to go in, though Nessa left them to rejoin Cousin Jane, they gathered round the school-room fire and chattered and laughed all the same, and laid plans for what they would do when they got away to Torquay with Frankie.

He was so happy in the prospect, poor little fellow! He had not played to-day; he had lain on the rug beside Nessa; but he quite forgot that. He felt as though he had been playing too, and with faintly flushed cheeks and sparkling eyes he sat curled up on the sofa listening in delight.

"Why, of course, you'll be able to swim like two fishes before you come back," he was acquiescing in answer to a remark of Murtagh's, when the door opened and Emma came in. The room was dark now, and the children thought it was Nessa.

"Do you hear, Nessa?" cried Winnie. "We intend to learn to swim at Torquay, and to swim all about the sea into the caves and places where nobody has ever been before."

"It's time for you to come and dress for dinner, Frankie," replied Emma's voice; "and," she added with some primness as Frankie rose reluctantly from the sofa, "you had better not make too many plans for Torquay."

She turned and left the room as she spoke, but Frankie sprang after her, exclaiming: "Emma, what do you mean about Torquay?" and her answer was quite audible as she walked down the passage.

"I mean that of course mamma will not allow Murtagh to be your only playmate for so many months if he persists in telling such stories. There is no knowing what he might teach you."

Murtagh's cheek flushed as he heard the words, and from the other children arose a chorus of:

"What a shame!"

"It can't be true!"

"There's something else we have to thank Mr. Plunkett for!"

"It's wicked and unjust," cried Winnie. "He knows as well as I do that you didn't do it. I don't know how he can dare to pretend he doesn't. It's enough to drive one mad; but there's one thing, Myrrh, if you don't go, I won't; Cousin Jane needn't think I will."

"It's not true; it's only Emma's rubbish," decided Bobbo.

"Let us go and ask Nessa," said Murtagh, with a curious kind of quietness in his voice, and while the others dashed off impatiently to Nessa's room he, thrusting his hands into his pockets, walked slowly after them.

CHAPTER XXIII

Ⅰ T WAS ONLY TOO TRUE. It was difficult to say with whom the idea had first originated, but after much talking with Emma and Mr. Plunkett, Cousin Jane had announced that she could not take Murtagh with her unless he were ready to confess his guilt. Mr. Blair was annoyed, but there was no help for it. It was true that Murtagh had not been altogether proved innocent. He could not be till Pat was found, and till he was everybody had of course a right to their own opinion.

The children were bitterly indignant, but Murtagh still said nothing. The injustice seemed to him at first too impossible to be true; and when he realized that it was true, the feelings it roused against Mr. Plunkett, were such he would have found it difficult to express. A sort of astonished contempt filled his mind. He had not thought before that Mr. Plunkett could be so bad as that, and if at times the thought of his disappointment roused in him hot indignation, this new feeling of sheer disgust made him shrink from even thinking much of Mr. Plunkett.

Frankie's disappointment was beyond expression. For perhaps the first time in his life he behaved like the spoilt child he was. He would not go to the sea at all, he said, or if he did he wouldn't take a bit of trouble to get well. He had set his heart on having his cousin with him, and his mother vainly proposed instead companion after companion. He didn't care for any of them, he said, and all the pleasure of his winter was gone.

Cousin Jane was one of those people who rarely understand the consequences of what they do, and she was greatly disturbed by Frankie's trouble. She had intended to punish Murtagh, not Frankie, and it had seemed to her quite simple to take Bobbo in Murtagh's place. But Bobbo and Winnie declared at once that they would not go anywhere with people who said Murtagh told stories, and when Cousin Jane appealed to Mr. Blair, he replied that he thought they had a right to decide for themselves.

In despair at her son's trouble Cousin Jane would have been glad to change her mind and say that Murtagh might come, but Mr. Plunkett and Emma both urged her to be firm. Mr. Plunkett alone would not perhaps have had sufficient influence, but she was accustomed to be ruled by Emma, and Emma was very determined.

Poor Cousin Jane!—it was a hard fate which had taken away her husband. Nature had intended her to have always some one to lean upon; and who can say how much happier her life would have been had she had a tenderer and more trustworthy counsellor than her sharp and accomplished daughter!

Frankie locked himself into his room and would not see anybody. His poor bewildered mother made herself wretched with thinking how ill he would be after such excitement, and finally retired almost in tears to her own room, declaring that she had never met such children, and that she wished she had never come to Castle Blair to be mixed up in all this trouble. Every one felt dreary and uncomfortable, and the children wandered disconsolately about the house, muttering their opinions of Mr. Plunkett, and wishing aloud that it wasn't Sunday, till Nessa suggested that they should go and pay their weekly visit to Mrs. Daly.

Anything to do was better than nothing, so they readily agreed; and when Nessa had them all to herself out of doors she soon succeeded in gently drawing their thoughts away from the subject which engrossed them.

She and Mrs. Donegan had been concocting certain plans for the benefit of Mrs. Daly and one or two other people in the village, and Nessa communicated them to the children. Falling readily into their notion of being bound up into a tribe, she suggested how nice it would be if the tribe could be of real use in the village, and the children, delighted to see a grown-up person entering seriously into a project which they had tried hard to persuade themselves was serious, were hearty in their acceptance of her proposals.

Wild, fierce little things as they seemed, they were something like lambs in lion's clothing. They were up in arms directly, and stormed like staunch little Home Rulers, as they were, at anything they considered unjust, but the slightest appeal to their sympathy was enough to make them forget all about themselves.

The walk was quite pleasant, and it was delightful to find Mrs. Daly sitting up in the sunshine, looking already much better for the wholesome dinner with which Nessa and Donnie provided her every day. After that they paid a very different visit; they went to see Mrs. O'Toole. The poor woman was in bitter grief, and she could not be comforted. An inadvertent mention of Mr. Plunkett's name suddenly roused a storm of rage that made Nessa turn pale and tremble, but the passionate abandonment of grief that followed would have moved to tears a harder heart than hers. Her sweet shy words of comfort were of little use. And when the children spoke hopefully of Pat being found and coming back, the poor mother cried out with a despairing wail: "An' that'll be the worst of all; oh, my heart's broken! my heart's broken!"

They had forgotten for the moment that if he came back it would be to come to prison. So they had to leave her in her desolation, and very sadly, very wearily the children went back to the house. How much of it all was their fault?

But Nessa had promised Mrs. Plunkett to go to the Red House that afternoon to see little Marion, so she left them to pay her visit.

She was not the only visitor at the Red House. Cousin Jane was there, and was there for no less a purpose than to see with Mr. Plunkett whether after all she could not take Murtagh with her.

Her mind was so divided between two opinions that she could not remain firm in either. She was in a most uncomfortable strait. Accustomed for years to use Emma as her brain she was in the habit of taking for granted that Emma's opinion was right, and with a simplicity and abnegation of self that would have been touching had they not been so fraught with mischief, she did always what Emma told her.

But though she was devoted to both her children, though she admired and respected Emma's cleverness, Frankie was the darling of her heart. She was almost ashamed sometimes of loving him so much. It seemed a little bit like treason to Emma. Even in the most secret recesses of her heart she would not for the world have instituted a comparison between them, but in a furtive sort of way, hiding the knowledge from herself, she yet loved Frankie with a love greater than she had given to any one.

She was a little bit afraid of Emma, for Emma used to laugh at her and sometimes even sneer. It never made her the least angry; of course, it was only natural, she thought, when Emma was so clever; but she was happier with Frankie; he was almost always gentle and caressing. Emma stirred her pride and her affection, but there were depths beneath that Frankie, and Frankie only, had ever moved. If Emma was her brain, Frankie was her heart.

She and Frankie had always been content together to do Emma's bidding, and when they did not quite like her plans they had confided their grievance to each other, and almost enjoyed their little mutual grumble; but now, when Frankie absolutely rebelled and Emma still insisted, their mother found herself in a state bordering upon distraction.

Her love for Frankie had never before led her to contradict Emma, and she really dared not. She would rather contradict Frankie himself, for she was not afraid of him. He would love her all the same, and after a time would understand and forgive her. But for all that she could not bear to think of Frankie's winter being spoilt, and with a great effort she had resolved that if Mr. Plunkett would support her she would for once oppose Emma and let Frankie have Murtagh.

This resolve had cost her four or five hours' fighting with herself in the solitude of her own room. Nothing but the remembrance of Frankie's locked door, and the dread that he might get ill and yet not let her in to nurse him, would finally have prevailed; but at last, as picture after picture passed before her mind of the terrible things he might do if he were ill and she not sitting by his bedside, she could bear it no longer, and with sudden determination had started up and gone to consult Mr. Plunkett. If only some one whom she trusted would strongly uphold her she thought she might find it easier to combat Emma's opinion.

She certainly needed somebody else's courage, for she had very little of her own. Even now, animated by all the strength of a sudden resolution, her heart beat like a frightened child's at the idea of meeting Emma, and being asked where she was going.

She reached the Red House without adventure, and finding herself thus far so brave, her hopes were raised quite high. But the little effervescing spirit of courage died quickly away under the influence of Mr. Plunkett's cold tones and grave looks.

In answer to her half-nervous, half-vehement suggestions he urged, with a calm propriety of just determination, the necessity for Murtagh's sake of some punishment being inflicted. Cousin Jane wished with all her heart that she had never said she believed Murtagh guilty, but she had said it over and over again; and though she would have liked to put that part of the question on one side and forget all about it, Mr. Plunkett would not allow her to do anything of the kind.

The arguments he brought forward did not really affect her in the least. Murtagh might be guilty; his character might be ruined by slipshod indulgence; but, in the first place, she could hardly grasp an idea so abstract as the ruin of a person's character by a course of treatment which did not actually drive them to drink and steal; and in the second place, if she had done so she would have thought it mattered very little compared with Frankie's pleasure; she had nothing to do with training Murtagh.

Still, though the arguments did not in the slightest degree change her wish to take Murtagh with her, they had their effect in this way. She felt that they ought to have changed it; that every one would expect them to change it. They were unanswerable, and when Emma used them she would have nothing to urge against them. All the reason was against her. Her little bit of courage vanished. She could not possibly face Emma unless some one would help her, and she dolefully resigned herself and Frankie to the will of the stronger powers.

The matter was not quite settled when Nessa entered. Quickly gathering the subject of the conversation, she ranged herself at once on Cousin Jane's side. But that, by some strange contradiction, had more effect than all Mr. Plunkett's arguments. Cousin Jane had been a little offended by seeing Nessa installed as mistress at Castle Blair. She had set her down in her mind as an unnatural sort of a girl, just one of John's sort, and directly Nessa advocated Murtagh's departure Cousin Jane began to understand the truth of all Mr. Plunkett urged against it.

She was scarcely conscious of what worked the change in her mind. It was just an effect which people she did not like always had upon her; and while Nessa was pleading Murtagh's cause with Mr. Plunkett, she found herself growing almost reconciled to leaving him behind.

At length she stood up to go, and made a last effort to compromise the matter by saying to Mr. Plunkett:

"Well, I shall tell them it is your doing. I'm sure I would never have the heart to do it by myself."

Mr. Plunkett was rather pleased that the children should know the punishment came through him, and he assented willingly. It was a great relief to Cousin Jane to find any one at all upon whom she could lay her responsibility, and on her return she took refuge in saying that she could not help it. Mr. Plunkett was determined they should not go. She had been down to him to ask him again, and she could not do any more.

Of all the children Frankie seemed to feel most keenly the slight put upon Murtagh, though after the first indignant outburst he avoided with a kind of shrinking pain any allusion to his departure. Unable to remain outside the heart of any one he loved, he understood and forgave his mother, and by his redoubled tenderness to Murtagh, and the wistful yearning looks with which he followed him about, he seemed to ask Murtagh to forgive her too. "It is not mother, you know," he said once; "it is Mr. Plunkett," and then he hurriedly changed the subject.

Greatly distressed by Frankie's trouble, Murtagh tried to console him, showing himself perfectly cordial with Cousin Jane, and pretending that he did not care so very much for the disappointment. Winnie, too, did her very best, but Frankie was not to be comforted. He seemed to have some secret reason for his depression, and though he followed their footsteps like shadow he paid no heed to their attempts at consolation.

The natural result of his trouble was that he became ill, and his mother in despair was twenty times on the point of changing her mind. But Emma told her that that was nonsense; as for Frankie's health, the best thing she could do was to get him away to the sea at once, and a very good thing it was that there he would be free from the excitement of Murtagh's presence; he had been ill ever since he came to Castle Blair.

That was very true; and then Frankie had already forgiven her, which Emma, she knew, would not do. So Cousin Jane, notwithstanding many tears and protestations of affection to Frankie, held to her resolution, and the days went by to their departure.

But Frankie grew more and more ill, and the sight of his grief rendered his little cousins more determinedly and bitterly indignant against Mr. Plunkett. There was no reason why they should not express as openly as they pleased their opinions of his conduct, and they railed against him in turn, as with each day their angry resentment of the injustice grew stronger.

Nessa was so troubled by their state of mind that she asked Mr. Blair to interfere so far at least as to establish a clear understanding that Cousin Jane might take the children if she chose. But he was tired of children and their concerns, and he only laughed at her a little, and told her that when people are in Ireland they must do as the

Irish—leave things to take care of themselves. It would all come right as soon as Cousin Jane was gone.

Royal was the only refuge. He was always good-humored, always ready to entice the children to play. He seemed to understand quite well that they were in trouble, and to want to comfort them. When they were talking angrily he would stand looking up into their faces with a sort of half-puzzled, half-coaxing expression, that seemed to say, "I can't understand a single word. What is the good of it all? come and play with me," and his invitation was almost always successful. Winnie seldom could resist him long.

The moment he saw signs of relaxing in her face he would wag his tail and bound away, looking back to see if she were coming. Then if she did not come at once he would stop suddenly and stand with his forepaws spread wide apart, his head down and his tail up, saying as plainly as action could say it, "You can't catch me, now just try if you can."

That invitation was always irresistible; the children would rush after him in a body, and generally dog and children were in another moment rolling over together in a heap. Then Royal would shake himself free, and bound off again to have the same rolling repeated further on, till the children forgot their troubles in a sheer romp.

The day before Cousin Jane's departure especially his success was unbounded. Nessa was sitting in the school-room window watching the children on the lawn, and she saw him try his process of consolation.

The children were talking together apparently about Frankie's going, for they looked exceedingly gloomy. Royal gamboled round the group trying to coax first one and then another to play with him. Winnie at last knelt down and throwing one arm round his neck seemed to be telling him their troubles. He stood quite still for a moment looking into her face. Then he sprang away, and stood wagging his tail and looking back so roguishly that Winnie was proof against him no longer.

She bounded after him, and in another minute was lying on the ground with Royal standing over her, playfully hitting him with her little brown fists, while he rolled her from side to side with his muzzle. The others rushed forward, and Royal in his turn was rolled over on the grass. He was up in a minute, and ready to revenge himself. The children's grievance was forgotten, and with merry peals of laughter they raced from side to side of the lawn, over the empty flower-beds, up to the house, down to the river's edge,—one minute attacking, the next running away from the dog.

But suddenly in the midst of the laughter there came a great splash in the river, and a sharp cry arose from three or four of the children:

"Fetch her, Royal; fetch her!"

Nessa knew that the river was not very deep; but the children were excited, and in one of the pools if they lost their heads—— In an instant she was on the bank. Quick as she was Royal was quicker. By the time she reached the children Winnie was standing dripping wet upon the grass—laughing, panting, sputtering the water out of her mouth, and rubbing it out of her eyes, while the others crowded round Royal with many exclamations of delight.

Nessa's anxious face was received with peals of laughter. She asked Winnie if she were hurt, but at that Winnie only laughed the more, till at last Rosie explained:

"She didn't tumble in; she did it on purpose. We wanted to see whether Royal would fetch her out."

"And then he did!"

"Isn't he a beauty! Did you ever know such a perfect dog?"

"It's just the same as if he had saved her life, because he thought she'd tumbled in by accident!"

"Murtagh said Newfoundland dogs would! Oh, Winnie, you are lucky to have him for your own."

"There now, Miss Rosie; who was right, you or Murtagh?"

"Did he bite, Winnie?"

All the children were speaking at once, pouring out a volley of cross questions and remarks, interspersed with laughter and caresses of Royal. But they managed to hear Nessa, as trying to forget her fright she replied laughingly:

"You are a set of reckless monkeys; come in and do penance now by changing your clothes."

And while Murtagh, Bobbo, and Rosie began all at once eagerly to describe what happened, Winnie, with little rivers running down from every fold of her dress and every lock of her hair, led the way towards the house.

Both her hands were occupied with trying to pull her clinging petticoats away from her knees in order to enable her to walk, but Royal trotted gravely beside her, looking at her from time to time to make sure she was not hurt, and wagging his tail with satisfaction as she lavished upon him every extravagant epithet of endearment that came to her lips. Donnie's feelings when she saw the wet frocks, for with hugging Royal the other children were nearly as wet as Winnie, did not disturb anybody in the least. They all knew what Donnie's scoldings meant; and as soon as they had changed into dry clothes they came down as merry as ever to crown Royal king of the school-room.

It was, however, only a transient gleam of brightness. They went out again after tea while Frankie was at dinner, but they found the merry fit was over. The gloom of Frankie's approaching departure surrounded them. Their attempt at a game was a failure, and they soon wandered in again to watch for him as he came out of the dining-room.

The evening passed sadly. Frankie was tired and depressed; Cousin Jane reproaching herself for having waited till so late in the season to take Frankie to Torquay, and unable to conceal her anxiety at the prospect of the approaching voyage; the children gloomily indignant.

Nessa was astonished that in Frankie's condition there could be any question of persisting in the journey. But though the doctor had said with that saddest of all kindness that he might stay if he wished it, Cousin Jane determinately persuaded herself that he was only worse because he had stayed too long in Ireland, and she clung with all a mother's desperate hope to the journey that was to work wonders for her boy. Poor Cousin Jane!—she would not, she could not understand the grief that was coming upon her.

By reason of the inconvenient hours of the trains the traveling party was obliged to start at an early hour in the morning, and at six o'clock the children were up to see it off.

The hall fire had not yet been made up for the day; yesterday's gray embers smouldered in the hearth; and in the dreary light of the one lamp Brown had put in the hall they stood and watched the boxes being brought down. The door was open, outside it was still dark, and a fine rain was falling which made the raw morning air damp and unpleasantly cold.

The children shivered as they waited, but Cousin Jane did not keep them long. She came down first with Frankie to let him say good-by to his cousins while Emma was occupied with last preparations. Poor Cousin Jane's natural good nature triumphed at the last moment. She seemed to have provided herself with half-crowns innumerable, and as she kissed all the children she insisted on shoveling big silver pieces into their hands. She said she hoped at all events to bring Frankie back for a long visit in the spring, and as she bid Murtagh good-by she added warmly:

"I am very sorry you're not coming with us, Murtagh, and I'm sure Frankie's as sorry as you are. Well, it's not my fault; I'd a great deal rather have taken you than have you all disappointed."

The last words were perhaps more true than judicious, but at the moment Emma came down, and Cousin Jane went to arrange the carriage for Frankie.

It turned out to be a long process, and while the others gathered round the carriage Frankie stood with Murtagh and Winnie in the deep window recess, silently looking out at the wet steps and the dark figures faintly illuminated by the yellow light of the carriage-lamps.

The three little hearts were very full, but not a word was spoken till at last Cousin Jane called: "Come now, sonnie! we're nearly ready."

At the sound of her voice Frankie turned slowly away from the window; then, throwing his arms round Murtagh's neck, he kissed him passionately three or four times. "Good-by," he whispered, "good-by!" But there seemed to be something else he wanted to say. His deep brown eyes were fixed upon Murtagh's face with a wistful, yearning earnestness that made Murtagh, with one of his sudden impulses of tenderness, pass his arm round Frankie's neck and whisper: "Never mind, you'll soon come back!"

Winnie, who had been watching the preparations with a half-angry feeling, suddenly felt a choking lump rise in her throat. She took one of Frankie's hands, but Frankie seemed scarcely to notice her, and drawing a long breath he continued in a rapid whisper:

"Myrrh, I must tell you now, because perhaps this is the last. I think I'm dying; and I'm very glad, because you'll be much richer. They told me about it when they wanted me to get well. And if I die before I come back you're to have my pony, and Winnie has Royal. And—and you won't forget all about me, because I do love you so!" His voice faltered, and neither Winnie nor Murtagh could speak. "I will always remember you there," he added in a still lower whisper, "being dead can't make me forget."

One last silent kiss from both the children, and he went slowly towards the carriage trying to hide his emotion from his mother and sister. Murtagh and Winnie forgot that any one was there, and tears trickled unheeded over their cheeks as they stood together on the threshold watching the little wasted figure descend the steps.

Royal was standing by the carriage. He understood the meaning of the boxes, and looked wistfully from his little master to Winnie as if uncertain which to forsake. Frankie stooped and kissed him. "Good-by, Royal," he said; "you are hers now; mind you take good care of her. Winnie," with a faint attempt to smile as he turned again to his cousins, "I know you'll take good care of him."

The carriages drove away, and Brown not noticing the two children shut the hall door. They stood on the wet steps looking through the darkness at the swiftly disappearing lights. They were too shocked and, as it were, stunned by Frankie's words to be able to realize all at once what they meant; but slowly, slowly, the full meaning dawned upon them. They were never to see little Frankie again. They had said their last good-by.

"Win, it can't be true! it can't be true!" exclaimed Murtagh.

"Oh, Myrrh, isn't it *dreadful* being children?" cried Winnie. "We can't go with him. Oh, I do hate Mr. Plunkett. I do hate him, so I do!" And Winnie, who seldom cried, threw herself down on the steps in a passion of tears.

CHAPTER XXIV

T HE END WAS NEARER than even the doctors had expected. Frankie caught cold on the journey, and two or three days after his departure a broken-hearted letter came from his poor mother saying that they were at an hotel in Dublin; they could get no further, for Frankie was dangerously ill. It was the first time she had ever admitted that there was danger in his illness, and when Mr. Blair gave the letter to Nessa to read, he said: "It was a matter of months before, now I am afraid it is a matter of days. Poor Jane!"

Poor Jane, indeed! Even while Mr. Blair was speaking, she was sitting in dumb despair in the darkened hotel bed-room holding her dead son's hand in hers. The end had come, the end of all her brightest hopes, the end of all her tenderest affections. Suddenly,—in a moment. And already of the old sweet time nothing was left but memory. How could she believe it? Ah, poor Jane, poor Jane!

But at Castle Blair they did not yet know this, and neither Mr. Blair nor Nessa had thought it necessary to communicate to the children the bad news they had received of little Frankie's state. On the contrary, Nessa kindly devoted herself to cheering and amusing them in order that they might feel as little as possible the disappointment of not accompanying their cousin.

And though she was little accustomed to the society of children, she had a wonderfully practical way of doing whatever she made up her mind had to be done. What she did she seemed to do by a sort of instinct, much as the birds sing, and the flowers grow; and somehow she generally succeeded.

In this instance she succeeded marvelously. Winnie and Murtagh began to forget the trouble into which Frankie's words had thrown them. When they were alone and quiet it came back to them, but they had repeated to no one what he had said, and somehow in the midst of all their occupations the words began to seem unreal. The trouble of Pat's absence was there too down underneath, but Nessa did not speak at all of those things. She laughed with the children, went for walks with them, took an interest in their occupations, and began as she said to reform them. She just wanted to divert their thoughts.

So it happened that three or four days after Frankie's departure, the children having been with Nessa and Royal for a scramble across the fields, came in quite rosy with racing, and in a mood to think of some improvements that they desired to make in the fire-place of the island hut.

"There's no time like the present," said Murtagh, and as the others were of his opinion they left Nessa to enter the house alone, and started off with Royal to spend the rest of the afternoon upon the island.

Nessa was glad to be alone. Good-natured as she was she was too little accustomed to children's society not to be a little fatigued by it, and to-day especially, for though she had not chosen to seem one bit less bright, she had thought often of Cousin Jane's sad letter about little Frankie.

She was thinking of it again now as she stood by the school-room window. The park was in dreary unison with depressed thoughts, for dying leaves hung damply to the branches, and mists were already rising to close the short day; winter had almost come. But Nessa did not pay much attention to the landscape. She was thinking of the bright gentle little boy who had so lately been with them, and she too felt awed at the thought of death. But she could not believe that he would die; it seemed impossible it was such a short time since he had been there talking and laughing with them all. His mother's anxiety made her think him worse than he was, and Uncle Blair always saw things sadly.

Nessa could not believe in sadness. No, no, it would not be, he would get well, he could not die when his mother loved him so. So she persuaded herself; but when, after standing a long while by the window she happened to look out, the gray dampness of the landscape made her shudder, she did not quite know why, and with a sudden impulsive movement she pulled down the blind. She came over to the fire and poked it into a blaze. Poor little fellow! But, yes, she felt certain he would get well. In Dublin he would be near the best doctors. That glimpse she had had of dim rolling sward with skeleton trees standing out against a heavy sky, had produced a singular effect; she could not quite shake it off; but it was foolish to be influenced by such things; she would get a book to read, and think no more about it.

She rang for Peggy to put the room in order, and went up-stairs to take her things off and to fetch a book. A quarter of an hour later she was comfortably established on the big brown sofa by the fire, and her unpleasant impressions were forgotten in a book that interested her immensely.

It was an odd book for her to be charmed by, but coming upon it the other day in the library she had stood nearly an hour by the book-case reading on from where she had opened, and though she had not been able to look at it since, she had not forgotten the almost painful charm it had had for her. It was only a collection of stories taken from Italian history. Nothing more unlikely to please her could well have been imagined. Three months ago she would have turned from it with a sort of horror; but a new side of her nature had been awakened since she had been in Ireland; and the wildness, the enthusiasm, the restless, passionate courage, roughly but vividly described in the pages of this book, responded not to new wants arising in her mind, but to new sympathies.

What she had opened on to-day was an account of the conquest of Sicily by Charles of Anjou. It told of the bitter slavery of the people, of the heroic efforts of Giovanni di Procida to free his beloved country, and then of the irresistible passion bursting out at last on the day of the Sicilian Vespers. Nessa would not have understood it a little while ago. Now she read with such absorbed attention that she forgot everything in this world save Sicilian wrongs.

But as she was coming to the very climax of the story she was startled out of her abstraction by Peggy's entrance with a tray of rattling tea-things.

"It wants ten minutes of dinner-time, Miss," remarked that maiden in a tone of respectful admonition.

"What!" exclaimed Nessa. "The whole afternoon gone already. And the children, too, they have not come in."

But there was no time for exclamations; climax or no climax, the nine pages that remained of her book had to be left till after dinner; and, as it was, her evening toilette had to be made with a truly fairy-like rapidity.

She was growing accustomed now to the erratic ways of her little cousins, and did not trouble herself about their prolonged absence. Even when after dinner she returned to the school-room and found tea still untouched, she only concluded that their fire-place had taken longer to build than they had expected.

Her mind was still full of her book, and having piled fresh wood upon the fire she settled down contentedly to finish it.

The children left her just time. She was reading the last lines, when a banging of doors, a sudden clatter of little feet across the hall, a confusion of voices and laughter mixed with the short playful barks of a dog, announced that they were coming. The next minute Bobbo burst open the school-room door and rushed in, followed by the two girls, all rosy—laughing, panting, and all trying to talk at the same time. Royal jumped round them and barked in chorus, till the sounds became so mixed that it was difficult to say who was barking and who was talking.

"Down, Royal; be quiet, my beauty!" cried Winnie at last, while Bobbo exclaimed: "Oh, Nessa, we've had such fun, and Royal behaved so splendidly. You never saw such a dog. He does every single thing Winnie tells. He's the best king of our tribe we could possibly have; he flew at them like—— Oh, it was glorious to see how they ran."

Here all the children again tried to tell what had happened, and Bobbo's voice was lost in the Babel that ensued.

Nessa had shut up her book on their entrance, and laughingly put her hands to her ears.

"How can I hear a single word," she exclaimed, "if you all talk at once?"

"All right; give me something to eat, and I'll be as quiet as a lamb," cried Bobbo, sitting down to the tea-table as he spoke and seizing upon some bread and butter. "Gollyloo! I *am* starving."

"But do just listen," cried Winnie. "It was such fun to see them. You'd have thought Royal was a wild bea— Oh, where's the milk!" she exclaimed, suddenly interrupting herself. "He must have some supper."

"Here's the milk," said Nessa. "And where is Murtagh? And what is it that Royal has done?"

"Oh, Murtagh! He's coming; he'll be here in a minute. Well—we were on the island, and we'd got some big stones out of the river, and we were building away when we heard some one coming. First we thought it was you, and we thought that was jolly, so we called out: 'Here we are, awfully busy. Are you going to help us?' But then Royal jumped up and began to growl, and a man called back again: 'I think we'll help ye with the wrong sides of our shovels;' and lo and behold! there were two of the men—Hickey and that red-headed donkey, Phelim,—with picks and shovels on their shoulders, and would you like to know what they wanted?"

Nessa looked her surprise and attention, but did not even attempt to guess the preposterous design.

"To pull down our hut!" shouted all the children together. "Our own very hut that we've had ever since we came here!"

Bobbo opportunely choked over a mouthful of toast, and Rosie patted his back, while Winnie, seizing the chance, continued: "Did you ever hear of such a thing in your life? There was a wall to be mended somewhere, they said, and Mr. Plunkett had told them to take the stones from our hut. But we soon let them see their mistake. We told them they might go to London for their stones if they liked, but they weren't going to have one of ours. Phelim began to laugh in his stupid, aggravating way, and he said: 'Oh, ay, we've found our master now, you know, and what he says has got to be. The quality is no account at all now alongside o' the agents.'

"So then Murtagh started up from the fire-place and he came to the door, and he said: 'All the agents in Ireland may go to the bottom of the sea for all I care. But if you touch one stone of this hut I'll set the dog upon you.' And Royal knew quite well what Murtagh was saying, for he wagged his tail and looked as pleased as possible. Phelim was frightened; but Hickey said he couldn't help it, and he came up nearer to the hut; and Murtagh called out to him to stay where he was. And Royal growled; he growled just like a *bear*, so he did. And Hickey would come on. So then Murtagh and me called out, 'At them, Royal; good dog!' and he sprang straight at them.

"They both turned and ran; but just as they got to the edge of the island he seized Phelim, and down he went with him into the river. Oh, Nessa, if you could have seen Phelim!" continued Winnie with a merry peal of laughter. "His great red head went down and his heels went up; there was a tremendous splashing and gurgling, and then he roared! he roared just like a child, and the very top of his voice, and Royal—Royal laughed at him! he did, really, upon my word; we all saw him; he regularly shook himself with laughing; because he got out of the water and stood on the bank, and Phelim sat there in the river just roaring till—till——" But the remembrance of the scene made Winnie laugh so much that her words became incoherent.

"Till Hickey pulled him out, and they both took themselves off," said Murtagh's voice behind her.

"And Royal?" said Nessa, laughing.

"Oh," said Winnie, recovering herself, "Royal was too much of a gentleman to have anything more to say to him, only when Hickey was going to help him up, Royal ran at Hickey; so then Hickey took to his heels, and so did Phelim, and Royal just stood on the shore and barked and barked as much as to say, 'You know what you have to expect if you come worrying my tribe.' Didn't you, my beauty?" and Winnie's story ended with a hug to Royal as she knelt down before him with his supper.

"But you had better take care," said Nessa, "or you will be getting Royal into trouble."

"Oh," said Winnie, "that doesn't matter. You're my own, aren't you, my precious one, and nobody can touch you without my leave."

While Winnie continued to speak, Murtagh had flung himself silently into a great arm-chair by the window, and Nessa saw by his face and manner that he was in one of his proud, angry moods. She attended to the wants of the other children who were ravenously hungry, and then seeing that he did not stir, she said: "Your tea is poured out, Murtagh."

"I don't want any tea, thank you," replied Murtagh from the depths of his arm-chair.

Then ashamed, perhaps, of the tone in which he had spoken, he sprang up and came to the table.

"But let me cut the bread and butter for them," he said, taking the loaf from her, "see what red marks the knife makes on your hands." He looked up as he spoke with a pleasant smile.

"Did you ever know any one like Mr. Plunkett?" remarked Rosie at the same moment. "Just imagine him wanting to take the stones of our hut!"

"He's not going to get them," said Murtagh shortly, his brow clouding over again.

"It's the most ridiculous idea I ever heard in my life!" exclaimed Winnie,—"knock down our hut that we've had ever since we've been here, to mend some silly old wall. They'll be knocking down this house next to build up Mr. Plunkett's. I think they've all gone mad."

"And besides," said Murtagh, "papa built that hut with his own hands when he was a little boy. He told us all about it before we came here. Pat O'Toole's father helped him, and they collected every single stone that's in it one by one out of the river. It took them more than six months getting all the stones, and building."

"Why don't you tell that to Uncle Blair?" said Nessa. "You may be quite sure nobody remembers who built it, or they would not pull it down to mend a wall. Shall I tell him for you this evening and ask him to explain to Mr. Plunkett?"

Murtagh's face relaxed a little, and Rosie exclaimed:

"Oh yes, do; then that will prevent another fight with Mr. Plunkett, and we shan't be all so miserably uncomfortable. I think it's much nicer to be a peaceful tribe. It is so like savages, fighting and fighting."

"Listen to Rosie talking good!" burst out Winnie contemptuously. "Do you suppose Nessa means we ought to try and not fight just to make ourselves more comfortable?"

Rosie reddened, but made some sharp reply, and then ensued one of their ordinary sparring matches, while Nessa paying no attention to them was busy at the fire toasting a slice of bread.

The sparring passed into a din of continuous remarks which every one made and nobody listened to; but Murtagh stood silent cutting bread till Nessa returned from the fire and a plate of buttered toast was laid on the table beside him, with a smiling, "After all, I believe you are hungry, Murtagh." Then he took a bit of toast, and continued in the same tone as his last remark:

"Papa knows the shape of every one of the biggest stones. He made a picture for us once of the inside of the hut, and he used to tell us stories in the evenings when there wasn't any one there, about his adventures when he went in the river looking for stones."

"And you know that three-cornered white one, just a little bit on the right-hand side, inside the door!" cried Winnie. "Well, he was very nearly drowned getting that. They thought he was drowned first, only Grannie O'Toole got him round (she's dead now, you know), and they never told papa's papa and mamma for fear they mightn't let him go in the river for any more."

"And then," said Murtagh, his anger rising again at the remembrance, "they think they're going to get it to put in some beastly wall. But Mr. Plunkett's greatly mistaken if he supposes I'm going to let him touch a single one of papa's stones."

"Not while we have Royal to protect us," said Winnie. "I'd rather stay up there day and night."

"There's one thing," put in Bobbo, "even if he did get the stones we could knock the wall down and take them back and hide them."

"He'll get a good many duckings from Royal before he gets a stone out of the hut," returned Murtagh fiercely. "And if he's held under a little too long by mistake it would be a good riddance," he added half under his breath.

"Murtagh!" exclaimed Nessa almost involuntarily, but in a tone that expressed her dismay.

"I *can't* help it," returned Murtagh, "he makes me feel—" And the tone of Murtagh's voice finished his sentence for him.

Nessa looked at him; she could not understand this energy of hate. But notwithstanding his anger there was in his face something so forlorn that she felt more sorry for him than shocked.

"Come and sit by the fire, and let us try and forget all about him just for the present. It is no use to talk about him, is it?" she said kindly. Murtagh flashed back a bright grateful glance as he responded to her invitation by throwing himself upon the hearth-rug, but he did not speak, and his brow soon clouded over again. Nessa began to chat with the others; but she wished to keep the conversation clear of Mr. Plunkett, and all subjects interesting to the children had a fatal tendency to come back to him sooner or later. The safest thing to do was to talk of herself.

"Do you know what I have been doing all this afternoon?" she remarked presently. "I have been reading the most wonderful— But no, you shall just guess. Guess what it was about."

"Easy to guess," said Winnie, "if you got it out of the library. Some horrible dry stuff or other out of a book a yard long. Don't you know what grown-up people always read?"

"No, it wasn't," said Nessa. "The book was not bigger than one of your story books, and—"

"Horrid squinny little print, then, and yellow paper all over stains," replied Winnie laughing and unceremoniously interrupting. "*I* know Uncle Blair's books; they make one feel dusty to look at them."

"No, it wasn't," replied Nessa shaking her head. "It had—well, yes, it had a dreadfully ugly binding, but lovely white paper."

"Long S's," suggested Murtagh, making the remark because it occurred to him, but showing no desire to enter into the conversation.

"Oh yes, yes," cried Winnie. "Long S's, and funny little pictures of girls with parasols over their heads and trousers down to their boots. Now wasn't it, Nessa?"

"No," said Nessa, laughing, "not one single long s, and the pictures were all of robber castles in the mountains, and men fighting, and women fainting, and shipwrecks, and dungeons."

"Oh, I say, how jolly!" exclaimed Bobbo. "That's something like a book. What was it all about?"

"Couldn't you tell us some of it?" said Rosie. "It's so nice being told stories."

"Oh yes," cried Winnie. "If it's something dreadful do please tell us. I feel just in the very humor to put out the candles and poke up the fire and have something awful— something that'll make our flesh regularly creep and our hair stand up."

The other children were apparently of Winnie's mind, so little Ellie was sent to bed, the table was hastily cleared to prevent Peggy coming in to interrupt, and they all gathered round the fire.

Nessa was not accustomed to story-telling, but she acquitted herself wonderfully well. Sure that the subject would charm the children, she was delighted to find something which would take them completely out of their every-day troubles. So she described at length the sunny beauty of Sicily, its fruitful fields and smiling landscapes; she pictured the charming peaceful life that the inhabitants might have led; and if she allowed her imagination to run away with her a little, she succeeded at all events in warmly interesting her audience.

Murtagh alone paid little attention. His thoughts were full of his own troubles, and he lay on his back on the hearthrug brooding over them with a bitterness that excluded every other feeling. Soon, however, Nessa came to the conquest of the island. Some sentences that he overheard aroused his interest. He began to listen, and before she had gone very far in her relation of the oppression and injustice to which the unfortunate Sicilians were then forced to submit, he had rolled himself over and was lying stretched out at her feet, his elbows planted firmly on the ground, his chin resting on his hands, and his burning black eyes fixed upon her face with an expression that might well have startled her had she seen it.

She did not see it, however; she was now quite occupied by her story, and without being aware of the fact she had become eloquent in her description of how by degrees the whole country cried out for freedom, till at last a man was found ready to devote himself to his country's cause.

Murtagh's face as she proceeded was a curious study. It seemed at first with restless indignation to reflect every passion she described, but when she began to speak of John of Procida, and entered upon his resolute and devoted efforts for the freedom of his country, there came over it an eager exalted look, a look of fixed and passionate sympathy, that never faded till she brought the story to its climax.

"I would rather read you the end," she said, pausing to look down at their flushed faces, and eager eyes, and towsled heads, ruddy in the firelight. "The book will tell it better than I can."

The book was still on the sofa; she had only to open it. The children, all wondering what was to come next, were too much interested to speak, and she read:

"In the year 1282, Easter Monday fell on the 30th of March. It was a beautiful spring day, and the people of Palermo, according to their custom on holidays, flocked out in hundreds to the meadows in the direction of the church of Montreal, intending to hear vespers and to witness also the marriage of a beautiful young girl, the daughter of one Roger Mastrangelo.

"Mixed among the crowd of Sicilians were many Frenchmen who had come out intending also to see the marriage and to join in the games that were to fill the evening. But, as usual, the French were behaving roughly to the Sicilian men and impudently to the women, causing the Sicilian faces to look black and angry.

"It was one of the vexatious laws of the French that no Sicilian should carry arms, and presently a Frenchman cried out:

" 'These rebellious Paterins must have arms hidden upon them or they would never dare to look so sulky. Let us search them.'

"The idea was instantly caught up, and in another moment the festival would have been disturbed by a general search, when an admiring murmur running through the crowd turned all thoughts to another direction. The bride was coming, and every one turned to look.

"Dressed in her pretty wedding finery, her gold ornaments glinting in the sunlight, she leaned upon her father's arm, while her lover and the friends who were asked to the wedding walked behind. Every one moved out of her way, the crowds round the church door opened a pathway in their midst for her to walk through, and blushing and smiling she advanced toward the church. Suddenly a Frenchman stepped out of the crowd, and crying out with a coarse laugh, 'I daresay she has got arms hidden about her somewhere,' he tore open her dress and thrust his hand into her bosom. Terrified and insulted the poor girl fainted into her lover's arms, but her father sprang upon the offender, and tearing his sword from him stabbed him with it, crying as he did so; 'Let the French die.'

"Then every Sicilian in the place echoed the shout, 'Let the French die.' They had broken at last from their slavery, and more like wild beasts than men they took their revenge. In a moment the French were overpowered. Their arms were dragged from them and they were killed with their own swords. Back into the town went the Sicilians shouting everywhere, 'Let the French die,' and before they laid down their arms that evening they had killed four thousand."

Murtagh's eyes were fixed eagerly upon Nessa, and as her voice ceased he drew himself up suddenly on to his knees and exclaimed:

"Oh, how I wish I had been there! I *would* have fought with all my might and main against those mean French thieves. Did John of Procida succeed in the end?"

"Yes," said Nessa. As she answered she looked at him and was startled by the almost feverish interest of his face. His cheeks were flushed, his eyes bright, and he continued with rapid passionate utterance:

"How could they bear it so long? How could they live not free in their own beautiful country? But John of Procida was true, he was brave, he knew that it is better to die than to live like slaves."

Murtagh was not speaking to any one. His words poured out one after the other as though the feeling in his mind had unconsciously framed itself into speech. What a strange excitable nature it was! Nessa half wished that she had not told him the story as she looked at him kneeling there in the fire-light with that fierce fervent look upon his face.

The other children looked at him in surprise; his enthusiasm had astonished them too.

"Why, Murtagh," said Rosie, "how awfully hot you look! your cheeks are as red as fire."

"Yes," said Nessa, bending forward and arranging with her fingers his hair that was standing up on end, "I think you are quite excited by my story."

"If you please, Miss," said Brown's respectfully subdued voice at the door, "tea has been in the drawing-room for a quarter of an hour, and Mr. Blair desired me to let you know."

Murtagh started up.

"Why, Nessa, I had no idea it was so late!" he said, with a certain amount of ordinary surprise in his voice, but his eyes still full of suppressed excitement. "Good night," and without more words he went.

His abrupt departure disturbed Nessa; she feared that with the intention of distracting his thoughts she had really excited him too much; and more than once while she chatted with her uncle that evening she found herself wondering whether Murtagh were asleep yet. A good night's rest would be the best remedy for all his troubles.

Her disquietude would not have lessened if she had been able to see into Murtagh's mind.

He had entered the school-room in a tumult of rage, indignation, and rebellion. Bitterly repentant for the scene in the haggart which had caused so much unhappiness, he believed that it was nothing but deliberate persecution on Mr. Plunkett's part to pretend still to consider him guilty. He could not imagine that any one could really think him capable of such a tissue of lies, of such abominable cowardice as his guilt would now imply; and there was something that roused all his indignation in the idea that Mr. Plunkett saw now a good opportunity for crushing him and was determined to hit him hard while he was down. It was cruel, unjust, ungenerous. "Why does he do it?" Murtagh had cried passionately to himself, "Why does he do it? I shall do something dreadful some day, I know I shall, if he goes on like this."

With his wild little heart stirred to these depths he had listened to Nessa's story. The barbaric independence, the despairing savage struggle for freedom of the oppressed and devoted Sicilians, had appealed to his imagination in a way that it would have done at no other time. His own spirit seemed to be put in action; his wrongs were somehow merged in theirs; and in the tempest of their vengeance he was whirled along, feeling almost as though he too were at last taking just revenge for all the injuries that rankled in his mind. The fierce, almost savage, satisfaction that he felt, would have horrified himself had he not been so strangely moved; but for nearly the whole of the last month he had been living in a state of high pressure which could not fail to have some strong effect. He had alternated between extremes of violent passion and heroic resolve, and his mind was torn and shaken by the storm.

Alone in his room he walked up and down in the darkness, absently undressing, and dropping the various articles of his clothing upon the floor. Absorbed as he was he could not have told his thoughts; they scarcely were thoughts at all; his mind was carried along by some stronger power. Nessa's story possessed him; he was living in that, and confusedly mixed up with it was the indignant remembrance of his own troubles.

At last he threw himself upon his bed, but too excited to sleep he tossed and turned for hours, seeing over and over again in the darkness all the details of the story. Unconsciously he fell into imagining himself the leader of the Sicilians; he felt the enthusiasm and the savage joy that must have burned in them. His cheeks grew hot, his eyes flashed, as with vivid fancy he saw the fighting round him; the only thing worth doing in this world seemed to be to die for freedom, and through all the excitement there flashed across his mind, from time to time, a feeling of something like impatient despair at the thought that there was nothing for him to do.

CHAPTER XXV

Towards morning Murtagh fell into a disturbed sleep; but almost before daybreak he was awakened by Bobbo, who exclaimed as he shook him by the shoulder:

"Get up, Myrrh! We'd better be on the island early if we want to save the hut."

In an instant Murtagh was out of bed. Save the hut! whatever else he might give in about he would never relinquish that,—their father's hut.

The passionate thoughts of the night before had now assumed the tangible form of a dogged determination to resist Mr. Plunkett, and a pleasant sense of anticipated triumph tingled through his veins as he hurriedly dressed himself. All the miserable abasement of yesterday's anger was gone. He was going to fight now!

With his head thrown back and a confident determined look upon his face he ran down the stairs, saying to Bobbo: "Call the girls, while I fetch Royal. We shall see who'll be master this time!"

Before it was fully light the four children were on the island. Rosie, with practical forethought, had possessed herself of such scraps of food as she could find in the kitchen and servants' hall, and now they lighted a fire and sat down by it to eat their miscellaneous breakfast.

"But what are you going to do, Murtagh?" inquired Rosie, with a note of fretful disappointment in her voice. It really was an unkind fate which had made her the sister of such a brother. She had not the least taste for adventures.

"You'll see when the time comes," replied Murtagh, whose ideas were in truth very vague. He felt only sure of one thing, which was that he meant to do something.

"I don't mind what it is," said Winnie; "I'm ready for anything!"

"So am I," said Bobbo, "only I vote we don't hurt the poor beggars if we can help it."

"No; because it's not their fault you know, Myrrh," decided Winnie.

"No; but we can't let them land here!" replied Murtagh determinately. "If they will get hurt we can't help it. Now look here, we had better collect a lot of bits of wood, and clods, and things, and pile them up in front here, where we can get at them easily. They are sure to come up this front way."

"Oh," cried Winnie in delight, "you're going to pelt them! Then let us get some of that stiff, yellow mud from the bank. It will do gloriously!"

But their warlike preparations seemed likely to be quite unnecessary. Time passed quietly on. No one came to disturb the peace of the island, and the children were beginning to think they might have spared themselves the trouble of their early watch, when the loose rattle of cart-wheels was heard coming along the road on the left bank of the river.

"Here they come!" cried Murtagh, springing from his seat by the fire and hurrying out to reconnoitre.

The others hastily followed. Through a gap in the bushes they saw two empty carts coming down the road. The driver of each was seated on the shaft smoking a short pipe, and in the corner of one of the carts were visible the handles of picks and mallets.

"Yes," exclaimed Murtagh, "it's them. Now we're in for it! Royal, old boy, are you ready?"

The faces of the other children beamed with excitement. Royal understood well enough that something unusual was the matter, for he answered Murtagh's appeal by a short yap and a pricking up of his ears which meant business. Even Rosie was so carried away by the excitement of the approaching battle as to exclaim in sympathy with Winnie's dancing eyes, "Isn't jolly?"

The carts stopped on the road, and the men taking their tools began leisurely to descend through the little wood into the bed of the river.

"Now then, steady!" said Murtagh. "I'll talk to them first." He advanced as he spoke along the little path, and standing at the edge of the river he called out in a loud firm voice to know what they wanted.

The men were evidently somewhat discomfited at finding the island already occupied, and Hickey replied evasively: "Sure, Mr. Murtagh, we didn't expect to find you up here."

"What do you want here?" repeated Murtagh.

"Well, Mr. Plunkett's sent us for a load o' them stones; and you know orders is orders, so you'll let us have them quiet, like a good young gentleman, won't you now? Ye've hed ye're bit o' play yesterday evenin', and there's no gettin' on with work when ye're hindered that way!"

"I told you yesterday that you shouldn't touch our hut," replied Murtagh, "and you shan't! Mr. Plunkett may get his stones from the quarry."

"It's no good standin' blathering here!" exclaimed Phelim roughly. "We've got to have the stones, and there's an end of it! Come on, Hickey; we got the measure of Mr. Plunkett's tongue last night, and I don't want no more of it!"

"Take that for your impudence!" cried Bobbo, who without waiting for more snatched a stick from the heap of missiles and flung it at Phelim's head.

The stick flew harmlessly past, but a shout from the other children echoed Bobbo's words, and a rapid volley of mud-balls, sticks, and clods of earth saluted the onward advance of the men. So true was the aim, and so hard and fast did the children pelt, that Hickey and Phelim ran for shelter round the point of the island, and tried to effect a landing on the other side.

But on the other side the water was deeper, and the only standing-room was on a belt of shingle close to the shore of the island. The children knew this well, and when the men emerged upon it from behind the protecting screen of bushes they were greeted with such a shower of missiles, that Phelim, whose courage had been considerably undermined by the sound of Royal's excited barking, turned and fled blindly into the water.

As he lost his footing and rolled over in the water deep enough to souse him completely, the children raised a prolonged shout of triumph, and redoubled their efforts to dislodge Hickey, who, while returning their attack with whatever he could lay his hands on, was good-humoredly swearing at them and imploring them to stop their fun.

Suddenly in the midst of all the hubbub, over the noise of the children's shouting, Royal's barking, Hickey's swearing, Phelim's lamenting, a stern—"What's the meaning of all this uproar?" made itself heard, and Mr. Plunkett in shooting costume burst through the bushes on the right bank of the river.

Missiles were flying in every direction, and the only immediate answer to Mr. Plunkett's question was a mud-ball, which hit him on the forehead, and a stick that carried away his hat.

He put his hand angrily to his head, and losing all his habitual command of language, exclaimed: "What the devil do you mean by this?"

"We mean," cried Murtagh, who was perfectly wild with excitement, "that we won't have our rights interfered with, and you may just as well know, once for all, that we won't have this hut touched if all the walls in Ireland go unmended."

"Don't be impertinent to me, sir; you'll have whatever you are told to have," returned Mr. Plunkett hotly.

"Where are you going?" he inquired of the men, who, taking advantage of the cessation of active hostilities, were slinking off towards the carts.

"Please, sir, them stones is no good at all at all," Hickey ventured in answer; "they're all rubbish, every one of them, not worth the carting."

"I didn't ask your opinion of the stones. I told you to fetch them. A set of lazy scoundrels! I believe you're every one of you in league to prevent anything being decently done," exclaimed Mr. Plunkett.

"League or no league, the hut shall not be touched!" reiterated Murtagh.

"We shall very soon see that," returned Mr. Plunkett. "Go on to the island, and pull it down at once," he added, turning to the men. "I stand here till the work is begun."

"I'll set the dog on the first one of you who attempts to land," said Murtagh resolutely.

"Do you hear what I say to you?" demanded Mr. Plunkett, as the men stood doubtfully eyeing Royal, who, apparently enraged by Phelim's appearance, was furiously barking.

"Please, sir, the dog's very savage; he nearly killed Phelim last night," said Hickey apologetically.

"You pair of cowards! do you mean to tell me you are afraid of the dog?" exclaimed Mr. Plunkett contemptuously.

The men did not answer, but neither did they show the slightest inclination to move, and Winnie called out derisively: "How much for standing there till the work is begun?"

"Do you wish me to begin it myself?" demanded Mr. Plunkett angrily of the two men. "I tell you that hut has to be pulled down before I leave this spot."

He moved along the bank as he spoke, and prepared to jump on to a little island of shingle that lay in the bed of the stream.

"If you come one step nearer I'll set Royal upon you," cried Murtagh, roused to the last pitch of defiance by Mr. Plunkett's determination.

He and Winnie were both of them holding on to Royal's collar, and it was only with difficulty that they could restrain the dog, who seemed ready to attack anything and everything in his excitement.

"If you set your wild dog upon me I give you fair warning that I will shoot him," retorted Mr. Plunkett.

"As if you dare!" cried Winnie incredulously.

Mr. Plunkett's only answer was to spring on to the shingle.

"At him, Royal!" cried Winnie and Murtagh in a breath, loosing their hold as they spoke. With a furious growl Royal bounded into the river. Almost instantaneously Mr. Plunkett raised his gun. There was a loud report, then a piteous whine; the little cloud of smoke cleared away; there was a broad red streak in the water; and Royal turned his dying eyes reproachfully to Winnie.

"Oh, Murtagh! He's done it, he's done it!" she cried, with a beseeching disbelief in her voice that went even to Mr. Plunkett's heart, and though the water was over her ankles she dashed across to the shingle bank.

"Help me to take him out, Murtagh. Don't you see the water's carrying him down? He can't help himself. Royal, darling, I didn't mean it; I didn't think he would. Where are you hurt? oh, why can't you speak?"

The current swept the dog towards her, she managed to throw her arms round his neck and to get his head rested upon her shoulder, while Bobbo and Murtagh going in to her assistance tried to lift his body. But he groaned so piteously at their somewhat clumsy attempt that they stopped, and all three stood still, and in speechless dismay watched the wounded dog. Royal seemed more content, and from his resting-place on Winnie's shoulder licked away the tears that were rolling down her face. But after a time the children's wet feet began to grow numb, and Winnie looked up and signed to Murtagh to try and move him now.

He groaned again. For a moment he seemed to struggle convulsively, his head fell off Winnie's shoulder, his eyes looked up appealingly to hers, his limbs suddenly straightened, and then he was quite quiet as the children supported him through the water, and tried tenderly to lift him on to the bank. He was too heavy for them, and Mr. Plunkett, his hot anger past, came forward saying almost humbly, "Let me help you;" but though the children none of them answered, they turned their faces from him in such an unmistakable manner that he fell back and signed to one of the men to go and help them in his place.

Thus Royal was lifted on to the right bank of the river; and Winnie, sitting on the ground, took his head into her lap, while Murtagh, Bobbo, and Rosie stood round and watched. But he never moved nor groaned; he was so unnaturally still that a dim terror entered into the children's minds. Winnie stooped down to kiss him; as she did so her fear became a certainty.

"Murtagh," she said, raising a white frightened face. "He—he's killed him."

Murtagh made no answer, but falling on his knees beside Royal he laid his cheek against the dog's muzzle to feel if there were any breath. Then his mournful eyes and sad shake of the head confirmed Winnie's words. Mr. Plunkett and the two men had known it for some minutes, but as Mr. Plunkett stood watching the group of children he felt a strange, unusual moisture rising to his eyes, and he turned and walked away.

As they realised that the dog was dead, really dead, Rosie and Bobbo began to cry; the other two sat dry-eyed gazing at Royal.

The men stood one side respecting their grief for a few moments, but then they came forward and began to make remarks and offer consolation.

"He was a beautiful creachure," said Hickey, "and indeed it would serve old Plunkett right if he got shot with the very same gun. But there, don't take on so, bless yer hearts; the master'll get yez another dog as fine as ever this was."

While Pat was speaking Phelim stooped down and idly taking one of Royal's paws shook it slowly backwards and forwards. Winnie put out her hand to prevent the sacrilege, and looking up at Murtagh said, "Take them away, Murtagh, all of them."

"We'd better take the dog with us and bury him," said Phelim; "a big dog like that'll want buryin'."

"No, no," cried Murtagh, with a quick glance towards Winnie which seemed to say he would have protected her from the words if he could. "Come away, all of you, and leave her alone."

And so Winnie was left sitting on the ground with her dead dog's head resting on her lap. Bobbo and Rosie returned to the house to tell the sad news to Nessa. The two men went to find Mr. Plunkett, but Murtagh wandered away by himself into the woods higher up the river.

The men having found Mr. Plunkett at home inquired what they were to do about the hut. Was it to be taken down?

"Yes, of course," returned Mr. Plunkett testily, feeling strongly inclined to say on the contrary that it might be left standing, but ashamed of what he considered a bit of inconsequent weakness.

CHAPTER XXVI

Murtagh in the mean time wandered alone through the woods above the island. The defence of the hut was quite forgotten, and every other feeling was cut short by horror. The shock of Royal's death had been so sudden, so totally inconceivable beforehand, that it was only with great difficulty he could realize it now. His mind seemed in a measure benumbed. He went backwards and forwards through the woods with his hands thrust deep into his pockets. Dead leaves fluttered down upon his bare head and lay in golden drift on either side as his feet cut furrows through the gathered layers, sunlight glinted through the branches, a few birds were singing in the clear air; but it might have been snowing for all Murtagh knew to the contrary.

Almost unconsciously a kind of instinct to be with Winnie in her trouble led his footsteps after a time back to where she had been left, and the first outward sounds which woke him from his abstraction were her violent sobs. A thin screen of branches had prevented him from seeing her as he came up, but now he looked through it and saw her lying upon the ground, her arms thrown round Royal, her face buried in his dark curly coat, and her whole body shaken with emotion.

"Royal, darling, you're not dead! You can't be dead, really!" she cried passionately. Then, as her own sobs were the only sound and Royal lay stiff and cold beneath them, she wailed out: "How could he do it? How could he murder you?"

"Win, don't cry so *dreadfully!*" cried Murtagh, breaking through the bushes and throwing himself down beside her. His own voice was choked, and he tried to put his arms round her and kiss her. But she did not lift up her face; he could find nothing but the back of her ear to kiss through her hair, and her sobs came with redoubled violence. He knelt beside her with one arm thrown over her back and looked around, feeling perfectly powerless to console her. The dull thuds of the picks and mallets which were demolishing the hut fell mechanically upon his ear, but he did not heed them.

Winnie sobbed on in utter abandonment of grief.

"Don't cry so, Win," he said again, laying his face down on her head.

After a minute Winnie replied between sobs: "Go away, please. I'd rather be here. You can't ever make him alive again!"

For one moment she raised a face so swollen and tear-stained that Murtagh was startled at the sight of it; but shaking back her hair she dropped again into her former position with such evident desire to be alone that Murtagh got up and went slowly into the wood.

He never remembered to have seen Winnie cry so, and he could not bear to think of her alone there without any comfort. He did not venture back to her again, but he wandered about near where she lay, trying to think of something to do to comfort her. And nothing seemed to be a bit of good; he never, never could make Royal alive again. Oh, that dreary, dreary day! The shadows began to lengthen, but still he stayed in the wood near Winnie, coming from time to time to peep through the branches and see if she still were there.

After a while she stopped sobbing, but she scarcely changed her position all day, and Murtagh began to feel in a state of half-frightened despair.

He did not like to speak to her, but at last he could bear it no longer, and after watching her for a long time he called almost timidly:

"Win!"

She did not move. He called her a little louder, then a third and a fourth time, but still she gave no kind of answer. His heart stood still with a vague fear, and, scarcely knowing what he expected to see, he went close and gently lifted some of the brown hair that fell in confusion over her shoulder. She was fast asleep. Her head still rested upon Royal's shaggy curls, one arm was thrown round him, and the little face looked so white upon its rough black pillow that Murtagh bent very close before he could feel sure that she was only asleep. Then he could hardly have explained the relief that he felt. He sat down to watch beside her, but after a little time he thought he would go and get Nessa to come before she wakened again, so he left her and went towards the house.

But the day was far from finished yet; there was worse to come.

As he got down into the pleasure ground he was met by Rosie, her face swollen and stained with crying.

"Oh, Murtagh!" she exclaimed. "Where have you been all day? I've been hunting for you everywhere to tell you. Poor Frankie's dead; it came by the telegraph to-day."

She burst out crying again as she spoke, but Murtagh did not. He looked at her blankly as though he did not take in the sense of the words, and then he said, "What?"

"Frankie's dead," she repeated, "and they never thought it would be so sudden; and oh, Murtagh, just think of his being here,—being the very last time."

"Where's Nessa?" said poor Murtagh, with a confused bewildered feeling that she would somehow contradict this.

"In the drawing-room," replied Rosie, and she turned and followed Murtagh as he walked rapidly along.

"Don't you want to cry, Murtagh?" she asked curiously after a minute, her own tears stopped by astonishment at Murtagh's way of receiving the news. "Bobbo is crying so, poor fellow, up in his own room. It is so dreadful too, isn't it, to think—" Here her tears overpowered her again and she spoke no more.

At the drawing-room door Murtagh was met by Nessa. He could not speak, and she, seeing that he knew all, just put her arms round him and kissed him tenderly.

For an instant he clung to her, and a great sob shook his body, but then he disengaged himself and looked up still dry-eyed.

"Winnie," he said; "come to her while she's asleep. And—and don't tell her, or she won't come away all night."

He turned and walked down the passage and across the hall expecting Nessa to follow him, but at the door he stopped, and looking at her dress said:

"You'll be cold. I'll go and fetch your—" He put his hands up to his temples with a dazed kind of expression as though he could not remember the words he wanted, and added with an effort—"your coat and things."

He rushed up the stairs and returned with Nessa's hat and jacket. He helped her into them, and then they set off together for the wood. Nessa stretched out her hand for his, and they went hand in hand the whole way, but something in Murtagh's manner prevented a word from being spoken.

It was almost dark when they reached the spot where Royal lay. They found Winnie still lying beside him, but she was awake now and seemed calmer. She sat up when she saw them; Nessa knelt down beside her and kissed her; and though her tears began to flow again they were quieter and more natural.

"You must come home now, dear," said Nessa after a little time, gently laying her cheek against the troubled face that rested upon her shoulder, and almost unconsciously tightening the clasp of her arms as she thought of the new trouble waiting at home.

Murtagh had stood watching them in silence, and now he only said: "We will cover him with branches." He picked a branch of fir as he spoke and gently laid it upon Royal's body. But there was in his tone such resolute putting on one side of his own grief, such perfect patient tenderness for Winnie, that Nessa could contain her tears no longer, and she fairly sobbed.

She recovered herself immediately, and her tears served to compose Winnie, who kissed her and got up and helped Murtagh to put the covering upon Royal. The last branch was soon laid upon his head, and then Winnie went slowly away with Nessa. But Murtagh stayed behind and plunged again into the wood, where flinging himself upon the ground, he gave way to all his grief. It was not only grief for Frankie which brought those short fierce sobs and then the long bursts of tears—tears that ran down unheeded into the ground on which he lay. It was everything altogether that made the child so supremely miserable.

How long he lay there he did not know, but night had come when at last sick and exhausted he sat up and leaned against a tree.

It was time to be going home, but he could not face the school-room full of children. He would sleep there, he thought; and he was lying down again at the foot of the tree, when it occurred to him that the hut would be a better place. So he got up, and with some difficulty, because of the darkness, he crossed the river and groped his way to where the little island path made an opening in the thick brushwood. He drew himself up the bank and advanced slowly, stretching out his hands to feel for the door. He groped about unable, of course, to find it, till presently his foot struck against something, a covered fire apparently, for a shower of sparks flew upwards. He jumped to one side, and a bright blaze flaming out displayed to his astounded eyes the scattered rubbish, which was all that remained of their beloved hut. The stones had been taken away, but the door and broken pieces of the roof lay there upon the ground.

So utterly astonished was he that at first he could scarcely believe his eyes. Then he remembered the sounds which had echoed through the woods in the earlier part of the day, and with a sudden revulsion of feeling he exclaimed aloud:

"The coward! he has taken advantage of——"

"Ay, and it isn't only your little play-place he's turned you out of," said a familiar voice behind him in the bushes, "but my father and mother's to be turned out of the place they've held backwards and forwards this hundred years, because they can't pay the rent since it's riz upon them last Michaelmas."

Murtagh started and turned round to see Pat O'Toole standing in the full blaze of the firelight.

"Oh, Pat, Pat!" he cried, springing towards him, "you've come back at last."

"I couldn't stop away at all," he replied. "I was up in the mountains, and one and another of the boys gave me food, but I used to come down o' nights, an' one night my mother was out fetching the goat, and the tears were running down as she walked along, and so I couldn't help it at all, but I just up and told her I was there. And look here, Mr. Murtagh," he continued, dropping his voice and coming closer, "the boys say he isn't a bit o' good, and now he's riz the rents there's the Dalys'll have to go out, an' the Cannons; and there's many'll die o' distress with the winter coming on, and the bad potatoes an' all; an' I've been watchin' for you because I thought ye'd help me. And look here, Mr. Murtagh, if ye'll get me a gun some way I'll shoot him, and ha' done with it."

Pat's voice sank into a fierce hoarse whisper as he ended, and his face was bent down close to Murtagh's. Murtagh did not answer at once; he could hardly believe that he was not dreaming, and Pat continued: "It's a benefactor you'll be to the country. There's many and many a one'll bless you far an' wide. There's Jim Cannon, brother to Cannon down beyant there, has his wife and children in the Union, and he's wanderin' about, daren't come home and do a bit o' decent work because Plunkett's informed against him for a Fenian.

"And there's Mike Coyle and his wife and children had to turn out and shift for themselves, because he wouldn't let the old man keep them with him at home in his own place. And there's my mother and father turned out of a place we've had from one to another this hundred year; and Johnny Worsted taken from his work, and his old father and mother dependin' upon him, and sent to prison for nothing in the world but knocking over a couple o' little hares. And look now, Mr. Murtagh," he added, dropping his voice again to a cautious whisper, "if he was killed out o' the way it'd all come right, and I told the boys how we were bound together in a tribe like, and you'd never fail us in a pinch. There's many and many a heart'll be made glad through the country. Isn't he oppressin' every one of us, and changin' all the old ways that was good enough for them as was better than him! And look at yerselves; isn't it just the same way with yez? Isn't he tyrannizin' over yez, and doesn't mind a word anybody spakes to him, but only havin' everything his own way? He doesn't care for any one's feelin's! Just look at the way he massacrated Miss Winnie's beautiful dog this mornin', and she nearly cried her heart out over it. But he don't care, he'd do it again to-morrow; and only took advantage of ye bein' thinkin' o' that, to come and pull down your hut that was built before ever he came here."

Murtagh listened now without attempting to interrupt. He had hated Mr. Plunkett before, but nothing had ever equaled the feelings with which he regarded him to-day. The shooting of Royal, their beautiful Royal, who was almost like another brother to them, was too cruel. And then when the news of Frankie's death had come and they were absorbed by their double misery, to take advantage of that to pull down their hut! There was something so revolting in such conduct that Murtagh could only think of the man with disgust as well as hate.

Pat's words stirred up all the fierce passion of last night, and the feelings with which he had heard Nessa's story surged up again in his heart. As he listened the blood went coursing swiftly through his veins. Was not this a way to end it all? All the country round was suffering as they were. The people looked to him to help them; would not this be doing something indeed for freedom! He never in the least realized what it was; how could he, a child of eleven? But it presented itself vaguely to him as a grand and terrible action. Something in him spoke loudly against Pat's reasoning, but so thoroughly was his whole nature warped by the excitement of the last month that he mistook his true instinct for cowardice, asking himself if John of Procida would have hesitated so.

And while his decision was hanging thus in the balance, Pat brought before him the picture of Winnie's grief and Mr. Plunkett's indifference. The remembrance flashed through his mind of Hickey's words in the morning—"It would serve old Plunkett right to be shot with the very same gun," and with a sudden gust of passion he decided.

"Yes," he said, "I'll do it! you shall have the very gun he shot Royal with."

"I knew ye'd help us!" replied Pat exultingly. "I told the boys you wouldn't fail us; ye have too much o' the real old spirit in ye."

It was done; he had given his promise; but if he had only hesitated one minute longer all might have been different. Pat had only just answered when a sound of scrambling on the other bank made Murtagh exclaim in a hurried whisper, "Hide!" and there was barely time for Pat to conceal himself in the bushes before Bobbo appeared followed by Nessa.

Poor little Nessa looked very white and tired, and a faint struggle to smile died away in the attempt.

"I was nervous," she said; "I could not go to bed while you were out, so Bobbo came with me. He thought you would be here. Will you not come in now?"

"Yes," said Murtagh, "I'll come, you go on first."

Nessa looked at him in some surprise. She had expected to find him prostrated with grief in some out-of-the-way corner, but here he was standing up by a blazing fire, his cheeks flushed, and his eyes bright with excitement. He really was incomprehensible.

"Our hut gone!" exclaimed Bobbo in dismay, standing still and surveying the ruins. "He can't have been so mean—! To take it to-day!" And with the remembrance of all the day's troubles the tears came into his eyes.

"Yes," said Murtagh. Then in a hurried loud voice he continued: "Never mind; let us go home. Get on the stones and help Nessa down."

His manner half-frightened Nessa; she wondered whether he were ill. She followed

Bobbo, however, and Pat putting his head out from his place of concealment whispered to Murtagh:

"To-morrow night, here."

"All right, here!" Murtagh replied, and he hastened after the others.

Nessa put her hand through his arm as they walked along. Murtagh knew that she meant it partly as a caress, and he almost wished she would not. He was in no mood for caresses. They spoke little. Murtagh asked what time it was, and was told it must be eleven now. They had waited till ten, Nessa said, before they started to look for him.

As they were nearing home Murtagh roused himself with an effort from his thoughts.

"Poor Nessa!" he said; "you must be nearly dead tramping about like this. Why did you come for me?—I'd have done very well out there."

"I couldn't have you out there. I did not know where you were; I was frightened." And there was a little tremble in Nessa's voice that melted away a good deal of Murtagh's excitement.

In the school-room he found a little table prepared for supper.

"You have eaten nothing all day," said Nessa, and she insisted upon his sitting down and trying to eat while she made some tea from a kettle that stood boiling on the hob.

To please her he tried to eat, and under the influence of her gentle ways and little tender cares he grew quieter and quieter. At last he asked hesitatingly "if she had told Winnie yet?"

"Yes," she replied. "It was no use to keep it for the poor child to hear in the morning. When she was in bed I told her."

Murtagh sat looking into the fire for a few minutes with tears glistening in his eyes, and then he asked:

"What did she—?"

'Poor little thing!—she could not believe it at first, and then, then it was very sad. She seemed to feel so much about Frankie having given her Royal; it made it worse for her. She has cried herself to sleep again now. I went in to look at her before we came out."

Nessa spoke a little hesitatingly, saddened by the recollection of Winnie's grief, and not knowing what effect her words would have upon Murtagh. But she was relieved to see tears flowing over his cheeks, they were more natural than his previous state of excitement.

"I think I'll go to bed," he said in a choked voice, getting up to say good night.

"Good night, dear!" and she held him tight in her arms for a moment as she kissed him.

Her tenderness brought back all the soft natural grief for his cousin, and when he was in bed he gave not a thought to Pat; but, like Winnie, cried himself to sleep with his mind full of thoughts of Frankie's dear loving ways.

CHAPTER XXVII

NEXT MORNING poor Royal was buried. Hickey asked the children where they would like his grave to be dug, and Winnie chose the point of the island.

With many tears he was taken across the river and laid in his last resting-place. The sobs that escaped from Winnie as the earth was thrown in upon him shook Murtagh's heart and stirred up again his bitter indignation against Mr. Plunkett, but he stood silent beside her till the last shovelful of earth was patted down into its place. Good-natured Hickey had begged a rose-tree from Bland, which he planted for them at the head of the grave; then he took his tools and trudged away, telling them not to fret. Bobbo called Rosie to see the desolation of the hut, and Winnie and Murtagh were left standing by the grave alone.

"Don't stay here, Win," said Murtagh, putting his arm round her neck. "It will make you so dreadfully miserable, as it did yesterday. Come away into the wood, and let us be together. And look here, Win," he added, the indignation breaking out at last. "There's one thing, you'll be well paid out. He's going to get what he deserves at last."

"That won't do any good," returned Winnie disconsolately. "But I hope he will," she added with sudden anger. "It will serve him right. Oh, Murtagh, how could any one be so cowardly and so cruel to shoot at him when he was in the water like that?—so close to him he couldn't possibly miss. And then—then Royal looked as if he thought I'd sent him in on purpose, and he couldn't understand when I told him we didn't; and—and Frankie said he knew I'd never let any one hurt him; and now Frankie's dead, and I can't tell him about it either; and oh, Myrrh, doesn't it seem as if everybody was dying?" The end of Winnie's sentence was almost lost in tears.

The two children had been moving away while she spoke with their arms round each other's necks, and now they wandered into the wood and spent the rest of the morning walking up and down together, their conversation a confused medley of grief, anger, and sad, loving recollections of the doings of their two dead.

Towards the end anger predominated. Murtagh repeated to Winnie all that Pat had told him of the sufferings of the people about. He told her, too, that Pat was in hiding at home; that he was going to be revenged on Mr. Plunkett, and that he (Murtagh) was going to help him. He did not tell her exactly what he was going to do, something within him prevented him from speaking of that. Winnie listened eagerly.

"I do hope he will succeed," she said; "and just fancy, Myrrh, if he does set all the people free, he will be just like John of Procida that Nessa was telling us about."

And for the moment Murtagh wished that he were himself the one who was to shoot Mr. Plunkett.

In the afternoon Nessa went to Ballyboden to buy what was necessary for the children's mourning, and Rosie eagerly accepted her invitation to go too, and help her in the choice. They took Ellie with them in the carriage, and the other three being left alone spent a half-sad, half-bitter afternoon wandering idly about together.

Theresa Curran, coming up to the Castle on a message, met them in the avenue, and curtsying deeply told them with some shyness that "they down at the village was all very glad to think it was Mr. Murtagh now would be master over them some day."

Murtagh did not understand what she meant, and when she explained that "sure, after the master, it'll belong to you and yours now," he exclaimed in angry surprise:

"You mean that you're glad! Aren't you ashamed to be so cruel and unkind?"

Theresa saw that she had made a mistake, and replied in some confusion: " 'Deed, an' we're all very sorry for him, poor little gentleman, but we'll be very glad to have you reign over us, Mr. Murtagh dear. There'll be a stop put then, maybe, to some o' the doings goes on now. Every one hunted out o' their homes, and no more account made of it than if they was wild animals."

Theresa's complaint was bitter enough, seeing that her mother was one of the people who were to be "hunted out o' their homes;" but it was only Irish wit that led her to make it at that moment. It seemed to her the readiest means of diverting Murtagh's attention from her piece of gaucherie, and she was not mistaken. Murtagh inquired at once who else was being turned out, and nearly an hour was spent in listening to Theresa giving the same account as Pat had given of the village discontent.

"There!" said Murtagh as she passed on; "they all say just the same thing."

"And I don't wonder," replied Bobbo; "when he could do what he did yesterday he could do anything. Why if it wasn't for him being so unjust poor Royal would be safe away with you, instead of—"

"I don't think he has ever done anything but make people unhappy all his life!" said Winnie, her tears overflowing again as she spoke. "Even poor little Frankie, he made him miserable the last time he was here, and if it hadn't been for him we might have been there at least to say good-by."

Still an hour afterwards, when Winnie and Bobbo feeling that they must do something, went to see the cows milked, and Murtagh was left alone, misgivings, which took the form of a natural shrinking from what he was going to do, assailed his mind. He tried to combat his doubts. This was a right and a great thing to do. It was a just retribution that Mr. Plunkett should be shot with the very gun he had used against Royal. All the people would be able to spend this winter in their homes. If Frankie could know things he would be glad.

Instinctive right was strong enough within him, however, to make it impossible for him to feel quite clear, and it was with a sense of relief that he saw the carriage coming up the avenue, and ran to the hall door to meet it.

There were a great many parcels to be taken out, and before they were all disposed of Winnie and Bobbo made their appearance.

"Oh, Winnie!" cried Rosie, "Nessa has chosen such pretty hats for us! Ellie is to have a little round one, but we are to have felts turned up at one side, with a long black feather going right down over our hair."

Winnie looked at her in astonishment. "I do believe," she began contemptuously; but whatever she had been going to say was apparently too bitter, for she broke off suddenly and turned away while her eyes filled with tears.

Rosie reddened so painfully that Nessa felt quite sorry for her, and giving her some parcels asked her to take them to her bed-room; Rosie escaped up-stairs, and Nessa soon followed to take off her things.

Then came tea, and Nessa came to the school-room to pour it out. She did not often honor the tea-table with her presence, but her coming was always a treat, and to-day she seemed only to think of what she could do to please the children. At another time

Murtagh would have appreciated her gentle kindness, but now the time for him to perform his promise to Pat was drawing so near, that he was too much excited to be able to feel anything save the strain of trying to be quiet and to appear unconcerned.

He had decided yesterday evening on leaving the island that the time to possess himself of the gun would be while Mr. Plunkett was down at supper. Supper at the Red House was a kind of tea-dinner, at seven o'clock, and as that hour approached all doubts were thrown aside, and his heart beat high in anticipation. He could not sit still through the whole of tea-time, but after drinking a cup of milk and shaking his head at all offers of food he presently pushed back his chair and went away.

It was already dusk, so he went out into the park, and hovered about near the Red House till the ringing of the supper-bell announced that his time had come. Then it was the work of a minute to climb on the roof of the dairy, and from thence into Mr. Plunkett's dressing-room, the window of which was shutterless. The room was, of course, quite dark, but Murtagh had matches in his pocket, and with trembling fingers lit the candle. He knew the gun was kept in a cupboard in the corner among walking-sticks and fishing tackle. He found it in its usual place, found also the cartridges belonging to it, possessed himself of both, extinguished the light, and noiselessly let himself down again on to the dairy roof. In another minute he was safe outside the garden, hurrying away towards the island.

It was the first time in his life that he had held a gun in his hands, and the touch of the steel barrel made him shudder. He was not quite free from doubt either as to whether it would not go off, but he was burning with excitement; and soon he stood amongst the ruins of the hut where, by the light of a more cautious fire than the one he had kicked into flames the night before, Pat sat waiting for him.

"There," he cried, putting the gun into Pat's hands. "Now when are you going to do it?"

"To-morrow evening'll be my chance. He's going to dine up at the Castle to-morrow, and on his way home is when I'm to do it," replied Pat. "Then I'm to throw the gun down beside him and go straight away off again, and being his own gun there's no one will be suspected."

But there seemed something treacherous to Murtagh in the idea of killing Mr. Plunkett in the dark, on his way home from dinner at the Castle.

"Oh no, Pat," he exclaimed, "I don't like that. Do it out in the field in the morning, and let him know what it's for. Couldn't you show me how to do it?"

"Whisht, sir; ye don't know anything about it," replied Pat, grasping the gun. "Leave it to me and I'll settle it right enough."

"Yes, but, Pat, you mustn't do it that cowardly way," persisted Murtagh.

"Now, Mr. Murtagh, ye're talking foolish," said Pat, who seemed to have grown years older in his short absence. "Whatever way we do it mustn't we do it sure an' certain? and if it's me's to do it mustn't I do it my own way? What good would it do ye for the polis to take me? Leave it to me and he'll know what it's for sure enough. Ye don't want to be goin' back off your word, do ye?"

"No, indeed, I don't!" cried Murtagh with vivid recollection of Winnie's grief and Theresa's stories.

"They said I'd never be able to do it right," pursued Pat; "but gettin' a gun was the only thing that bothered me; now my mother'll stop where she is and die in the old home; and it isn't only her—there's many'll say a prayer for ye for this evening's work, Mr. Murtagh. They say what he wants is to turn us all out and get foreigners in bit by bit. It's an Englishman he's put into Dolan's farm. But if we mayn't live at home in our own place where is it we'll live at all? We're made no more account of than if we was rats and mice."

Then followed detail after detail that only served to inflame Murtagh's heated brain the more. Neither of the boys really knew anything of what he was talking about. They only heard that people had to pay more than they had ever paid before for their homes, and that in some cases they were turned out of them altogether. They did not hear that where rents had been raised it was in consequence of expensive and necessary improvements; where tenants had been turned out it was always for a solid reason. Rigorous justice had been dealt to all. But the people did not like such ways, and Pat repeated to Murtagh the grumblings of the worst and most discontented among them.

Murtagh could have sat there all night listening to his stories, but it would not do for him to attract attention by being late again this evening; so after a time he bade Pat good night and hurried homewards. In his present state of excitement he could not venture into the school-room, but sending Peggy in to say that he had gone to bed he went straight to his own room.

CHAPTER XXVIII

He TOSSED AND TUMBLED all night long, wakening Bobbo sometimes, and frightening him by the wild things he called out in his sleep, and next morning when he woke he was in such a state of nervous exaltation as made even Bobbo's companionship almost too painful to be borne. Only now did he fully realize that his share in this enterprise was done, and the greatness of the catastrophe he was helping to bring about seemed to begin to dawn upon him as the time for its fulfillment approached. His heart thumped against his side; his lips and hands were hot and dry. How was he to spend his day in the companionship of the others without betraying himself?

He knew that he could not keep away from them all day without causing remark and perhaps search; so he tried to force himself to feel calmer, and when the breakfast-bell summoned him to the dining-room he went in and took his usual seat at the table.

But so startling was his appearance that Nessa exclaimed anxiously: "Murtagh dear, you are ill!"

His uncle looked up, and was shocked too at the face that his eyes rested upon.

"Why, my boy," he said kindly, "what is the matter with you? Do you feel pain anywhere?"

"I am quite well, thank you," said Murtagh. He had felt as if he could not make his lips frame the short sentence, but the words came out in a clear, loud tone that astonished him. His uncle continued to look anxiously at him. Nessa said no more, but put a cup of tea beside his plate, laying her hand for one instant on his head as she passed back to her own seat. Her touch thrilled through him in a way that was almost pain. He drank some of the tea, and then his heart began to beat less rapidly; so that when his uncle asked him if he had slept well he was able to answer more naturally: "Yes, thank you."

"Awfully queerly!" said Bobbo; "you were shouting out all sorts of things all the time!"

His uncle made no remark, and breakfast proceeded in silence. But when it was over Mr. Blair called Nessa back as she was leaving the room and told her that she had better send for the doctor and let him see Murtagh.

"It can do no harm, at all events," he said, "and the child looks ill."

Breakfast had done Murtagh good, but he was in a state of feverish unrest. He made an effort to control himself, and talked loud, and tried to "chaff" the children when they hazarded surmises as to what might be the matter with him; but he was glad at last to take refuge in saying that he did not feel very well, and throwing himself upon the school-room sofa he lay for the rest of that miserable morning with his eyes fixed upon its brown moreen back.

Every distant banging of a door, every step in the passage, every sudden raising of voices, caused his heart almost to stand still with expectation, for in his excitement yesterday evening he had not quite clearly understood whether Pat did or did not intend to change the plan of action he had described. All he knew was that he had done his share, he had given the gun, and now at any moment Mr. Plunkett might be killed with it.

He did not shrink, but as the time approached his mind had become so filled with the horror of the deed that he felt not one grain of the exultation he had expected. Still he did *not* shrink. If any one had offered to undo for him all that he had done he would not have accepted the offer, for he clung to his belief that this was a great action. But though he would not have gone back, there came once or twice underneath all a pricking doubt which for the moment turned his state of expectation into agony.

Could it be that he was all wrong? Yesterday evening Pat had crushed the dawning of this thought by the assertion that it was a doubt only worthy of a child, and by the tales of injustice with which he had so adroitly proceeded to fill Murtagh's mind. But his description of the way the gun was to be used was altogether different from anything Murtagh had conceived, and it was impossible quite to shake off the conviction that it must be cowardly to shoot at a man in the dark when he suspects no danger.

Twice during the morning this conviction grew so strong as almost to make the whole truth flash upon Murtagh, but he rejected it. It was impossible. Pat's way of doing it might be cowardly, but the deed itself must be great, and as one after another of Pat's and Theresa's stories came back into his mind he felt persuaded again that he was right.

The morning passed away; the terrible news that Murtagh lay expecting did not come; and it was just luncheon time when Rosie, returning from a message to Nessa's room, remarked that Mr. Plunkett had been looking over papers in the study all day, and that some lunch had just gone up for him on Uncle Blair's tray. Then it had not happened yet, and it could not happen for some time to come. Murtagh scarcely knew if he were relieved to hear it, but the strain of momentary expectation was gone, and he began to feel tolerably sure now that Pat intended to keep to the plan he had described.

The doctor came after lunch, but he could make nothing of Murtagh's state, and went away saying that he would call again to-morrow.

As Mr. Blair had seemed anxious, Nessa went to the study to tell him what the doctor had said, and after a time, Murtagh, who had remained standing by the drawing-room window, heard through the open door the sound of Mr. Plunkett's voice and Mr. Blair's as they advanced with her towards the hall door. They were not thinking of him apparently, for they were talking of some business matter. Mr. Plunkett went out, and Mr. Blair called after him: "Seven o'clock dinner, remember, Plunkett."

Yes, and after that seven o'clock dinner! As Murtagh stood watching Mr. Plunkett walk briskly away over the grass all his horror of the way Pat had chosen for the execution of his plan came back upon him in full force. Surely, surely, it was treacherous to kill a man in the dark, when he was on his way home from your very own house. He stood immovable, his eyes fixed upon Mr. Plunkett, his head feeling as though it were really turning with conflicting thoughts, till Mr. Plunkett disappeared behind some distant bushes. Then some words of his uncle's fell upon his ears. He was talking to Nessa in the hall.

"Yes, all things considered," he was saying, "it is strange, isn't it, little one, that that man should be risking his life every day for Murtagh's benefit?"

Murtagh could hardly believe his senses. What was his uncle talking about?

Nessa apparently did not understand either.

"How do you mean for Murtagh?" she asked.

"I thought I had told you how he constantly receives threatening letters in consequence of the improvements he is making in the estate. Many of these improvements will bear no fruit till long after my time, and now that poor little Frankie is gone Murtagh is the person who will profit by them. I remarked that to Plunkett to-day, when he was talking to me about this ejectment business, and I asked him why he went on with it. He said, 'It is my duty, sir.' " Mr. Blair had spoken slowly, and he ended with a little sigh.

"But surely, Uncle Blair," asked Nessa, as Mr. Blair moved away, "they could never really shoot him?"

"I believe," replied Mr. Blair, "that if it were not well known that he always carries a loaded pistol he would be shot at to-morrow. Now the risk is too great, for they know that if they miss him he is not likely to miss them. His perfect fearlessness is greatly in his favor."

"Oh dear, what a terrible, dreadful, place!" sighed Nessa, as her uncle left her standing in the hall. She hated to hear of these things; they made her feel as though she would like just to lock herself up in her bedroom and stay there all the rest of her natural life.

On his side of the drawing-room door Murtagh stood horror-stricken at the revelation that Mr. Plunkett was deliberately risking his life for his benefit, at the time that he was consenting to a plot to kill Mr. Plunkett. He understood only in the vaguest manner how it came about that it was for his benefit; still his uncle's words were not to be mistaken, and the mere fact that Mr. Plunkett knew the danger and braved it deliberately, was in itself enough to arouse in that impulsive little heart something akin to sympathy. Every generous feeling in him was set at war with what Pat was going to do, but still he felt with an acuteness of suffering beyond his years that the cause of the people was just the same. If it had been right before that Mr. Plunkett should die, it was right now. What should he do? It had become odious in him to have helped Pat, but Pat was just as right as ever, and in passionate defence of him he entered the hall, exclaiming:

"Nessa, you and Uncle Blair don't know how he does things. You don't know how he turns the people out of their houses, and sends them to prison for nothing, and sees them starving in the winter-time and doesn't care. No wonder they hate him. No wonder they want to kill him! Every one says if Uncle Blair would go about himself things would be very different. He may make money, but oh! I wish it could never be for me. I would rather starve than have that money that's robbed from them."

"He is not robbing them," exclaimed Nessa, opening her great gray eyes indignantly; "and even if he were it's too dreadful hating like that and watching to kill people. I'd rather be oppressed all my life than be guilty of a cowardly murder."

"It's only what the Sicilians did," answered Murtagh. "It's not right that a tyrant should go on doing what he pleases."

"It's not what the Sicilians did," returned Nessa; "they fought a brave hand-to-hand struggle; they did not secretly murder a man who was going fearlessly about amongst them; and what they did do they did only after having tried every other means in their power. Besides, they fought against real tyranny, and Mr. Plunkett is not tyrannizing over these people; I know he is not, Murtagh. Uncle Blair has told me about it lots of times. He's trying all he can to make things better for the people, only they are so unreasonable; they expect to have everything done for them, and they don't want to give anything in exchange. It is quite fair when a lot of expensive improvements have been made that the rent should be raised; and then when people are drunken and worthless and won't take care of their land of course they *have* to be turned out. Mr. Plunkett may be disagreeable," she added, "but I don't see why they need hate him for that. We hate people, I suppose, when they are wicked; but he isn't wicked; they are wicked when they can think for one minute of such mean, cowardly revenge."

"You don't know, Nessa. He is wicked. He must be wicked. You'll drive me perfectly mad if you talk like that. I believe everything's all wrong together and nothing ever can be right."

And with this confused utterance of the despair that was fast possessing him Murtagh would have rushed away out of doors, but Nessa caught him in her arms, and thinking that her indignation had hurt him, exclaimed penitently:

"Murtagh dear, I didn't mean you. Of course I never meant that for one minute. I know very well that whatever else you are you could never be cruel and cowardly."

He did not speak; he had no right to her faith, no right to her love. He disengaged himself as quickly as he could and rushed away, he didn't care where—anywhere, anywhere to escape from the thoughts that came hurrying upon him now. But he made one last effort still to combat them. Nessa did not know, Mr. Blair did not know all that went on. They only heard Mr. Plunkett's account; he had heard the people's side. He called to mind story after story to fortify himself in his refusal to believe Nessa; but more than ever did he hate the manner in which Pat had decided to do the deed.

If only he had had the slightest idea where Pat was to be found he would have gone to him, and insisted that it should be done openly. But he had not. He only knew that he was not to be on the island. They had decided that it was an unsafe place to stay because of the children. Mrs. O'Toole might know. Murtagh went to her, but she declared that she knew nothing about Pat's hiding-place; and whether she knew or not no power of Murtagh's could draw the information from her. In despair he returned to the park. There was nothing to be done but to let things take their course. After all wasn't Pat perhaps right; since he was to do it hadn't he a right to choose his own way? Wasn't it weak to want to stop it now?

Scarcely knowing where he went Murtagh nevertheless kept near the Red House, declaring to himself that things must now take their course, but at the same time feeling as though he in some measure protected Mr. Plunkett by keeping close to him.

At last he threw himself upon the ground under a hedge, and he had not been there many minutes when steps and voices on the other side roused him from his miserable struggle.

He sat up, discovered that he was sitting under the hedge of Mr. Plunkett's back garden, and as he began to take note of external things he became aware that Mr. Plunkett was walking along the path on the other side of the hedge carrying his little daughter in his arms. There were gaps in the thickness of the hedge, and Murtagh could see the pair quite distinctly. The child's head rested lovingly upon her father's shoulder, the golden hair scattered a little over his sleeve. One arm was round his neck, and the delicate little face was illumined by that look of perfect contentment which is almost more beautiful than a smile.

"How nice it is that you are so strong, Fardie," she said caressingly as they passed close by Murtagh.

"Are you comfortable, dear?" asked Mr. Plunkett.

"Yes, very," she replied with a little sigh of pleasure.

They took one turn in silence down the path and back again. Then little Marion spoke again, but this time there was a troubled sound in her voice.

"Don't be late to-night, father, will you?"

"Not very, my pet," replied Mr. Plunkett, "but you must be sound asleep long before I come."

"I'll shut up my eyes and try, Fardie, but I can't go to sleep when you're out because——" And here the little voice trembled and stopped short.

"Because what, dear?" said Mr. Plunkett, bending his head a little so that his cheek touched her forehead.

"Because I think such dreadful things when I'm in the dark, and I get so dreadfully, dreadfully frightened, Fardie, lest those wicked men might kill you!"

The last words came out in a low tone, as though she feared that uttering them might make what she dreaded more probable, and putting her other arm up round her father's neck she clung to him tightly.

"Who let you hear of such things?" exclaimed Mr. Plunkett in the stern voice that Murtagh knew well.

"Mother often cries when you're out," said Marion; "and she says perhaps you'll be brought in dead! But, Fardie, you mustn't, because I *couldn't* bear it!"

Mr. Plunkett did not speak immediately; then he said:

"My little daughter, you mustn't mind everything you hear people say, but if such a thing ever did happen you will be my own brave child, won't you?—and you will like to think afterwards that your father died at his work!"

"No, no, Fardie, I couldn't be brave then!" cried Marion. "I couldn't stay alive with only mother! You won't let them do it? Promise, father!"

At that moment "mother's" voice made itself heard, calling: "Marion, Marion, come in! How could you keep her out so late, James?"

"No, no, my pet; they shan't do it if I can help it!" replied Mr. Plunkett, kissing her and hastily setting her down. "Now put all such ideas out of your head, and run in to your mother; she's calling you."

The child went slowly away and Mr. Plunkett looking after her said sadly:

"My poor little one, I suppose it will come upon you some day soon; and yet, God knows, I am doing the best I can for them!"

He spoke to himself, but the words were loud enough to reach Murtagh's ears, and they told him more than years of explanations could have done.

For the moment he felt as if he could almost have loved Mr. Plunkett. He dashed out of the ditch and away across the park. Find Pat he must and would. He saw it all in its true light now! How could he have helped in such a fiendish plan?

It was easier to determine to find Pat than to find him. Murtagh went back again to Mrs. O'Toole, but she either could not or would not help him. In the woods by the island, on every island in their part of the river, in the shrubberies, in every clump of trees that dotted the park, he searched but searched in vain; and while he looked it grew dark.

But though he hurried from place to place he was comparatively calm now. He had quite made up his mind what to do, and his energy was the energy of resolution. Pat evidently intended to keep to the late hour he had named, and before any mischief could be done he must come into the park and station himself between the Castle and the Red House. There Murtagh was almost sure that he could not miss him, and since it seemed impossible to find him now there was nothing to be done but to wait. He was not going to betray Pat by warning Mr. Plunkett if he could help it, and having thoroughly searched the park he watched Mr. Plunkett without any fear as he crossed it on his way to dinner.

Then he entered the house, and fetching himself a cup of milk and some bread from the servants' hall he sat quietly enough upon the door-step while he ate it. Mr. Plunkett would not return home till ten o'clock. Murtagh knew that he always took his leave when the clock struck that hour, so there was a long anxious time to wait before Pat was likely to be found, and as Murtagh sat upon the step he planned with an almost curious calmness all that must come after.

Pat must be helped somehow. The only way would be, Murtagh thought, to tell his uncle all. First he thought of going to Nessa, but a more manly instinct made him decide that he would go straight to his uncle. Then he hoped things would be put properly right for Pat, and it was with a lighter heart than he had had for a long time that he got up to continue his search.

But the night was pitch dark, and towards half-past nine he was still unsuccessful. He was keeping careful watch upon the time, and the suspense now grew painfully intense, for he knew that if he had not discovered Pat when the stable clock rung out a quarter to ten, there would be nothing for it but to warn Mr. Plunkett. Was Pat not coming at all? and if not, where and how should he ever find him?

At last he began to call gently, "Pat, Pat!" and after a minute a cautious, "Whisht, sir!" from some bushes on his right told him that Pat was there.

He bounded forward. "I began to think that I should never find you!" he exclaimed. "Here, give me the gun! Oh, Pat, to think how awfully near we were doing it!"

But Pat started back, holding the gun tightly, and asked in a tone different from any he had ever used to Murtagh before, "What is it you're meaning?"

"We were dreadfully wicked, really; he's not half so bad as we thought, and it would have been just a cowardly murder," said Murtagh, his voice conveying the horror that he felt.

"I don't care what it is," said Pat. "I'm going to do it this night."

"You shan't touch him," replied Murtagh. "You don't understand. He isn't half so bad as we thought. This isn't the way; give me the gun."

"Look here, Mr. Murtagh, I don't want to hurt ye," replied Pat in a fierce whisper, "but if ye offer to touch that gun I'll have to give ye a knock that'll keep you quiet till it's all over."

"Are you mad, Pat? I tell you we were all wrong." And Murtagh stretched out his hand for the gun.

"Right or wrong, it's all one to me. I won't stir out o' this till he's as dead as a door-nail."

"You shan't touch him with that gun; I got it, and I'll have it back," replied Murtagh. As he spoke he seized the gun, and half-succeeded in wrenching it from Pat's grasp. Pat struck out at him a blow that made him reel back and loose his hold for a moment, but he sprang forward and seized the gun again. Pat tried to wrench it from him; Murtagh hung on with all his strength; the gun went off in the struggle, and the loud report rang through the park. Almost instantaneously there was a second report. Something whizzed through the bushes, and before Murtagh had time to realize what had happened Pat had fled and he was standing alone with the gun in his hands, a curious stiff sensation numbing his left arm. He felt half-stunned, and all he could think at first was that Pat was gone, and that something strange had happened. He stood there for a few seconds; then he sprang out of the bushes and hurried towards the house.

The hall was full of light and commotion. The children were out upon the steps, the servants had come from the kitchen, Nessa and Mr. Blair stood by Mr. Plunkett, who in a perfectly calm voice was desiring Brown to bring him a lantern.

"I heard no sound after I fired," he added, turning to Mr. Blair, "but if any one is wounded we must get a doctor for him, and if—if it should be worse—"

"I trust it is not, I trust it is not," interrupted Mr. Blair, "but if it should be so, Plunkett, remember we were fully agreed beforehand that what you have done was the right thing to do."

"It is all right," cried Murtagh, "you haven't hurt him, and here's your gun; you're quite safe now."

His arm was hurting, and his head swam, so that he staggered and almost fell as he held out the gun to Mr. Plunkett.

"And he never fired at you at all; it was when I was trying to get the gun from him that it went off. But oh, do be *kinder* to the people. They don't know anything about just; and he doesn't understand now; they *can't* understand."

And the tension of that awful day over at last, the excitement died suddenly out of

Murtagh's face, and Mr. Plunkett had just time to catch him in his arms as he fell fainting to the floor.

CHAPTER XXIX

He RECOVERED CONSCIOUSNESS to find himself on the drawing-room sofa, with Nessa and Mrs. Donegan anxiously applying restoratives, while Mr. Blair and the children stood round. The moment the wound in his arm had been perceived, Mr. Plunkett had himself saddled a horse and gone to fetch a doctor.

"Go away, please, all of you," said Murtagh, as soon as he could speak. "I want to speak to Uncle Blair. Nessa may stay."

Mrs. Donegan and the children looked reluctant, but Mr. Blair turned them all out except Winnie. She was sitting curled up on a footstool by the head of the sofa, and she did not stir.

"Murtagh and me's the same," she said. "I know what he's going to say." And as Murtagh put out his hand to keep her, Uncle Blair shut the door.

"Please promise first," said Murtagh, "that you won't tell anybody else."

"If it's about the man who made this attempt to-night, Murtagh, I'm afraid I can't promise," replied Mr. Blair, reluctant to refuse, but with a remembrance of Mr. Plunkett's energy in his mind. "He must be prosecuted; you yourself will, I fear, be obliged to answer questions in a court of justice."

"But you *must* promise," said Murtagh, a feverish flush spreading over his cheek. "Make him promise, Nessa. I know I have no right, but it's the only way. It can't possibly be put right if he doesn't."

"Do promise him," said Nessa, looking entreatingly at her uncle, and then glancing anxiously at Murtagh. "Surely you can manage somehow." And most unconstitutionally Mr. Blair did manage.

"It was more my fault than his, because he couldn't have done it if I hadn't got him the gun yesterday," began Murtagh. But he suddenly closed his eyes, unable to proceed. Nessa put a spoonful of brandy between his lips and he revived a little.

"Don't say anything more, my boy," said his uncle, astonishment at Murtagh's statement entirely swallowed up in anxiety; "I understand you don't want him punished."

"I can't tell you now," continued Murtagh, "I feel so funny; but you must help him soon, or he'll do it again. He doesn't understand. He's hiding now. His mother—I—I can't remember; Winnie'll know."

He looked anxiously at Winnie, and his eyes closed again, but he was not unconscious; and Nessa, while she attended to him, said almost impatiently:

"Tell us what it is, Winnie. This excitement is very bad for him." All the Irishmen in Christendom seemed to her at that moment of no importance compared to the chances of fever setting in with this wounded arm.

"I don't quite know," said Winnie, taking hold of Murtagh's hand and looking up at her uncle; "but I think what he means is he wants you to help Pat O'Toole. He's been in hiding ever since the fire, you know, and I suppose——" Here Winnie hesitated a little. "I suppose he has tried to do this, and that's why Murtagh doesn't want the others to know; and his mother knows where he is. And I expect Murtagh means if you could help him regularly, get him some work or something, and make him come back."

"Yes," said Murtagh, opening his eyes suddenly, and looking feverish and excited again; "only quick, quick, or he'll do it again. He doesn't understand, he doesn't understand, and it's all my fault. Nessa said it was; didn't she, Winnie?" His voice was loud, and he evidently did not quite know what he was saying.

"Hush, hush, my boy," said his uncle. "It shall be all right; I promise you I will go myself to Mrs. O'Toole to-morrow." Murtagh seemed to hear what his uncle said, for he looked content, and dropped back on the pillow from which he had been attempting to rise; but then he fainted again, and though proper remedies soon revived him the coming of the doctor was anxiously watched for.

He came and examined first the wound in Murtagh's arm. Mr. Plunkett's bullet had passed through the fleshy part of the arm, and though the loss of blood had been considerable the wound was not important. But the exposure and excitement of the last three days had brought more serious effects in their train, and the doctor looked very grave, when, after examining the boy, he began to give careful directions to Nessa.

He would come early next day, he said, and all might be well, but he feared it was his duty to warn them that the case might be a very serious one.

His fears were but too well founded, and not many days later a telegram went from Mr. Blair to his brother Launcelot telling him that Murtagh was dangerously stricken with brain fever.

       *   *   *   *   *

But he was not to die. November, December, and January passed away, and one mild day early in February he was well enough to sit in the big arm-chair by the open school-room window, while Winnie sat on the window-sill, swinging her legs outside, and fed her ducks once more with a merry heart. It had been a sad winter for her and Rosie and Bobbo, but their independent ways had proved of some use, and they had given real help in the long time of anxious nursing. Mr. Plunkett had taken his turn of sitting up at night, and had shown himself a valuable nurse. And all smaller sorrows had been merged in the one great trouble.

With Murtagh ill the children could think of little else; but Mr. Blair had been roused by the events preceding the boy's illness to act for once with energy. He had kept his promise of going without delay to Mrs. O'Toole, and he had known how to draw from her the information she had refused to Murtagh. Pat had been produced, and Mr. Blair knowing Mr. Plunkett well, had trusted him with the whole story.

Mr. Plunkett justified the trust. Honor would have forbidden any attempt to punish the boy, and Mr. Blair saw that in this instance the ends of policy also would be better served by generous treatment; but it was neither policy nor the strict requirements of honor alone which moved Mr. Plunkett to take the tone he did when he talked with Mr. Blair, and to listen with unwonted gentleness even to Nessa when she suggested that one of the best ways of saving Pat from further mischief would be to find work for him elsewhere.

It was not the effect of the danger from which he had escaped; that would probably have made him simply hard and indignant; but Pat's confession had opened his eyes to many things. Unexpected kindness, together with Murtagh's dangerous illness, had filled Pat with remorse. He had confessed not only his full share in this last enterprise, but his unaided burning of Mr. Plunkett's hayricks; and it was in hearing of Murtagh's entire innocence with respect to that misfortune, that Mr. Plunkett's self-confidence received a shock of which the effect was to him considerable. The fact that it was only a child whom he had misjudged and unfairly tried to punish, did not make a difference to him as it would have done to most people. He had been unjust; and whether the injustice had been committed towards a child, a man, or a chimpanzee, had, according to his way of looking at it, nothing to do with the question.

He was accustomed to respect himself, to think himself right, and now he found that he had been wrong,—more wrong than the child he had despised. He may have been proud, but he was not a man to shirk anything. He vividly realized the ruin into which the two boys had nearly rushed, and while he made no attempt even in his own mind to exculpate them altogether he remembered that they were children, and blamed himself unsparingly for the treatment which had roused them to such a pitch of passion.

He would have thought little of Pat had it not been for Murtagh. He had nothing to reproach himself with so far as Pat was concerned. At any other time he would have said the boy had only got what he deserved when he was caned for an impertinence. But the revelation of his injustice to Murtagh had strangely shaken his trust in himself. He had been wrong with him, perhaps he had often been wrong with other people too.

The very fact that no one else thought of attaching a shadow of blame to him, made him perhaps judge himself all the more severely; and it was with almost childlike humility that he thought how nearly he had killed Murtagh at the very moment when the boy, moved by some unaccountable impulse of forgiveness, was fighting in his defence.

Looking back over his feelings he was forced to acknowledge to himself that he had never for a moment felt forgivingly towards Murtagh. The child had been greater than he; he freely and humbly acknowledged it. He did not know that he owed his life to little Marion's love, but he turned to it in his trouble. Whatever he had done to others he had never judged her too harshly, and her clinging arms about his neck comforted him now when, though even Marion scarcely knew it, he was in need of comfort. And perhaps the gentle little spirit upon which at this time he was leaning influenced his actions more than either of them knew, for he certainly could not have been expected to feel particularly tender towards Pat; and yet Nessa was surprised by the kindness with which he entered into their plans for him, and relieved them of the trouble of making arrangements.

He advised Mr. Blair to apprentice the lad to a trade in Dublin, where he would be removed from the influence of his bad companions, and he himself took the trouble to find a respectable household in which the boy might live; so that when the cloud of delirium passed from Murtagh's brain and he asked with almost his first connected words for Pat O'Toole, Nessa was able to tell him truly that Pat was quite safe and was doing well.

But that had been some weeks ago. Mr. Plunkett had been in England on business since then. Murtagh had grown daily stronger; and surrounded by Nessa's tender cares, and by the household rejoicing which attended his recovery, he found his convalescence a pleasant time.

He had spent more than one day in the big arm-chair, looking out with all an invalid's pleasure at the returning life which the spring sunshine was bringing to the land; and as he sat and watched the purple shadows of the trees and hedges contrasting with the faint green of the winter grass, or gazed at the bright sky above where little white clouds disported themselves in the clear blue air, he had many thoughts that he would have found it hard to express to any one. Never had the crocuses seemed so bright or the snow-drops so beautiful as they seemed this year; and when one day the children brought him in a spray of bursting hawthorn and a bunch of lord and lady leaves from the hedges, tears of pleasure came into his eyes at the sight.

Life was very peaceful and beautiful in those early spring days. Nessa's presence seemed to have brought a spring of gentleness to the children's hearts, and the joy in Murtagh's recovery shed sunshine through the house. The boys too were near the realization of one of their chief hopes. They were to go to school. For Mr. Launcelot Blair on hearing from his brother an account of all that happened had written to say that he was coming home on leave, and that one of his first cares should be to find a private tutor to whom Murtagh and Bobbo might go to be prepared for being sent next year to Eton.

"From all that you tell me of them," he wrote, "I believe that the discipline of a public school is what they want. They have been so left to themselves that they judge nothing by an ordinary standard, and a lot of rough school-boys will knock common sense into them a great deal faster than you or I could do it."

To the boys no prospect could be more delightful. They had longed to go to school; and though the preliminary tutor had never entered into their dreams, they acknowledged that it might be as well to be somewhat more advanced in their studies before they exposed their little stock of learning to the world, and they accepted him very cheerily, determining to work hard now they had something to work for.

One thing still remained to be done. To-day Murtagh was to see Mr. Plunkett for the first time since his recovery. He felt some natural nervousness at the prospect of the interview, but convinced of his fault, he had, since he had been able to think about it, looked forward anxiously to making the only reparation in his power, and no false shame came to trouble him when he thought of the explanation and apology he owed to Mr. Plunkett.

And now, while King and Senior squabbled over a tempting piece of brown bread too large for either of them to swallow, and Murtagh lay back in the chair, amused but scarcely taking the trouble to laugh, a big Newfoundland poked his black muzzle between and carried off the morsel.

"Why, Win," exclaimed Murtagh, roused by the sudden apparition to a more energetic display of interest, "where did he come from? Did papa get him for you?"

Winnie did what Murtagh never expected to see her do when anything touched, however remotely, upon Royal,—began to laugh.

"No," she said. "Guess who did."

"I don't know," replied Murtagh.

"No, and you never would guess if you tried till Doomsday, so I may as well tell you. Old Plunkett! And, Murtagh," she added, with a sudden change of manner, "he was really sorry. He told me all about it, how it was because he was so very angry. And I thought about you getting in such rages, and—" Winnie paused as though she were fighting out again the struggle to accept the dog.

"What's his name?" asked Murtagh.

"Jim," replied Winnie. "I thought I ought to call him after him, you know; but I really *couldn't* call him 'James dear.' And besides," she added, dropping her voice, "I didn't want it to be a bit like—" She stopped short and her eyes filled with tears.

At that moment steps were heard advancing along the passage: Winnie dashed the tears out of her eyes, and as she glanced up at Murtagh she saw by the faint flush upon his cheek that he guessed who was coming.

"Are you going to say anything to him about—?" she asked.

Murtagh nodded.

"Then I'll be off," she replied, jumping as she spoke from the window-sill to the flower-border beneath. "Come along; Guck, Guck, Guck." And the harsh sound of her duck-call filled the air as she walked away, the white flock waddling after her.

Murtagh was glad of it. It seemed to cover his nervousness a little as the door opened and Mr. Plunkett entered alone. Poor child!—he was very weak still, and his heart beat fast and his hands trembled as he watched Mr. Plunkett advance across the long room. But it was only for a moment. When Mr. Plunkett took one of the wasted hands in his, and asked him kindly how he was, he recovered himself, and answered: "Oh, much better, thank you; they are all so kind, they make me well."

Then after a little pause, the flush mounting again to his cheek: "I wanted to see you because I wanted to tell you I am very, very sorry I was so near—being so dreadfully wicked." And the effort to speak of it brought tears to his eyes. They were driven back again at once, but Mr. Plunkett saw them. He had not expected any apology; he had been thinking how wasted and shadowy the boy still looked. He was taken by surprise, and he suddenly flushed and looked more confused than Murtagh.

Not that he did not think an apology was owing to him; but Murtagh had scarcely ever spoken even civilly to him before, and the brown eyes raised to his looked so humble and beseeching through their shimmering veil of tears, that he found himself remembering only all the hard things he had said and done to the boy.

"Don't say anything more," he said, looking straight before him out of the window; "perhaps there were faults on both sides."

Murtagh did not quite hear, for Mr. Plunkett did not speak with his usual distinct utterance, but he was encouraged to continue:

"I didn't know how wicked it was. I thought it would be a great thing to do, because I thought—" He hesitated a little, not quite sure how much Mr. Plunkett would bear. "I thought you were oppressing the people, and it would set them free. And then Nessa said you weren't, and then little Marion— It was so dreadful; I knew about how wicked it was then, but I never, never would have tried if I'd known at first."

"Marion!" said Mr. Plunkett, turning his head. "What had she to do with it?"

"I was in the ditch near your garden, and you were carrying her, and she had her arms round you, and she seemed to love you so. It seemed almost like papa," said

Murtagh, his voice dropping at the recollection. "It would have been so dreadful if anything happened to you then. And then you said, 'God knew you were doing the best you could for the people;' and I felt quite sure you were speaking the truth, and you really were trying, and you were only just making mistakes; and it seems so cruel people getting hurt for making mistakes."

Mr. Plunkett did not speak at once. He knew himself to be one of the best agents in Ireland, and yet he had listened without a smile as Murtagh, in childish good faith, described how he had been tried, found wanting, and forgiven by so ignorant a little judge. Perhaps the boy's words stirred something within him that was not often moved. Perhaps with the remembrance of the death to which both he and the child had been so near there came a thought of another tribunal at which he would one day be tried, found wanting, and yet, he hoped, forgiven; for after a moment he turned and said:

"I have made mistakes with you; but we must start fresh, and perhaps we shall get on better now."

And before Murtagh had recovered from his surprise Mr. Plunkett had wrung his hand and left the room. For a moment or two Murtagh was too much astonished to understand. Then he felt that he was forgiven, really forgiven, as he had never expected to be. The old life was wiped out, and with a rush of happy exultation he realized that this was indeed a fresh start.

Nessa entered the room with a bunch of white crocuses and some ivy leaves that she had just brought in from the garden.

"Oh, Nessa," he exclaimed, "I am so happy!"

"Are you, dear?" she said, with a glad smile, kneeling down beside him and laying the crocuses on his knees.

"Yes," he said. "Everything seems so good and bright. Only when I look at it all," he added slowly, "I wonder how I could ever—have thought like I used to think."

Nessa did not answer. She wondered too as she gazed out across the sunny grass to the bridge. Winnie was standing on the ivy-covered parapet, with one hand swinging her hat, and with the other supporting a pigeon which she was feeding with bits of bread from between her lips; Jim sat patient on the gravel; the white ducks clamored round her; and another pigeon was spreading his tail and pluming himself upon the parapet at her feet. The water sparkled; the sky beyond was blue; the voices of the other children playing somewhere out of sight floated in happy bursts upon the air. It was all beautiful enough to make anybody wonder how wickedness could be.

Murtagh's eyes followed Nessa's. They both looked at Winnie in silence for a moment, and then he continued, turning to Nessa:

"But I am glad I have been ill. It has made me seem to understand things better. I have been thinking and thinking, often when you didn't think I was thinking of anything. And I seem to feel now,"—he blushed a little, but went on firmly,—"that even if people are wicked and disagreeable it can't do one bit of good hating them. I mean," he said, fixing his eyes with a fervent earnest look upon hers, "I feel it is so that I don't think I ever can forget it."

"Yes," said Nessa softly. "If God were to hate us even when we are wicked what should we do? It often comes over me with a sort of rush of gladness, how that when we make mistakes, and get tired, and go wrong, He is still there watching over us, loving us all the time, never getting impatient. And you know," she added a little shyly, "we are told to try and be as like God as we can."

THE END

9

Jackanapes

By JULIANA HORATIA EWING

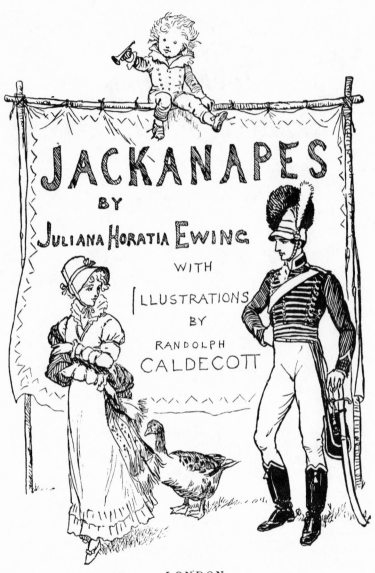

JACKANAPES

BY

JULIANA HORATIA EWING

WITH

ILLUSTRATIONS

BY

RANDOLPH CALDECOTT

LONDON
SOCIETY FOR PROMOTING CHRISTIAN KNOWLEDGE,
NORTHUMBERLAND AVENUE, CHARING CROSS, W.C.;
43, QUEEN VICTORIA STREET, E.C.;
26, ST. GEORGE'S PLACE, HYDE PARK CORNER, S.W.
BRIGHTON: 135, NORTH STREET.
NEW YORK: E. & J. B. YOUNG & CO.

MRS. EWING (1841–1885) properly receives respectful attention (but perhaps not respectful enough) in all accounts of Victorian children's literature. A storyteller from her nursery days, she was the most conscious literary artist of any writer we have yet considered. She wrote many fairy tales, and many tales of real life, usually in the form of the long short story or short novel. A woman of pronounced and not untypical opinions, she sometimes put her causes into her children's fiction.

Her father, the Reverend Alfred Gatty, was a Yorkshire village parson, and her mother, Margaret Gatty (daughter of Admiral Nelson's chaplain aboard the *Victory*), was herself a successful and celebrated writer for young people. In addition to fiction, Mrs. Gatty wrote between 1855 and 1871 five volumes of *Parables from Nature*, a collection of tales in which she drew upon her knowledge of nature to illustrate the truths of Scripture. By introducing animals, birds, and plants as characters, and by a generous use of humor, she made these stories not only readable but very popular. Major contemporary artists illustrated them: Tenniel, Millais, Holman Hunt, Burne-Jones.

The Gattys' second daughter, Juliana, whose nickname at home was Judy, was the official spinner of yarns for all her sisters and brothers. Her mother early used Judy's name in the titles of her own collected short stories; *Aunt Judy's Tales* (1859) and *Aunt Judy's Letters* (1861) were two of Mrs. Gatty's most popular books. All the stories were put into the mouth of a beloved but sternly moralizing elder sister, who would tolerate no frivolous remark without an answering lecture, who preached submission at every turn (especially to the most unpleasant and apparently unreasonable of God's decisions for us), and who tried to reconcile her young listeners to the deaths of those they loved. Although ostensibly told by "Aunt Judy," the stories were in fact written by her mother, and reflect the sombre religion of the older generation. When Juliana Ewing began to write on her own she would demonstrate that, though a devout Broad Church woman, with some Tractarian leanings, and with her mother's fondness for edifying youthful deathbeds, she was a far freer spirit.

In 1866, Mrs. Gatty founded *Aunt Judy's Magazine*, to which her daughter regularly contributed. In its pages most of Juliana's writing first appeared during the nineteen years until she died. Juliana Gatty married in 1867 Major Alexander Ewing of the Army Pay Department, an excellent musician and composer of hymns, and a man of many intellectual interests. The Ewings had no children. They spent two years in New Brunswick, where they studied Hebrew together in their leisure moments, and eight at the British Army camp at Aldershot, where they lived in a military hut or bungalow, before a brief tour of duty at Manchester and York. In 1879, ill health prevented Mrs. Ewing from accompanying her husband to Malta, and later to Ceylon. It persisted after he returned to England in 1883, and she died in 1885.

As a child, she was inspired by the fairy tales—Grimm, Andersen, and Bechstein— that she had been reading, but her invention was often stimulated by a woodcut or other picture to create a wholly new narrative. Captain Marryat's *Children of the New Forest*, a children's story of the English Civil Wars, with strong Royalist sympathies, helped to imbue her with the Tractarian reverence for Charles I, saint and martyr. In proper Tractarian fashion, she spent her first earnings on new hangings for her father's church. She loved acting in private theatricals, sketched and painted in watercolor, wrote verses for hymns, and was devoted to wildflowers and animals. In New Brunswick she studied the flora, and afterwards she not only wrote a story about the trillium (*The*

Blind Hermit and the Trinity Flower) but tried to introduce the plant itself into England. Favorite dogs played a major part in her life and in her writings. In the absence of Anna Sewell's *Black Beauty* (1877) from this collection, *Jackanapes* shows much of the same love of horses. The dog, too, was drawn from life.

Almost any one of Mrs. Ewing's best stories might have served here as an example of her writing. In *The Peace Egg* (1872), the children of an army officer unwittingly restore harmony to their own family by performing an English Christmas mystery-play, which the Gatty children had seen in Yorkshire. When the story became popular, Mrs. Ewing published the play itself with notes on its folklore. *Lob-lie-by-the-Fire* (1873), the story of a gypsy child, is full of fine irony and of implicit satire on the behavior of adults—most unusual in children's stories of the period. *Six to Sixteen* (1875), the autobiography of a young girl whose parents have died in India, and who lives with uncongenial relatives and attends a repressive school, deeply affected the young Rudyard Kipling, who read it as a child of ten, when his own parents were far off in India and he hated the people who were looking after him. All his life he remembered *Six to Sixteen,* and in his sixties he wrote of it, "I owe more in a circuitous way to that tale than I can tell. I knew it then as I know it still, almost by heart." And Mrs. Ewing quite clearly influenced the style of Kipling's own early tales and stories of childhood. A reader of Kipling who comes upon Mrs. Ewing's stories for the first time finds himself listening to familiar cadences; the make of the sentences, the rhythm of the dialogue, seems Kiplingesque. But that is to put the cart before the horse. It is *Wee Willie Winkie* or *Kim* that is Ewingesque, although nobody seems to have noticed it.

Daddy Darwin's Dovecote (1881) is a beautifully told sentimental rural idyll of a workhouse boy who successfully pleads to be taken on as apprentice to an aged bachelor keeper of doves, works hard, fulfills all his promises, and eventually comes into his inheritance and marries his childhood sweetheart. Deceptively simple, the story is full of symbolism. The beautiful pigeons are, without artificial straining for effect, made to stand for freedom and the highest of human aspirations. *The Story of a Short Life* (published in *Aunt Judy's Magazine* in 1882, although not reprinted as a book until a few days before Mrs. Ewing's death in 1885) is written with equal skill but hardly with equal taste. It is a real tearjerker, the story of a well-born English boy, proud of his goodly heritage, whose family motto is *Laetus Sorte Mea* ("Happy in my lot"). Exactly resembling a remote ancestor killed at seventeen fighting for Charles I, the hero, who longs to become a soldier, is hopelessly crippled when he tries to save his dog from an accident. His parents allow him to spend his last days at Asholt (Aldershot) in the bungalow of his uncle, the commanding officer there. He reduces officers and enlisted men alike to tears, and eventually dies as the troops at his request are singing a favorite hymn in the nearby chapel. Writing to defend the military life against its contemporary critics, Mrs. Ewing nonetheless put her hero into a velvet suit with a lace collar, the same dress that Frances Hodgson Burnett would use the very next year for the mawkish Cedric Erroll, Lord Fauntleroy. One can hardly doubt that Mrs. Burnett pilfered Cedric's sugary if upright character as well as his costume from his unfortunate and equally incredible predecessor. The prose rhythms that the young Kipling would soon be taking as his own resound particularly loudly from the pages of *The Story of a Short Life.*

Of all Mrs. Ewing's stories, however, *Jackanapes* is the most famous. It succeeds where *The Story of a Short Life* fails. It was the first story for which she secured the collaboration of the distinguished artist Randolph Caldecott as illustrator. Previously he had illustrated his own books for children, less important for their texts than for his pictures; but after *Jackanapes* he remained Mrs. Ewing's collaborator for the six years until she died. Caldecott's drawings, with their straightforward yet subtle sense of the English countryside, and the simple beauty of the people, young and old, of their clothes, of their horses and dogs, became an indispensable part of Mrs. Ewing's public's pleasure in her writing.

Jackanapes was inspired by events in Zululand. In 1879 at Isandlhwana, the Zulus massacred a British force, and soon afterwards the son of the former French emperor Napoleon III, the "Prince Imperial," an observer with the British armies, was killed by the Zulus when he failed to mount his horse in time and the British forces with him had already made good their escape. These tragic episodes were much discussed in England, and Mrs. Ewing heard some people criticize the officer who had been assigned to accompany the prince for "abandoning" him, while others—chiefly businessmen—maintained that at such moments the rule was "devil take the hindmost." Mrs. Ewing felt compelled to refute these views and to reaffirm the importance of fulfilling one's military obligations. But she did not wish to seem to pronounce on the specific case.

So she set *Jackanapes* in the remote past: the hero's father is killed at Waterloo, just before Jackanapes is born, and he himself dies in some unspecified battle twenty-odd years later, giving his life to save a fellow officer and childhood friend. His death is hard going for the modern reader. Mrs. Ewing's point, that heroic unselfishness is essential and no waste, is unfashionable now. And she drives it home with a sledgehammer:

> . . . there be things—oh, sons of what has deserved the name of Great Britain, forget it not!—"the good of" which and "the use of" which are beyond all calculation of wordly goods and earthly uses: things such as Love, and Honour, and the Soul of Man, which cannot be bought with a price, and which do not die with death. And they who would fain live happily EVER after, should not leave these things out of the lessons of their lives.

In reading *Jackanapes*, we must perhaps abandon our own standards of patriotism, morality, and taste; but this is what the reading and criticism of Victorian literature often demand of us. Against the bourgeois who failed to understand the values of the British Army, or who seemed to deride them, Mrs. Ewing ably defended the ancient ideals of the Bible and of *Pilgrim's Progress*, from which she drew the epigraphs for two of her chapters.

More striking is her self-conscious and successful artistry. From a thoughtful reading of John Ruskin's *Elements of Drawing*, she had reached the conclusion that the "Laws of Principality, Repetition, Continuity, Contrast, Harmony, etc." there set forth were applicable to writing. The trouble with most English fiction, she felt, was that it failed to tell a good story artistically. So in *Jackanapes*, the hero stands out as the only important figure (Law of Principality), while all the other characters, including the beloved pony and horse, the two Lollos, help accentuate his noble characteristics. Again and again Mrs. Ewing returns to the Village Green (Law of Repetition) as a center of peace and repose amidst the tragedies and violence of life. The Grey Goose gabbles out inanities that match those of the peace-at-any-price politician; the blond and blue-eyed and vigorous young Jackanapes—the future soldier—is seen in comparison with the maimed and wounded hero of past wars (Law of Contrast). And when the yellow-haired little boy pursues the yellow gosling, one "yellow thing" chasing the other across the green and into the pond, the pictorial intention is obvious, and triumphantly achieved. Foreground, middle distance, background: the personages of *Jackanapes* are carefully, but not obviously, disposed in a painterly fashion.

None of the characters says anything that fails to advance the story; Mrs. Ewing uses language economically. She holds sentiment and action in balance. Few writers of fiction amongst the Victorians thought of themselves as striving to create works of art, and no writer for children known to me except Mrs. Ewing made the conscious and principled effort to do so. In *Jackanapes* the effort was crowned by success. Modern readers—unlike Charlotte Yonge—will be prepared to overlook the horrendous fact that Jackanapes's mother had eloped with his father before being forgiven by her own family: to us the story seems suitable in its entirety.

The text of Jackanapes, *with illustrations by Randolph Caldecott, is reprinted from the first edition (London: Society for Promoting Christian Knowledge, 1886).*

"If I might buffet for my love, or bound my horse for her favours,
I could lay on like a butcher, and sit like a Jackanapes, never off!"
King Henry V., Act v., Scene 2

CHAPTER I

Last noon beheld them full of lusty life,
Last eve in Beauty's circle proudly gay,
The midnight brought the signal sound of strife,
The morn the marshalling in arms—the day
Battle's magnificently stern array!
The thunder-clouds close o'er it, which when rent
The earth is covered thick with other clay,
Which her own clay shall cover, heaped and pent,
Rider and horse:—friend, foe,—in one red burial blent.

Their praise is hymn'd by loftier harps than mine:
Yet one would I select from that proud throng.
——to thee, to thousands, of whom each
And one as all a ghastly gap did make
In his own kind and kindred, whom to teach
Forgetfulness were mercy for their sake;
The Archangel's trump, not glory's, must awake
Those whom they thirst for.
BYRON

T WO DONKEYS AND THE GEESE lived on the Green, and all other residents of any social standing lived in houses round it. The houses had no names. Everybody's address was,

"The Green," but the Postman and the people of the place knew where each family lived. As to the rest of the world, what has one to do with the rest of the world, when he is safe at home on his own Goose Green? Moreover, if a stranger did come on any lawful business, he might ask his way at the shop.

Most of the inhabitants were long-lived, early deaths (like that of the little Miss Jessamine) being exceptional; and most of the old people were proud of their age, especially the sexton, who would be ninety-nine come Martinmas, and whose father remembered a man who had carried arrows, as a boy, for the battle of Flodden Field. The Grey Goose and the big Miss Jessamine were the only elderly persons who kept their ages secret. Indeed, Miss Jessamine never mentioned any one's age, or recalled the exact year in which anything had happened. She said that she had been taught that it was bad manners to do so "in a mixed assembly."

The Grey Goose also avoided dates, but this was partly because her brain, though intelligent, was not mathematical, and computation was beyond her. She never got farther than "last Michaelmas," "the Michaelmas before that," and "the Michaelmas before the Michaelmas before that." After this her head, which was small, became confused, and she said, "Ga, ga!" and changed the subject.

But she remembered the little Miss Jessamine, the Miss Jessamine with the "conspicuous" hair. Her aunt, the big Miss Jessamine, said it was her only fault. The hair was clean, was abundant, was glossy, but do what you would with it it never looked quite like other people's. And at church, after Saturday night's wash, it shone like the best brass fender after a Spring cleaning. In short, it was conspicuous, which does not become a young woman—especially in church.

Those were worrying times altogether, and the Green was used for strange purposes. A political meeting was held on it with the village Cobbler in the chair, and a speaker who came by stage coach from the town, where they had wrecked the bakers' shops, and discussed the price of bread. He came a second time, by stage, but the people had heard something about him in the meanwhile, and they did not keep him on the Green. They took him to the pond and tried to make him swim, which he could not do, and the whole affair was very disturbing to all quiet and peaceable fowls. Ater which another man came, and preached sermons on the Green, and a great many people went to hear him; for those were "trying times," and folk ran hither and thither for comfort. And then what did they do but drill the ploughboys on the Green, to get them ready to fight the French, and teach them the goose-step! However, that came to an end at last, for Bony was sent to St. Helena, and the ploughboys were sent back to the plough.

Everybody lived in fear of Bony in those days, especially the naughty children, who were kept in order during the day by threats of, "Bony shall have you," and who had nightmares about him in the dark. They thought he was an Ogre in a cocked hat. The Grey Goose thought he was a Fox, and that all men of England were going out in red coats to hunt him. It was no use to argue the point, for she had a very small head, and when one idea got into it there was no room for another.

Besides, the Grey Goose never saw Bony, nor did the children, which rather spoilt the terror of him, so that the Black Captain became more effective as a Bogy with hardened offenders. The Grey Goose remembered *his* coming to the place perfectly. What he came for she did not pretend to know. It was all part and parcel of the war and bad times. He was called the Black Captain, partly because of himself, and partly because of his wonderful black mare. Strange stories were afloat of how far and how fast that mare could go, when her master's hand was on her mane and he whispered in her ear. Indeed, some people thought we might reckon ourselves very lucky if we were not out of the frying-pan into the fire, and had not got a certain well-known Gentleman of the Road to protect us against the French. But that, of course, made him none the less useful to the Johnsons' Nurse, when the little Miss Johnsons were naughty.

"You leave off crying this minnit, Miss Jane, or I'll give you right away to that horrid wicked officer. Jemima! just look out o' the windy, if you please, and see if the Black Cap'n's a-coming with his horse to carry away Miss Jane."

And there, sure enough, the Black Captain strode by with his sword clattering as if it did not know whose head to cut off first. But he did not call for Miss Jane that time. He went on to the Green, where he came so suddenly upon the eldest Master Johnson, sitting in a puddle on purpose, in his new nankeen skeleton suit, that the young gentleman thought judgment had overtaken him at last, and abandoned himself to the howlings of despair. His howls were redoubled when he was clutched from behind and swung over the Black Captain's shoulder, but in five minutes his tears were stanched, and he was playing with the officer's accoutrements. All of which the Grey Goose saw with her own eyes, and heard afterwards that that bad boy had been whining to go back to the Black Captain ever since, which showed how hardened he was, and that nobody but Bonaparte himself could be expected to do him any good.

But those were "trying times." It was bad enough when the pickle of a large and respectable family cried for the Black Captain; when it came to the little Miss Jessamine crying for him, one felt that the sooner the French landed and had done with it the better.

The big Miss Jessamine's objection to him was that he was a soldier, and this prejudice was shared by all the Green. "A soldier," as the speaker from the town had observed, "is a bloodthirsty, unsettled sort of a rascal; that the peaceable, home-loving, bread-winning citizen can never conscientiously look on as a brother, till he has beaten his sword into a ploughshare, and his spear into a pruninghook."

On the other hand there was some truth in what the Postman (an old soldier) said in reply; that the sword has to cut a way for us out of many a scrape into which our bread-winners get us when they drive their ploughshares into fallows that don't belong to them. Indeed, whilst our most peaceful citizens were prosperous chiefly by means of cotton, of sugar, and of the rise and fall of the money-market (not to speak of such saleable matters as opium, firearms, and "black ivory"), disturbances were apt to arise in India, Africa, and other outlandish parts, where the fathers of our domestic race were making fortunes for their families. And, for that matter, even on the Green, we did not wish the military to leave us in the lurch, so long as there was any fear that the French were coming.*

---

*"The political men declare war, and generally for commercial interests; but when the nation is thus embroiled with its neighbours the soldier ... draws the sword, at the command of his country. . . . One word as to thy comparison of military and commercial persons. What manner of men be they who have supplied the Caffres with the firearms and ammunition to maintain their savage and deplorable wars? Assuredly they are not military. . . . Cease then, if thou would'st be counted among the just, to vilify soldiers."—W. NAPIER, Lieut.-General, *November*, 1851

To let the Black Captain have little Miss Jessamine, however, was another matter. Her Aunt would not hear of it; and then, to crown all, it appeared that the Captain's father did not think the young lady good enough for his son. Never was any affair more clearly brought to a conclusion.

But those were "trying times;" and one moonlight night when the Grey Goose was sound asleep upon one leg, the Green was rudely shaken under her by the thud of a horse's feet. "Ga, ga!" said she, putting down the other leg, and running away.

By the time she returned to her place not a thing was to be seen or heard. The horse had passed like a shot. But next day, there was hurrying and skurrying and cackling at a very early hour, all about the white house with the black beams, where Miss Jessamine lived. And when the sun was so low, and the shadows so long on the grass that the Grey Goose felt ready to run away at the sight of her own neck, little Miss Jane Johnson, and her "particular friend" Clarinda, sat under the big oak-tree on the Green, and Jane pinched Clarinda's little finger till she found that she could keep a secret, and then she told her in confidence that she had heard from Nurse and Jemima that Miss Jessamine's niece had been a very naughty girl, and that that horrid wicked officer had come for her on his black horse, and carried her right away.

"Will she never come back?" asked Clarinda.

"Oh, no!" said Jane decidedly. "Bony never brings people back."

"Not never no more?" sobbed Clarinda, for she was weak-minded, and could not bear to think that Bony never never let naughty people go home again.

Next day Jane had heard more.

"He has taken her to a Green."

"A Goose Green?" asked Clarinda.

"No. A Gretna Green. Don't ask so many questions, child," said Jane; who, having no more to tell, gave herself airs.

Jane was wrong on one point. Miss Jessamine's niece did come back, and she and her husband were forgiven. The Grey Goose remembered it well, it was Michaelmas-tide, the Michaelmas before the Michaelmas before the Michaelmas—but, ga ga! What does the date matter? It was autumn, harvest-time, and everybody was so busy prophesying and praying about the crops, that the young couple wandered through the lanes, and

got blackberries for Miss Jessamine's celebrated crab and blackberry jam, and made guys of themselves with bryony-wreaths, and not a soul troubled his head about them, except the children, and the Postman. The children dogged the Black Captain's footsteps (his bubble reputation as an Ogre having burst), clamouring for a ride on the black mare. And the Postman would go somewhat out of his postal way to catch the Captain's dark eye, and show that he had not forgotten how to salute an officer.

But they were "trying times." One afternoon the black mare was stepping gently up and down the grass, with her head at her master's shoulder, and as many children crowded on to her silky back as if she had been an elephant in a menagerie; and the next afternoon she carried him away, sword and *sabre-tache* clattering war-music at her side, and the old Postman waiting for them, rigid with salutation, at the four cross roads.

War and bad times! It was a hard winter, and the big Miss Jessamine and the little Miss Jessamine (but she was Mrs. Black-Captain now), lived very economically that they might help their poorer neighbours. They neither entertained nor went into company, but the young lady always went up the village as far as the *George and Dragon*, for air and exercise, when the London Mail* came in.

One day (it was a day in the following June) it came in earlier than usual, and the young lady was not there to meet it.

But a crowd soon gathered round the *George and Dragon*, gaping to see the Mail Coach dressed with flowers and oak-leaves, and the guard wearing a laurel-wreath over and above his royal livery. The ribbons that decked the horses were stained and flecked with the warmth and foam of the pace at which they had come, for they had pressed on with the news of Victory.

---

*The Mail Coach it was that distributed over the face of the land, like the opening of apocalyptic vials, the heart-shaking news of Trafalgar, of Salamanca, of Vittoria, of Waterloo.... The grandest chapter of our experience, within the whole Mail Coach service, was on those occasions when we went down from London with the news of Victory. Five years of life it was worth paying down for the privilege of an outside place.—DE QUINCEY

Miss Jessamine was sitting with her niece under the oak-tree on the Green, when the Postman put a newspaper silently into her hand. Her niece turned quickly—

"Is there news?"

"Don't agitate yourself, my dear," said her aunt. "I will read it aloud, and then we can enjoy it together; a far more comfortable method, my love, than when you go up the village, and come home out of breath, having snatched half the news as you run."

"I am all attention, dear aunt," said the little lady, clasping her hands tightly on her lap.

Then Miss Jessamine read aloud—she was proud of her reading—and the old soldier stood at attention behind her, with such a blending of pride and pity on his face as it was strange to see:—

> "Downing street,
>   *June* 22, 1815, 1 a.m."

"That's one in the morning," gasped the Postman; "beg your pardon, mum."

But though he apologised, he could not refrain from echoing here and there a weighty word. "Glorious victory,"—"Two hundred pieces of artillery,"—"immense quantity of ammunition,"—and so forth.

> "The loss of the British Army upon this occasion has unfortunately been most severe. It had not been possible to make out a return of the killed and wounded when Major Percy left headquarters. The names of the officers killed and wounded, as far as they can be collected, are annexed.
>
>   "I have the honour——"

"The list, aunt! Read the list!"

"My love—my darling—let us go in and——"

"No. Now! now!"

To one thing the supremely afflicted are entitled in their sorrow—to be obeyed—and yet it is the last kindness that people commonly will do them. But Miss Jessamine did. Steadying her voice, as best she might, she read on, and the old soldier stood bareheaded to hear that first Roll of the Dead at Waterloo, which began with the Duke of Brunswick, and ended with Ensign Brown.* Five-and thirty British Captains fell asleep that day on the Bed of Honour, and the Black Captain slept among them.

    *   *   *   *   *   *

There are killed and wounded by war, of whom no returns reach Downing Street.

Three days later, the Captain's wife had joined him, and Miss Jessamine was kneeling by the cradle of their orphan son, a purple-red morsel of humanity, with conspicuously golden hair.

"Will he live, Doctor?"

"Live? God bless my soul, ma'am! Look at him! The young Jackanapes!"

---

*"Brunswick's fated chieftain" fell at Quatre Bras, the day before Waterloo, but this first (very imperfect) list, as it appeared in the newspapers of the day, did begin with his name, and end with that of an Ensign Brown.

CHAPTER II

And he wandered away and away
With Nature, the dear old Nurse.
LONGFELLOW

THE GREY GOOSE remembered quite well the year that Jackanapes began to walk, for it was the year that the speckled hen for the first time in all her motherly life got out of patience when she was sitting. She had been rather proud of the eggs—they were unusually large—but she never felt quite comfortable on them; and whether it was because she used to get cramp, and go off the nest, or because the season was bad, or what, she never could tell, but every egg was addled but one, and the one that did hatch gave her more trouble than any chick she had ever reared.

It was a fine, downy, bright yellow little thing, but it had a monstrous big nose and feet, and such an ungainly walk as she knew no other instance of in her well-bred and high-stepping family. And as to behaviour, it was not that it was either quarrelsome or moping, but simply unlike the rest. When the other chicks hopped and cheeped on the Green about their mother's feet, this solitary yellow brat went waddling off on its own responsibility, and do or cluck what the speckled hen would, it went to play in the pond.

It was off one day as usual, and the hen was fussing and fuming after it, when the Postman, going to deliver a letter at Miss Jessamine's door, was nearly knocked over by the good lady herself, who, bursting out of the house with her cap just off and her bonnet just not on, fell into his arms, crying—

"Baby! Baby! Jackanapes! Jackanapes!"

If the Postman loved anything on earth, he loved the Captain's yellowed-haired child,

so propping Miss Jessamine against her own door-post, he followed the direction of her trembling fingers and made for the Green.

Jackanapes had had the start of the Postman by nearly ten minutes. The world—the round green world with an oak tree on it—was just becoming very interesting to him. He had tried, vigorously but ineffectually, to mount a passing pig the last time he was taken out walking; but then he was encumbered with a nurse. Now he was his own master, and might, by courage and energy, become the master of that delightful, downy, dumpty, yellow thing, that was bobbing along over the green grass in front of him. Forward! Charge! He aimed well, and grabbed it, but only to feel the delicious downiness and dumpiness slipping through his fingers as he fell upon his face. "Quawk!" said the yellow thing, and wobbled off sideways. It was this oblique movement that enabled Jackanapes to come up with it, for it was bound for the Pond, and therefore obliged to come back into line. He failed again from top-heaviness, and his prey escaped sideways as before, and, as before, lost ground in getting back to the direct road to the Pond.

And to the Pond the Postman found them both, one yellow thing rocking safely on the ripples that lie beyond duck-weed, and the other washing his draggled frock with tears, because he too had tried to sit upon the Pond, and it wouldn't hold him.

CHAPTER III

... If studious, copie fair what time hath blurred,
Redeem truth from his jawes; if souldier,
Chase brave employments with a naked sword
Throughout the world. Fool not; for all may have,
If they dare try, a glorious life, or grave. . . .

In brief, acquit thee bravely: play the man.
Look not on pleasures as they come, but go.
Defer not the least vertue: life's poore span
Make not an ell, by trifling in thy woe.
If thou do ill, the joy fades, not the pains.
If well: the pain doth fade, the joy remains.
GEORGE HERBERT

YOUNG MRS. JOHNSON, who was a mother of many, hardly knew which to pity more; Miss Jessamine for having her little ways and her antimacassars rumpled by a young Jackanapes; or the boy himself, for being brought up by an old maid.

Oddly enough, she would probably have pitied neither, had Jackanapes been a girl. (One is so apt to think that what works smoothest works to the highest ends, having no patience for the results of friction.) That Father in GOD, who bade the young men to be pure, and the maidens brave, greatly disturbed a member of his congregation, who thought that the great preacher had made a slip of the tongue.

"That the girls should have purity, and the boys courage, is what you would say, good Father?"

"Nature has done that," was the reply; "I meant what I said."

In good sooth, a young maid is all the better for learning some robuster virtues than maidenliness and not to move the antimacassars. And the robuster virtues require some fresh air and freedom. As, on the other hand, Jackanapes (who had a boy's full share of the little beast and the young monkey in his natural composition) was none the worse, at his tender years, for learning some maidenliness—so far as maidenliness means decency, pity, unselfishness and pretty behaviour.

And it is due to him to say that he was an obedient boy, and a boy whose word could be depended on, long before his grandfather the General came to live at the Green.

He was obedient; that is he did what his great aunt told him. But—oh dear! oh dear!—the pranks he played, which it had never entered into her head to forbid!

It was when he had just been put into skeletons (frocks never suited him) that he became very friendly with Master Tony Johnson, a younger brother of the young gentleman who sat in the puddle on purpose. Tony was not enterprising, and Jackanapes led him by the nose. One summer's evening they were out late, and Miss Jessamine was becoming anxious, when Jackanapes presented himself with a ghastly face all besmirched with tears. He was unusually subdued.

"I'm afraid," he sobbed; "if you please, I'm very much afraid that Tony Johnson's dying in the churchyard."

Miss Jessamine was just beginning to be distracted, when she smelt Jackanapes.

"You naughty, naughty boys! Do you mean to tell me that you've been smoking?"

"Not pipes," urged Jackanapes; "upon my honour, Aunty, not pipes. Only segars like

Mr. Johnson's! and only made of brown paper with a very very little tobacco from the shop inside them."

Whereupon, Miss Jessamine sent a servant to the churchyard, who found Tony Johnson lying on a tombstone, very sick, and having ceased to entertain any hopes of his own recovery.

If it could be possible that any "unpleasantness" could arise between two such amiable neighbours as Miss Jessamine and Mrs. Johnson—and if the still more incredible paradox can be that ladies may differ over a point on which they are agreed—that point was the admitted fact that Tony Johnson was "delicate," and the difference lay chiefly in this: Mrs. Johnson said that Tony was delicate—meaning that he was more finely strung, more sensitive, a properer subject for pampering and petting than Jackanapes, and that, consequently, Jackanapes was to blame for leading Tony into scrapes which resulted in his being chilled, frightened, or (most frequently) sick. But when Miss Jessamine said that Tony Johnson was delicate, she meant that he was more puling, less manly, and less healthily brought up than Jackanapes, who, when they got into mischief together, was certainly not to blame because his friend could not get wet, sit a kicking donkey, ride in the giddy-go-round, bear the noise of a cracker, or smoke brown paper with impunity, as he could.

Not that there was ever the slightest quarrel between the ladies. It never even came near it, except the day after Tony had been so very sick with riding Bucephalus in the giddy-go-round. Mrs. Johnson had explained to Miss Jessamine that the reason Tony was so easily upset, was the unusual sensitiveness (as a doctor had explained it to her) of the nervous centres in her family—"Fiddlestick!" So Mrs. Johnson understood Miss Jessamine to say, but it appeared that she only said "Treaclestick!" which is quite another thing, and of which Tony was undoubtedly fond.

It was at the Fair that Tony was made ill by riding on Bucephalus. Once a year the Goose Green became the scene of a carnival. First of all, carts and caravans were rumbling up all along, day and night. Jackanapes could hear them as he lay in bed, and could hardly sleep for speculating what booths and whirligigs he should find fairly established, when he and his dog Spitfire went out after breakfast. As a matter of fact, he seldom had to wait so long for news of the Fair. The Postman knew the window out of which Jackanapes' yellow head would come, and was ready with his report.

"Royal Theayter, Master Jackanapes, in the old place, but be careful o' them seats, sir; they're rickettier than ever. Two sweets and a ginger-beer under the oak-tree, and the Flying Boats is just a-coming along the road."

No doubt it was partly because he had already suffered severely in the Flying Boats, that Tony collapsed so quickly in the giddy-go-round. He only mounted Bucephalus (who was spotted, and had no tail,) because Jackanapes urged him, and held out the ingenious hope that the round-and-round feeling would very likely cure the up-and-down sensation. It did not, however, and Tony tumbled off during the first revolution.

Jackanapes was not absolutely free from qualms, but having once mounted the Black Prince, he stuck to him as a horseman should. During the first round he waved his hat, and observed with some concern that the Black Prince had lost an ear since last Fair; at the second, he looked a little pale, but sat upright, though somewhat unnecessarily rigid; at the third round he shut his eyes. During the fourth his hat fell off, and he clasped his horse's neck. By the fifth he had laid his yellow head against the Black

Prince's mane, and so clung anyhow till the hobby-horses stopped, when the proprietor assisted him to alight, and he sat down rather suddenly and said he had enjoyed it very much.

The Grey Goose always ran away at the first approach of the caravans, and never came back to the Green till there was nothing left of the Fair but footmarks and oyster-shells. Running away was her pet principle; the only system, she maintained, by which you can live long and easily, and lose nothing. If you run away when you see danger, you can come back when all is safe. Run quickly, return slowly, hold your head high, and gabble as loud as you can, and you'll preserve the respect of the Goose Green to a peaceful old age. Why should you struggle and get hurt, if you can lower your head and swerve, and not lose a feather? Why in the world should any one spoil the pleasure of life, or risk his skin, if he can help it?

> " 'What's the use?'
> Said the Goose,"

Before answering which one might have to consider what world—which life—and whether his skin were a goose-skin; but the Grey Goose's head would never have held all that.

Grass soon grows over footprints, and the village children took the oyster-shells to trim their gardens with; but the year after Tony rode Bucephalus there lingered another relic of Fair-time, in which Jackanapes was deeply interested. "The Green" proper was originally only part of a straggling common, which in its turn merged into some wilder waste land where gipsies sometimes squatted if the authorities would allow them, especially after the annual Fair. And it was after the Fair that Jackanapes, out rambling by himself, was knocked over by the Gipsy's son riding the Gipsy's red-haired pony at break-neck pace across the common.

Jackanapes got up and shook himself, none the worse, except for being heels over head in love with the red-haired pony. What a rate he went at! How he spurned the ground with his nimble feet! How his red coat shone in the sunshine! And what bright eyes peeped out of his dark forelock as it was blown by the wind!

The Gipsy boy had had a fright, and he was willing enough to reward Jackanapes for not having been hurt, by consenting to let him have a ride.

"Do you mean to kill the little fine gentleman, and swing us all on the gibbet, you rascal?" screamed the Gipsy-mother, who came up just as Jackanapes and the pony set off.

"He would get on," replied her son. "It'll not kill him. He'll fall on his yellow head, and it's as tough as a cocoanut."

But Jackanapes did not fall. He stuck to the red-haired pony as he had stuck to the hobby-horse; but oh, how different the delight of this wild gallop with flesh and blood! Just as his legs were beginning to feel as if he did not feel them, the Gipsy boy cried "Lollo!" Round went the pony so unceremoniously, that, with as little ceremony, Jacka-napes clung to his neck, and he did not properly recover himself before Lollo stopped with a jerk at the place where they had started.

"Is his name Lollo?" asked Jackanapes, his hand lingering in the wiry mane.

"Yes."

"What does Lollo mean?"

"Red."

"Is Lollo your pony?"

"No. My father's." And the Gipsy boy led Lollo away.

At the first opportunity Jackanapes stole away again to the common. This time he saw the Gipsy-father, smoking a dirty pipe.

"Lollo is your pony, isn't he?" said Jackanapes.

"Yes."

"He's a very nice one."

"He's a racer."

"You don't want to sell him, do you?"

"Fifteen pounds," said the Gipsy-father; and Jackanapes sighed and went home again. That very afternoon he and Tony rode the two donkeys, and Tony managed to get thrown, and even Jackanapes' donkey kicked. But it was jolting, clumsy work after the elastic swiftness and the dainty mischief of the red-haired pony.

A few days later Miss Jessamine spoke very seriously to Jackanapes. She was a good deal agitated as she told him that his grandfather the General was coming to the Green, and that he must be on his very best behaviour during the visit. If it had been feasible to leave off calling him Jackanapes and to get used to his baptismal name of Theodore before the day after to-morrow (when the General was due), it would have been satisfactory. But Miss Jessamine feared it would be impossible in practice, and she had scruples about it on principle. It would not seem quite truthful, although she had always most fully intended that he should be called Theodore when he had outgrown the ridiculous appropriateness of his nickname. The fact was that he had not outgrown it, but he must take care to remember who was meant when his grandfather said Theodore.

Indeed for that matter he must take care all along.

"You are apt to be giddy, Jackanapes," said Miss Jessamine.

"Yes, aunt," said Jackanapes, thinking of the hobby-horses.

"You are a good boy, Jackanapes. Thank GOD, I can tell your grandfather that. An obedient boy, an honourable boy, and a kind-hearted boy. But you are—in short, you

are a Boy, Jackanapes. And I hope"—added Miss Jessamine, desperate with the results of experience—"that the General knows that Boys will be Boys."

What mischief could be foreseen, Jackanapes promised to guard against. He was to keep his clothes and his hands clean, to look over his catechism, not to put sticky things in his pockets, to keep that hair of his smooth—("It's the wind that blows it, Aunty," said Jackanapes—"I'll send by the coach for some bear's-grease," said Miss Jessamine, tying a knot in her pocket-handkerchief)—not to burst in at the parlour door, not to talk at the top of his voice, not to crumple his Sunday frill, and to sit quite quiet during the sermon, to be sure to say "sir" to the General, to be. careful about rubbing his shoes on the door-mat, and to bring his lesson-books to his aunt at once that she might iron down the dogs' ears. The General arrived, and for the first day all went well, except that Jackanapes' hair was as wild as usual, for the hairdresser had no bear's grease left. He began to feel more at ease with his grandfather, and disposed to talk confidentially with him, as he did with the Postman. All that the General felt it would take too long to tell, but the result was the same. He was disposed to talk confidentially with Jackanapes.

"Mons'ous pretty place this," he said, looking out of the lattice on to the Green, where the grass was vivid with sunset, and the shadows were long and peaceful.

"You should see it in Fair-week, sir," said Jackanapes, shaking his yellow mop, and leaning back in his one of the two Chippendale arm-chairs in which they sat.

"A fine time that, eh?" said the General, with a twinkle in his left eye. (The other was glass.)

Jackanapes shook his hair once more. "I enjoyed this last one the best of all," he said. "I'd so much money."

"By George, it's not a common complaint in these bad times. How much had ye?"

"I'd two shillings. A new shilling Aunty gave me, and elevenpence I had saved up, and a penny from the Postman—*sir!*" added Jackanapes with a jerk, having forgotten it.

"And how did ye spend it—*sir?*" inquired the General.

Jackanapes spread his ten fingers on the arms of his chair, and shut his eyes that he might count the more conscientiously.

"Watch-stand for Aunty, threepence. Trumpet for myself, twopence, that's fivepence. Ginger-nuts for Tony, twopence, and a mug with a Grenadier on for the Postman, fourpence, that's elevenpence. Shooting-gallery a penny, that's a shilling. Giddy-go-round, a penny, that's one and a penny. Treating Tony, one and twopence. Flying Boats (Tony paid for himself), a penny, one and threepence. Shooting-gallery again, one and fourpence; Fat Woman a penny, one and fivepence. Giddy-go-round again, one and sixpence. Shooting-gallery, one and sevenpence. Treating Tony, and then he wouldn't shoot, so I did, one and eight-pence. Living Skeleton, a penny—no, Tony treated me, the Living Skeleton doesn't count. Skittles, a penny, one and ninepence. Mermaid (but when we got inside she was dead), a penny, one and tenpence. Theatre, a penny (Priscilla Partington, or the Green Lane Murder. A beautiful young lady, sir, with pink cheeks and a real pistol), that's one and elevenpence. Ginger beer, a penny (I *was* so thirsty!) two shillings. And then the Shooting-gallery man gave me a turn for nothing, because, he said, I was a real gentleman, and spent my money like a man."

"So you do, sir, so you do!" cried the General. "Why, sir, you spend it like a prince. And now I suppose you've not got a penny in your pocket?"

"Yes I have," said Jackanapes. "Two pennies. They are saving up." And Jackanapes jingled them with his hand.

"You don't want money except at fair-times, I suppose?" said the General.

Jackanapes shook his mop.

"If I could have as much as I want, I should know what to buy," said he.

"And how much do you want, if you could get it?"

"Wait a minute, sir, till I think what twopence from fifteen pounds leaves. Two from nothing you can't, but borrow twelve. Two from twelve, ten, and carry one. Please remember ten, sir, when I ask you. One from nothing you can't, borrow twenty. One from twenty, nineteen, and carry one. One from fifteen, fourteen. Fourteen pounds nineteen and—what did I tell you to remember?"

"Ten," said the General.

"Fourteen pounds nineteen shillings and tenpence then, is what I want," said Jackanapes.

"Bless my soul, what for?"

"To buy Lollo with. Lollo means red, sir. The Gipsy's red-haired pony, sir. Oh, he *is* beautiful! You should see his coat in the sunshine! You should see his mane! You should see his tail! Such little feet, sir, and they go like lightning! Such a dear face, too, and eyes like a mouse! But he's a racer, and the Gipsy wants fifteen pounds for him."

"If he's a racer, you couldn't ride him. Could you?"

"No—o, sir, but I can stick to him. I did the other day."

"You did, did you? Well, I'm fond of riding myself, and if the beast is as good as you say, he might suit me."

"You're too tall for Lollo, I think," said Jackanapes, measuring his grandfather with his eye.

"I can double up my legs, I suppose. We'll have a look at him to-morrow."

"Don't you weigh a good deal?" asked Jackanapes.

"Chiefly waistcoats," said the General, slapping the breast of his military frock-coat. "We'll have the little racer on the Green the first thing in the morning. Glad you mentioned it, grandson. Glad you mentioned it."

The General was as good as his word. Next morning the Gipsy and Lollo, Miss Jessamine, Jackanapes and his grandfather and his dog Spitfire, were all gathered at one end of the Green in a group, which so aroused the innocent curiosity of Mrs.

Johnson, as she saw it from one of her upper windows, that she and the children took their early promenade rather earlier than usual. The General talked to the Gipsy, and Jackanapes fondled Lollo's mane, and did not know whether he should be more glad or miserable if his grandfather bought him.

"Jackanapes!"

"Yes, sir!"

"I've bought Lollo, but I believe you were right. He hardly stands high enough for me. If you can ride him to the other end of the Green, I'll give him to you."

How Jackanapes tumbled on to Lollo's back he never knew. He had just gathered up the reins when the Gipsy-father took him by the arm.

"If you want to make Lollo go fast, my little gentleman——"

"*I* can make him go!" said Jackanapes, and drawing from his pocket the trumpet he had bought in the fair, he blew a blast both loud and shrill.

Away went Lollo, and away went Jackanapes' hat. His golden hair flew out, an aureole from which his cheeks shone red and distended with trumpeting. Away went Spitfire, mad with the rapture of the race, and the wind in his silky ears. Away went the geese, the cocks, the hens, and the whole family of Johnson. Lucy clung to her mamma, Jane saved Emily by the gathers of her gown, and Tony saved himself by a somersault.

The Grey Goose was just returning when Jackanapes and Lollo rode back, Spitfire panting behind.

"Good, my little gentleman, good!" said the Gipsy. "You were born to the saddle. You've the flat thigh, the strong knee, the wiry back, and the light caressing hand, all you want is to learn the whisper. Come here!"

"What was that dirty fellow talking about, grandson?" asked the General.

"I can't tell you, sir. It's a secret."

They were sitting in the window again, in the two Chippendale arm-chairs, the General devouring every line of his grandson's face, with strange spasms crossing his own.

"You must love your aunt very much, Jackanapes?"

"I do, sir," said Jackanapes warmly.

"And whom do you love next best to your aunt?"

The ties of blood were pressing very strongly on the General himself, and perhaps he thought of Lollo. But Love is not bought in a day, even with fourteen pounds nineteen shillings and tenpence. Jackanapes answered quite readily, "The Postman."

"Why the Postman?"

"He knew my father," said Jackanapes, "and he tells me about him, and about his black mare. My father was a soldier, a brave soldier. He died at Waterloo. When I grow up I want to be a soldier too."

"So you shall, my boy. So you shall."

"Thank you, grandfather. Aunty doesn't want me to be a soldier for fear of being killed."

"Bless my life! Would she have you get into a feather-bed and stay there? Why, you might be killed by a thunderbolt, if you were a butter-merchant!"

"So I might. I shall tell her so. What a funny fellow you are, sir! I say, do you think my father knew the Gipsy's secret? The Postman says he used to whisper to his black mare."

"Your father was taught to ride as a child, by one of those horsemen of the East who swoop and dart and wheel about a plain like swallows in autumn. Grandson! Love me a little too. I can tell you more about your father than the Postman can."

"I do love you," said Jackanapes. "Before you came I was frightened. I'd no notion you were so nice."

"Love me always, boy, whatever I do or leave undone. And—God help me—whatever you do or leave undone, I'll love you! There shall never be a cloud between us for a day; no, sir, not for an hour. We're imperfect enough, all of us, we needn't be so bitter; and life is uncertain enough at its safest, we needn't waste its opportunities. Look at me! Here sit I, after a dozen battles and some of the worst climates in the world, and by yonder lych gate lies your mother, who didn't move five miles, I suppose, from your aunt's apron-strings,—dead in her teens; my golden-haired daughter, whom I never saw."

Jackanapes was terribly troubled.

"Don't cry, grandfather," he pleaded, his own blue eyes round with tears. "I will love you very much, and I will try to be very good. But I should like to be a soldier."

"You shall, my boy, you shall. You've more claims for a commission than you know of. Cavalry, I suppose; eh, ye young Jackanapes? Well, well; if you live to be an honour to your country, this old heart shall grow young again with pride for you; and if you die in the service of your country—God bless me, it can but break for ye!"

And beating the region which he said was all waistcoats, as if they stifled him, the old man got up and strode out on to the Green.

CHAPTER IV

"Greater love hath no man than this, that a man lay down his life for his friends."
—JOHN XV. 13

TWENTY AND ODD YEARS LATER the Grey Goose was still alive, and in full possession of her faculties, such as they were. She lived slowly and carefully, and she lived long. So did Miss Jessamine; but the General was dead.

He had lived on the Green for many years, during which he and the Postman saluted each other with a punctiliousness that it almost drilled one to witness. He would have completely spoiled Jackanapes if Miss Jessamine's conscience would have let him; otherwise he somewhat dragooned his neighbours, and was as positive about parish matters as a ratepayer about the army. A stormy-tempered, tender-hearted soldier, irritable with the suffering of wounds of which he never spoke, whom all the village followed to his grave with tears.

The General's death was a great shock to Miss Jessamine, and her nephew stayed with her for some little time after the funeral. Then he was obliged to join his regiment, which was ordered abroad.

One effect of the conquest which the General had gained over the affections of the village, was a considerable abatement of the popular prejudice against "the military." Indeed the village was now somewhat importantly represented in the army. There was the General himself, and the Postman, and the Black Captain's tablet in the church, and Jackanapes, and Tony Johnson, and a Trumpeter.

Tony Johnson had no more natural taste for fighting than for riding, but he was as devoted as ever to Jackanapes, and that was how it come about that Mr. Johnson bought

him a commission in the same cavalry regiment that the General's grandson (whose commission had been given him by the Iron Duke) was in, and that he was quite content to be the butt of the mess where Jackanapes was the hero; and that when Jackanapes wrote home to Miss Jessamine, Tony wrote with the same purpose to his mother; namely, to demand her congratulations that they were on active service at last, and were ordered to the front. And he added a postscript to the effect that she could have no idea how popular Jackanapes was, nor how splendidly he rode the wonderful red charger, whom he had named after his old friend Lollo.

     *   *   *   *   *

"Sound Retire!"

A Boy Trumpeter, grave with the weight of responsibilities and accoutrements beyond his years, and stained, so that his own mother would not have known him, with the sweat and dust of battle, did as he was bid; and then pushing his trumpet pettishly aside, adjusted his weary legs for the hundredth time to the horse which was a world too big for him, and muttering, " 'Taint a pretty tune," tried to see something of this, his first engagement, before it came to an end.

Being literally in the thick of it, he could hardly have seen less or known less of what happened in that particular skirmish if he had been at home in England. For many good reasons; including dust and smoke, and that what attention he dared distract from his commanding officer was pretty well absorbed by keeping his hard-mouthed troop-horse in hand, under pain of execration by his neighbours in the melée. By-and-by, when the newspapers came out, if he could get a look at one before it was thumbed to bits, he would learn that the enemy had appeared from ambush in overwhelming numbers, and that orders had been given to fall back, which was done slowly and in good order, the men fighting as they retired.

Born and bred on the Goose Green, the youngest of Mr. Johnson's gardener's numerous offspring, the boy had given his family "no peace" till they let him "go for a soldier" with Master Tony and Master Jackanapes. They consented at last, with more tears than they shed when an elder son was sent to gaol for poaching, and the boy was perfectly happy in his life, and full of *esprit de corps*. It was this which had been wounded

by having to sound retreat for "the young gentleman's regiment," the first time he served with it before the enemy, and he was also harassed by having completely lost sight of Master Tony. There had been some hard fighting before the backward movement began, and he had caught sight of him once, but not since. On the other hand, all the pulses of his village pride had been stirred by one or two visions of Master Jackanapes whirling about on his wonderful horse. He had been easy to distinguish, since an eccentric blow had bared his head without hurting it, for his close golden mop of hair gleamed in the hot sunshine as brightly as the steel of the sword flashing round it.

Of the missiles that fell pretty thickly, the Boy Trumpeter did not take much notice. First, one can't attend to everything, and his hands were full. Secondly, one gets used to anything. Thirdly, experience soon teaches one, in spite of proverbs, how very few bullets find their billet. Far more unnerving is the mere suspicion of fear or even of anxiety in the human mass around you. The Boy was beginning to wonder if there were any dark reason for the increasing pressure, and whether they would be allowed to move back more quickly, when the smoke in front lifted for a moment, and he could see the plain, and the enemy's line some two hundred yards away.

And across the plain between them, he saw Master Jackanapes galloping alone at the top of Lollo's speed, their faces to the enemy, his golden head at Lollo's ear.

But at this moment noise and smoke seemed to burst out on every side, the officer shouted to him to sound retire, and between trumpeting and bumping about on his horse, he saw and heard no more of the incidents of his first battle.

Tony Johnson was always unlucky with horses, from the days of the giddy-go-round onwards. On this day—of all days in the year—his own horse was on the sick list, and he had to ride an inferior, ill-conditioned beast, and fell off that, at the very moment when it was a matter of life or death to be able to ride away. The horse fell on him, but struggled up again, and Tony managed to keep hold of it. It was in trying to remount that he discovered, by helplessness and anguish, that one of his legs was crushed and broken, and that no feat of which he was master would get him into the saddle. Not able even to stand alone, awkwardly, agonizingly unable to mount his restive horse, his life was yet so strong within him! And on one side of him rolled the dust and smoke-cloud of his advancing foes, and on the other, that which covered his retreating friends.

He turned one piteous gaze after them, with a bitter twinge, not of reproach, but of loneliness; and then, dragging himself up by the side of his horse, he turned the other way and drew out his pistol, and waited for the end. Whether he waited seconds or minutes he never knew, before some one gripped him by the arm.

"*Jackanapes! GOD bless you!* It's my left leg. If you *could* get me on——"

It was like Tony's luck that his pistol went off at his horse's tail, and made it plunge; but Jackanapes threw him across the saddle.

"Hold on anyhow, and stick your spur in. I'll lead him. Keep your head down, they're firing high."

And Jackanapes laid his head down—to Lollo's ear.

It was when they were fairly off, that a sudden upspringing of the enemy in all directions had made it necessary to change the gradual retirement of our force into as rapid a retreat as possible. And when Jackanapes became aware of this, and felt the lagging and swerving of Tony's horse, he began to wish he had thrown his friend across his own saddle, and left their lives to Lollo.

When Tony became aware of it, several things came into his head. 1. That the dangers of their ride for life were now more than doubled. 2. That if Jackanapes and Lollo were not burdened with him they would undoubtedly escape. 3. That Jackanapes' life was infinitely valuable, and his—Tony's—was not. 4. That this—if he could seize it—was the supremest of all the moments in which he had tried to assume the virtues which Jackanapes had by nature; and that if he could be courageous and unselfish now——

He caught at his own reins and spoke very loud——

"Jackanapes! It won't do. You and Lollo must go on. Tell the fellows I gave you back to them, with all my heart. Jackanapes, if you love me, leave me!"

There was a daffodil light over the evening sky in front of them, and it shone strangely on Jackanapes' hair and face. He turned with an odd look in his eyes that a vainer man than Tony Johnson might have taken for brotherly pride. Then he shook his mop, and laughed at him.

"*Leave you?* To save my skin? No, Tony, not to save my soul!"

CHAPTER V

Mr. VALIANT *summoned. His will. His last words.*

Then, said he, "I am going to my Father's. . . . My Sword I give to him that shall
succeed me in my Pilgrimage, and my Courage and Skill to him that can get it." . . . And
as he went down deeper, he said, "Grave, where is thy Victory?"
So he passed over, and all the Trumpets sounded for him on the other side.
BUNYAN'S *Pilgrim's Progress*

COMING OUT OF a hospital-tent, at headquarters, the surgeon cannoned against, and
rebounded from, another officer; a sallow man, not young, with a face worn more by
ungentle experiences than by age; with weary eyes that kept their own counsel, iron-
grey hair, and a moustache that was as if a raven had laid its wing across his lips and
sealed them.

"Well?"

"Beg pardon, Major. Didn't see you. Oh, compound fracture and bruises, but it's all
right. He'll pull through."

"Thank GOD."

It was probably an involuntary expression, for prayer and praise were not much in
the Major's line, as a jerk of the surgeon's head would have betrayed to an observer. He
was a bright little man, with his feelings showing all over him, but with gallantry and
contempt of death enough for both sides of his profession; who took a cool head, a
white handkerchief and a case of instruments, where other men went hot-blooded with
weapons, and who was the biggest gossip, male or female, of the regiment. Not even the
Major's taciturnity daunted him.

"Didn't think he'd as much pluck about him as he has. He'll do all right if he doesn't
fret himself into a fever about poor Jackanapes."

"Whom are you talking about?" asked the Major hoarsely.

"Young Johnson. He——"

"What about Jackanapes?"

"Don't you know? Sad business. Rode back for Johnson, and brought him in; but,
monstrous ill-luck, hit as they rode. Left lung——"

"Will he recover?"

"No. Sad business. What a frame—what limbs—what health—and what good looks!
Finest young fellow——"

"Where is he?"

"In his own tent," said the surgeon sadly.

The Major wheeled and left him.

*   *   *   *   *

"Can I do anything else for you?"

"Nothing, thank you. Except—Major! I wish I could get you to appreciate Johnson."

"This is not an easy moment, Jackanapes."

"Let me tell you, sir—*he* never will—that if he could have driven me from him, he
would be lying yonder at this moment, and I should be safe and sound."

The Major laid his hand over his mouth, as if to keep back a wish he would have been ashamed to utter.

"I've known old Tony from a child. He's a fool on impulse, a good man and a gentleman in principle. And he acts on principle, which it's not every——some water, please! Thank you, sir. It's very hot, and yet one's feet get uncommonly cold. Oh, thank you thank you. He's no fire-eater, but he has a trained conscience and a tender heart, and he'll do his duty when a braver and more selfish man might fail you. But he wants encouragement; and when I'm gone——"

"He shall have encouragement. You have my word for it. Can I do nothing else?"

"Yes, Major. A favour."

"Thank you, Jackanapes."

"Be Lollo's master, and love him as well as you can. He's used to it."

"Wouldn't you rather Johnson had him?"

The blue eyes twinkled in spite of mortal pain.

"Tony *rides* on principle, Major. His legs are bolsters, and will be to the end of the chapter. I couldn't insult dear Lollo, but if you don't care——"

"Whilst I live——which will be longer than I desire or deserve——Lollo shall want nothing, but——you. I have too little tenderness for——my dear boy, you're faint. Can you spare me for a moment?"

"No, stay—Major!"

"What? What?"

"My head drifts so—if you wouldn't mind."

"Yes! Yes!"

"Say a prayer by me. Out loud please, I am getting deaf."

"My dearest Jackanapes—my dear boy——"

"One of the Church Prayers—Parade Service, you know——"

"I see. But the fact is—GOD forgive me, Jackanapes—I'm a very different sort of fellow to some of you youngsters. Look here, let me fetch——"

But Jackanapes' hand was in his, and it wouldn't let go.

There was a brief and bitter silence.

" 'Pon my soul I can only remember the little one at the end."

"Please," whispered Jackanapes.

Pressed by the conviction that what little he could do it was his duty to do, the Major—kneeling—bared his head, and spoke loudly, clearly, and very reverently—

"The Grace of our Lord Jesus Christ——"

Jackanapes moved his left hand to his right one, which still held the Major's—

"—The Love of GOD."

And with that—Jackanapes died.

CHAPTER VI

"Und so ist der blaue Himmel grösser als jedes
Gewölk darin, und dauerhafter dazu."
JEAN PAUL RICHTER

J ACKANAPES' DEATH was sad news for the Goose Green, a sorrow just qualified by honourable pride in his gallantry and devotion. Only the Cobbler dissented, but that was his way. He said he saw nothing in it but foolhardiness and vainglory. They might both have been killed, as easy as not, and then where would ye have been? A man's life was a man's life, and one life was as good as another. No one would catch him throwing his away. And, for that matter, Mrs. Johnson could spare a child a great deal better than Miss Jessamine.

But the parson preached Jackanapes' funeral sermon on the text, "Whosoever will save his life shall lose it; and whosoever will lose his life for My sake shall find it;" and all the village went and wept to hear him.

Nor did Miss Jessamine see her loss from the Cobbler's point of view. On the contrary, Mrs. Johnson said she never to her dying day should forget how, when she went to condole with her, the old lady came forward, with gentlewomanly self-control, and kissed her, and thanked GOD that her dear nephew's effort had been blessed with success, and that this sad war had made no gap in her friend's large and happy home circle.

"But she's a noble, unselfish woman," sobbed Mrs. Johnson, "and she taught Jackanapes to be the same, and that's how it is that my Tony has been spared to me. And it must be sheer goodness in Miss Jessamine, for what can she know of a mother's feelings? And I'm sure most people seem to think that if you've a large family you don't know one from another any more than they do, and that a lot of children are like a lot of store-apples, if one's taken it won't be missed."

Lollo—the first Lollo, the Gipsy's Lollo—very aged, draws Miss Jessamine's bath-chair slowly up and down the Goose Green in the sunshine.

The Ex-postman walks beside him, which Lollo tolerates to the level of his shoulder. If the Postman advances any nearer to his head, Lollo quickens his pace, and were the Postman to persist in the injudicious attempt, there is, as Miss Jessamine says, no knowing what might happen.

In the opinion of the Goose Green, Miss Jessamine has borne her troubles "wonderfully." Indeed, to-day, some of the less delicate and less intimate of those who see everything from the upper windows, say (well behind her back) that "the old lady seems quite lively with her military beaux again."

The meaning of this is, that Captain Johnson is leaning over one side of her chair, whilst by the other bends a brother officer who is staying with him, and who has manifested an extraordinary interest in Lollo. He bends lower and lower, and Miss Jessamine calls to the Postman to request Lollo to be kind enough to stop, while she is fumbling for something which always hangs by her side, and has got entangled with her spectacles.

It is a twopenny trumpet, bought years ago in the village fair, and over it she and Captain Johnson tell, as best they can, between them, the story of Jackanapes' ride across the Goose Green; and how he won Lollo—the Gipsy's Lollo—the racer Lollo— dear Lollo—faithful Lollo—Lollo the never vanquished—Lollo the tender servant of his old mistress. And Lollo's ears twitch at every mention of his name.

Their hearer does not speak, but he never moves his eyes from the trumpet, and when the tale is told, he lifts Miss Jessamine's hand and presses his heavy black moustache in silence to her trembling fingers.

The sun, setting gently to his rest, embroiders the sombre foliage of the oak-tree with threads of gold. The Grey Goose is sensible of an atmosphere of repose, and puts up one leg for the night. The grass glows with a more vivid green, and, in answer to a ringing call from Tony, his sisters, fluttering over the daisies in pale-hued muslins, come out of their ever-open door, like pretty pigeons from a dovecote.

And, if the good gossips' eyes do not deceive them, all the Miss Johnsons, and both the officers, go wandering off into the lanes, where bryony wreaths still twine about the brambles.

$$*\qquad*\qquad*\qquad*\qquad*$$

A sorrowful story, and ending badly?

Nay, Jackanapes, for the End is not yet.

A life wasted that might have been useful?

Men who have died for men, in all ages, forgive the thought!

There is a heritage of heroic example and noble obligation, not reckoned in the Wealth of Nations, but essential to a nation's life; the contempt of which, in any people, may, not slowly, mean even its commercial fall.

Very sweet are the uses of prosperity, the harvests of peace and progress, the fostering sunshine of health and happiness, and length of days in the land.

But there be things—oh, sons of what has deserved the name of Great Britain, forget it not!—"the good of" which and "the use of" which are beyond all calculation of worldly goods and earthly uses: things such as Love, and Honour, and the Soul of Man, which cannot be bought with a price, and which do not die with death. And they who would fain live happily EVER after, should not leave these things out of the lessons of their lives.

THE END